D1432988

ART LAW

ART LAW
Rights and Liabilities of Creators and Collectors

Successor to
ART WORKS: LAW, POLICY, PRACTICE

I

Franklin Feldman
MEMBER, NEW YORK BAR

Stephen E. Weil
MEMBER, NEW YORK BAR

with the collaboration of
Susan Duke Biederman
MEMBER, NEW YORK BAR

LITTLE, BROWN AND COMPANY
BOSTON   TORONTO

Library of Congress Catalog Card No. 85-81680

ISBN 0-316-09296-7

MV

Published simultaneously in Canada
by Little, Brown & Company (Canada) Limited

Printed in the United States of America

To our respective spouses:

Naomi (F.F.)

Liz (S.E.W.)

Danny (S.D.B.)

SUMMARY OF CONTENTS

•

CONTENTS

•

Volume II

BIOGRAPHIES

•

Franklin Feldman, a partner in the law firm of Stroock & Stroock & Lavan, New York, received his B.A. from New York University in 1948 and graduated from Columbia Law School in 1951. He was editor-in-chief of the Columbia Law Review.

Mr. Feldman is a lecturer in Law at Columbia Law School, a former chairman of the Art Committee of the Association of the Bar of the City of New York, and a former president of the International Foundation for Art Research, Inc. He is also a life member of the Art Students League and in 1983 was an artist-in-residence at Yaddo in Saratoga Springs, New York.

Stephen E. Weil has been deputy director of the Smithsonian Institution's Hirshhorn Museum and Sculpture Garden since 1974. He received a B.A. from Brown University in 1949 and graduated from Columbia Law School in 1956. From 1967 to 1974, he was administrator of the Whitney Museum of American Art in New York City.

Mr. Weil has been a senior museum associate and faculty member of the Museum Management Institute at the University of California, Berkeley, since its inception in 1979. Among his other professional activities, he has chaired the planning committee for the annual ALI-ABA course of study on Legal Problems of Museum Administration and served for seven years on the Executive Committee of the American Association of Museums. *Beauty and the Beasts,* a collection of his essays on museums, art, the law, and the market, was published by the Smithsonian Institution Press in 1983.

Susan Duke Biederman is an attorney in private practice in New York City with a speciality in art law, representing institutions and individuals in the visual, performing, and literary arts fields.

Mrs. Duke Biederman received her B.A., Phi Beta Kappa, in 1975 from the University of California at Los Angeles and her Doctor of Laws degree in 1978 from the Law School of the University of Chicago, where she studied current problems in the visual arts world with the late Harold Rosenberg. She has guest-lectured at Parsons School of Design and elsewhere, and was recently selected by the National Conference of State Legislatures to prepare its 1986 Arts and the States Update, a state-by-state analysis of art law.

ACKNOWLEDGMENTS

•

A work such as this, taking nearly five years from initial discussion to completion, can only be accomplished with the contributions of numerous people. Special acknowledgment and thanks are due Richard A. Altman, Esq., Richard Andrews, Robert Anthoine, Esq., Shea Bergin, Rhoda L. Berkowitz, Huntington T. Block, Ben W. Bolch, Joseph Bresnan, Mary E. Case, the late Ralph F. Colin, Esq., Elizabeth Croog, Esq., Edward J. Damich, Esq., William W. Damon, Russell J. DaSilva, Esq., Gladys Distler, Gilbert S. Edelson, Esq., Jeremy Epstein, Esq., Joseph Fudali, Marge Goldwater, Hon. Richard N. Gottfried, Gustave Harrow, Esq., Fritz Hatton, C. Elton Hinshaw, Deborah DePorter Hoover, Esq., Heather Horan, Mary Ann Jacoby, Esq., Charles Jurrist, Esq., Audrey S. Kauders, John B. Koegel, Esq., Alvin S. Lane, Esq., Marshall A. Leaffer, James B. Lyon, Esq., Marie C. Malaro, Esq., Gordon H. Marsh, Esq., Dr. Michael McCann, John Henry Merryman, Esq., Marie A. Moravec, Carol Moreno, Jennifer Moyer, Norman Narotzky, David A. Newberg, Esq., Philip Palmer, Esq., John G. Petrovich, Esq., Aimée Brown Price, Monroe E. Price, Esq., Anthony J. Radich, Marie A. Reilly, Edward J. Ross, Esq., Monona Rossol, Alan S. Samuels, Gretchen Sarno, Donna Shandley, Robert Shireman, Theodore E. Stebbins, Jr., Peter R. Stern, Esq., Marjorie E. Stone, Esq., Judith L. Teichman, Esq., Jill Troner, Nicholas D. Ward, Esq., Robert A. Weiner, Esq., Beverly M. Wolff, Esq., and Agnes Zimmerman.

Several others must be mentioned singularly. We are most fortunate in having Little, Brown and Company as our publisher, and, in particular, Thomas W. Lincoln as our editor. This book would simply not have come into existence without Tom and his wide array of support, encouragement, solutions, and help. If the field of legal writing has a Max Perkins, it is he. John Bergin, our manuscript editor, gave us critical guidance in his astute and patient copyediting; his comments, encouragement, and humor were invaluable.

Finally, acknowledgment must be made to our spouses for allowing us the time and frequent absences from family life that such a work demands, and for giving constant encouragement and support, without which this book would never have been contemplated, much less finished. We dedicate it to them.

Franklin Feldman
Stephen E. Weil
Susan Duke Biederman

July 1, 1986

PERMISSIONS

•

The authors gratefully acknowledge the permissions granted to reproduce the following materials.

Anthoine, Robert, The Collector of Taxes vs. The Collector of Objects, 59 Taxes 917, 919-922 (1981). This article appeared originally in the December 1981 issue of Taxes — The Tax Magazine, published and copyrighted © 1981, by Commerce Clearinghouse, Inc., in Chicago, and appears here with its permission and that of the author.

Berkowitz, Rhoda L., & Leaffer, Marshall A., 8 Art & L. 249 (1984). The authors are professors of Law at the University of Toledo, College of Law. Reprinted with permission.

Bolch, Ben W., & Damon, William W., & Hinshaw, C. Elton, An Economic Analysis of the California Art Royalty Statute, 10 Conn. L. Rev. 689 (Spring 1978). Mr. Bolch is president of The Bolch Group, Inc., a financial investment firm located in Atlanta, Georgia; he is a former professor of Economics at Vanderbilt University. Mr. Damon is a professor of Economics at Vanderbilt University. Mr. Hinshaw is an associate professor of Economics at Vanderbilt University and the secretary of the American Economics Association. Reprinted with permission.

Christie's Consignment Agreement: Conditions of Acceptance and Conditions of Sale. Reprinted with the permission of Christie, Manson & Woods International, Inc.

Colin, Ralph F., Statement on Behalf of the Art Dealers Association of America on the Subject of Artists Sharing in Profits of Resale (July 21, 1977). Reprinted with permission.

Damich, Edward J., The New York Artists' Authorship Rights Act: A Comparative Critique, 84 Colum. L. Rev. 1733 (1984). Copyright © 1984 by the Directors of the Columbia Law Review Association, Inc. All rights reserved. This article originally appeared in 84 Colum. L. Rev. 1733 (1984). Reprinted by permission.

DaSilva, Russell J., Droit Moral and the Amoral Copyright: A Comparison of Artists' Rights in France and the United States, 28 Bull. Copyright Socy. U.S.A. 1 (1980). Copyright © by Russell J. DaSilva. Mr. DaSilva received his J.D. in 1979 from the Harvard Law School and is associated with the law firm of Milbank, Tweed, Hadley & McCloy in New York City. Reprinted with permission.

Hoover, Deborah DePorter, Title Disputes in the Art Market: An Emerging Duty of Care for Art Merchants, 51 Geo. Wash. L. Rev. 443 (No. 3, 1983). Reprinted with permission.

INTRODUCTION

•

In the preface to our 1974 compendium *Art Works: Law, Policy, Practice* (Practising Law Institute), we said:

> A generation ago, most legal problems involving art works were resolved by recourse to some generalized body of law. The rules regulating the sale of an etching by Picasso were largely the same as those covering a sack of potatoes. . . . Today, American law as it relates to art works is in the course of becoming particular. At every level—from international treaty to local ordinance—works of fine art and those who make, sell and collect them, are singled out for special legal treatment.

Now, a half generation later still, this trend continues to accelerate at an exceptional rate. The need for a fresh treatment of the subject is manifest. Two of the principal areas in which bodies of law unique to the visual arts are emerging most rapidly concern the rights of artists and the rights of collectors. They are to a degree interwoven — artists' rights such as copyright, moral right, and resale rights have either been expanded or newly established almost wholly in derogation of the rights hitherto enjoyed by collectors.

The first volume of this work focuses on the rights of artists. Foremost among these is the right of the artist to use works of art as a medium of personal expression. This has rarely been attacked directly. Thought is free, and — aside from those instances in which the actual creation of the work would infringe a copyright or violate a protective statute such as 18 U.S.C. 711 (the "Smokey Bear" statute) — most efforts to restrict artists from communicating to the public have been directed at the display or other dissemination of their work rather than at its initial creation. Sometimes these efforts have been successful, sometimes not. The artist's right to free expression, as well as the rights of others — art critics, particularly — to express themselves *about* the artist's work, is the subject of Chapter 1.

Chapter 2 deals with reproduction rights, with special attention paid to the far-reaching effects on artists of the Copyright Revision Act of 1976.

Chapters 3, 4, 5, and 6 all deal with the situation of the artist after he has first launched a work into the stream of commerce. Chapter 3 focuses on the relationship of artists to dealers; it argues that the artist is best served when this relationship is memorialized in some written contractual form. The spread of state legislation protective of artists in their relationship to dealers is also examined in this chapter. Chapter 4 deals with artworks commissioned for specific clients, with particular attention paid to public works of art and their siting. Recent controversies, including the *Tilted Arc* case in New York, are discussed in detail. Chapter 5 deals with the moral right, first examining the European origin of this once-alien concept, and then tracing its American development through the passage of various statutes in California, New York, Massachusetts, and, to a lesser degree, Maine. We have every reason to believe that the moral right is an idea whose time has come and that an understanding of these statutes is crucial. Chapter 6 covers resale rights. Here recent efforts to introduce this concept to the United States are examined, including California's Resale Royalty Act. The very notion of a resale royalty continues to roil the art community to a degree virtually unmatched by any other current issue.

Chapter 7 touches on other legislation protective of artists. Included here are "live-work" statutes and the regulation of toxic art supplies. Both are nascent, yet potentially important, sources of artists' rights.

Chapter 8 deals with the death of the artist. Litigation of one sort or another has often followed the deaths of many of this country's best-known artists, among them Franz Kline, David Smith, and Mark Rothko; the decisions in all these cases are reproduced and analyzed here. Also considered briefly in this chapter is the possibility that works of art might be used to pay all or a portion of the estate tax due at the artist's death.

In the second volume, our focus shifts from the rights of artists to the rights of collectors, both individual and institutional. Chronicled by the case law we have gathered is an inordinate number of disputes between art collectors and dealers, art dealers and creditors, art collectors and museums, one art expert and another, and still more. The possible permutations appear almost endless. Collectors both buy and sell works of art. So do dealers, but dealers also give opinions about them. So do people who work for museums, but museums, in addition, also borrow works of art. Sometimes they also misplace them. And so on.

Notwithstanding this enormous variety of litigants and subject matter, two key themes run throughout these cases: authorship and title. What are the consequences, if any, when a painting that was sold on the basis of its execution by the hand of artist *A* (and, accordingly, was fairly priced at $*XXX*) is suddenly said to have been executed instead by the hand of artist *B* (and, accordingly, was unconsciously overpriced at that same $XXX)? And what are the legal consequences, if any, when a work of art acquired by *C* in good faith from *D* turns out to actually have been — or may still be — the property of *V*, from whom it was stolen by *X*, *Y*, and *Z*? To sort this tangle out in some manageable way, we have divided the coverage of the rights of collectors into six chapters.

Chapter 9 deals with private transactions, principally those between collectors and art dealers. It begins with coverage of early English cases and then goes on to trace the application of the Uniform Commercial Code to transactions involving works of art. Finally, it examines recent state legislation specifically intended to regulate the art market, including warranty and print disclosure statutes.

Chapter 10 deals with public transactions — with the purchase and sale of works of art through the medium of public auction. The gap between what should be a simple transaction and the often hideous legal complexities of a mistaken attribution, flaw in title, or a misplaced expectation concerning the auctioneer's duties makes this a topic of increasing controversy.

Chapter 11 deals with claims made against collectors by third parties. Most frequently, these are claims that a work of art acquired by the collector is *actually* the property of the claimant. An understanding of statutes of limitations is vital here, and we have included materials on this topic in the second part of Chapter 11.

Chapter 12 addresses two situations where the parties' roles are reversed; here the collector may be the claimant against a third party other than the dealer or auction house from whom the artwork was obtained. The first of these involves the loan of art to museums where the work may be unreturnable or where the terms of the loan have been obscured by time. The second involves opinions by experts, appraisers, or others concerning works of art. Here again are considered the many permutations of the nature, timing, and control of such opinions.

Chapter 13 presents a detailed treatment of the charitable deduction for gifts of artworks under federal tax law. The proper valuation of such gifts has been a source of chronic difficulty and, in the view of some commentators, an invitation for abuse. Recent developments in case law and the radically tightened substantiation rules adopted in 1985 are reviewed extensively.

Finally, in Chapter 14 we consider those aspects that works of art acquire when viewed as an investment. Here we have traveled the greatest possible distance from the point at which this book begins — the work of art as a medium for personal expression. In the cases reproduced and discussed in this chapter, the reader will find works of art viewed in ways that strip them almost wholly bare of any aesthetic or communicative qualities.

In these volumes we have attempted to present art law in its many guises. As with any field of endeavor torn between the contradictions of the creative process and the demands of the marketplace, art law presents special and increasingly complex problems to the varied members of the visual arts community.

In a few instances, where the law has not changed significantly, we have carried materials from *Art Works: Law, Policy, Practice* into this new work with little or no change. Also, with reference to that earlier book, it covered several subjects that we felt free to omit in this successor work because they have since been so thoroughly covered in individual treatises by other authors. These include the laws pertaining to the international movement of art and much of the art law relevant to museum collections. Readers interested in exploring these subjects further are referred to Paul M. Bator's *The International Trade in Art* (University of Chicago Press ed. 1983) and Marie C. Malaro's *A Legal Primer on Managing Museum Collections* (Smithsonian Institution Press 1985). We have also omitted coverage of many of the tax rules as they relate to artists. These have been treated extensively by various monographs published by Volunteer Lawyers for the Arts, New York City.

What should be clear from the cases, commentary, and other materials to be found in this work is that our Anglo-American jurisprudence now increasingly accords a "special legal treatment" to artists and to works of art. Art is out of the ordinary, and — to an ever greater degree in the eyes of the law — so are those who create it.

Until recently, we believed this recognition of art's special legal status to be basically a twentieth-century phenomenon. Serendipitous discovery of an early nineteenth-century case[1] from Halifax, Nova Scotia, indicates that its origins may have been earlier.

At issue was a shipment of 21 paintings and 52 prints that had been seized on the high seas and brought to Halifax by the British during the War of 1812. The works of art had been placed aboard the American flag vessel *Marquis de Somereules* in Italy and were destined for the Pennsylvania Academy of Fine Arts as gifts from Joseph Allen Smith, a citizen of South Carolina and an early patron of the Academy. A petition for their release was submitted to the Honorable Sir Alexander Croke, Justice of

---

[1] The Marquis De Someruedes, Stewart's Vice-Admiralty Reports 482 (N.S. 1813).

the Court of Vice Admiralty in Halifax. By a decree dated April 21, 1813, Mr. Justice Croke ordered the works of art released to the Academy. He wrote:

> The same law of nations, which prescribes that all property belonging to the enemy shall be liable to confiscation, has likewise its modifications and relaxations of that rule. The arts and sciences are admitted amongst all civilized nations, as forming an exception to the severe rights of warfare, and as entitled to favour and protection. They are considered not as the peculium of this or of that nation, but as the property of mankind at large, and as belonging to the common interests of the whole species.[2]

More noble sentiments about the arts have rarely been expressed. That they formed the basis for a judicial decree in 1813 is not without significance.

Given the turbulence of the art marketplace, it is not surprising that the creation and ownership of the "property of mankind" has generated so much legal controversy. The trend continues unabated. Our intent in this work has been to both chronicle and anticipate the growth of art law as a separate jurisprudence.

---

[2] *Id.* at 483.

ART LAW

CHAPTER ONE

The Right of Expression

•

§1.1. The Artist's Right of Expression

§1.2. Limitations on the Artist's Right of Expression

§1.3. Expressions by Others

§1.1. THE ARTIST'S RIGHT OF EXPRESSION

§1.1.1. Is Visual Speech a Protected Form of Speech?

Important, if not primary, among a fine artist's concerns is whether works of art, their creation, and their placement are protected forms of speech. When an artwork is attacked under a statute prohibiting the physical use of the American flag, for example, or a work of public art is claimed to be a nuisance by a community that considers it offensive and wants it removed, are the creations entitled to the same constitutional protection that the First Amendment provides to the spoken and written speech of literature, journalism, and political discourse? The question is not simply one of immunity from potential harassment; in a sense, it goes to the very dignity of what artists do. Are they mere decorators of surfaces and environments, or are they engaged in a form of communication that ought to be treated by the law in ways comparable to other forms of communication?

The protection of visual speech is, at best, a deeply unsettled area of art law. This section of the chapter presents instances in which works of art have found protection under the same legal theories that are generally regarded as governing other forms of expression. Section 1.2 then examines situations in which the type of First Amendment analysis customarily applied to other forms of expression was not afforded visual speech. We have a sense, if not yet a settled conviction, that the courts have been more likely to undertake such an analysis when the artist or exhibitor was able to plausibly demonstrate that the artwork either had political content or at least dealt with some matter of public concern. If this is so, then it can be anticipated that at the other extreme the courts would be most resistant to employing such constitutional scrutiny when dealing with art that is primarily self-expressive, decorative, or just convivial. Consider, for example, the unwillingness of the court to make such an inquiry in *Close v. Lederle* (see §1.2.2 *infra*).

The unsettled state of jurisprudence is compounded by some recently emerged forms of art. Consider graffiti art. While generally accepted today as an authentic form of expression, what happens when this type of visual expression collides wth a local anti-graffiti statute? Or consider certain site-specific art. Such works are often viewed by the art community as religiously wedded to the environment for which they were "specifically" created. From the artist's point of view, efforts to alter that environment may appear to violate the work. Public art in which process plays an intrinsic role — the work of Bulgarian-born artist Christo Javacheff (Christo), for example — sets up still another conflict. Often the processes necessary for a work's production may require a stiff and lengthy public review; in these instances, stubborn opposition often results between necessary bureaucratic safeguards and the artist's desire to retain the traditional freedom of the studio.

While much remains to be resolved concerning the visual artist's right of expression, the situation of critics and others who comment on works of art is considerably more certain. In general, the courts have tended to treat such commentary as opinion. By doing so, they have permitted a wide latitude of expression. Issues relating to comments *about* art are discussed in §1.3.

As for the larger question of whether art should be treated as a protected form of speech, we unequivocally believe that it should. What we advocate is not an absolute shield whereby all creative works and processes are exempt from review merely by virtue of being labeled art. Rather, we ask only that they routinely be entitled to the same careful analysis the courts now generally reserve for other forms of speech. The *Yorty v. Chandler* case (see §1.1.9 *infra*) points in that direction and is particularly illuminating concerning what the appropriate parameters may well be.

§1.1.2. *People v. Radich:* An Early Test of Free Speech

In our opinion, no facts could more sharply focus the question of whether artworks are entitled to consideration as "symbolic speech" than those surrounding the 1966 arrest, and conviction the following year, of New York City art dealer Stephen Radich. His crime? To display the sculptural constructions of Marc Morrel. The charge? That Radich had "cast contempt on the flag of the United States of America" because some of Morrel's constructions were partly composed of American flags. He was found guilty of violating New York's flag desecration law. The 1970 decision of New York's Court of Appeals affirming his conviction follows. Most noteworthy is Chief Judge FULD's dissent — an opinion prophetic of the federal court decision that would clear Radich some four years later.

PEOPLE v. RADICH
26 N.Y.2d 114, 308 N.Y.S.2d 846, 257 N.E.2d 30 (1970), *aff'd by an equally divided* Court, 401 U.S. 531 (1971)

GIBSON, J. The issue is whether defendant's conviction of a violation of New York's flag desecration statute was in contravention of his right of free speech under the First Amendment to the Constitution of the United States. The particular penal provision found to have been violated provides, in substance, that any person who shall publicly mutilate, deface, defile, or defy, trample upon, or cast contempt upon the flag of the United States of America, either by words or act, shall be guilty of a misdemeanor (former Penal Law, §1425, subd. 16, par. *d*, now General Business Law, §136, subd. *d*). The constitutional question in respect of the proscribed defilement by an "act," rather than by "words," was expressly left open in *Street v. New York* (394 U.S. 576, 594), which reversed our affirmance of a conviction under this same statute (*People v. Street*, 20 N.Y.2d. 231). We have concluded that the conviction in the case now before us infringed no constitutional guarantee.

The defendant, the proprietor of an art gallery in the City of New York, publicly displayed and exposed for sale, certain "constructions," comparable to sculptures, which had been fashioned by an artist as expressive of protest against the Vietnam war and which, in each case, prominently incorporated the American flag.

The complaint, upon which defendant was charged and convicted, alleged, among other violations of the statute, that defendant publicly displayed the flag of the United States of America in the form of the male sexual organ, erect and protruding from the upright member of a cross; also, in the form of a human body, hanging from a yellow noose; and, again, wrapped around a bundle resting upon a two-wheeled vehicle, shown by photographs in evidence to resemble a gun caisson.[1]

For the purposes of this opinion it seems necessary to discuss only the first of the constructions complained of. Testifying in his own behalf, the defendant said that this was protest art; and that during the exhibition of the constructions, background music, consisting of war protest songs, was played from a tape. Asked, on cross-examination, as to the use of the flag for the purpose of protest, he said that the object extending from the vertical member of the cross and wrapped in a small flag was representative of a human penis; that tassels at the base of this protrusion repre-

---

[1] The allegations, in full, were that "the defendant did have on public display and for public viewing, the flag of the United States of America, in the following manner: 1 — in the form of a male sexual organ, protruding from the body of form, in the anterior portion of the body of the form and depicting the erected male penis, protruding from a form of a cross. 2 — the flag of the United States of America, wrapped in a chained bundle. 3 — The standard of the United States on the form of an alleged elephant. 4 — The Union of the flag of the United States of America, depicted in the form of an octupus [*sic*]. 5 — The American flag attached to a gas meter. 6 — The American flag wrapped around a bundle attached to a two wheeled vehicle. 7 — The American flag in the form of a body, hanging from a yellow noose."

sented "probably . . . decorative or pubic hair, depending on what one decides it looks like to him." [2] Asked as to the particular expression and protest intended to be conveyed, the witness said that perhaps the penis represents the sexual act, which by some standards is considered an aggressive act; that organized religion is also symbolized by the figure, which seems to suggest that organized religion is supporting the aggressive acts suggested.

Only recently this court had occasion to give extended consideration to section 1425 of the former Penal Law and specifically to paragraph *d* of subdivision 16 thereof. In *People v. Street* (20 N.Y.2d 231, revd. 394 U.S. 576, *supra*) we affirmed the conviction of a defendant who, upon hearing of the shooting of the civil rights leader James Meredith, took an American flag to a street corner, burned it, saying, "We don't need no damn flag," and made other statements to people who gathered to watch these actions, one of these being the arresting policeman, to whom defendant said: "If they let that happen to Meredith, we don't need an American flag." The crux of the defense was that defendant's acts and speech were proper forms of protest legitimized by the First Amendment. Synopsizing Chief Judge FULD's opinion upholding the conviction, we find the position of the court to be this: While nonverbal expression may be a form of speech within the protection of the First and Fourteenth Amendments, the same kind of freedom is not afforded to those who communicate ideas by conduct as to those who communicate ideas by pure speech; that the State may legitimately proscribe many forms of conduct and no exception is made for activities to which some would ascribe symbolic significance; that, in sum, the cases show that the constitutional guarantee of free speech covers the substance rather than the form of communication, but that if the substance is being conveyed by a form violative of the public health, safety or well-being, then the First Amendment protection is subordinated to the general public interest. With regard specifically to the flag desecration statute it was squarely held that it was a valid statute in that, regardless of the major motivating factor behind its enactment, there was a clear legislative purpose to prevent a breach of the peace; that the Supreme Court long ago in *Halter v. Nebraska* (205 U.S. 34, 41) stated: "[I]nsults to a flag have been the cause of war, and indignities put upon it, in the presence of those who revere it, have often been resented and sometimes punished on the spot." This court said that

---

[2] The "construction" was described in the majority opinion of the Criminal Court as " in the form of a large cross with a bishop's mitre on the headpiece, the arms wrapped in ecclesiastical flaps and an erect penis wrapped in an American flag protruding from the vertical standard." (53 Misc.2d 718.)

our statute was designed to prevent the outbreak of such violence by discouraging contemptuous and insulting treatment of the flag in public.

The Chief Judge's opinion then noted that concededly defendant's acts arose out of indignation and a sense of outrage; that the act was one of incitement and as such threatened the public peace, a result which the State is legitimately interested in preventing. With regard to Street's purpose—to express indignation and protest—the parallel to the case before us is clear. Here, the expression, if less dramatic, was given far wider public circulation and, in consequence, perhaps, a measurable enhancement of the likelihood of incitement to disorder, by the placement of one of the constructions in a street display window of defendant's gallery on Madison Avenue in the City of New York, and the exhibition and exposure for sale of the companion pieces in the public gallery and mercantile establishment within. Implicit in the invitation to view was the opportunity thereby afforded to join in the protest, or in counterprotest, with the consequent potential of public disorder; or so the trier of the facts could properly find.

The Supreme Court's reversal of *Street* (394 U.S. 576, *supra*) seems not to have questioned or disturbed the rationale enunciated here by Chief Judge FULD. The majority felt that since it could not be determined what part of Street's conviction rested on the fact that he was charged with uttering constitutionally protected words and what part upon his act of setting fire to the flag, the conviction could not be upheld. The majority expressly left open the question concerning the validity of the conviction insofar as it was sustained on the basis that Street could be punished for flag burning "even though the burning was an act of protest" (p.594).[3]

The dissenters considered that the few words that Street uttered were part of the act of symbolic conduct, from which they could not be separated, and thus posed an issue which the majority opinion should have met.[4]

---

[3] Thus, Mr. Justice Harlan, writing for the majority, said:

[W]e reiterate that we have no occasion to pass upon the validity of this conviction insofar as it was sustained by the state courts on the basis that Street could be punished for his burning of the flag, even though the burning was an act of protest. Nor do we perceive any basis for our Brother White's fears that our decision today may be taken to require reversal whenever a defendant is convicted for burning a flag in protest, following a trial at which his words have been introduced to prove some element of that offense.

(*Street v. New York*, 394 U.S. 576, 594.)

[4] The salient points of dissent may be quoted as follows: Chief Justice WARREN: "Since I am satisfied that the constitutionality of appellant's conduct should be resolved in this case and am convinced that this conduct can be criminally punished, I dissent." Mr. Justice Black: "The talking that was done took place 'as an integral part of conduct in violation of a valid criminal statute' against burning the American flag in public. I would therefore affirm this conviction." Mr. Justice

While it seems well established that a clear violation of a valid statute may not be saved on First Amendment grounds, it is necessary in this case eventually to reach a somewhat different question, which is, whether or not the act said to constitute the violation is tempered by the application of the First Amendment. In other words, while burning, spitting upon and stomping upon the flag are clearly and inherently disrespectful, do we reach a point where other acts may be performed with regard to the flag which do not so easily admit of the requisite contemptuousness; where the intent behind the act may be of the purest sort, but where the results of the act may nevertheless have the effect which, as Chief Judge FULD found in *Street*, the statute was validly designed to prevent — the arousement of passions likely to lead to disorder? Before considering that problem, and in aid of its solution, it would be well to examine several significant recent cases.

In *Hoffman v. United States* (256 A.2d 567 [Ct. of App., D.C., 1969]), the defendant, who was to testify before the House Un-American Activities Committee, upon approaching the House Office Building was arrested for desecrating the flag, in that he was wearing a shirt that resembled the American flag. He was convicted of breaching that part of the statute which proscribed defilement of the flag. On appeal to the District of Columbia Court of Appeals, Hoffman argued that the statute was vague, that he was entitled to First Amendment protection and that his acts did not constitute defilement since he undertook no physical destruction of the flag. On the vagueness question the court held that the statute admitted of that degree of reasonable certainty as to what could constitute a violation, so that it could not be said that a person possessing a reasonable degree of intelligence could not understand what conduct would be disrespectful to the flag and what conduct would not. The First Amendment argument was rather summarily disposed of, the court relying on the recently decided case of *United States v. O'Brien* (391 U.S. 367), a draft card burning case hereinafter discussed. Finally, the court held that wearing the flag, or part of it, as a shirt was a rather clear act of defilement in that the flag was thus dishonored; that the idea of dishonorment was the key to the question whether the flag was defiled. The court concluded (256 A.2d 567, 570)

that the use of the word "defile" in the subject Statute was intended to include public conduct which brings shame or disgrace upon the flag by its use for an

---

White: "For myself, without the benefit of the majority's thinking if it were to find flag burning protected by the First Amendment, I would sustain such a conviction." Mr. Justice Fortas: "Protest does not exonerate lawlessness. And the prohibition against flag burning on the public thoroughfare being valid, the misdemeanor is not excused merely because it is an act of flamboyant protest." (394 U.S. 576, 605-617.)

unpatriotic or profane purpose. It is our opinion that the wearing of a shirt which resembles the American flag, under the circumstances of this case, is a physical act which defiles the flag in violation of 18 U.S.C. §700. Such a use of the flag would "degrade and cheapen the flag in the estimation of the people, as well as to defeat the object of maintaining it as an emblem of national power and national honor." *Halter v. Nebraska*, 205 U.S. 34,42.

Similarly, in *People v. Cowgill* (78 Cal. Rptr. 853, app. dsmd. 396 U.S. 371), the California court affirmed the conviction of a defendant for wearing a vest fashioned from a cut-up American flag, in violation of a flag defilement statute, the court posing and then answering affirmatively the question left open in *Street* (*supra*), whether the States have power to protect the flag from acts of desecration and disgrace.

It is necessary to make reference, also, to the draft card burning cases of *United States v. Miller* (367 F.2d 72, *cert. den.* 386 U.S. 911) and *O'Brien v. United States* (376 F.2d 538). In *O'Brien*, the First Circuit held that a 1965 amendment to title 50 (§462, subd. [b]) of the United States Code, proscribing destruction of draft cards, was an unconstitutional abridgement of freedom of speech. The Supreme Court disagreed in *United States v. O'Brien* (391 U.S. 367, *supra*). The only dissent was that by Justice Douglas. The court, through Chief Justice WARREN, noted that the statute on its face deals with conduct having no connection with speech.

> It prohibits the knowing destruction of certificate issued by the Selective Service System, and there is nothing necessarily expressive about such conduct. . . . A law prohibiting destruction of Selective Service certificates no more abridges free speech on its face than a motor vehicle law prohibiting the destruction of drivers' licenses, or tax law prohibiting the destruction of books and records.

(391 U.S. 367, 375.) It should be noted that O'Brien publicly burned his card on the South Boston courthouse steps, a crowd having been attracted by his and his companions' activities. The draft card statute, like the flag statutes, had a legitimate reason behind its enactment.

One of O'Brien's contentions was that the action he took with his draft card was a communication of ideas by conduct and that this conduct expressed his position as regards the war and the draft. As to this the court stated:

> However, even on the assumption that the alleged communicative element in O'Brien's conduct is sufficient to bring into play the First Amendment, it does not necessarily follow that the destruction of a registration certificate is constitutionally protected activity. . . . a governmental regulation is sufficiently justified if it is within the constitutional power of the Government; if it furthers an important or substantial governmental interest; *if the governmental interest is unrelated to the suppression of free expression*; and if the incidental restriction on alleged First Amendment freedoms is no greater than is essential to the furtherance of that interest.

(391 U.S. 367, 376-377; emphasis supplied.) Of those requisites the flag desecration statute need only be considered with respect to the one above emphasized.

The discussion thus far enables us to reach certain conclusions. It becomes clear, upon considering Chief Judge FULD's statement in *Street* (20 N.Y.2d 231, *supra*), along with the authorities there cited, and the more recent cases discussed just above, that a person with the purest of intentions may freely proceed to disseminate the ideas in which he profoundly believes, but he may not break a valid law to do it. The flag statute has been repeatedly held valid from the *Halter* case (*supra*) on down, even through *Hoffman v. United States* (*supra*) and *People v. Cowgill* (*supra*), where the flag was not, in either case, burned, spit or trampled upon, but was used, in each case, to further political or ideological viewpoints by employment as an article of clothing. There appears no significant difference between those situations and the one we are here considering. The defendant may have a sincere ideological viewpoint, but he must find other ways to express it. Whether defendant thinks so or not, a reasonable man would consider the wrapping of a phallic symbol with the flag an act of dishonor; he would consider the hanging effigy a dishonor; and to a lesser and more debatable extent it might be found that wrapping the flag in chains, attaching it to a gas meter, and fashioning the other representations involved, were acts dishonoring the flag. The exhibitor who, as in this case, engages to join the artist in the commercial exploitation of the supposed expression of protest stands in no better position.

There appears to be one further question with respect to the First Amendment which the *O'Brien* court (391 U.S. 367, *supra*) was not especially concerned with, having found the draft card law based upon the valid reason that registrants should be required to retain their cards simply to facilitate administration of the act. This question concerns itself with the requirement in *O'Brien*, emphasized above, that the governmental interest be unrelated to the suppression of free expression.

The *Halter* case (205 U.S. 34, *supra*), at which any investigation of the validity of flag statutes must begin, was decided at a time before the Supreme Court was as concerned with First Amendment rights as it is today. Thus, the effect of *Stromberg v. California* (283 U.S. 359), the case cited by the majority in reversing the *Street* conviction (394 U.S. 576, *supra*), deserves consideration. Miss Stromerg [*sic*] conducted a daily ceremony at a children's summer camp during which the children raised the Soviet flag and recited a pledge of allegiance to it. The California statute made it a criminal offense to display a red flag (1) as a symbol of opposition to organized government, or (2) as an invitation to anarchistic action, or (3) as an aid to propaganda of a seditious character. Miss Stromberg was convicted under the statute, although it was not made clear which of the three criteria were involved in the breach. The court reversed on the ground that if defendant was convicted for flying the flag as a symbol of opposition, her First Amendment right to freedom of expression had been breached.

However, the statutes prohibiting certain kinds of exhibition of foreign flags, and statutes requiring the salute to our flag (cf. *Board of Educ. v. Barnette*, 319 U.S. 624) are clearly designed for no other purpose than communicative suppression whereas a flag desecration statute is aimed at keeping the public peace. While it is true that violations of the flag desecration statute will probably not occur apart from the expression of an idea, the prime reason for the statute was not to insure suppression of such ideas, but rather to insure preservation of the public peace. The *Halter* case (205 U.S. 34, *supra*) still expresses the law as rephrased in *Street* (20 N.Y.2d 231, 236, *supra*), where it is stated: "In any event, whatever motivated the Legislature to act, the statutory purpose is clear — it is to prevent a breach of the peace." Some enlightenment may also be gained from the implication to be drawn from the *Stromberg* case (283 U.S. 359, *supra*) that had defendant's conviction rested specifically on either or both of the statutory prohibitions relating to anarchistic or seditious actions, it might have been upheld. We thus conclude that the statute before us does not breach the *O'Brien* requirement (391 U.S. 367, 377, *supra*) that the governmental interest served by it must be unrelated to the suppression of free expression; and we affirm the lower court's conclusion that the legitimate public interest which the statute is designed to protect was threatened by the violation of which defendant was convicted.

Appellant's additional contentions are insubstantial and may be dealt with summarily. The statute is not unconstitutionally vague; and at least two of the "constructions" clearly cast the flag into dishonor. (*Hoffman v. United States*, 256 A.2d. 567, *supra*; *People v. Cowgill*, 78 Cal. Rptr. 853, app. dsmd. 396, U.S. 371, *supra*.)

Another argument is addressed to the factor of intent; but even if we assume that defendant had an honest political intent in exhibiting these constructions, or that he had no intent at all, that element is not essential to a conviction of violating a statute which is *malum prohibitum*. (*People v. Werner*, 174 N.Y. 132, 134; *People v. Kibler*, 106 N.Y. 321, 322-323.)

No less tenuous is appellant's claim of denial of equal protection, predicated on the provision exempting from the operation of the statute "a certificate, diploma, warrant, or commission of appointment to office, *ornamental picture*, article of jewelry, stationery . . . or newspaper or periodical, on any of which shall be printed . . . said flag . . . disconnected and apart from any advertisement" (former Penal Law, §1425, subd. 16; emphasis supplied); and equally insubstantial is his contention based on the grammatical imperfection apparent in paragraph *d* of subdivision 16, it being clear beyond dispute that "flag" is the intended object, as it is the explicit object of every other act inhibited by the statute. The judgment should be affirmed.

Chief Judge Fuld (dissenting). I cannot agree with the majority that sufficient legitimate public interest is served by preventing the sale and exhibition of works of art—such as those which formed the predicate for the conviction of the defendant Radich—to justify interference with his right to free expression.

The defendant was the proprietor of a second-floor art gallery on Madison Avenue in New York City. He exhibited for sale seven sculptures, termed "constructions," by an artist named Marc Morrel, in which the latter made use of American flags, or what appeared to be parts of such flags, in various provocative shapes and forms to express protest, particularly against the Vietnam War. (See *Life* Magazine, March 31, 1967, p.22.) The defendant was charged with defiling and casting contempt upon the flag of the United States, in violation of section 1425 (subd. 16) of the former Penal Law.[1]

At the trial, the Art News Editor of the *New York Times* testified that he considered the sculptures or constructions to be works of art, more specifically, a form of "protest art" which (he added) was in line with established artistic tradition. The defendant also testified; observing that this "protest art" was exemplified by the works of such artists as Michelangelo, Goya and Picasso, he went on to say that, although the works express a political viewpoint, neither he, nor the artist intended to defile or cast contempt upon the flag. It was his belief, he asserted, that the artist, far from intending to do so, was seeking, rather, to convey the idea

---

[1] Insofar as relevant, subdivision 16 of section 1425 (now General Business Law, §136) provided:

16. Any person, who . . .
    d. Shall publicly mutilate, deface, defile, or defy, trample upon, or cast contempt upon . . . by . . . act, or
    f. Shall publicly carry or display any emblem, placard or flag which casts contempt, either by word or act, upon the flag of the United States of America, . . .
    Shall be deemed guilty of a misdemeanor; . . .
    The words flag, standard, color, shield or ensign, as used in this subdivision or section, shall include any flag, standard, color, shield or ensign, or any picture or representation, of either thereof, made of any substance, or represented on any substance, and of any size, evidently purporting to be . . . said flag, standard, color, shield or ensign, of the United States of America . . . or a picture or a representation . . . thereof, upon which shall be shown the colors, the stars, and the stripes, in any number of either thereof, or by which the person seeing the same without deliberation may believe the same to represent the flag, colors, standard, shield or ensign of the United States of America . . .
    This subdivision shall not . . . be construed to apply to a[n] . . . ornamental picture . . . on . . . which shall be printed, painted or placed, said flag, standard, color, shield or ensign disconnected and apart from any advertisement.

that others were condemning the flag by committing aggressive acts in its name.

The court, in affirming the conviction, places primary reliance upon *People v. Street* (20 N.Y.2d 231, revd. on other grounds, 394 U.S. 576) in which we held that the State may legitimately circumscribe certain acts which are contemptuous of the flag. (See *People v. Street*, 24 N.Y.2d 1026, 1028.) However, there is nothing in our opinion in that case which suggests that the mere fact that a person chooses to express himself by other than verbal means removes him entirely from the protections of the First Amendment. On the contrary, we wrote as follows (20 N.Y.2d, at p.235):

> It is the teaching of the cases that the constitutional guarantee of free speech covers the substance rather than the form of communication and that the right to employ a particular mode of expression will be vindicated only if it has been outlawed, not because of any legitimate State interest, but solely for the purpose of censoring the underlying idea or thought.

In other words, in the absence of a showing that the public health, safety or the well-being of the community is threatened, the State may not act to suppress symbolic speech or conduct having a clearly communicative aspect, no matter how obnoxious it may be to the prevailing views of the majority. (See, e.g., *Tinker v. Des Moines School Dist.*, 393 U.S. 503, 505, 509; see, also, Note, 68 Col. L. Rev. 1091; cf. *Cowgill v. California*, U.S. 371, per Harlan, J., concurring in dismissal of appeal.)

Quite obviously, the act which was prosecuted in the *Street* case — the public burning of a flag on a street corner in a section of Brooklyn at a time when feelings undoubtedly ran high following the shooting of James Meredith — posed a threat to public order which the State could legitimately act to prevent. Indeed, in *Street*, we likened the public mutilation of the flag to "shouting epithets at passing pedestrians" (20 N.Y.2d, at p.237), a situation patently fraught with danger to the public peace. The same may not, however, be said of the art forms which the defendant before us displayed in the quiet surroundings of his upstairs art gallery on Madison Avenue in midtown Manhattan. In our modern age, the medium is very often the message, and the State may not legitimately punish that which would be constitutionally protected if spoken or drawn, simply because the idea has been expressed, instead, through the medium of sculpture.

Unlike the situation in the recent case of *Cowgill v. California* (396 U.S. 371, *supra*),[2] the artist in the present case unquestionably made use of the

---

[2] In *Cowgill*, where there was no showing that the use of a cut-up, mutilated American flag was motivated by a desire to express a particular philosophy or point of view — where, in other words, the display had no "recognizable communicative aspect" — the court held that no substantial First Amendment question was presented. (See *Cowgill v. California*, 396 U.S. 371, *supra*.)

flag for the purpose of expressing his political philosophy or views, his dissatisfaction with, and opposition to, the Vietnam War and other activities carried on by the Government. The challenged "constructions" were, in effect, but three-dimensional political cartoons. It is quite true that one's political motives may not be relied upon to justify participation in an activity which is otherwise illegal. But it is equally true that an activity which is otherwise innocent may not be treated as criminal solely because of its political content.

Subdivision 16 expressly exempts from prosecution the display of the flag in or on an "ornamental picture" and, presumably, this exemption would apply to other forms of art as well. It is evident that the only reason why these works of Morrel were singled out for prosecution was not because the flag was used in the sculptures but solely because of the particular political message which those sculptures were intended to convey. In a very real sense, therefore, it was not the artist's *act* of making use of the flag which is being punished but solely the *protest* or the political views he was seeking thereby to express.

I have spoken principally of the artist who made the constructions in questions. There is even less justification for proceeding against the owner of the gallery in which the works were being exhibited for sale, particulary in view of the absence of any proof that he himself actually intended to defile or cast the flag in contempt. Although it is true that intent need not be an element of a crime—provided it be considered *malum prohibitum*—this is not the case where the challenged conduct involves the expression of political views. The First Amendment is designed not merely to prevent prosecutions but to actively encourage and foster the free dissemination of ideas. Thus, even activity which is not, in itself, subject to the protection of the First Amendment may not be prosecuted in a manner which will have an inhibiting effect upon the free dissemination of ideas. (See, e.g., *Smith v. California*, 361 U.S. 147, 152 *et seq.*)[3]

In sum, I do not understand how it may reasonably be said that the mere display of Morrel's constructions in an art gallery, distasteful though they may be, poses the type of threat to public order necessary to render such an act criminal. This prosecution, in my view, is nothing more than political censorship falling far outside our holding in *People v. Street*. It should not be constitutionally sustained.

The judgment appealed from should be reversed.

---

[3] In the *Smith* case (361 U.S. 147), the court held that a bookseller could not be prosecuted for the sale of obscene material unless he was shown to be aware of the contents of the books. The rationale behind that decision—that absolute liability for the dissemination of unprotected material would chill the distribution of legitimate works which were subject to constitutional protection—is, it seems to me, equally applicable here.

Judges Scileppi, Bergan, Breitel and Jasen concur with Judge Gibson; Chief Judge FULD dissents and votes to reverse in a separate opinion in which Judge Burke concurs.

Judgment affirmed.

§1.1.3. *United States ex rel. Radich v. Criminal Court of the City of New York:* Free Speech Prevails

Radich's New York conviction was appealed to the U.S. Supreme Court, which affirmed it (Justice Douglas not participating) by a 4-4 vote. Radich thereafter applied for habeas corpus relief in the U.S. District Court for the Southern District of New York. After an initial procedural setback—and after having been unquestionably assisted by two cases that the Supreme Court had meanwhile decided, setting aside flag desecration convictions in Massachusetts and Washington—Radich was vindicated in 1974. In the opinion that follows, the court found that the New York statute, as applied to Radich, violated the First and Fourteenth amendments. Nearly seven years had elapsed since his arrest.

UNITED STATES EX REL. RADICH v. CRIMINAL COURT OF THE CITY OF NEW YORK
385 F. Supp. 165 (S.D.N.Y. 1974)

OPINION

CANNELLA, D.J. The writ of habeas corpus is granted. On May 5, 1967, the petitioner, Stephen Radich, was convicted in the Criminal Court of the City of New York of casting contempt on the American flag in violation of then §1425(16)(d) of the New York Penal Law, now recodified as §136(d), of the McKinney's Consol. Laws, c.20, New York General Business Law.[1] *People v. Radich,* 53 Misc. 2d 717, 279 N.Y.S.2d

---

[1] The statute, §136(d) of the New York General Business Law, provides in pertinent part:

Any person who . . .
  d. Shall publicly mutilate, deface, defile, or defy, trample upon, or *cast contempt upon* [the flag] either by words or act . . . Shall be guilty of a misdemeanor [emphasis added].

This statute, which finds its origin in the Uniform Flag Act, has counterparts in many other states. See, e.g., Rosenblatt, Flag Desecration Statutes: History and Analysis, 1972 Wash. U.L.Q. 193 (1972); Note, Flag Desecration: Illegal Conduct or Protected Expression?, 22 Case W. Res. L. Rev. 555, 556-559 (1971). Compare, the Federal Flag Statute, 18 U.S.C. §700 (a),

Whoever knowingly casts contempt upon any flag of the United States by publicly

680 (Crim. Ct. 1967) (2-1 decision). He was sentenced to pay a $500 fine or serve sixty days in the workhouse. On appeal the conviction was affirmed. *People v. Radich*, 57 Misc. 2d 1082, 294 N.Y.S.2d 285 (App. T. 1st Dept. 1968) (per curiam), *aff'd*, 26 N.Y.2d 114, 308 N.Y.S.2d 846, 257 N.E.2d 30 (1970) (5-2 decision). Petitioner then sought review in the Supreme Court of the United States. The Court, after hearing oral argument on the merits, "affirmed by an equally divided Court" the judgment of the New York Court of Appeals (Mr. Justice Douglas, although present for oral argument, did not participate in the decision). *Radich v. New York*, 401 U.S. 531, 91 S. Ct. 1217, 28 L. Ed. 2d 287 (1971).[2]

Immediately upon the affirmance by the Supreme Court, petitioner commenced the instant action in this Court seeking relief in the nature of habeas corpus pursuant to 28 U.S.C. §2241 *et seq*. On December 3, 1971, in an unreported decision, the Court denied relief upon the ground that the affirmance of Radich's conviction by an equally divided Supreme Court constituted an actual adjudication by that Court of the merits of petitioner's constitutional claims, thus serving to bar subsequent federal habeas corpus relief pursuant to 28 U.S.C. §2244 (c). The Court of Appeals for the Second Circuit reversed and remanded for a determination on the merits, finding that an affirmance by an equally divided Supreme Court did not constitute an actual adjudication of petitioner's constitutional claims within the meaning of the habeas statute. *United States ex rel. Radich v. Criminal Court of the City of New York*, 459 F.2d 745 (1972). In light of its decision in *Neil v. Biggers*, 409 U.S. 188, 93 S. Ct. 375, 34 L. Ed. 2d 401 (1972),[3] the Supreme Court denied certiorari, *Ross v. Radich*, 409 U.S. 1115, 93 S. Ct. 893, 34 L. Ed. 2d 698 (1973). The petitioner has been released on one dollar bail pending the adjudication of his claims.[4]

---

mutilating, defacing, defiling, burning, or trampling upon it shall be fined not more than $1,000 or imprisoned for not more than one year, or both

and its legislative history. H.R. Rep. No. 350, 90th Cong., 1st Sess. (1967); S. Rep. No. 1287, 90th Cong., 1st Sess. (1968) *with* the present New York formulation. See also, Smith v. Goguen, 415 U.S. 566, 582 n.30, 94 S. Ct. 1242, 39 L.Ed. 2d 605 (1974).

[2] The full text of the Supreme Court's opinion in Radich v. New York reads as follows:

PER CURIAM
The judgment is affirmed by an equally divided court.
Mr. Justice Douglas took no part in the consideration or decision of this case.

[3] In Neil v. Biggers, the Court specifically held that its earlier equally divided affirmance on direct appeal did not serve as an actual adjudication on the merits barring subsequent habeas corpus relief.

[4] It is now settled beyond dispute that petitioner is "in custody" within the meaning of the federal habeas corpus statute, 28 U.S.C. §2241 *et seq*. Hensley v. Municipal Court, 411 U.S. 345, 93 S. Ct. 1571, 36 L. Ed. 2d 294 (1973).

THE FACTS

In December of 1966, petitioner, the proprietor of an art gallery on Madison Avenue in New York City displayed in his gallery certain "constructions," comparable to sculptures, which had been created by an artist named Marc Morrel. These constructions were partly composed of United States flags or portions thereof, and partly of other objects including a Vietcong flag, a Russian flag, a Nazi swastika and a gas mask. Three of the thirteen three-dimensional art forms which had been displayed in the gallery were singled out for particular attention by the state courts: an object resembling a gun caisson wrapped in a flag, a flag stuffed into the shape of a six-foot human form hanging by the neck from a yellow noose, and a seven-foot "cross with a bishop's mitre on the head-piece, the arms wrapped in ecclesiastical flags and an erect penis wrapped in an American flag protruding from the vertical standard." [5]

At trial, the complaining police officer testified that on December 27, 1966, from a vantage point on Madison Avenue, he had observed the construction which appeared to be a human form hanging from a yellow noose in the window of Radich's second floor gallery. He further testified that upon entering the gallery the following day with a police photographer in order to serve petitioner with a criminal summons he had observed this construction, as well as the others. [6] There was no testimony adduced from any witness of disturbance or disorder in or around the premises of the gallery.

The petitioner and Mr. Hilton Kramer, the art news editor of The New York Times, testified for the defense. Both stated that in their expert opinions the constructions were, under contemporary standards, works of art. In addition, petitioner testified that he had not intended to cast contempt upon or show disrespect for the American flag by virtue of his exhibition of the constructions; that the constructions were intended solely to express protest against the American involvement in Vietnam

---

[5] People v. Radich. 53 Misc. 2d at 718, 279 N.Y.S.2d 682.

[6] The contents of the criminal summons which served as predicate for Radich's prosecution are as follows:

[T]he defendant did have on public display and for public viewing, the flag of the United States of America, in the following manner; 1 — in the form of a male sexual organ, protruding from the body of form, in the anterior portion of the body of the form and depicting the erected male penis, protruding from a form of a cross. 2 — the flag of the United States of America, wrapped in a chained bundle. 3 — [T]he standard of the United States on the form of an alleged elephant. 4 — [T]he Union of the flag of the United States of America, depicted in the form of an octupus [sic]. 5 — [T]he American flag attached to a gas meter. 6 — [T]he American flag wrapped around a bundle attached to a two wheeled vehicle. 7 — [T]he American flag in the form of a body, hanging from a yellow noose.

People v. Radich, 26 N.Y.2d at 118 n.1, 308 N.Y.S.2d at 848 n.1, 257 N.E.2d at 31 n.1.

and against war in general.[7] Radich further testified that during the exhibition of these sculptures anti-war protest music, audible throughout the entire gallery, was played from a tape recorder.[8]

Petitioner was convicted by a three-judge panel in the New York City Criminal Court. That court, Judge Basel dissenting, concluded that Radich had "cast contempt" upon the American flag by virtue of his exhibition of the Morrel constructions in violation of subsection 16(d) of former §1425 of the Penal Law (now §136(d) of the General Business Law). The court found the constructions not to come within the ambit of protection afforded to speech by the First Amendment, and that the state, by means of the statute and the prosecution of the petitioner, had properly exercised its police power to restrict acts which might pose an "immediate threat to public safety, peace, or order."[9] In addition, the criminal court rejected petitioner's contention that the statute was unconstitutionally vague, concluding instead that the offense charged was "malum prohibitum," no criminal intent to violate the statute was prerequisite for conviction.[10] Judge Basel dissented, finding the "casting contempt" portion of the statute unconstitutionally vague.[11] The Appellate Term of the Supreme Court for the First Department affirmed petitioner's conviction without opinion.[12]

On appeal, the New York Court of Appeals affirmed the conviction by a divided bench (5-2).[13] That court found the statute neither vague nor requiring a *mens rea* as predicate for criminal liability, and rejected petitioner's First Amendment claims as well.[14] The majority, impliedly accepted the constructions as symbolic speech[15] and, thus, finding them to

---

[7] Trial Transcript, reprinted in Appendix to Appellant's Brief in Radich v. New York, 401 U.S. 531, 91 S. Ct. 1217, 28 L. Ed. 2d 287 (1971), at p.82a.

[8] *Id.* at 80a.

[9] 53 Misc. 2d at 720-721, 279 N.Y.S.2d at 684-685.

[10] *Id.* at 721, 279 N.Y.S.2d at 685.

[11] *Id.* at 721-725, 279 N.Y.S.2d at 686-689.

[12] People v. Radich, 57 Misc. 2d 1082, 294 N.Y.S.2d 285 (App. T. 1st Dept. 1968) (per curiam).

[13] 26 N.Y.2d 114, 308 N.Y.S.2d 846, 257 N.E.2d 30 (1970).

[14] *Id.* at 124-125, 308 N.Y.S.2d at 854, 257 N.E.2d 30.

[15] The New York Court of Appeals stated:

The discussion thus far enables us to reach certain conclusions. It becomes clear . . . that a person with the purest of intentions may freely proceed to disseminate the ideas in which he profoundly believes, but he may not break a valid law to do it. . . . The defendant may have a sincere ideological viewpoint, but he must find other ways to express it.

Id. at 123, 308 N.Y.S.2d at 852, 257 N.E.2d at 35. And later in its opinion, the court declared:

be within the purview of the First Amendment, applied the analysis suggested by United States v. O'Brien,[16] concluding therefrom that the governmental interest served by the statute (the preservation of the public peace) was unrelated to the suppression of free expression and that petitioner, by his display of the constructions had dishonored and cast contempt upon the United States flag.[17] Chief Judge FULD, joined by Judge Burke, dissented.

> I do not understand how it may reasonably be said that the mere display of Morrel's constructions in an art gallery, distasteful though they may be, poses the type of threat to public order necessary to render such an act criminal. This prosecution, in my view, is nothing more than political censorship. . . . It should not be constitutionally sustained.[18]

The decision of the New York Court of Appeals was affirmed by an equally divided United States Supreme Court.[19]

DISCUSSION

On the instant petition, Radich challenges his state conviction upon the First and Fourteenth Amendment grounds, specifically, that: (a) the involved statute violates the First Amendment in that casting contempt on the American flag may not constitutionally be made a crimi-

---

While it is true that violations of the flag desecration statute will probably not occur apart from the expression of an idea, the prime reason for the statute was not to insure suppression of such ideas, but rather to insure preservation of the public peace.

Id. at 124, 308 N.Y.S.2d at 853, 257 N.E.2d at 36.

[16] In United States v. O'Brien, 391 U.S. 367, 376, 88 S. Ct. 1673, 1678, 20 L. Ed. 2d 672 (1967), Mr. Chief Justice Warren declared:

We cannot accept the view that an apparently limitless variety of conduct can be labelled "speech" whenever the person engaging in the conduct intends thereby to express an idea.

He thereafter suggested a four-pronged test for the analysis of governmental action in symbolic speech cases.

[W]e think it is clear that a government regulation is sufficiently justified if it is within the constitutional power of the Government; if it furthers an important or substantial governmental interest; if the governmental interest is unrelated to the suppression of free expression; and if the incidental restriction on alleged First Amendment freedoms is no greater than is essential to the furtherance of that interest.

Id. at 377, 88 S. Ct. at 1679.

[17] We thus conclude that the statute before us does not breach the *O'Brien* requirement . . . that the governmental interest served by it must be unrelated to the suppression of free expression; and we affirm the lower court's conclusion that the legitimate public interest which the statute is designed to protect was threatened by the violation of which defendant was convicted.

26 N.Y.2d at 124, 308 N.Y.S.2d at 854, 257 N.E.2d at 36.

[18] *Id.* at 129, 308 N.Y.S.2d at 857, 257 N.E.2d at 39.

[19] 401 U.S. 531, 91 S. Ct. 1217, 28 L. Ed.2d 287 (1971).

nal offense; (b) the statute is unconstitutionally overbroad and vague; and (c) the statute violates the equal protection clause of the Fourteenth Amendment in that it arbitrarily bars sculpture which casts contempt on the flag while permitting other forms of expression, such as pictures, photographs and cartoons which cast contempt on the flag.[20] As the Court finds the recent decision of the Supreme Court in *Spence v. Washington*, 418 U.S. 405, 94 S. Ct.2727, 41 L. Ed. 2d 842 (1974) to provide a workable framework within which petitioner's First Amendment challenges can be analyzed, it is content in the conclusion that the New York statute is unconstitutional "as applied" to Radich, reserving to later courts the resolution of the broader constitutional questions which have been presented.[21] See also, *Cline v. Rockingham County Superior Court*, 502 F.2d 789 (1 Cir. 1974).

In recent years, numerous courts, both state and federal, have been called upon to determine the relationship between statutes prohibiting acts of flag desecration and the First Amendment's guarantee of freedom of speech. Such consideration has produced diverse results, as both the state and federal judiciary have been unable to either agree upon the standard to be applied, or uniformly determine which conduct is to be protected and which is to be proscribed.[22] The commentators, on the

---

[20] Petition at ¶12. See also, Brief for Appellant in Radich v. New York, 401 U.S. 531, 91 S. Ct. 1217, 28 L. Ed. 2d 287 (1971), at 3-4.

[21] As the Court finds such an "as applied" analysis wholly sufficient to do justice in this habeas corpus case, consideration of petitioner's challenge to the statute as overbroad, as well as the other questions which he has directed to the statute itself, is unwarranted. Cf., Ashwander v. TVA, 297 U.S. 288, 341, 56 S. Ct. 466, 80 L. Ed. 688 (1936) (Brandeis, J., concurring). As the Court recently declared:

> [T]he plain import of our cases is, at the very least, that facial overbreadth adjudication is an exception to our traditional rules of practice and that its function, a limited one at the outset, attenuates as the otherwise unprotected behavior that it forbids the State to sanction moves from "pure speech" towards conduct and that conduct — even if expressive — falls within the scope of otherwise valid criminal laws that reflect legitimate state interests in maintaining comprehensive controls overharmful, constitutionally unprotected conduct. Although such laws, if too broadly worded, may deter protected speech to some unknown extent, there comes a point where that effect — at best a prediction — cannot, with confidence, justify invalidating a statute on its face and so prohibiting a State from enforcing the statute against conduct that is admittedly within its power to proscribe. . . . To put the matter another way, particularly where conduct and not merely speech is involved, we believe that the overbreadth of a statute must not only be real, but substantial as well, judged in relation to the statute's plainly legitimate sweep.

Broadrick v. Oklahoma, 413 U.S. 601, 615, 93 S. Ct. 2908, 2917, 37 L. Ed. 2d 830 (1973). See also, Goguen v. Smith, 471 F.2d 88, 105 (1 Cir. 1972) (Hamley, J., concurring), *aff'd on other grounds*, 415 U.S. 566, 94 S. Ct. 1242, 39 L. Ed. 2d 605 (1974).

[22] See, cases collected in Mr. Justice White's concurring opinion in Smith v. Goguen, 415 U.S. 566, 583-584 n.1, 94 S. Ct. 1242, 39 L. Ed. 2d 605 (1974). See

other hand, while similarly unable to agree upon a uniform standard for balancing the guarantees of the First Amendment against the interests of the state in prohibiting acts of flag desecration, have almost uniformly opposed the imposition of criminal sanctions for conduct such as that engaged in by Radich.[23] Although the Supreme Court has had several opportunities in years past to consider and define the limits of the protection afforded by the First Amendment to acts of flag desecration, including the direct appeal of petitioner's conviction,[24] it was not until the term just passed that the Court provided direction for lower courts in resolving these controversies.

In the first flag related decision of the 1973 Term, *Smith v. Goguen*, 415 U.S. 566, 94 S. Ct. 1242, 39 L. Ed. 2d 605 (1974), the Court affirmed a First Circuit decision which had granted habeas corpus relief to a state prisoner who had been convicted of violating a Massachusetts statute making it a crime to "treat contemptuously" the flag of the United States. The district court [25] and the court of appeals [26] had concluded that the contempt provision of the Massachusetts flag misuse statute was both unconstitutionally vague and impermissibly overbroad. The Supreme Court affirmed on vagueness grounds alone, finding that the statute failed to draw reasonably clear lines between the kinds of nonceremonial

---

also, cases collected in People v. Vaughan, 514 P.2d 1318, 1320 nn. 2 and 3 (Sup. Ct. Colo. 1973); State v. Farrell, 209 N.W.2d 103, 105-106 (Sup. Ct. Iowa 1973) and Nimmer, The Meaning of Symbolic Speech under the First Amendment, 21 U.C.L.A. L. Rev. 29, 48 nn.73-74 (1973) [hereinafter "Nimmer"].

[23] See, e.g., T. Emerson, The System of Freedom of Expression 88 (1970); Nimmer, *supra*; Rosenblatt, *supra* note 1; Mittlebeeler, Flag Profanation and the Law, 60 Ky. L.J. 885 (1972); Comment, Flag Desecration as Constitutionally Protected Symbolic Speech, 56 Iowa L. Rev. 614 (1971); Comment, Flag Desecration Statutes in Light of United States v. O'Brien and the First Amendment, 32 U. Pitt. L. Rev. 513 (1971); Comment, New York Flag Desecration Statute — Abridgement of First Amendment Rights — Symbolic Protest through Artistic Expression, 16 N.Y.L.F. 493 (1970); Note, 22 Case W. Res. L. Rev. 555, *supra* note 1; Note, Flag Desecration Under the First Amendment: Conduct or Speech, 32 Ohio St. L. J. 119 (1971); Note, Freedom of Speech and Symbolic Conduct: The Crime of Flag Desecration, 12 Ariz. L. Rev. 71 (1970); Note, Flag Burning, Flag Waving and the Law, 4 Valparaiso U. L. Rev. 345 (1970); Note, The Bill of Rights and National Symbols: Flag Desecration, 1970 Wash. U. L. Q. 517 (1970); Note, Symbolic Conduct, 68 Colum. L. Rev. 1091 (1968); Note, Constitutional Law — Freedom of Speech — Desecration of National Symbols as Protected Political Expression, 66 Mich. L. Rev. 1040 (1968).

[24] See, e.g., Radich v. New York, 401 U.S. 531, 91 S. Ct. 1217, 28 L. Ed. 2d 287 (1971) (per curiam); Cowgill v. California, 396 U.S. 371, 90 S. Ct. 613, 24 L. Ed. 2d 590 (1970) (per curiam); Street v. New York, 394 U.S. 576, 89 S. Ct. 1354, 22 L. Ed. 2d 572 (1969).

[25] 343 F. Supp. 161 (D. Mass. 1972).

[26] 471 F.2d 88 (1 Cir. 1972).

treatment of the flag which are criminal and those which are not.[27] Justice Powell, writing for the Court, specifically declined an invitation to address the substantive First Amendment arguments advanced.[28] Mr. Justice White concurred in the result; the Chief Justice and Justices Blackmun and Rehnquist dissented.

In June of this year, subsequent to its decision in *Smith,* the Supreme Court, in *Spence v. Washington,* 418 U.S. 405, 94 S. Ct. 2727, 41 L. Ed. 2d. 842 (1974), reversed the state court conviction of an individual who had

---

[27] Petitioner urges that this Court find the New York statute "void for vagueness," as well as impermissibly overbroad. While such a contention gains vitality in light of the Supreme Court's decision in *Smith,* but see, 415 U.S. at 582-583 n.31, 94 S. Ct. 1242, the Court does not reach the issue here.

In rejecting petitioner's "void for vagueness" argument, the New York Court of Appeals stated: "The statute is not unconstitutionally vague; and at least few of the "constructions" clearly cast the flag into dishonor." 26 N.Y.2d at 125, 308 N.Y.S.2d at 854, 257 N.E.2d at 36. The State, in response to petitioner's present argument, asserts that whatever facial vagueness might heretofore have plagued the statute has been divested by the judicial gloss found both in *Radich* and the subsequent case of People v. Keough, 31 N.Y.2d 281, 338 N.Y.S.2d 618, 290 N.E.2d 819 (1972). While it may be said that these decisions speak to the relationship between the enforceability of the statute and the constitutionally necessary requirement of a "likelihood of incitement to disorder," the Court does not perceive them to address the vagueness which might be found inherent in the statutory phrase "cast contempt." It is to this term that petitioner addresses his vagueness challenge and it is this question that the Court does not here reach, in light of the conclusion that the statute is unconstitutional as applied to Radich.

It should be noted, however, that the "treats contemptuously" phrase contained in the Massachusetts statute which was held impermissibly vague by the Court in *Smith* has been distinguished from the "cast contempt" language employed in the New York formulation. See, e.g., State v. Royal, 305 A.2d 676, 679 (Sup. Ct. N.H. 1973) (discussed in Mr. Justice White's concurring opinion in Smith v. Goguen, 415 U.S. at 588-589 n.3, 94 S. Ct. 1242; but see, Commonwealth v. Young, 325 A.2d 315 (Pa. Super. 1974) (declaring unconstitutional a Pennsylvania statute worded identically to that of New York).

Additionally, it may be said that the New York statute retains vitality as presently formulated and as construed by the cases in certain limited instances. For example, in the case of Van Slyke v. State, 489 S.W.2d 590 (Tex. Cr. App. 1973), *appeal dismissed,* 418 U.S. 907, 94 S. Ct. 3198, 41 L. Ed. 2d 1154 (1974), the defendant was convicted under the Texas flag desecration statute for purporting to masturbate into the American flag while seated on a raised platform in the commons room at Rice University, at a time when numerous persons were present, one of whom attempted to physically take the flag from Van Slyke. Cases embracing facts of this sort well comport with the analysis set forth in the ensuing paragraphs of this decision and present the type of conduct against which the state may justifiably act; breach of the peace may well be perceived as imminent in such circumstances.

[28] 415 U.S. at 582-583 n.32, 94 S. Ct. 1242. Justices White, Blackmun and Rehnquist discussed the First Amendment issues in their separate opinions, 415 U.S. at 583, 590 and 591, 94 S. Ct. 1242.

been found guilty of violating a Washington statute proscribing improper uses of the flag. Spence, a college student, had hung a United States flag from his apartment house window. The flag was in an upside down position and had attached upon both of its sides a peace symbol fashioned of removable black tape. At trial, Spence testified that he had put the symbol on the flag in protest against the then recent invasion of Cambodia by United States forces and the killings at Kent State University. It was conceded by the state that the sole reason for the arrest was his placing of the peace symbol on the flag and exposing it to public view in that condition. The Supreme Court, in a per curiam opinion (three Justices dissenting), reversed the conviction. The Court found that Spence's use of the flag constituted the expression of an idea through activity, and that his conduct was sufficiently imbued with cummunicative elements as to bring it within the ambit of speech protected by the First Amendment. The Court then held that no state interest which arguably supported the prosecution had been sufficiently impaired by Spence's activity as to warrant the imposition of criminal sanctions. Hence, the Court in *Spence* may be said to have adopted a two-step analysis. First, a determination of whether flag related conduct is within the protections of the First Amendment, and, second, whether, upon the record of the given case, the interests advanced by the state are so substantial as to justify infringement of constitutional rights. Mr. Justice Blackmun concurred in the result and Mr. Justice Douglas separately concurred for reasons advanced by the Supreme Court of Iowa in *State v. Kool*, 212 N.W.2d 518 (1973).

In addition to the decisions in *Smith* and *Spence*, the Supreme Court, during the 1973 Term, summarily disposed of five other appeals involving the flag and its relationship with the First Amendment.[29] Several of these summary decisions involved convictions pursuant to statutes similar to that at bar and the action of the Supreme Court with respect to these cases, when read together with the decision in *Spence*, well illuminates the path upon which this Court will now travel.

SYMBOLIC SPEECH

In Spence, the Court recognized that certain "activity [is] sufficiently imbued with elements of communication [as] to fall within the

---

[29] Heffernan v. Thomas, 418 U.S. 908, 94 S. Ct. 3199, 41 L. Ed. 2d 1154 (1974), *vacating and remanding*, 473 F.2d 478 (2 Cir. 1973); Van Slyke v. Texas, 418 U.S. 907, 94 S. Ct. 3198, 41 L. Ed. 2d 1154 (1974), *dismissing appeal from*, 489 S.W.2d 590 (Tex. Cr. App. 1973); Sutherland v. Illinois, 418 U.S. 907, 94 S. Ct. 3198, 41 L. Ed. 2d 1154 (1974), *vacating and remanding*, 9 Ill. App. 3d 824, 292 N.E.2d 746 (1973); Farrell v. Iowa, 418 U.S. 907, 94 S. Ct. 3198, 41 L. Ed. 2d 1154 (1974), *vacating and remanding*, 209 N.W.2d 103 (Sup. Ct. Iowa 1973); Cahn v. Long Island Vietnam Moratorium Committee, 418 U.S. 906, 94 S. Ct. 3197, 41 L. Ed. 2d 1153 (1974), *aff'g.*, 437 F.2d 344 (2 Cir. 1970).

scope of the First and Fourteenth Amendments. . . ."[30] At the same time, the Court reiterated that " '[w]e cannot accept the view that an apparently limitless variety of conduct can be labeled "speech" whenever the person engaging in the conduct intends thereby to express an idea.' " [31] Thus, as point of departure for this Court's analysis of the constitutionality of petitioner's state court conviction, it must be determined whether or not his exhibition of the Morrel constructions is entitled to protection under the First Amendment. Such determination is to be made by objectively viewing "the nature of [petioner's] activity, combined with the factual context and environment in which it was undertaken;" [32] a standard requiring "intent to convey a particularized message" and, from the surrounding circumstances a "likelihood . . . that the message would be understood by those who viewed it." [33] That petitioner's display of the Morrel constructions was symbolic speech, that is non-verbal communicative conduct or expression intended to espouse an idea or express a certain viewpoint, is, when viewed both with regard to the symbol employed and the context in which that symbol was so employed, plainly apparent to this Court.[34]

---

[30] 418 U.S. at 409, 94 S. Ct. at 2730.

[31] *Id.*

[32] *Id.*

[33] *Id.*

[T]he following criteria seem helpful in defining the symbolic conduct. First, the conduct should be assertive in nature. This will generally mean that the conduct is a departure from the actor's normal activities and cannot adequately be explained unless a desire to communicate is presumed. Second, the actor must have reason to expect that his audience will recognize his conduct as communication. Third, communicative value does not depend on whether the idea sought to be expressed can be verbalized. The symbolism or medium may be an idea in itself.

Note, 68 Colum. L. Rev., *supra* note 23, at 1117. See also, Smith v. United States, 502 F.2d 512 (5 Cir. 1974); Nimmer at 37 ("[S]ymbolic speech requires not merely that given conduct results in a meaning effect, but that the actor causing such conduct must intend such a meaning effect by his conduct."); Comment, 56 Iowa L. Rev., *supra* note 23, at 620-621. Compare, United States v. Donner, 497 F.2d 184 (7 Cir. 1974), *petition for cert. filed,* 43 U.S.L.W. 3095 (July 9, 1974) (No. 74-98).

[34] The display of the Morrel constructions was so "closely akin to 'pure speech'" because of the artistic, political and controversial significance of the sculptures, that had this case not been presented to the State Courts as a "symbolic speech" case and this Court now free to write upon a *tabula rasa,* the Court might well be persuaded to analyze Radich's activity in terms of "pure speech" alone. Such analysis notwithstanding, the Court here applies a symbolic speech analysis "with the realization that if the statute cannot meet those standards for constitutionality, it is a fortiori unconstitutional if viewed as affecting pure speech." Goguen v. Smith, 471 F.2d at 100 n.18 (citing Tinker v. Des Moines School District, 393 U.S. 503, 89 S. Ct. 733, 21 L. Ed. 2d 731 (1969)). As one commentator has stated: "Displaying art, no matter how repulsive, is nothing if it

The American flag has long been recognized as a symbol possessed of a "very special meaning." [35] As was stated in *Spence*:

> The Court for decades has recognized the communicative connotations of the use of flags. . . . In many of their uses flags are a form of symbolism comprising a "primitive but effective way of communicating ideas . . . ," and "a shortcut from mind to mind." [Citations omitted][36]

Other federal courts which have considered the symbolic nature of the American flag have been eloquent in defining its expressive qualities,[37] and this Court need not engage in lengthy discourse upon the symbolic character of the flag as it finds the communicative qualities of our national standard to be as well recognized as they are obvious. Indeed, as Chief Judge Coffin has noted, were the flag not possessed of such com-

---

is not communication. The artist who uses the flag does so precisely because of what its symbolism will call up in the minds of those who study his *work*," Note, 32 Ohio St. L.J., *supra* note 23, at 146. See also, Rosenblatt, *supra* note 1, at 219-223 (discussing flag related conduct as art).

[35] Goguen v. Smith, 471 F.2d at 99. See also, West Virginia State Bd. of Educ. v. Barnette, 319 U.S. 624, 632-633, 63 S. Ct. 1178, 87 L. Ed. 1628 (1943); Mittlebeeler, *supra* note 23, at 924.

[36] 418 U.S. at 410, 94 S. Ct. at 2730 (quoting from *Barnette* 319 U.S. at 632, 63 S. Ct. 1178, 87 L. Ed. 1628).

As Mr. Justice White declared in his concurring opinion in *Smith*, 415 U.S. at 587, 94 S. Ct. at 1254: "One need not explain fully a phenomenon to recognize its existence and in this case to concede that the flag is an important symbol of nationhood and unity, created by the nation and endowed with certain attributes." See also, Mr. Justice Rehnquist's dissenting opinion in *Smith*, 415 U.S. at 601-603, 94 S. Ct. 1242.

[37] [W]e think it is self-evident that most, if not all, conduct associated with the United States flag is symbolic speech. Such conduct is normally engaged in with the intent to express some idea. Further, such conduct is invariably successful in communicating the idea. There is nothing equivocal about a flag-draped casket or a flag flying at half-mast at the death of a dignitary. Nor in this day and time is anyone likely to mistake the nature of the ideas expressed by a young person who desecrates his country's flag at an anti-war gathering.

Crosson v. Silver, 319 F. Supp. 1084, 1086 (D. Ariz. 1970) (three-judge court).

As the three-judge court in Parker v. Morgan, 322 F. Supp. 585, 588 (W.D.N.C. 1971) stated,

> If the flag says anything at all, and we agree it often may in a given context, we think it says everything and is big enough to symbolize the variant viewpoints of a Dr. Spock and a General Westmoreland. With fine impartiality the flag may head up a peace parade and at the same time and place fly over a platoon of soldiers assigned to guard it.
> . . . Sometimes the flag represents government. Sometimes it may represent opposition to government. Always it represents America — in all its marvelous diversity.

See also, Joyce v. United States, 147 U.S. App. D.C. 128, 454 F.2d 971, 973-976 (D.C. Cir. 1971), *cert. denied*, 405 U.S. 969, 92 S. Ct. 1188, 31 L. Ed. 2d 242 (1972).

municative nature "[i]f it did not speak by itself as a symbol of the United States of America, we doubt that any state would have sought to protect its message from verbal or physical abuse. . . ." [38] by means of statutes such as that now at bar.

In addition to the symbolic nature of which the American flag is possessed standing alone, "the context in which [this] symbol is used for purposes of expression is important, for the context may give meaning to the symbol." [39] In the instant case, the context and environment in which Radich displayed the Morrel constructions is revealing. He did so at the time of this nation's most significant involvement in the Vietnam conflict, as a means of signifying his dissent and protest against the American action. The playing of recorded anti-war protest music in the gallery during the exhibition further intensified the symbolic and communicative nature of the display. In such an environment, in the context and tenor of those times, "it would have been difficult for the great majority of citizens to miss the drift of [petitioner's] point at the time that he made it" by the display of the sculptures. [40] It must be concluded that Radich's exhibition

was not an act of mindless nihilism. Rather, it was a pointed expression of anguish . . . about the then current . . . foreign affairs of his government. An intent to convey a particularized message was present, and in the surrounding circumstances the likelihood was great that the message would be understood by those who viewed it. [41]

---

[38] Goguen v. Smith, 471 F.2d at 99. See also, Cline v. Rockingham County Superior Court, 367 F. Supp. 1146, 1149 (D.N.H. 1973), aff'd on other grounds, 502 F.2d 789 (1 Cir. 1974).

[39] 418 U.S. at 410, 94 S. Ct. at 2730.

[40] Id.

[41] Id.

[D]enial of First Amendment protection for communicative conduct unnecessarily alienates those who do not possess verbal skills. Implicit in the notion that the First Amendment gives a man the right to say what he wants is the idea that a man must be able to form his own beliefs and opinions, that he is to be allowed to express his thoughts and beliefs in his own way, and that any suppression of either the formation or the expression of these beliefs and opinions is an affront to his dignity. Perhaps the artist in People v. Radich who wrapped a construction resembling a dead body in an American flag had not the eloquence to express in words his disgust and revulsion with America and its participation in what he believed to be an unjustified war.

Note, 68 Colum. L. Rev., supra note 23, at 1107. See also, Emerson, supra note 23, at 88.

[U]ltimately it is difficult to avoid the conclusion that desecration of the flag, however obnoxious it may be to some of us, is realistically intended as expression and nothing else. It should therefore be treated as such. For those who may be shocked by this conclusion it is well to remember that loyalty to the flag, like loyalty to the country, cannot be coerced.

Petitioner's display of the Morrel constructions was, therefore, symbolic speech "of a nature closely akin to 'pure speech,' " hence embued with the protections of the First Amendment.

THE INTERESTS OF THE STATE OF NEW YORK

Having thus concluded that petitioner's exhibition of the sculptures constituted speech and communicative expression coming within the purview of the First Amendment, the Court next turns to consider those state interests which might be advanced to support his conviction and the resulting suppression of expression. In *Spence*, the Court, drawing upon its earlier opinion in *Street v. New York*,[42] addressed itself to three principal interests which conceivably could be called upon to justify state action against flag desecration: (1) prevention of breach of the peace; (2) protection of the sensibilities of passersby; and (3) preservation of the American flag as an unalloyed symbol of our country.[43] In addition to these three primary interests, the Supreme Court noted certain additional factors which are as pertinent to the instant case as they were to the case then before the Court.

> First, this was a privately-owned flag. In a technical property sense it was not the property of any government. . . . Second, appellant displayed his flag on private property. He engaged in no trespass or disorderly conduct. Nor is this a case that might be analyzed in terms of reasonable time, place or manner restraints on access to a public area.[44]

Similarly, there is no evidence in the state court record which would demonstrate that the flags employed in the Morrel constructions were other than privately-owned flags and, it is clear, that the constructions were displayed in Radich's own art gallery; upon private property.

PRESERVATION OF THE FLAG AS AN UNALLOYED SYMBOL

In *Spence*, the Court discussed the state's interest in preserving the flag "as an unalloyed symbol of our country" in the following terms:

> Presumably, this interest might be seen as an effort to prevent the appropriation of a revered national symbol by an individual, interest group, or enter-

---

[42] 394 U.S. 576, 590-594, 89 S. Ct. 1354, 22 L. Ed. 2d 572 (1969).

[43] 418 U.S. at 412, 94 S. Ct. at 2731.

[44] *Id.* at 408, 94 S. Ct. at 2729. Compare the dissenting opinions of Mr. Justice Rehnquist in Smith v. Goguen, 415 U.S. at 591, 94 S. Ct. 1242 and Spence v. Washington, 418 U.S. at 416, 94 S. Ct. at 2733 and Mr. Justice Fortas in Street v. New York, 394 U.S. at 616, 89 S. Ct. 1354 *with* Nimmer at 52-53; Comment, 32 U. Pitt. L. Rev., *supra* note 23, at 523-524, "Many flags, however, are not government property, and the continued existence or non-existence of a privately-owned flag according to the tastes of its owner can have no imaginable relation to the inner working of government. The government interest, then, must lie elsewhere."

prise where there was a risk that association of the symbol with a particular product or viewpoint might be taken erroneously as evidence of governmental endorsement. Alternatively, it might be argued that the interest asserted by the state court is based on the uniquely universal character of the national flag as a symbol. For the great majority of us, the flag is a symbol of patriotism, of pride in the history of our country, and of the service, sacrifice and valor of the millions of Americans who in peace and war have joined together to build and to defend a Nation in which self-government and personal liberty endure. It evidences both the unity and diversity which are America. For others the flag carries in varying degrees a different message. "A person gets from a symbol the meaning he puts into it, and what is one man's comfort and inspiration is another's jest and scorn." [Citation omitted] It might be said that we all draw something from our national symbol, for it is capable of conveying simultaneously a spectrum of meanings. If it may be destroyed or permanently disfigured, it could be argued that it will lose its capability of mirroring the sentiments of all who view it.

But we need not decide in this case whether the interest advanced by the court below is valid. We assume arguendo that it is. The statute is nonetheless unconstitutional as applied to appellant's activity. There was no risk that appellant's acts would mislead viewers into assuming that the government endorsed his viewpoint. To the contrary, he was plainly and peacefully protesting the fact that it did not. Appellant was not charged under the desecration statute . . . nor did he permanently disfigure the flag or destroy it. He displayed it as a flag of his country in a way closely analogous to the manner in which flags have always been used to convey ideas.[45]

---

[45] 418 U.S. at 412-415, 94 S. Ct. at 2731-2732 [footnotes omitted]. Other Justices (and this Court were it not constrained by the weight of precedent) have taken the view that preservation of the physical integrity of the flag is a sufficient basis upon which states may act to curtail the exercise of First Amendment rights in the flag desecration context.

> I would not question those statutes which proscribe mutilation, defacement or burning of the flag or which otherwise protect its physical integrity, without regard to whether such conduct might provoke violence. Neither would I find it beyond congressional power, or that of state legislatures, to forbid attaching to or putting on the flag any words, symbols or advertisements. All of these objects, whatever their nature, are foreign to the flag, change its physical character, and interfere with its design and function. There would seem to be little question about the power of Congress to forbid the mutilation of the Lincoln Memorial or to prevent overlaying it with words or other objects. The flag is itself a monument, subject to similar protection.

Smith, 415 U.S. at 587, 94 S. Ct. at 1254 (White, J., concurring). See also, Mr. Justice Rehnquist's dissenting opinion in *Smith*, 415 U.S. at 591, 94 S. Ct. 1242, as well as his later dissent in *Spence*, 94 S. Ct. at 2733.

It is interesting to compare the analysis of the several Justices with the thoughts of Professor Nimmer, as expressed in the following passage.

> For Americans, probably to a much greater degree than for other peoples, the flag constitutes a sacred embodiment of patriotic sentiments. Is the preservation of the sanctity of this symbol a state interest which will support flag desecration statutes? Clearly this is an anti- not a non-speech interest. A symbol *qua* symbol is essentially a

In so assuming arguendo the Court stated.

> If this interest is valid, we note that it is directly related to expression in the context of activity like that undertaken by appellant. For that reason and because no other governmental interest unrelated to expression has been advanced or can be supported on this record, the four-step analysis of *United States v. O'Brien*, 391 U.S. 367, 377 [88 S. Ct. 1673, 1679, 20 L. Ed. 2d 672] . . . is inapplicable.[46]

Notwithstanding the fact that petitioner has been convicted under the New York desecration statute of casting contempt upon the flag, it can not be said that his display of the Morrel constructions exhibited the flag

---

component of speech. The fact that one entity *symbolizes* another (in this case a flag symbolizes the nation) means simply that the former carries a message of identification with the latter. To preserve respect for a symbol *qua* symbol is to preserve respect for the meaning expressed by the symbol. It is, then, fundamentally an interest in preserving respect for a particular idea. An act of flag desecration is a counter symbol, which may express hostility, or at least constitute a contradiction of the sanctity of the idea expressed by the flag symbol. A flag desecration statute is, then, in essence a governmental command that one idea (embodied in the flag symbol) is not to be countered by another idea (embodied in the act of flag desecration). That, of course, is precisely what the First Amendment will not permit. The Court in *Street* expressly held that "respect for our national symbol" is not an interest which may be protected against words that deprecate such respect. If the only governmental interest at stake is the prohibition of communications that deprecate respect for the flag, then it can make no difference that the message of deprecation is expressed by symbolic acts rather than words. In either event the governmental interest to be protected is not, in the *O'Brien* phrase, an "interest unrelated to the suppression of free expression," and hence must succumb to the First Amendment.

Nimmer at 56-57. See also, Comment, 32 U. Pitt. L. Rev., *supra* note 23, at 528; Note, 12 Ariz. L. Rev., *supra* note 23, at 85.

[46] 418 U.S. at 414, 94 S. Ct. at 2732 n.8. Compare the statement of the text *with* the views expressed by Mr. Justice Rehnquist in his dissenting opinion in *Smith*, 415 U.S. at 598-600, 94 S. Ct. 1242.

Other courts have also considered the state's interest in preserving the physical integrity of the flag, as well as the flag as a national symbol. Some have found such interest to be sufficient ground upon which a criminal conviction for flag desecration might be predicated; others have dismissed this factor as insufficient to warrant abridgment of constitutional rights; while still others, applying an *O'Brien* test, have arrived at diverse results, finding either that such interest was so inexplicably intertwined with the ideas expressed by means of the flag related conduct as not to form a sufficient independent basis for denying constitutionally guaranteed rights or not so inexplicably intertwined as to prevent its invocation. See, cases cited and accompanying text, Goguen v. Smith, 471 F.2d at 100 nn.19-21. See also, United States v. Crosson, 462 F.2d 96 (9 Cir. 972); Cline v. Rockingham County Superior Court, 367 F. Supp. at 1150-1151; Jones v. Wade, 338 F. Supp. 441 (N.D. Tex. 1972), *rev'd on other grounds*, 479 F.2d 1176 (5 Cir. 1973); Crosson v. Silver, 319 F. Supp. at 1087; People v. Vaughan, 514 P.2d at 1323; State v. Farrell, 209 N.W.2d at 106; State v. Royal, 305 A.2d at 680. The latter view is apparently that which was adopted by the Court in *Spence* and it is specifically adopted by this Court in the instant case.

in a fashion from which "it could be argued that it will lose its capability of mirroring the sentiments of all who view it." The constructions and their display would have been valueless as communication and meaningless as protest were the flag not invoked by the artist in the fashion and form in which it was. Unlike the flag which is burned, destroyed or otherwise substantially and permanently disfigured, thereby divesting it of its "capability of mirroring the sentiments of all who view it," Morrel's use of the flag simply transferred the symbol from traditional surroundings to the realm of protest and dissent.[47] This shifting of context did not rape the flag of its universal symbolism. Those who are accustomed to emotions of pride when viewing the flag atop this courthouse, might well have been moved to revulsion when confronted with Morrel's works in the gallery. Others, perhaps, were deeply moved and made proud of our "constitutionally guaranteed 'freedom to be intellectually . . . diverse or even contrary' "[48] when viewing the constructions; persons in whom the flag would otherwise stir no emotion. "A person gets from a symbol the meaning he puts into it, and what is one man's comfort and inspiration is another's jest and scorn."[49]

The quality of the flag as a symbol embraced within Morrel's sculptures was the expression intended by their exhibition. Unlike the consumption of the flag when it is burned as the *vehicle* for expression of an idea, the flag as displayed by petitioner in his gallery was itself the idea, the sine qua non for the artist's endeavors. The symbol was not consumed by the sculptures, but rather, flourished in all of its communicative majesty, unalloyed and undiminished. "It is the character, not the cloth, of the flag which"[50] the State of New York has interest in preserving and, here, the symbolic character of the flag was neither trammeled upon nor dimmed.

PROTECTION OF THE SENSIBILITIES OF PASSERSBY

The second factor which was stated, analyzed and rejected by the Court in *Spence*, "that the State may have desired to protect the

---

[47] The distinction made between flag burning and like acts and the display for which petitioner stands convicted is made for purposes of illustrating the closeness of the present case to *Spence*, rather than similarity to the usual case which arises under desecration statutes like §136(d) of the General Business Law. These views are not intended to express an opinion by this Court concerning the suggestion of several Justices, see, n.45, *supra*, that the state's interest in preserving the physical integrity of the flag is alone sufficient ground to proscribe mutilation, defacement or burning of the flag.

[48] Street v. New York, 394 U.S. at 593, 89 S. Ct. at 1366.

[49] West Virginia State Bd. of Educ. v. Barnette, 319 U.S. at 632-633, 63 S. Ct. at 1182-1183.

[50] 418 U.S. at 421, 94 S. Ct. at 2736 (Rehnquist, J., dissenting).

sensibilities of passersby," is similarly unavailing to the State of New York in the instant case.

"It is firmly settled that under our Constitution the public expression of ideas may not be prohibited merely because the ideas are themselves offensive to some of their hearers." [Citation omitted] Moreover, appellant did not impose his ideas upon a captive audience. Anyone who might have been offended could easily have avoided the display.[51]

Similarly, in the matter at bar, petitioner did not thrust his ideas upon a captive audience, but rather displayed the constructions in the privacy of his second floor art gallery. Nor can it be said that the construction which was displayed in the gallery window and visible to persons located on the street below was so unavoidable as to require its suppression.

PRESERVATION OF THE PUBLIC PEACE

In affirming the lower courts' conviction of the petitioner, Judge Gibson, speaking for the New York Court of Appeals, stated, "the prime reason for the statute [based upon the legislative history] was not to insure suppression of . . . ideas, but rather to insure preservation of the public peace."[52] The Judge concluded that

---

[51] 418 U.S. at 412, 94 S. Ct. at 2731. See also, Papish v. Univ. of Mo., 410 U.S. 667, 670, 93 S. Ct., 1197, 35 L. Ed. 2d 618 (1973) (per curiam); Gooding v. Wilson, 405 U.S. 518, 92 S. Ct. 1103, 31 L. Ed. 2d 408 (1972); Cohen v. California, 403 U.S. 15, 91 S. Ct. 1780, 29 L. Ed. 2d 284 (1971); Street v. New York, 394 U.S. at 592, 89 S. Ct. 1354; Long Island Vietnam Moratorium Committee v. Cahn, 437 F.2d at 349; Nimmer at 55-56; Comment, 56 Iowa L. Rev., *supra* note 23, at 626-627 ("this interest in protecting sensibilities is therefore neither frequently nor seriously considered with respect to First Amendment communication"). Compare, State v. Waterman, 190 N.W.2d 809, 812 (Sup. Ct. Iowa 1971).

The record discloses, nonetheless, that the government's interest in protecting the sensibilities of witnesses to the act who might be shocked by it is very real. As Mrs. Martineau put it, "I was more or less crushed." Alvina Fitzgerald, also a desk clerk at the hotel, testified: "It just made me sick." It is only a short step from this feeling of revulsion to an act of retribution.

[52] 26 N.Y.2d at 124, 308 N.Y.S.2d at 853, 257 N.E.2d at 36. Elsewhere in his opinion, Judge Gibson compared petitioner's conduct with that involved in the earlier case of People v. Street, 20 N.Y.2d 231, 282, N.Y.S. 2d 491, 229 N.E.2d 187, *rev'd*, 394 U.S. 576, 89 S. Ct. 1354, 22 L. Ed. 2d 572 (1969):

The Chief Judge's opinion [in Street] then noted that concededly defendant's acts arose out of indignation and a sense of outrage; that the act as one of incitement and as such threatened the public peace, a result which the State is legitimately interested in preventing. With regard to Street's purpose — to express indignation and protest — the parallel to the case before us is clear. Here, the expression, if less dramatic, was given far wider public circulation and, in consequence, perhaps, a measureable enhancement of the likelihood of incitement to disorder, by the placement of one of the constructions in a street display window of defendant's gallery on Madison Avenue in the City of New York, and the exhibition and exposure for sale of the companion pieces in the public

a reasonable man would consider the wrapping of a phallic symbol with the flag an act of dishonor; he would consider the hanging effigy a dishonor; and to a lesser and more debatable extent it might be found that wrapping the flag in chains, attaching it to a gas meter, and fashioning the other representations involved, were acts dishonoring the flag,[53]

acts which would arouse passions in the average man likely to lead to disorder, thereby warranting abridgement of petitioner's First Amendment rights. This Court finds that such a standard[54] which views the act of display as solely sufficient to allow for the imposition of criminal sanctions, apparently upon the premise that the act creates a possible or hypothetical danger to the public peace, is insufficient predicate upon which the exercise of constitutional rights may be chilled.

This Court has read and reviewed the transcript of petitioner's trial in the New York City Criminal Court and is unable to find in it any objective evidence whatever which would sustain the conclusion that a breach of the peace was either likely to occur, or an imminent result of petitioner's exhibition of the Morrel constructions. There is no evidence that any crowd had gathered outside of the gallery nor is there proof that any disturbance or altercation had occurred within the premises. The display of the Morrel pieces had been in progress for approximately two weeks prior to the time that the state acted, and, aside from an expression of outrage by one group which resulted in a civil law suit,[55] there is absolutely no proof of any reaction whatsoever by any individual who viewed the sculptures. Thus, as in *Spence*, the notion that the state acted in preservation of the public peace "is totally without support in the record."

There is no question but that preservation of the public peace is a valid interest which the state may invoke in order to justify prosecutions for flag desecration. *Spence* and the earlier Supreme Court case of *Street v. New York* so state.[56] Those other cases which have considered the validity

---

gallery and mercantile establishment within. Implicit in the invitation to view was the opportunity thereby afforded to join in the protest, or in counterprotest, with the consequent potential of public disorder; or so the trier of the facts could properly find.

Id. at 119, 308 N.Y.S.2d at 849, 257 N.E.2d at 32. Compare, the court's statement with Note, 66 Mich. L. Rev., *supra* note 23, at 1050-51.

[53] *Id.* at 123, 308 N.Y.S.2d at 852-853. Compare the text with Note 1970 Wash. U. L.Q., *supra* note 23, at 525-26.

[54] At what point, if ever, does a "reasonable man" break the law and breach the peace?

[55] United States Flag Foundation, Inc. v. Radich, 53 Misc. 2d 597 N.Y.S.2d 233 (Sup. Ct. 1967).

[56] 418 U.S. at 412, 94 S. Ct. at 2731. Street v. New York, 394 U.S. at 590-592, 89 S. Ct. 1354. Cf., *Smith*, 415 U.S. at 583, 94 S. Ct. 1242 (White, J., concurring).

of this interest have so concluded.[57] The commentators do not disagree.[58] Rather, the question at bar is to what extent must the state demonstrate the factual existence of this interest, i.e., how imminent must a breach of the peace be, before it can validly act to punish an individual for exercising his First Amendment rights.

Numerous courts have concluded, as did the New York Court of Appeals in *Radich*, that acts of flag descration are, of themselves, always so inherently inflammatory as to pose so great a danger to the public peace as warrants the state to act.[59] Other courts have adopted the view that an act of flag desecration standing alone is insufficient provocation to justify the imposition of criminal sanctions or abridge First Amendment rights; other objective evidence which demonstrates the imminence of public unrest or a clear and present danger that a breach of the peace is likely must be adduced before a state may constitutionally act in a given case.[60] A fair reading of *Spence*,[61] and those other cases which

---

[57] See, cases collected at nn.59 & 60, *infra*.

[58] See, note 23, *supra*.

[59] See, e.g., Sutherland v. DeWulf, 323 F. Supp. 740 (S.D. Ill. 1971); People v. Sutherland, 292 N.E.2d at 749; State v. Farrell, 209 N.W.2d at 107; State v. Royal, 305 A.2d at 680; State v. Mitchell, 32 Ohio App. 2d 16, 288 N.E.2d 216 (Ct. App. 1972); State v. Waterman, 190 N.W.2d at 812; People v. Cowgill, 274 Cal. App. 2d Supp. 923, 78 Cal. Rptr. 853, 855 (App. Dep't. Super. Ct. 1969).

[60] See, e.g., Goguen v. Smith, 471 F.2d at 103-104, *aff'g*, 343 F. Supp. at 165; Cline v. Rockingham County Superior Court, 367 F. Supp. at 1151-1153; Crosson v. Silver, 319 F. Supp. at 1088; Thomas v. Smith, 334 F. Supp. 1203, 1211 (D. Conn. 1971) (three-judge court), *aff'd*, 473 F.2d 478 (2 Cir. 1973), *vacated and remanded*, 418 U.S. 908, 94 S. Ct. 3199, 41 L. Ed. 2d 1154 (1974); Hodsdon v. Buckson, 310 F. Supp. 528, 536 (D. Del. 1970), *rev'd on other grounds*, 444 F.2d 533 (3 Cir. 1971); People v. Vaughan, 514 P.2d at 1323; State v. Kool, 212 N.W.2d at 521; State v. Kasnett, 34 Ohio St. 2d 193, 297 N.E.2d 537 (1973); People v. Von Rosen, 13 Ill. 2d 68, 147 N.E.2d 327 (1958).

As the Court stated in State v. Kool, *supra* (adopted by Mr. Justice Douglas in *Spence*, 418 U.S. at 416, 94 S. Ct. at 2733):

> This is not to say we are completely sure that no one would be violent. Someone in Newton might be so intemperate as to disrupt the peace because of this display. But if absolute assurance of tranquility is required, we may as well forget about free speech. Under such a requirement, the only "free" speech would consist of platitudes. That kind of speech does not need constitutional protection.
>
> . . . [W]e will uphold incursion upon symbolic expression on the basis of probable violence only when we are convinced that violence really is probable.

[61] Two of the cases which were summarily disposed of by the Supreme Court last term deserve special attention. The first, State v. Farrell, 209 N.W.2d 103 (Sup. Ct. Iowa 1973), involved the burning of an American flag in a dormitory courtyard at the University of Iowa in February of 1971, at a time when a crowd had gathered around the desecrators. Defendant was convicted under a statute almost identical to that at bar and her conviction was affirmed by the Iowa

have delimited the bounds of First Amendment freedoms, results in the conclusion that the latter view is the only one which is constitutionally

---

Supreme Court. That court viewed the several state interests asserted in support of the conviction through the eyes of an *O'Brien* test. It concluded "all of the above noted state interests heretofore accorded recognition, save and except preventing breaches of the peace, have been criticized or condemned both by courts and legal commentators alike." *Id.* at 106. As to the state's interest in preservation of the public peace the court stated, "The presence or absence of an actual peace disturbance is immaterial, since the physical act of burning a United States flag is conduct which could reasonably be expected to provoke a breach of peace." *Id.* at 107. The Supreme Court, 418 U.S. 907, 94 S. Ct. 3198, 41 L. Ed. 2d 1154 (1974), vacated and remanded the cause for further consideration in light of its decision in *Spence.*

The second case, People v. Sutherland, 9 Ill. App. 3d 824, 292 N.E.2d 746 (1973), involved the prosecution of several individuals under a statute identical to that of New York for burning a flag upon the lawn adjacent to the Federal Building in Rock Island, Illinois. After the fire had been started, a passing motorist stopped his car, double parked, and proceeded to stomp on the flag to put out the fire. The appellate court relied upon the state's interest in prevention of breaches of the peace and preservation of public order to sustain the conviction. It stated

> The defendants also argue that the likelihood of a breach of the peace was not established. We disagree. It appears to us that the desecration of the flag by burning it in a public place is highly likely to cause a breach of the peace. . . . Violence might have resulted in the case before us if the defendants had not been girls.

Id. at 827, 292 N.E.2d at 749. Again, the Supreme Court vacated the state court's decision and remanded the case. 418 U.S. 907, 94 S. Ct. 3198, 41 L. Ed. 2d 1154 (1974). It so acted both in light of *Spence* and *Smith.*

Although these summary actions by the Court are not to be accorded the weight of precedent, they are instructive and give indication of the Court's thinking.

> An appeal in which the Supreme Court vacates the judgment and remands the cause for reconsideration in light of another case is not considered at length here, for like many other types of summary dispositions, it is not a final view of the Court on the merits of the case. Nor do such dispositions have intrinsic value as precedent. But such dispositions do suggest an "out" for the Court in certain appeal cases that it would otherwise be obliged to decide summarily or hear fully. The use of an "in light of" reference is usually a citation to a relevant case, recently decided, and unavailable to the lower court at the time of its decision — such as a recent Supreme Court decision. A remand "in light of" such a case gives the lower court another opportunity to resolve the dispute before the Supreme Court is obliged to pass on the merits.

Note, Summary Disposition of Supreme Court Appeals: The Significance of Limited Discretion and a Theory of Limited Precedent, 52 B.U.L. Rev. 373, 420 (1972). See also, R. Stern and E. Gressman, Supreme Court Practice §5.12 at 220 (4 ed. 1969).

At the least, these decisions demonstrate that the rationale of *Spence* is to be considered applicable in desecration cases and, *Farrell* and *Sutherland* can be viewed, to a limited extent, as supportive of this Court's thesis that possible or hypothetical breaches of the peace are insufficient grounds upon which the abridgment of First Amendment rights can be justified.

sanctioned;[62] the state's interest in preventing a breach of the peace cannot be said to arise merely in its assertion.

As Mr. Justice Holmes long ago stated, "[e]very idea is an incitement." [63] So too, every act of flag desecration and every employment of the flag in other than ordinary contexts must be viewed as a provocation, a calling out to others to react and counteract, to express support or disdain. As every expression of ideas may not be trammeled upon in derogation of the First Amendment, so too, conduct regarding the flag, which is "sufficiently imbued with elements of communication to fall within the scope of the First and Fourteenth Amendments," may not be suppressed solely because it is done or because someone might find the act so reprehensible as to become violent. As has been stated:

---

[62] As Professor Nimmer has stated:

The state interest in avoiding violent and other unlawful acts is, of course, completely legitimate. But it is not necessarily a non-speech interest, in the sense of an interest unrelated to meaning effect, i.e., the content of the communication. In the context of flag desecration, it is precisely the particular idea conveyed by the act of desecration that it is feared will lead to a violent or unlawful reaction. Thus, insofar as the governmental objective is the suppression of the communication of an idea in order to avoid resulting violence, it is an anti-speech interest, i.e., an interest in the suppression of speech. Applying the foregoing analysis, it follows that if this particular governmental interest is focused upon, flag desecration must be regarded as symbolic speech. This, however, merely establishes that the First Amendment is prima facie applicable. As is well established in verbal speech context, the mere possibility that speech may lead to violent or other unlawful acts does not justify abridgment of that speech. But if such acts can be shown to be both likely and imminent as a result of the speech (whether verbal or symbolic), the speech itself may be suppressed. May it, then, be concluded that *every* act of flag desecration produces such likelihood and such imminence? Contemporary familiarity with all manner of flag uses, many of which might technically fall afoul of the flag desecration statutes, must surely confirm that not all flag desecration results or is likely to result in violent or unlawful acts. Even in its most provocative form, flag burning, there is not such certainty of reaction. Those in sympathy with the flag burner are as likely to consider his act a culmination of the festivities as they are to consider it a forerunner of more explosive conduct. Those who are offended by flag burning, if they happen to be observers, might be inclined to resort to violent retaliation against the burner, but judging from the not infrequent campus experiences of this sort within the past few years, such retaliatory conduct is very far from certain. Moreover, we then enter the tenuous sphere where speech is suppressed by the government in order to avoid threatened violence not by the speaker or his supporters but by a hostile audience. Though there are some older cases that support this approach, the more recent Supreme Court opinions appear to have narrowed this justification for the suppression of speech, limiting it perhaps to the "fighting words" context i.e., those words "likely to provoke the average person to retaliation, and thereby cause a breach of the peace." It is now clear that "fighting words" are limited to those "personally abusive epithets" which constitute "a direct personal insult." Expression of an unpatriotic point of view, no matter how offensive to the viewer, does not fall within the "fighting words" category.

It may be concluded, then, that the state interest in avoiding violent and other unlawful acts resulting from flag desecration in itself renders flag desecration a form of symbolic speech, and does not justify the suppression of such speech.

Nimmer at 53-55 (footnotes omitted).

[63] Gitlow v. New York, 268 U.S. 652, 673, 45 S. Ct. 625, 69 L. Ed. 1138 (1925) (Holmes, J., dissenting).

[A] function of free speech under our system of government is to invite dispute. It may indeed best serve its high purpose when it induces a condition of unrest, creates dissatisfaction with conditions as they are, or even stirs people to anger. Speech is often provocative and challenging. It may strike at prejudices and preconceptions and have profound unsettling effects as it presses for acceptance of an idea. That is why freedom of speech, though not absolute, *Chaplinsky v. New Hampshire* [315 U.S. 568, 62 S. Ct. 766, 86 L. Ed. 1031] . . . , is nevertheless protected against censorship or punishment, unless shown likely to produce a clear and present danger of a serious substantive evil that rises far above public inconvenience, annoyance, or unrest. [Citations omitted] There is no room under our Constitution for a more restrictive view. For the alternative would lead to standardization of ideas either by legislatures, courts, or dominant political or community groups.[64]

So too, New York's undifferentiated fear[65] that the display of the Morrel constructions in Radich's gallery might provoke a reasonable person to commit unlawful and disruptive acts is insufficient under the Constitution.

While it is not the duty of this Court in the present case to determine the extent of the objective evidence which must be shown before a state may constitutionally suppress an act of flag desecration, whether the anticipated disorder be imminent or probable or whether such potential disorder present a clear and present danger to the public peace,[66] the Court can unhesitatingly state that New York's unsupported assertion that a breach of peace might have resulted from the exhibition of the Morrel constructions, is not a permissible basis for imposition of criminal sanctions.[67] Where the constitutionally guaranteed right to freedom of

---

[64] Terminiello v. Chicago, 337 U.S. 1, 4-5, 69 S. Ct. 894, 896, 93 L. Ed. 1131 (1949). Compare, Feiner v. New York, 340 U.S. 315, 71 S. Ct. 303, 95 L. Ed. 295 (1951). See also, Hess v. Indiana, 414 U.S. 105, 94 S. Ct. 326, 38 L. Ed. 2d 303 (1973) (per curiam); Tinker v. Des Moines School District, 393 U.S. at 508-509, 89 S. Ct. 733, 21 L. Ed. 2d 731.

[65] Compare, Smith v. United States, 502 F.2d 512, at 518 (5 Cir. 1974).

[66] Compare, State v. Kool, 212 N.W.2d at 521 with People v. Vaughan, 514 P.2d at 1323.

[67] Several of the commentators have suggested that flag desecration should be viewed not as a separate crime, but rather as simply one degree or variety of the offenses of breach of peace, disturbing the peace or like crimes. See, e.g., Mittlebeeler, *supra* note 23, at 928; Note, 4 Valparaiso U.L. Rev., *supra* note 23, at 357-58. While such a view does not well comport with the position adopted in the opinions of Justices White and Rehnquist in *Smith* and *Spence*, see, n.45, *supra*, it is worthy of note in light of the strong position adopted by many of the other courts which have accepted preservation of the public peace as the sole justification for suppression of flag-related activity. The legislature of New York might well be advised to re-evaluate the present statute in light of such analysis or, at least, to make comparison of §136(d) with the federal statute, see, n.1, *supra*, as well as a form of statute which has been formulated by one of the commentators.

speech and the free dissemination of ideas, be they popular or unpopular, is to be chilled or abridged, the state must demonstrate more than a mere speculative or hypothetical possibility of disorder; it must present to the trier of facts objective evidence which would lead to the conclusion that, at the very least, a disorder was in fact likely and imminent.

> [O]ur task in a given case, and in this case, is to weigh the likelihood of violence against the right of free expression. The danger is that we will overuse "likelihood of violence" in order to be on the safe side. But the framers of the constitutional guarantees must have known they were taking some risk when they inserted the free speech clauses, for many utterances of unpopular ideas are fraught with the possibility of retaliatory action. . . . We must not water down the guarantees by undifferentiated fear or apprehension. *For our part, we will uphold incursions upon symbolic expression on the basis of probable violence only when we are convinced that violence is really probable.*[68]

Our Constitution and the guarantees which are embodied in it are the supreme symbol and law of our nation. Its values and meaning surpass all other symbols and law. In seeking to afford our citizenry the right to speak freely, to assert views which may be unpopular to the majority, and, even, to deprecate those symbols which others hold dear, the framers consciously chose to construct a society and a nation in which the free dissemination of ideas, the thoughts of all free-thinking men, even the smallest dissenting voice, might be heard without fear of prosecution. This is our birthright as Americans. The "freedom to differ is not limited to things that do not matter much. That would be a mere shadow of freedom. The test of its substance is the right to differ as to things that touch the heart of the existing order."[69] Although such freedom is not absolute, it may not lightly be abrogated.

The flag and that which it symbolizes is dear to us, but not so cherished as those high moral, legal and ethical precepts which our Constitution teaches. When our interests in preserving the integrity of the flag conflict with the higher interest of preserving, protecting and defending the Constitution, the latter must prevail, even when it results in the expression of ideas about our flag and nation which are defiant, contemptuous or unacceptable to most Americans.

For its own part, this Court does not subscribe to the views espoused

---

No person shall willfully and in public burn, trample upon, tear, or otherwise physically destroy the United States flag or the flag of this State where such act causes a breach of the public peace or where there is an immediate danger of such act causing a breach of the public peace.

Note, 22 Case W. Res. L. Rev., *supra* note 1, at 573-74.

[68] State v. Kool, 212 N.W.2d at 521 [emphasis added].

[69] West Virginia State Bd. of Educ. v. Barnette, 319 U.S. at 642, 63 S. Ct. at 1187.

by the petitioner by means of his display of the Morrel constructions, but his right to express his mind is guaranteed by our Constitution and, on the state of this record, the Court finds no cause for the state's abridgement of that right.

CONCLUSION

It is the opinion and decision of this Court that the conviction of petitioner, Stephen Radich, in the Criminal Court of the City of New York, as affirmed by the Appellate Courts of the State of New York, served to deprive him of his rights under the First and Fourteenth Amendments to the Constitution of the United States and that §1425(16)(d) of the New York Penal Law, now §136(d) of the New York General Business Law, is unconstitutional as applied to him.

Let the writ of habeas corpus issue forthwith upon the submission of an appropriate order.

§1.1.4. Ronnie Cutrone's Flag Paintings

In the early 1980s, artist Ronnie Cutrone executed a number of paintings directly on American flags. The late Morton Neumann, a Chicago collector who had purchased one of these, subsequently asked the artist whether his painting, entitled *Space Invader*, could legally be displayed in public. Cutrone, in turn, referred the inquiry to the Volunteer Lawyers for the Arts in New York City. The following response, prepared by legal intern Nancy Wein, summarizes the state of the law at that time:

Ronnie Cutrone asked us to respond to your inquiry of whether his painting "Space Invader" can be displayed publically. After reviewing all of the facts and examining a reproduction of the work, we have concluded that "Space Invader" can be displayed in public.

Most speech, including symbolic speech, is protected under the First Amendment. Freedom of speech is one of the freedoms most valued by the courts, and speech loses its protection only in extreme circumstances, e.g., if it is obscene or likely to induce immediate violence. Artists are protected under the First Amendment because speech includes all forms of self-expression.

The United States Supreme Court has laid down criteria for analyzing whether use of the American flag is protected or not under the First Amendment, i.e., whether such use is speech. (*Spence v. Washington*, 418 U.S. 405: a peace symbol superimposed on an American flag held to be protected speech.) These criteria include: (1) the nature of the work, (2) the context and environment in which the flag was used, (3) the intent of the individual using the flag, (4) the likelihood that the individual's message will be conveyed to the public and (5) the purpose of the flag desecration statute.

State and Federal courts have protected many uses of the American flag for purposes of art and social comment. For example, exhibiting a photograph of a nude woman draped with an American flag was protected (*People v. Keough*,

31 N.Y. 2nd 281), as were three-dimensional works of a flag in the forms of a phallic symbol, a flag in the shape of a human form hanging from a noose, and a gun caisson wrapped in a flag (*U.S. ex rel Radich v. Criminal Court of the City of New York*, 385 F. Supp. 165).

In our opinion, based on our examination of the foregoing decisions, "Space Invader" is a legitimate use of the flag. Cutrone intended to produce a work of art. Video games and missiles both are relevant to contemporary society, and Cutrone's work is meaningful because he incorporated these contemporary symbols into an image together with the American flag, a traditional symbol of the United States.

Furthermore, Cutrone's use does not conflict with the purpose of the federal flag desecration statute: he has preserved the flag as a symbol of the United States, the work is not obscene, and it will not incite viewers to immediate violence.

In our opinion, Cutrone's painting, "Space Invader," does not desecrate the American flag; it is a legitimate and protected use of the flag, and it may be displayed publically.[1]

That same year, the display at South Carolina's Greenville County Museum of Art of another of Cutrone's works, entitled *Fruits of the Spirit* — a work in which a Woody Woodpecker-like figure had been painted on an American flag — became the center of a local controversy. Following a series of protests by American Legion members and others, State Representative Dill Blackwell asked the South Carolina attorney general if he would give an opinion as to whether the public display of the painting violated the state's flag desecration law (applicable equally to the flags of the United States, South Carolina, and the Confederacy). The attorney general declined to do so.

Strong support for the museum and the artist's right of expression came from a local paper, the *Greenville Piedmont*,[2] which published an editorial asserting that the issue raised a constitutional question and that the painting was a protected form of speech. Of the veterans who demanded that the artist's work be removed, the editorial said:

[T]hey do not have the right to demand that his expression be squashed. Such an action is the rawest kind of censorship, which when once launched knows no bounds. No one is in a better position to understand this principle than the men and women who have taken to the battlefield to preserve it.

---

§1.1. [1] Reproduced from Opinion Letter, May 11, 1983. Prepared by legal intern Nancy Wein for the Volunteer Lawyers for the Arts, New York City.

[2] Nov. 3, 1983, at A4.

§1.1.5. *Latin American Advisory Council v. Withers:* A Mural Is More Than a Sign

In *Withers*, which follows, we find the artist appearing as one of several plaintiffs rather than as a defendant. Again the issue is whether a work of art—in this case a proposed mural "depicting the struggles of Mexican-American laborers"—is a form of expression entitled to constitutional protection. The court found that it was and enjoined the application of a zoning ordinance under which the community's officials had attempted to block the mural's execution.

LATIN AMERICAN ADVISORY COUNCIL v. WITHERS
No. 74 Civ. 2717 (N.D. Ill. Nov. 22, 1974) (mem. and order)

This action comes now on Plaintiffs' motion for a preliminary injunction to restrain Defendants from interfering with the painting of a mural and to prohibit them from using a city zoning ordinance to frustrate this artistic endeavor.

FACTS
The Plaintiffs include members of a community organization whose design is to promote Hispanic culture and an artist whom the Council has engaged to paint a mural depicting the struggles of Mexican-American laborers. To accomplish this end, the Plaintiffs leased the outside wall of a restaurant in Blue Island, Illinois and secured a grant from a state cultural agency to finance the project.

The Defendants—the Mayor, Building Commissioner, and other officials of Blue Island—have attempted to stop the Plaintiffs from going forward with their art work. The City Council of Blue Island on September 9, 1974 voted to deny permission to the Plaintiffs to paint the mural. The City Building Inspector originally told Blue Island police to arrest anyone working on the mural and, on September 12, he sent notice to the owner of the building that the proposed mural would be in violation of the Blue Island Zoning Ordinance of 1971.

Defendants' purported authority to prohibit this mural are city ordinances which regulate the size and location of signs. "Sign" is defined by Section 131 of Article III of the Blue Island Zoning Ordinance:

SIGN: A "sign" is a name, identification, description, display, illustration, or device which is affixed to or represented directly or indirectly upon a building, structure, or land in view of the general public, and which directs attention to a product, place, activity, person, institution, or business. It does not include any official traffic sign, emblem, or insignia of a nation, state, county, municipality, school, or religious group.

Sections 132 and 134 further define "sign" in subclasses of Advertising Signs and Business Signs. An "Advertising Sign" is defined in Section 132 as a "[s]ign which directs attention to a business, service or activity not necessarily conducted, sold or offered upon the premises where such a sign is located." "Advertising signs" in the zone where Plaintiffs' mural is to be painted may not exceed a length of twenty-five feet. The Plaintiffs' painting, however, is planned to be substantially longer than that.

DECISION

The Blue Island Ordinances regulating signs do not cover this situation. The Plaintiffs' mural does not "[d]irect attention to a product, place, activity, person or institution"; it seeks to portray an idea and it is exactly this kind of expression which the First Amendment protects from government interference. Defendants here are misapplying an ordinance which regulates only commercial communication and are threatening Plaintiffs' free exercise of their communicative right.

Under these circumstances, federal injunctive relief is proper to safeguard Plaintiffs' First Amendment rights from infringement by Defendants' ill-founded application of its zoning ordinances. Although Defendants state their intentions of testing the zoning ordinances in a State suit for a mandatory injunction compelling Plaintiffs to remove what has been painted from the wall, there were no State proceedings of any kind pending at the time the federal complaint was filed. As the Supreme Court reemphasized in *Steffel v. Thompson*, 94 S. Ct. 1209, 1217 (1974), it is the duty of federal courts to enforce constitutional rights and "[p]rinciples of equity, comity and federalism have little force in the absence of a pending state proceeding." Even though Defendants assert they have made no further attempts to harass or arrest Plaintiffs, they admit that "[t]here may have been some initial threats along these lines." A declaratory judgment of the ordinances' inapplicability and an order restraining Blue Island officials from using it to stop the mural will remove the cloud of illegality under which Plaintiffs have been forced to work.

Abstention, moreover, is inappropriate here. There is no ambiguity; there is no fair way a state court could construe this mural to meet the zoning ordinance's definition of a "Sign." In these circumstances a federal court may not shirk its responsibility to protect rights secured by the Constitution. *Kusper v. Pontikes*, 94 S. Ct. 303 (1974).

ORDER

Plaintiffs' motion for a preliminary injunction is granted. I declare that the Blue Island Zoning restrictions on signs do not apply to the Plaintiffs' mural and order the Defendants not to use those ordinances to threaten, harass, or, in any way, frustrate Plaintiffs from painting it.

So ordered.

§1.1.6. *Silberman v. Georges:* **Opinions, Even When Painted, Cannot Be Stopped**

Attempts to restrain visual expression have also been made with allegations of libel. Thus it was with Paul Georges' painting *The Mugging of the Muse*, a work that was indisputably intended to criticize the aesthetic views of several of the painter's fellow New York artists. Claiming that they had been held up to ridicule and scorn because what Georges had depicted allegorically was intended to be taken literally, the artists brought suit. A jury found in their favor, but on appeal the lower court was reversed and the case dismissed. The appellate court found *The Mugging of the Muse* to be nothing more than "rhetorical hyperbole." If such is not actionable when expressed through words, the court said, then it is no more so when expressed by visual means. The appellate court decision in *Georges* follows.

SILBERMAN v. GEORGES
91 A.D.2d 520, 456 N.Y.S.2d 395 (1st Dept. 1982)

Judgment, Supreme Court, New York County, entered January 29, 1982, unanimously reversed, on the law, and the complaint dismissed, with costs (one bill). This defamation case should not have gone to the jury, the "statement" made by defendant in his obviously allegorical and symbolic painting being one of critical opinion only at most and constituting no accusation of criminal or antisocial conduct. Further, the fair meaning of the picture does not exceed appropriate comment, nor was there any showing of malice whatever. In addition, plaintiffs were not damaged in any way by defendant's expression. It is to be noted that the trial justice himself had grave doubt, as demonstrated by his expressions on a motion to set aside the jury's verdict for plaintiffs, that a case had been made out. The difficulty was that, though appropriate respect was accorded the jury's function in deciding issues of fact, the court should have decided the question of law of whether plaintiffs had, at a minimum, presented sufficient evidence to raise a question of fact to go to a jury. *Steinman v. DiRoberts*, 23 A.D.2d 693, 257 N.Y.S.2d 695.

The instrument by which plaintiffs-respondents claim to have been libeled is a painting called "The Mugging of the Muse," exhibited [for which read "published"] before the Alliance of Figurative Artists prior to the commencement of this action. The plaintiffs and defendant, all three of them artists known in the world of painting, had been friends for some time. They had come to a parting of the ways as the culmination of a dispute over refinements of their respective views of aspects of their art. Against the background of this prologue, defendant painted the offending picture, and presented it at one or more showings, and also permitted its magazine publication, to — it is claimed — the injury of plaintiffs.

The picture shows an apparent attempt at assassination on a city street by three males, armed with knives, upon a barefoot woman, scantily draped in a red cloth, the appearance of which suggests that it might be a bath towel. This scene is observed by a blue-winged cherub, standing between a hydrant, from which is spewing forth a fluid of the same color as the towel, and a brick wall, the lower aspect of which is covered by a yellowish overlay. The only other details are a collared brown, otherwise nondescript dog confronting the attackers, and a bent stanchion bearing a "no standing" sign. A crepuscular background of purplish hue contrasts with nearer overhead lighting, suggesting a street corner lamp. The only clue found within the picture, which might suggest identity of any of the actors, is supplied by masks on the faces of the two "downstage" assassins, claimed by plaintiffs to depict them. Quite obviously the trial jury found by its verdict that this was so intended by defendant. Indeed, part of the evidence at trial had been that, at a slide presentation of the subject picture, the audience had reacted with a gasp of recognition when that slide flashed upon the screen. There is no serious question of fact that the resemblance between the masks and the plaintiffs was more than coincidental and that they were the persons depicted. Defendant avers that, in any event, the portrayal was allegorical only and constituted no more than an expression of opinion. Plaintiffs claim that, to the contrary, the depiction held them up to ridicule and scorn, that they had been equated with muggers and robbers and accused of criminal conduct, that their reputations had been impaired, and that they had been cast in a derogatory and socially unacceptable light. This does not comport with any reasonable interpretation of the evidence in the case. The picture, viewed as though written words, may be described as "no more than rhetorical hyperbole." See *Greenbelt Cooperative Publishing Assn., Inc. v. Bresler*, 398 U.S. 6, 14, 90 S. Ct. 1537, 1542, 26 L. Ed. 2d 6. And the very presence of the cherub and the bloody hydrant underscores the fanciful nature of the presentation.

For the purpose of this disposition there is no necessity to consider the question of whether libel may be committed through a picture as it might be via a writing. We assume that one may be deemed the equivalent of the other. The picture could not be intended, viewed by any reasonable person, as an accusation by defendant that either plaintiff had actually participated in an assault or related crime such as attempted homicide, or had any intention of so doing. It is undoubtedly an allegory in that it uses persons and symbols to convey a hidden meaning which must be extracted by a ratiocinative process, possibly entirely speculative. In its worst possible aspect, it accuses plaintiffs of engaging in destruction of something symbolized by the lady in red. In the context provided by the factual background and the use of the word "Muse," that figure could be representative only of the arts; therefore, the painting states that plaintiffs' artistic beliefs and activities are destructive of the arts. It says nothing more. Far worse commentary is written almost daily by newspaper and magazine critics of every aspect of the arts and is deemed to be no more than expression of opinion.

Further, there was no proof of injury to plaintiffs. The picture's effect might well have been extreme embarrassment, the probable result of any well-aimed critical shaft, but that is not cognizable injury. See *Salamone v. MacMillan Publishing Company,* 77 A.D.2d 501, 429 N.Y.S.2d 441. Nor is a showing of intent on defendant's part to assure that plaintiffs would be recognized as his targets indicative of malice; neither gross irresponsibility nor reckless disregard can be inferred from the fact that defendant, while in work on his picture, gave no attention to warnings that its characters portrayed plaintiffs. *Gertz v. Welch,* 418 U.S. 323, 349, 94 S. Ct. 2997, 3011, 41 L. Ed. 2d 789. The painting, viewed as though it were a writing, did not "expose a person to hatred, contempt or aversion, or to induce an evil or unsavory opinion of him in the minds of a substantial number of the community . . ." *Mencher v. Chesley,* 297 N.Y. 94, 100, 75 N.E.2d 257. No such inference was demonstrated. Indeed, special damages were neither pleaded nor proven in this case, nor was there a claim of libel per se, and, on this basis alone, it should not have gone to the jury. *Moran v. Hearst,* 50 A.D.2d 527, 375 N.Y.S.2d 113, *aff'd,* 40 N.Y.2d 1071, 392 N.Y.S.2d 253, 360 N.E.2d 932.

§1.1.7. Can the Visual Arts Be Social Commentary? *Georges, Salamone,* and *The Milky Way*

Following the publication of the Appellate Division's decision in *Silberman v. Georges* that the depiction of two men in an allegorical painting could not constitute a cause of action for libel, an article appeared in the Columbia Journal of Art and the Law entitled *Art as Libel: A Comment on* Silberman v. Georges. The article was coauthored by a member of the law firm that had represented Georges in the action and the author of an amicus brief submitted on behalf of the defendant by the Volunteer Lawyers for the Arts.[3] While largely an extensive review of the *Georges* litigation, the article is useful for the following history of art in the service of social commentary:

---

[3] Dorsen & McMahon, Art as Libel: A Comment on Silberman v. Georges, 9 Art & L. 1 (1984).

Throughout history, paintings have been used to advocate ideas, to make social and political comment and criticism, and to influence attitudes. Art has served to promote both the religious and political ideas of those in power. Michelangelo's Sistine Chapel frescos (particularly the effective and frightening *Last Judgement*) and Peter Paul Rubens' paintings glorifying the reign of Marie de Medici are but two examples of such art. Critical and social commentary also appears in the paintings of Hieronymus Bosch, Pieter Bruegel the Elder, Rembrandt, William Hogarth, Honoré Daumier and others. Picasso's *Guernica*, which hung in New York's Museum of Modern Art for many years, is a powerful expression of the horrors of war and a condemnation of those responsible for it; so is Francisco Goya's *The Third of May, 1808*. Goya also employed scathing satire in his unflattering portrait of *The Family of Charles IV* for the purpose of criticizing the policies and activities of the monarch.[4]

Other works of art, when challenged, have received the usual legal analysis afforded written or oral speech. *Salamone v. Macmillan Publishing Company*[5], a libel action in which an appellate court reversed a lower court and unanimously granted defendant's motions for summary judgment, is one such case. At issue was whether a cartoon parody of a fictional work in which a real person was labeled a child molester could be found to be libelous. Plaintiff Salamone failed to prove special damages, believability of the statement to anyone, or loss of reputation; hence, no defamation.

An interesting twist involving art as social commentary and a court's express decision to separate its personal opinion of a disputed work from its analysis of the law occurred in *Pillsbury Co. v. Milky Way Productions, Inc.*[6]

Milky Way, like *Georges*, involved social commentary expressed through image. The defendant in *Milky Way* published a picture of figures resembling the trade characters "Poppin Fresh" and "Poppie Fresh" engaged in sexual intercourse and fellatio in Screw magazine. Plaintiff sued for, inter alia, copyright infringement, trademark infringement, and the tarnishment of its advertising jingle.

While the court found that several of plaintiff's copyrights had indeed been infringed, ultimately it found defendant's unauthorized use protected by "fair use." In its analysis of the defense, the court found that rather than attempting to capitalize financially, the defendants were intending to make "social commentary."[7] It went on to say that "Al-

---

[4] *Id.* at 10 (footnotes omitted).

[5] 97 Misc. 2d 346, 429 N.Y.S.2d 441 (1st Dept. 1980).

[6] 215 U.S.P.Q. 124 (N.D. Ga. 1981) (BNA).

[7] *Id.* at 131.

though the portrayal is offensive to the court, the court has no doubt that Milky Way intended to make an editorial comment on the values epitomized by these trade characters." [8] Hence, the use of the visual arts as a vehicle for social commentary was again explicitly recognized.

§1.1.8. *Sefick v. City of Chicago:* A Blanket Snow Job

Whereas the preceding cases involved efforts to restrain visual expression under the color of one law or another, the *Sefick* case, which follows, arose from a virtually naked attempt to censor. At issue was a so-called installation piece based on a portrayal of Chicago's former Mayor Michael Bilandic and his wife Heather. In ordering that the City of Chicago honor its commitment to exhibit this work, the court had no hesitation in determining that it "constituted speech within the meaning of the First Amendment."

SEFICK v. CITY OF CHICAGO
485 F. Supp. 644 (N.D. Ill. 1979) (mem. and order)

ASPEN, D.J. Plaintiff John Sefick has brought this action challenging a decision by defendant Rose Farina to revoke permission to display certain of his sculptures at the lobby of the Richard J. Daley Civic Center in Chicago. Sefick alleges that the permit revocation violated his freedom of speech rights as guaranteed by the First and Fourteenth Amendments to the United States Constitution. He seeks both injunctive and monetary relief.[1] On the date the complaint was filed, the plaintiff moved for a temporary restraining order to compel defendants to display his exhibit. This motion was denied on November 21, 1979.[2] Thereafter, on November 26, 1979, the Court held a consolidated proceeding at

---

[8] *Ibid.*

[1] Federal jurisdiction against the City of Chicago, the Council on Fine Arts, and defendants Cummings and Byrne is premised on 42 U.S.C. §1983, and the jurisdictional grant contained in 28 U.S.C. §1343. The plaintiff also invokes the Court's jurisdiction under the declaratory judgment provisions of 28 U.S.C. §§2201-2202.

[2] By granting a temporary restraining order at that stage of the litigation, the Court effectively would have rendered the issues in this case moot. The plaintiff's exhibit surely would have run for its scheduled period prior to the time when the Court could have issued a ruling on the merits. Conversely, the plaintiff could show no immediate and irreparable harm so as to justify the extraordinary remedy of a temporary restraining order.

which the trial on the merits as well as an application for preliminary injunctive relief was heard.[3] The facts as developed at trial are as follows.

John Sefick is an employee of the United States Probation and Parole Office. As an avocation, Sefick has done considerable work in the art genre known as "installation" or "environmental" sculpture.[4] Since 1968, Sefick has exhibited his works in a number of public and private establishments throughout the Chicago metropolitan area.

On October 24, 1978, Sefick wrote to Rose Farina of the Chicago Council on Fine Arts concerning the possibility of exhibiting his work at the Richard J. Daley Civic Center lobby for an exhibition of his work. Attached to this letter of inquiry were a listing of Sefick's prior exhibitions and a letter of reference from Cynthia Alton Fielding, Assistant Coordinator of Exhibits at the Chicago Public Library Cultural Center.[5] Sefick included neither a picture nor a description of the tableau he proposed to exhibit at the Daley Center.[6] Farina, who wields sole authority for the scheduling of programs and exhibits at the Daley Center, expressed interest in Sefick's offer.[7] In September, 1979, she notified Sefick that space in the Daley Center had been reserved for an exhibition

---

[3] Fed. R. Civ. P. 65(a)(2) provides in relevant part: "Before or after the commencement of the hearing of an application for a preliminary injunction, the court may order the trial of the action on the merits to be advanced and consolidated with the hearing of the application."

[4] This art medium involves the placement of sculpted figures in tableaus. The figures may be made from a variety of materials, and may vary with respect to size, degree of caricaturization, and use of moving parts. Tape recordings are often used in these tableaus. It is common for such tableaus, both through the sculptures and recordings, to convey messages concerning social or political issues and events.

Sefick's numerous works are life-size, plaster cast models which usually are accompanied by tape recordings. Expert testimony by Jane Allen, editor of the New Art Examiner and an expert in Twentieth Century Art, established that Sefick's works are typical of the "environmental" sculpture genre.

[5] Prior to his contract with Farina, Sefick had written to Fielding seeking permission to display his work at the Public Library Cultural Center. Although Fielding rejected Sefick's request due to a limited amount of available exhibition space, she recommended that he contact Farina about obtaining permission to exhibit his work in the Daley Center.

[6] As indicated in Farina's testimony, the process by which exhibits are scheduled for display at the Daley Center is an informal one. There is no standard application form; artists merely contact Farina by letter with requests for exhibition space. Farina herself then determines what information she requires in order to render a decision on a proposed exhibit.

[7] Farina testified that although she may receive suggestions from Commission members or their staff as to possible exhibits, she alone determines which proposed exhibits are given space at the Daley Center. She further stated that no decision of hers ever has been vetoed by the Mayor or by the Council on Fine Arts.

of his work for the three weeks from November 5, 1979, through November 23, 1979. At no time prior to the issuance of this permit did Farina request further information concerning the nature of the tableau Sefick proposed to exhibit at the Daley Center.

Shortly after Sefick learned that his proposal had been approved, he provided Farina with more detailed information about the exhibits so that the Council on Fine Arts could issue press releases to publicize the display. Sefick notified Farina that a different tableau would be used for each of the three weeks of the exhibition:

First Week

A Judge and his Court. Three life-size plaster figures arranged in a court setting. A Chief Judge, court reporter, and clerk are about to bring court to order.

Second Week

A Chicago Transit Authority passenger rides a Chicago subway car. This is also life-size with a tape recording.

Third Week

A Chicago portrayal of Grant Woods' famous painting American Gothic in plaster. The life-size figures are contemporaries of Chicago Society. Husband, wife and child make up the setting.

In this letter to Farina, Sefick also observed that "[m]ost of his works have a critical social commentary to them." Prior to the date of exhibition, Susan Fastwolf, an aide to Farina, tried to obtain additional information about the exhibit from Sefick. Sefick, however, testified that at the time he had not determined many of the details he would add to the tableaus. Accordingly, he was unable to further supplement the information he had provided Farina. Neither Fastwolf nor Farina insisted on more complete disclosure of the contents of the exhibit; nor did they demand to view the tableaus prior to their public display at the Daley Center.

On November 4, 1979, Sefick set up his tableau entitled "A Judge and his Court" in the area assigned to him in the Daley Center. The display varied from the description provided Farina in that the sculptures were accompanied by a tape recording satirizing the court system. The exhibit, however, remained on display from November 5 through November 10 without complaint either by the judiciary located at the Daley Center courtrooms, the general public, or the Council on Fine Arts.

On November 11, 1979, Sefick removed his "A Judge and his Court" display and set up in its place a tableau entitled "Chicago Transit Authority." This display varied from the prior description in that it was accompanied by a title. The tableau was also accompanied by a tape recording satirizing the problems often encountered by riders of public transportation. This exhibit was displayed from November 12 through November 17 without complaint.[8]

On November 18, 1979, Sefick removed the Chicago Transit Authority display and replaced it with the tableau scheduled for the third week, entitled "The Bilandics." Sefick testified that not until the prior evening had he decided to include a tape recording with the exhibit. The sculptures, along with the tape recording, satirized the handling by then-mayor Michael Bilandic of the snow removal operation necessitated by the record snowfall that victimized the city of Chicago during the winter of 1979. The tableau depicted Bilandic seated in an easy chair with his wife, Heather, sitting on the arm of the chair. The tape recording continuously played the following statement:

> Heather, Heather, I think it is still snowing out there, Heather. I think it is still snowing. God, it must be around eight feet now, isn't it, Heather? At least eight feet. Maybe another log on the fire, Heather. Maybe another log on the fire. On the fire, another log on the fire, Heather. It is beginning to snow again. Another log on the fire, Heather. I think it is beginning to snow once again. My God, it must be eight feet out there now, Heather. I don't know what to do. What do you think we should do, Heather?[9]

Farina first saw the exhibit early on Monday morning, November 19. At the time, she had received no comments, positive or negative, concerning this tableau. Upon viewing the tableau, however, she contacted Sefick and informed him that it was unsuitable for display in the Daley Center and would have to be removed. Later that morning, Farina wrote a letter to Sefick reiterating her displeasure with the tableau and her desire that it be removed by the end of the day. Meanwhile, Farina placed a blanket over the exhibit to prevent others from viewing it.

In her letter to Sefick, Farina indicated that her decision to revoke the permit for the tableau display was based on the failure of Sefick to provide complete and accurate information about the nature of the display scheduled for the third week. In her testimony at trial, Farina noted

---

[8] On November 14, Sefick contacted Farina to inquire about the removal of the "Chicago Transit Authority" title from the tableau. Farina indicated that the sign had not been securely fastened in place, and she had removed it for fear that it might come loose and damage the sculptures. As a result of the conversation, the title was replaced in front of the tableau.

During the course of the conversation Sefick and Farina spoke about the progress of the exhibition. At no time during this conversation did Sefick provide additional information about the tableau scheduled for the third week; nor did Farina demand that she be shown the tableau prior to the public display.

[9] As reflected by Farina's testimony, many persons are of the opinion that Bilandic's handling of the snow removal operation contributed to his defeat in the Democratic mayoral primary in February, 1979. The Court, of course, expresses no view as to the correctness of that opinion.

three particular aspects in which the description was at variance with the tableau actually displayed: (1) there had been no prior indication that the exhibit would be titled; (2) there had been no prior indication that the exhibit would focus on a particular individual; and (3) there had been no prior notification that a tape would accompany the tableau. In addition, Farina testified that she found the tableau unsuitable for display because she believed it singled out particular individuals and subjected them to ridicule.

When first contacted, Sefick did not contest the decision to revoke his permit for the display. Later, however, he reconsidered his acquiescence to Farina's demand that the display be terminated. As a result, he retained counsel and filed this suit to compel the defendants to exhibit the tableau for the agreed upon period of time.

The plaintiff's position is quite straight-forward. He argues that the artistic expression of social and political views is protected speech under the first amendment. Accordingly, the permit revocation, which the plaintiff contends was based on Farina's objection to the content of the third week's tableau, is unconstitutional. The defendants, on the other hand, assert that the issuance or revocation of a permit to display art is a discretionary decision that does not implicate first amendment concerns. Further, they assert that the decision was not based on the content of the display, but rather on the variance of the tableau with the earlier description provided by Sefick.[10] Thus, in determining the propriety of the revocation, the Court must first address two preliminary issues: (1) whether the first amendment applies to this revocation of Sefick's permit to exhibit his tableau; and (2) whether the revocation was based on the content of the tableau or on the failure of Sefick to inform Farina of the precise nature of the exhibit.

A. APPLICATION OF THE FIRST AMENDMENT

The Court believes that the art form involved in this case constitutes speech within the meaning of the first amendment and thus is entitled to constitutional protection.[11] The exhibit consisted not only of

---

[10] Other defendants in the case assert additional grounds for denying relief. Defendants Byrne and Cummings seek dismissal from the suit on the ground that at most they are only vicariously liable for Farina's actions and therefore are not subject to suit under the reasoning of Monell v. Department of Social Services of the City of New York, 436 U.S. 658, 98 S. Ct. 2018, 56 L. Ed. 2d 611 (1978). The Court notes that the complaint failed in any way to allege conduct which would subject these defendants to liability under *Monell*. Accordingly, the complaint is dismissed as to Byrne and Cummings. In addition, the parties have agreed to dismiss the Council on Fine Arts from this litigation. Therefore, the balance of this opinion will address the liability of the City of Chicago and Farina.

[11] The concept of constitutionally protected speech has been expanded beyond the bounds of mere oral expression. See Southeastern Promotions, Ltd.

figures depicting a fireplace scene but also included a tape recording of a conversation between the figures. The initial issue before the Court is whether the decision to revoke Sefick's permit to exhibit his work and subsequently cover the figures has first amendment implications.[12]

The public display area in the Daley Center has been voluntarily opened to art exhibits. The defendants were under no constitutional compulsion to provide this public forum. However, it is widely recognized that once this forum has been provided, constitutional guarantees come into play:[13]

> There is an "equality of status in the field of ideas," and government must afford all points of view an equal opportunity to be heard. Once a forum is opened up to assembly or speaking by some groups, government may not prohibit others from assembling or speaking on the basis of what they intend to say.

Police Dept. of the City of Chicago v. Mosley, 408 U.S. 92, 96, 92 S. Ct. 2286, 2290, 33 L. Ed. 2d 212 (1972).

In those circumstances which do not involve obscenity, libel, speech calculated to create a clear and present danger to other individuals, or regulations involving the manner, time, and place of speech, a governmental entity ordinarily cannot select which issues are worth discussing or which views should be heard when public facilities are involved. *Id.* The Court disagrees with the defendant's contention that the permit is a mere license and thus revocable at will, even if the licensor is the government.[14] Once the defendants have opened up the forum and, as is the

---

v. Conrad, 420 U.S. 546, 95 S. Ct. 1239, 43 L. Ed. 2d 448 (1975) (theatre; rock-musical Hair), and Joseph Burstyn, Inc. v. Wilson, 343 U.S. 495, 72 S. Ct. 777, 96 L. Ed. 1098 (1952) (films), and Cohen v. California, 403 U.S. 15, 91 S. Ct. 1780, 29 L. Ed. 2d 284 (1971) (words and inscription on a jacket).

[12] At oral arguments counsel for the plaintiff conceded that, although he disagreed with the state of the case law, it was his opinion that had the defendants initially refused the application by the plaintiff, a lawsuit based on that refusal could not properly have been brought. Due to the willingness of counsel on both sides to narrow the issues, the Court will not address this question.

[13] Southeastern Promotions, Ltd. v. Conrad, 420 U.S. 546, 95 S. Ct. 1239, 43 L. Ed. 2d 448 (1975), held that a municipal board's rejection of an application to use a public forum due to the content of the play constituted an improper prior restraint under a system lacking in constitutionally required minimal procedural safeguards. Also relevant in this regard is Police Dept. of the City of Chicago v. Mosley, 408 U.S. 92, 92 S. Ct. 2286, 33 L. Ed. 2d 212 (1972), where the Supreme Court found that an anti-picketing statute violated the equal protection clause of the fourteenth amendment by discriminating in the use of a forum by allowing only those views which were found acceptable.

[14] At trial, counsel for defendants argued that there "is a right in a party who is giving a permissive sponsorship to withdraw that sponsorship if they find this offensive. That the party happens to be a governmental entity that is giving the

case here, given permission to display an exhibit, the plaintiff's right of expression cannot be "infringed by the denial of or placing conditions upon a benefit or privilege." *Minarcini v. Strongsville City School District,* 541 F.2d 577, 582 (6th Cir. 1976).

The fact that a governmental entity has no obligation to provide a forum but when it does is subject to constitutional mandates has been recognized and applied in a number of situations. In *Minarcini,* 541 F.2d at 582, the court found that once a library was created, the school board could not remove certain books without regard to constitutional guarantees:

> Neither the State of Ohio nor the Strongsville School Board was under any federal constitutional compulsion to provide a library for the Strongsville High School or to choose any particular books. Once having created such a privilege for the benefit of its students, however, neither body could place conditions on the use of the library which were related solely to the social or political tastes of school board members.

In another school-related case, *Right to Read Defense Committee of Chelsea v. School Committee of the City of Chelsea,* 454 F. Supp. 703 (D. Mass. 1978), a school committee had ordered a teenage literary anthology removed from the library. The court found that the removal constituted an infringement of the students' first amendment rights:

> Clearly, a school committee can determine what books will go into a library and, indeed, if there will be a library at all. But the question presented here is whether a school committee has the same degree of discretion to order a book removed from a library.
> . . . It is a familiar constitutional principle that a state, though having acted when not compelled, may consequentially create a constitutionally protected interest.

Id. at 711, 712.

The plaintiff's constitutional rights are involved in defendant's revocation of the permit and subsequent closing of the exhibit. The defendants have voluntarily provided a public forum and invited the plaintiff to display his form of art at a public facility. In doing so, a "constitutionally protected interest" has been created, an interest which must be accorded full first amendment protection. Thus, the cancellation of the Bilandic tableau exhibit is permissible only to the extent it passes muster under first amendment principles.

B. MOTIVE FOR REVOCATION OF THE PERMIT

As indicated above, the defendants argue that the revocation was based not on the content of the tableau, but rather upon the variance

---

sponsorship is of no consequence and gives no greater rights to the artist being displayed under that sponsorship." In the light of *Mosley, supra,* note 13, this contention cannot be accepted by the Court.

between the exhibit and the prior description given by Sefick. The facts as developed at trial, however, lead to a contrary conclusion.

First, it must be observed that the defendants overstate the degree of variance between the Bilandic tableau and the earlier description provided by Sefick. It is true that Sefick did not indicate that his portrayal of Grant Woods' painting, "An American Gothic," would depict the Bilandics. Nor did he indicate that the tableau would bear a title or be accompanied by a tape recording. Sefick's description, however, did state that the tableau would consist of "life-size figures [who] are contemporaries of Chicago Society." Clearly, this contemplated the identification of specified individuals in the tableau.[15] Moreover, Sefick had notified Farina that his works often contain critical social commentary. Thus, it is disingenuous for the defendants to assert that they were surprised that the third week's tableau contained political content, particularly since the first two tableaus displayed also contained social-political content.

Second, the evidence at trial indicated that both of Sefick's tableaus, displayed during the first two weeks, varied to some degree from the descriptions provided to Farina. The "Judge and his Court" exhibit contained a satirical tape recording, although prior communications between Sefick and Farina had not expressly stated that this would be the case. The "Chicago Transit Authority" tableau bore a title of the scene depicted, contrary to the prior description given. Despite these variations from the earlier description, the first two tableaus were allowed to remain on display for the full duration of their scheduled exhibition. Only the final tableau, "The Bilandics," was removed from display.[16]

The foregoing leads to the inescapable conclusion that Farina's decision to revoke permission for Sefick's final tableau was based predominantly, if not exclusively, on the content of that tableau. All of the displays varied from the prior description. All of them contained satirical

---

[15] If the identification of particular individuals was contrary to the policy of the Council on Fine Arts, then Farina could have denied permission to exhibit the tableaus before November 19. It should have been irrelevant that the Bilandics, rather than some other less well-known couple, were to be identified by the tableau. The fact that Farina did not cancel the exhibition until she learned that the tableau identified the Bilandics suggests that in fact there is no general policy against the identification of individuals.

[16] In her testimony, Farina suggested that the failure by Sefick to provide complete information justified revocation of the permit because it denied her the information necessary to make a judgment as to "logistics." She failed, however, to specify precisely what difficulty she encountered as a result of the incomplete information. Moreover, she failed to explain why the incomplete information with respect to the first two tableaus did not require cancellation of the exhibition as well. The Court must conclude that concern for "logistics" played no role in Farina's determination to remove the exhibit from display.

or critical social-political commentary. Furthermore, the defendants had notice that the final week's tableau would identify specific individuals. The primary distinguishing feature between the third tableau and the first two exhibited was that the former tableau identified Michael Bilandic and satirized a purported attitude toward a Chicago snowstorm. It was on this basis that Farina decided to remove the exhibit from public view.[17] Therefore, it is this attempt to regulate the content of the display that must be judged under first amendment principles.

C. PERMISSIBILITY OF THE REVOCATION

The deep-rooted traditions of the first amendment reflect "a profound national commitment to the principle that debate on public issues should be uninhibited, robust, and wide-open," even though such speech "may well include vehement, caustic, and sometimes unpleasantly sharp" comments. *New York Times Company v. Sullivan*, 376 U.S. 254, 270, 84 S. Ct. 710, 721, 11 L. Ed. 2d 686 (1964). To effectuate this commitment, the first amendment must be sufficiently broad to curtail government restriction of expression "because of its message, its ideas, its subject matter, or its content." *Police Department of the City of Chicago v. Mosley*, 408 U.S. 92, 95, 92 S. Ct. 2286, 2290, 33 L. Ed. 2d 212 (1972). Thus, "[s]elective exclusions from a public forum may not be based on content alone, and may not be justified by reference to content alone." *Mosley*, 408 U.S. at 96, 92 S. Ct. at 2290. This does not mean, of course, that the government is completely powerless to regulate speech. Rather, it requires the government to show that the regulation is in furtherance of a substantial governmental interest, and not merely the product of disagreement with the message of the speaker. *Young v. American Mini Theatres, Inc.*, 427 U.S. 50, 67-68, 96 S. Ct. 2440, 2450-2451, 49 L. Ed. 2d 310 (1976); *Mosley*, 408 U.S. at 98-99, 92 S. Ct. at 2291-2292. In this case, it is evident that the cancellation of the exhibition was based on Farina's objection to the social-political content of the Bilandic tableau. Without more, the defendants' actions would violate the first amendment. The defendants, however, contend that cancellation was necessary to serve other important governmental interests.

The defendants argue that cancellation of the exhibition was justified under the "captive audience" theory. They assert that since the tableau was placed in a heavily trafficked corridor in a public building, the defendants legitimately could act to protect unwitting passers-by from the objectionable message. In support of this view, defendants cite *Close*

---

[17] Farina herself admitted as much during her testimony. She stated that she found the Bilandic tableau inappropriate because it singled out identifiable individuals for ridicule, and that had she known of the content of the exhibit from the outset, she never would have approved Sefick's proposal.

v. Lederle, 424 F.2d 988 (1st Cir.), *cert. denied,* 400 U.S. 903, 91 S. Ct. 141, 27 L. Ed. 2d 140 (1970). There, the defendant university had invited an artist to exhibit his works in a Student Union corridor. Due to the sexual explicitness of the paintings, however, the university cancelled the exhibit on the fifth day of a scheduled 24-day display. The court approved this action, finding that the defendant had the right to protect the captive audience which regularly passed through this corridor against this " 'assault upon individual privacy.'" *Close,* 424 F.2d at 990.

This Court, however, does not find *Close* to be persuasive precedent. The *Close* decision preceded the analysis in *Cohen v. California,* 403 U.S. 15, 21, 91 S. Ct. 1780, 1786, 29 L. Ed. 2d 284 (1971), in which the Court limited application of the captive audience theory to those instances in which "substantial privacy interests are being invaded in an essentially intolerable manner." [18] The facts of *Close* are such that the action of the university might well be justifiable even in light of *Cohen.* The situation presented by the instant case, however, is distinguishable from *Close* in several respects. [19] The sexual explicitness of the message in *Close* implicated far more serious privacy interests than does the social-political message conveyed by Sefick's tableau. [20] Furthermore, the manner in which Sefick conveyed his message was far less intrusive than was the case in *Close.* In that case, the large-scale depiction of genitalia in a corridor made it difficult for passers-by to avoid viewing this sensitive subject. Here, the most objectionable part of the exhibit is probably the tape portraying a hypothetical conversation between the Bilandics concerning the snowfall last winter. Given the size and acoustical nature of

---

[18] In that case, the Court reversed Cohen's conviction for breach of the peace based on his strolling through a Los Angeles courthouse while wearing a jacket bearing the inscription "Fuck the Draft." The Court held that

> if Cohen's "speech" was otherwise entitled to constitutional protection, we do not think the fact that some unwilling "listeners" in a public building may have been briefly exposed to it can serve to justify this breach of the peace conviction where, as here, there was no evidence that persons powerless to avoid appellant's conduct did in fact object to it, and where that portion of the statute upon which Cohen's conviction rests evinces no concern . . . with the special plight of the captive auditor.

403 U.S. at 22, 91 S. Ct. at 1786.

[19] Initially, it should be noted that in *Close* the court found that there was "no suggestion . . . that plaintiff's art was seeking to express political or social thought." 424 F.2d at 990. In light of this finding, the court considered plaintiff's constitutional interest in his speech minimal. On the other hand, it is clear in this case that Sefick's tableau of the Bilandics possessed social-political content; indeed, content was the motivating factor in the removal of the exhibition.

[20] Farina's testimony indicated that she received no complaints about the tableau prior to her cancellation of the exhibition. This brings the case within the *Cohen* reasoning, in which the court found it relevant that there had been no complaints about the message emblazoned on Cohen's jacket.

the Daley Center, it is unlikely that the tape recording would be heard except by those who sought to listen to it.[21] See *Packer Corporation v. Utah*, 285 U.S. 105, 110, 52 S. Ct. 273, 274, 76 L. Ed. 643 (1932). In light of the foregoing, the Court concludes that the captive audience theory cannot justify the cancellation of the exhibit in this case.[22] *Gambino v. Fairfax City School Board*, 429 F. Supp. 731, 735 (E.D. Va.), *aff'd*, 564 F.2d 157 (4th Cir. 1977).

Defendants also assert that cancellation of the exhibit was necessary to prevent the impression that the City of Chicago had adopted the message conveyed by Sefick's tableau. According to Farina's testimony, the purpose of the Daley Center program is to "turn a public building into a living building by encouraging the art community of Chicago, performing the visual artists, to exhibit or perform." Farina indicated, however, that her acceptance of an artist's proposal to display his or her work never has been viewed as an endorsement of any substantive messages contained in the art. Indeed, Farina at no time expressed concern that the critical satires of the judiciary system or of the Chicago Transit Authority contained in Sefick's first two tableaus would be thought to represent official city viewpoints. Thus, the Court finds this "sponsorship" theory inadequate to support the cancellation of the exhibit. See *Gambino v. Fairfax City School Board*, 429 F. Supp. at 736.

Finally, the defendants urge that the power to cancel exhibits such as the Bilandic tableau is necessary if the city is to be able to avoid suits for slander and libel. In closing argument, however, counsel for the defendants disavowed any contention that the message contained in the Bilandic tableau was libelous.[23] The Court cannot accept the proposition

[21] Farina's actions in revoking the permit and covering the sculpture has predictably proved counter-productive to her stated desire to limit the viewing of the sculpture. Her suppression of the exhibition has created the attendant media publicity which undoubtedly has caused more persons to learn of the sculpture and has fostered wider dissemination of the message contained in plaintiff's art work than there would have been had she permitted the exhibition to run its course.

[22] Indeed, the evidence suggests that the cancellation of the exhibit was motivated more by Farina's concern for the privacy interests of the Bilandics than by concern for a captive audience of public passers-by. It is questionable even whether the Bilandics share Farina's concern. They have heard and read much harsher words about themselves than the rather benign criticism suggested by plaintiff's sculpture. Significantly, the Bilandics have not objected to Farina or to other city officials as to the showing of the exhibit. Nor have they sought to intervene in this law suit.

[23] The plaintiff has urged the Court to find that the Bilandics are public figures within the meaning of *Gertz v. Welch*, 418 U.S. 323, 94 S. Ct. 2997, 41 L. Ed. 2d 789 (1974). In view of the fact that defendants have abandoned the argument that Sefick's display was libelous, the Court declines to express an opinion on this issue.

that cancellation of this admittedly non-libelous[24] art tableau is necessary to preserve the city's right to cancel future exhibits which may be
libelous. This position conflicts with the first amendment maxim that any
regulation of speech, to be permissible, must be narrowly drawn. *Mosley*,
408 U.S. at 99, 92 S. Ct. at 2292. Therefore, the Court must reject this
proposition as a basis for cancelling Sefick's exhibition.

CONCLUSION

Plaintiff's sculpture is protected by the first amendment. Defendants have revoked permission to exhibit the sculpture because of
their apparent objection to the social and political nature of the art work.
By cancelling the exhibition at the lobby of the Richard J. Daley Civic
Center, defendants have violated plaintiff's first amendment constitutional rights.

For this reason, the Court finds in favor of the plaintiff John Sefick and
against defendants Rose Farina and City of Chicago. Judgment is entered
on this finding. Pursuant to this judgment, it is ordered that defendants
exhibit plaintiff's sculpture for five consecutive days at the Daley Civic
Center lobby in the same manner and place as was exhibited at the time
of its covering by defendants, that this exhibition be scheduled within the
next 60-day period, and that defendants notify plaintiff within 10 days
as to the dates scheduled for exhibition in accordance with this order. It is
further ordered that defendants exercise all due care in handling plaintiff's sculpture before, during, and after exhibition.

§1.1.9. *Yorty v. Chandler:* The Art of Caricature

When nineteenth century caricaturist Honoré Daumier used his
satiric pen to create an image unflattering to King Louis Philippe, the
French monarch was able to restrain him with a substantial fine and a jail
sentence. In *Yorty*, which follows, we can see how the First and Fourteenth amendments to the Constitution can operate to prevent such a
result in the United States. Important here is the court's explicit recognition that the standards relevant to the publication of a visual image — in
this case, a political cartoon — may be the same as those applicable to the
publication of printed words. Notwithstanding the extravagance of such

---

[24] As noted above, any message of ridicule or satire contained in plaintiff's
sculpture is exceedingly mild. Mayor Bilandic not only is the immediate past
mayor but is currently active politically. Political cartoons and satirical commentary by newspaper columnists and television commentators as to prominent
political personalities generally and as to Mayor Bilandic particularly make plaintiff's sculpture by comparison appear to be almost good-natured ribbing.

an image, it may still be protected as nothing more than "rhetorical hyperbole."

YORTY v. CHANDLER
13 Cal. App. 3d 467, 91 Cal. Rptr. 709 (1971)

FLEMING, A.J. Libel action for $2,000,000 by Samuel W. Yorty against Otis Chandler, Los Angeles Times, The Times-Mirror Company (sued as Times Mirror Corporation), and Paul Conrad, in which plaintiff complains of a cartoon drawn by Conrad and published on the editorial page of the Los Angeles Times. The trial court ruled on demurrer that the cartoon was not defamatory and entered judgment for defendants.

The cartoon was published under the following circumstances: in mid-November 1968 Richard M. Nixon, having been elected President of the United States, was engaged in the selection of nominees for appointment to his cabinet. At a press conference Samuel W. Yorty, Mayor of the City of Los Angeles, publicly expressed interest in such an appointment, and, in particular, appointment as Secretary of Defense. According to the allegations of plaintiff's complaint, President-elect Nixon was then considering Mayor Yorty for appointment to a cabinet post, and that fact was known to defendants.

On 19 November 1968 the Los Angeles Times published on its editorial page the following cartoon and caption: [omitted. Description follows.]

The cartoon depicts Mayor Yorty seated at his office desk talking on the telephone. Four white-coated medical orderlies with doleful expressions on their faces stand beside the desk. One orderly is holding a straight jacket behind his back while another beckons to Mayor Yorty with his finger. The caption reads, "I've got to go now . . . I've been appointed Secretary of Defense and the Secret Service men are here!"

In claiming that the cartoon was defamatory, the complaint asserts:

> In publishing said cartoon, Defendants and each of them, intended to mean and convey to the readers of the editorial page of the LOS ANGELES TIMES, that Plaintiff was claiming that he had been appointed Secretary of Defense by President-elect RICHARD NIXON, and that he was further claiming that he was qualified to serve in such capacity; and that in making such a claim, he was insane and should be placed in a straight jacket. The defendants, in publishing said cartoon, intended to insinuate to [their] readers that Plaintiff was unfit to serve as Secretary of Defense and, that in believing he was so qualified, he was mentally ill.

Plaintiff thus interprets the cartoon as a factual report that Mayor Yorty suffered from the delusion that he had been appointed Secretary of Defense and that because of his delusion he was insane and needed to be placed in a straight jacket.

The sole question is whether the cartoon is reasonably susceptible to the interpretation placed upon it in plaintiff's complaint. The trial court concluded it was not, ruled as a matter of law that the cartoon was not libelous, and dismissed the complaint. Plaintiff appeals.

First, some consideration of the subject matter of this suit, the political cartoon. Ever since stone-age man began to draw on the walls of his cave, caricature has been used as a device to express opinion on matters of current interest. Examples of the art of caricature in ancient Egyptian and Roman times still abound. With the advent of printing, caricature became a form of social and political commentary, and in one of its aspects began to manifest itself as critical opinion on public issues and public figures. Thus the political cartoon was born. In America the first political cartoon was designed by Benjamin Franklin, and by the time of the Civil War the political cartoon had become a standard adjunct to public life. In the 1870's Thomas Nast proved the effectiveness of the political cartoon by a devastating series of drawings which helped break the corrupt political regime of "Boss" Tweed and the Tammany Ring. From Daumier and Tenniel to Low and Herblock the political cartoon has occupied a central position in the presentation of critical comment on events and personages of the times.

The genius of a well-conceived political cartoon lies in its ability to communicate in graphic form a statement of editorial opinion which might otherwise require paragraphs of written material to express. To say so much with so little, the political cartoonist makes extensive use of symbolism, caricature, exaggeration, extravagance, fancy, and make-believe. For example, if a federal official made a "fact-finding" trip to a vacation spot at public expense, a political cartoonist might criticize that official's conduct by drawing a distorted likeness of the official taking money from the pocket of an unwary Uncle Sam. Because the use of symbolism in political cartooning is well-understood, the drawing would be interpreted by its viewers as editorial comment on the waste of public funds involved in the trip, and no reasonable viewer would consider it a factual report that the official had picked someone's pocket, much less that of an elderly gentleman with a wispy white beard who was dressed in an American flag.

A cartoon, of course, remains subject to the law of libel (Civ. Code, §45), and, like any other form of depiction or representation, it may be found libelous if it maliciously presents as fact defamatory material which is false. For example, a political cartoon which falsely depicts a public official selling franchises for personal gain, or a judge taking a bribe, or an attorney altering a public record, or a police officer shooting a defenseless prisoner, will not be exempt from redress under the laws of libel merely because the charge is depicted graphically in linear form rather than verbally in written statement. (*Snively v. Record Publishing*

Co., 185 Cal. 565, 198 P.1; *Newby v. Times-Mirror Co.*, 173 Cal. 387, 160 P. 233; *Gloria v. A Colonia Portuguesa*, 128 Cal. App. 640, 18 P.2d 87.) On the other hand, a cartoon which depicts a fanciful, allegorical, anthropomorphical, or zoomorphical scene will not be considered libelous merely because it depicts a public person as a flower, a block of wood, a fallen angel, or an animal. Because a political cartoon presents critical opinion in imaginative and symbolic form, in claimed instances of defamation a court must ferret out the underlying themes of the cartoon and then determine whether these can reasonably be considered libelous. (*Blake v. Hearst Publications*, 75 Cal. App. 2d 6, 170 P.2d 100.)

The present cartoon is said by plaintiff to have made two basic assertions: First, an assertion that the Mayor was unqualified for high national office. Second, an assertion that the Mayor, in believing he was qualified for high national office, demonstrated mental incompetency to such a degree that he required the restraint of a straight jacket. Defendants concede the first assertion and defend their right to make it. Defendants deny the second assertion and deny that any reasonable viewer would interpret the cartoon as having made such a statement.

On the first point, it is settled law that mere expression of opinion or severe criticism is not libelous, even though it adversely reflects on the fitness of an individual for public office. (*Howard v. Southern Cal. etc. Newspapers*, 95 Cal. App. 2d 580, 213 P.2d 399.) Here, the cartoon was published on the editorial page of the Los Angeles Times at a time President-elect Nixon was engaged in choosing nominees for his cabinet and after Mayor Yorty had publicly expressed interest in appointment as Secretary of Defense. The cartoon was a form of editorial comment on these events and pointedly expressed the opinion of the Los Angeles Times that the Mayor's view of his own political stature was so far removed from reality, that his reach for national office so exceeded his grasp, that his aspirations for political preferment so outran his qualifications, that these ambitions could popularly be described as insane, mad, or crazy. To recognize the right of the Los Angeles Times to publish an unflattering and derogatory opinion of the Mayor's qualifications for high national office at a time he was under consideration for such an appointment is not to accept that opinion as gospel writ, but merely to hold that in a free country the Los Angeles Times, like everyone else, has a right to express its views on who should be appointed to public office, even though its views are those of a political adversary and are presented in rhetorical hyperbole. (Calif. Const., art. I, §9; *Eva v. Smith*, 89 Cal. App. 324, 264 P. 803; *Taylor v. Lewis*, 132 Cal. App. 381, 22 P.2d 569; *Corman v. Blanchard*, 211 Cal. App. 2d 126, 27 Cal. Rptr. 327; *Howard v. Southern Cal. etc. Newspapers*, 95 Cal. App.2d 580, 213 P.2d 399.) On this point we find pertinent the comments of the court in *Eva v. Smith*, *supra* (89 Cal. App. pp.328-330, 264 P. pp.804-805):

It is claimed that . . . the article was published to disparage plaintiff; its plain import being to characterize him as the type of man who should not be returned to public office. Taking the article as a whole . . . it amounts to no more than a criticism of plaintiff's qualifications for office and one which defendant was entitled to make. . . . An individual who seeks or accepts public office invites and challenges public criticism so far as it may relate to his fitness and qualifications. . . . The right of criticism rests upon public policy and those who seek office should not be supersensitive or too thin-skinned concerning criticism of their qualifications. . . . In so far as the articles might imply that, in the opinion of defendant, plaintiff was unfitted for the office he was seeking to be returned to, no complaint can be made, for defendant had the right to express his opinion in this respect.

On the second point, plaintiff contends that the Los Angeles Times, in expressing its views on Mayor Yorty's fitness for a cabinet post, published a false report that he was in fact insane and needed the physical restraint of a straight jacket. If in fact defendants had published such a report unquestionably the publication could be found libelous. For example, in *Goldwater v. Ginzburg*, D.C., 261 F. Supp. 784 (2d Cir. 1969), 414 F.2d 324, *cert. den.* 396 U.S. 1049, 90 S. Ct. 701, 24 L. Ed. 2d 695 (1970), a publication reported that Senator Goldwater was "mentally unbalanced," a "dangerous lunatic," a "coward," a "compensated schizophrenic," and charged that he suffered from "nervous breakdowns," "paranoia," "chronic psychosis," etc. These statements were considered by the court to involve more than subjective opinion and were ruled libelous, subject to proof of their falsity and proof of knowing or reckless disregard for the truth by the publisher. (See also cases cited in 23 A.L.R.3d 652.) At bench, however, what defendants published was not a factual report of news intended to circulate at face value but a cartoon intended to present an editorial comment on the Mayor's qualifications for high national office. From the cartoon no reasonable person would assume more than that in the opinion of the Los Angeles Times the Mayor was not qualified for the post of Secretary of Defense, President-elect Nixon would not appoint him, and it was foolish of the Mayor to aspire to an appointment for which he was not qualified. No reasonable person would interpret the cartoon as a report that Mayor Yorty had actually made the statement shown in the caption or that he was in fact mentally deranged or insane. Clearly, the cartoon was using the surface imagery and stage properties of mental incompetency to express the underlying idea of unrealistic aspirations and extravagant hopes. In that respect its symbolism was not new to political cartooning. For example, a Currier and Ives lithograph published during the election of 1860 depicts utopian supporters of Abraham Lincoln marching with him to the "Lunatic Asylum" and carries the caption "The Republican Party Going to the Right House" (Hess & Kaplan, "The Ungentlemanly Art, a History of American Political Cartoons" (1968) p.75).

The popular usage of words denoting mental incompetency, such as *insane, mad,* or *crazy,* to express the idea of excessive optimism, extravagant expectation, overweening ambition, foolish hope, distraction with eager desire, goes back in the English language to the time of Milton and Shakespeare.[1] Clearly, it was the latter idea which the cartoon intended to and did convey. In *Correia v. Santos,* 191 Cal. App.2d 844, 13 Cal. Rptr. 132, one radio broadcaster charged another with being driven by "vanity of power" to "insanity." The court declared that

> When these statements are considered as a part of the whole broadcast and are given the meaning which would be attributed to them by the average listener, it is apparent that the object of the broadcaster was not to describe the plaintiff as a person who was mentally ill but as one who was unreasonable in his actions and demands.

(191 Cal. App. 2d at p.853, 13 Cal. Rptr. at p.137.) In *Cowan v. Time, Inc.,* 41 Misc. 2d 198, 245 N.Y.S.2d 723 (Sup. Ct. N.Y.), an article entitled "Some Idiots Afloat" showed a photograph of plaintiff and others in an overloaded boat. The court concluded that in the context of the article the word "idiot" only charged plaintiff with carelessness in boating.

Plaintiff, however, while conceding that the cartoon might be interpreted as charging him with no more than foolish and unrealistic expec-

---

[1] MAD: Webster's New International Dictionary, Second Edition, defines "mad" both as "exhibiting unsoundness or disorder of the mind," and as "foolish, vain, especially, rashly or ruinously foolish." The Oxford English Dictionary says: "1. Suffering from mental disease," and "2. Foolish; unwise." Shakespeare used the word in both senses in 1602.

Hamlet, Act V, scene 1, 165-170:

Hamlet: Ay, marry, why was he sent into England?

Clown: Why, because he was mad; he shall recover his wits there; or, if he do not, 'tis no great matter there.

Hamlet: Why?

Clown: 'Twill not be seen in him there; there the men are as mad as he.

CRAZY: Webster's New International Dictionary, Second Edition, gives three current definitions: "Full of cracks or flaws," "insane," and "distracted with eager desire, excitement, or the like; inordinately desirous or obsessed." The Oxford English Dictionary says "crazy" is often "used by way of exaggeration in sense: Distracted or 'mad' with excitement, vehement desire, perplexity." In 1617 Chamberlain wrote of a man "noted to be crazy and distempered." And in 1641 Milton wrote of "the floting carcas of a crasie and diseased Monarchy."

INSANE: Webster's New International Dictionary, Second Edition, defines "insane" to mean not only "exhibiting unsoundness or disorder of the mind," but also as "characterized by . . . the utmost folly; chimerical; unpractical; and an *insane* plan, attempt, etc." The Oxford English Dictionary defines "insanity" both as "unsoundness of the mind" and as "Extreme folly or want of sound sense." Thus in 1862 Spencer wrote of the "insanities of idealism," and in 1869 Coleridge wrote of an "insane and excessive passion for athletics."

tations, argues that the cartoon is also susceptible to a literal interpretation which charges him with mental disorder, and he contends that since the cartoon is susceptible of two interpretations — one innocent, one defamatory — it is for a jury and not a court to make the choice between conflicting interpretations (*Mellen v. Times-Mirror Co.*, 167 Cal. 587, 593, 140 P. 277; *MacLeod v. Tribune Publishing Co.*, 52 Cal. 2d 536, 546, 343 P.2d 36). Hence, he argues, the trial court usurped the fact-finding function of a jury when it held the cartoon non-libelous as a matter of law. In debatable instances of libel the correctness of this view is not open to question. But here, there can be only one reasonable interpretation of the cartoon, and that interpretation is non-libelous. In such circumstances a court is required to rule as a matter of law that the material is not defamatory, and it is not allowed to submit the issue to a jury. This has always been the rule in California (*Mellen v. Times-Mirror Co.*, 167 Cal. 587, 593, 140 P. 277; *Arno v. Stewart*, 245 Cal. App. 2d 955, 959, 54 Cal. Rptr. 392; *Corman v. Blanchard*, 211 Cal. App. 2d 126, 132, 27 Cal. Rptr. 327; *Howard v. Southern Cal. etc. Newspapers*, 95 Cal. App. 2d 580, 586, 213 P.2d 399; *Harris v. Curtis Publishing Co.*, 49 Cal. App. 2d 340, 346, 121 P.2d 761; *Eva v. Smith*, 89 Cal. App. 324, 264 P. 803), and in recent years it has also become part of the guaranty of free speech under the First and Fourteenth Amendments of the federal constitution (*Greenbelt Co-op Publishing Ass'n v. Bresler*, 398 U.S. 6, 90 S. Ct. 1537, 26 L. Ed. 2d 6; *New York Times Co. v. Sullivan*, 376 U.S. 254, 84 S. Ct. 710, 11 L. Ed. 2d 686).

In *Greenbelt Co-op Publishing Ass'n v. Bresler, supra,* plaintiff Bresler was seeking to obtain from the city council of Greenbelt a zoning variance on land owned by him, and at the same time the city was seeking to buy a different tract of land from him on which to construct a new high school. Bresler refused to agree to sell the high school property unless he were given a zoning variance on his other land, and at a city council meeting he was charged by persons from the community with "blackmail." Defendant, a weekly newspaper, reported these charges. In reversing a jury verdict for plaintiff and holding as a matter of constitutional law that the references to " blackmail" were not defamatory, the Supreme Court said:

> For the reasons that follow, we hold that the imposition of liability on such a basis was constitutionally impermissible — that as a matter of constitutional law, the word "blackmail" in these circumstances was not slander when spoken, and not libel when reported in the Greenbelt News Review. . . . It is simply impossible to believe that a reader who reached the word "blackmail" in either article would not have understood exactly what was meant: it was Bresler's public and wholly legal negotiating proposals that were being criticized. No reader could have thought that either the speakers at the meeting or the newspaper articles reporting their words were charging Bresler with the commission of a criminal offense. On the contrary, even the most careless

reader must have perceived that the word was no more than rhetorical hyperbole, a vigorous epithet used by those who considered Bresler's negotiating position extremely unreasonable. . . . To permit the infliction of financial liability upon the petitioners for publishing these two news articles would subvert the most fundamental meaning of a free press, protected by the First and Fourteenth Amendments.

(*Greenbelt Co-op Publishing Ass'n v. Bresler*, 398 U.S. at pp.13-14, 90 S. Ct. at pp.1541-1542.)

These comments in *Bresler* have a parallel application to the cause at bench, and we paraphrase them thus: It is simply impossible to believe that a viewer of the cartoon would not have understood exactly what was meant: it was Mayor Yorty's public aspiration for appointment as Secretary of Defense which was being ridiculed. No reader could have thought that either the cartoonist or the editor of the Los Angeles Times was charging Mayor Yorty with mental derangement or mental incompetency. On the contrary, even the most careless reader must have perceived that the cartoon was no more than rhetorical hyperbole, a vigorous expression of opinion by those who considered Mayor Yorty's aspiration for high national office preposterous. To penalize defendants for publishing this political cartoon would subvert the most fundamental meaning of a free press, protected by the First and Fourteenth Amendments.

We conclude that under both state and federal law the trial court correctly determined that the cartoon was not reasonably susceptible to a defamatory meaning and that consequently plaintiff had failed to state a cause of action.

The judgment of dismissal is affirmed.

ROTH, P.J., concurs.

COMPTON, A.J. (concurring). I concur in the result reached by Justice Fleming in his very scholarly and learned analysis of the subject matter at hand, but for somewhat different reasons.

Because of what appears to me to be a continuing escalation in the frequency and viciousness of both physical and verbal attacks on duly elected public officials, I feel compelled to add some comments of my own.

The Los Angeles Times' right to express, in cartoon form, its opinion concerning the Mayor's qualifications for public office is protected by the First Amendment to the United States Constitution. On the other hand, as Justice Fleming points out, the political cartoon is not protected if it is libelous and maliciously presents false and defamatory material. In other words, a cartoonist or an artist who undertakes, in pictorial form, to criticize an individual must be held to the same standards as though he used the printed word.

I am persuaded also that in determining whether or not a matter is defamatory, the fact that it is presented as a subjective opinion rather than a statement of fact is not completely controlling.

This is especially true where, as here, the issue is the imputation of mental illness. As a practical matter the question of an individual's sanity under the present state of the art is always determined on the basis of opinion — whether it be the opinion of a psychiatrist or the opinion of a layman, as those opinions are accepted under our rules of evidence.

As Justice Fleming so clearly points out, if the defendants in this case had published a false report that the Mayor was in fact insane and needed the physical restraint of a straight jacket, such a report could be found libelous. (See *Goldwater v. Ginzburg*, D.C., 261 F. Supp. 784 (2d Cir. 1969), 414 F.2d 324, *cert. den.* 396 U.S. 1049, 90 S. Ct. 701, 24 L. Ed.2d 695 (1970).) In this area I see no distinction between a so-called statement of fact and an expression of opinion.

The question presented on this appeal is whether the cartoon in question is susceptible of a defamatory interpretation, i.e., an imputation of mental illness in the real sense. If the cartoon is so susceptible, it is defamatory whether it is viewed in terms of the Times saying "The Mayor is insane" or "In our opinion the Mayor is insane."

It is one thing for the Los Angeles Times to express an opinion that the Mayor because of a lack of administrative ability, a lack of experience or qualification, or for a myriad of other reasons, was not a qualified candidate for political office, but it is quite another thing to falsely opine that his lack of fitness for political office was premised on mental imbalance.

Our affirmance of the trial court's decision deprives the plaintiff of an opportunity to have that question decided by a jury. For that reason we should be very careful about reaching the conclusion that "no reasonable viewer" could assume that the matter was defamatory.

Standing alone, the cartoon *is* susceptible of a defamatory meaning. Straight jackets and men in white coats are commonly associated in the popular mind with violent insanity. It is possible for a "reasonable viewer" to equate what was depicted in this cartoon with the type of words which were condemned in *Goldwater v. Ginzburg*.

In my view the cartoon in question is cured of any possible defamatory interpretation *only* when viewed in light of the retraction, by which the Times specifically disavowed any imputation of actual mental incompetency.

My concurrence in affirming the judgment is premised on the fact that the retraction sufficiently dispels the defamatory nature of the cartoon and that the plaintiff did not plead any special damages.

Justice Fleming points to a Currier and Ives lithograph of 1860 depicting President Lincoln on his way to an insane asylum as some precedent for reading out of the present cartoon any defamatory interpretation. Apparently that lithograph was never challenged. The fact that one libel goes unchallenged does not provide a sound basis for exculpating a second or similar libel.

Additionally, I discern a trend in the laws of libel comparable to the very frightening developments which we have witnessed in the obscenity field. Our courts have continued to pay lip service to the principle that obscenity does not enjoy First Amendment protection. At the same time, however, individual decisions holding matters not to be obscene have so raised the threshold of what *is* obscene that the original principle has become a hollow shell.

Similarly, reiterating the principle that libel does not enjoy First Amendment protection while at the same time sanctioning progressively vicious and scurrilous false attacks upon public officials will render the laws of defamation meaningless.

The protection of the freedom of a responsible press does not require that we insulate from liability for libel the artists whose pens drip venom and whose skill in drawing and cartooning far exceeds their sense of responsibility, respect for the truth and the depth of their understanding of public issues.

In my opinion the defendants in this action escaped possible liability only because of a prompt and adequate retraction.

§1.1.10. Freedom of Expression, Obscenity Exemptions, and Sunday Statutes

State legislatures throughout the country have adopted several types of statutes in recognition of the artist's need for laws supportive of the ability and right to create. Most states have passed either broad, policy-type enactments regarding the freedom of artistic expression or adopted exceptions to state obscenity laws for artistic works. A third, more specific but far less widespread development in support of the artist's ability to create is also occurring in the form of legislation authorizing artist live-work spaces.[9]

Nearly half the states assign to their arts councils or commissions the job of guarding the freedom of artistic expression.[10] While most define

---

[9] A fourth type of such laws is the Sunday Statutes, i.e., laws that permit the sale of artworks (usually only originals) on Sunday despite the blanket prohibition of other "commercial" activities. See, e.g., La. Rev. Stat. Ann. §51:192.A(9) (West 1986) and S.C. Code Ann. §53-1-50(11) (Law. Co-op. Supp. 1985).

[10] See Ala. Code §41-9-45(4) (1982); Alaska Stat. §44.27.050(4) (1985); Ariz. Rev. Stat. Ann. §41-982(B)(4) (1985); Conn. Gen. Stat. Ann. §10-370 (West 1977 & West Supp. 1984); Fla. Stat. Ann. §265.285(2)(f) (West 1985); Ga. Code Ann. §50-12-23(4) (1982); Ind. Code Ann. §4-23-2-2(d) (Burns 1982); Md.

the duty as being to "encourage and assist freedom of artistic expression essential for the well-being of the arts,[11] several states go further: South Dakota denies its Council the right to "Control . . . the content or expression of any of the fine art forms,[12] while Minnesota instructs its Board of Arts to "avoid any actions which infringe on the freedom of expression. . . .[13] See also Connecticut, Maryland, New Hampshire, and Oklahoma, which all specifically instruct their councils not to "limit" the freedom of expression.[14]

Almost as many states as attempt to safeguard the freedom of artistic expression specifically exempt either artworks or arts institutions from their lewdness statutes.[15] These exemptions take one of several forms: Works are either deemed to have sufficient artistic value[16] (a quality for which evidence is frequently deemed admissible),[17] or the institution, or individual working with that institution, is exempt.[18] The state of Colorado, for example, exempts from the provisions of its statute "[t]he exhi-

---

Code Ann., Art. 41 §398 (1982); Mich. Comp. Laws Ann. §2.124(4) (1981); Minn. Stat. Ann. §139.10(2)(a) (West 1979 & West Supp. 1985); Miss. Code Ann. §39-11-7(4) (1972); Mo. Ann. Stat. §185.040(4) (Vernon Supp. 1986); Mont. Code Ann. §22-2-106(4) (1985); Neb. Rev. Stat. §82-312(4) (1981); N.H. Rev. Stat. Ann. §19-A:1 (1970); N.J. Rev. Stat. Ann. §52:16A-26(c) (1970); N.D. Cent. Code §54-54-05.4 (1982); Okla. Stat. Ann. tit. 53, §62 (West 1969); R.I. Gen. Laws §§22-16-2(3) & 42-75-7(4) (1984 & 1985); S.D. Codified Laws Ann. §1-22-6 (1985); and Wyo. Stat. §9-2-903(a)(v) (1982).

[11] See, e.g., Ala. Code §41-9-45(4) (1982).

[12] S.D. Codified Laws Ann. §1-22-6 (1985).

[13] Minn. Stat. Ann. §139.10(2)(a) (West 1979 & West Supp. 1985).

[14] Conn. Gen. Stat. Ann. §10-370 (West 1977 & West Supp. 1984); Md. Code Ann., Art. 41 §398 (1982); N.H. Rev. Stat. Ann. §19-A:1 (1970); and Okla. Stat. Ann. tit. 53, §162 (West 1969).

[15] See Colo. Rev. Stat. §§18-7-104(a) & (b) (Supp. 1985); Ga. Code Ann. §16-12-80(b)(2) (1984); Iowa Code Ann. §728.7 (1979); Minn. Stat. Ann. §617.241(a) (West Supp. 1985); Mo. Ann. Stat. §§573.010 & 573.050 (Vernon 1979 & Vernon Supp. 1986); Mont. Code Ann. §45-8-201 (3)(b) (1985); Neb. Rev. Stat. §§28-813(1)(c) & 28-815(1) (1979); Nev. Rev. Stat. §201-237 (1985); N.H. Rev. Stat. Ann. §§650:1 (IV(c)) & 650:5 (III & IV) (Supp. 1983); Okla. Stat. Ann., tit. 21 §1021.1 (West 1983); Or. Rev. Stat. §§167.085(2) & 167.089 (1985); R.I. Gen. Laws §11-31-1 (1981); S.C. Code Ann. §16-15-280(5) (Law. Co-op. 1985); S.D. Codified Laws Ann. §§22-24-27(4)(c) & 22-24-37(2) (1979); Tenn. Code Ann. §§39-6-1101(5)(c) & 39-61-1117 (3) (1982); Utah Code Ann. §§76-10-1201(11)(iii) & 76-10-1203(1)(c) (1978); Vt. Stat. Ann. tit. 13, §§2801(6)(c) & 2805(b)(3) & 2805(c) (Supp. 1985); Va. Code §§18.2-372 & 18.2-383(2) (1982); W. Va. Code §61-8A-1(7)(c) (1984).

[16] See, e.g., Mont. Code Ann. §45-8-201(2)(b)(iii) (1985).

[17] See Mont. Code Ann. §45-8-201(3)(b) (1985).

[18] See, e.g., Nev. Rev. Stat. §201.237 (1985).

bition . . . by any accredited . . . museum. . . .[19] The Iowa legislature created perhaps the most interesting exemption. Its statute provides that "[n]othing in this chapter prohibits the attendance of minors at an exhibition or display of works of art. . . ."[20]

§1.2. LIMITATIONS ON THE ARTIST'S RIGHT OF EXPRESSION

§1.2.1. *People v. Gonzales:* Nudes May Be Obscene

As may be inferred from *Gonzales*, which follows, the mere assertion that visual representations — photographs of nude women, for example — may be "art" is not in itself enough to put them within the ambit of constitutionally protected speech. While nudity per se may not constitute obscenity, there remain in force, nonetheless, obscenity laws under which the sale or distribution of certain visual representations may have criminal consequences. The Supreme Court has changed its view of what may be deemed obscene several times, but there has always been some point beyond which visual representations may not transgress. (See, however, §1.1.10 *supra* in which are listed various state lewdness statutes that specifically exempt artworks or arts institutions from their coverage.)

PEOPLE v. GONZALES
107 N.Y.S.2d 968 (Mag. Ct. N.Y. County 1951)

PLOSCOWE, City Mag. This Court is called upon to determine whether certain pictures are within the prohibitions of Sec. 1141 of the Penal Law which forbids the sale or distribution of any "obscene, lewd, lascivious, filthy, indecent or disgusting . . . picture . . . photograph, . . . figure or image." Although three different prosecutions are involved herein, the pictures which are the basis of each prosecution are similar. They are snapshots of women, face and form, generally in the nude in various poses, some of which are frankly provocative. The pictures in the case of *People v. Finkelstein* are a strip tease series. An attractive model is shown in various stages of undress until complete nudity is achieved. In the *Gonzales* and *Rosenzweig* cases, some of the pictures feature two and even three models in various poses in the nude.

---

[19] Colo. Rev. Stat. §18-7-104(a) (Supp. 1985).
[20] Iowa Code Ann. §728.7 (West 1979).

The pictures are apparently sold openly to anyone who has the price. In *People v. Gonzales*, they were bought by the police officer in plainclothes, at a store that specializes in the sale of magic and novelty articles but whose windows also feature art books containing poses of nude women and playing cards on whose covers are nudes. In *People v. Rosenzweig*, the pictures were sold to the police officer in a general bookstore which specializes in cheap books. In *People v. Finkelstein*, the pictures were bought at a bookstore, which from its window display, on the day on which it was examined by the Court, featured sexy books. The Court noted such titles in the window as "Free Lovers," "Sinful Cities of the Western World," the "Slaughtered Lovelies," the "Magnificent Courtesan," "French Love Passion," "The Art of Kissing," "How to Make Love," "Psychopathia Sexualis," etc.

The Court was advised that pictures similar to those involved in the instant prosecution are sold in many different stores through the Times Square Area.

One school of thought believes that the law is wrong in attempting to prohibit any form of expression which takes a pictorial or printed form. It is alleged that the evils of censorship far outweigh the gains which may be achieved in the repression of pornographic literature or pictorial pornography. A city magistrate with specific allegations of violations of Sec. 1141 of the Penal Law before him, need take no part of this dispute. His duty is to determine whether as a prima facie matter, the books or pictures which are the object of the prosecution are "obscene, lewd, lascivious, filthy, indecent or digusting," and therefore, violate Sec. 1141 of the Penal Law. Unfortunately, the aforementioned words are not self-defining, nor is a recourse to a dictionary of any help, since the words are synonymous. One must turn to the decisions of our higher Courts and see what content has been given to these words and whether they prohibit the specific material which forms the basis for the prosecutions.

In determining whether the pictures before the court are "obscene, lewd and lascivious" within the meaning of Sec. 1141 of the Penal Law, one can start with the proposition that nudity per se is not obscenity. The reproduction of a Goya nude may titillate, fascinate and stimulate, yet, such reproduction does not violate the statute. The prohibitions of 1141 of the Penal Law do not extend to bona fide artistic expression, even where such expression takes the form of reproducing Rubens famous painting of satyrs chasing buxom and robust nudes. (See Life for October 1, 1951, pp.64-65.) Public sophistication has also advanced to the stage where a man displaying a September Morn Calendar will not be clapped into jail, even though September Morn is a far inferior artistic production to a Goya or a Rubens.

No argument can be made in the cases before us that the pictures are works of art. They are not even good photography. When one sees men pawing over such pictures in stores in the Times Square area, as this Court has done, it is obvious that their appeal is frankly sexual. They meet the test of obscenity laid down in *People v. Berg*, 1934, 241 App. Div. 543, 272 N.Y.S. 586, 588, which interpreted the statute in connection with an obscene book and came to the conclusion that book was obscene which resulted in "The exciting of lustful and lecherous thoughts and desires," or, "tends to stir sexual impulses or to lead to sexually impure thoughts." The pictures which are the basis of the present prosecutions are intended to "excite lustful and lecherous thoughts and to stir sexual impulses." If they did not do this, they would not be sought after and bought. If they could not stir sexual impulses, there would be no reason for the strip tease, or the pictures which portray models holding out their breasts in provocative fashion, or the pictures which make such a prominent display of the female buttocks and the anal region.

While the sale of photographs of female nudes has become quite common in New York, storekeepers should be reminded that certain cases are still law. Their nude merchandise may therefore be subject to seizure and they may be subject to criminal prosecutions for violating the obscenity statutes. In *People v. Fellerman*, 1934, 243 App. Div. 64, 276 N.Y.S. 198, the conviction of a defendant for selling a nudist magazine containing pictures of persons in nudist camps was sustained by the Apellate Division. Similar convictions have been upheld in other jurisdictions. *King v. Commonwealth*, 1950, 313 Ky. 741, 233 S.W.2d 522; *Gore v. State*, 1949, 79 Ga. App. 696, 54 S.E.2d 669; *Hadley v. State*, 1943, 205 Ark. 1027, 172 S.W.2d 237; *Benjamin v. U.S.*, D.C. Mun. App., 74 A.2d 64. Contra *State v. Lerner*, Ohio Com. Pl., 81 N.E.2d 282.

In Freedman v. New York Society for the Suppression of Vice, 248 App. Div. 517, 290 N.Y.S. 753, 755, *affirmed* 274 N.Y. 559, 10 N.E.2d 550; the Appelate Division stated that pictures in a book called "Let's Go Naked," exposed in the window of a store, violated both 1141 and 1141a of the Penal Law. The fact that strips of paper covered the private parts of the individuals portrayed did not make the pictures any the less obscene, for according to this opinion. "The strips of paper . . . tended to accentuate rather than to diminish the lewd and lascivious character of the publication." In *People v. Smith*, 1937, 252 App. Div. 622, 300 N.Y.S. 651, 652, the Appellate Division affirmed the convictions of a defendant for selling a book containing a collection of 88 photographs "mostly of female figures in the nude." The book as "displayed in the window of a store managed by the defendant where artists supplies and materials were sold. No attempt was made, however, to confine the sale of the book to those interested in the graphic arts. [T]he book was offered for sale to all prospective purchasers indiscriminately. It was displayed in a window facing on the highway in such a manner as to be open to view to the young as well as the old, to the strong-minded as well as the weak, but *particularly to those the statute was expressly designed to protect — the young and the impressionable.*

> The photograph exposed in the window was that of a woman reclining, in the nude, on what appears to be a couch, with the lighting effects so arranged that the woman's busts and private parts were brought into prominence, and the woman so posed that unquestionably the display was intended to be that of a "provocative picture."

The above description is appicable to many of the so-called art books which are offered for sale and prominently displayed throughout the Times Square Area. But at least these books purport to serve the purposes of art. Not such pretense can be made for the pictures which are the basis of the instant prosecutions.

If, as we believe, the aforementioned cases authoritatively lay down the law of this state, much greater police activity in connection with pictures of female nudes and so-called art books would appear to be indicated. In any event, it is clear that as a prima facie matter, the pictures in the prosecutions before us, are sufficiently "obscene, lewd, and lascivious" to warrant a denial of a motion to dismiss the prosecution on the ground that the pictures do not violate 1141 of the Penal Law.

§1.2.2. *Close v. Lederle:* **The Captive Audience**

Since the 1970s Chuck Close has been widely recognized for his meticulously painted, oversized portraits of art world luminaries. *Close*, which follows, arose from an incident that took place early in the artist's career while he was an instructor at the University of Massachusetts. As the case vividly demonstrates, constitutional protection of visual, artistic expression hinges almost entirely on a threshold finding that it is a form of speech. Here, the court (all but scornfully) rejected such a contention, leaving the artist unable to prevent the dismantling of his exhibition. Query, would the result have been the same if Close's paintings had addressed the Vietnam War instead of merely portraying "clinically" explicit nudes? The *Sefick* case (see §1.1.8 *supra*) makes an interesting comparison.

Another case involving a canceled art exhibition on a university campus was *Appelgate v. Dumke*.[1] While the plaintiff/artist asserted that he had a constitutional right to exhibit his sculpture, the court disposed of the matter without reaching the question.

---

§1.2. [1] 25 Cal. App. 3d 304, 101 Cal. Rptr. 645 (1972).

CLOSE v. LEDERLE
424 F.2d 988 (1st Cir. 1970)

ALDRICH, C.J. Plaintiff, an art instructor at the University of Massachusetts, was asked by a superior if he would care to have an exhibition of his paintings on the walls of a corridor used from time to time for such purposes in the Student Union, a university building. He said that he would. The exhibition, which had been arranged for but not seen by the superior in charge, proved to be controversial. Several administrative meetings were held, attended by the university president, the provost, and other officials, and after it had been up for five of the twenty-four days scheduled, the exhibition was removed. Claiming that this was an invasion of his constitutional rights, plaintiff sued for a mandatory injunction ordering the officials to make the space available for the equivalent of the unexpired period. The district court, after trial, granted the relief and defendants appeal.

Basically, the district court held that "embarrassment" and "annoyance," causing defendants to conclude that the exhibition was "inappropriate" to the corridor, was insufficient to warrant interference with plaintiff's right of free speech. This holding was not grounded upon a finding that defendants were unreasonable in their opinion. The court refused autoptic profference of the exhibition, apparently taking the position that, at least in the absence of express regulations as to what was impermissible, defendants had no right to censor simply on the basis of offensiveness which fell short of unlawful obscenity.

We disagree. We first consider the nature and quality of plaintiff's interest. Plaintiff makes the bald pronouncement, "Art is as fully protected by the Constitution as political or social speech." It is true that in the course of holding a motion picture entitled to First Amendment protection, the Court said in *Joseph Burstyn, Inc. v. Wilson*, 1952, 343 US 495, at 501, 72 S. Ct. 777, at 780, 96 L. Ed. 1098 that moving pictures affect public attitudes in ways "ranging from direct espousal of a political or social doctrine to the subtle shaping of thought which characterizes all artistic expression." However, this statement in itself recognizes that there are degrees of speech.

There is no suggestion, unless in its cheap titles, that plaintiff's art was seeking to express political or social thought. Cf. *People v. Radich*, 26 N.Y. 114, 308 N.Y.S.2d 846, 257 N.E.2d 30. Cases dealing with students' rights to hear possibly unpopular speakers, e.g., Brooks v. Auburn University, D. Ala., 1969, 296 F. Supp. 188, *aff'd* 5 Cir., 412 F.2d 1171; *Dickson v. Sitterson*, M.D. N.C., 1968, 280 F. Supp. 486; *Smith v. University of Tennessee*, E.D.Tenn., 1969, 300 F. Supp. 777; *Snyder v. Board of Trustees*, N.D. Ill., 1968, 286 F. Supp. 927, involve a medium and subject matter entitled to greater protection than plaintiff's art.[1] Even as to verbal communication the extent of the protection may depend upon the subject matter. See *New York Times v. Sullivan*, 1964, 376 U.S. 254, 84 S. Ct. 710, 11 L. Ed. 2d 686; *Garrison v. Louisiana*, 1964, 379 U.S. 64, 85 S. Ct. 209, 13 L. Ed. 2d 125. We consider plaintiff's constitutional interest minimal.

In this posture we turn to the question whether defendants have demonstrated a sufficient counterinterest to justify their action. The corridor was a passageway, regularly used by the public, including children.[2] Several of the paintings were nudes, male or female, displaying the genitalia in what was described as "clinical detail." A skeleton was fleshed out only in this particular. One painting bore the title, "I'm only 12 and already my mother's lover wants me." Another, "I am the only virgin in my school."

The defendants were entitled to consider the primary use to which the corridor was put. *LeClair v. O'Neil*, D. Mass., 1969, 307 F. Supp. 621. See C.A. Wright, *The Constitution on the Campus*, 22 Vand. L. Rev. 1027, 1040-1043 (1969). On the basis of the complaints received, and even without such, defendants were warranted in finding the exhibit inappropriate to that use. Where there was, in effect, a captive audience, defendants had a right to afford protection against "assault upon individual privacy," see *Redrup v. New York*, 1967, 386 U.S. 767, 769, 87 S. Ct. 1414, 18 L. Ed. 2d 515, short of legal obscenity. Cf. Emerson, *Toward a General Theory of the first Amendment*, 72 Yale, L.J. 877, 938 (1963). To quote from Professor Wright, *supra*, at 1058,

> There are words that are not regarded as obscene, in the constitutional sense, that nevertheless need not be permitted in every context. Words that might properly be employed in a term paper about Lady Chatterley's Lover or in a novel submitted in a creative writing course take on a very different coloration if they are bellowed over a loudspeaker at a campus rally or appear prominently on a sign posted on a campus tree.

Freedom of speech must recognize, at least within limits, freedom not to listen.

---

[1] The cited cases all rest to some extent upon principles of vagueness and overbreadth. We may doubt, however, the value of doctrines based on "chilling effect" and prejudice from lack of fair warning when no penalty is involved beyond an order to desist. In any event, the degree to which specificity will be required should correspond to the importance of the speech interest asserted. In the case at bar the absence of a regulation against offensive exhibitions, and the failure to describe what would be considered offensive, does not impress us as significant.

[2] While the presence of children might be thought to show defendants inescapably reasonable, cf. Ginsberg v. New York, 1968, 390 U.S. 629, 88 S. Ct. 1274, 20 L. Ed. 2d 195, we do not deem it necessary to make such a finding, and rest our decision on broader priniciples.

In hyperconcern with his personal rights plaintiff would not only regard his interest in self-expression as more important than the interests of his unwilling audience, but asks us to add nearly three weeks of such exposure to the five days he has already received. With all respect to the district court, this is a case that should never have been brought.

Judgment reversed. Complaint dismissed.

§1.2.3. *Nenner v. Davis:* **Protector of the Public at Large**

Nenner relies on the holding of the *Close* court: Those mounting an exhibition have a right superior to the rights of the participating artists when there might be a "captive audience" that should be shielded from the works involved. In *Close*, the artworks were "clinically" explicit nudes; in *Nenner*, the work, *Crucified Coyote*, consisted of a stuffed coyote nailed to an 11-foot wooden cross in the style of a crucifix. The artist's explanatory message follows:

CRUCIFIED COYOTE

This work is a reaction to certain Judeo-Christian concepts which inadvertently alienated humanity from animals and the rest of nature when individual worth became a major religious tradition. Unfortunately, we were elevated so high as to be above and beyond the reach of an empathy we once had with the earth. Although there is biblical reference to the veneration of nature as we were deigned its stewards in these texts, the maxim has gone largely ignored. It is possible that when western religion and its reflective culture moved away from paganism and older biblical teachings, it moved too fast, too impulsively, too thoughtlessly and too far. In evidence is our recent rediscovery of what the ancients knew so well; our species can never survive without caring for all other life it shares the earth with.

Whereas holy figures in Judeo-Christian religions are limited to human form, other religions such as Buddhism, Hinduism and most "primitive" religions include animals as dieties. The people of these religions are deeply linked to the earth, much more so than we, and therefore consider animals in a higher place in their lives than we do. For example, when American Indians kill deer for essential food, they pray for the soul of that deer and thank the deer god for giving up that deer for their survival. We, on the other hand, treat the earth and its wild inhabitants as cheap labor only to be exploited. We have no strong beliefs which consider the dignity and well-being of other life we both practically and spiritually depend upon. We steal from the earth its rich bounties rarely attempting to leave it as we found it, or to repair the wounds we have inflicted upon it. As a result, the world gives up at least one species to extinction each day. In a few years it will be at an hourly rate.

In the eleventh hour we are slowly reassuming our stewardship of nature. More and more of us are working toward this end. Perhaps what you experience here will work to accelerate that process.

Paulette Nenner, 28 February 1981

That message, said reviewers in such publications as The Village Voice, was powerfully conveyed.[2]

As New York City's Commissioner of Parks and Recreation, however, Gordon J. Davis felt that the work on exhibition posed a serious danger to some people within his jurisdiction; i.e., children who might view it without intending to while using a different area of the park — not, it should be noted, while *within* the exhibition space.

Does *Nenner* go too far? Does it ignore the political content of the artwork, which is entitled to First Amendment analysis? Does it overlook that Davis' concerns could have been allayed by a means less restrictive than dismantling the exhibit, such as restricting the site and posting a sign at the entrance?

NENNER v. DAVIS

No. 5892/81 (Sup. Ct. N.Y. County, Spec. Term Pt. 1, April 14, 1981)

Petitioner commenced this Article 78 proceeding seeking an order directing respondent Gordon Davis, Commissioner of the Department of Parks and Recreation of the City of New York (Commissioner) to restore an artwork executed by her in an art exhibit currently being held in the Bird House and Arsenal at the Central Park Zoo.

The exhibit is being conducted under the auspices of the New York City Parks Department in conjunction with the New York City Department of Cultural Affairs under the theme of "Animals in the Arsenal." The Commissioner authorized the presentation of the exhibit as an official parks function upon condition that all works of art to be displayed would be submitted to him for review and approval.

The petitioner's work entitled "Crucified Coyote," consists of a dead stuffed coyote that is nailed to an eleven-foot wooden cross formed in the style of a crucifix. This work was not submitted to the Commissioner or his Parks Department aides by the co-curators of the exhibit.

The Commissioner first viewed the object, without notice, shortly before a preview reception to which the press, artists and others were invited. Prior to the public opening, the work was displayed in a prominent place where it could readily be seen by park users including children, not intending to view the exhibition.

The Commissioner immediately objected to the inclusion of the object as being unauthorized and inappropriate but, after discussion, he permitted it to remain for the remainder of the preview showing. Thereafter, on the next day, he ordered it removed and suggested that it would

---

[2] Village Voice, June 3-9, 1981, at 78.

possibly be exhibited at a different place. He offered the services of his Department in trying to locate such a different place.

Petitioner claims she has been denied her constitutional right of freedom of speech and that the Commissioner's action has resulted in an abridgement of her right of freedom of expression. She further claims that she has an absolute right to exhibit her work because public funds have been expended to sponsor the exhibition in a public place.

The Commissioner avers that it is within his power as Commissioner of Parks to exercise the authority vested in him by virtue of Chapter 533 of the New York City Charter to use his discretion and judgment in running the Parks Department for the good of the public at large.

Based upon the record before it this court finds the Commissioner has clearly acted within the scope of his authority.

Further, he has shown extraordinary sensitivity and understanding in his efforts to find a different location for the display of the "Crucified Coyote."

Further, the court is not convinced that petitioner has been denied her constitutional right of freedom of speech and expression.

In order to state a claim for constitutional deprivation, the petitioner must demonstrate that she has a constitutional right which has been abridged. Although there is a right to free expression of ideas, there is no concomitant right to command a particular medium to display or publish a particular idea. *[Avins] v. Rutgers State University*, 385 F.2d 151,153 (3rd Cir., 1967) *cert. denied.*

In *[Avins]*, the court upheld the right of the editors of the Rutgers University Law Review to reject a proposed law review article on the grounds that it was within the rightful discretion of the editors to accept or reject it notwithstanding the fact that Rutgers University receives supporting funds from the State of New Jersey.

In *Close v. Lederle*, 424 F.2d 988-991, (C.C.A.1 1970) *cert. denied*, the court upheld a state university's right to remove an artist's paintings from a university art exhibition. Several of the paintings were nudes, male and female, displaying genitalia in "clinical detail." The paintings were displayed in a corridor of the Student Union, a public passageway regularly used by the public, including children. The court reasoned that the university officials were entitled to consider the primary use of the corridor as a public thoroughfare and during such use, the public was made, in effect, a captive audience and the officials had a right to afford protection against assault on individual privacy.

Here, but for the action of the Commissioner, the "Crucified Coyote" would have been situated where the public, including children, would be exposed to the sight of the object in question, without entering the exhibition hall. Accordingly, the Commissioner was justified in removing the object and affording protection against the assault upon the individual privacy of the members of the public.

Under these circumstances, this court would be loathe to override the actions of the Commissioner.

The petition is dismissed.

§1.2.4. *Piarowski v. Illinois Community College:* Art That Offends

Hard cases make bad law. *Piarowski*, which follows, is just such a case. At issue was an artist's right to show his work free of restraint. For the civil libertarians who would normally come to his support, the difficulty was that his work was — in the eyes of some — racially offensive. The situation was not wholly unlike that in which the American Civil Liberties Union found itself called upon to defend the right of Nazi sympathizers to parade in Skokie, Illinois, in the late 1970s.

While the court ultimately determined that the artist's First Amendment rights had not been violated, this finding was so entangled with extra-constitutional considerations as to make the decision virtually useless as a guide for the resolution of future controversies. *Piarowski* nonetheless stands as a brilliant demonstration of just how intractable a real-life fact situation may be.

PIAROWSKI v. ILLINOIS COMMUNITY COLLEGE
759 F.2d 625 (7th Cir. 1985)

POSNER, C.J. Prairie State College is a junior college owned by the State of Illinois and located just to the south of Chicago; it has 6,000 students. Albert Piarowski is the chairman of its art department. The president and other top officials of the college, defendants along with the college in this federal civil-rights suit under 42 U.S.C. §1983, ordered Piarowski to remove from a public exhibit in the college three works of art that he had created and was displaying there. He claims that by doing this the defendants (whose action, none deny, was state action) violated his rights under the First Amendment, made applicable to the states by interpretation of the Fourteenth Amendment. After a bench trial, the district court gave judgment for the defendants, and Piarowski appeals. Although the underlying dispute is not rare in the art world, see DuBoff, The Deskbook of Art Law, ch. VIII (1977), we have found only two cases that resemble this. In *Close v. Lederle*, 424 F.2d 988 (1st Cir. 1970), an art instructor at a state university, after being invited to exhibit his paintings in a busy corridor, was made to remove them because they were sexually explicit; the First Circuit found no violation of the First Amendment. *Appelgate v. Dumke*, 25 Cal. App. 3d 304, 101 Cal. Rptr. 645 (1972), has similar facts, but went off on waiver grounds.

On the main floor of Prairie State College's principal building is a large open area, the "mall." A room 27 feet by 21 feet in size, the "gallery," adjoins the mall near the entrance to the building. No wall separates the gallery from the mall; the gallery is thus an alcove off the mall. A cafeteria, a book store, and a number of other facilities also open onto the mall, and the part of the mall that adjoins the gallery doubles as a student lounge. The mall is the college's main gathering place and thoroughfare; the classrooms are on the upper floors of the same building.

Piarowski and another member of the art department are the gallery coordinators, meaning that they are in charge of arranging art exhibits for the gallery — exhibits of student work picked by members of the faculty, exhibits of the work of outside artists invited by the coordinators, and finally exhibits of art work by members of the faculty. The college has set no criteria for picking works to be exhibited in the gallery, leaving the matter to the coordinators' judgment.

On March 3, 1980, the "Art Department Faculty Exhibition," an annual affair to which the coordinators invite all the members of the department to contribute (there are four full-time members), opened with works by all four members. Each had decided which of his works to exhibit. Piarowski contributed eight stained-glass windows. Five were abstract; three were representational and became the focus of controversy. One depicts the naked rump of a brown woman, and sticking out from (or into) it a white cylinder that resembles a finger but on careful inspection is seen to be a jet of gas. Another window shows a brown woman from the back, standing, naked except for stockings, and apparently masturbating. In the third window another brown woman, also naked except for stockings and also seen from the rear, is crouching in a posture of veneration before a robed white male whose most prominent feature is a grotesquely outsized phallus (erect penis) that the woman is embracing.

Although when described in words the three stained-glass windows (especially the third) sound pretty obscene, the defendants do not argue that the windows are obscene in the legal sense. The windows are not very realistic; seem not intended to arouse, titillate, or disgust; and are not wholly devoid of artistic merit, or at least artistic intention. They are in the style of Aubrey Beardsley, the distinguished *fin de siècle* English illustrator. Two of Piarowski's windows are imitations of two of Beardsley's illustrations for *Lysistrata*, Aristophanes' comedy, itself sexually explicit, about wives who go on a sex strike in an effort to end the Peloponnesian War. On his deathbed Beardsley ordered his illustrations for *Lysistrata* destroyed as obscene, Weintraub, Aubrey Beardsley: Imp of the Perverse 258 (1976), but the order was not carried out; and though some of the illustrations, with their immense and graphic phalluses, see, e.g., Wilson, Beardsley, pl. 38 (3d ed. 1983), might well be considered indecent even today, the originals are on public display in — with nice irony — the Victoria and Albert Museum. See Weintraub, *supra*, at 199 n.1. The window with the phallus is based on a forged Beardsley drawing entitled "Adoration of the Penis."

Piarowski testified that he never intended the women in the windows to be taken to be Negro women; he used brown glass (he said amber, but the women in two of the windows are darker than that) for contrast. The women could, indeed, be taken to be Polynesian rather than Negro (but they are too dark to be Greek). Of course the "Adoration of the Penis" window would not have been less offensive if the man had been dark and the woman light.

The three windows were clearly visible from the mall, and they provoked a number of complaints from students, cleaning women, and black clergymen, though it is not clear that the clergymen actually saw the windows. Prairie State College serves a community in which Aubrey Beardsley is not a household word; almost half the students are night students, three-fourths are part-time rather than full-time students, and the college has no admission requirements. Anyway the exhibit did not mention Beardsley. After ten days the defendants ordered Piarowski to remove the windows. They suggested he exhibit them in a room on the fourth floor (the floor on which the art department's classrooms are located) that in its one year in use as an exhibit room had been used only for exhibiting photography. The room is smaller than the gallery (10 feet by 25 feet) but large enough to hold all of Piarowski's windows and indeed the whole exhibit. Although the room was being used for another exhibit at the time and it appears, though not clearly, that it would not have been free till the summer (the college is in session during the summer), the defendants may not have known that the room was in use — there is nothing in the record on this question. And they may, for all we know, have been willing to move the photography exhibit somewhere else. Their directive to Piarowski left room for counterproposals: ". . . the three stained glass pieces . . . are to be removed from the mall of the college as soon as possible. If you feel that an alternative place for exhibiting these pieces is needed, the gallery on the fourth floor will be acceptable. Thank you for your cooperation." No counterproposals were forthcoming. Piarowski did not even tell the defendants that the fourth-floor room was occupied. Apparently his objection to exhibiting the windows in that room was not that it was unavailable but that it was out of the way and, more important, that the exhibit should not be broken up.

When Piarowski refused to remove the windows, one of the defendants removed them. That was on Friday, March 14. On Monday the art department voted to close the exhibit rather than break it up and it closed two weeks after it had opened, which is to say a week before it was scheduled to close. In retrospect the defendants might have been wiser to have suffered the exhibit to continue intact for another week and have thereby avoided this lawsuit.

Piarowski intended no political statement by the content and coloring used in his windows, no disparagement of women or blacks, no commentary on relations between the sexes or between the races. The windows were art for art's sake. But the freedom of speech and of the press protected by the First Amendment has been interpreted to embrace purely artistic as well as political expression (and entertainment that falls far short of anyone's idea of "art," such as the topless dancing in *Doran v. Salem Inn, Inc.,* 422 U.S. 922, 932-934, 95 S. Ct. 2561, 2568-2569, 45 L. Ed. 2d 648 (1975)), unless the artistic expression is obscene in the legal sense. See, e.g., *Miller v. California,* 413 U.S. 15, 34-35, 93 S. Ct. 2607, 2620-2621, 37 L. Ed. 2d 419 (1973). And if the college had opened up the gallery to the public to use as a place for expression it could not have regulated that expression anyway it pleased just because the gallery was its property, *Perry Education Ass'n v. Perry Local Educators' Ass'n,* 460 U.S. 37, 45, 103 S. Ct. 948, 955, 74 L. Ed. 2d 794 (1983), or because the artist happened to be a member of the college's faculty. Cf. *Pickering v. Board of Education,* 391 U.S. 563, 568, 88 S. Ct. 1731, 1734, 20 L. Ed. 2d 811 (1968); *Knapp v. Whitaker,* 757 F.2d 827 (7th Cir. 1985). The artist's status as an employee would give the college more control over his activities than over a stranger's, cf. *id.,* at 842; *McMullen v. Carson,* 754 F.2d 936, 938-939 (11th Cir. 1985); *Clark v. Holmes,* 474 F. 2d 928 (7th Cir. 1972) (per curiam), but not unlimited control.

But the public was not allowed to exhibit in the gallery; unlike the municipally operated theater in *Southeastern Promotions, Ltd. v. Conrad,* 420 U.S. 546, 95 S. Ct. 1239, 43 L. Ed. 2d 448 (1975), where outside producers put on plays for the entertainment of the general public, the gallery was not generally available for outsiders to use to display their work. That Piarowski sometimes invited artists from outside the college to exhibit their work in the gallery no more made the gallery a public forum than a teacher's inviting a guest lecturer to his classroom would make the classroom a public forum. The record is silent on how often the work of outside artists was exhibited. The district judge found that the gallery was never used by outsiders, which is clearly wrong. But Piarowski strays from the record, too, when he says in his brief that outsiders were "regularly invited" to exhibit in the gallery—there just is no evidence of that. Occasional use by outsiders, which is all that this record shows, is not enough to make a college art gallery a public forum. See *Perry Education Ass'n v. Perry Local Educators' Ass'n, supra,* 460 U.S. at 47, 103 S. Ct. at 956.

Although *Widmar v. Vincent,* 454 U.S. 263, 102 S. Ct. 269, 70 L. Ed. 2d 440 (1981), held that a state university could not bar religious student groups from its facilities while letting secular student groups use them,

the student groups were autonomous; their relationship to the university administration was the same as that of the theatrical producers in *Southeastern Promotions* to the municipal theater. Prairie State College has not given student groups free access to the gallery, and Piarowski is not a student; indeed, as chairman of the art department and gallery coordinator, he is a part of the college administration. Faculty, unlike students, are employees, and it would make nonsense of the concept of public forum to say that because the employees of a public employer naturally have the use of the employer's property, which is where they work, it is a public forum. They are not members of the public.

We may assume, however, that public colleges do not have carte blanche to regulate the expression of ideas by faculty members in the parts of the college that are not public forums. We state this as an assumption rather than a conclusion because, though many decisions describe "academic freedom" as an aspect of the freedom of speech that is protected against governmental abridgment by the First Amendment, see, e.g., *Sweezy v. New Hampshire*, 354 U.S. 234, 250, 77 S. Ct. 1203, 1213, 1 L. Ed. 2d 1311 (1957) (plurality opinion); *id.* at 262-263, 77 S. Ct. at 1217-1818 (concurring opinion); *Keyishian v. Board of Regents*, 385 U.S. 589, 603, 87 S. Ct. 675, 683, 17 L. Ed. 2d 629 (1967); *Dow Chem. Co. v. Allen*, 672 F.2d 1262, 1274-1276 (7th Cir. 1982); *Gray v. Board of Higher Education*, 692 F.2d 901, 909 (2d Cir. 1982); Note, *Academic Freedom in the Public Schools: The Right to Teach*, 48 N.Y.U.L. Rev. 1176 (1973), the term is equivocal. It is used to denote both the freedom of the academy to pursue its ends without interference from the government (the sense in which it used, for example, in Justice Powell's opinion in *Regents of the University of California v. Bakke*, 438 U.S. 265, 312, 98 S. Ct. 2733, 2759, 57 L. Ed. 2d 750 (1978), or in our recent decision in *EEOC v. University of Notre Dame Du Lac*, 715 F.2d 331, 335-336 (7th Cir. 1983)), and the freedom of the individual teacher (or in some versions — indeed in most cases — the student) to pursue his ends without interference from the academy; and these two freedoms are in conflict, as in this case. The college authorities were worried that Piarowski's stained-glass windows, created by the chairman of the college's art department and exhibited in an alcove off the college's main thoroughfare, would convey an image of the college that would make it harder to recruit students, especially black and female students. If we hold that the college was forbidden to take the action that it took to protect its image, we limit the freedom of the academy to manage its affairs as it chooses. We may assume without having to decide that the college's interest was not great enough to have justified forbidding Piarowski to display the windows anywhere on campus, but it may have been great enough to justify ordering them moved to another gallery in the same building. *Young v. American Mini Theatres, Inc.*, 427 U.S. 50, 96 S. Ct. 2440, 49 L. Ed. 2d 310

(1976), after all, upheld an ordinance regulating the location of "adult" movie theaters; and the plurality opinion states that sexually explicit though nonpornographic art can be regulated more broadly than political speech. See *id.* at 70, 96 S. Ct. at 2452. It cannot on that account be suppressed altogether; but as *Young* suggests, relocation is not suppression, and if reasonable is not fobidden.

This conclusion holds even if we are wrong to think the gallery not a public forum. If it was one, then so was the photography gallery on the fourth floor, and any other room in the main building that would have been suitable for the exhibit; and all together could be viewed as a single public forum for the exhibition of art. A decision as to where within a public forum to display sexually explicit art is less menacing to artistic freedom than a decision to exclude it altogether.

The concept of freedom of expression ought not be pushed to doctrinaire extremes. No museum or gallery, public or private, picks the most prominent place in the museum to display those works in its collection that are most likely to offend its patrons; and even though the consequence of its decision is to discourage — though very mildly we should think — the production of art calculated to shock, to outrage, to *épater le bourgeois*, we do not think the decision has constitutional significance. If Piarowski had given to the man's face in his pastiche of "Adoration of the Penis" the unmistakable likeness of the chairman of the college's board of trustees, we doubt that we would be hearing the argument that the First Amendment prevents any tampering with the siting of a work of art; it would be reasonable in such a case for the college to order the stained-glass window moved to a less conspicuous spot on the campus — especially when the window had been created by an employee of the college, and not just by any employee but by the chairman of the art department and gallery coordinator. Coming closer to the actual facts of this case, if Piarowski had entitled the windows, "Typical Prairie State Coeds," we do not think the college would have been forbidden to order the windows moved to a more discreet location. Or if a member of the art department had submitted such a work of art for display at an exhibit, Piarowski would not have violated the First Amendment by refusing, in his capacity as gallery coordinator, to display it in a conspicuous place. If Claes Oldenburg, who created a monumental sculpture in the shape of a baseball bat for display in a public plaza in Chicago, had created instead a giant phallus, the city would not have had to display it next to a heavily trafficked thoroughfare. The first-floor gallery in Prairie State College's main building is a place of great prominence and visibility, implying college approval rather than just custody, and the offending windows could be seen by people not actually in the gallery. There is no constitutional right to exhibit sexually graphic works of art in a gallery that is missing an outside wall.

At argument Piarowski's able counsel conceded that there would have been no violation of the First Amendment if the defendants had put up venetian blinds to screen the gallery from the mall. This concession acknowledges, quite properly in our view, the existence of some scope for a managerial judgment concerning access to sexually frank pictorial art, even a judgment influenced by the offensive nature of the art. Cf. *Avins v. Rutgers,* 385 F.2d 151 (3d Cir. 1967). But we are told that while Piarowski could not have compelled the college to allow him to exhibit offensive art works in the most prominent place of exhibition, once they were exhibited they could not be ordered moved, even to another gallery in the same building; that having delegated the organizing of exhibits in the gallery to Piarowski and another art professor, the college was constitutionally required to forgo any participation in those decisions — even though Piarowski, when forced to decide whether to exhibit his own work, had a potential conflict of interest between his career objectives as an artist and his managerial responsibilities as a gallery administrator.

Neither the distinction between location and relocation nor the concept of irrevocable delegation is a persuasive ground for reversing the district court. What the parties call the gallery is not to be compared to the National Gallery of Art in Washington, D.C. A room of modest dimensions, it is not even the entire exhibit space of the college, for we know that photographic art is exhibited in a different, although smaller, room on a separate floor. As for the idea that there is a ratchet in play, such that the college could have prevented Piarowski from exhibiting the three stained-glass windows in the gallery in the first place but could not order them removed, we cannot imagine what policy of the First Amendment would be served by making sequence determine outcome. The college authorities did not have to ignore the controversy created by Piarowski's windows. If the college had done nothing it might have been thought to be endorsing the windows by allowing them to be displayed so prominently right off the main thoroughfare, and near the main entrance, of the college. Piarowski's positions as chairman of the art department and gallery coordinator, to the extent known, would enhance the impression of official approval. And while hanging venetian blinds might have limited the audience for the stained-glass windows less than moving them to a less conspicuous exhibition site, we do not think the Constitution requires drawing such fine lines. If the gallery had had two rooms, a front and a back, and the defendants instead of putting up venetian blinds had told Piarowski to move his windows to the back room, the abridgment of free expression would have been trivial. Instead the college had (at least) two rooms, in the same building, suitable for exhibits — only the rooms were not contiguous. The difference between a walk and an elevator ride is not of constitutional dimensions.

If showing Piarowski's work separately from that of the other artists represented in the exhibit might have reduced the exhibit's quality, Piarowski could have suggested moving the entire exhibit to another room, which he did not do. But the premise is in any event dubious. Since the exhibit was simply a group of self-selected works by the members of the department, it is not obvious that it had an artistic integrity to be violated. Piarowski testified that the three objectionable windows were "totally different" from his five other windows (which were abstract rather than representational), although he wanted them exhibited together in order to demonstrate the versatility of stained glass as an artistic medium.

To hold the defendants liable to Piarowski for ordering his work relocated would have disturbing implications for the scope of federal judicial intervention in the affairs of public museums and art galleries. Distinguished public galleries such as the Metropolitan Museum of Art in New York and the National Gallery of Art in Washington would have to worry that if they refused to flaunt their most offensive works of art they might be held to have violated the constitutional rights of artist, donor, or viewer. Nor would it be right to equate Piarowski and the art department to the museum, and the college administrators to a state agency telling the museum what it can and can't exhibit, and where. The gallery was a single room in the college. Piarowski was no more its proprietor than a junior curator at the Metropolitan Museum of Art is the proprietor of the displays he arranges. It cannot be right that if any authority whatever is delegated to a curator, the owner of the museum — the college in this case — is helpless to correct the curator's errors of taste. The precept that in museum management "good taste is the first refuge of the witless," Museum of the City of New York, Explorations of the Ways, Means, and Values of Museum Communication With the Viewing Public 53 (1969) (remarks of Harley Parker); but see Burcaw, Introduction to Museum Work 177 (1975), is not yet engraved in constitutional law.

We emphasize that the college did not offer Piarowski the fourth-floor gallery as an alternative site on a take-it-or-leave-it basis, and may not have known it was already occupied. The college was apparently open for counterproposals, but none were forthcoming. The idea of venetian blinds — even of a disclaimer of college sponsorship or endorsement — was not forthcoming. Piarowski did not tell the defendants that the fourth-floor gallery was occupied, which might have caused the defendants to rethink their edict of removal, especially since the exhibit had only 10 days left to run when the storm arose. Common sense tells us that the chairman of the art department must have known better than anyone else in the college which if any alternative sites might be acceptable to show his art; and if none were acceptable, he should have said so, and did not. He seems to have been more interested in becoming a martyr to artistic freedom than in finding another room in the building to exhibit his work, or persuading the defendants to back off by demonstrating to them the absence of any reasonable alternatives, though we hesitate to conclude that he waived his First Amendment rights like the artist in *Appelgate v. Dumke, supra*.

This is an easier case than *Close v. Lederle, supra*, where the issue was removal, not relocation, though there was a finding there, and not here, that children used the corridor in which the offensive art was hung. If the defendants had said to Piarowski, you cannot exhibit such work anywhere on campus, Piarowski might have been discouraged from creating similar work in the future; for Prairie State College is the most natural site for a member of its art department to exhibit his work. The discouragement is much less, and hence the abridgment of freedom of expression is less, when the college says to him, you may exhibit your work on campus — just not in the alcove off the mall. Although this location maximized the artist's audience, the impact, both on his incentive to create controversial works of art and on the accessibility of those works to the viewing public, of moving it to another place (and we do not mean the broom closet) in the same building would have been slight.

Sefick v. City of Chicago, 485 F. Supp. 644 (N.D. Ill. 1979), which questioned *Close* en route to invalidating the revocation by the City of Chicago of permission to display sculptures in the lobby of a city building, is distinguishable from the present case both because the motive for revocation was political (the sculptures satirized the city's mayor) and because the issue, as in *Close*, was removal rather than relocation. Not every trivial alteration of the site of an art exhibit — not every modest yielding to public feeling about sexually explicit and racially insulting art — is an abridgment of freedom of expression.

When we consider that the expression in this case was not political, that it was regulated rather than suppressed, that the plaintiff is not only a faculty member but an administrator, that good alternative sites may have been available to him, and that in short he is claiming a First Amendment right to exhibit sexually explicit and racially offensive art work in what amounts to the busiest corridor in a college that employs him in a responsible administrative as well as academic position, we are driven to conclude that the defendants did not infringe the plaintiff's First Amendment rights merely by ordering him to move the art to another room in the same building. The judgment of the district court dismissing the complaint is therefore

Affirmed.

§1.2.5. Christo's *Gates*: Public Space versus Public Art

By his *Report and Determination in the Matter of Christo: The Gates*, dated February, 1981 and running 107 pages (excluding exhibits and appendices), Gordon J. Davis, then Commissioner of the New York

City Department of Parks and Recreation, rejected a controversial proposal by Christo and Jeanne-Claude, his wife and partner, to install a work of art in Central Park to be called *The Gates*. Christo's proposal called for the installation of between 11,000 and 15,000 steel-supported, golden-orange banners on 25 miles of park pathways to be installed for a two-week period during the fall of an unspecified year between 1982 and 1985. The artist envisioned "a celebration of the processional, ceremonial walkways of the park" achieved by "activating their overhead space." [3] He explained his concept further:

> By involving the entire topography of Central Park, *The Gates* will be uniquely and equally shared by many different groups, thereby becoming a true Public Work of Art, revealing the rich variety of the people of New York City. Walking through *The Gates*, following the walkways, *The Gates* will be a golden ceiling creating warm shadows. When seen from the buildings surrounding Central Park, *The Gates* will seem a golden river appearing and disappearing and through the foliage of the trees and highlighting the footpaths.[4]

He planned on financing the project in its entirety (at an estimated cost, including insurance, of $5,221,000) just as he had with his other temporary public artworks, such as *Valley Curtain, Running Fence, Stacked Oil Drums,* and the 1985 wrapping of the Pont Neuf in Paris. *The Gates,* however, was not to be. Finding that the project would be, "after all, in the wrong place, at the wrong time, and in the wrong scale," [5] Commissioner Davis denied Christo's permit application, going on to explain, "In all these respects the defects of the physical project mirror the defects of the artist's grasp and understanding of Central Park." [6] The commissioner felt that "*The Gates* simply cannot and should not be forced to fit into New York's greatest public space." [7]

At the heart of Davis' decision was not an aesthetic determination; rather, as guardian of the physical space of Central Park, he felt an obligation to protect the park's structure from "the substantial unknown risks inevitable in such a venture." [8] Indeed, Davis expressed regret that

---

[3] Glueck, City Rejects Christo Plan for Central Park 'Gates' N.Y. Times, Feb. 26, 1981, at C15.

[4] See Davis, Report and Determination in the Matter of Christo: *The Gates*, (Exhibit 7) (Feb. 1981).

[5] *Id.* at 101-102.

[6] *Id.* at 102.

[7] *Ibid.*

[8] *Ibid.*

he had to deny the permit; he said the "decision is made more in sorrow than in anger" due to "what *The Gates'* [sic] offers as public art." [9]

Is this a valid balancing act — public space versus public art, the result of which may be to deny the ability to create because of a prospective work's site specificity? If after the inordinately extensive environmental impact studies done in *The Gates* project are submitted and the public official makes a meritorious decision based on this balance, perhaps it could be considered valid. What if the decision is not based on an environmental considerations, however, but on aesthetics? This problem has arisen in the vociferous dispute now raging over Richard Serra's *Tilted Arc* in lower Manhattan. There the community that was intended to be enhanced by the work has objected to it and gone on to win round one. The acting administrator of the agency responsible for the work's selection, the General Services Administration, has decided to explore an alternate site for *Tilted Arc*. (For an extensive discussion of *Tilted Arc* as a troubled public commission, see Chapter 4.)

Clearly a tension exists between the rights of the majority of users of public space and the right of the individual artist to use it. That there is no absolute right to exhibit in a particular place seems equally clear. [10] In *Silvette v. Art Commission of the Commonwealth of Virginia*, [11] the court, in refusing to accept that plaintiff's First Amendment rights had been violated because the defendant had refused to accept his work without their recommended modifications, said:

> Of course an artist has the right to paint as he chooses. It does not follow, however, that he has the right to compel the Commonwealth to accept and display any or all of his paintings tendered as gifts.
>
> A somewhat similar situation was presented and determined by the Third Circuit, in *Avins v. Rutgers*, the State University of New Jersey, 3 Cir., 385 F.2d 151 (1967), wherein the author of a rejected article he had submitted to the Rutgers Law Review asserted that the rejection of his work . . . violated his

---

[9] *Ibid.*

[10] The United States is not alone in facing the difficult issue of how to deal with grand-scale public art. As reported in the International Herald Tribune of May 11, 1985, London has recently tussled with the same question. Robert Pollak, a 30-year old Czech-born artist, sought to float 1,000 bikini underpants on the Serpentine in London's Hyde Park. He envisioned that the floating briefs would be reminiscent of Claude Monet's waterlily paintings. The Royal Parks Authority originally rejected the project, but the British arts minister, Lord Gowrie, reportedly intervened and urged that permission be granted. Gowrie's assistant, John Dowling, is quoted as saying that the lord "considered it an acceptable form of art, although an unusual form."

[11] 413 F. Supp. 1342 E.D. Va. 1976.

constitutional right of freedom of speech. The Court of Appeals, after noting that the right of freedom of speech does not open every avenue to one who desires to use a particular outlet for expression, concluded ". . . [H]e does not have the right, constitutional or otherwise, to commandeer the press and columns of the Rutgers Law Review for the publication of his article, at the expense of the subscribers to the Review and the New Jersey taxpayers, to the exclusion of other articles deemed by the editors to be more suitable for publication. . . ."

An artist is in a somewhat analogous position—He cannot compel the acceptance of his painting any more than an author can force the publication of his article.[12]

§1.2.6. New York City Graffiti Law: What of Graffiti Art?

If the artist has no absolute right to display work in a particular location (see §1.2.5 *supra*), what of art so tied to its location that it simply cannot effectively exist elsewhere? What of laws that specifically preclude certain artistic creation, such as flag statutes (as in *Radich*, see §1.1.2 *supra*) or anti graffiti laws? We have included New York City's graffiti law in this connection.

NEW YORK CITY GRAFFITI LAW
N.Y. Admin. Code Ch. 18, tit.A, §435-13.2 (1976)

§435-13.2 Defacing property; aerosol paint cans, prohibited.—

a. **Legislative intent.**—The use of broad-tipped pens, spray cans or other marking devices used in connection with writing graffiti on the walls and other places of public buildings, on subways and buses has reached proportions requiring serious punishment for the perpetrators. The defacing of such public property and the use of foul language in many of the writings is harmful to the general public and is violative of the good and welfare of the people of the city of New York.

1. That the need for legislative intervention is necessary and advisable to regulate the distribution and sale of aerosol cans of paint and similar products used in writing graffiti. Punishment by fine or imprisonment insofar as our youthful offenders are concerned has failed to halt this vandalism. It is the intent of the council that any person guilty of writing graffiti on public buildings should be punished so that the punishment shall fit the crime.

We, accordingly, recommend to the judiciary, when an offender has

---

[12] *Id.* at 1346.

been convicted of violating this local law that he be sentenced to remove graffiti under the supervision of an employee of the public works office, New York city transit authority or other officer or employee designated by the court.

b. No person shall write, paint or draw any inscription, figure or mark of any type on any building public or private, or any other property real or personal owned, operated or maintained by a public benefit corporation, the city of New York, or by any person, firm or corporation or any agency or instrumentality thereof, without the express permission of the owner or operator of said property.

c. Absent express permission to the contrary, it shall be unlawful for any person to carry an areosol can of paint in any public building or other public facility with intent to use same in violation of this local law unless such areosol can is delivered completely enclosed in a sealed container, which areosol can cannot be utilized unless the seal is broken and cannot be resealed by the purchaser.

d. **Violations** — Any person who violates this section shall be guilty of a class B misdemeanor punishable by a fine of not more than five hundred dollars or imprisonment for not more than three months, or both.

e. **Separability** — If any clause, sentence, paragraph, section or part of this section shall be adjudged of competent jurisdiction to be invalid, such judgment shall not affect, impair or invalidate the remainder thereof, but shall be confined in its operation to the clause, sentence, paragraph, section or part thereof directly involved in the controversy and in which such judgment shall have been rendered.

§1.2.7. Limitations on the Use of People as Subjects in Art — Privacy and Right of Publicity Statutes

Had the miscreants whom Paul Georges depicted as mugging the muse (see *Silberman v. Georges* reproduced at §1.1.6 *supra*) borne the likenesses of Pablo Picasso and Henri Matisse rather than two local New York City artists, the burgeoning recognition of a so-called right of publicity might have provided their heirs with an alternative basis for bringing an action against the artist. In many respects, the burden of proof would have been easier. The gravamen of the offense would not have been that these individuals' likenesses were used in some defamatory way but simply that they had been used without prior authorization.

Although sometimes described as an extension of the right of privacy, the right of publicity appears to be developing more as a property right rather than a personal one. The right of privacy is, at bottom, the right to be free from, for instance, unwanted or unwarranted publicity; it is the right to be left alone. We include New York's statute in §1.2.8. *infra* as an example of legislation concerning this right. It is a limited law that ceases with an individual's death. The right of publicity, by contrast, centers on the freedom to exploit (and to exclude others from exploiting) the commercial value that may be inherent in, for instance, one's own name, voice, signature, photograph, image, or likeness. In their 1979 article, *Privacy, Publicity and the Portrayal of Real People by the Media*,[13] Felcher and Rubin describe it as a person's "right to profit from [his] general notoriety."

To the extent that this resembles a property right, the question must inevitably arise as to whether such a right — unlike the right of privacy — survives an individual so that it may subsequently be enforced by his heirs or transferees. The courts have been divided on this question. In New York, the right of publicity has been treated as a property right and, accordingly, as descendible. In California, however, the opposite result has obtained. There a state appellate court in *Lugosi v. Universal Pictures*[14] found that the family of the late Bela Lugosi had no right to prevent Universal Pictures from using the actor's name or likeness in producing "Dracula" T-shirts, toys, and other memorabilia. Whatever rights Lugosi may have originally had, the court said, could only have been exercised by him during his lifetime. Section 970 of the California Civil Code, however, was adopted in 1984 to reverse this outcome. Today, subject to certain filing requirements, the right of publicity can be preserved and protected for up to 50 years following an individual's death, provided that the name, voice, signature, photograph, or likeness of that particular individual had "commercial value at the time of his or her death." The statute is not wholly prospective; protection is offered for individuals who may have died as long ago as January 1, 1935.

What does this mean for visual artists? To what extent may they be putting themselves at risk by including in their work the unauthorized likenesses of such iconic figures as Charlie Chaplin, Marilyn Monroe, Malcolm X, or Pablo Picasso? Concerning a painting, artists should not need to worry. Unlike §3344, California's basic right of privacy statute that makes no exception for any kind of art, subdivision (n)(3) of the State's right of publicity statute specifically exempts "single and original works of fine art." Fine art works made in multiples, however — e.g., graphic works (consider, for instance, Andy Warhol's silkscreen print of

---

[13] 88 Yale L.J. 1577 (1979).
[14] 25 Cal. App. 3d 813, 603 P.2d 425, 160 Cal. Rptr. 323 (1979).

Marilyn Monroe) or an edition of bronze portrait busts — may be more problematic. Unless the motivation behind their publication can be demonstrated as political, in which case they would be exempt under another section of the statute, it appears that the creation of such works of art might now be per se the basis for an action for damages.

Since Nashville is to recorded music what Hollywood is to films, it should be no surprise that Tennessee also adopted a right of publicity statute[15] in the same year as California. (What's sauce for a Lugosi should be a comparable condiment for a Presley.) The Tennessee statute applies to both the quick and the dead. While it makes no specific exception for works of fine art, it is by no means clear that these would be deemed of a "commercial purpose" — the principal sort of use that the Act seeks to control.

Three other features of the Tennessee statute ought be noted. First, unlike the California law, its coverage is not limited to the likenesses or images of celebrities, i.e., those whose "names, voice, signature, photograph, or likeness had commercial value at the time of [their] death." It covers everybody. Secondly, there is no requirement for filing in order to activate the right. Thus, the heirs of an individual whose likeness nobody suspected might otherwise have a commercial value would be entitled to relief if the individual's likeness should, in fact, be used from some commercial purpose. Finally, the statute appears to create a right of publicity that might run in perpetuity, provided the right continues to be exercised. Section 4(b) provides that:

> The exclusive right to commercial exploitation of the property rights is terminated by proof of the non-use of the name, likeness, or image of any individual for commercial purposes by an executor, assignee, heir or devisee to such use for a period of two (2) years subsequent to the initial ten (10) year period following the individual's death.

Kentucky has also enacted such a statute.[16] After recognizing that the right of privacy terminates upon death, this rather short statute goes on to say that the right of publicity, a "right of protection from appropriation of some element of an individual's personality for commercial exploitation," [17] does not terminate upon death. Rather, the name or likeness of a public figure shall not be used for commercial profit for 50 years from the date of death without written consent of the executor or administrator of the estate.

---

[15] Personal Rights Protection Act of 1984, Tenn. Code. Ann. §47-25-1101 to 47-25-1108 (1985).

[16] Ky. Rev. Stat. §391.170 (1984).

[17] *Ibid.*

To better understand how these new California, Tennessee, and Kentucky enactments will be applied to works of art — as well as to see how this right of publicity will continue to unfold in states without statutes — we must await judicial interpretations. Nonetheless, artists ought be cautious lest this expanding right of publicity further curtails the range of visual references that they are free to employ. In the end, such constraints on the use of images drawn from day-to-day life are stifling to free expression. If art is indeed a form of speech, it ought not be so easily restricted as appears to have happened with the right of publicity — fundamentally commercial in its genesis. The conversion of so wide a range of images into private property can only be impoverishing for contemporary art and artists.[18]

§1.2.8. New York Civil Rights Law §§50-51: The Right of Privacy

Noteworthy about the New York Right of Privacy Statute, which follows, is that it invokes both a civil and criminal penalty for invasions of the right of privacy.[19]

RIGHT OF PRIVACY STATUTE
N.Y. Civ. Rights Law §50 (McKinney 1976) & §51 (McKinney Supp. 1986)

§50
A person, firm or corporation that uses for advertising purposes, or for the purposes of trade, the name, portrait or picture of any living person without having first obtained the written consent of such person, or if a minor of his or her parent or guardian, is guilty of a misdemeanor.

§51. ACTION FOR INJUNCTION AND FOR DAMAGES
Any person whose name, portrait or picture is used within this state for advertising purposes or for the purposes of trade without the written consent first obtained as above provided may maintain an equitable action in the supreme court of this state against the person, firm or corporation so using his name, portrait or picture, to prevent and restrain

---

[18] For a general overview of the law prior to the adoption of the several state statutes, see Horowitz, An Analysis of the Right of Privacy, 6 Art & Law 941 (1981).

[19] For an interesting analysis of the New York statute in a photography case, see Camera Arts, Oct. 1982, at 26. See also, Mass. Gen. Laws Ann. c.214 §3A (West Supp. 1985); R.I. Gen. Laws §§9-1-28 and 9-1-28.1 (1985); and Okla. Stat. Ann. tit. 21, §§839.1 to 839.3 (West 1983) (which has an interesting exemption for a photographer that permits him to exhibit "specimens" of his work in or about his establishment without violating the statute.)

the use thereof; and may also sue and recover damages for any injuries sustained by reason of such use and if the defendant shall have knowingly used such person's name, portrait or picture in such manner as is forbidden or declared to be unlawful by §50 of this article, the jury, in its discretion, may award exemplary damages. But nothing contained in this article shall be so construed as to prevent any person, firm or corporation from selling or otherwise transferring any material containing such name, portrait or picture in whatever medium to any user of such name, portrait or picture, or to any third party for sale or transfer directly or indirectly to such a user, for use in a manner lawful under this article; nothing contained in this article shall be so construed as to prevent any person, firm or corporation, practicing the profession of photography, from exhibiting in or about his or its establishment specimens of the work of such establishment, unless the same is continued by such person, firm or corporation after written notice objecting thereto has been given by the person portrayed; and nothing contained in this article shall be so construed as to prevent any person, firm or corporation from using the name, portrait or picture of any manufacturer or dealer in connection with the goods, wares and merchandise manufactured, produced or dealt in by him which he has sold or disposed of with such name, portrait or picture used in connection therewith; or from using the name, portrait or picture of any author, composer or artist in connection with his literary, musical or artistic productions which he has sold or disposed of with such name, portrait or picture used in connection therewith.

§1.3. EXPRESSIONS BY OTHERS

§1.3.1. *Fisher v. The Washington Post Co.:* **Can an Art Critic Defame?**

The topic of the first two sections of this chapter is the artist's right to create — i.e., when it is protected and when it is not. The vehicle often used to attempt to suppress speech is the law of libel and slander. In this section, we again look to this area of the law, but this time as it relates to those who comment *about* art rather than create it.

FISHER v. THE WASHINGTON POST CO.
212 A.2d 335 (D.C. App. 1965)

QUINN A.J. Appellant is the owner of a local art gallery. In the spring of 1963 he planned an exhibition of paintings by the artist Irving Amen and he sent a letter to appellee Ahlander, art critic for appellee Washington Post, asking her to review the show. Subsequently, on May 19, 1963, the following paragraph appeared in Mrs. Ahlander's column:

The Fisher Galleries are showing about 20 oils by the noted printmaker, Irving Amen. The paintings are warm in color and expressionist in tendency, but lack the distinction of the prints. They are so badly hung among many commercial paintings that what quality they might have is completely destroyed. The Fisher Galleries should decide whether they are a fine arts gallery or a commercial outlet for genuine "handpainted" pictures. The two do not mix.

Claiming that this article was defamatory, malicious, and injurious to his business reputation, appellant instituted a libel action in which he sought $10,000 damages. After three days of hearing evidence on appellant's case, the court granted appellee's motion for a directed verdict, finding that the article in question came within the doctrine of fair comment and that there was insufficient evidence of malice to go to the jury. This appeal followed.

Fair comment or criticism on a matter of public interest is not actionable so long as the comment is not motivated by malice.[1] The social values inherent in a free interchange of opinion far outweigh the injury which such discussion might cause to a person in the public eye. So long as the comment is the speaker's actual opinion, based on fact, about a matter of public interest, the words are protected unless they are grounded in malice or go beyond a discussion of the public works or acts of the subject of the opinion.[2] Thus, critical comments about works of literature,[3] musical performances,[4] practices of art experts,[5] vivisectionists,[6] and even store owners[7] have been found to be within the fair comment doctrine. So, too, are comments about the manner in which an art gallery presents its paintings, for the public is as much interested in the display as in the paintings themselves. Just as the music or drama critic may comment on the concert hall's acoustics or the play's sets, the art critic may comment on the paintings' surroundings. Moreover, appellant himself actively sought out the review of his show. As the court said in *Brewer v. Hearst Pub. Co., supra* n.2, "In doing so, he invited criticism and free expression by others of their opinion of his conduct and cause. He should not be heard to complain if the criticism so invited is not gentle."[8]

Appellant asserts that it was error for the trial court to apply the fair

---

[1] Potts v. Dies, 77 U.S. App. D.C. 92, 132 F.2d 734 (1942).

[2] Brewer v. Hearst Pub. Co., 185 F.2d 846 (7th Cir. 1950).

[3] Sullivan v. Meyer, 78 U.S. App. D.C. 367, 141 F.2d 21 (1944).

[4] Cherry v. Des Moines Leader, 114 Iowa 298, 86 N.W. 323 (1901).

[5] Porcella v. Time, Inc., 300 F.2d 162 (7th Cir. 1962).

[6] Brewer v. Hearst, *supra* n.2.

[7] Afro-American Publishing Company, Inc. v. Jeffe, D.C. Cir. (No. 18363, May 27, 1965).

[8] 185 F.2d at 850.

comment doctrine because the libel went to the conduct of his trade and business. Fair comment is a complete defense to a suit for libel and the words are not made actionable by the fact that the complaining party is injured in his business reputation.[9] It follows that critical comments may have adverse financial effects upon artists or their exhibitors, but to allow suit on the basis of such injury would be to emasculate the fair comment doctrine completely.

The fair comment defense goes only to opinions expressed by the writer and does not extend to misstatements of fact.[10] Appellant contends that Mrs. Ahlander's statements that the pictures were "badly hung" and that there were "many commercial paintings" in the gallery were misdescriptions of fact and that the article was thus not within the fair comment doctrine. Whether pictures are badly hung at an exhibit and whether a painting is "commercial" in quality are clearly matters for critical opinion. Indeed, appellant himself conceded in his brief and at trial that opinions could differ on such matters. Such statements are "neither false nor demonstrably true"[11] and are protected by the doctrine of fair comment so long as they have a factual basis.

Appellant next contends that in order for opinion to be protected by the fair comment doctrine, the facts upon which it is based must be stated or referred to so that the reader might draw his own conclusions. While this is the rule of some authorities,[12] others have stated that the criticism is not actionable if it is based on facts otherwise known or available to the public.[13] This is the view adopted by the Restatement of Torts §606:

> . . . To be privileged comment under the rule stated in this Section, therefore, the facts upon which the opinion is based must be stated or they *must be known or readily available* to the persons to whom the comment or criticism is addressed, as in the case of a newspaper criticism of a play or a review of a book. . . . [Emphasis supplied.]

And it appears to be the rule applied in at least one case in this jurisdiction. In *Sullivan v. Meyer, supra* n.3, a news story stated that plaintiff was "the author of a defeatist, anti-Jewish book." At the trial for libel the entire 195-page book was read to the jury, although, of course, it was not contained in the article itself. The United States Court of Appeals affirmed the jury verdict that there was no defamation because the charges

---

[9] Porcella v. Time, Inc., *supra* n.5.

[10] Washington Times Co. v. Bonner, 66 App. D.C. 280, 86 F.2d 836, 110 A.L.R. 393 (1936).

[11] Potts v. Dies, *supra*, 77 U.S. App. D.C. at 93, 132 F.2d at 735.

[12] A. S. Abell Company v. Kirby, 227 Md. 267, 176 A.2d 340, 90 A.L.R.2d 1264 (1962); Cohalan v. New York Tribune, 172 Misc. 20, 15 N.Y.S.2d 58 (1939).

[13] See Annotation, 90 A.L.R.2d 1279 and cases cited therein.

were true, but it further stated that the trial court incorrectly ruled the issue of fair comment out of the case and could have directed a verdict for the defendant after having read the book. Thus the court indicated that opinion could be fair comment even if the facts upon which it is based are not included along with the opinion.

We believe that this is the better view, for criticism in the art world may be based on such intangibles as experience, taste, and feeling. It is often impossible for the critic to explain the basis for his opinion; to require him to do so would tend to discourage public discussion of artistic matters. So long as the facts are available to the public, the criticism is within the doctrine of fair comment. The Amen show was open to the public both before and after publication, and the facts upon which Mrs. Ahlander based her conclusions were readily accessible to any who wanted to test them.

Whether the article in question is fair comment and criticism on a matter of public interest is a question of law and the trial court was correct in not allowing the issue to go to the jury.[14] Evidence was introduced showing that the criticism had some factual basis and it does not matter that the jury could have disagreed with the conclusions drawn therefrom.[15] Thus, the only question which might have gone to the jury was whether the article was motivated by malice on the part of Mrs. Ahlander. But the record shows only innuendo and speculation which could not lead to a finding of malice. Since there was insufficient evidence on the issue to go to the jury, the court correctly directed a verdict for appellees.

Finally, appellant contends that the trial court erred in stating that he was bound by the testimony of Mrs. Ahlander, whom he called as an adverse witness. While this was error, it was harmless, for in actuality the court allowed appellant to cross-examine and attempt to rebut her testimony. In any case, even without Mrs. Ahlander's testimony there was insufficient evidence of malice to go to the jury.

Affirmed.

§1.3.2. *Porcella v. Time, Inc.:* A California Fairytale

Porcella, which follows, would in all likelihood be disposed of today on constitutional grounds rather than by recourse to the Illinois law of libel, with its defenses of fair comment and innocent construction. As such, this case resembles *Fisher* (§1.3.1 *supra*). *Porcella* has additional

---

[14] Sullivan v. Meyer, *supra* n.3; Potts v. Dies, *supra* n.1; Porcella v. Time, Inc., *supra* n.5; Brewer v. Hearst Pub. Co., *supra* n.2.

[15] Cohalan v. New York Tribune, *supra* n.12.

interest, however, for the light it sheds on the American art market during the 1950s. The case involved a Life magazine article alleged to be libelous, which, after describing how inflated valuations can be used to increase the value of charitable contributions, concluded:

> So far in the U.S. there are no legal penalties for such dealings. The quasi experts are not held responsible for their authentications. The auction houses are not required to back up the authenticity of the works they sell. And with the art market enjoying its biggest boom, the flood of dubious "masterpieces," both old and new, is sure to continue." [1]

Change is slow, but it does come. Now the appraiser who knowingly prepares an incorrect valuation of an artwork for submission to the IRS may be prosecuted for the crime of preparing a false income tax return.[2] Under the 1984 amendments to the Internal Revenue Code, even an appraiser who unknowingly makes an assessment that is subsequently determined to be egregiously incorrect may be in essence "blacklisted" from doing any further appraisals for taxpayers. Also, it is no longer entirely true that auction houses are not held to the authenticity of the works they sell. (See the discussion of this issue in Chapter 10.) Still wholly apt, however, is the Porcella court's observation about art experts in general: "We know of no governmental control of this profession, or requirement that a diploma or other authorization from any seat of learning must [be] held."

PORCELLA v. TIME, INC.
300 F.2d 162 (7th Cir. 1962)

Before SCHNACKENBERG, CASTLE and KILEY, Circuit Judges.

SCHNACKENBERG, C.J. Amadore Porcella, a citizen of the Republic of Italy, plaintiff, appeals from a judgment of the district court granting the motion of Time, Inc., a New York corporation, defendant, dismissing plaintiff's cause at his costs, on the ground that his complaint fails to state a claim upon which relief may be granted.

The parties are in agreement that the substantive law of Illinois governs in this case.

According to his brief, plaintiff, an art expert, brought this action for libel against defendant, publisher of Life, a weekly magazine, to recover damages resulting from an article published in the issue of December 7, 1959, wherein allegedly libelous language concerning plaintiff in his professional capacity as an art expert imputed to him lack of skill and

---

§1.3. [1] What Is So Rare as a Rare Find? Life, Dec. 7, 1959.

[2] See, for example, United States v. Wolfson, 573 F.2d 216 (5th Cir. 1978).

competence, as well as dishonesty, trickery and misconduct, to the injury and damage of plaintiff's reputation as an art expert.

The court ruled that the language is not libelous within the meaning of the innocent construction rule, and that the language complained of constituted fair comment.[1]

According to plaintiff, the article pertained to the discovery of certain paintings in California which were attributed to certain old masters by plaintiff in his capacity and profession as an art expert.

WHAT IS SO RARE AS A RARE FIND?
California produces the latest reasons
for viewing "Old Masters"
suspiciously

The news item from California was a rarity even in that land of overnight fairy-tale fortunes. Ten paintings, owned by Italian immigrants in Pasadena, were said to be Old Masters worth millions of dollars —"the greatest art find of the century!" This was the latest of a long line of "fabulous discoveries" that have burst upon the art world in recent years. The California canvases had long been in the Naples family of Maria and Alfonso Follo. When Maria married a GI, she brought them to her new home in Pasadena and tucked them away in a closet and under a bed.

A year ago Alfonso Follo, a TV repairman who had come to live with his sister, dropped in at the neighborhood electrical supply store of Charles and Jay di Renzo and invited them to come up and see the family paintings some time. The Di Renzos came, saw and promptly made a deal with the Follos to help sell the art. Their first step: to find an expert to identify the paintings. They telephoned one Amadore Porcella, an Italian who had just authenticated a Raphael in Chicago.

Hurrying out to Pasadena, Porcella took one ecstatic look at the paintings and pronounced them masterpieces. One, he said, was a long-lost painting by the 17th Century Italian master, Caravaggio, and he valued it at more than $1 million. Porcella then called in his friend, Alexander Zlatoff-Mirsky, a Chicago art restorer, for some heavy work. After a few weeks of working with "powerful solvents," Zlatoff-Mirsky declared the paintings almost as good as new and ready for unveiling.

Shortly after the "masterpieces" were made public, ominous doubts began to gather about their authenticity. A Pasadena expert said he had seen the paintings several years ago and found them worthless. A New York scholar said the long-lost Caravaggio was known through authentic copies and bore no resemblance to the Pasadena work. Finally an Italian priest disclosed that the Follos' so-called Caravaggio was in fact a copy of a minor 17th Century painting which hangs in Naples. The California fairy tale was showing signs of being just that.

---

[1] In this opinion, unless otherwise indicated, the word "article" refers to the alleged libelous article.

BUSY TEAM AND ITS THRIVING OUTLET

Discovering a trove of valuable Old Masters would be a once-in-a-lifetime stroke of luck for most mortals. But Porcella and Zlatoff-Mirsky have, as one of their friends observed, a "remarkable talent" for it. Just in the course of the past year they have authenticated more than a dozen "masterpieces."

The pair's instinct for art showed up early. Porcella started out to be a painter in Rome. At the age of 17, he explains, he switched to art criticism. Around 1934 he worked briefly at the Vatican gallery (compiling a guidebook of the art collection). Since then he has written a number of books and "authenticated" innumerable paintings. Zlatoff-Mirsky worked as a painter in Russia until the 1930s when he migrated to Chicago and took up the more remunerative profession of restoring art.

In 1958 the two "experts" met for the first time in New York. Soon after, Porcella went to Chicago and settled down in Zlatoff-Mirsky's studio to inspect the paintings which the Russian was restoring. In a short time they identified "millions of dollars" worth of art, tagged with such top-drawer names as Leonardo da Vinci, Rembrandt and Raphael.

The dual role of source and thriving outlet for most of the team's discoveries is played by the Sheridan Art Galleries, a Chicago auction house which specializes in old and modern "masterpieces." For the past 20 years their highly prized consultant and art restorer has been none other than Zlatoff-Mirsky. Recently the gallery's reputation was slightly tarnished when two buyers proved that the paintings they bought there were fakes. The gallery refunded the complainants' money, later sold one of the paintings for an even higher price.

THE INS AND OUTS OF AUTHENTICATING

Active as they are, Professor Porcella and his colleague Zlatoff-Mirsky have not cornered the art "discoveries" market. Rival authenticators continue to turn up, armed with new-found treasures and long-lost masterpieces. Some of them are reputable authorities. Others are "experts" with elusive or spurious credentials. Whatever their background, many authenticators seem to be in the business at least as much for love of money as love of art.

How much an authenticator makes depends generally on the importance of the painter's name and the authenticator's evaluation of the particular painting. An expert is inclined to charge more for recognizing a Leonardo than a Lastman. Often the price of authenticating a painting far exceeds the amount paid for the work. Porcella received $2,000 for authenticating a work that was bought for half that price. . . . Professor Erik Larsen received $550 for certifying a painting that originally cost his client $20. . . .

To enhance their prestige and give validity to their judgment, authenticators often publish books or articles reproducing their "discoveries." But their talent for writing is apt to show up best in the flamboyant certificates they compose for their "masterpieces."

The more unscrupulous authenticators have found a bonanza in providing income tax outs. A buyer who pays $1,000 for an old painting may call upon an "expert" to evaluate his purchase. For a comfortable fee, the "expert" values the painting at many times its actual worth. The buyer then donates the painting to a museum or some other institution, thereby getting a sizable write-off on his income tax for his charitable donation.

So far in the U.S. there are no legal penalties for such dealings. The quasi experts are not held responsible for their authentications. The auction houses are not required to back up the authenticity of the works they sell. And with the art market currently enjoying its biggest boom, the flood of dubious "masterpieces," both old and new, is sure to continue.

Several photographs and printed explanations appeared with the article.[2]

---

[2] These explanations (designated alphabetically) are:

(a) THE "DISCOVERY" in Pasadena was labeled Caravaggio's long-lost painting of Mary Magdalene by the Follos' so-called experts. Other well-known authorities say that the stiff figure and the murky landscape are unlike the art of Caravaggio.

(b) THE ORIGINAL from which the Pasadena painting was probably copied hangs in the art gallery of the Gerolomini Friars in Naples. It was not done by Caravaggio, according to Father Antonio Bellucci . . . but probably by an undistinguished contemporary name Gian Battista Caracciolo, who was called "Battistello." The work has hung in this gallery for 300 years. The subject of the Magdalene was popular with painters of the Baroque period.

(c) ALTHOUGH A COPY, this is what Caravaggio's still-lost Magdalene looked like. It was made by [a] Dutch artist a few years after Caravaggio painted his picture. This is in Barcelona. Another copy made in 1612 by a Flemish artist, is in Marseilles.

(d) OWNERS OF "MASTERPIECES" are Alfonso Follo . . . , his sister Maria and her husband Chester Hataburda. . . . Here they talk to lawyer Lester Olson about their personal dispute with their partners, the di Renzos.

(e) DISPLAY of name artists at the Sheridan Art Galleries in Chicago is supervised by the director, Jack Shore. . . . The paintings have been labeled as . . . a "Poussin," "Rembrandt," and "Steen"; . . . "Correggio," "Metsys" and a "Leonardo da Vinci" which is held by Shore.

(f) REPAIR SHOP for "masterpieces" is the studio of Alexander Zlatoff-Mirsky . . . who sports artist's beret when he is on the job. He is surrounded by paintings which he discovered and Porcella authenticated. They include a "Rubens" . . . , "El Greco" . . . , "Van Dyck". . . .

(g) AUTHENTICATOR Amadore Porcella inspects a painting in his Rome apartment. In foreground are photographs of controversial paintings in Pasadena.

(h) COMPARISON of Pasadena painting which Porcella attributes to Luca Giordano with an authentic Giordano in Florence reveals few similarities, many striking differences. Pasadena picture . . . , showing centaur carrying off Hercules' wife, seems based on Giordano's Rape of Persephone. . . . But ungainly poses, theatrical faces and claw-like hands in Pasadena work indicate it was done by an unskilled follower of the 17th Century master.

(i) AUCTION VICTIM, Richard Feigen, bought painting . . . which Sheridan Art Galleries attributed to modern master, Paul Klee. Feigen, a Chicago art dealer, checked work with two Klee experts who identified it as a forgery. He then returned picture to the Sheridan galleries and got his money back.

(j) BUYER J. P. De Laney hired Porcella and Larsen to identify purchase. Porcella labeled it Giorgione; Larsen, a del Piombo. Others doubt both labels.

(k) DISCOVERER Maurice Goldblatt attributes latest "find" to Raphael's father, Giovanni Santi. Goldblatt has authenticated art for Sheridan galleries.

(l) MEDIUM was called into the act by Antonio Follo, brother of the Pasadena Follos, to give advice on his family's paintings. In a table-tipping session in Naples, medium

The question arises in this case as to what extent public comment may be made about plaintiff in the practice of his profession as an art expert, in the course of which, as he alleges in his complaint, he renders "expert counsel, advice, opinions, evaluations and authentications pertaining to paintings, drawings and related works of art, to art museums, art collectors, art dealers and persons possessing such works of art." Plaintiff claims "a reputation for professional skill, competency and proficiency as an art expert in the eyes of the public."

We know of no governmental control of this profession, or requirement that a diploma or other authorization from any seat of learning must have been held by plaintiff.

Certainly plaintiff would be entitled, as any other person would be, to redress against any false statements of fact maliciously published in regard to him. However, in his complaint, as explained in his brief, *ante* 1, plaintiff's denial of the truth of the statements in the article has been limited to those charging or implying that plaintiff is not a qualified and recognized art expert and those imputing to plaintiff, as an art expert, a lack of skill, competence and fitness, as well as dishonesty, trickery and misconduct.

It is these statements which plaintiff charges defendant "wilfully, recklessly and maliciously wrote, edited . . . published. . . ."

In addition to plaintiff's own admission that he occupied a position in a public field, it is obvious that as an expert he was able in the appraising of works of art to not only have an effect upon the market for the paintings and the prices paid therefor, but he also was in a position to appraise art donated by patrons for charitable purposes, who thereby would be the beneficiaries of tax deductions under the tax laws of the United States. In the latter activity he was in a position to leave his imprint upon the federal government's collection of revenue from the public.

Our analysis of the alleged libelous article convinces us that, insofar as the complaint charged it to be false, it is an expression of the publisher's comments and opinions upon the activities of plaintiff as an art expert with a description of the entire setting in which he was active. It might well be characterized as a satirical recital by an author who made no effort to conceal his belief that there were some authenticators of paint-

---

. . . professed to have made contact with 18th Century prince. Prince said that the paintings are worth "millions of dollars."

(m) BEAMING BENEFICIARIES of an "art treasure" are children of Mr. and Mrs. Alex Schiffelbian Jr. of Center Moriches, N.Y., whose future education is partly tied to painting of Magdalene on wall. Schiffelbians bought painting in furniture shop in Northport for $20. They showed it to Professor Erik Larsen of Georgetown University who declared it as long-lost Van Dyck worth at least $15,000. Other experts reject his attribution — underlining the problems in this controversial field.

ings less reliable than others. The article, insofar as it offended plaintiff, merely expressed the author's opinion, rather than made a false statement of any fact. Plaintiff was engaged in a field which he admits (and even boasts) was in the public domain and, as such, he was subject to comment by the public press as to his activities in that field.[3] Certainly there are no facts alleged to even suggest any personal animus between him and defendant in this case.

Because of the public nature of plaintiff's activities and the controversial question as to the genuineness of the alleged work of old masters, it is for the court to decide whether the publication was reasonably capable of the meaning ascribed to it by plaintiff. *Kulesza v. Chicago Daily News, Inc.,* 311 Ill. App. 117, 125, 35 N.E.2d 517.

In *Brewer v. Hearst Publishing Co.,* 185 F.2d 846, at 850 we said:

> The publications in the instant case are fair comment and criticism on a matter of public interest and as such are not actionable. The essential elements of fair comment in order to be deemed not actionable are: (1) that the publication is an opinion; (2) that it relates not to an individual but to his acts; (3) that it is fair, namely that the reader can see the factual basis for the comment and draw his own conclusions; and (4) that the publication relates to a matter of public interest.

Moreover, in the case at bar, we are required to apply the rule recognized in Illinois as the innocent construction rule.

As we said in *Crosby v. Time, Inc.,* 254 F.2d 927, at 929:

> The so-called innocent construction rule, that is, if language is capable of innocent construction it should be read and declared non-libelous, is firmly established in Illinois. *La Grange Press v. Citizen Pub. Co.,* 252 Ill. App. 482, 485; *Dilling v. Illinois Publishing and Printing Co.,* 340 Ill. App. 303, 306, 91 N.E.2d 635; *Parmelee v. Hearst Pub. Co., Inc.,* 341 Ill. App. 339, 343, 93 N.E.2d 512; *Epton v. Vail,* 2 Ill. App. 2d 287, 119 N.E.2d 410. In the latter case, the Court in dismissing a complaint stated (opinion not published):
>
> "The language must receive an innocent construction when susceptible of such interpretation and cannot by innuendo be extended beyond a reasonable construction. [Citing cases.]"

---

[3] In Dilling v. Illinois Publishing & Printing Co., 340 Ill. App. 303, 91 N.E.2d 635, 637, which was a libel action, the court said:

> According to the allegations of her complaint, plaintiff sought public support and patronage, thus inviting public criticism. The fact that defendants were reporting and commenting on a matter of public interest appears from the complaint. Hence, defendants' right of fair comment in a matter of public interest was properly presented for determination by their motion to dismiss, and it was unnecessary to plead this right as an affirmative defense. Manifestly the executive committee of the California American Legion does not share plaintiff's views on Americanism. In our view this expression of difference of opinion as reported in the article here complained of is not actionable per se.

More recently, in *John v. Tribune Company,* Jan. 23, 1962, 181 N.E.2d
105, the Illinois Supreme Court said:

> We further believe the language in defendant's articles is not libelous of
> plaintiff when the innocent construction rule is consulted. That rule holds that
> the article is to be read as a whole and the words given their natural and
> obvious meaning, and requires that words allegedly libelous that are capable
> of being read innocently must be so read and declared nonactionable as a
> matter of law. Although this court has not heretofore expressed the rule, it has
> been adopted and applied by our Appellate Courts and by Federal Courts
> sitting in Illinois.

We hold that the district court correctly ruled that the article is not
libelous within the meaning of the innocent construction rule and that
the language complained of constituted fair comment.

For these reasons the judgment from which this appeal has been taken
is affirmed.

Judgment affirmed.

KILEY, C.J. (concurring). I concur in the result reached in the majority
opinion. My concurrence is confined to the adequate ground of the fair
comment rule. I expressly refrain from joining in the application of the
innocent construction rule as stated by the Illinois Supreme Court in *John
v. Tribune Company,* 181 N.E.2d 105, decided January 23, 1962.

§1.3.3. *Fisher v. The Washington Post Co.:* The Law of Libel as Applicable to Art Criticism and Other Opinions

Until it was rendered obsolete by the broader constitutional view
of libel that the Supreme Court began to formulate in the mid-1960s, the
doctrine under which *Fisher* was decided — i.e., that there was a privilege (particularly for the professional reviewer or critic whose views
had been specifically solicited) to express an opinion on a matter of public
interest "so long as the comment is not motivated by malice" — did
yeoman service in protecting art critics against defamation actions by
aggrieved artists.

Another noteworthy occasion on which the doctrine was invoked
involved a dispute — in retrospect, almost farcical — between two of the
more prominent members of the New York art world, the painters Ad
Reinhardt and Barnett Newman. Notwithstanding the ultimate somber-
ness of his paintings, Reinhardt's writings and other observations about
art were infused with great wit. Still vividly remembered are the acerbic
"art comics" and "satires" that he drew for the liberal tabloid newspaper
P.M. and the magazine Art News in the 1940s and 1950s.

During the summer of 1953, Reinhardt delivered a paper entitled *The
Artist in Search of an Academy, Part Two: Who Are the Artists?* at a sympo-

sium in Woodstock, New York. The paper was subsequently published the following year in the summer issue of the College Art Journal, a quarterly publication of the College Art Association. Grouping his fellow contemporary artists into various categories, Reinhardt described one such group as follows:

> Fourth, the latest up-to-date popular image of the early fifties, the artist-professor and traveling-design-salesman, the Art-Digest-philosopher-poet and Bauhaus-exerciser, the avant-garde-huckster-handicrafts-man and edu-cational-shop-keeper, the holy-roller-explainer-entertainer-in-residence-(Albers, Bolotowsky, Chermayeff, Diller, Ferren, Greene, Holtzman, Holty, Morris, Motherwell, Newman, Wolff, Vytlacil, etc.).[3]

Then, summing up his various categories (but naming no further names), he added: "Are these the 'artists'? Are Professional jobbers, Pepsi-cola-humanists, careerist-Romancers, Professional-button-holers and their followers, the 'fine' artists?"[4]

Newman sued Reinhardt and the College Art Association for libel. He claimed that the references to him were untrue, that they were malicious, and that, by innuendo, they suggested that he was, among other things, a charlatan, a fake, an incompetent, and an egotistical, dishonest, and ludicrous individual, without the integrity required of an artist dedicated to the creation of his work, and that he exploited art for commercial and social purposes. The defendants answered that the article implied none of these things but that Reinhardt's words, in any event, were privileged as fair comment and criticism on a matter of public interest. Given the long personal friendship between the two artists, they also denied that there had been any malice.

The trial judge permitted Newman to present his case, but then dismissed the suit on the grounds that the evidence offered by Newman and his wife — they were the only two witnesses — failed to support the causes of action pleaded in the complaint. Subsequently, without a written opinion, the Appellate Division of the Supreme Court of New York unanimously affirmed the trial court's dismissal of Newman's suit.

Sturdy as the "fair comment" defense proved to be, the authors of newspaper, magazine, and other forms of criticism have enjoyed even stronger protection still since the Supreme Court "federalized" the law of libel in *New York Times Co. v. Sullivan*,[5] and more particularly since it drew a sharp distinction between actionable "facts" and nonactionable

---

[3] Reinhardt, The Artist in Search of an Academy, Part Two: Who Are the Artists?, 1954 College Art J. 314, 315 (summer).

[4] *Ibid.*

[5] 376 U.S. 254, 84 S. Ct. 710, 11 L. Ed. 2d 686 (1964).

"opinions" in *Gertz v. Robert Welch, Inc.*[6] So long as critics confine themselves to opinions, the presence or absence of malice is no longer relevant. They are virtually immune from prosecution for libel. As the Court said in *Gertz*, "Under the First Amendment there is no such thing as a false idea. However pernicious an opinion may seem, we depend for its correction not on the conscience of judges and juries but on the competition of other ideas."[7]

What legal recourse then remains for the painter, playwright, or filmmaker who feels aggrieved by what he or she considers a defamatory review? One theoretical strategy might be to assert that the utterances complained of are facts rather than opinions. If this were demonstrated along with a showing of malice, a recovery might still be possible. The difficulty of such a case in practice, however, can be gleaned from *Mr. Chow of New York v. Ste. Jour Azur S.A.*[8] While this involved neither art nor drama nor even films — it was, rather, an aggressively prosecuted lawsuit concerning fried rice and sweet and sour pork — it powerfully suggests that there are virtually no circumstances under which straight aesthetic criticism can serve as "a breeding ground for successful libel actions."[9]

The case concerned a highly unfavorable review of a New York City Chinese restaurant published in the 1981 French edition of the *Gault/Millau Guide to New York*. The restaurant's owner sued for libel. Following a full trial, the judge instructed the jury that, as a matter of law, six statements included in the review were statements of fact and that if any one of them was proven false, defamatory, and to have been made with malice, it would support a finding of libel. The jury returned a general verdict for the plaintiff and awarded nominal damages. Shortly thereafter, a unanimous decision of the Second Circuit Court of Appeals reversed the lower court and ordered the complaint dismissed.

Illustrative of the court of appeals' approach is its handling of two of the statements that the trial judge had determined to be statements of fact: that "the sweet and sour pork contained more dough . . . than meat" and that the rice was "soaking . . . in oil"[10] The court based its opinion on the Supreme Court's holding in *Greenbelt Cooperative Publishing Assn. v. Bresler*[11] that the constitutional protection afforded state-

---

[6] 418 U.S. 323, 94 S. Ct. 2997, 41 L. Ed. 2d 789 (1974).
[7] *Id.* at 339-340, 94 S. Ct. at 3007, 41 L. Ed. 2d at 805.
[8] 759 F.2d 219 (2d Cir. 1985).
[9] *Id.* at 228.
[10] *Id.* at 222.
[11] 398 U.S. 6, 90 S. Ct. 1537, 26 L. Ed 6 (1970).

ments of opinion was not lost simply because an opinion is expressed through the use of figurative or hyperbolic language The Court of Appeals found that, from the perspective of an ordinary reader, the reviewer's language — particularly in a publication known "for being interesting and fun to read" [12] — would clearly be understood as expression of opinion. The reviewer obviously believed that the pork was too doughy and the rice too oily.

> Read reasonably, the statements are incapable of being proved false. For example, the proper amount of oil in fried rice is clearly a matter of personal taste. What is too oily for one person may be perfect for some other person. The same can be said for . . . the amount of dough in sweet and sour pork. . . . Perhaps Mr. Chow could prove the reviewer's personal tastes are bizarre and his opinions unreasonable, but that does not destroy their entitlement to constitutional protection.[13]

Important here is that it was the embodiment of these statements in a *review* that, in the court's analysis, made it so likely that the ordinary reader would consider them to be opinions. Citing *Ollman v. Evans*[14] for the proposition that regard should be given to "the different social conventions or customs inherent in different types of writing," [15] the court also quoted with approval the following holding in *Greer v. Columbus Monthly Publishing Corp.:*[16] "By its very nature, an article commenting upon the quality of a restaurant or its food, like a review of a play or movie, constitutes the opinion of the reviewer." [17]

For art reviewers, no less than for drama or film critics, this appears to be extremely broad protection. Whether it may nonetheless have its limits is still open to exploration. What if, for example, a critic does not merely offer opinions about the quality of the works of art being shown at an art gallery but then goes on to make assertions about the management policies or practices by which such a gallery is operated?

In December 1982, Regina Hackett, the art critic of the Seattle Post-Intelligencer, wrote a wrap up column about the preceding year's activities in Seattle's museums and commercial art galleries. One establishment that she commented on was the Foster/White Gallery:

> Many galleries became more conservative in their exhibition programs, steering clear of unknowns and concentrating on artists with name familiarity. Galleries in this category include . . . Foster White.

---

[12] 759 F.2d at 229.

[13] *Ibid.*

[14] 750 F.2d 970 (D.C. Cir. 1984).

[15] 759 F.2d at 226, *quoting Ollman,* 750 F.2d at 984.

[16] 4 Ohio App. 3d 235, 448 N.E.2d 157 (1982).

[17] 759 F.2d at 227, *quoting Greer,* 4 Ohio App. 3d at 238, 448 N.E.2d at 161.

Commercial gallery owners who continue to take their chances and let their artists experiment without insisting they turn in work that was sure-fire salable were few. . . . Even some established and critically acclaimed artists had difficulty convincing Foster White's gallery director to let them show work that wasn't overwhelmingly salable.[18]

In January 1983, Hackett reviewed an exhibition entitled "Functional Art—Future Traditions" at Foster/White. Observing that art is whatever artists say it is, she went on to remark:

Art is not, however, whatever art dealers say it is. This crucial difference makes Foster White's functional art show an insult to those who care about art. . . .

Foster White . . . is leading its artists by their noses into what may be called the new practicality. In the process this gallery betrays a basic disrespect for art on its own terms. The gallery message is clear: Paintings that explore light, color and form just don't cut it anymore in the marketplace. To give them consumer appeal, why not turn them into bedspreads? . . .

[O]verall the show is not an art show, and Foster White shouldn't be celebrating its 10th anniversary by pretending that it is. It's tough enough to be an artist already. If Foster White's new direction prevails, soon visual artists will be asked for paintings that are self-cleaning floors and poets will be expected to provide recipes for bread in their verses.[19]

Shortly thereafter, Donald Isle Foster, the gallery's owner, commenced a suit against Hackett and her employer, The Hearst Corporation, claiming that the two articles were libelous and injurious to the plaintiffs' business relationships with "artists, sculptors, craftsmen, and purchasers and patrons of art and art objects."[20] Among the defenses pleaded were the traditional one of fair comment, and the more contemporary one of constitutional privilege. Regarding both, they also pleaded an absence of malice.

Following several strenuous rounds of discovery (criss-crossed by legal questions as to Hackett's right to protect the confidentiality of her sources), the case was settled in March 1984. As part of the settlement, the Seattle Post-Intelligencer ran a clarification by Hackett. Without retreating from any of her earlier statements, she acknowledged that they merely represented her "views as a critic" and were in no way intended "to imply that Foster/White would never show any art that was experimental or wasn't overwhelmingly salable" or that the gallery "literally forced artists to participate" in its functional art exhibition.[21]

---

[18] Seattle Post-Intelligencer, Dec. 29, 1982, at D1.
[19] Seattle Post-Intelligencer, Jan. 20, 1983, at C9.
[20] *Ibid.*
[21] Seattle Post-Intelligencer, March 9, 1984, at 4.

Shorn thus of any factual inferences, Hackett's observations could once again be safely anchored in the constitutionally protected harbor of opinion. What we are still left to ponder is whether a court, on such a set of facts, might find the plaintiff's case little more than an effort to use libel laws to silence a hostile critic, or whether some useful distinction is to be drawn between a critic's comments on the management practices of an arts organization and that same critic's personal response to the art that such an organization presents. Put otherwise, do exactly the same rules of immunity hold for criticizing a museum as for criticizing the artworks that it shows? We don't yet know.

CHAPTER TWO

Reproduction Rights

•

A. INTRODUCTION TO COPYRIGHT LAW

§2.1. An Overview

§2.2. The Visual Arts: Where Copyright Problems Might Arise
Berkowitz & Leaffer, *Copyright and the Art Museum*

B. WORKS OF FINE ART

§2.3. The Copyright Cases Introduced
§2.4. The Severability of Copyright from the Work of Art

§2.5. Must Fine Art Be Original to Be Copyrighted?

D. PATENTS: ADDITIONAL PROTECTION FOR THE ARTIST

§2.11. Pros and Cons of Patents

A. INTRODUCTION TO COPYRIGHT LAW

§2.1. An Overview

The concept of copyright—the legal term for controlling the reproduction of an author's work—enjoys a critical role in art law, being frequently linked in discussion with ideas about the nature of a work of art, the authorship of artwork, the essence of moral right, resale rights, and constitutional protections.

Copyright law, of course, comprises a substantial body within the corpus of intellectual property, and a treatise-length discussion of its myriad facets and complexities is beyond the scope of this chapter.[1] We have focused our attention here on those issues of copyright law that continue to be of most immediate concern to visual artists and collectors.

Included in this chapter is a review of basic copyright principles — the conceptual "building blocks" that are essential to a basic understanding of the scope of protection offered by copyright law to artworks. These basic concepts are illuminated with a series of cases that touch upon the most critical issues involving the visual arts. The cases often raise as many questions as they answer — a phenomenon often true of copyright law in general. However, their value in indicating the fundamental concerns of the artist and collector remains undiminished.

---

§2.1. [1] See M. Nimmer, Nimmer on Copyright (1985); see also W. Strong, The Copyright Book: A Practical Guide (2d ed. 1982).

§2.1.1. The Statutory Basis of Copyright

The U.S. Constitution is the fundamental source of copyright protection in this country. Article I, §8 provides that Congress shall have the power to "promote the Progress of Science and useful Arts, by securing for limited Times to Authors and Inventors the exclusive Right to their respective Writings and Discoveries." As will be demonstrated in this chapter, the constitutional grant of copyright law was long ago extended to works created by a visual artist, and in recent years new and intriguing questions have been repeatedly raised and litigated. The federal Copyright Act of 1909,[2] and more recently, the Copyright Revision Act of 1976[3] provide the statutory basis for American copyright law. As with any major revision, the earlier Act continues to apply to works created before its effective date, January 1, 1978. Furthermore, although most law has arisen under these Acts, a number of basic copyright decisions were decided under their predecessors; these remain sound jurisprudence today.

The Copyright Revision Act of 1976, representing a significant modification of the 1909 Act, did not have as its principal focus the visual arts. Nonetheless, a number of its provisions deal with the special problems facing artists and, almost necessarily, the rights of those who acquire art, whether by gift, purchase, will, or devise. Furthermore, recent amendments to the federal tax statutes — principally the Economic Recovery Act of 1981 (ERTA) — contain provisions relevant to the copyright interests of the artist and of those who may acquire rights through him.

§2.1.2. Ownership of Copyright as Distinct from the Tangible Object

What unique rights does the ownership of copyright give the owner? Copyright is a property right and as such is subject to some of the same attributes as ownership of tangible personal property. However, because copyright is an intangible right, it has acquired some special attributes.

The most basic of these is that ownership of a copyright is distinct from ownership of the material object in which the copyright is embodied. Transfer of a material object does not of itself convey any right in copyright in that object, nor, in absence of an agreement, does transfer of a copyright convey a property right in the object itself. Thus under the

---

[2] 17 U.S.C. §101.
[3] 17 U.S.C. §404(c).

Copyright Revision Act, in contrast to the basic rule at common law,[4] if an artist sells a painting, the copyright in the work is not transferred. If the purchaser wishes to own the copyright in the work, he must obtain a specific transfer of the copyright.

§2.1.3. Divisibility

Copyright is often referred to as a "bundle of rights" that attach to the material object. Divisibility is a corollary of this concept.

The Copyright Revision Act expressly provides that copyright is divisible — that is, one or more parts of this bundle of rights that constitute copyright may be transferred to a party, or parties, while retaining other parts.[5] Thus, an artist can sell his original painting to a collector, after having sold the first right of reproduction to a publisher, and retain the right to reproduce the painting for Christmas cards, ash trays, or other multiples. The statute provides that the term "copyright owner" with respect to "any one of the exclusive rights comprised in a copyright, refers to the owner of that particular right."[6]

§2.1.4. Notice

Notice is the formal indication of copyright ownership placed on the work. The Copyright Revision Act prescribes a specific form of notice that must be placed on every published work. Section 401 provides that whenever a work protected under the statute is "published" in the United States or elsewhere the following form of notice shall be placed on all publicly distributed copies of the work:

(1) The symbol © (the letter C in a circle), or the word "Copyright," or the abbreviation "Copr."; and
(2) The year of the first publication of the work. . . . The year date may be omitted where a pictorial, graphic, or sculptural work . . . is reproduced in or on greeting cards, post-cards, stationery, jewelry, dolls, toys, or any useful articles; and
(3) The name of the owner of copyright in the work, or an abbreviation by which the name can be recognized, or a generally known alternative designation of the owner.[7]

---

[4] See, e.g., Pushman v. New York Graphic Society, Inc., 287 N.Y. 302, 39 N.E.2d 249 (1942), reprinted at §2.4.2 *infra*.

[5] Copyright Revision Act of 1976 §101.

[6] *Ibid.*

[7] Copyright Revision Act of 1976 §401.

The notice is required to be affixed to the copies "in such a manner and location as to give reasonable notice of the claim of copyright." [8]

There is an anachronism in the date of notice requirement. Under the prior statutes, which had provided for an across-the-board term of copyright (28 years plus renewal) dating from first publication, there was a logic to requiring the publication date. The new statute, however, affords an indeterminate copyright term — namely, the period ending 50 years after the artist's death — unless the work is made for hire. Accordingly, there is no relationship between the publication date and the duration of the term. In the case of made-for-hire artwork, the duration of copyright is 75 years from publication or 100 years after creation. Therefore, the date in the notice may be unrelated to any of the relevant time periods. As a result, a third party curious as to whether a work has entered the public domain is without guidance.

The statute does, however, attempt to alleviate the problem associated with omission of the notice. Section 405 provides that the omission of the copyright notice does not invalidate the copyright in a work if (1) the notice has been omitted from no more than a relatively small number of copies distributed to the public (obviously offering no protection in the usual case to the visual artist) or (2) registration for the work has been made before or is made within five years after publication without notice, and a reasonable effort is made to add notice to all copies distributed to the public in the United States after the omission has been discovered. This protective provision would seem to be of little help to the painter who sells a work without the requisite notice. Although the work might have been registered — without the date of notice — prior to publication, the artist is nevertheless required to make a "reasonable effort" to add the notice to the work after publication. The chances of a painter retrieving a work in order to add the copyright notice after the work has been sold are remote at best. On the other hand, it may be that the effort in itself would be sufficient.

Notwithstanding the apparent incongruity of the new statute concerning inclusion of the date in the copyright notice on a published work, there is at least one provision that ties the holder of copyright to the date of publication. That provision specifies that a grant of copyright interest may be terminated either at the end of a thirty-five year period that runs

---

[8] *Ibid.* A continuing source of uncertainty is the extent to which a foreign artist, who has not placed a notice on his published work (because the foreign law may not have required it), may enforce his foreign copyright in the United States. A recent case, Hasbro Bradley, Inc. v. Sparkle Toys, Inc., 780 F. 2d 189 (2d Cir. 1985), suggests that he may not. Notice is required to prevent it from falling into the public domain.

"from the date of publication of the work" under the grant or "at the end of forty years from the date of execution of the grant, whichever term ends earlier." [9]

§2.1.5. Publication

The concept of publication remains an important element in copyright. As stated in the preceding discussion about notice, every published work must include the statutory notice for copyright to be retained. Accordingly, the determination of what constitutes publication and when it occurs remains vital.

Professor Melville B. Nimmer in his treatise on copyright took the view that under the Copyright Revision Act of 1976 the public display of a work of art, or of copies thereof, without concurrent public sale or public offer of sale does not constitute publication.[10] In his opinion, "the ambiguity of the pre-1978 law on this point was removed by the explicit definition of 'publication' under Section 101 of the current Act." [11]

This view is supported by the comments of Congressman Kastenmeier, Chairman of the House subcommittee that reported out the bill that became the current Copyright Act. He stated in the House debate:

> . . . I would like to discuss several questions which have been raised concerning the meaning of several provisions of S. 22 as reported by the House Judiciary Committee and of statements in the committee's report, No. 94-1476. One of these questions involves the meaning of the concept of "publication" in the case of a work of art, such as a painting or statue, that exists in only one copy. It is not the committee's intention that such a work would be regarded as "published" when the single existing copy is sold or offered for sale in the traditional way—for example, through an art dealer, gallery, or auction house. On the other hand, where the work has been made for reproduction in multiple copies — as in the case of fine prints such as lithographs — or where multiple reproductions of the prototype work are offered for purchase by the public—as in the case of castings from a statue or reproductions made from a photograph of a painting—publication would take place at the point when reproduced copies are publicly distributed or when, even if only one copy exists at that point, reproductions are offered for purchase by multiple members of the public.[12]

The Senate and House reports contain identical language on this subject. That language reads as follows:

---

[9] Copyright Revision Act of 1976 §203.

[10] See 1 M. Nimmer, Nimmer on Copyright §4.09 (1985).

[11] *Ibid.*

[12] 122 Cong. Rec. H10874-5 (daily ed. Sept. 22, 1976).

It should be noted that, under the definitions of "publication" in section 101, there would no longer be any basis for holding, as a few court decisions have done in the past, that the public display of a work of art under some conditions (e.g., without restriction against its reproduction) would constitute publication of the work. And, as indicated above, the public display of a work of art would not require that a copyright notice be placed on the copy displayed.[13]

There is a serious question in our minds, however, as to whether this is necessarily so. The Copyright Revision Act of 1976 defines "publication" and "publicly" in its elaborate set of definitions.[14] The language, relevant to visual art, reads as follows:

"Publication" is the distribution of copies . . . of a work to the public by sale . . . or by rental, lease or lending. The offering to distribute copies . . . to a group of persons for purposes of further distribution . . . or public display, constitutes publication. A public performance or display of a work does not of itself constitute publication.

To perform or display a work "publicly" means —

(1) to perform or display it at a place open to the public or at any place where a substantial number of persons outside of a normal circle of a family and its social acquaintances is gathered. . . .[15]

Under §106 of the Act the copyright owner has the exclusive right to "reproduce the copyrighted work"[16] and to "display the copyrighted work publicly."[17] Section 109(b) of the Act, however, undercuts the exclusive right of public display. It provides the following:

Notwithstanding the provisions of section 106(5), the owner of a particular copy lawfully made under this title, or any person authorized by such owner, is entitled, without the authority of the copyright owner, to display that copy publicly, either directly or by the projection of no more than one image at a time, to viewers present at the place where the copy is located.

The key question, then, is whether a public display without a statutory notice constitutes a publication and hence places the work in the public domain.

It appears that Nimmer and Kastenmeier are not wholly in accord on this question. Kastenmeier suggests that public display of an artwork does not constitute a publication regardless of whether the work is accompanied by an offer of sale. Nimmer suggests, however, that an offer of sale at a public display would constitute publication.

Neither Nimmer nor Kastenmeier, however, makes reference to the

---

[13] S. Rep. No. 473, 94th Cong., 1st Sess. 126 (1975); H.R. Rep. No. 476, 94th Cong., 1st Sess. 144 (1975).

[14] See Copyright Revision Act of 1976 §101.

[15] *Ibid.*

[16] Copyright Revision Act of 1976 §106(1).

[17] *Id.* at §106(5).

impact, if any, of the definition of "publicly" or of §109(b) on the meaning of "publication."

The implication of the definition of "publicly" is to provide a safe harbor to persons who display a work, or permit a work to be displayed, before a limited audience. Obviously, one who purchases a painting — with or without a copyright notice — can display it in his home and in view of his personal acquaintances, and by virtue of §109(b) may display it publicly. But how safe is the harbor? First, even under Nimmer's view, the conclusion is predicated on their not being an "offer of sale" of the work; most paintings exhibited at galleries, and certainly auction houses, however, are offered for sale. Second, if an offering cannot safely be made with a display, one must determine how many persons constitute a "substantial" number and whether the count must be taken on one or a number of successive occasions. Third, one must decide what constitutes a place open to the public. Perhaps an opening of an exhibit by invitation only would not run the risk of constituting a publication, or of its being publicly displayed, but the balance of the time during which an exhibit is open to public view may be enough to constitute a public display and thereby a publication. Moreover, since the word "copies" includes "the material object . . . in which the work is first fixed" and "pictorial, graphic, and sculptural works" require a copyright notice "when published," [18] it would seem that a public display took place and therefore if there was an offering of sale of the work, there probably was "publication."

Furthermore, although copyright is not necessarily lost if a notice has been omitted, protection requires the omission on "no more than a relatively small number of copies . . . distributed to the public" or registration made within five years after publication and a reasonable effort to add notice to all copies after the omission has been discovered.[19] Inasmuch as an original painting may have no copies it would be extremely difficult for an artist to comply with this provision.

The statute is not clear as to when, if at all, a public display accompanied by an offer of sale would constitute a publication. Also, it is not clear what the impact of §109(b) in a case where the public display accompanied by an offer of sale has not been authorized by the copyright holder. Is that to be deemed a divestive publication? It seems that such a public display should not destroy the copyright owner's right.

Parenthetically, although the courts developed the concept of "limited publication" as against "general publication," it does not appear that

---

[18] *Id.* at §104.
[19] *Id.* at §405.

under the present Copyright Act this doctrine would be very helpful if there were no restrictions on disclosure of the work or its copying.[20] Accordingly, it would appear that if any artist wishes to protect his copyright, he would be well advised to place the statutory notice on each work.

§2.1.6. Works Made for Hire

There are, of course, artists who are employed on a continuing basis, but many work on commission. Works for hire made on commission are covered in §201 of the Copyright Revision Act. The Act provides that in the case of a work made for hire, the employer or other person for whom the work was prepared is considered the author and owns all rights held in the copyright. This is a frightening idea for most artists.

The term "work made for hire" is among those defined in §101 of the Act. It is defined as follows:

(1) a work prepared by an employee within the scope of his employment; or
(2) a work specially ordered or commissioned for use as a contribution to a collective work, as a part of a motion picture or other audio-visual work, as a translation, as a supplementary work, as a compilation, as an instructional text, as a test, as answer material for a test, or as an atlas, if the parties expressly agree in a written instrument signed by them that the work shall be considered a work made for hire. For the purpose of the foregoing sentence, a "supplementary work" is a work prepared for publication as a secondary adjunct to a work by another author for the purpose of introducing, concluding, illustrating, explaining, revising, commenting upon, or assisting in the use of the other work, such as forewords, afterwords, pictorial illustrations, maps, charts, tables, editorial notes, musical arrangements, answer material for tests, bibliographies, appendices, and indexes, and an "instructional text" is a literary, pictorial, or graphic work prepared for publication and with the purpose of use in systematic instructional activities.

It is clear that if a traditional employment relationship exists and a written instrument does not provide otherwise, the employer, not the artist, owns the copyright. In all other cases (except when a piece is specially ordered or commissioned as part of a collective work or falls into one of the seven other specific categories, *and* when the parties agree in writing that the work is a work for hire) the copyright apparently belongs to the artist. The recent cases of *Aldon Accessories, Ltd. v. Spiegel* and *Peregrine v. Lauren Corp. (see* §§2.7.1. and 2.7.3 *infra)*, however, suggest that these distinctions are not so clear.

---

[20] See 1 M. Nimmer, Nimmer on Copyright §4.13[B] (1985).

The real problem here is determining whether an employment situation exists. Most vexing in resolving this issue is the distinction between the traditional common law "master-servant" relationship and the relationship of the independent contractor to his employer. Authority is divided on this issue.

Prior to the 1976 Copyright Act, the Court of Appeals for the Second Circuit had held that the work made for hire provision was not limited to the traditional common law relationship but extended to an independent contractor relationship where the commissioning party had control of the work.[21] Some authorities believed that subdivision (1) of the work made for hire definition in the 1976 statute was restricted to the narrow master-servant relationship.[22] This view, however, has been rejected by the Second Circuit Court of Appeals in the *Aldon Accessories* case and by the Colorado District Court in the *Peregrine* case. (See §§2.7.1 and 2.7.2.) We point out that the brochure prepared by the Copyright Office in 1977 (shortly after enactment of the statute) states that the term "other person" apparently was included to make it clear that the person who commissions a work that falls within the §101 definition of a work made for hire shall be regarded as the author. The earlier case of *Roth v. Pritikin*[23] indicated that an independent contractor would have different rights depending on whether the 1976 statute or the predecessor statute applied.

§2.1.7. Termination

As noted in our discussion on notice (see §2.1.4 *supra*), the Copyright Acts of 1909 and 1976 provide for different terms of copyright protection. Other than these automatic expirations provided therein, what rights do the original owners of a copyright have to terminate any grant or transfer they may have made? Section 203 of the 1976 Act contains the following rather extraordinary provision:

§203. TERMINATION OF TRANSFERS AND LICENSES GRANTED BY THE AUTHOR
(a) Conditions for Termination. — In the case of any work other than a work made for hire, the exclusive or nonexclusive grant of a transfer or license of copyright or of any right under a copyright, executed by the author on or after January 1, 1978, otherwise than by will, is subject to termination under the following conditions:

---

[21] See Picture Music, Inc. v. Bourne, Inc., 457 F.2d 1213 (2d Cir. 1972). See also Yardley v. Houghton Mifflin Co. at §2.6.6 *infra*.

[22] Latman & Ginsberg, N.Y.L.J. 1 (Nov. 18, 1983).

[23] 710 F.2d 934 (2d Cir.), *cert. denied*, 104 S. Ct. 394 (1983).

(1) In the case of a grant executed by one author, termination of the grant may be effected by that author or, if the author is dead, by the person or persons who, under clause (2) of this subsection, own and are entitled to exercise a total of more than one-half of that author's termination interest. In the case of a grant executed by two or more authors of a joint work, termination of the grant may be effected by a majority of the authors who executed it; if any of such authors is dead, the termination interest of any such author may be exercised as a unit by the person or persons who, under clause (2) of this subsection, own and are entitled to exercise a total of more than one-half of that author's interest.

(2) Where an author is dead, his or her termination interest is owned, and may be exercised, by his widow or her widower and his or her children or grandchildren as follows:

   (A) the widow or widower owns the author's entire termination interest unless there are any surviving children or grandchildren of the author, in which case the widow or widower owns one-half of the author's interest;

   (B) the author's surviving children, and the surviving children of any dead child of the author, own the author's entire termination interest unless there is a widow or widower, in which case the ownership of one-half of the author's interest is divided among them;

   (C) the rights of the author's children and grandchildren are in all cases divided among them and exercised on a per stirpes basis according to the number of such author's children represented; the share of the children of a dead child in a termination interest can be exercised only by the action of a majority of them.

(3) Termination of the grant may be effected at any time during a period of five years beginning at the end of thirty-five years from the date of execution of the grant; or, if the grant covers the right of publication of the work, the period begins at the end of thirty-five years from the date of publication of the work under the grant or at the end of forty years from the date of execution of the grant, whichever term ends earlier. . . .

(5) Termination of the grant may be effected notwithstanding any agreement to the contrary, including an agreement to make a will or to make any future grant. . . .

A few observations should be made with respect to this provision. First, this right to terminate cannot be waived by the artist or his family. Subdivision (5) states that termination of the grant may be effected "notwithstanding any agreement to the contrary, including an agreement to make a will or to make any future grant." Second, the procedures set out for terminating a grant must be scrupulously followed: Notice to terminate must be effected within the five-year period commencing thirty-five years from the grant and served not less than two or more than ten years from the effective date of termination, and a copy of the notice must be recorded in the Copyright Office before the effective date of termination. Third, the right of termination does not apply to a work made for hire. Obviously, if a person is dealing with the purported owner of the copyright, he must be certain that the rights he is being granted may not be subject to termination prior to the contemplated term during which the copyright is to be exploited.

With respect to visual art, this right may be more theoretical than real. Inasmuch as the original, created art may exist in only one unique form, and by hypothesis the copyright to the work (and probably the work itself) was transferred thirty-five years earlier, it would seem that only the most astute artist (or artist's family) would be sufficiently knowledgeable to effect the termination.

§2.1.8. Renewals

Because the terms of copyright created under the 1909 Act may overlap January 1, 1978 (the effective date of the 1976 Act), renewal can remain a vital issue for the visual artist or collector. Most important, it may still be necessary to renew a copyright. If a work was in its first term of copyright as of January 1, 1978, a renewal is imperative to extend copyright protection another 47 years. Renewal must be made during the last year of the initial copyright period and must be made by the proper claimant; namely, the artist or his family, except in the case of a work made for hire for which the proper claimant would be the employer or its assignee or successor.

§2.1.9. Transfers

Like any other property right, copyright may be freely transferred from one person to another. What constitutes an effective transfer is denoted in the Copyright Act.

Transfers of copyright, other than by operation of law, are not valid unless the instrument of conveyance is in writing.[24] This provision makes it clear that, unless the artist expressly transfers the right to copyright in a particular work, the sale of the tangible object (a painting or sculpture) does not carry with it the copyright in the work.

A transfer of copyright may, but need not, be recorded in the Copyright Office in order to give the public "constructive notice" [25] of the facts stated in the document. This is adequate only if (1) registration has been

---

[24] Copyright Revision Act of 1976 §204.
[25] *Id.* at §205(c).

made for the work and (2) the work is specifically identified, so that after the documentation is indexed by the register of copyrights, it would be revealed by a reasonable search under the work's title or registration number. Thus, a blank assignment of "all copyrights that I may own" would not provide appropriate constructive notice.[26]

As under prior law, although registration is not a prerequisite to obtaining copyright, it is a prerequisite to instituting an infringement suit. Suit may be instituted *only* after registration for a cause of action that arose prior to registration.[27] Thus, to institute a suit in the name of the copyright holder of record, any assignment should be recorded before the suit is commenced. Recordation also provides the safest method of preserving one's copyright interests in situations relating to priority among conflicting transfers.[28]

Finally, "transfer of copyright ownership" in §205(f) includes every conceivable form of transfer (including mortgage) except the grant of a nonexclusive license.[29]

§2.1.10. Probate Rights and Charitable Deduction

There is an important area that, while strictly speaking is not wholly embodied in copyright law, is sufficiently pertinent to merit discussion in this section. It is the subject of probate rights in copyright and the charitable deduction for contributions of works of art.[30]

Any of the exclusive rights of copyright may be bequeathed. As discussed above, it is possible to transfer the material object (i.e., the painting or sculpture) to one person and the copyright to another. Furthermore, if a work were not specifically bequeathed, a residuary beneficiary would receive the rights to the painting included in an estate and the copyrights thereto. The right of termination of the copyright interest does not, however, go to the residuary beneficiary. As §203 provides, after the author's death the right of termination may be exercised only by a specific class of beneficiary: the widow or widower, unless there are children or grandchildren.

There is another aspect of probate relating to copyright. Generally a gift tax or estate tax deduction cannot be claimed if there is a gift to charity with a retained interest unless the transfer is of fractional interest, in

---

[26] *Id.* at §205.

[27] *Id.* at §205(d).

[28] *Id.* at §205(e).

[29] *Id.* at §101.

[30] For a more complete discussion of the deductibility of charitable contributions, see Chapter 13.

which case the deduction is limited to the fraction that is given. Furthermore, a split charitable transfer to a charity will qualify for a deduction only if the gift can be placed in the form of a guaranteed annuity or can pay out a fixed annual percentage of its fair market value. Art works generally cannot meet that test.

Prior to 1982 a charitable deduction was not allowable if an individual gave the original artwork to charity and retained the copyright interest attributable to the work. Section 423 of ERTA however, amended §§2055(e) and 2522(c) of the Internal Revenue Code to permit, under certain circumstances, a deduction for an inter vivos or testamentary gift of an artwork, but not its copyright, to a charitable organization. As amended, §2055(e) permits an estate tax deduction for persons dying after December 31, 1981, if there is a qualified contribution with a retained copyright interest, i.e., a transfer to a "qualified organization if the use of the property by the organization is related to the purpose or function constituting the basis for its exemption under Section 501 [of the Internal Revenue Code]." The related-use issue could present a problem for certain collectors who wish to give valuable paintings (while retaining the copyright interest) to a charity that is unable to meet the related-use test. A gift to a private nonoperating foundation will not meet the requirements of this provision.

If the collector never had a copyright interest because the artist retained it, or if the collector is making a gift of both the work of art and copyright, he would not be making a split interest transfer and presumably should not be bothered by the related use test of §2055. A related question is whether the retention of the copyright will affect the fair market value of the gift. A House Committee Report suggests that it will not. It states the following:

> [R]ecent changes in copyright law treat the tangible object (i.e., the original artwork) and the intangible copyright as separate items of property. These two items of property typically are not transferred together. As a result, the value of each item of property can be determined separate from sales of similar properties. Moreover, the use or exploitation of the art work or copyright generally does not affect the value of the other property. Accordingly, the value of the art work (determined from comparable sales) which is used to determine the amount of the charitable deduction should provide a high degree of correlation with the value of property received by charity.[31]

Recently, regulations clarifying this point have been issued by the IRS.[32]

---

[31] H.R. Rep. No. 201, 97th Cong., 1st Sess. 184 (1981).

[32] See Lerner, Final Sec. 2055(e)(4) Regs May Result in Loss of Charity Deduction for Artist's Estate, J. Taxn. 300 (May 1985), discussing the final regulations issued by the IRS.

It has been pointed out that the statute speaks of a qualified contribution of a *work of art*. The statute does not mention a contribution of a copyright interest, however. Therefore, if a decedent (collector) transferred a copyright interest alone, no charitable deduction would lie since such a transfer would be a split-interest transfer not in unitrust form.

Moreover, if an artist transfers an artwork but retains the copyright interest, his heirs could not obtain a separate charitable deduction for a gift of the copyright inasmuch as a copyright is not a capital asset under §1221(3) of the Internal Revenue Code. The benefit of §2055 to artists is not in obtaining an additional charitable deduction but in permitting their heirs to exploit the retained copyright interest.[33]

§2.2. THE VISUAL ARTS: WHERE COPYRIGHT PROBLEMS MIGHT ARISE

The article that follows, while ostensibly directed to museums, provides a useful introduction to copyright problems relevant to the visual arts. Its scope is much broader than its title, and the article is an effective bridge between the concepts introduced in the first section of this chapter and the case law that follows.

BERKOWITZ & LEAFFER, COPYRIGHT AND THE ART MUSEUM
8 ART & L. 249 (1984)

1. INTRODUCTION
1.1. Introductory Example
Perhaps more than any other institution, the art museum is a daily setting for a wide range of copyright problems. Consider the following sequence of events: an art museum is having an exhibition of the work of a prominent photo-realist painter.[1] At the time, the museum is

---

[33] See generally, Lerner, Representing Artists, Collectors and Dealers 90 (1983).

[1] Photo-Realism, or photographic realism, is a style of painting developed in the late 1960's.

A painting was made to resemble the impression of a sharply focused photograph, the sharpness and precision of detail being evenly distributed over the whole with no subordination in deference to variations of psychological interest.

The Oxford Companion to Twentieth-Century Art at 433, (H. Osborne ed. 1983). Some artists who paint in this style include Richard Estes, Chuck Close, Don Eddy and Audrey Flack. L. Meisel, Photo-Realism (1980).

considering for purchase two of the artist's works, one painted in 1970 and another painted in 1979. The exhibition will consist of works on loan from other museums, works on loan from private collections, and one painting from the museum's own collection. Photographers hired by the museum have taken photographs of the artist at work and several of his paintings. These will be used for promotion of the exhibition and for didactic purposes. In a small gallery located next to the exhibition, the museum staff has prepared an audio-visual program about the artist, accompanied by music. The museum staff has prepared a catalogue for the exhibition containing photographs of the paintings, as well as critical essays contributed by several scholars, including the museum's curator of contemporary art. In the bookstore, the museum will sell the catalogue, postcards of several paintings from the exhibition, and a poster advertising the exhibition.

During the exhibition, a dance troupe from the local university will perform a program in the museum's auditorium. It has prepared a program of modern dance choreographed to contemporary music, and set against a background of changing slide images of photo-realist paintings.

1.2. Importance of Copyright in the Museum Context

This typical sequence of events, involving an exhibition of contemporary art, illustrates how administrators of an art museum almost daily confront the law of copyright.

Among the many questions arising from this introductory example are:

Are the works under purchase consideration subject to copyright protection?[2] Are they affected by the New Copyright Act which came into effect in 1978?[3]

What are the copyright implications in displaying[4] the works of art on loan from museum or private collections and reproducing[5] them in posters, publicity materials[6] and the exhibition catalogue?

---

[2] For discussion of publication and forfeiture problems under the 1909 Copyright Act [Act of March 4, 1909, Ch. 320, 35 Stat. 1075] and the 1976 Copyright Act [17 U.S.C. §§101-810 (1982)], see *infra* §4 (notes 77-102 and accompanying text).

[3] For a discussion of copyright infringement generally, see *infra* §10 (notes 265-79 and accompanying text).

[4] For a discussion of exclusive rights generally, see *infra* §8 (notes 167-70 and accompanying text); for the display right in particular see *infra* §§8.12-8.13 (notes 214-20 and accompanying text).

[5] For discussion of reproduction and adaption rights, see *infra* §§8.2-8.4 (notes 171-84 and accompanying text).

[6] For discussion of fair use as a defense to infringement, see *infra* §11 (notes 280-93 and accompanying text).

Are photographs copyrightable?[7] If so, who owns the copyright on the photographs commissioned by the museum,[8] the photographers or the museum? Similarly, who owns the copyright for the exhibition catalogue, the museum or the contributing scholars? Would the contribution by the museum's own employee present different ownership questions?[9]

What formalities should the museum take in protecting its copyright as to affixation of notice and registration?[10] How long does the copyright last?[11]

What are the copyright problems involved in performing the modern dance with its musical and visual accompaniment?[12]

Obviously museum administrators need a solid understanding of copyright law and an awareness for situations where copyright problems might arise.[13] With this article we wish to provide the museum administrator and the non-specialist attorney with an overview of copyright law as it affects the museum environment.[14] We also wish to show that copyright considerations in the art museum context transcend the immediate concerns of acquisition and exhibition.

By our introductory example, it is apparent that from a copyright perspective, the art museum is much more than a place which houses and exhibits works of art.[15] In addition to these functions, the art museum both creates and uses copyrighted works to educate the public about art

---

[7] For discussion of copyrightability, see *infra* §§2-3 (notes 24-76 and accompanying text).

[8] For discussion of ownership, generally, see *infra* §9 (note 221 and accompanying text).

[9] For discussion of works made for hire, see *infra* §9.5 (notes 240-56 and accompanying text); for collective works, see *infra* §9.6 (notes 257-59 and accompanying text).

[10] For discussion of formalities generally, see *infra* §5 (notes 103-28 and accompanying text); for notice and affixation, see *infra* §5.2 (notes 116-28 and accompanying text); for registration, see *infra* §5.1 (notes 103-15 and accompanying text); and for recordation, see *infra* §§9.3-9.4, (notes 230-39 and accompanying text).

[11] For discussion of duration, see *infra* §6, (notes 129-41 and accompanying text); and for discussion of renewal, see *infra* §7 (notes 142-66 and accompanying text).

[12] For discussion of performance right see *infra* §§8.7-8.11 (notes 195-213 and accompanying text).

[13] Questions concerning copyright may be of concern to others in the museum in addition to the director and his immediate administrative staff. These include the registrar, curators, particularly the curator of contemporary art, the librarian, the slide librarian and the education staff.

[14] For an introduction to some of these problems, see S. Weil, Beauty and The Beasts: On Museums, Art, The Law, and The Market (1983); M. Phelan, Museums and The Law, (1982) 77-91; and Ward, Copyright in Museum Collections: An Overview of Some of the Problems, 7 J. of Coll. & U.L. 297 (1980-81).

[15] For a description of the types and frequency of educational and cultural

and artists. Its staff creates copyrighted works, such as catalogues, gallery guides, articles for museum publications,[16] and audio-visual materials.[17] The museum also commissions outside experts to create works such as the photographs[18] and the dance program referred to in our introductory example.

The museum is also a central location where events in the performing arts take place, sometimes to complement an exhibition, and other times as a regular museum program.[19] The museum administrator must recognize copyright problems relating to musical, dance,[20] and dramatic performances, both for the classroom and general public.

---

programs offered by museums, see Museums, USA; A Survey Report (1975) [hereinafter cited as *Museums, USA*]. See generally The Art Museum As Educator (1978); Museums, Adults and the Humanities (1981); America's Museums: The Belmont Report (1969); and E. Alexander, Museums in Motion (1979) at 193-229 [hereinafter cited as *Museums in Motion*].

[16] G. Hamilton, Education and Scholarship, On Understanding Art Museums at 127-128 [hereinafter cited as Hamilton].

[17] Audio-visual components of a museum exhibition can be important to establish historical context or to include aspects of a theme which would not be suitable for normal gallery spaces, e.g., films of dance for an art and dance exhibition. In addition, individual narration systems or "recorded tours" may give the viewer didactic information not included in labels. Telephone interview with Rose Glennon, Coordinator of Gallery Education, The Toledo Museum of Art, June 25, 1983. For museum utilization of audio-visual equipment, see also Miller & Crosman, A Cure for Videophobia, 55 Museum News at 38 (March-April, 1977) and Newman, Video Discs: The Emerging Picture, 59 Museum News at 28 (Jan.-Feb., 1981) discussing the possible use of video discs for archival storage and distribution of "books" of slides, in addition to gallery and classroom.

[18] Photographs are specifically included in the classification of "pictorial, graphic and sculptural works" of the Copyright Act, 17 U.S.C. §101 (1982). Copyright was initially extended to artistically conceived photographs in Burrow-Giles Lithographic Co. v. Sarony, 111 U.S. 53 (1883). Through the years, most photographs were held to be sufficiently original to satisfy copyright requirements. See 1 M. Nimmer on Copyright, §2.08[E](1978) [hereinafter cited as Nimmer].

[19] A survey conducted for The National Endowment for the Arts showed that 41% of art museums scheduled performing arts presentations on a regular or occasional basis, see Museums, USA at 41. For example, during the 1981-82 season, the Metropolitan Museum of Art held 241 concerts and lectures. The Metropolitan Museum of Art Annual Report for the Year 1981-82 at 59. See also Museum Sponsorship of the Performing Arts, 53 Museum News at 24 (June 1975); Gravesmill,Museums and The Performing Arts, 45 Museum News at 29 (Jan. 1967); National Endowment for the Arts, Audience Studies of The Performing Arts and Museums: A Critical Review (1978).

[20] Choreographic works are specifically included in the listing of "works of authorship," 17 U.S.C. §102(a)(1982), although no definition is included under §101. See Traylor, Choreography, Pantomime and the Copyright Revision Act of 1976, 16 New Eng. L. Rev. 227 (1981); and Note, Moving to a New Beat: Copyright Protection for Choreographic Works, 24 U.C.L.A. L. Rev. 1287 (1977).

Today's art museum is a big business which both creates and uses copyrighted works. It cannot ignore the legal environment of its activities. It publicizes its events[21] and hires photographers and other personnel to develop advertising materials. Many museum shops are lucrative ventures which sell art reproductions, postcards, posters, tee-shirts, and books.[22] What is surprising is that many museum administrators either ignore or are unaware of certain pervasive copyright considerations. We direct this article to the administrators of museums and to their non-specialist counsel as a comprehensive review of the major aspects of copyright law affecting the art museum.[23]

2. WHAT IS COPYRIGHT?

Copyright law creates a system of property rights for the protection of art, literature, and music. Unlike other kinds of property, land or

---

[21] Many museums send out calendars of programs to members. These may include photographs of works of art and activphotographs from museum programs. See Cruger, Eventful Calendars, 57 Museum News at 40 (Jan.-Feb., 1979). Both the text and the photographs are copyrightable subject matter. See *infra* notes 49-63 and accompanying text.

[22] For example, in 1982, gross revenues from merchandise operations for The Metropolitan Museum of Art amounted to $22,578,788. The Metropolitan Museum of Art, Annual Report for the Year 1981-82 at 70. Revenues for the same period from the sales shop of the Philadelphia Museum were $665,601. Philadelphia Museum of Art, 106th Annual Report 1981-82 at 43. For the Dallas Museum of Fine Arts, revenues from the museum shop were $420,806. Dallas Museum of Fine Arts, Report for the Fiscal Year October 1, 1981-September 30, 1982. See also Taylor, The Art Museum in the United States in On Understanding Art Museums at 48-9; and Trucco, The Shopping Boom at Your Local Museum, 76 Art News 56, (October 1977). The Museum Store Association, an organization of approximately 600 members, publishes a journal, MUST, devoted to issues of interest to museum stores. One concern, particularly with the expansion of the types of merchandise carried in these stores, has been the maintenance of tax exempt status. Museum stores sales must be related to the tax exempt purpose of the institution, §501(c)(3) IRC. See Gilbert, Coming to Terms With the Tax Man, 61 Museum News at 18 (Sept.-Oct. 1982); and Liles and Roth, The Unrelated Business Income Problems of Art Museums, 10 Conn. L. Rev. 638 (1978).

[23] For the non-specialist lawyer who may be unfamiliar with copyright law, the leading source is a four-volume treatise, Nimmer on Copyright. Shorter, but useful works are N. Boorstyn, Copyright Law (1981) [hereinafter cited as Boorstyn]; A. Latman, The Copyright Law: Howell's Copyright Law Revised and the 1976 Act, (5th ed. 1978), [hereinafter cited as Latman]; and W. Strong, The Copyright Book (1981) [hereinafter cited as Strong]. For a focus on copyright law and fine arts, see T. Crawford, The Visual Artist's Guide to the New Copyright Law (1978); Millinger, Copyright and The Fine Artist, 48 Geo. Wash. L. Rev. 354 (1980); Brenner, A Two-Phase Approach to Copyrighting the Fine Arts, 24 Bull. Copyright Soc'y 85 (1976); and Gottlieb, Pictorial, Graphic and Sculptural Works Under the New Copyright Act in Current Developments in Copyright Law at 415 (1980).

objects, copyright occupies no physical space; it is an intangible property right conferred on certain kinds of expressive information called works of authorship.[24] Although a copyright is essentially intangible, it springs into existence when an author, e.g., an artist, a composer, a choreographer, embodies the work of authorship in a relatively permanent form. In the language of the current Copyright Act, "copyright subsists in original works of authorship fixed in a tangible medium of expression. . . ."[25] We will now discuss the meaning of these key requirements for copyrightability: fixation and tangible medium of expression. We will later turn to the question of originality and authorship.[26]

2.1. Fixation

From the above definition, copyright protection begins when an author has fixed his work[27] in a tangible medium of expression. A copyright is not granted by the government, as is a patent,[28] but comes into being when an author places his artistic expression in a material object. The object could be a piece of paper, a canvas, a tape, or a block of marble. This concept is one of the most misunderstood of copyright law because many believe that a copyright protection begins when the Copyright Office registers the work. Although there are many excellent reasons for registering a claim for copyright in the Copyright Office, it[29] is the act of the author placing his work in a tangible medium of expression, rather than the act of registration, which creates the copyright.

---

[24] Works of authorship include the following:

(1) literary works;
(2) musical works, including any accompanying words;
(3) dramatic works, including any accompanying music;
(4) pantomimes and choreographic works;
(5) pictorial, graphic, and sculptural works;
(6) motion pictures and other audiovisual works; and
(7) sound recordings

17 U.S.C. §102(a) (1982). The introductory example includes a variety of works of authorship, e.g., the exhibition catalogue (literary work), the musical accompaniments for audio-visual program and dance (musical work), the modern dance (choreographic work), the paintings, photographs, postcards and posters (pictorial works), the audio-visual program (audio-visual works), the recordings of the music (sound recording). This statutory listing is not exhaustive and Congress has the power to include, by legislation, new types of works of authorship. H.R. Rep. No. 94-1476, 94th Cong., 2d Sess. 124 (1976) at 51 [hereinafter cited as H.R. Rep.].

[25] 17 U.S.C. §102(a) (1982).

[26] See *infra* notes 49-76 and accompanying text.

[27] For stylistic convenience, words of the masculine gender are intended to include the feminine.

[28] 35 U.S.C. §1 (1982).

[29] See *infra* notes 103-115 and accompanying text.

What constitutes a tangible medium of expression? In the language of the Copyright Act, there are two basic varieties of objects in which works are embodied: copies[30] and phonorecords.[31] Phonorecords encompass tapes, discs or similar objects in which sound is recorded, whereas the term "copy"[32] defines a residue category which includes all things, other than phonorecords, in which works are placed. For example, a work of music may be embodied on a phonorecord in tape or disc form or in a copy by notation on a sheet of paper. Whether an object is called a copy or a phonorecord is of little importance. What is important is that one must conceptually distinguish the material object from the work of authorship, that is, the copyright.

When one refers to "media of expression," what most often comes to mind are books, tapes, canvasses and the like. As with the development of sound recording in the early twentieth century, technological advances often produce new forms of expression. The current Copyright Act takes into account those yet to be discovered media of expression.[33] A newly discovered medium will qualify as copy or phonorecord as long as it meets the requirement of tangibility.

As stated above, a copyrighted work must be tangible as well as fixed.[34] To meet the requirement of tangibility, the artist must render his

---

[30] "Copies" are material objects, other than phonorecords, in which a work is fixed by any method now known or later developed, and from which the work can be perceived, reproduced, or otherwise communicated, either directly or with the aid of a machine or device. The term "copies" includes the material object, other than a phonorecord, in which the work is first fixed.

17 U.S.C. §101 (1982).

[31] "Phonorecords" are material objects in which sounds, other than those accompanying a motion picture or other audiovisual work, are fixed by any method now known or later developed, and from which the sounds can be perceived, reproduced, or otherwise communicated, either directly or with the aid of a machine or device. The term "phonorecords" includes the material object in which the sounds are first fixed.

17 U.S.C. §101 (1982).

[32] Argues Nimmer, "An unnecessary complexity in a necessarily complex statute could have been avoided by defining copies to include all material objects in which works of authorship are fixed, regardless of whether or not the work itself consists of sound." 1 Nimmer, §2.03[C] at 2-32.

[33] "Copyright protection subsists . . . in original works of authorship fixed in any tangible medium of expression, now known *or later developed*. . . ."17 U.S.C. §102(a) (1982) (emphasis added). As the House Report states, "Authors are continually finding new ways of expressing themselves, but it is impossible to foresee the forms that these new expressive methods will take. The bill does not intend . . . to freeze the scope of copyrightable technology. . . ." H.R. Report at 51.

[34] See *supra* note 33. Works that are not fixed in a tangible medium of expression are left to protection under state common law copyright. Even though state

work in a sufficiently permanent and stable form. There are many works which involve great creativity, such as a sand sculpture, a fence running along the countryside,[35] a window display in a store, or a stage set, but which do not exist in a relatively permanent form. None of these works would meet the tangibility requirement.[36] Similarly, a museum curator's installation of an exhibition may entail great planning and imagination,[37] and, as with the other examples, be the subject of written commentary;[38] but, because there is no stable embodiment of a work of authorship, it is not subject to copyright protection.

2.2. Material Object and Copyright

As stated, one must conceptually seperate ownership of the material object and ownership of the copyright. The copyrighted work may be a literary work printed on pages of a book, pigment painted on a

---

law is a possible form of protection, it is an inadequate substitute for protection under federal law. Rights in an unfixed work are much more difficult to protect because their very nature and existence are difficult to prove. Further, state courts vary in their attitudes toward their own copyright laws and the outcome of a suit based on state common law principles is difficult to predict. See Dunlap, Copyright Protection for Oral Works — Expansion of the Copyright Law into the Area of Conversations, 20 Bull. Copyright Soc'y 285 (1973).

[35] Perhaps the best known sculptor of "temporary monuments" is Christo, the originator of packaging art, who has wrapped cars, buildings and islands, in addition to sections of coastline. See Alloway, Christo (1969); Christo: Oceanfront (1975).

[36] For arguments that displays and environmental works of art, such as Christo's "Running Fence," fulfill the constitutional and statutory requirements of copyright, see Note, Copyright Protection for Short-Lived Works of Art, 51 Fordham L. Rev. 90 (1982).

[37] Installation of an exhibition, either a temporary one or one that is more permanent, may involve extensive work, including selection of objects, planning the layout and arranging the objects, lighting, label preparation, and the development of audio-visual and other didactic materials. The ultimate goal may be to "provide fresh ways of looking at objects that enhance their impact and meaning." Museums in Motion at 182. For the extensive amount of work which exhibition installation design can entail see, e.g., Ciulla and Montgomery, Creative Compromise: The Curator and the Designer, 55 Museum News 31 (March-April 1977).

[38] For criticism of otherwise widely praised installation of American Art at Yale University Art Gallery, where, for example, chairs were hung from walls, where they could be seen as objects, rather than as pieces of furniture: "A wall of chairs can be a thing of beauty in itself . . . but chairs were meant to be sat on, and were designed to be seen from different angles than high on a wall." Hamilton, *supra* note 4, at 122. The installation of the photo-realist exhibition's overall design and layout is not copyrightable, the photographs and didactic labels used as part of the installation are copyrightable works of authorship.

canvas, or a musical work pressed into the grooves of a phonorecord. Books, canvasses and phonorecords are sold to the public, but their acquisition does not confer ownership of the copyright in a literary, artistic, or musical work.[39]

A misunderstanding of this basic principle can lead to unfortunate results for the art museum. Even if the museum owns a painting, bought at great expense, it does not hold the copyright on the painting unless it is specifically transferred by the artist.[40] The museum may believe erroneously that ownership of the object includes ownership of the copyright and therefore the right to reproduce the work on a poster or postcard for sale in the museum shop. Many museums make this error because of a fundamental misunderstanding of the intangible nature of copyright, by failing to separate conceptually ownership of the copyright from ownership of the material object. Perhaps they make this mistake because many works of art are unique and valuable. But the museum, absent a specific grant, no more owns the copyright on the painting that if it were to acquire the copyright in a literary work by buying a paperback book at a bookstore.

Returning to the introductory example, concerning the acquisition of the two paintings, the museum should consider acquiring both the paintings and their copyrights. Most often, the artist will have no object to transferring the canvas and its copyright, but as artists become more sensitive to copyright, the two aspects of ownership, material object and copyright, may become the subject of separate negotiation.

2.3. Idea and Expression

An owner of a copyright owns certain rights to an intangible intellectual creation, but not all creations of the mind enjoy copyright protection. One such major limitation is that copyright does not protect

---

[39] Ownership of a copyright, or of any of the exclusive rights under a copyright, is distinct from ownership of any material object in which the work is embodied. Transfer of ownership of any material object, including the copy or phonorecord in which the work is first fixed, does not of itself convey any rights in the copyrighted work embodied in the object; nor, in the absence of an agreement, does transfer of ownership of a copyright or of any exclusive rights under a copyright convey property rights in any material object.

17 U.S.C. §202 (1982).

[40] [C]opyright ownership and ownership of a material object in which the copyrighted work is embodied are entirely separate things. Thus, transfer of a material object does not of itself carry any rights under copyright, and this includes transfer of the copy or phonorecord . . . the photographic negative, the unique painting or statue . . . in which the work was first fixed.

H.R. Report at 124. For a discussion of the change this requirement of specific transfer had made in the common law, see *infra*, notes 260-64 and accompanying text.

ideas, only the expression of ideas.[41] This is one of the most elusive concepts in copyright law, but one which affects all aspects of copyrightable subject matter. Once public, an idea becomes public property free for anyone to use. It makes no difference how intricate, clever, or beneficial the idea may be. Examples are systems of bookkeeping,[42] abstract outlines of fictional plots[43] and historical discoveries of fact.[44] Similarly,

---

[41] "In no case does copyright protection for an original work of authorship extend to any idea, procedure, process, system, method of operation, concept, principle or discovery, regardless of the form in which it is described, explained, illustrated, or embodied in such work." 17 U.S.C. §102(b) (1982).

[42] See Baker v. Selden, 101 U.S. 99 (1879), a landmark decision of the U.S. Supreme Court, which held that a system of bookkeeping, illustrated by ruled lines and blank columns was not copyrightable. While the expression of the idea was copyrightable, e.g., the book, the underlying idea, e.g., the bookkeeping system, was not. See 1 Nimmer, §2.18[B], [C], for a discussion of the Baker v. Selden doctrine; and 37 C.F.R. §202.1(b), (c) (1982), for a codification of these principles. Where the expression of an idea is limited in form, it has been held not to be copyrightable. See Morrissey v. Procter & Gamble Co., 379 F.2d 675, 678 (1st Cir. 1967), denying copyright protection to sweepstake contest rules.

When the uncopyrightable subject matter is very narrow, so that the topic necessarily requires . . . , if not only one form of expression, at best only a limited number, to permit copyrighting would mean that a party . . . could exhaust all possibilities of future use of the substance.

See also Taylor Instrument Co. v. Fawley-Brost Co., 139 F.2d 98 (7th Cir. 1943) (chart for recording temperatures held not copyrightable); and Aldrich v. Remington Rand, 152 F. Supp. 732 (N.D. Tex. 1942) (forms for keeping tax records held not copyrightable). But, cf., Harcourt, Brace & World, Inc. v. Graphic Controls Corp., 329 F. Supp. 517 (S.D.N.Y. 1971) (holding that printed answer sheets, created for use in conjunction with student achievement and intelligence tests and designed to be graded mechanically were copyrightable); and Continental Casualty Co. v. Beardsley, 253 F.2d 702 (2d Cir. 1958) (blanket bond forms held copyrightable).

[43] See, e.g., Nichols v. Universal Pictures Corp., 45 F.2d 119 (2d Cir. 1930), in which the author of the play, "Abie's Irish Rose," sued the producer of the movie, "The Cohens and the Kellys." Both were comedies dealing with religious inter marriage. Judge Learned Hand held for the defendant on the grounds that the theme of the play fell in the realm of unprotected "ideas." See also cases cited in Latman, supra note 23, at 32; and Warner Bros., Inc. v. Am. Broadcasting Co., 654 F.2d 204 (2d Cir. 1981) (holding that the television comedy, "The Greatest American Hero" did not infringe the copyright in cartoon strips and movies of "Superman" because the theme of a character with superhuman powers who battles the forces of evil is not copyrightable although the expression of such an idea could be). For an excellent discussion of the protection of literary dramatic characters, see Authors League Symposium on Copyright, 29 J. of Copyright Soc'y 611 (1982).

[44] While historical facts themselves, even newly discovered ones, may not be entitled to copyright, it may be argued that their selection and arrangement in a particular work provides sufficient originality to warrant protection. This problem displays the inherent tension in copyright law between the underlying and

one might devise an elaborate theory of art, [45] discover a new work by an Old Master, [46] or devise an ingenious method for installing an exhibition. These intellectual creations would, however, be considered as belonging to the realm of ideas and therefore unprotectable under copyright law. There is a limited basis for protecting an idea under state law by privately disclosing it under circumstances which expressly or through implication indicate confidentiality. [47] But such contractual protection of an idea only

---

competing policies of protecting the interests of an author who may have spent great time and effort on his product, and the benefit to the public in the wide dissemination of facts. See generally Gorman, Copyright Protection for the Collection and Representation of Facts, 76 Harv. L. Rev. 1569 (1963); Gorman, Fact or Fancy? The Implications for Copyright, 29 J. of Copyright Soc'y 560 (1982); and Denicola, Copyright in Collections of Facts: A Theory for The Protection of Nonfiction Literary Works, 81 Colum. L. Rev. 516 (1981). The question of the copyrightability of research often arises when a second work, e.g., a telvision movie, is based upon facts uncovered in an earlier work. See, e.g., Rosemont Enterprises, Inc. v. Random House, Inc., 366 F.2d 303 (2d Cir. 1966), cert. denied, 385 U.S. 1009 (1967) (the life story of Howard Hughes); Miller v. Universal City Studios, 650 F.2d 1365 (1981) (kidnapped victim who was buried alive); and Hoehling v. Universal City Studios, 618 F.2d 972 (2d Cir. 1980) (the destruction of the Hindenberg). This decision is extensively criticized in Guinsburg, Sabotaging and Reconstructing History: A Comment on the Scope of Copyright Protection in Works of History after Hoehling v. Universal Studios, 29 J. Copyright Soc'y 647 (1982). Holding that these works are collections of facts, rather than the expression of ideas, copyright protection has been denied to maps, Amsterdam v. Triangle Publications, Inc., 189 F.2d 104 (1951); Moore v. Lighthouse Pub. Co., 429 F. Supp. 1304 (S.D. Ga. 1977); and directories, New York Times Co. v. Roxburg Data Interface, 434 F. Supp. 217 (D.N.J. 1977), but cf., Schroeder v. William Morrow & Co., 566 F.2d 3 (7th Cir. 1977) (gardening directory held copyrightable when made by substantial independent effort and selection).

[45] See, e.g., A. Breton, What Is Surrealism? (1934), reprinted in Theories of Modern Art (1968), at 402-27. Breton's concepts of the origins of surrealism would not have been copyrightable and would therefore be freely appropriable by other writers. Of course, the actual expression of his ideas could be protected under copyright.

[46] E.g., in 1954, a ceiling sketch, "Allegory of The Planets and Continents," by Giovanni Battista Tiepolo (1696-1770) was discovered in the Hendon Hall Hotel in London. E. Fahy, Paints, Drawing in The Wrightsman Collection, The Metropolitan Museum of Art at 239-40 (1973).

[47] See, e.g., Desny v. Wilder, 46 Cal. 2d 715, 299 P.2d 257 (1956) (writer alleged express promise by movie producer to pay for story if used). The California Supreme Court stated, "The person who can and does convey a valuable idea to a producer who commercially solicits the service or who voluntarily accepts it knowing that it is tendered for a price should likewise be entitled to recover." Id. at 734, 299 P.2d at 267. See also Davies v. Krasna, 245 Cal. App. 2d 535, 54 Cal. Rptr. 37 (1966); Donahue v. Ziv Television Programs, 245 Cal. App. 2d 593, 54 Cal. Rptr. 130 (1966); and Minniear v. Tors, 266 Cal. App. 2d 495, 72 Cal. Rptr. 287 (1968).

extends to the parties subject to the disclosure and not to third parties who find out about it some other way.[48]

3. COPYRIGHTABLE SUBJECT MATTER
3.1. Originality and Authorship

The Copyright Act confers protection on original works of authorship fixed in a tangible medium of expression. We have already discussed the concept of fixation, tangibility and the medium of expression. We now turn to the question of what is an original work of authorship.

The copyright law sets forth broad categories of works of authorship which include literary works, drama, pure and applied art, audio-visual works and sound recordings.[49] The art museum in one way or another might make use of the entire range of this subject matter. Our purpose in this section, though, is not to discuss the intricacies of the various forms of copyrightable subject matter, but rather to focus on the concepts of "originality" and "authorship" which concern all categories of copyrightable works, whether a literary work, audio-visual, or pictorial work.[50]

Originality and authorship are concepts whose meanings have developed through the years by their construction in courts of law.[51] Generally, an original work of authorship is one which owes its origin to an author, while demonstrating at least a minimal amount of creativity.[52] The original work of authorship need not be novel, as long as the author's work is independently created. Thus, it is entirely possible that copyright protection could be enjoyed by two identical works if the second author had not copied from the first.[53]

The other aspect of originality, that of minimal creativity, embodies no conception of artistic merit. Very early in the century an oft-cited Supreme Court case established the above proposition.[54] This case, which concerned the copyrightability of a circus poster, explicitly established that courts should not inject their view on what constitutes artistic merit

---

[48] For extensive discussion of protection under state law, see 3 Nimmer, §16.03.

[49] 17 U.S.C. §102(a) (1982).

[50] For an analysis of the requirement of "originality" as applies to the visual arts, see Oppenheimer, Originality in Art Productions, 26 J. of Copyright Soc'y 1 (1978).

[51] See H.R. Report at 51.

[52] See infra notes 64-76 and accompanying text.

[53] See infra note 268 and accompanying text.

[54] Bleistein v. Donaldson, 188 U.S. 239 (1903).

when deciding questions of copyrightability.[55] Since that time, both the courts and Copyright Office have uniformly refused to exercise their conception of artistic quality in determining questions of originality.[56]

---

[55] It would be a dangerous undertaking for persons trained only to the law to constitute themselves final judges of the worth of pictorial illustrations, outside of the narrowest and most obvious limits. At the one extreme some works of genius would be sure to miss appreciation. . . . At the other end, copyright would be denied to pictures which appealed to a public less educated than the judge.

Id. at 251-52.

[56] See, e.g., Alfred Bell & Co. v. Catalda Fine Arts, Inc., 191 F.2d 99, 103 (2d Cir. 1951) ("No matter how poor artistically the 'author's' addition, it is enough if it be his own.") This constraint is incorporated into the new copyright law. According to the House Report,

[t]he phrase, "original works of authorship," which is purposely left undefined, is intended to incorporate without change "the standards of originality" established by the courts under the present copyright statute. This standard does not include requirements of novelty, ingenuity, or esthetic merit, and there is no intention to enlarge the standard of copyright protection to require them. . . .

H.R. Rep. at 51.

Considerations of creativity and originality aside, a troublesome question through the years has been the availability of copyright protection under the classification "work of art" for works of applied art, as compared to works of fine art. This is particularly difficult when the object combines both "utilitarian" and "artistic" features, because utilitarian articles fall outside copyright protection. In the leading case of Mazer v. Stein, 347 U.S. 201 (1954) the Supreme Court held that the statuette of a dancing figure which constituted the base of a lamp constituted a "work of art." However, in 1978, the U.S. Court of Appeals in Esquire, Inc. v. Ringer, 591 F.2d 796 (D.C. Cir. 1978), *cert. denied*, 440 U.S. 908 (1979), refused copyright protection as "works of art" to outdoor lighting fixtures. The Court held that the overall shape of a utilitarian object is not copyrightable and distinguished *Mazer* on the grounds that the dancing figures were capable of existing as a work of art independent of the utilitarian article in which they were incorporated.

Although the original Senate version (S. 22) of the 1976 Copyright Act contained a provision for copyright of design, this was deleted in the final version of the bill. However, the 1976 Act did add language to the definition of "pictorial, graphic and sculptural works," stating:

Such works shall include works of artistic craftsmanship insofar as their form but not their mechanical or utilitarian aspects are concerned; the design of a useful article, as defined in this section, shall be considered a pictorial, graphic, or sculptural work only if, and only to the extent that, such design incorporates pictorial, graphic, or sculptural features that can be identified separately from and are capable of existing independently of, the utilitarian aspects of the article.

17 U.S.C. §101 (1976). See also, H.R. Report at 54-55. The distinction between works of utilitarian design and works of art was further confused by the decision in Kieselstein-Cord v. Accessories by Pearl, Inc., 632 F.2d 989 (2d Cir. 1980) granting copyright protection to two belt buckle designs. The court, referring to the concept that "separability" may occur either physically or conceptually held that "[t]he primary ornamental aspect of the . . . buckles is conceptually separable from their subsidiary utilitarian function" at 993. In sum, in spite of Blei-

Although the quality of art is not an issue in determining copyright-ability, a certain quantum of originality, or creative authorship, is re-quired.[57] This is largely a de minimis standard and easy to meet, but copyright has been denied to fragmentary words or phrases,[58] slogans,[59] slight variations of musical compositions,[60] and a paraphrase of standard business forms.[61] On the other hand, almost any trivial variation will satisfy the standard for creativity. Thus courts have found[62] originality in

---

stein's pronouncement that courts of law should not discriminate against various art forms, industrial design which is precluded from protection is a notable exception. Although industrial design at this time appears in large part outside the realm of copyright, design patent is an alternate form of protection. See 35 U.S.C. §171 (1982). Obtaining design patent protection, however, is both time-consuming and expensive and application is subject to intense scrutiny by the Patent office as to meeting the rigorous standards of patentibility, novelty and non-obviousness. Draft, Second Supplementary Report of the Register of Copy-rights on The General Revision of the U.S. Copyright Law, Chapter VII (1975). Therefore, a museum such as the Museum of Modern Art, which collects works of contemporary design, must be aware of possible copyright and patent impli-cations. For recent articles in this area see generally Denicola, Applied Art and Industrial Design: A Suggested Approach to Copyright in Useful Articles, 67 Minn. L. Rev. 707 (1983); Paul, Functional Works of Art: Copyright, Design Patent, or Both?, 3 Comm/Ent. L.J. 83 (1980); and Note, Works of Applied Art: An Expansion of Copyright Protection, 56 So. Cal. L. Rev. 241 (1982).

[57] "Copyright protection subsists . . . in *original works of author-ship*. . . . "17 U.S.C. §102(a) (1982) (emphasis added). "In order to be accept-able as a pictorial, graphic, or sculptural work, the work must embody some creative authorship in its delineation or form." 37 C.F.R. §202.10(a) (1982).

[58] E.g., Alberto-Culver Co. v. Andrea Dumon, Inc., 466 F.2d 705 (7th Cir. 1972) (holding that the phrase "most personal sort of deodorant" is not copy-rightable.) See also 37 C.F.R. §202.1 (1982), in which, under "Materials not subject to copyright," "words and short phrases such as names, titles and slo-gans" are included. A new "label" for a school of painting, for example, such as "minimalism" or "photo-realism" would not be entitled to copyright protection. But see, 1 Nimmer, §2.01[B] at 2-15, for arguments that even a short phrase, if sufficiently creative, might be entitled to copyright protection.

[59] Slogans can be protected under certain circumstances under the law of unfair competition. See generally, McCarthy, Trademarks and the Law of Unfair Competition (1973) at §7.5.

[60] See, e.g., Shapiro, Bernstein & Co. v. Miracle Record Co., 91 F. Supp. 473 (N.D. Ill. 1950); and McIntyre v. Double-A Music Corp., 179 F. Supp. 160 (S.D. Cal. 1959). But cf. Wihtol v. Wells, 231 F.2d 550 (7th Cir. 1956) (holding that composition based on folk song was copyrightable.)

[61] See, e.g., Donald v. Zack Meyers' T.V. Sales and Service, 426 F.2d 1027, 1031 (5th Cir. 1970), cert. denied, 400 U.S. 992 (1971) (holding that the plaintiff's legal form was not entitled to protection, the court stated, "We reward creativity and originality with a copyright but we do not accord copyright protection to a mere copycat.")

[62] See, e.g., Kitchens of Sara Lee, Inc. v. Nifty Foods Corp., 266 F.2d 541, 545 (2d Cir. 1957) (The pictures of the cakes used by plaintiff on its labels although

such banal creations as the label on a box of cake and plastic flowers.[63]

3.2. Originality and Derivative Works: Reproductions of Works of Art

Much artistic work is consciously based on one or more preexisting works. Examples are art reproductions,[64] musical arrangements, dramatizations, and abridgments which either embody or recast these preexisting or underlying works in some way. This kind of work, known as a derivative work,[65] is a protectible work under copyright, but is protectable only as to the new authorship added to the preexisting work.[66] The creator of a derivative work cannot claim copyright in the underlying work, and if the underlying work is subject to copyright protection, the derivative work author must obtain consent to create the derivative work or copyright will be infringed.[67]

Both the concepts of originality and derivative work authorship are

---

possibly not achieving the quality of a Leonardo "Still Life" nevertheless have sufficient commercial artistry to entitle them to protection against obvious copying.) But cf. Bailie v. Fisher, 258 F.2d 425 (D.C. Cir. 1958) (holding that a standing cardboard star does not fall within the historical and ordinary conception of a work of art.)

[63] See, e.g., Prestige Floral v. California Artificial Flower Co., 201 F. Supp. 287 (S.D.N.Y. 1962). But cf. Gardenia Flowers, Inc. v. Joseph Markovits, Inc., 280 F. Supp. 776 (S.D.N.Y. 1968) (holding that plaintiff's artificial corsages lacked the creativity and originality necessary for a work of art under the Copyright Act.)

[64] Art reproductions are specifically included in the definition of "pictorial, graphic and sculptural works." See 17 U.S.C. §101 (1982). Note that the registrability of a work of art is not affected by the number of copies reproduced, 37 CFR §202.10(a) (1982).

[65] A "derivative work" is a work based upon one or more preexisting works, such as a translation, musical arrangement, dramatization, fictionalization, motion picture version, sound recording, art reproduction, abridgment, condensation, or any other form in which a work may be recast, transformed, or adapted. A work consisting of editorial revisions, annotations, elaborations, or other modifications which, as a whole, represent an original work of authorship, is a "derivative work."

17 U.S.C. §101 (1982). See generally Goldstein, Derivative Rights and Derivative Works in Copyright, 30 J. of Copyright Soc'y 209 (1983).

[66] "The subject matter of copyright as specified by section 102 includes compilations and derivative works, but protection for a work employing preexisting material in which copyright subsists does not extend to any part of the work in which such material has been used unlawfully." 17 U.S.C. §103(a) (1982).

[67] The copyright in a compilation or derivative work extends only to the material contributed by the author of such work, as distinguished from the preexisting material employed in the work, and does not imply any exclusive right in the preexisting material. The copyright in such work is independent of, and does not affect or enlarge the scope, duration, ownership, or subsistence of, any copyright protection in the preexisting material.

17 U.S.C. §103(b) (1982).

important to the art museum, particularly for art reproductions such as may be used for posters, postcards, photographic slides, and sculpture.[68] These uses of copyrighted works constitute a major source of income for both the museum and the artist. One can only sell, rent or reproduce a work of art and it is this latter function which can earn steady income for the artist and the museum.

Who owns the copyright, if any, in reproduction of a work of art? Because a reproduction of a work of art is basically a derivative work, the museum as a reproducer must obtain the consent of the copyright owner to reproduce the work and create a non-infringing derivative work. As in any work, the museum as copyright claimant must add an original contribution not found in the preexisting work.

The general de minimis standard of originality applies to an art reproduction as to any other work. The author need only add something irreducibly his own, but no more than a trivial variation on the preexisting work. For example, engravings of public domain paintings,[69] as well as three-dimensional scale-model reproductions have been held copyrightable.[70] Although there appears to be some discrepancy in how far the courts will go in conferring copyright on art reproductions,[71] the

---

[68] For an interesting argument that restorations of works of art should qualify as derivative works for copyright protection, see Mandel, Copyrighting Art Restorations, 28 J. of Copyright Soc'y. 273 (1981).

[69] See, e.g., Alfred Bell & Co. v. Catalda Fine Arts, Inc., 191 F.2d 99 (2d Cir. 1951) (holding that mezzotint engravings of "old master" paintings, for example, Gainsborough's "Blue Boy" were copyrightable as they were "versions" of the paintings, distinguishable from them, and the mezzotint process involved originality (i.e., skill and judgment) on the part of the engraver. Lithographic reproductions of these mezzotints, therefore, constituted enfringement of copyright).

[70] See, Alva Studios, Inc. v. Winninger, 177 F. Supp. 265 (S.D.N.Y. 1959). The work involved was a small scale reproduction of Rodin's "Hand of God," (which was in the public domain), produced by Alva in arrangement with the Department of Fine Arts of The Carnegie Institute, owner of the Rodin sculpture. The court held that Alva's reproduction was copyrightable as its work "embodies and resulted from its skill and originality in producing an accurate scale of reproduction of the original." *Id.* at 267. The court emphasized the difference in size between the original sculpture and the Alva model, the different treatment of the base of the sculpture and the quality control exercised by the museum's curatorial staff.

[71] See, L. Batlin & Son, Inc. v. Snyder, 536 F.2d 486 (2d Cir. 1976), a case involving plastic replicas of antique iron "Uncle Sam" banks. The court held that the copyright statute's requirement of originality was not met as the variations were merely trivial. It distinguished *Alva* as dealing with the reproduction involving complexity and exactitude not present in this case. The Batlin decision was relied upon by the court in Gracen v. Bradford Exch. 698 F.2d 300 (7th Cir. 1983), deciding inter alia the copyrightability of paintings and drawings made of Wizard of Oz characters and based on stills from the movie. The court held that the plaintiff's work was not an original derivative work."[A] derivative work

historical tendency has been expansive. For this reason, the museum should always claim copyright in any reproduction that appears in a poster, postcard, advertisement, brochure, or three-dimensional model.[72]

Museums make art reproductions of both public domain works and works which are protected by copyright. In each instance the museum has created a derivative work and can protect only what it has added either to the public domain work or to the copyrighted work. This can result in a rather thin copyright, depending upon how much the museum has added. As for the public domain work, anyone can make his own reproduction of it. For example, if the museum reproduces El Greco's

---

must be substantially different from the underlying work to be copyrightable." 698 F.2d at 305. As the court pointed out, the concept of originality serves an important legal function to prevent overlapping claims.

> Suppose Artist A produces a reproduction of the Mona Lisa, a painting in the public domain, which differs slightly from the original. B also makes a reproduction of the Mona Lisa. A, who has copyrighted his derivative work, sues B for infringement. B's defense is that he was copying the original, not A's reproduction. But if the difference between the original and A's reproduction is slight, the difference between A's and B's reproductions will also be slight, so that if B had access to A's reproductions, the trier of fact will be hard-pressed to decide whether B was copying A or copying the Mona Lisa itself. 698 F.2d at 304.

Cf. Eden Toys v. Florelee Undergarment Co., 697 F.2d 27 (2d Cir. 1982), holding that gift wrap design based on sketches of Paddington Bear was copyrightable because the "cleaner look" of the gift wrap design satisfied the minimal requirements for originality under the Copyright Act.

The courts have clearly been inconsistent in their treatment of art reproductions. This inconsistency will continue into the foreseeable future because of the basic dilemma between protecting "sweat of the brow" but at the same time requiring de minimis level of creativity. The extent of the variations in *Alva* and *Batlin* was similar, but the expertise and the amount of effort expended by the reproducer was strikingly different. Once again, the court has smuggled in concepts of artistic quality despite the stated goals of *Bleistein* to the contrary.

[72] This reproduction could take the form of a photograph. A close question, however, is whether a photograph of a painting displays sufficient originality to qualify for copyright. According to Nimmer, a photograph of a two-dimensional object, for example, a painting or drawing, may lack this quantum of originality; however, such a work may claim copyright as a reproduction of a work of art. 1 Nimmer, §2.08[E] at 2-111. Alternatively, a photograph of a sculpture or other three-dimensional object, which involves the photographer's judgment in selecting camera angles and lighting, is a clearer case of sufficient original authorship. For cases involving originality in photographs, see Gross v. Seligman, 21 F. 930 (2d Cir. 1914) (where photographer, after sale of photograph and copyright, took later picture with same model and pose but with addition of a smile on her mouth and a cherry in her teeth, held an infringement); and the related case of Franklin Mint Corp. v. Nat'l Wildlife Art Exch., 575 F.2d 62 (3d Cir. 1978) (holding that later painting by artist of same subject not infringement, as similarity reflected the common theme).

"View of Toledo," a work in the public domain, anyone else could reproduce the same painting. What he could not do is copy the museum's reproduction of that work, because this would necessarily entail copying the original aspects of authorship contributed by the museum.[73] To quote Justice Holmes, "Others are free to copy the original. They are not free to copy the copy."[74]

Suppose the museum has reproduced a work currently protected by copyright. The same principles of originality apply here, except that the museum can claim copyright only in those original aspects added by the reproduction. Of course, the museum, to avoid being an infringer, must obtain consent of the copyright owner to make the reproduction.[75] Note that even after the museum has created the reproduction, the artist could allow others to make their own reproductions, although no one could copy the museum's reproduction without its consent. As a corollary, when the underlying work falls into the public domain, the whole world may copy it. The museum's copyright in its reproduction, however, will not be affected by the underlying work falling into the public domain, and its copyright in its derivative work will continue for the full duration.[76]

4. PUBLICATION
4.1. Importance of Publication

For works created after January 1, 1978, federal copyright protection begins on creation, when an author fixes his work in a tangible medium of expression.[77] Works created before this critical date present a more complicated situation. For these works the duration of the copy-

---

[73] If, for example, the museum produced a postcard of one of its paintings which was in the public domain and copyrighted the card, a jigsaw puzzle manufacturer could not base a puzzle on the postcard, even if the original painting could be copied. See, e.g., Habersham Plantation Corp. v. Country Concepts, 209 U.S.P.Q. 711 (N.D. Ga. 1980), granting injunction for alleged copyright infringement of photographs of furniture in a catalogue. The furniture itself could be copied, the photographs could not. This case illustrates that copying in a different medium (Country Concepts' catalogue contained line drawings based on Habersham's photographs) also constitutes infringement. See *infra* note 172 and accompanying text.

[74] Bleistein v. Donaldson Lithographing Co., 188 U.S. at 249.

[75] See infra notes 171-73 and accompanying text.

[76] See *supra* notes 64-76 and accompanying text.

[77] A work is "created" when it is fixed in a copy or phonorecord for the first time; where a work is prepared over a period of time, the portion of it that has been fixed at any particular time constitutes the work as of that time, and where the work has been prepared in different versions, each version constitutes a separate work.

17 U.S.C. §101 (1982).

right is still measured by the 1909 Act,[78] certain terms of which are essential for a thorough grasp of copyright law.

Unlike the current Act, the 1909 Act measured federal protection not on creation but on publication.[79] The event of publication constituted the dividing line between state common law protection and federal copyright. Publication also determined how long a particular work could endure. As long as the work was not published, it could theoretically endure forever under state common law copyright.[80]

The 1976 Act has greatly reduced the fundamental importance of publication by extending federal protection from the moment of creation.[81] But publication and the provisions of the 1909 Act continue to be important.[82] This is because the new Act does not protect any work which has gone into the public domain before January 1, 1978.[83] Before the effective date of the new Act, an author had to affix proper notice to all copies of the work when published. Failure to affix proper notice would inject the work into the public domain.[84] This aspect of copyright

---

[78] Act of March 4, 1909, Ch. 320, 35 Stat. 1075.

[79] 17 U.S.C. §10 (1909) (Superseded 1976).

[80] Under the theory of state common-law copyright, unpublished works, for example, the manuscript of a book, came under perpetual copyright protection. See generally Brown, Unification: A Cheerful Requiem for Common Law Copyright, 24 U.C.L.A. L. Rev. 1070 (1977).

[81] Section 301 of the 1976 Copyright Act provided a major change from the earlier law.

> Instead of a dual system of "common law copyright" for unpublished works and statutory copyright for published works . . . the bill adopts a single system of Federal statutory copyright from creation. . . . By substituting a single Federal system for the present anachronistic, uncertain, impractical, and highly complicated dual system, the bill would greatly improve the operation of the copyright law and would be much more effective in carrying out the basic constitutional aims of uniformity and the promotion of writing and scholarship.

H.R. Report at 129. For major arguments in favor of a single system, see H.R. Report at 129-30.

[82] For example, copyright notice must include the year of first publication (§402(b)(2)); the term of copyright for anonymous and pseudonymous works and works made for hire is measured from the year of first publication (§302(c)); registration in the Copyright Office must occur within five years of first publication in order for the registration certificate to constitute prima facie evidence of the validity of the copyright (§410(c)). For a comprehensive listing of the instances where publication continues to be important, see 1 Nimmer, §4.01[A] and Latman at 143-44.

[83] This Act . . . does not provide copyright protection for any work that goes into the public domain before January 1, 1978. . . ." 17 U.S.C. Note prec. §101 (1982).

[84] See, e.g., Letter Edged in Black Press, Inc. v. Pub. Bldg. Comm'n of Chicago, 320 F. Supp. 1303 (N.D. Ill. 1970) (maquette of Picasso sculpture displayed to public without copyright notice affixed resulted in loss of protection for the sculpture).

has proven to be an insidious trap for the unwary, and many an author has dedicated his work to the public domain without wishing to do so.[85] For example, if an artist had distributed copies of his painting by photograph to the public without proper copyright notice before January 1, 1978, the work would enter the public domain forever and nothing could be done to revive the work to copyright status once it had entered the public domain. Thus, the museum, in acquiring the copyright to a work created before January 1, 1978, must be concerned about its publication history in order to determine if the copyright is valid. Alternatively, a museum may be interested in using a particular work, as for example, to reproduce it as a postcard or in a poster. If the artist has published his work without proper notice, the museum as well as the public can make use of the work any way it wishes.

What constitutes publication?[86] Paradoxically, this enormously important concept is not defined under the 1909 Act. Publication doctrine has developed rather inconsistently through case law.[87] The 1976 Act has attempted to codify this decisional law, defining publication as:

> the distribution of copies or phonorecords of a work to the public by sale or other transfer of ownership or rental, lease, or lending. The offering to distribute copies or phonorecords to a group of persons for purposes of further distribution, public performance, or public display constitutes publication. A public performance or display of a work does not of itself constitute publication.[88]

The above definition does not involve any question of subjective intent on the artist's part. Thus, publication may occur even if the copyright owner does not realize as matter of law that the acts he is committing or consenting to constitute publication. In sum, as long as the copyright owner voluntarily sells, leases, loans or gives away the original or tangible copies of the work to the general public, publication occurs. Further, even if a sale or other disposition of the work has not taken place, publication will occur if an authorized offer is made to dispose of the work in any manner.[89]

4.2. Publication in Commercial Art Galleries

Questions of publication often occur in the art gallery context. Suppose the artist in our example placed in the painting completed in

---

[85] For example, the failure of the artist Robert Indiana to copyright his widely adapted "Love." The Visual Artist and Law (Rev. Ed. 1974).

[86] Note that the term "publication" in copyright law is a legal one, as distinct from the every day usage of the word.

[87] See discussion in 1 Nimmer, §4.04, and Strauss, Protection of Unpublished Works, in 1 Studies on Copyright 189 (Arthur Fisher Mem. Ed. 1963).

[88] 17 U.S.C. §101 (1982).

[89] See 1 Nimmer, §4.04 (4-19) and cases cited therein.

1970 in a gallery for sale that year. Typically, the artist may not have affixed proper copyright notice to the painting.[90] If the gallery reproduced the work for sale in an advertising brochure, publication would have occurred. Here, because neither the gallery nor the artist affixed proper notice, the work would forever be placed in the public domain. Nothing could revive its status as a copyrighted work.

But what of a sale of that painting to a member of the general public without its having been reproduced? This presents a difficult question in the law of publication, both under the 1909 and the 1976 Acts: whether a sale of a painting in its original form to a member of the general public is a copy for purposes of publication.[91] This should be compared with a sale of a painting by the artist out of his studio without offering the painting to the general public. Here, publication has clearly not occurred.

4.3. Publication by Non-Commercial Display of Works of Art

Another problem of publication under the 1909 Act concerns the display of a work of art without an accompanying offer to sell.[92] Does such a display constitute a publication sufficient to divest common law copyright? The law is not entirely clear on this issue, but indicates that publication depends on the circumstances of the display. Generally, such

---

[90] See *infra* note 122.

[91] Arguably it is. Even though the 1976 Act defines publication as the "distribution of *copies* . . . of the work to the public by sale or other transfer of ownership . . . ," in other words, uses the plural of "copy," implying more than one material embodiment, prior case law has found publication by the sale or distribution of a single copy. See, e.g., Pierce & Business Mfg. Co. v. Werckmeister, 72 Fed. 54 (1st Cir. 1896); Burke v. Nat'l Broadcasting Co., 598 F.2d 688 (1st Cir. 1979).

The term "copy" is another instance of copyright language differing from everyday use. Most would infer from "copy" that an original work must preexist the creation of the copy. However, §101 of the 1976 Copyright Act defines copies as including the material object in which the work is *first* fixed (emphasis added). Rep. Kastenmeir, who chaired the House Committee, which reported out the bill, noted the problem of the meaning of publication in the case of a work of art, such as a painting, which exists in only one copy. He stated on the floor of the House,

It is not the committee's intention that such a work would be regarded as "published" when the single existing copy is sold or offered for sale in the traditional way—for example, through an art dealer, gallery, or auction house. On the other hand, where the work has been made for reproduction in multiple copies—as in the case of fine prints such as lithographs—or where multiple reproductions of the prototype work are offered for purchase by the public—as in the case of castings from a statue or reproductions made from a photograph of a painting—publication would take place at the point when reproduced copies are publicly distributed or when, even if only one copy exists at that point, reproductions are offered for purchase by multiple members of the public.

122 Cong. Rec. H.10, 874-75 (daily ed. Sept. 22, 1976).

[92] See generally Jonakait, Do Art Exhibitions Destroy Common-Law Copyright in Works of Art? 19 Copyright L. Symp. (ASCAP) 81 (1971).

a display or exhibit did not constitute a publication if the public were admitted to view the work of art with the understanding, express or implied, that no copying would take place and that these restrictions were enforced by the museum.[93]

In sum, the above examples show how important it is for anyone acquiring a work of art to determine the circumstances relating to the publication of a work created before 1978. Often this is impossible to do without the proper records, particularly when a work has been resold several times. Nevertheless, the museum should take pains to unearth publication history before acquiring copyright to a work or it may be unpleasantly surprised to find that the work has been injected into the public domain. To repeat, the current Act will not revive a work that has gone into the public domain by acts committed before 1978.[94]

4.4. Continuing Importance of Publication

Although the current Copyright Act has greatly reduced the importance of publication, this event is still of great significance in the law of copyright for a number of reasons. First, the Copyright Act specifically requires notice on all published copies of the work and the notice confers certain procedural and substantive rights under the Copyright Act.[95] For example, the registration certificate can constitute *prima facie* evidence of the validity of the copyright if the work is registered within five years of the first publication.[96] In addition, statutory damages and

---

[93] The leading case for the proposition that where circumstances of an exhibition indicated that care was taken to deter copying, publication did not take place is American Tobacco Co. v. Werckmeister, 207 U.S. 284 (1907). See also, Carns v. Keefe Bros., 242 Fed. 745 (D. Mont. 1917) (holding that statue of elk was displayed in unrestricted circumstances which amounted to publication, in spite of putative copyright notice); Morton v. Raphael, 334 Ill. App. 399, 79 N.E.2d 522 (1948) (holding that murals on walls of hotel room were published when they could be seen by anyone who visited the hotel); and Scherr v. Universal Match Corp., 297 F. Supp. 107 (S.D.N.Y. 1967), *aff'd on other grounds,* 417 F.2d 497 (2d Cir. 1969) (statute published when displayed without restriction as to either persons or on the copying or photographing of the statue).

[94] See, e.g., Lynn Goldsmith v. Peter Max, 213 U.S.P.Q. 1008 (S.D.N.Y. 1981) (holding that photograph of Mick Jagger used in later collage by defendant artist had been injected into the public domain prior to 1978, and therefore not entitled to protection under the 1976 Act).

[95] "Whenever a work protected under this title is published in the United States or elsewhere by authority of the copyright owner, a notice of copyright as provided by this section shall be placed on all publicly distributed copies from which the work can be visually perceived, either directly or with the aid of a machine or device." 17 U.S.C. §401(a) (1982).

[96] "In any judicial proceedings the certificate of a registration made before or within five years after first publication of the work shall constitute prima facie evidence of the validity of the copyright and of the facts stated in the certificate." 17 U.S.C. §410 (c) (1982).

attorney's fees are available for published works if registration is effected within three months after first publication.[97]

Thus, publication and notice formalities continue to be of importance under the current Copyright Act. Even though it is much more difficult to inject a work into the public domain, the museum should ensure that notice is affixed to all works on which it owns a copyright interest, particularly on those published. In addition, the museum should promptly register all works in which it has an ownership interest.[98]

4.5. Forfeiture of Copyright Under the Current Act

How then can copyright be forfeited under the current Act for works created after January 1, 1978? It is difficult, but possible, to forfeit copyright.[99] One can inject a work into the public domain if notice is omitted from a substantial number of copies[100] and if registration of the work is not made within five years of the publication. In addition to registration, a reasonable effort to add notice to the copies is required to save the copyright on a work.[101]

To illustrate the above principles, let us return to our introductory

---

[97] 17 U.S.C. §412 (1982).

[98] See *infra* notes 103-15 and accompanying text.

[99] See generally Levine & Squires, Notice, Deposit and Registration: The Importance of Being Formal, 24 U.C.L.A. L. Rev. 1232 (1977) [hereinafter cited as Levine & Squires].

[100] The omission of the copyright notice . . . from copies or phonorecords publicly distributed by authority of the copyright owner does not invalidate the copyright in a work if —

(1) the notice has been omitted from no more than a relatively small number of copies or phonorecords distributed to the public;

17 U.S.C. §405(a)(1) (1982).

[101] [R]egistration for the work has been made before or is made within five years after the publication without notice, and a reasonable effort is made to add notice to all copies or phonorecords that are distributed to the public in the United States after the omission has been discovered;

17 U.S.C. §405(a)(2) (1982).

Thus, if notice is omitted from more than a "relatively small number" of copies . . . , copyright is not lost immediately, but the work will go into the public domain if no effort is made to correct the error or if the work is not registered within five years.

H.R. Report at 147.

See Florists' Transworld Delivery Ass'n v. Reliable Glassware, 213 U.S.P.Q. 808 (N.D. Ill. 1981) (denying defendant's motion for summary judgment and set for trial on question of reasonable effort where plaintiff, upon discovering that 1,200,000 vases packed for shipment lacked notice, mailed labels with notice to each flower shop with instructions to affix label to each vase).

It is open to debate whether deliberate omission of notice irrevocably injects the work into the public domain or may be rectified by later reasonable effort. See conflicting decisions in O'Neill Developments v. Galen Kilbur, Inc., 524 F. Supp. 710 (N.D. Ga. 1981) (holding that deliberate omission may be cured); and Bea-

example. Suppose the museum decides to purchase the photo-realist painting finished in 1979 and its copyright. Assume that the artist consigned the painting to a gallery and gave the gallery the right to offer the painting for sale to the public as the gallery saw fit. In so doing, the gallery produced a brochure with a photograph of the painting and disseminated to the public without placing notice of copyright anywhere on the brochure. Shortly thereafter, the museum acquired the painting with its copyright. Here to avoid injecting the work into the public domain, the museum should promptly (certainly no more than five years after the publication) register the claim to copyright and make a reasonable effort to affix notice to copies of the brochure that could yet be distributed to the public.

As the example illustrates, to avoid unnecessary difficulties the museum should affix notice to all works it owns and promptly register them. It should do so in a mechanical way and should establish a formal administrative procedure to accomplish this goal. It should register not only works of art, but any work that the museum produces, such as brochures, catalogues, or audio-visual programs. Unfortunately, it appears that not many museums have instituted clear administrative procedures for copyright matters.[102]

5. FORMALITIES
5.1. Registration

Registration of a claim to copyright is permissive, confers no ownership right, and has no durational consequence.[103] But registration does confer valuable benefits,[104] is relatively inexpensive,[105] and is easy

---

con Looms, Inc. v. S. Lichtenberg & Co., 552 F. Supp. 1305 (S.D.N.Y. 1982) (holding only unintentional omissions qualify under §405(a)(2). See also discussion in 2 Nimmer §7.13[B](3) and Patton and Hogan, The Copyright Notice Requirement—Deliberate Omission of Notice, 5 Comm/Ent L.J. 225 (1982-83).

[102] The lack of thorough copyright procedures is indicated in Weber-Karlitz, Survey: Museums, Artists & Copyrights, 2 Cardozo Arts & Eng. L.J. 121 (1983), particularly the summary of museum responses.

[103] At anytime during the subsistence of copyright in any published or unpublished work, the owner of copyright or of any exclusive right in the work may obtain registration of the copyright claim by delivering to the Copyright Office the deposit specified by this section, together with the application and fee specified by sections 409 and 708. Subject to the provisions of section 405(a), such registration is not a condition of copyright protection.

17 U.S.C. §408 (1982)

[104] See, e.g., *supra* notes 111-15 and accompanying text.

[105] A $10 fee is charged for each registration. 37 C.F.R. §202.3(c)(2) (1982). See Copyright Office Circular R4, Copyright Fees Effective January 1, 1978. For museums and others who might utilize registration frequently, the Copyright Office allows the maintenance of a Deposit Account, obviating the need to send a separate check with each registration. See Copyright Office Circular R5, How to Open and Maintain a Deposit Account in The Copyright Office.

to execute. Accordingly, the museum should systematically and promptly register all significant works in which it has a copyright interest.[106] Moreover, the ease and simplicity of registration does not necessitate the use of an attorney; administrative personnel can handle registration formalities. The Copyright Office has issued short and self-explanatory registration forms specified for the type of work being registered.[107] One or two deposit copies must accompany the registration form[108] and copyright registration is effective once the application, fee

---

[106] According to the Copyright Office regulations, an application for copyright may be submitted by "any author or other copyright claimant of a work, or the owner of any exclusive right in a work . . ." 37 C.F.R. §202.3(c)(1) (1982). Even if a museum owns only the right of reproduction to a work, rather than the entire copyright (see *infra* note 222 and accompanying text), the museum, if the author has not already done so, can register the copyright. If the museum is unclear whether or not a particular work was registered, it is possible to initiate a copyright investigation. For a fee, the Copyright Office will make a search of its records. See Copyright Office Circular R22, How to Investigate The Copyright Status of a Work. For the importance of recordation of assignments and licenses, see *infra* notes 230-39 and accompanying text.

[107] Of particular interest to a museum would be: Form VA, for a work of the visual arts (for paintings, sculpture, prints, including derivative works such as postcards and photographic slides); Form TX, for non-dramatic literary works (for example, exhibitions, catalogue, quarterly bulletin); and Form SR, for sound recordings (e.g., audio-visual sound track for gallery tour).

[108] [T]he owner of copyright or of the exclusive right of publication in a work published with notice of copyright in the United States shall deposit, within three months after the date of such publication —

(1) two complete copies of the best edition; or
(2) if the work is a sound recording, two complete phonorecords of the best edition, together with any printed or other visually perceptible material published with such phonorecords . . .

17 U.S.C. §405(a) (1982).

Unlike the simplicity of sending two copies of an exhibition catalogue, it would clearly be impractical for an artist or a museum to send a copy of a work of art. By statutory authority (17 U.S.C. §408 (1982)), the Copyright Office has provided that in the case of pictorial or graphic or sculptured works of art, identifying material may be deposited instead of a copy. 37 C.F.R. §202.20(c)(2)(iv), (ix) (1982). See also Copyright Office Circular R40b, Deposit Requirements for Registration of Claims to Copyright in Visual Arts Material. Copyright Office Circular R40a, Specifications for Visual Arts Identifying Material, sets out the requirements for such material, e.g., photographic transparencies of a particular size, reproducing actual colors used, if the work is a pictorial or graphic work. Note that the Copyright Office regulations exempt picture postcards from deposit. 37 C.F.R. §202.19(c)(2) (1982). The Copyright Office has published lists of criteria to be applied in determining the best edition of each of several types of material, e.g., for printed textual matter, hard cover rather than soft cover. See Copyright Office Circular R76, Best Edition of Published Copyrighted Works for The Collections of The Library of Congress.

and deposit copy are received.[109] The Office examines the application and deposit copies to see that they are in proper form; it neither evaluates the worth of the claim nor compares the claim with earlier works.[110]

What will the museum obtain in return for the ten dollar registration fee and the time spent on filling out the forms? The benefits are many. Registration is an essential step in preventing forfeiture of copyright for a work published without notice.[111] Second, registration is required before bringing an infringement suit.[112] Third, registration within five years of publication establishes prima facie proof of copyright and validity.[113] Fourth, registration within three months of publication may allow the copyright owner to recover certain monetary remedies in an action for infringement.[114] Finally, registration confers constructive notice of the contents of certain filed documents.[115] From the above, it is clear that prompt registration is well worth the small amount of time and expense required.

Applying these principles to our introductory example, there are many opportunities for filing claims for registration in the Copyright Office. The museum should consider filing for the 1970 and 1979 paintings, the photographs, the exhibition catalogue, the posters and the audio-visual program, to name a few. The museum may or may not wish to register all

---

[109] "The effective date of a copyright registration is the day on which an application, deposit, and fee, which are later determined by the Register of Copyrights or by a court of competent jurisdiction to be acceptable for registration, have all been received in the Copyright office." 17 U.S.C. §410(d) (1982).

[110] See Kaplan, The Registration of Copyright, in 17 Studies on Copyright 325 (Arthur Fisher Mem. Ed. 1963).

[111] "The omission of the copyright notice . . . does not invalidate the copyright in a work if . . . (2) registration for the work has been made before or is made within five years after the publication without notice. . . ."17 U.S.C. §405(a) (1982).

[112] "[N]o action for infringement of the copyright in any work shall be instituted until registration of the copyright claim has been made in accordance with this title. . . ." 17 U.S.C. §411(a) (1982).

[113] "In any judicial proceedings the certificate of a registration made before or within five years after first publication of the work shall constitute prima facie evidence of the validity of the copyright and of the facts stated in the certificate." 17 U.S.C. §410(c) (1982).

[114] In any action under this title . . . no award of statutory damages or of attorney's fees . . . shall be made for . . . any infringement of copyright commenced after first publication of the work and before the effective date of its registration, unless such registration is made within three months after the first publication of the work.

17 U.S.C. §412 (1982).

[115] "Recordation of a document in the Copyright Office gives all persons constructive notice of the facts stated in the recorded document, but only if . . . (2) registration has been made for the work." 17 U.S.C. §205(c) (1982).

of these works, but if proper administrative procedures are in place, it could do so promptly and efficiently.

5.2. Notice and Methods of Affixation

To prevent the possibility of a work involuntarily entering the public domain, the museum should affix copyright notice to all published copies.[116] If notice is defective or incomplete, it may constitute no notice at all.[117] In addition to proper notice, the other preventive measure to avoid forfeiture of copyright is prompt registration of the work.[118] Consequently, museum personnel should understand the proper methods to affix notice and develop procedures for the systematic registration of works.

Notice of copyright consists of three elements: ©, or copyr., or copyright; the name of the owner of the copyright; and the date of first publication.[119] A typical notice may look like this: © John Doe, 1983. As

---

[116] Although recognizing the burden on copyright owners to place notice on their works, the drafters of the 1976 Act determined that notice serves several principal functions: (1) it places in the public domain, material no one has an interest in copyrighting, (2) it informs the public whether a particular work has been copyrighted, (3) it identifies the copyright owner, and (4) it gives the date of publication. H.R. Report at 143. See generally Roth, Is Notice Necessary?: An Analysis of The Notice Provisions of The Copyright Law Revision, 27 Copyright L. Symp. (ASCAP) 245 (1982); Levine & Squires, *supra* note 99, at 1236-1253; Note, Copyright Notice Placement for The Visual Artist, 7 Colum. J. of Art and L. 281 (1983); and Crawford, The New Copyright Law: Help in Half-Measures, 65 Art in America (Sept.-Oct. 1977) at 11, 12, 15 criticizing requirement of notice).

[117] Care should be taken by anyone affixing notice to see that it is in proper form. Certain errors in fixation of notice are considered by the Copyright Act to constitute a complete omission of notice and therefor subject the copyright owner to forfeiture. For example, §406(b) "The year date is more than one year later than the year in which publication first occurred, the work is considered to have been published without any notice." Similarly, under §406(c), omission of name or date from publicly distributed copies is also considered omission of notice with the same possible result of forfeiture.

The second variety of incorrect notice does not subject the copyright owner to forfeiture, but can be used as a defense to an infringement action if the alleged infringer shows that he was misled by the incorrect notice. See §405(b), §406(a) and §406(b). For a discussion of infringement see *infra* notes 265-79 and accompanying text.

[118] See *supra* note 111 and accompanying text.

[119] The notice appearing on the copies shall consist of the following three elements:

(1) the symbol © (the letter C in a circle), or the word "Copyright," or the abbreviation "Copr."; and
(2) the year of first publication of the work . . . ; and
(3) the name of the owner of copyright in the work, or an abbreviation by which the name can be recognized, or a generally known alternative designation of the owner.

17 U.S.C. §401(b) (1982).

for position of notice, the current Act provides that notice shall be affixed in a manner and location to afford reasonable notice of the claim to copyright.[120] Of particular interest to the museum, the Register of Copyrights has issued a regulation indicating the position and manner of notice appropriate for various categories of works such as pictorial, graphic and sculptural works, audio-visual works and literary works.[121] The museum should have a copy of this regulation on hand if any questions of proper notice should arise.

Museums and artists have traditionally omitted notice from works of art, perhaps because they were unaware of the requirement, or perhaps they thought that copyright notice would deface the painting or sculpture.[122] These beliefs are not justified; notice is easy to apply and need not affect the visual image of the work. For two-dimensional works, notice must be durably affixed, directly or by label, to the front or back of the work or to other material to which the copies are permanently housed.[123] The same applies to three-dimensional works except that notice must be placed on a visible portion of the work.[124] It is interesting to note that the year date may be omitted on pictorial and graphic works that are reproduced in useful articles such as postcards, stationery, jewelry, dolls and toys.[125]

Of importance to the museum is the appropriate placement of notice on material with repetitive designs such as wrapping or writing paper. This issue was unclear under the 1909 Act.

---

[120] 17 U.S.C. §401(c) (1982).

[121] 37 C.F.R. §201.20 (1982). It should be noted that these regulations are not to be interpreted in a limiting way:

A notice placed or affixed in accordance with the regulations would clearly meet the requirements, but, since the Register's specifications are not to "be considered exhaustive," a notice placed or affixed in some other way might also comply with the law if it were found to "give reasonable notice" of the copyright claim.

H.R. Report at 144.

[122] A 1973 survey revealed that of 206 artists questioned, 71.8% did not place copyright notice on their works. Many were simply unaware of possible copyright protection, as were the gallery owners to whom they looked for information concerning legal rights. Other factors impeding copyright use were fears that notice would deface the work of art or commercialize it, and that copyright would deter future buyers. Sheehan, Why Don't Fine Artists Use Statutory Copyright?, 22 Bull. Copyright Soc'y 242 (1975). See also Note, Statutory Copyright — A Valuable Right for The Visual Artist, 7 Ga. L. Rev. 134 (1972).

[123] 37 C.F.R. §201.20(i)(1) (1982).

[124] 37 C.F.R. §201.20(i)(2), (3) (1982).

[125] "The year date may be omitted where a pictorial, graphic, or sculptural work, with and accompanying text matter, if any, is reproduced in or on greeting cards, postcards, stationery, jewelry, dolls, toys, or any useful articles. . . ." 17 U.S.C. §401(b)(2) (1982).

For example, was one required to place notice on each design or could notice be placed on the margin or selvage of the fabric?[126] The current Act has clarified this problem, and consistent with the policy of flexibility,[127] the Register's regulations allow notice on the reproduction itself, on the margin or selvage, on tags, or labels or containers housing the material.[128]

6. DURATION

6.1. Works Created After 1978

The duration of a copyright is complicated because one must take into account both the 1909 Act and the current Act.[129] We shall first

---

[126] See, e.g., Peter Pan Fabrics, Inc. v. Martin Weiner Corp., 274 F.2d 487 (2d Cir. 1960) (where copyright notice placed on selvage of fabric was removed from view by dress manufacturers, court held that in the case of a deliberate copyist the absence of notice must be proven by the copyist who must show that the notice could have been embodied in the design without impairing its market value). Cf. Dejonge & Co. v. Breuker & Kessler Co., 235 U.S. 33 (1914) (holding that where sheet of gift wrapping paper contained twelve squares of design, the copyright notice should have been affixed to each square).

[127] Unlike the prior act, under which insufficient and/or unintended omission of notice could prove fatal for protection, the 1976 Act is much more flexible. The drafters recognized that there were other inducements for notice than outright forfeiture.

The provisions [effect of omission of copyright] make clear that the notice require- ments . . . are not absolute and that, unlike the law now in effect, the outright omis- sion of a copyright notice does not automatically forfeit protection and throw the work into the public domain. This not only represents a major change in the theoretical framework of American copyright law, but it also seems certain to have immediate practical consequences in a great many individual cases. . . . Thus, if notice is omitted from more than a "relatively small number" of copies . . . , copyright is not lost immediately, but the work will go into the public domain if no effort is made to correct the error or if the work is not registered within five years.

H.R. Report at 146-47. It is for court interpretation to determine what constitutes a "relatively small number of copies." See, e.g., Original Appalachian Artworks, Inc. v. Toy Loft, Inc. 684 F.2d 821 (11th Cir. 1982) (holding that the sale of 400 out of 40,000 dolls without copyright notice constituted the "relatively few" indicated under §405(a)(1) of the 1976 Act and that the inadvertent omission of the co-author's name did not render the registration invalid.) But cf. James DeWitt King v. Winston A. Burnette, Copyright L. Rep. (CCH), §25,489 (D.C. 1982)(holding that artist's sculpture, though registered for copyright, entered the public domain because 300 to 500 of the 1,335 replicas which he had authorized to be sold and distributed were published without copyright notice and there was no showing that he had made a reasonable effort to add notice to the distributed copies). Note in this case that the artist had registered the work prior to distribu- tion. The Copyright Act is silent on this situation.

[128] 37 C.F.R. §201.20(i)(4) (1982).

[129] See generally Cohen, Duration, 24 U.C.L.A. L. Rev. 1180 (1977); Rothen- berg, Old Copyrights, Old Copyright Lawyers and the New Copyright Act, 29 J. of Copyright Soc'y 395 (1982).

discuss duration under the current Act which bases the term of copyright on when the work was created, i.e., fixed in a tangible medium of expression. For works created after 1978, the basic term of copyright begins on creation and lasts for the life of the author plus fifty years.[130] As a result, how long a copyright lasts will depend on the longevity of the author, rather than on an arbitrary amount of time.[131] To illustrate, suppose that an artist finishes paintings in 1978, 1979 and 1980, dying in 1980. The duration of copyright for these works will last until 2030, fifty years after the death of the author. Thus, for individually created works, the Copyright Act establishes a basic term of life plus fifty years and this will account for all works which are not anonymous, psuedonymous, or works made for hire.[132]

---

[130] "Copyright in a work created on or after January 1, 1978, subsists from its creation and, except as provided by the following subsections, endures for a term consisting of the life of the author and fifty years after the author's death." 17 U.S.C. §302(a) (1982).

[131] There are many instances where the date of the author's death would be unknown. Section 302(d) provides that any person having an interest in a copyright may record in the Copyright Office a statement of the date of death of the author of the copyrighted work, or a statement that the author was still alive on a particular date. The Register of Copyrights is then required to maintain current obituary records.

Section 302(e) provides a method of establishing a presumption as to an author's death. After a specified period of time, a person may obtain from the Copyright Office a certified statement that their records do not indicate that the author is living or died less than fifty years before. The person is then entitled to a presumption that the author has been dead more than fifty years and reliance in good faith on this presumption is a complete defense to an action for infringement of copyright.

[132] An "anonymous work" is a work on the copies or phonorecords of which no natural person is identified as author. . . .

A "pseudonymous work" is a work on the copies or phonorecords of which the author is identified under a fictitious name. . . .

A "work for hire" is

(1) a work prepared by an employee within the scope of his or her employment; or
(2) a work specially ordered or commissioned for use as a contribution to a collective work, as a part of a motion picture or other audiovisual work, as a translation, as a supplementary work, as a compilation, as an instructional text, as a test, as answer material for a test, or as an atlas, if the parties expressly agree in a written instrument signed by them that the work shall be considered a work made for hire. For the purpose of the foregoing sentence, a "supplementary work" is a work prepared for publication as a secondary adjunct to a work by another author for the purpose of introducing, concluding, illustrating, explaining, revising, commenting upon, or assisting in the use of the other work, such as forewords, afterwords, pictorial illustrations; maps, charts, tables, editorial notes, musical arrangements, answer material for tests, bibliographies, appendixes, and indexes, and an "instruction text" is a literary, pictorial, or graphic work prepared for publication and with the purpose of use in systematic instructional activities.

17 U.S.C. §101 (1982).

This latter category, works made for hire, is economically significant because many works are created in the course of one's employment.[133] For these works, along with anonymous and pseudonymous works, a different duration applies. Here, the term is seventy-five years after publication or one hundred years after creation, whichever is shorter.[134] For example, an exhibition catalogue prepared by a museum staff member as an employment duty in 1980 would have a term of copyright expiring in 2080; but if the work were published in 2000, the term would last until 2075. This would constitute the basic term of copyright no matter how long the life of the museum staff member.

Considering events which will take place fifty or more years in the future gives the question of duration of copyright under the current Act an air of unreality. But duration is of more immediate concern for works created before 1978.

6.2. Works Created and Published Before 1978

Under the 1909 Act, the term of copyright begins on the publication of a work. The 1909 Act set up a system of two copyright terms, a first term of twenty-eight years and a renewal term of twenty-eight years, for a total of fifty-six years. The second or renewal term was not automatically granted, and a copyright owner was required to file a renewal claim in the Copyright Office. Failure to do so during the twenty-seventh and twenty-eighth years would cause the work to enter the public domain.[135] These renewal provisions still apply to all works coyrighted under the 1909 Act in their first term of copyright.[136] For example, the copyright of the photo-realist painting published in 1970 must be renewed in 1997. Although the current Act has extended the second or renewal term from twenty-eight to forty-seven years,[137] the second term must be timely and properly claimed.[138] Because of these renewal provisions, the museum administrator should take an inventory of all works whose first copyright term of twenty-eight years will soon expire.[139] Following this inventory,

---

[133] See *infra* notes 240-56 and accompanying text.

[134] 17 U.S.C. §302(c) (1982).

[135] 17 U.S.C. §24 (1909) (superseded 1976).

[136] "Any copyright, the first term of which is subsisting on January 1, 1978, shall endure for twenty-eight years from the date it was originally secured. . . ." 17 U.S.C. §304(a) (1982).

[137] 17 U.S.C. §304(a) (1982).

[138] [I]n default of the registration of such application for renewal and extension, the copyright in any work shall terminate at the expiration of twenty-eight years from the date copyright was originally secured." 17 U.S.C. §34(a) (1982).

[139] The museum should take notice of a special situation which exists for works originally copyrighted between September 19, 1920, and renewed between September 19, 1934, and September 19, 1948. A series of interim bills were enacted

a renewal registration should be filed in the Copyright Office for the museum to benefit from another forty-seven years of copyright protection. Even if there is some doubt about ownership of the renewal term, the museum should file a renewal registration as a precaution for the copyright to continue to be protected.

The above discussion involves works in their first term of copyright when the new Act became effective. But what of works that were already in their second term as of 1978? Here, the current Copyright Act has extended the renewal term another nineteen years to comprise a renewal term of forty-seven years.[140] Nothing need be done to acquire this additional duration. In effect, all works in their first or second term on the effective date of the current Act can now enjoy seventy-five years of copyright protection.

6.3. Works Created But Not Published Before 1978

The last durational problem concerns works which were created, but not published before 1978. These works typically include letters, diaries, manuscripts, and works of art in a museum collection which were never sold, exhibited, or reproduced for public distribution. The copyright for these works will endure for the life of the author plus fifty years, but protection will not terminate, regardless of the death date of the author, until 2002. If these unpublished works are published before 2002, protection under copyright will last an extra twenty-five years until 2027.[141] Although 2002 seems many years off, the museum should con-

---

by Congress to keep their renewal period alive, in the expectation that a copyright revision act would imminently be passed. The last such interim law maintained renewals through December 31, 1976. See Latman at 89 and H.R. Report at 139-40, for listing of relevant Public Law numbers. The 1976 Act, by §304(b), increased the renewal term for seventy-five years from the date the copyright was originally secured. Therefore, these copyrights which were extended earlier, are extended again by lesser amounts, but in no case for longer than a total term of seventy-five years. The copyright on works published in 1906 went into the public domain in 1981.

[140] The duration of any copyright, the renewal term of which is subsisting at any time between December 31, 1976, and December 31, 1977, inclusive, or for which renewal is registration is made between December 31, 1976, and December 31, 1977, inclusive, is extended to endure for a term of seventy-five years from the date copyright was originally secured.

17 U.S.C. §304(b) (1982).

[141] Copyright in a work created before January 1, 1978, but not theretofore in the public domain or copyrighted, subsists from January 1, 1978, and endures for the term provided by section 302. In no case, however, shall the term of copyright in such a work expire before December 31, 2002; and, if the work is published on or before December 31, 2002, the term of copyright shall not expire before December 31, 2027.

17 U.S.C. §303 (1982).

sider systematically publishing such works to benefit from the additional duration. For example, black and white photographs of these works placed in a publicly distributed bulletin would serve this purpose.

7. RENEWAL AND TERMINATION OF TRANSFERS
7.1. Renewal

An enormous number of copyrighted works were published before 1978, many of which are now in their first or second term of copyright. For works in their first term, the acquisition of the renewal term is an important consideration and is a subject fraught with traps for the unwary.

One may erroneously believe that the formalities of renewal registration no longer apply after 1978. This misunderstanding may have the effect of inadvertently ejecting a work into the public domain. A renewal registration must be filed in the Copyright Office to claim the renewal term.[142] If a renewal registration is not timely filed, copyright is permanently lost.[143] The registration for renewal must be filed within the year preceding the termination of the first term of copyright.[144]

Who owns the second renewal term is an area of potential confusion. Unless specifically contracted for, the second renewal term reverts to the author.[145] Thus, if the museum is interested in the second renewal term, it should make this a matter of express written contract with the author.

If the author lives until the second renewal term begins, such contractual arrangements are honored by the courts.[146] But, what if the author

---

[142] See Form RE and Copyright Office Circular 15, Renewal of Copyright.

[143] "[I]n default of the registration of . . . application for renewal and extension, the copyright in any work shall terminate at the expiration of twenty-eight years from the date copyright was orginally secured." 17 U.S.C. §304(a) (1982). "The Copyright Office has no discretion to extend the renewal time limits." 37 C.F.R. §202.17 (1982).

[144] 17 U.S.C. §304(a) (1982). Protection is extended to the end of the calendar year in which the twenty-eighth year ends. "All terms of copyright . . . run to the end of the calendar year in which they would otherwise expire." 17 U.S.C. §305 (1982). Therefore, if the museum purchased a painting which was copyrighted in May , 1960, the renewal must be filed before December 31, 1988. This avoids the confusion engendered by the 1909 Act which ran the first term from "the date of first publication." 17 U.S.C. §24 (1909, superceded 1978). The purpose of this change was to make the duration easier to compute, H.R. Report at 142.

[145] "[T]he author of such work . . . shall be entitled to a renewal and extension of the copyright . . . for a further term of forty-seven years. . . ." 17 U.S.C. §304(a) (1982).

[146] See, e.g., Fred Fisher Music Co. v. M. Witmark & Sons, 318 U.S. 643 (1943) (holding that an author (here the composer of "When Irish Eyes Are Smiling") can validly assign his right to renewal of his copyright by an agreement made prior to the expiration of the original copyright term). These are considered

dies before the second renewal term begins? Here, the Copyright Act sets forth the rights of ownership and despite all previous contractual arrangements, the renewal right automatically goes to the surviving spouse and children, or to as many of them as are living, or as a group, rather than to one who has bought the copyright from the author.[147] The effect of this rule is that a transferee will be deprived of copyright ownership if the author of the work dies before the renewal begins. For example, if the artist of the photo-realist painting has published his work in 1970 and has sold it to the museum along with the copyright, renewal must be claimed in 1997-98. If the artist has transferred both terms of copyright and is still alive in 1998 when the renewal begins, the museum will accede to the second term. If, however, the artist dies before 1998, then the renewal term will revert to the widow or children, or to both.[148]

The purpose of this provision is to allow the author's family to benefit from a work which may have become famous at a later time.[149] Thus, the two separate terms of copyright were designed to protect artists and their

---

questions of contract and controlled by state law. See, e.g., Dolch v. United California Bank, 702 F.2d (9th Cir. 1983) (denying federal jurisdiction in case involving claim of invalidity of assignment of renewal rights for lack of consideration).

[147] "[T]he widow, widower, or children of the author, if the author be not living . . . shall be entitled to a renewal and extension of the copyright. . . ." 17 U.S.C. §304(a) (1982).

[148] If there is only a surviving spouse and no children, she or he will receive the entire termination interest. If there are surviving children or grandchildren as well, then the spouse receives one-half of the artist's interest and the children and grandchildren take one-half interest *per stirpes*. For example, if the artist and his wife had three children, one child having died leaving two children, these two grandchildren of the artist would share a one-sixth interest in the termination interest. 17 U.S.C. §304 (c)(A), (B) and (C) (1982). In order for the termination to be effected, it must be carried out by persons who are entitled to exercise more than one half of the author's interest. 17 U.S.C. §304(c)(1) (1982). Therefore, if there are children and/or grandchildren, the widow must be joined with at least one other person before she can act. These provisions, dealing with renewal in the case of death of the author, are identical to the provisions of the statute relating to termination of transfer in works created after 1978. See 17 U.S.C. §203 (1982) and *infra* notes 150-66 and accompanying text. See also H.R. Report at 125 and General Guide to the Copyright Act of 1976 (1977) at 6:2, 6:3. For some of the intricacies posed by the language of this section, see DeSylva v. Ballentine, 351 U.S. 570 (1956) (holding: (1) that widow and children succeed to the right of renewal as a class, each being entitled to share the renewal term; and (2) in order to determine whether an illegitimate child came within the term "children," reference must be made to state law). If there is no surviving spouse, child or grandchild, then the right to renewal rests in the author's executors, or in the absence of a will, his or her next of kin. 17 U.S.C. §304(a) (1982).

[149] See generally, Ringer, Renewal of Copyright, in 1 Studies on Copyright 503 (Arthur Fisher Mem. Ed., 1963).

families who may have signed away valuable rights under economic duress or ignorance. To avoid the reversion of the renewal term, it became common practice for a transferee to seek out the author's wife and children to persuade them to sell their rights if the author died before the vesting of the renewal term.

7.2. Termination of Transfer

The renewal provisions only apply to works published before 1978 in their first term of copyright. For works created after 1978, renewal no longer applies. In its place, serving the same protective function, a termination of transfer is allowed by the current Act. A termination of transfer[150] may be exercised by the author or his heirs between the thirty-fifth and fortieth years after the date of the grant.[151] Because this termination right is a special privilege given by the Copyright Act, it cannot be bargained away.[152] The termination right extends to all works except works made for hire.[153] The other major limitation to termination is that it applies only to grants given by a living author made after December 31, 1977;[154] grants by will are not subject to termination.[155]

The major affirmative obligation imposed on the artist and his heirs is that notice of termination must be given in writing, specifying the date of termination within the appropriate five-year period.[156] One must give

---

[150] A transfer is a sale of a copyright interest, for example, an exclusive license for the right of reproduction of a painting might be sold by the artist to a calendar manufacturer.

[151] "Termination of the grant may be effected at any time during a period of five years beginning at the end of thirty-five years from the date of execution of the grant. . . ." 17 U.S.C. §203(a)(3) (1982).

[152] The provisions of section 203 are based on the premise that . . . the proposed law should substitute for [revisionary provisions] a provision safeguarding authors against unremunerative transfers. A provision of this sort is needed because of the unequal bargaining position of authors, resulting in part from the impossibility of determining a work's value until it has been exploited.

H.R. Report at 124.

[153] "In the case of any work other than a work made for hire, the . . . grant of a transfer . . . is subject to termination. . . ." 17 U.S.C. §203(a) (1982).

[154] "In the case of any work, other than a work made for hire, the exclusive or nonexclusive grant . . . executed by the author on or after January 1, 1978. . . ." 17 U.S.C. §203(a) (1982).

[155] "[T]he . . . grant of a transfer . . . executed by the author . . . otherwise than by will, is subject to termination. . . ." 17 U.S.C. §203(a) (1982).

[156] The termination shall be effected by serving an advance notice in writing . . .

(A) The notice shall state the effective date of the termination, which shall fall within the five-year period. . . .

17 U.S.C. §203(a)(4) (1976).

notice at least two years, but not more than ten years, before the termination date.[157] If, for example, the artist transferred copyright ownership for the painting created in 1979 to the museum in 1980, the artist or his heirs may terminate the transfer between 2016 and 2021 by filing the appropriate written notice no less than two, but not more than ten years, before the date of termination. Note that the responsibility for termination is placed upon the artist or his heirs; the museum is not obligated to alert the transferor of his right to terminate. Thus, if the artist or his heirs failed to exercise their termination rights in a timely manner, the museum will benefit from the entire duration of copyright. Involving all copyrighted works except for those made for hire, the termination right will eventually prove to be one of the most economically significant provisions of the current Act.[158]

Inasmuch as this discussion refers to events taking place some decades in the future, it may seem like a purely theoretical exercise. Yet such is not the case. Termination of transfer is of immediate concern because it applies to the second renewal term of copyright which has been extended from twenty-eight to forty-seven years.[159] The additional nineteen years of protection are now subject to termination with several qualifications. The right to terminate applies only to transfers made before January 1, 1978.[160] It will not apply to works made for hire[161] or grants made by will.[162] It is thus now possible for an author's surviving spouse or children to terminate any transfer of a copyright interest, allowing them to reclaim all or part of the additional nineteen years of the second renewal term.[163]

---

[157] "[T]he notice shall be served not less than two or more than ten years before that date." 17 U.S.C. §203(a)(4) (1976).

[158] For discussions of this highly complex topic, see generally Curtis, Caveat Emptor in Copyright: A Practical Guide to the Termination of Transfers Under the New Copyright Code, 25 Bull. Copyright Soc'y 19 (1977); Nimmer, Termination of Transfers Under the Copyright Act of 1976, 125 U. Pa. L. Rev. 947 (1977); and Stein, Termination of Transfers and Licenses Under the New Copyright Act: Theory Problems for the Copyright Bar, 24 U.C.L.A. L. Rev. 1141 (1977). For focus on the problems arising for the derivative work if the proprietor of the underlying work terminates the transfer, see Ellingson, The Copyright Exception for Derivative Works and The Scope of Utilization, 56 Ind. L.J. 1 (1980); Mimms, Reversion and Derivative Works Under the Copyright Acts of 1909 and 1982, N.Y.L. Sch. L. Rev. 595 (1980).

[159] 17 U.S.C. §304(b) (1982).

[160] 17 U.S.C. §304(c) (1982).

[161] *Id.*

[162] *Id.*

[163] "Where an author is dead, his or her termination interest is owned, and may be exercised, by his widow or her widower and his or her children or grandchildren. . . ." 17 U.S.C. §304(c)(2) (1982).

The mechanics of termination for these works are similar to termination for post-1978 works. Termination may take effect at any time during the five-year period beginning either fifty-six years from the date that copyright in the work was first secured, or January 1, 1978, whichever date is later.[164] The terminating party must give written notice not more than ten years, and not less than two years, before the date of termination is to take effect.[165] Notice procedures must comply with Copyright Office regulations.[166]

Because the possibility of termination of copyright always exists, the museum must adjust to economic realities. It should inventory works whose second renewal term is to expire in the near future. For example, works renewed in 1958 in which the museum owns the copyright are subject to termination by the author or his heirs by giving the prescribed written notice in 1986. Such written notice will reclaim the extra nineteen years of protection and unless the museum renegotiates, it will no longer be able to make use of the work. As in the case of post-1978 terminations, there is no affirmative duty for the museum to notify the artist about the termination right. Similarly, the museum will not have to concern itself about termination of grants given by will or works made for hire, which are not subject to termination.

8. EXCLUSIVE RIGHTS

8.1. In General

Copyright springs into existence when a work of authorship is created and its ownership vests in an author. We now turn to what it means to own a copyright and what are the practical benefits of that ownership. Generally, a copyright consists of a bundle of rights, known as the exclusive rights. The Copyright Act enumerates five exclusive rights:[167] the reproduction right, the adaptation right, the distribution

---

[164] 17 U.S.C. §304(c)(3) (1982).

[165] 17 U.S.C. §304(c)(4)(A) (1982).

[166] 17 U.S.C. §304(c)(4)(B) (1982). For regulations promulgated by the Copyright Office, see 37 C.F.R. §201.10 (1982).

[167] [T]he owner of copyright under this title has the exclusive rights to do and to authorize any of the following:

(1) to reproduce the copyrighted work in copies or phonorecords;
(2) to prepare derivative works based upon the copyrighted work;
(3) to distribute copies or phonorecords of the copyrighted work to the public by sale or other transfer of ownership, or by rental, lease, or lending;
(4) in the case of literary musical, dramatic, and choreographic works, pantomimes, and motion pictures and other audiovisual works, to perform the copyrighted work publicly; and
(5) in the case of literary, musical, dramatic, and choreographic works, pantomimes, and pictorial, graphic, or sculptural works, including the individual images of a motion picture or other audiovisual work, to display the copyrighted work publicly.

17 U.S.C. §106 (1982).

right, the performance right and the display right.[168] Copyright ownership is therefore not absolute: every unauthorized use of copyrighted
work is not an infringement of copyright. A use of a copyrighted work is
an infringing use if, and only if, it falls within the scope of the enumerated rights.[169]

---

[168] The enumerated rights recognized under §106 do not include the concept
of moral rights. An extensive review of moral rights, or *droit moral*, that is, the
continuing interest of the artist in his work after sale, is beyond the scope of this
article. "Moral rights" is an umbrella term, and is generally said to include, inter
alia, the right of paternity or authorship, the right of integrity or protection
against distortion or mutilation, and the right of honor or reputation. Although
widely recognized in civil law countries, moral rights have not been specifically
recognized in this country with the exception of California, see *infra* discussion in
text. See generally Roeder, The Doctrine of Moral Right: A Study in the Law of
Artists, Authors and Creators, 53 Harv. L. Rev. 554 (1940); Merryman, The
Refrigerator of Bernard Buffet, 27 Hastings L. Rev. 1023 (1976); 2 Nimmer,
§8.21. Over the years, several bills dealing with moral rights have been introduced in Congress. The most recent is H.R. 1521, Visual Artists' Moral Rights
Amendment of 1983, introduced by Rep. Barney Frank. This bill would amend
the copyright law so that the artist or the artist's representative, independent of
the copyright, would have the right to protect his work from distortion, mutilation, or alteration done without his consent. This right would endure for the same
period as the copyright, life of the author plus fifty years. Some commentators
maintain that libel laws, the expanding concept of the right to privacy and
restrictions on unfair competition provide adequate protections. See, e.g., Treece,
American Law Analogues of the Author's Moral Right, 16 Am. J. Comp. L. 487
(1968); Note, Protection of Artistic Integrity: Gilliam v. American Broadcasting
Companies, 90 Harv. L. Rev. 473 (1976); Comment, Moral Rights for Artists
Under the Lanham Act, 18 Wm. & Mary L. Rev. 595 (1977); Comment, The
Monty Python Litigation of Moral Right and The Lanham Act, 125 U. Pa. L. Rev.
611 (1977).

California recently passed the California Art Preservation Act, Cal. Civ. Code
§987 (West Supp. 1981), incorporating the moral rights doctrines of right of
privacy and integrity. This act allows an artist who suffers a wrong to his work in
California to bring a civil action and request injunctive relief and damages. For
review of the act, see Gantz, Protecting Artists' Moral Rights: A Critique of the
California Art Preservation Act as a Model for Statutory Reform, 49 Geo. Wash.
L. Rev. 873 (1981); Francione, The California Art Preservation Act and Federal
Preemption by the 1976 Copyright Act—Equivalence and Actual Conflict, 18
Cal. W.L. Rev. 189 (1982); Comment, The California Art Preservation Act: A
Safe Hamlet for "Moral Rights" in the U.S., 14 U.C.D. L. Rev. 975 (1981); Note,
Artworks and American Law: The California Art Preservation Act, 61 B.U. L.
Rev. 1201 (1981).

[169] For example, the Copyright Act gives a performance right to a literary or
dramatic work, but not to a pictorial, graphic or sculptural work. If, for example,
the program of modern dance presented during the photo-realist exhibition contained several "tableaux vivants" of copyrighted paintings, these would arguably be performances of the pictorial works and therefore there would be no
infringement of the owner's exclusive rights. However, the background projec-
tions of changing slide images would constitute a display of these pictorial works
and permission of the copyright owner would be necessary.

The museum must accordingly take into account both exclusive rights and their limitations to avoid problems of infringement,[170] while making use of works to their fullest extent.

8.2. The Reproduction Right

The right to reproduce the copyrighted work is in some ways the most basic of the exclusive rights. The reproduction right is infringed when an author's work is placed without his consent in a tangible form in a material object.[171] It makes no difference that the work is reproduced in a photograph; infringement may occur even though a different medium and dimension are involved.[172] Similarly, one may infringe the reproduction right by making an unauthorized recording of a literary work in book form or a transcript of a musical work on sheet music from a tape recording. For infringement to occur, the copying does not have to be verbatim, as long as it is substantially similar to the copyrighted work.[173]

8.3. Limitations on the Reproduction Right: Library Photocopying

The reproduction right is subject to important limitations which may apply to a museum which operates a library or archive open to the general public or researcher in a specialized field of interest.[174] This exception to the reproduction right provides that under certain circum-

---

[170] "Anyone who violates any of the exclusive right of the copyright owner as provided by sections 106 through 118, . . . is an infringer of the copyright." 17 U.S.C. §501(a) (1982).

[171] "[A] copyrighted work would be infringed by reproducing it in whole or in any substantial part, and by duplicating it exactly or by imitation or simulation." H.R. Report at 61.

[172] See, e.g., King Features Syndicate v. Fleisher, 299 Fed. 533 (2d Cir. 1924) (toys based on copyrighted cartoons); Time, Inc. v. Bernard Geis Assoc., 293 F. Supp. 130 (S.D.N.Y. 1968) (sketches based on photograph); Habersham Plantation Corp. v. Country Concepts, 209 U.S.P.Q. 711 (N.D. Ga. 1980) (line drawings based on photographs). This same principle is true for infringement of derivative works. See, e.g., Eden Toys v. Florelee Undergarment Co., 697 F.2d 27, 35 (2d Cir. 1982) ("No one may copy another's novel additions in a derivative work, even if the copier employs a medium different from that used by the holder of the derivative copyright.") The unauthorized use of photographers' images in paintings has been the subject of some controversy. See Morris, When Artists Use Photographs: Is It Fair Use, Legitimate Transformation or Rip-Off?, 80 Art News 102 (Jan. 1981).

[173] "Wide departures or variations from the copyrighted works would still be an infringement as long as the author's 'expression' rather than merely the author's 'ideas' are taken." H. R. Report at 61. For discussion of what constitutes "substantial similarity," see infra note 270 and accompanying text.

[174] See generally Treece, Library Photocopying, 24 U.C.L.A. L. Rev. 1025 (1977); Young, Copyright and the New Technologies — The Case of Library Photocopying, 28 Copyright L. Symp. (ASCAP) 51 (1982). Written principally for librarians are: J. Miller, Applying the New Copyright Law: A Guide for Educators and Librarians (1979) and Copyright Office Circular R21, Reproduction of Copyrighted Works by Educators and Librarians.

stances, a library open to the public may qualify for the privilege of reproducing and distributing one copy of a work without infringing copyright. The library must make the distribution without any purpose of direct or indirect commercial gain and the reproduction must bear copyright notice.[175] The library can make no more than one copy or phono-record of the work at a time, thus precluding systematic reproduction and distribution activities. Consequently, the museum library could send a photocopy of an article in a journal or a reprint to a researcher without infringing copyright if the above provisions were followed. Significantly, the library's right to reproduce does not extend to musical works, pictorial, graphic, or sculptural works except those appearing as illustrations, or to certain kinds of audio-visual works.[176]

The provisions apply to library photocopying for a patron's use of a work. Other provisions relate to the library's own use of a work; the current Act allows the library to reproduce an unpublished work for archival preservation and to reproduce a published work for replacement which has been damaged, lost, stolen, or is deteriorating.[177] The replacement privilege for published works applies only if the library cannot obtain the work at a fair price after making a reasonable effort.[178]

---

[175] [I]t is not an infringement of copyright for a library or archives, or any of its employees acting within the scope of their employment, to reproduce no more than one copy or phonorecord of a work, or to distribute such copy or phonorecord, under the conditions specified by this section, if —

(1) the reproduction or distribution is made without any purpose of direct or indirect commercial advantage;
(2) the collections of the library or archives are (i) open to the public, or (ii) available not only to researchers affiliated with the library or archives or with the institution of which it is a part, but also to other persons doing research in a specialized field; and
(3) the reproduction or distribution of the work includes a notice of copyright.

17 U.S.C. §108(a) (1982).

Section 108(e) requires that the library display warnings of copyright in accordance with the prescribed regulations. The text of the warning appears in 37 C.F.R. §201.14(b) (1982). Section 108(i) requires that the Register of Copyrights report every five years to Congress concerning this library photocopy. The latest report, Library Reproduction of Copyrighted Works, was submitted to Congress in January, 1983. 25 Pat., Trademark & Copyright J. (BNA) 229 (1983).

[176] 17 U.S.C. §108(h) (1982). It would appear that a museum library would be prohibited under this section from copying a full-page reproduction, e.g., a drawing reproduced in a catalogue raisonnee, but it could photocopy a page in which an illustration accompanied explanatory text.

[177] 17 U.S.C. §108(c) (1982).

[178] The scope and nature of a reasonable investigation to determine that an unused replacement cannot be obtained will vary according to the circumstances of a particular situation. It will always require recourse to commonly known trade sources in the United States, and in the normal situation to the publisher or other copyright owner (if such owner can be located at the address listed in the copyright registration), or an authorized reproducing service.

H.R. Report at 75-76.

8.4. The Adaptation Right

The adaptation right,[179] or the right to make derivative works, is related to the reproduction and performance rights. The adaptation right is infringed when one makes an unauthorized derivative work. Examples include art reproductions, translations, musical arrangements, dramatizations or any other mode by which a preexisting work is recast, transformed or adapted.[180] The standard for infringement, as in any copyright case, is one of substantial similarity.[181] Thus, if one were to write a play based on a novel and the play substantially embodied the novel, the copyright owner could bring an action for the infringement of the adaptation and reproduction right. If the play were performed, the performance right, as well as the other two rights, would be infringed. The exclusive rights in many cases thus overlap and the infringement of the adaptation right almost invariably involves infringement of the reproduction right, performance right,[182] or both.

There is one instance where the adaptation right alone is subject to infringement. This may occur when the copyright owner has licensed another to reproduce or perform the copyrighted work, but has not specifically licensed the right to make derivative work.[183] For example, a museum may have acquired the right to reproduce a copyrighted paint-

---

[179] 17 U.S.C. §106(2) (1982).

[180] For discussion of copyrightability of derivative works, see *supra* notes 64-76 and accompanying text.

[181] See *infra* note 270. "To be an infringement the 'derivative work' must be 'based upon the copyrighted work. . . .' Thus, to constitute a violation of section 106(2), the infringing work must incorporate a portion of the copyrighted work in some form." H.R. Report at 62.

[182] The exclusive right to prepare derivative works . . . overlaps the exclusive right of reproduction to some extent. It is broader than the right, however, in the sense that reproduction requires fixation in copies or phonorecords, whereas the preparation of a derivative work, such as a ballet, pantomime, or improvised performance, may be an infringement even though nothing is ever fixed in tangible form.

H.R. Report at 62.

[183] The leading case is Gilliam v. Am. Broadcasting Co., 538 F.2d 14 (2d Cir. 1976)(holding that American Broadcasting Company, which received a license to show Monty Python films, had infringed the copyright held by that group when they edited them for broadcast).

One who obtains permission to use a copyrighted script in the production of a derivative work, however, may not exceed the specific purpose for which permission was granted. . . . Whether intended to allow greater economic exploitation of the work . . . or to ensure that the copyright proprietor retains a veto power over revisions desired for the derivative work, the ability of the copyright holder to control his work remains paramount in our copyright law.

Id. at 20-21. See also Nat'l Bank of Commerce v. Shaklee, 503 F. Supp. 533 (W.D. Texas 1980) (holding that licensee infringed copyright of plaintiff, columnist Heloise, by inserting advertisements for their products in her books).

ing; but what if the museum reproduces only part of the painting, including it as a full-page detail in an engagement calendar or cookbook?[184] Here, many courts would likely construe the contract narrowly and find the museum to have infringed the adaptation right because it was specifically granted the reproduction right only and no more. Thus, the museum should expressly acquire the adaptation right depending upon the use it wishes to make of a copyrighted work.

8.5. The Distribution Right

The third exclusive right enumerated by the Copyright Act is the distribution right.[185] By the distribution right, the copyright owner has the right to control the first public distribution of the work either by sale, gift, loan, or rental. The distribution right is often infringed along with other exclusive rights, most often the reproduction right. Such would occur if one were to make and sell unauthorized prints of a work of art. Sometimes the infringement of the distribution right may occur alone. This type of infringement arises most commonly in the record and music industry when pirated records or video cassettes acquired from a third party are sold at retail. Although the retail seller may not know that the works were improperly made, they would still be infringing the distribution right by selling the pirated copies.[186] As in all cases of infringement, innocence is no defense.[187] Similarly, the museum could infringe the distribution right if it sold posters, postcards, or sculpture reproduced without authorization from the copyright owner. Infringement would occur even though the objects were bought from a third party and inno-

---

[184] Many museums publish calendars [and] cookbooks, illustrated with works from their collections. See, e.g., Grove, Museum Cookbooks: For Fun and Profit, 53 Museum News 52 (June 1975). The illustrations are often appropriate details from paintings, to complement the theme of the book, e.g., flowers or food.

[185] 17 U.S.C. §106(3) (1982).

[186] "[A]ny resale of an illegally 'pirated' phonorecord would be an infringement. . . ." H.R. Report at 79.

[187] Innocent intent, although relevant to questions of remedy, will not be a defense to actions for statutory copyright infringement. See, e.g., Buck v. Jewell-LaSalle Realty Co., 283 U.S. 191, 198 (1930) ("Intention to infringe is not essential under the Act"); Platt & Munk Co. v. Playmore, Inc., 218 F. Supp. 267 (S.D.N.Y. 1962); and Plymouth Music Co. v. Magnus Organ Corp., 456 F. Supp. 676 (S.D.N.Y. 1978).

"[A] plea of innocence in a copyright action may often be easy to claim and difficult to disapprove. . . . Copyright would lose much of its value if third parties such as publishers and producers were insulated from liability because of their innocence as to the culpability of the persons who supplied them with the infringing material" (footnotes omitted). 3 Nimmer, §13.08 at 13-110. Innocent intent is a defense to charges of criminal infringement, which, of course, requires culpable *mens rea*. See *infra* note 274.

cently sold without the museum knowing the circumstances of reproduction.[188]

8.6. Limitations on the Distribution Right: The First-Sale Doctrine

A basic exception to the distribution right is known as the first-
sale doctrine. This limitation on the distribution right authorizes the
owner of a particular copy or phonorecord, which has been lawfully
made, to sell or otherwise dispose of its possession.[189] Thus a museum
which owns a work of art may resell it to another as long as it was bought
from an individual who had lawful ownership. Of course ownership of
the copy of the work does not include ownership of the copyright in the
work itself. The first-sale doctrine therefore applies only to the right to
resell the work and not to exploit it in any other way, except perhaps to
display the work under certain circumstances as will be later discussed.[190]

The first-sale doctrine allows the copyright owner the privilege of
making a profit on the first sale of his work, but not on a further resale or
rental of the work. As it applies to artists, this doctrine reveals a particularly American notion about the ownership of tangible property. By
comparison, countries such as France and Germany allow the artist to

---

[188] For cost-sharing reasons primarily, many of the temporary exhibitions at
museums today are traveling ones, organized by one or perhaps more institutions
and shown at several. The organizing museum often prepares materials such as
exhibition catalogues, posters, postcards, etc. to be sold at each participating
museum. While museums often pay careful attention to copyright questions
involved in loans of works of art, little regard is given to possible copyright
infringements in the material sold during the traveling exhibition, perhaps in the
mistaken belief that any infringement would be the problem of the organizing
museum and not the "innocent third party."

189

  (a) Notwithstanding the provisions of section 106(3), the owner of a particular copy or
     phonorecord lawfully made under this title, or any person authorized by such
     owner, is entitled, without the authority of the copyright owner, to sell or otherwise
     dispose of the possession of that copy or phonorecord. . . .
  (c) The privileges prescribed by subsections (a) and (b) do not, unless authorized by the
     copyright owner, extend to any person who has acquired possession of the copy or
     phonorecord from the copyright owner, by rental, lease, loan, or otherwise, without
     acquiring ownership of it.

17 U.S.C. §109(a), (c) (1982).

190

  (b) Notwithstanding the provisions of section 106(5), the owner of a particular copy
     lawfully made under this title, or any person authorized by such owner, is entitled,
     without the authority of the copyright owner, to display that copy publicly, either
     directly or by the projection of no more than one image, to viewers present at the
     place where the copy is located.

17 U.S.C. §109(b) (1982). See *infra* notes 214-20 and accompanying text.

recover a portion of the profit from the resale of a work as it passes from owner to owner.[191] Influenced by the European experience and responding to pressure from artists rights' groups, in 1976 California passed a Resale Royalties Act which allowed an artist to recover 5% of the total price payable for the sale of his pictorial, graphic, or sculptural work sold for more than $1,000.[192] For the Resale Royalties Act to apply, the resale must, however, occur in California. If the resale occurs elsewhere, the seller must be a resident of California at the time of sale.[193] Thus the museum may have to consider the California act when acquiring a work of art in California or from a California resident. Because of its narrow scope, the California Resale Royalties Act will have limited application,[194] but it may be representative of a general movement to depart from the strictures of the first-sale doctrine. . . .

8.12. The Display Right

The right to display[214] the copyrighted work has obvious importance to anyone involved in the visual arts. As in the performance right, the display right only involves public display of the work and is subject to

---

[191] For discussion of resale royalties rights abroad, see, e.g., Sherman, Incorporation of the *Droit de Suite* Into United States Copyright Law, 18 Copyright L. Symp. (ASCAP) 50 (1970); Schulder, Art Proceeds Act: A Study of the *Droit de Suite* and a Proposed Enactment for the United States, 61 Nw. U.L. Rev. 19 (1966); Hauser, The French *Droit de Suite:* The Problem of Protection for the Underprivileged Artist under the Copyright Law, 11 Copyright L. Symp. (ASCAP) 1 (1962); and Price, Government Policy and Economic Security for Artists: The Case of The *Droit de Suite,* 77 Yale L.J. 1333 (1968).

[192] Cal. Civ. Code §986 (West Supp. 1980).

[193] The Act has been widely criticized as benefitting only a few artists, those with a secondary market (not the great majority of artists); as being in reality a sales tax which will reduce the amount of money which museums and collectors would spend on art; as a psychological barrier to the purchase of art; and as the creator of uneconomic administrative burdens. See Ashley, Critical Comment on California's *Droit de Suite,* Civil Code Section 986, 29 Hastings L.J. 249 (1977); Elsen, California Artist's Resale Law: Failure of Innocence, 65 Art In America 15 (Mar.-April 1977); and Bolch, Damon and Hinshaw, An Economic Analysis of the California Art Royalty Statute, 10 Conn. L. Rev. 689 (1978).

[194] The Act has also been questioned regarding preemption by federal copyright law. See, e.g., 2 Nimmer, §8.22[B] (1981); Katz, Copyright Preemption Under the Copyright Act of 1976: The Case of *Droit de Suite,* 47 Geo. Wash. L. Rev. 200 (1978). In 1980, applying the Copyright Act of 1909, the U.S. Court of Appeals for the Ninth Circuit upheld the constitutionality of the Act. Morsburg v. Balyon, 621 F.2d 972 (9th Cir. 1979), *cert. denied,* 449 U.S. 983 (1980). For an analysis of the 1976 Copyright Act as applied to the California Act, see Note, The California Resale Royalties Act as a Test Case for Preemption Under the 1976 Copyright Law, 81 Colum. L. Rev. 1315 (1981).

[214] 17 U.S.C. §106 (1982). The right to display is codified for the first time in the 1976 Act. H.R. Report at 63.

some of the same educational limitations as the performance right discussed in the previous section.[215] To display a work is to show a copy of it
directly or by a device. A motion picture, for example, is displayed when
frames are shown non-sequentially; when shown in sequence, however,
the motion picture is considered performed.[216]

8.13. Limitations on the Display Right

One limitation to the display right, apart from the face-to-face
teaching exemption, is closely related to the first-sale doctrine.[217] This
allows the owner of a lawfully made copy of a work to display it directly
or by projection of no more than one image at a time to viewers present at
the place where the copy is located.[218] Thus if the museum owns a
painting, even if it does not own the copyright on the painting, it may
show the painting to the public directly or by projection, as long as the
display takes place on museum grounds and is not further projected to
distant locations.

The privilege to display or to authorize others to display the copy
applies only to those who own the work. Therefore the museum which is
lent a painting may only display it at the museum and cannot authorize
others to display it. Of course the right to display does not include any
other use of the painting, such as reproduction in an exhibition catalogue.[219] Here the museum must acquire permission from the copyright

------

[215] See *supra* notes 195-213 and accompanying text. 17 U.S.C. §101 (1982).

[216] According to §101 of the Act: "To 'display' a work means to show a copy of
it, either directly or by means of a film, slide, television image, or any other device
or process or, in the case of a motion picture or other audio-visual work, to show
individual images nonsequentially."

According to the House Report: "Since 'copies' are defined as including the
material object 'in which the work is first fixed,' the right of public display applies
to original works of art as well as to reproductions of them." H.R. Report at 64.

[217] See *supra* notes 189-94 and accompanying text.

[218] 17 U.S.C. §109(b) (1982).

[219] The House Report, in its discussion of §109(b), raises the question of the
right of an artist, who has sold a painting, but not the copyright, to restrain the
new owner from displaying the work of art publicly for example in galleries.
The drafters answer the question by stating that §109(b) adopts the general
principle that the lawful owner should be able to put his copy on public display
without the consent of the copyright owner. If, however, they would contract to
the contrary, this would appear to be enforceable. H.R. Report at 79.

This limitation on the right of display is limited to viewers "present at the
place where the copy is located." Nimmer, pointing out some ambiguities in the
language of the exception, asks: "If viewers observe a painting projected on a
screen in one room of a large museum, while the 'copy' being projected is in
another room at the opposite end of the museum, are the viewers 'present at the
place where the copy is located'?" Referring to this House Report discussion of
the place located as "a situation in which viewers are present in the same physical

owner if it wishes to reproduce a work given to it on loan from another person or museum, even though the third party may own the copy of the work.[220] Of course if the lender owns the copyright as well as the copy, no such complications will arise.

9. OWNERSHIP

Copyright ownership initially vests in the author of the work, who is given as copyright owner a bundle of rights known as the exclusive rights.[221] The exclusive rights of reproduction, adaptation, distribution, performance and display set forth the boundaries of copyright ownership, specifying what constitutes infringement on the one hand and how the copyright owner can economically exploit his property on the other.

9.1. Divisibility of Ownership

The current Copyright Act recognizes the principle of divisibility which allows the copyright owner to split up his ownership in an infinite number of ways by sale, gift or lease.[222] For example, the copyright owner of a sculpture may sell the right of reproduction and distribution to

---

surrounding as the copy, even though they cannot see the copy directly" (H.R. Report at 80), Nimmer concludes that this museum display would fall within the exception. 2 Nimmer §8.20[B] at 8-244.

[220] This is true whether the museum is the owner of the work but does not own the copyright, is lent the work by an owner who does not own the copyright, or is lent the work by an owner who does own the copyright, but is authorizing nothing more than display. The drafters of the act were concerned that the exception to the right of display not affect the copyright owner's market for reproduction and distribution of copies. H.R. Report at 80.

[221] 217 U.S.C. §201(a) (1982).

[222]

(1) The ownership of a copyright may be transferred in whole or in part by any means of conveyance or by operation of law, and may be bequeathed by will or pass as personal property by the applicable laws of intestate succession.

(2) Any of the exclusive rights comprised in a copyright, including any subdivision of any of the rights specified by section 106, may be transferred as provided by clause (1) and owned separately. The owner of any particular exclusive right is entitled, to the extent of that right, to all of the protection and remedies accorded to the copyright owner by this title.

17 U.S.C. §201(d) (1982). This is the first statutory recognition of the principle of divisibility of copyright. "This provision means that any of the exclusive rights that go to make up a copyright . . . can be transferred and owned separately." H.R. Report at 123. See generally Kaminstein, Divisibility of Copyrights, Study No. 11 in 1 Studies in Copyright at 623 (Arthur Fisher Mem. Ed. 1963). See also Note, Divisibility of Copyright: Its Application and Effect, 19 Santa Clara L. Rev. 171 (1979); Note, Divisibility of Copyright: A Bill of Rights for Authors, 14 Cal. W.L. Rev. 590 (1979).

a publishing company while retaining the right of adaptation for himself and, at the same time, give an exclusive license for the display of his work to a museum for one year. Each of these transferees now becomes owner of a copyright interest along with the original author and, unless there is a limitation placed on the transfer, the new owner of the copyright interest can further sell or lease his interest in the work. In addition, he may also bring copyright infringement actions in his own name against those who are improperly using his property right.[223]

Although desirable, it may not always be possible for the museum to acquire the full copyright along with the work of art. If not, the museum at the least should negotiate an assignment or license authorizing the specific use it wishes to make of the work, e.g., reproduction for purposes of publicity and education. We now turn to the manner in which copyright interests are transferred.

9.2. Assignments and Licenses

One must distinguish among the several ways in which the copyright owner may exploit his copyright interest. The entire copyright interest might be assigned to another who now becomes the copyright owner. Similarly, the copyright owner can also assign his interest in one or more of the exclusive rights, such as the reproduction and performance rights, while either retaining some rights for himself or selling or leasing them to others. The copyright owner can also convey less than a complete ownership interest in a work. Such a transfer is called a license which is either an exclusive license, if the licensor agrees not to give the same right to someone else, or a nonexclusive license, if the licensor retains the right to license the same rights to others.[224] For example, a museum as the copyright owner may license a publisher the right to reproduce the work in a poster to be sold in certain retail outlets only during a five-year period. By an exclusive license, the museum would agree not to give another the same right.[225]

---

[223] It is thus clear, for example, that a local broadcasting station holding an exclusive license to transmit a particular work within a particular geographic area and for a particular period of time, could sue, in its own name as copyright owner, someone who infringed that particular exclusive right.

H.R. Report at 123.

[224] See generally 3 Nimmer, §§10.01-10.15 (Assignments, Licenses, and Other Transfers of Rights).

[225] Museum licensing arrangements with manufacturers for the production of goods based on works of art in the collection and to be carried in its own and other stores, as well as by mail-order catalogues, can be a lucrative source of revenue for the museum. These products can range from traditional items such as greeting cards and posters, to tee-shirts, bed linens and needle-point canvasses. See generally Hodes & Gross, Museums in the Commercial Marketplace: The Need for

The distinction between assignments and exclusive licenses on the one hand and non-exclusive licenses on the other is important. Assignments and exclusive licenses are considered transfers of copyright[226] and under the Copyright Act, to be effective, must be manifested in a signed writing.[227] Alternatively, non-exclusive licenses can be conveyed orally as informally as an agreement over the telephone. Nevertheless, it is highly recommended that one effect a written document for all assignments or licenses.[228]

What form should the writing take? Just about any format will suffice, such as a letter stating the terms of the assignment or license. The written agreement should explictly set forth the royalty provisions, the length of the time of the conveyance, the circumstances of termination, if any, the name to be carried on the notice of copyright, and the responsibilities for maintaining an infringement suit against third parties.[229]

9.3. Recordation and Ownership Priorities

For a nominal fee the Copyright Act permits recordation of all documents pertaining to copyright ownership no matter what their form.[230] The museum should make use of this privilege for all important

---

Licensing Agreements, 10 Conn. L. Rev. 620 (1978) [hereinafter cited as Hodes & Gross]; and Faul, Licensing Programs — A Second Life for Museum Collections, 54 Museum News 26 (Nov.-Dec., 1975).

[226] A "transfer of copyright ownership" is an assignment, mortgage, exclusive license, or any other conveyance, alienation, or hypothecation of a copyright or of any of the exclusive rights comprised in a copyright, whether or not it is limited in time or place of effect, but not including a non-exclusive license.

17 U.S.C. §204(a) (1982).

[227] 17 U.S.C. §204(a) (1982).

[228] One reason for this recommendation is that it may not be clear whether a particular agreement is an exclusive or non-exclusive license. See, e.g., Library Publications v. Medical Economics, 548 F. Supp. 1231 (E.D. Pa. 1982), where plaintiff had alleged breach of non-exclusive license to distribute a book published by the defendant, the court held the license was exclusive and as such, invalid as it was not in writing.)

[229] Strong, the Copyright Book: A Practical Guide (1981) at 41-42. For a sample licensing agreement drafted specifically for museums, see Model Museum Licensing Agreement, Appendix A in Hodes & Gross, *supra* note 225, at 631. This agreement includes sections on manner of reproduction and quality control directed to particular museum concerns with the safety of their valuable works of art and with the quality of resulting products. The objects produced by license reflect the quality of the original work and also reflect the museum's aesthetic reputation.

[230] Any transfer of copyright ownership or other document pertaining to copyright may be recorded in the Copyright Office. . . . 17 U.S.C. §205(a) (1982).

See 37 C.F.R. §201.4 (1982) for regulation of the Copyright Office pertaining to the recordation of transfers.

transfer documents, whether assignments, exclusive licenses, or non-exclusive licenses. Recordation, specifically identifying the work, will give notice to the world of the facts set forth in the recorded documents. This means that even if a third party did not have actual notice of the document, he is presumed to have had that information.[231] This important constructive notice aspect of recordation applies only if the underlying work is registered.[232] For optimum effectiveness, recordation should accompany registration.

Perhaps the most important aspect of recordation is that it establishes priority of ownership.[233] Suppose, for example, that the artist conveyed to the museum the copyright on the photo-realist painting in December, 1983, and then conveyed the copyright on the same painting to a third party in January, 1984. The museum, as first transferee, under the terms of the Copyright Act, is allowed a grace period of one month (two months if the agreement was executed outside the country) to record the work in the Copyright Office.[234] When the one-month grace period terminates, it then becomes a race between the two transferees to record, and if the museum is last to record, it will be deprived of its ownership right. The museum may still possibly obtain damages against the artist on the contract, but it has lost its chance to own the copyright in the painting. Note that these priority provisions apply only if the work, in this case the painting, was registered in addition to the recordation of the document. If no one has registered the work, these statutory priority provisions will not apply and the court will decide priority on proof submitted by the parties.

There are two exceptions to the above priority rules. First, priority will not be given to one who has received a transfer in bad faith,[235] as for example, to someone who actually knows about the prior transfer. The second major exception concerns a transfer not involving valuable consideration such as a gift or bequest.[236] In these two situations the later

---

[231] "Recordation of a document in the Copyright Office gives all persons constructive notice of the facts stated in the recorded document. . . ." 17 U.S.C. §205(c) (1982).

[232] 17 U.S.C. 205(c) (1982).

[233] As between two conflicting transfers, the one executed first prevails if it is recorded, in the manner required to give constructive notice under subsection (c), within one month after its execution, in the United States or within two months after its execution outside the United States, or at any time before recordation in such manner of the later transfer. Otherwise the later transfer prevails if recorded first in such manner, and if taken in good faith, for valuable consideration or on the basis of a binding promise to pay royalties, and without notice of the earlier transfer.

17 U.S.C. §205(e) (1982).

[234] Id.

[235] Id.

[236] Id.

transferee will not prevail over the first, even if he records in the proper manner. Later transferees, even if they are first to record, who receive an ownership right either in bad faith or for nothing cannot therefore prevail over a prior transferee.

Prompt registration and recordation is also important in ownership rights between a first transferee, assignee or exclusive licensee and later a non-exclusive licensee. For example, suppose the artist transferred the entire copyright to the photo-realist painting to a museum, but then gave a third party a non-exclusive license for reproduction and distribution. Here, the non-exclusive license would continue to be effective despite the transfer to the museum if it is evidenced by a written agreement signed by the artist and if the license were taken in good faith before recordation of the transfer.[237] Thus, the museum which neglected to record the transfer would own the copyright, but could do nothing to prevent the non-exclusive licensee from continuing to reproduce and distribute the work.

9.4. Recordation as a Prerequisite to Infringement Suit

Both registration and recordation are prerequisites to infringement suits. To prevent another from using the copyrighted work, a copyright owner must first register the work and record the transfer.[238] Sometimes the work will already have been registered and all that need be done is to record the transfer. Just as often, particularly in the art world, many copyright owners have failed to take advantage of registration. Thus if the museum enters into an agreement to transfer copyright, it should check the records in the Copyright Office for evidence of registration and recordation of other grants covering the copyrighted work.[239]

The museum should therefore, no more than one month after execution of the transfer document, make certain that the document is re-

---

[237] A non-exclusive license, whether recorded or not, prevails over a conflicting transfer of copyright ownership if the license is evidenced by a written instrument signed by the owner of the rights licensed or such owner's duly authorized agent, and if—

(1) the license was taken before execution of the transfer; or
(2) the license was taken in good faith before recordation of the transfer and without notice of it.

17 U.S.C. §205(f) (1982).

[238] No person claiming by virtue of a transfer to be the owner of copyright or of any exclusive right under a copyright is entitled to institute an infringement action under this title until the instrument of transfer under which such person claims has been recorded in the Copyright Office, but suit may be instituted after such recordation on a cause of action that arose before recordation.

17 U.S.C. §205(d) (1982).

[239] See *supra* note 106 relating to search of records at the Copyright Office.

corded in the Copyright Office. Because registration is a prerequisite to effective recordation, the museum may have to file simultaneously for registration as well. Again, there is a need for procedures within the museum to administer these simple ownership formalities which play such an important role in establishing one's effective rights in a copyrighted work.

9.5. Works Made for Hire

Having discussed the ways in which an owner of copyright can exploit his ownership in a work, we now turn to the question of who is an author. In general, the source of ownership is the author of the work, its maker or originator. Many works, however, are not created by an individual privately, but are motivated by an employer pursuant to employment duties or created on commission. In our opening example the curator of contemporary art has written a contribution to the photo-realist exhibition catalogue. Other staff have developed an audio-visual program to accompany the exhibition. Works like these, created in the course of one's employment, are called works made for hire.[240] Here, unless the parties have expressly agreed otherwise, ownership vests in the employer who is considered the author.[241]

Other works, such as the critical essays written by outside scholars and the special dance program, were created on commission. As will be discussed, only certain categories of commissioned works qualify as "works made for hire." A work made for hire differs from other works in several important ways. First, the employer need to nothing to secure ownership of the work; the employer should simply register the work in its own name. [242] Second, the duration for a work made for hire differs from other works.[243] Instead of the life of the author plus fifty years, the term for a work made for hire is seventy-five years from publication or 100 years from creation, whichever is shorter.[244] Third, a work made for hire is not subject to termination rights as are other works.[245]

---

[240] For definition, see *supra* note 132 and accompanying text. See generally O'Meara, Works Made "For Hire" Under The Copyright Act of 1976 — Two Interpretations, 15 Creighton L. Rev. 523 (1981-82); Angel & Tannenbaum, Works Made For Hire Under S.22, 22 N.Y.L. Rev. 209 (1976). See also Simon, Faculty Writings: Are They "Works Made for Hire" Under the 1976 Copyright Act?, 9 J. of Coll. and U.L. 485 (1982-83).

[241] 17 U.S.C. §201(b)(1982). For legislative history of this section, see H.R. Report at 121.

[242] 17 U.S.C. §408 (1982). Moreover, a statement to the effect that the work is a work made for hire must be included in the application for copyright registration. 17 U.S.C. §409(4) (1982).

[243] 17 U.S.C. §302(c) (1982).

[244] *Id.*

[245] See 17 U.S.C. §203(a) (1982), regarding termination of transfer. It states, "In the case of any work other than a work made for hire. . . ."

How does one decide whether a work has been created in the scope of employment? For example, what of a curator who works at home on a catalogue covering an aspect of the museum's collection or on an article for a journal?[246] This question is often more difficult to answer in practical situations, that is, the standard is more easily stated than applied. A work created within the employment relationship is one created at the insistence and expense of the employer. Close factual questions arise in construing this standard and actual cases turn on such elements as whether the employee was creating something related to his employment duties,[247] whether the employer had the right to direct and supervise his work,[248] and whether the employer was the motivating factor in the creation of the work.[249] If the above factors are present the law

---

[246] The benefits of publication for museum personnel are many: enhanced professional reputation, dissemination of scholarly ideas, even fees or royalties. As long as the practices of museums in this area are varied, and the law is unclear, it is advisable for a museum to promulgate written guidelines concerning staff writings. This is recommended by the Code of Ethics of the American Association of Museums (1978). For a review of the questions to be considered in such a policy and an articulate argument that it would ultimately aid museums in attracting and retaining highly qualified staff to allow them to keep proprietary and copyright interests in their writings, see Knoll & Drapiewski, Knowing Your Copyrights, 55 Museum News 49 (Mar.-April 1977).

[247] See, e.g., Public Affairs Assoc. v. Rickover, 268 F. Supp. 444 (D.C. 1967) (speeches delivered by Admiral Rickover held to be his private property for which he might obtain the copyright. The court emphasized that the invitations were delivered to him directly, and that the speeches were prepared on his own time and concerned a subject removed from his official duties), on remand from the U.S. Supreme Court, 369 U.S. 111 (1961).

[248] See, e.g., Donaldson Publishing Co. v. Bregman, Vocco and Conn., Inc. 375 F.2d 639 (2d Cir. 1967); Olympia Press v. Lancer Books, Inc., 267 F. Supp. 920 (S.D.N.Y. 1967); and Aitken v. Empire Construction Co., 542 F. Supp. 252 (D. Neb. 1982) (holding for architect as owner of copyright for plans, rather than contractor, court said that although contractor could direct the result that the architect was to accomplish, it could not direct the means, which the architect as a trained professional, was required to use). The work for hire doctrine has been held applicable to a volunteer, who prepared a manual for a town and then tried to claim the copyright. The court held that the crucial factor for purpose of the copyright laws was whether the town had the right to direct and supervise the manner in which the employee [volunteer] did his work. Town of Clarkstown v. Reeder, 566 F. Supp. 137 (S.D.N.Y. 1983).

[249] See, e.g., Picture Music, Inc. v. Bourne, Inc., 457 F.2d 1213 (2d Cir. 1972), cert. denied, 409 U.S. 997 (1972) (where copyright in song, "Who's Afraid of the Big Bad Wolf," claimed by adaptor, the court found that the composition was motivated by Walt Disney (who had control of the original work) and adaptor's supervisor, Irving Berlin, and therefore was a work done for hire); Siegel v. Nat'l Periodical Publisher, 508 F.2d 909 (2d Cir. 1967) (work made for hire not applicable to Superman, as it was developed before the employment relationship began); Excel Promotions Corp. v. Babylon Beacon, Inc., 207 U.S.P.Q. 616 (E.D.N.Y. 1979) (copyright in advertisements prepared by employees of a news-

establishes a presumption that the work is a work made for hire, with initial ownership vesting in the employer.[250] To reverse the presumption, the employer and employee may, by written contract, agree otherwise.[251] But note that the contrary is not true; if a work is not created in the scope of employment, the parties cannot agree to characterize the work as one for hire. In such cases the museum would have to seek a formal written assignment of the work to obtain copyright ownership.[252]

Works created in one's employment are clearly works made for hire, but what of specially commissioned works? For example, the museum may hire a public relations firm to develop certain promotional materials for its various activities. These specially commissioned works look like works made for hire, and under the 1909 Act, it was generally presumed that they were.[253] The current Act, however, has now reversed the presumption and has explicitly set forth nine circumstances where a commissioned work becomes a work made for hire, but only if the parties expressly agree in writing to create a work made for hire.[254] These nine

---

paper for a firm advertising in the paper held to be owned by the firm as it was at their insistence and expense that the work was done).

[250] "The presumption that initial ownership rights vest in the employer for hire is well established in American copyright law. . . ." H. R. Report at 121.

[251] 17 U.S.C. §201(b) (1982).

[252] See, e.g., Shapiro, Bernstein & Co. v. Jerry Vogel Music Co., 221 F. 2d 569 (2d Cir. 1955) (where lyrics were written on a special job assignment and writer later assigned his copyright to the company which hired him).

[253] See, e.g., Picture Music, Inc. v. Bourne, Inc., 457 F.2d 1213 (2d Cir. 1972), cert. denied, 409 U.S. 997 (1972); Brattleboro Publishing Co. v. Winmill Publishing Corp., 369 F.2d 565 (2d Cir. 1966); Yardley v. Houghton Mifflin Co., 108 F.2d 28 (2d Cir. 1939). Some problems may be raised regarding commissioned works created after the enactment of the 1976 Act but prior to its effective date of January 1, 1978. Which act should apply: the 1909 Act under which the employer is deemed the author or the 1976 Act which would award copyright to the artist if the work does not fall within the specified categories or the requirement of writing is not met? See Beckett, The Copyright Act of 1976: When Is It Effective, 24 Bull. Copyright Soc'y 391, 398 (1977).

[254] "[A] work specially ordered or commissioned for use . . . , if the parties expressly agree in a written instrument signed by them that the work shall be considered a work made for hire." 17 U.S.C. §101 (1982). As stated in the House Report,

> The basic problem is how to draw a statutory line between those works written on special order or commission that should be considered as "works made for hire," and those that should not. The definition now provided by the bill represents a compromise which, in effect, spells out those specific categories of commissioned works that can be considered "works made for hire" under certain circumstances.

at 121. For works denied classification as "works made for hire" because they fell outside one of the nine specified categories, see, e.g., Aitken v. Empire Constr. Co. 542 F. Supp. 252 (D. Neb. 1982) (architectural plans); Mister B Textiles, Inc.

circumstances are: as a contribution to a collective work, as part of a motion picture or other audio-visual work, as a translation, as a supplementary work, as a compilation, as an instructional text, as a test, as answer material for a test, or as an atlas.[255] Thus, if the museum commissions a work which does not fall into one of these categories, it is not a work made for hire even if the parties expressly agree in writing that it is. For example, the scholarly essays would likely be regarded as works made for hire because they fit into one of the nine enumerated categories as contributions to a collective work. Alternatively, the commissioned dance program does not fall within any of the nine categories and cannot be made a work made for hire. The museum, to become owner of the copyright, must obtain an assignment by written agreement. The rules relating to works made for hire illustrate how the current Copyright Act makes it difficult for the author to be dispossessed of ownership rights in his copyright.[256] As a result, the museum, when commissioning a work, should obtain an assignment of the copyright if there is any doubt about the status of the piece as a work made for hire.

9.6. Collective Works

From time to time a museum may solicit contributions from a number of sources and assemble them into a collective whole, such as an anthology, periodical issue, or exhibition catalogue. These works, known as collective works,[257] are a form of derivative work. The ownership of the copyright on the individual contributions to a collective work remains with the individual author and is not a work made for hire unless the parties expressly agree in writing.[258]

---

v. Woodcrest Fabrics, Inc., 523 F. Sup. 21 (S.D.N.Y. 1981) (fabric design); May v. Morganelli-Heumann and Assoc., 618 F.2d 1363 (9th Cir. 1980) (architectural drawings).

For denial of commissioned photographs of status as "work made for hire" because of lack of written instrument, see Childers v. High Society Magazine, 557 F. Supp. 978 (S.D.N.Y. 1983).

[255] 17 U.S.C. §101 (1982).

[256] At least, the right to terminate transfer at the appropriate time. There is evidence, however, that publishers still use "work made for hire" contracts with free lance artists by means of the categories "contributions to collective works" and "supplementary works." See Comment, Free Lance Artists, Works for Hire, and the Copyright Act of 1976, 15 U.C.D. L. Rev. 703, 714 (1982).

[257] "A 'collective work' is a work, such as a periodical issue, anthology, or encyclopedia, in which a number of contributions, constituting separate and independent works in themselves, are assembled into a collective whole." 17 U.S.C. §101 (1982).

[258] Copyright in each separate contribution to a collective work is distinct from copyright in the collective work as a whole, and vests initially in the author of the contribution. In the absence of an express transfer of the copyright or of any rights under it, the

What if a contributor to the photo-realist catalogue refuses to confer a work made for hire status on his individual contribution? The museum still remains the creator of a collective work and, as a collective work owner, has the right to reproduce and distribute the individual contribution as part of the current collective work, a revised edition, or in another collective work in the same series. But the museum cannot reproduce and distribute reprints of the individual contribution without the consent of the author.[259] The museum should resolve ownership rights at the outset when forming a collective work by either creating a work made for hire, obtaining copyright ownership, or obtaining an exclusive or non-exclusive license to make reprints of the individual contribution.

9.7. The *Pushman* Doctrine

We have already emphasized the fundamental principle in copyright law of the distinction between ownership of the material object and ownership of the copyright.[260] An outright sale of the material object such as a book, canvas, or master tape-recording of a musical work does not transfer copyright. One possible exception to the above principle that applies to certain works transferred before 1978 is a situation which involves the transfer of an unpublished work of art, one which has not yet acquired federal statutory copyright. Under the *Pushman* Doctrine, named after a case arising in New York State, [261] an artist was presumed to have transferred common law copyright at the time the original work of art was sold unless the artist specifically reserved copyright ownership.[262] The new law has clearly overruled the *Pushman* Doctrine,[263] and even before the current Act became effective, two important states in the art world, California and New York, enacted statutes reversing the presumption that an unconditional sale of an unpublished work of art transferred copyright along with the material object.[264]

---

owner of copyright in the collective work is presumed to have acquired only the privilege of reproducing and distributing the contribution as part of that particular collective work, any revision of that collective work, and any later collective work in the same series.

17 U.S.C. §201(c) (1982). For legislative history of this section, see H.R. Report at 122.

[259] 17 U.S.C. §201(c) (1982).

[260] 17 U.S.C. §202 (1982).

[261] Pushman v. New York Graphic Soc'y, 287 N.Y. 302, 39 N.E.2d 249 (1942).

[262] "[A]n artist must, if he wishes to retain or protect the reproduction right, make some reservation of that right when he sells the painting." *Id.* at 308, 39 N.E.2d at 251.

[263] See H.R. Report at 124, stating that the presumption of transfer is reversed under the new Act.

[264] N.Y. Gen. Bus. Law §§223-24 (McKinney 1968); Cal. Civ. Code §982(c) (West Supp. 1976).

10. COPYRIGHT INFRINGEMENT

Having discussed various aspects of copyrightable subject matter and ownership, we now turn directly to what constitutes the illegal use of a copyrighted work. Infringement of copyright is defined as the violation of any one of the exlusive rights.[265] Other than the distribution right, the rights of reproduction, adaptation, performance and display involve, in different ways, the copyright owner's authority to prevent others from copying his work without consent. In essence, to prove copyright infringement one must show that another has actually copied from the work[266] and that he has copied a material amount of the work.[267] Alternatively, copyright infringement does not occur when a third party has independently duplicated the work.[268] The classic example of this principle involves a photographer who has taken a picture of

---

[265] 17 U.S.C. §501(a) (1982).

[266] In the absence of direct proof of copying, which is extremely difficult to obtain, infringement may be proved by showing that the defendant had access to the copyrighted work and that there is substantial similarity between them. Sid and Marty Krofft Television Prods. Inc. v. McDonald's Corp., 562 F.2d 1157, 1172 (9th Cir. 1977) ("Access is proven when the plaintiff shows that the defendant had an opportunity to view or copy the plaintiff's work"); Novelty Textile Mills, Inc. v. Joan Fabrics Corp., 558 F.2d 1090 (2d Cir. 1977) (defendant's designers actually viewed the upholstery fabric design of the plaintiff); Universal City Studios v. Kamar Industries, 217 U.S.P.Q. 1162 (S.D. Tex. 1982) (defendant's products were based on character, E.T., movie had been released prior to manufacture of products and defendant held to have access); Jack Lenor Larsen v. Dakotah, Inc., 452 F. Supp. 99 (S.D.N.Y. 1978) (defendant saw photographs of plaintiff's fabric designs in a department store); Jason v. Fonda, 698 F.2d 966 (9th Cir. 1982) (bare possibility of access is insufficient to create a genuine issue of material fact where plaintiff alleged that the movie "Coming Home " had been based on her privately printed book which was sold in Southern California). The copying may be done subconsciously and not deliberately, and still be infringement. Bright Tunes Music Corp. v. Harrisongs Music, Ltd., 420 F. Supp. 177 (S.D.N.Y. 1976) (George Harrison's "My Sweet Lord" held an infringement of "He's So Fine.")

[267] The more striking the similarity is, the less likely that the work was independently duplicated. Boorstyn, *supra* note 23 at 290.

[268] "Absent copying there can be no infringement of copyright." Mazer v. Stein, 347 U.S. 201 (1954) at 218 (footnote omitted). See also Herbert Rosenthal Jewelry Corp. v. Kalpakian, 446 F.2d 738 (9th Cir. 1971) (In this case both plaintiff and defendant made jeweled bees. Court stated that there was evidence that defendant, who had designed other jeweled pins in the form of living creatures, had independently created his bee); Franklin Mint Corp. v. Nat'l Wildlife Art Exch. 575 F.2d 62, 65 (3d Cir. 1978) ("Since copyrights do not protect thematic concepts, the fact that the same subject matter may be present in two paintings does not prove copying or infringement"). Moreover, in this case, the artist, who had painted both works which were the subject of controversy, painted a third picture on the same theme "while in the courtroom and without referring to either of his earlier paintings." *Id.* at 66. The court held that each painting was a separate artistic effort.

the same scene and from the same point of view as in a prior copyrighted photograph. His independent, although identical creation, is not copyright infringement.

Although the principle of independent creation limits the scope of copyright protection, other principles broaden its scope. In this regard, innocent or unintentional copying is no defense to copyright infringement.[269] For example, if someone on the museum staff copied from a book thought to be in the public domain, infringement will have occurred. The intent of the infringer might carry some weight as to the scope of recovery and the extent of damages, but not in establishing infringement.

Also broadening the scope of infringement is the principle that infringement of copyright encompasses acts other than verbatim or literal copying. To constitute infringement, the amount copied must be substantial[270] and material when compared to the copyrighted work as a whole, but copyright infringement will include such acts transcending verbatim similarity such as paraphrasing,[271] or taking the general pattern of a work.[272] Regardless of what kind of copying has occurred, the

---

[269] See *supra* note 187. One may also be held liable on the theory of contributory infringement when "one who, with the knowledge of the infringing activity, induces, causes or materially contributes to the infringing conduct of another." Gershwin Publishing Corp. v. Columbia Artist Management, Inc., 443 F.2d 1159, 1162 (2d Cir. 1971). See also Original Appalachian Artworks v. Cradle Creations, 684 F.2d 821 (11th Cir. 1982) (pattern book for making dolls that were substantially similar to plaintiff's copyrighted dolls held to constitute contributor infringement).

[270] Nimmer has devised two basic forms of "substantial similarity," comprehensive nonliteral similarity, where the essence or structure of one work is copied by another, and fragmented literal similarity where there has been verbatim copying of a small amount of the original work. These two forms present very different problems for the courts: for the first, to determine when the line between idea and expression has been crossed and for the latter, to determine at which point the amount copied becomes substantial. 3 Nimmer §13.03[A].

[271] See, e.g., Meredith Corp. v. Harper & Row, Publishers, 378 F. Supp. 686 (S.D.N.Y. 1974), *aff'd*, 500 F.2d 1221 (2d Cir. 1974) (infringing psychology textbook was in large portion a recognizable paraphrase of an earlier work).

[272] The principle that the "pattern" of a work is protected was first expressed by Z. Chaffee in Reflections on Copyright Law, 45 Colum. L. Rev. 503 (1945).

I like to say that the protection covers the "pattern" of the work. . . . For example, the idea of Irish-Jewish marriage in a play may be borrowed. With this theme, some resemblance in characters and situations is inevitable, but the line of infringement may not yet be crossed. On the other hand, the pattern of the play — the sequence of events and the development of the interplay of the characters — must not be followed scene by scene. Such a correspondence of pattern would be an infringement although every word of the spoken dialogue was changed.

Id. at 511 (footnote omitted).

question to be decided in every case of copyright infringement is whether the copy comes so near the original as to give the impression created by the original. As long as the ordinary observer[273] would recognize the copy as having been taken from the original, it does not matter whether the copying is verbatim, a paraphrase, or the taking of the general pattern of the work.

Copyright infringement actions,[274] which can involve great time and expense, should not be brought unless the matter is a serious instance of infringement and the parties cannot work out a settlement. For the copyright owner who has won an infringement action, the damages can be substantial. A prevailing plaintiff in an infringement action can obtain both actual damages as a result of the infringement and the defendant's profits.[275] In lieu of these remedies, the Copyright Act provides for statutory damages which are based on set amounts per infringement at the court's discretion.[276] In addition, the prevailing plaintiff can obtain in-

---

[273] The determination of substantial similarity is thus to be made by the impression upon the ordinary observer or audience. "[T]he ordinary observer, unless he set out to detect the disparities [in the two fabric designs in question] would be disposed to overlook them, and regard their aesthetic appeal as the same." Peter Pan Fabrics Corp. v. Martin Weiner Corp., 274 F.2d 487 (2d Cir. 1960). See cases cited in 3 Nimmer §13.03[E] at 13-40, note 92 and subsequent criticism. One result of this test is that expert testimony on the question of similarity has been held irrelevant. Arnstein v. Porter, 154 F.2d 464 (2d Cir. 1946), *cert. denied*, 230 U.S. 851 (1947).

[274] A discussion of criminal prosecution for copyright infringement, as provided for in §506 of the Act, is beyond the scope of this article. See generally Lindenberg-Woods, The Smoking Revolver: Criminal Copyright Infringement, 27 Bull. Copyright Soc'y 63 (1979); and, Comment, Criminal Copyright Infringement and Step Beyond: 17 U.S.C. §506 (1976), 60 Neb. L. Rev. 114 (1981).

[275] The copyright owner is entitled to recover the actual damages suffered by him or her as a result of the infringement, and any profits of the infringer that are attributable to the infringement and are not taken into account in computing the actual damages. In establishing the infringer's profits, the copyright owner is required to present proof only of the infringer's gross revenue, and the infringer is required to prove his or her deductible expenses and the elements of profit attributable to factors other than the copyrighted work.

17 U.S.C. §504(b) (1982).

[276]

(1) Except as provided by clause (2) of this subsection, the copyright owner may elect, at any time before final judgment is rendered, to recover, instead of actual damages and profits, an award of statutory damages for all infringements involved in the action, with respect to any one work, for which any one infringer is liable individually, or for which any two or more infringers are liable jointly and severally, in a sum of not less than $250 or more than $10,000 as the court considers just. For the purposes of this subsection, all the parts of a compilation or derivative work constitute one work.
(2) In a case where the copyright owner sustains the burden of proving, and the court finds, that the infringement was committed willfully, the court in its discretion may

junctive relief[277] and in appropriate circumstances can have the infringing articles impounded or destroyed.[278] Finally, costs and attorney's fees can be given to the prevailing party at the court's discretion.[279]

11. FAIR USE

The major defense[280] to an action of copyright infringement is the defense of fair use.[281] This equitable doctrine creates a privilege to use

---

increase the award of statutory damages to a sum of not more than $50,000. In a case where the infringer sustains the burden of proving, and the court finds, that such infringer was not aware and had no reason to believe that his or her acts constituted an infringement of copyright, the court in its discretion may reduce the award of statutory damages to a sum of not less than $100. . . .

17 U.S.C. §504(c) (1982).

[277] "Any court having jurisdiction of a civil action arising under this title may . . . grant temporary and final injunctions on such terms as it may deem reasonable to prevent or restrain infringement of a copyright." 17 U.S.C. §502(a)(1982).

See, e.g., Brennan v. Hearst Corp., Copyright L. Rep. (CCH) ¶25,295 (1981) (defendant enjoined from distributing book which contained picture substantially similar to plaintiff's copyrighted drawing of grapes and leaves).

[278]

(a) At any time while an action under this title is pending, the court may order the impounding, on such terms as it may deem reasonable, of all copies or phonorecords claimed to have been made or used in violation of the copyright owner's exclusive rights, and of all plates, molds, matrices, masters, tapes, film negatives, or other articles by means of which such copies or phonorecords may be reproduced.

(b) As part of a final judgment or decree, the court may order the destruction or other reasonable disposition of all copies or phonorecords found to have been made or used in violation of the copyright owner's exclusive rights, and of all plates, molds, matrices, masters, tapes, film negatives, or other articles by means of which such copies or phonorecords may be reproduced.

17 U.S.C. §503 (1976). For a description of the historical development of these provisions and their interpretation by the courts, see Alexander, Discretionary Power to Impound and Destroy Infringing Articles: An Historical Perspective, 29 J. Copyright Soc'y 479 (1982).

[279] 17 U.S.C. §505 (1976).

[280] Other defenses include forfeiture of copyright, nonoriginality, lack of copyrightable subject matter, abandonment of copyright, de minimis use and the first amendment. See generally Leavens, In Defense of Unauthorized Use: Recent Developments in Defending Copyright Infringement, 44 Law & Contemp. Probs. 3 (1981).

[281] 17 U.S.C. §107 (1976). This is the first statutory recognition of a judicially created doctrine, "one of the most important and well-established limitations on the exclusive right of copyright owners. . . ." H.R. Report at 65.

See generally Latman, Fair Use of Copyrighted Works, Study No. 14, 2 Studies in Copyright (Arthur Fisher Mem. Ed. 1963); Seltzer, Exemptions and Fair Use in Copyright: The "Exclusive Rights" Tensions in The New Copyright Act, 24 Bull. Copyright Soc'y 215 (1977); and Schulman, Fair Use and the Revision of the Copyright Act, 53 Iowa L. Rev. 832 (1968); Perlman and Rhinelander, Wil-

another's work in a reasonable manner even though the use might technically constitute an infringement. Fair use is not easily defined, but the current Act has set forth basic guidelines or factors to be considered in determining fair use. These are the purpose and character of the use, including whether such use is of a commercial nature or is for non-profit educational purposes;[282] the nature of the copyrighted work;[283] the amount and substantiality of the portion used in relation to the work as a whole;[284] and the effect of the use on the potential market for the work.[285] The Copyright Act does not indicate what particular weight is to be given to these factors, nor does it indicate how the factors interrelate.[286] But perhaps the most important of the factors is the last, that is,

---

liams Wilkins Co. v. United States: Photocopying, Copyright and the Judicial Process, The Sup. Ct. Rev. 355 (1975).

[282] See, e.g., Triangle Publications, Inc. v. Knight-Ridder Newspapers, Inc., 626 F.2d 1171, 1175 (5th Cir. 1980) (holding that "any commercial use tends to cut against a fair use defense").

[283] "[I]t seems clear that the scope of the fair use doctrine should be considerably narrower in the case of the newsletters than in that of either mass-circulation periodicals or scientific journals." H.R. Report at 73.

[284] See, e.g., Walt Disney Prod. v. Air Pirates, 581 F.2d 751 (9th Cir. 1978), cert. denied, 439 U.S. 1132 (1979) (defendants claimed that their parody of Disney characters was protected by fair use; the court held that by copying the images in their entirety, the defendants' excessive copying precluded fair use); Quinto v. Legal Times of Washington, Inc., 506 F. Supp. 554, 560 (D.C.D.C. 1981) ("The admitted reprinting of approximately 92% of plaintiff's story precludes the fair use defense. . .").

[285] See, e.g., Meeropol v. Nizer, 560 F.2d 1061 (2d Cir. 1977), cert. denied, 434 U.S. 1013 (1978); (in case brought by sons of Julius and Ethel Rosenberg against Louis Nizer, author of book on the trial of the Rosenbergs, Nizer claimed his incorporation of copyrighted letters in the book constituted fair use. The court held that the effect of the use of the letters on their future market was a matter for trial); Roy Export Co. v. Columbia Broadcasting Sys., 503 F. Supp. 1137 (S.D.N.Y. 1980) (applying concept of effect on the market to a derivative work); Iowa State Univ. Research Found. v. Am. Broadcasting Co., 621 F.2d 57, 61 (2d Cir. 1980) ("The fair use doctrine is not a 'license for corporate theft'").

[286] According to the drafters of the Act, these are not exact rules, but guidelines, and the courts must be free to make decisions on a case-by-case basis. H.R. Report at 66. However, in the area of classroom use, more specific provisions were incorporated in the House Report. These are Guidelines for Classroom Copying in Not-For-Profit Educational Institutions and Guidelines for Educational Uses of Music. They were agreed to by interested organizations and were included in the House Report as "reasonable interpretations of the minimum standards of fair use." H.R. Report at 72. See Hayes, Classroom Fair Use: A Reevaluation, 26 Bull. Copyright Soc'y 101 (1978). The controversy over classroom photocopying was recently publicized when a group of publishers sued New York University, several individual faculty members and a private photo-copying facility used by them for copyright infringement. (Addison-Wes-

does the new work compete with and supplant the need for the original?[287] If so, chances are that fair use has not occurred.

In general, fair use occurs when one is using another's work in the context of a new work, usually for purposes of criticism, comment, news reporting, teaching, scholarship or research.[288] Examples are a photograph of a painting in the review of a museum exhibition; a quotation in a scholarly work or for purposes of review and criticism;[289] incidental reproduction in a newscast;[290] summary or quotations in an address or news article;[291] use in parody or burlesque.[292] Other typical examples

---

ley Publishing Co. v. New York University). Although the matter reached a settlement, the president of the Association of American Publishers stated:

> we wish to make clear that the publishing community does not consider the overall issue of college and university photocopying has been fully resolved.
>   We and our members will actively pursue further arrangements [such as those agreed to in the settlement] at other campuses and related copying facilities.

26 Pat., Trademark & Copyright J. (BNA) 145 (1983.)

[287] See 3 Nimmer, §13.05[A](4) and §13.05[B] for an analysis of this factor in terms of the function of each work.

[288] 17 U.S.C. §107 (1982).

[289] In this situation, the functional differences are distinctive. One would not read quotations in a review rather than see a play, or look at a photograph of a painting rather than viewing the original in the museum.

[290] See, e.g., Italian Book Corp. v. Am. Broadcasting Co., 458 F. Supp. 65 (S.D.N.Y. 1978); Pac. and S. Co. v. Carol Duncan, Copyright L. Rep. (CCH) ¶25,421 (N.D. Ga. 1982).

[291] See, e.g., Suid v. Newsweek Magazine, 503 F. Supp. 146 (D.C. 1980) (16-word quotation not infringement). But cf. Harper & Row v. Nation Enterprises, 557 F. Supp. 1067 (S.D.N.Y. 1983) (extensive quotations of material from soon-to-be published Gerald Ford memoirs not protected by fair use).

[292] The defense of fair use as applied to works of parody and satire has been raised in many infringement actions, e.g., Loew's Inc. v. Columbia Broadcasting Sys., 131 F. Supp. 165 (S.D. Cal. 1955), aff'd sub nom Benny v. Loew's Inc., 239 F.2d 532 (9th Cir. 1956), aff'd by an equally divided court, 356 U.S. 43 (1958) (holding that comedian Jack Benny's parody "Autolight" of the movie "Gaslight" was not entitled to fair use defense); Walt Disney Prods. v. Air Pirates, 591 F.2d 751 (9th Cir. 1978), cert. denied, 439 U.S. 1132 (1979) (limiting holding in Gaslight case); Elsmere Music, Inc. v. Nat'l Broadcasting Co., 623 F.2d 252 (2d Cir. 1980) (holding that Saturday Night Live's "I Love Sodom" a fair use of "I Love New York"). Issues raised by parody fair use include the benefits of parody (e.g., social criticism), the weight to be given to the amount taken from the original work and the effect of marketability on the original. See, Light, Parody, Burlesque and the Economic Rationale for Copyright, 11 Conn. L. Rev. 615 (1979); Comment, Piracy or Parody: Never the Twain, 38 U. Colo. L. Rev. 550 (1966); Comment, Parody and Fair Use: The Critical Question, 57 Wash. L. Rev. 163 (1981). While pictorial works may be less susceptible to parody than literary

where fair use might arise in the museum context are reproduction of works of art for documentary files, to accompany a notice that a work has been removed from its usual location in the museum, or as small illustrations on gallery guides. What is usually precluded from fair use is wholesale and systematic copying.[293]

Because of its inherent vagueness, the doctrine of fair use should not be abused by the museum trying to justify a wide variety of copying. A more solid justification is to be found under the exceptions to the exclusive rights, which are much more concrete than fair use and will form a more predictable basis in determining the allowable use of a copyrighted work.

12. CONCLUSION

Copyright law, by its nature sets up a tension between creators and disseminators of works of art. The art museum embodies this conflict. As disseminator, the art museum is the best vehicle by which the public has access to, and may learn about works of art. As creator, it has monetary and aesthetic interests in protecting its own copyrightable works.

The administrator and his counsel should be conscious of the museum's delicate position as creator and user. Awareness of copyright law and its underlying policies will allow them to obtain the information necessary to employ staff time efficiently, to avoid legal complications, and to make the economic decisions most beneficial to the museum.

---

or musical ones, paintings such as Grant Wood's "American Gothic" have formed the basis of many a cartoon.

[293] It is important to emphasize that this is the case even if the use is for a non-profit, educational purpose. Museums should not be indifferent to infringing practices on the grounds that they are non-profit institutions acting for the public good. See, e.g., Wihtol v. Crow, 309 F.2d 777 (8th Cir. 1962) (church choir director who made musical arrangement of copyrighted hymn held infringer); Encyclopaedia Britannica Education Corp. v. Crooks, 447 F. Supp. 243 (W.D.N.Y. 1978) (taping of plaintiff's entire copyrighted films for showing in schools too excessive for fair use defense); Marcus v. Rowley, 217 U.S.P.Q. 691 (9th Cir. 1983) (booklet on cake decorating prepared for public classroom use held to infringe similar booklet when majority of pages were copied verbatim and no attempt made to obtain copyright permission or credit plaintiff for the use of her material. The court refused to apply the defense of fair use because of the wholesale copying, in spite of the fact that the plaintiff suffered no monetary loss and the defendant showed no profit). But cf. Williams & Wilkins Co. v. United States, 487 F.2d 1345 (Ct. Cl. 1973), aff'd, 420 U.S. 376 (1975).

B. WORKS OF FINE ART

§2.3. THE COPYRIGHT CASES INTRODUCED

The law of copyright is extensive and there are many cases on the subject. Those that follow touch the key elements the courts have delineated in applying this law — a law undoubtedly conceived to protect "writings" in a more conventional sense — to all forms of visual images regardless of their communicative value.

Once it was decided that constitutional protection of writings extended to visual images (despite Justice Douglas' query as to whether this was the intention of the law (see §2.10.1 *infra*)), it was necessary to decide a number of critical questions. How much creative effort was necessary to command constitutional protection? Very little, the courts decided. What type of notice was required? Here, as with other writings, very little. Where on the image was the appropriate place for the placement of the notice? Great flexibility became the rule. Where did intellectual effort end and commercial exploitation begin? Still a difficult line to draw.

One of the intriguing aspects of copyright law as applied to visual art is that very often copying is little more than a form of flattery. In most situations there are no substantial sums involved and the unauthorized reproduction provides the creator of the original artwork with more exposure than would otherwise have been generated. For example, if one were to write an essay for a literary magazine or produce a painting without great distinction, an unauthorized copy thereof might exalt the original author's ego but have no effect on his pocketbook or that of the copier.

There are however situations where there are substantial economic benefits in controlling the copies. For example, in the Picasso case (*Letter Edged in Black Press*, see §2.6.4 *infra*) there was no doubt that the right to sell picture postcards of a Picasso sculpture provided substantial economic benefits. Similarly, when a number of years ago a manufacturer copied the Robert Indiana *Love* design, substantial profits inured to the manufacturer. The copyright vehicle — as contrasted with the moral right and *droit de suite* concepts — may, therefore, in appropriate cases, provide a mechanism for fashioning very significant monetary rewards.

Another aspect of copyright law touched on in the following cases is the extent to which the right of copyright can itself prevent the creator from producing images similar to those that he has previously produced. Can copyright protection act as a sword as well as a shield? In this connection the *Gross v. Seligman* (see §2.8.2. *infra*), *Franklin Mint Corp v. National Wildlife Art Exchange* (see §2.8.3 *infra*), and the *Factor v. Stella* (see §2.8.4 *infra*) cases are instructive. It would indeed be paradoxical if the person who initially created an image could be prevented from repeating himself. If that restriction is embodied in copyright, to what extent can realistic and practical limits be effectively imposed?

§2.4. The Severability of Copyright from the Work of Art

§2.4.1. *AMERICAN TOBACCO CO. v WERCKMEISTER:* THE NATURE OF COPYRIGHT AND THE SIGNIFICANCE OF PUBLICATION

The *Werckmeister* case, which follows, decided by the U.S. Supreme Court almost eighty years ago, can be read for a variety of teachings. It is one of the earliest discussions of the Supreme Court about the nature of copyright, it is indicative of the procedure utilized in the late nineteenth century to transfer an interest in a copyright, and it provides early jurisprudence on protecting an interest in a copyrighted work — i.e., limits on the right to copy a work displayed in a public gallery. Probably its most significant addition to the law, however, was the recognition that copyright in an artwork represented a right separate and apart from ownership of the tangible object itself. In copyright law — the law of reproduction — there can be a number of different persons who will have a separate interest in the same work — e.g., the person who has the right of first publication; the person with the right to make derivative works; another with the sole right to use the work in a limited way or territory; yet another with rights for a movie or television advertisement only; and, of course, the owner of the physical object itself, who will have specific rights as well.

AMERICAN TOBACCO CO. v. WERCKMEISTER
207 U.S. 284, 28 S. Ct. 72, 52 L. Ed. 208 (1907)

DAY, J. This is a writ of error to the circuit court of appeals for the second circuit, seeking reversal of a judgment affirming the judgment of the United States circuit court for the southern district of New York in favor of the defendant in error, adjudging him to be entitled to the possession of 1196 sheets, each containing a copy of a certain picture called "Chorus," the same representing a company of gentlemen with filled glasses, singing in chorus. The painting was the work of an English artist, W. Dendy Sadler. The defendant in error claimed to be the owner of a copyright taken out under the law of the United States. . . .

In January, 1894, by agreement between the artist and Werckmeister, the defendant in error, it was agreed that the painting should be finished by March 1, and then sent to Werckmeister to be photographed and returned to Sadler in time to exhibit at the Royal Academy in 1894. The painting was sent to Werckmeister at Berlin, where it was received on March 8, 1894, and was returned to Sadler in London on March 11, 1894. On April 2, 1894, the artist Sadler executed and delivered the following instrument:

> I hereby transfer the copyright in my picture "Chorus" to the Photographische Gesellschaft, Berlin (The Berlin Photographic Company,) for the sum of £200. London, April 2, 1894.
>
> (Signed)   W. DENDY SADLER

Werckmeister was a citizen of the German Empire, doing business in Berlin, Germany, under the trade name of "Photographische Gesellschaft," and did business in New York city under the name of the "Berlin Photographic Company."

The Photographische Gesellschaft of Berlin, by letter dated March 31, 1894, received on April 16, 1894, deposited the title and description of the painting and a photograph of the same in the office of the Librarian of Congress, the intention being to obtain a copyright under the act of Congress. (Rev. Stat. 4956) U.S. Comp. Stat. 1901, p.3407. After the painting was returned to London it was exhibited by Sadler at the exhibition of the Royal Academy at London, and was there on exhibition for about three months; the exhibition opening the first Monday of May and closing the first Monday of August, 1894. The exhibition was opened to the public on week days, from 8 A.M. to 7 P.M. upon the payment of the admission fee of 1 shilling, and during the last week was open evenings, the entrance charge being 6 pence. There was a private view for the press on May 2, and on May 3 up to 1 o'clock, and the remainder of the day was for the Royal private view. There was also a general private view on May 4. The members and the associate members of the Royal Academy and the artists exhibiting at the exhibition and their families were entitled at all times to free admission, and they, as well as the public, visited the exhibition in large numbers.

During the time that the painting was shown at the exhibition it was not inscribed as a copyright, nor were any words thereon indicating a copyright, nor on the substance on which it was mounted, nor on the frame, as required by the copyright act ((18 Stat. at L. 78, chap. 301) U.S. Comp. Stat. 1901, p.3411), if the original painting is within the requirements of the law in this respect.

The painting, while on exhibition, was for sale at the Royal Academy, but with the copyright reserved, which reservation was entered in the gallery sale book. They bylaws of the Royal Academy provided "that no permission to copy works on exhibition shall on any account be granted." The reasons for the bylaw, as it appears upon minutes of the Academy, are as follows: "That so much property in copyright being intrusted to the guardianship of the Royal Academy, the council feel themselves compelled to disallow, in future, all copying within their walls from pictures sent in exhibition."

The photogravures of the painting were placed on sale in June, 1894, or in the autumn of 1894; those photogravures were inscribed with the notice of copyright.

Mr. Sadler, the artist, afterwards, in October, 1899, sold the painting to a Mr. Cotterel, residing in London, England, since which time, so far as has been shown, it has been hanging in the dining room of the house of that gentleman.

On June 20, 1902, Werckmeister commenced an action, by the service of a summons, against the American Tobacco Company, plaintiff in error, and on the same day a writ of replevin was issued out of the circuit court of the United States for the southern district of New York, directed to the marshal of the same district, requiring him to replevin the chattels described in an annexed affidavit. Under the writ the marshal seized upon the premises of the American Tobacco Company 203 pictures. On July 23, 1902, Werckmeister caused another writ of replevin to issue out of the same court, directed to the marshal of the western district of New York, under which writ the marshall seized 993 pictures.

An amendment to the complaint set forth the seizure of the pictures. The copies seized were adjudged to be forfeited to the plaintiff, Werckmeister, and to be of the value of $1,010. . . .

This case involves important questions under the copyright laws of the United States, upon which there has been diversity of view in the Federal courts.

Before taking up the errors assigned it may aid in the elucidation of the questions involved to briefly consider the nature of the property in copyright which it is the object of the statutes of the United States to secure and protect. A copyright, as the term imports, involves the right of publication and reproduction of works of art or literature. A copyright, as defined by Bouvier's Law Dictionary, Rawles's edition, volume 1, p.436, is: "The exclusive privilege, secured according to certain legal forms, of printing, or otherwise multiplying, publishing, and vending copies of certain literary or artistic productions." And further, says the same author, "the foundation of all rights of this description is the natural dominion which everyone has over his own ideas, the enjoyment of which, although they are embodied in visible forms or characters, he may, if he chooses, confine to himself or impart to others." That is, the law recognizes the artistic or literary productions of intellect or genius, not only to the extent which is involved in dominion over and ownership of the thing created, but also the intangible estate in such property which arises from the privilege of publishing and selling to others copies of the thing produced.

There was much contention in England as to whether the common law recognized this property in copyright before the statute of Anne; the controversy resulting in the decision in the House of Lords in the case of *Donaldson v. Becket*, 4 Burr, 2408, the result of the decision being that a majority of the judges, while in favor of the common-law right, held the same had been taken away by the statute. See *Wheaton v. Peters*, 8 Pet. 591-656, 8 L. ed. 1055-1079; *Holmes v. Hurst*, 174 U.S. 82, 43 L. ed. 904, 19 Sup. Ct. Rep. 606.

In this country it is well settled that property in copyright is the creation of the Federal statute passed in the exercise of the power vested in Congress by the Federal Constitution in article 1, §8, "to promote the progress of science and useful arts by securing for limited times to authors and inventors the exclusive right to their respective writings and discoveries." See 8 Pet. 591, *supra; Banks v. Manchester*, 128 U.S. 244, 252, 32 L. ed. 425, 428, 9 Sup. Ct. Rep. 36; *Thompson v. Hubbard*, 131 U.S. 123, 151, 33 L. ed. 76, 86, 9 Sup. Ct. Rep. 710.

Under this grant of authority a series of statutes have been passed, having for their object the protection of the property which the author has in the right to publish his production, the purpose of the statute being to protect this right in such manner that the author may have the benefit of this property for a limited term of years. These statutes should be given a fair and reasonable construction with a view to effecting such purpose. The first question presented in oral argument and upon the briefs involves the construction of §4962 as amended (U.S. Comp. Stat., 1901, p.3411), which is as follows:

> That no person shall maintain an action for the infringement of his copyright unless he shall give notice thereof by inserting in the several copies of every edition published, on the title page or the page immediately following, if it be a book; or if a map, chart, musical composition, print, cut, engraving, photograph, painting, drawing, chromo, statue, statuary, or model or design intended to be perfected and completed as a work of fine arts, by inscribing upon some visible portion thereof, or of the substance on which the same shall be mounted, the following words, viz: 'Entered according to act of Congress, in the year _____, by A.B. in the office of the Librarian of Congress, at Washington'; or, at his option, the word 'copyright,' together with the year the copyright was entered, and the name of the party by whom it was taken out, thus: 'Copyright 18__, by A.B.'

It is the contention of the plantiff in error that the original painting was not inscribed as required by the act, and therefore no action can be maintained, and it is insisted that the inscription upon the photogravures offered for sale is not sufficient.

It must be admitted that the language of the statute is not so clear as it might be, nor have the decisions of the courts been uniform upon the subject. In *Werckmeister v. Pierce & B. Mfg. Co.*, 63 Fed. 445, Judge Putman held that the failure to inscribe the copyright notice upon the original painting did not affect the copyright. That judgment was reversed by the circuit court of appeals for the first circuit by a divided court. 18 C.C.A. 431, 33 U.S. App. 399, 72 Fed. 54.

In the case of Werckmeister v. American Lithographic Co., 142 Fed. 827, Judge Holt reached the same conclusion as Judge Putman, and in the case at bar the circuit court of appeals for the second circuit approved of the reasoning of Judges Putman and Holt and disagreed with the majority of the judges of the circuit court of appeals for the first circuit.

Looking to the statute, it is apparent that if read literally the words "inscribed on some visible portion thereof," etc., apply to the antecedent terms "maps, charts, musical composition, print, cut, engraving, photograph, painting," etc., and the words of the first part of the sentence, requiring notice to be inserted in the several copies of every edition published, apply literally to the title page or the page immediately following, if it be a book.

But in construing a statute we are not always confined to a literal reading, and may consider its object and purpose, the things with which it is dealing, and the condition of affairs which led to its enactment, so as to effectuate rather than destroy the spirit and force of the law which the legislature intended to enact.

It is true, and the plaintiff in error cites authorities to the proposition, that where the words of an act are clear and unambiguous they will control. But, while seeking to gain the legislative intent primarily from the language used, we must remember the objects and purposes sought to be attained.

We think it was the object of the statute to require this inscription, not upon the original painting, map, photograph, drawing, etc., but upon those published copies concerning which it is designed to convey information to the public which shall limit the use and circumscribe the rights of the purchaser.

As we have seen, the purpose of the copyright law is not so much the protection of the possession and control of the visible thing, as to secure a monopoly having a limited time, of the right to publish the production which is the result of the inventor's thought.

We have been cited to no case, nor can we find any direct authority in this court upon the question. But the opinion of Mr. Justice Miller in *Burrow-Giles Lithographic Co. v. Sarony*, 111 U.S. 53, 28 L. ed. 349, 4 Sup. Ct. Rep. 279, is pertinent. The court there considered whether Congress had the constitutional right to protect photographs and negatives by copyright, and the second assignment of error relates to the sufficiency of the words "Copyrighted 1892 by N. Sarony," when the copyright was the property of Napoleon Sarony. In treating this question the learned judge used this very suggestive language (111 U.S. p.55):

> With regard to this latter question, it is enough to say that the object of the statute is to give notice of the copyright to the public, by placing *upon each copy,* in some visible shape, the name of the author, the existence of the claim of exclusive right, and the date at which this right was obtained.

If the contention of the plaintiff in error be sustained the statute is satisfied only when the original map, chart, etc., or painting is inscribed with the notice, and this is requisite whether the original painting is ever published or not. We think this construction ignores the purpose and object of the act, which Mr. Justice Miller has said, in the language just quoted, is to give notice of the copyright to the public, — that is, to the persons who buy or deal with the published thing.

It is insisted that there is reason for the distinction in the statute between books, and maps, charts, paintings, etc., in that a book can only be published in print and becomes known by reading, while paintings, drawings, etc., are published by inspection and observation.

It may be true that paintings are published in this way, but they are often sold to private individuals and go into private collections, while the copies, photographs, or photogravures, may have a wide and extended sale.

It would seem clear that the real object of the statute is not to give notice to the artist or proprietor of the painting or the person to whose collection it may go, who need no information, but to notify the public who purchase the circulated copies of the existing copyright, in order that their ownership may be restricted.

There does not seem to be any purpose in requiring that an original map, chart, or painting shall be thus inscribed, while there is every reason for requiring the copies of editions published to bear upon their face the notice of the limited property which a purchaser may acquire therein.

This construction of the statute which requires the inscription upon the published copies is much strengthened by the review of the history of copyright legislation which is contained in Judge Putman's opinion in *Werckmeister v. Pierce & B, Mfg. Co.,* 63 Fed. 445; that legislation, before the statute of 1874, in which paintings were for the first time introduced, shows the uniform requirement of notice upon copies. The apparent incongruities in the statute, in the light of its history, have grown up from enlarging the scope of the law, from time to time by the introduction of new subjects of copyright and engrafting them on the previous statutes. The same argument which requires original paintings to be inscribed would apply to all other articles in the same class in the present law, as maps, charts, etc., which were formerly classed with books, so far as requiring notice upon copies is concerned.

Such original maps and charts, etc., may and usually do remain in the possession of the original makers, and there is no necessity of any notice upon them, but the copyright is invalid, as the plaintiff in error insists, unless the original is itself inscribed with the notice of copyright.

For the learned counsel for plaintiff in error says: "If the painting or like article is ripe for copyright, it is ripe for the inscription of the notice. The statute requires the inserting of notice in published things only in respect to published editions of books. The term 'published' is not used in connection with paintings, statues, and the like." And it is urged there can be no such thing as an "edition" of a painting, and copies of published editions are the only copies mentioned in the statute. But this phrase survives from former statutes, which dealt only with books, maps, charts, etc. When paintings and other things not capable of publication in "editions" were introduced into the statute, the language was not changed so as to be technically accurate in reference to the new subjects of copyright.

But the sense and purpose of the law was not changed by this lack of verbal accuracy, and we think, while the construction contended for may adhere with literal accuracy and grammatical exactness to the language used, it does violence to the intent of Congress in passing the law, and that the requirement of "inscription upon some visible portion thereof" should be read in connection with the first part of the sentence, which requires notice to be inserted in the several copies of every edition published, on the title page if it be a book, upon some visible portion of the copy if it be a map, chart, painting, etc.

As we have said in the beginning, the statute is not clear. But read in the light of the purpose intended to be effected by the legislation, we think its ambiguities are best solved by the construction here given, and that the circuit court of appeals made no error in this respect.

Again, it is contended that under the facts stated Werckmeister was but the licensee of Sadler, and, as such, not within the terms of the statute (§4952, as amended 1891 (26 Stat. at L. 1106, chap. 565), U.S. Comp. Stat. 1901, p.3406), which is as follows:

> The author, inventor, designer, or proprietor of any book, map, chart, dramatic or musical composition, engraving, cut, print, or photograph or negative thereof, or of a painting, drawing, chromo, statute, statuary, and of models or designs intended to be perfected as works of the fine arts, and the executors, administrators, or assigns of any such person, shall, upon complying with the provisions of this chapter, have the sole liberty of printing, reprinting, publishing, completing, copying, executing, finishing, and vending the same, and, in the case of dramatic composition, of publicly performing or representing it or causing it to be performed or represented by others, and authors or their assigns shall have the exclusive right to dramatize and translate any of their works for which copyright shall have been obtained under the laws of the United States.

But we think the transfer in this case accomplished what it was evidently intended to do — a complete transfer of the property right of copyright existing in the picture. There is no evidence of any intention on the part of Sadler to retain any interest in this copyright after the sale to Werckmeister; and when the painting was offered for sale at the Royal Academy it was with a reservation of the copyright.

It would be giving an entirely too narrow construction to this instrument to construe it to be a mere license or personal privilege, leaving all other rights in the assignor. That it was the purpose of the parties to make a complete transfer is shown by the instrument executed, when read in the light of the attendant circumstances.

In this connection it is argued that under the statute above quoted (§4952, as amended March 3, 1891) an author cannot, before publication, assign the right or privilege of taking a copyright independent of the "transfer of the copyrightable thing itself," and it is contended that the terms "author," "inventor," "designer," refer to the originator of the book, map, chart, painting, etc., and that the term "proprietor" refers to the person who has a copyrightable thing made for him under such circumstances as to become the proprietor; as, for instance, one who causes a digest to be compiled or a picture to be painted.

But we think this statute must be construed in view of the character of the property intended to be protected. That it was intended to give the right of copyright to others than the author, inventor, or designed is conclusively shown in the use of the terms "proprietor" and "assigns" in the statute.

It seems clear that the word "assigns" in this section is not used as descriptive of the character of the estate which the "author, inventor, designer, or proprietor" may acquire under the statute, for the "assigns" of any such person, as well as the persons themselves, may, "upon complying with the provisions of this chapter," have the sole liberty of printing, publishing, and vending the same. This would seem to demonstrate the intention of Congress to vest in "assigns," before copyright, the same privilege of subsequently acquiring complete statutory copyright as the original author, inventor, designer, or proprietor has. Nor do we think this result is qualified because the statute gives to assigns, together with the right to publishing vending, etc., the right of "completing, executing, and finishing" the subject matter of copyright.

And a strong consideration in construing this statute has reference to the character of the property sought to be protected. It is not the physical thing created, but the right of printing, publishing, copying, etc., which is within the statutory protection. While not, in all respects, analogous, this proposition finds illustration in *Stephens v. Cady*, 14 How. 528, 14 L. ed. 528, in which it was held, where the copyright for a map had been taken out under the act of Congress, a sale upon execution of the copperplate engraving from which it was made did not pass the right to print and sell copies of the map. Mr. Justice Nelson, delivering the opinion of the court, said:

But, from the consideration we have given to the case, we are satisfied that the property acquired by the sale in the engraved plate, and the copyright of the map secured to the author under the act of Congress, are altogether different and independent of each other, and have no necessary connection. The copyright is an exclusive right to the multiplication of the copies, for the benefit of the author or his assigns, disconnected from the plate, or any other physical existence. It is an incorporeal right to print and publish the map; or, as said by Lord Mansfield in *Millar v. Taylor*, 4 Burr. 2396, "a property in notion, and has no corporeal tangible substance."

And the same doctrine was thus stated by Mr. Justice Curtis in *Stevens v. Gladding*, 17 How. 447, 15 L. ed. 155:

and upon this question of the annexation of the copyright to the plate it is to be observed, first, that there is no necessary connection between them. They are distinct subjects of property, each capable of existing, and being owned and transferred, independent of the other.

While it is true that the property in copyright in this country is the creation of statute the nature and character of the property grows out of the recognition of the separate ownership of the right of copying from that which inheres in the mere physical control of the thing itself, and the statute must be read in the light of the intention of Congress to protect this intangible right as a reward of the inventive genius that has produced the work. We think every consideration of the nature of the property and the things to be accomplished supports the conclusion that the statute means to give to the assigns of the original owner of the right to copyright an article the right to take out the copyright secured by the statute, independently of the ownership of the article itself.

It is further contended that the exhibition in the Royal Gallery was such a publication of the painting as prevents the defendant in error from having the benefit of the copyright act. This question has been dealt with in a number of cases, and the result of the authorities establishes, we think, that it is only in cases where what is known as a general publication is shown, as distinguished from a limited publication under conditions which exclude the presumption that it was intended to be dedicated to the public, that the owner of the copyright is deprived of the benefit of the statutory provision.

Considering this feature of the case, it is well to remember that the property of the author or painter in his intellectual creation is absolute until he voluntarily parts with the same. One or many persons may be permitted to an examination under circumstances which show no intention to part with the property right and it will remain unimpaired.

The subject was considered and the cases reviewed in the analogous case of *Werckmeister v. American Lithographic Co.*, 68 L.R.A. 591, 134 Fed. 321, in a full and comprehensive opinion by the late Circuit Judge Townsend, which leaves little to be added to the discussion.

The rule is thus stated in Slater on the Law of Copyright and Trade Marks (p.92): "It is a fundamental rule that to constitute publication there must be such a dissemination of the work of art itself among the public as to justify the belief that it took place with the intention of rendering such work common property."

And that author instances as one of the occasions that does not amount to a general publication the exhibition of a work of art at a public exhibition where there are bylaws against copies, or where it is tacitly understood that no copying shall take place, and the public are admitted to view the painting on the implied understanding that no improper advantage will be taken of the privilege.

We think this doctrine is sound and the result of the best-considered cases. In this case it appears that paintings are expressly entered at the gallery with copyrights reserved. There is no permission to copy; on the other hand, officers are present who rigidly enforce the requirements of the society that no copying shall take place.

Starting with the presumption that it is the author's right to withhold his property, or only to yield to a qualified and special inspection which shall not permit the public to acquire rights in it, we think the circumstances of this exhibition conclusively show that it was the purpose of the owner, entirely consistent with the acts done, not to permit such an inspection of his picture as would throw its use open to the public. We do not mean to say that the public exhibition of a painting or statue, where all might see and freely copy it, might not amount to publication within the statute, regardless of the artist's purpose or notice of reservation of rights which he takes no measure to protect. But such is not the present case, where the greatest care was taken to prevent copying.

[The Court then discussed certain procedural questions.]

Finding no error in the judgment of the Circuit Court of Appeals, the same is affirmed.

§2.4.2. *Pushman v. New York Graphic Society, Inc.:* Common Law Copyright

The decision in *Pushman v. New York Graphic Society, Inc.*, which follows, is of historical interest. Decided prior to the New York statute that expressly overruled it and before the current Copyright Act reversed the decision's position on a nationwide basis, it represented the then prevailing common law view that the sale of an artist's painting carried with it the common law copyright. It did indicate, however, that when a painting is sold the underlying intent of the parties is critical, insisting that an artist must "make some reservation of that right when he sells the painting." Then, agreements reduced to writing offered (as they continue to do) the best protection for both parties.

PUSHMAN v. NEW YORK GRAPHIC SOCIETY, INC.
287 N.Y. 302, 39 N.E.2d 249 (1942)

DESMOND, J. Plaintiff, who is an artist, brought this suit in 1940 for an injunction to enjoin the defendants from making reproductions of a painting executed by plaintiff and which he had sold outright to the University of Illinois in 1930, for $3,600. This painting was not copyrighted under the copyright laws of the United States. Special Term denied the injunction and dismissed the complaint on the merits, writing an opinion and decision in which it is said that the only question in the case is as to whether an artist after giving an absolute and unconditional bill of sale of his painting, still retains such a common law copyright in it as to be able to prevent commercial reproduction. Appellate Division, First Department, one of the justices dissenting, affirmed without opinion.

Plaintiff, Pushman, has an international reputation as an artist, for his execution of still life subjects in color. He has been painting for fifty years; his original works command substantial prices and many of them are held by museums and collectors. In 1930 he completed the painting, entitled "When Autumn is Here," which is the subject of this action. He turned the painting over for sale to Grand Central Art Galleries which seems to be a mutual organization of artists for sale of their works, as agent for them. All the evidence is that the plaintiff did not state that he was seeking to reserve reproduction rights in his painting and that he made no such reservation at any time up to and including the sale to the University. There is evidence here of a general practice of this gallery whereby whenever it sold a painting to a purchaser who was in the reproduction business, which of course would not include the University, the Gallery negotiated a separate written agreement between the artist and the purchaser covering reproduction rights. Pushman never expressly authorized the Gallery to sell the rights to reproduce this painting nor did he forbid it. Shortly after this painting was sent to the Gallery for sale, the manager of the Gallery took it and a number of others to the University of Illinois where he exhibited them publicly for sale. The University chose seven of these paintings, including the one by plaintiff here in suit. The University would not pay plaintiff's asking price of $5,000 and so the Gallery sold it to the University for $3,600. All this took place in 1930. The painting remained at the University until 1940 when the University sold to the defendant, New York Graphic Society, Inc., the right to make reproductions. The trial proofs had been made by defendants and the reproductions were about to be put on the market when plaintiff learned of the project and brought this suit.

Both parties bear down hard on the leading case of *Parton v. Prang* (18 Fed. Cases, No. 10784). That suit, very similar to this, was decided on the pleadings. The artist plaintiff Parton who was seeking, like plaintiff here, to enjoin the reproduction of one of his paintings by a defendant who had bought the painting from a dealer, lost the suit. True, it was argued in that case that the artist had lost his rights to object because of certain negotiations with the defendant, but the court, leaving that question undecided, held positively that

> if the sale was an absolute and unconditional one, and the article was absolutely and unconditionally delivered to the purchaser, the whole property in the manuscript or picture passes to the purchaser, including the right of publication, unless the same is protected by copyright, in which case the rule is different

(18 Fed. Cases at page 1278). In *Parton v. Prang* there was cited *Turner v. Robinson* (10 Irish Chancery Rep. 121, 143), which case is considered authoritative and wherein it is said: "it would be a waste of time to add more than that the copyright is incident to the ownership, and passes at the Common Law with a transfer of the work of art." In Weil on Copyright Law, at page 116, the author cites the Prang case for the proposition that prima facie a transfer of a work of art "will be deemed to be intended to carry the common law copyright with it unless a contrary intention be manifested." In *Drone on the Law of Property in Intellectual Productions*, it is said at page 106 that the "unconditional sale of a painting is a transfer of the entire property in it." In *Dam v. Kirk La Shelle Co.* (175 Fed. Rep. 902, 904), in this circuit (not in point on the facts) it is said that "a sale or assignment without reservation would seem necessarily to carry all the rights incidental to ownership."

The most recent case called to our attention is *Yardley v. Houghton Mifflin Co.* (108 Fed. Rep. (2d) 28, Second Circuit; *certiorari denied*, 309 U.S. 686). That case concerns a painting copyrighted by the artist. In building a public school in New York city, the contractor was obligated to furnish a mural painting for the wall of one of the rooms. The artist was selected by the city but paid by the contractor. Nothing was said in the contract as to who was to own the copyright but when the painting was actually installed it had already been copyrighted by the artist. The court held that in the absence of any reservation, the copyright passed to the city and that the city owned and could sell the right to reproduce. I do not believe that this case is distinguishable because that painting was commissioned by the purchaser, or because the purchaser was a municipal corporation.

We are, of course, concerned here with the so-called common law copyright, not statutory copyright. This common law copyright is sometimes called the "right of first publication." There is no question but that it is a different and independent right from the usual right of ownership of an article of personal property (*Stephens v. Cady*, 14 How., (U.S.) 528, 530). The Stephens case quotes Lord Mansfield as saying it is "a property in notion, and has no corporeal tangible substance." There is no doubt that in New York State the separate common law copyright or control of the right to reproduce belongs to the artist or author until disposed of by him and will be protected by the courts (Oertel v. Wood, 40 How. Prac. 10; *Howitt v. Street & Smith Publications, Inc.* 276 N.Y. 345, 350). Such is the holding of the case of *Werckmeister v. Springer Lithographing Co.* (63 Fed. Rep. 808),which says (at p.811) that the painting itself may be transferred without a transfer of the common law rights of publishing or restricting publication, and that the ownership of the painting itself does not necessarily carry with it the common law copyright. The same thing is held in *Caliga v. Inter Ocean Newspaper Co.* (157 Fed. Rep. 186, 188; *affd.*, 215 U.S. 182). Palmer v. DeWitt (47 N.Y. 532) is not direct authority either way on the case before us.

We are not helped here by the cases which say that an artist's separate common law copyright does not necessarily pass with the sale of the painting. The question is whether it did pass with the sale of this painting. We think it follows from the authorities above cited that it did so pass and that an artist must, if he wishes to retain or protect the reproduction right, make some reservation of that right when he sells the painting. The Parton case above cited has always been considered as so holding. There are seemingly contrary expressions in some cases, such as the dictum in *Stephens v. Cady* (14 How. (U.S.) at p.531), that the right to reproduce "will not pass with the manuscript unless included by express words in the transfer." Appellant cites also other authorities which say that the sale of a work of art does not carry with it the right of reproduction "unless such was the evident intent of the parties." But this begs the question. What was the intent of the parties? The whole tenor of the Prang case, as we read it, is that an ordinary, straight out bill of sale shows an intention to convey the artist's whole property in his picture. Here there is no substantial proof of a contrary intent.

We are not entering into a separate discussion as to whether by this sale and the public exhibition the artist is to be held to have "published" the work so that his common law right is lost. Special Term so held (see Keene v. Kimball, 16 Gray (Mass.), 545; *Baker v. Taylor*, Fed Case No. 782). Nor need we examine into the equities, as did Special Term. Our conclusion is that under the cases and the texts, this unconditional sale carried with it the transfer of the common law copyright and right to reproduce. Plaintiff took no steps to withhold or control that right. "The Courts cannot read words of limitation into a transfer which the parties do not choose to use" (*Dam v. Kirk La Shelle Co.*, 175 Fed. Rep. 902, 904).

The judgment of the Appellate Division should be affirmed, with costs.

LEHMAN, CH. J., LOUGHRAN, FINCH, RIPPEY, LEWIS and CONWAY, JJ., concur.

Judgment affirmed.

§2.5. MUST FINE ART BE ORIGINAL TO BE COPYRIGHTED?

§2.5.1. *Alva Studios, Inc. v. Winninger:* How Creative Is "Original"?

A threshold question in dealing with an infringement of a copyright is whether the work claimed to have been infringed is "original." Can a work be original if it is copied from another work that is in the public domain? The *Alva Studios* case, which follows, deals with that question. For other cases that deal with essentially the same question, but with different sets of facts, see *Gracen v. The Bradford Exchange*, at §2.5.3 *infra*, and *L. Batlin & Son, Inc. v. Snyder*, at §2.10.3 *infra*. The necessary inquiry is how original must one be to create an object that justifies constitutional and legislative protection? For a related case dealing with the extent of the required originality, see *Fitzgerald v. Hopkins*, at §2.5.2 *infra*. As for the difference between copyright and patents, see the discussion at §2.11 *infra*.

ALVA STUDIOS, INC. v. WINNINGER
177 F. Supp. 265 (S.D.N.Y. 1959)

RYAN, C. J. Plaintiff in this suit for copyright infringement moves for an injunction *pendente lite*.

Plaintiff is a New York corporation and has its studios and offices in New York City. It reproduces three-dimensional works of art, the originals of which are owned by various museums throughout the United States and several foreign countries. Plaintiff is authorized by these museums to reproduce these works of art and pays royalties to them for this privilege. Plaintiff works in collaboration with the museum which owns the particular work being reproduced, and the curatorial staff of each such museum exercises close control over the quality and detail of a scaled reproduction of its sculpture works.

Defendant Winninger sells decorative accessories under the trade name of Wynn's Warehouse. Defendant Austin Productions is a New York corporation, engaged in the business of manufacturing and selling decorative accessories.

The plaintiff alleges of its works in its complaint that: "These reproductions are made through the use of special techniques, skills and judgment developed by plaintiff and are hand finished to duplicate as closely as possible the exact shape, patina, color and texture of the original."

The complaint further alleges that: "Prior to December 12, 1958 plaintiff caused to be created by its officers and employees a reproduction of a certain three-dimensional work of art approximately 18½ inches in height, which it designated 'Hand of God.'"

The plaintiff's product is not an exact replica, however, in that the original work has been reduced in size by the plaintiff. Describing the originality of the work in suit, plaintiff avers that "Rodin's 'Hand of God' is one of the most intricate pieces of sculpture ever created. Innumerable planes, lines and geometric patterns are all interdependent in this multidimensional work. In reduction they all have to be carried over with supreme exactness into smaller scale."

It is in the successful accomplishment of this reduction in size that plaintiff claims, with apparent support, that the originality and validity of the copyright of his work rests. It takes "an extremely skilled sculptor" many hours working directly in front of the original. If there is a small discrepancy in any part of this reduction, the "overall appearance would be altered."

A certificate of registration of copyright claim in a reproduction of Auguste Rodin's sculpture, "The Hand of God,"[was] issued to the plaintiff on April 17, 1959. The "replica" — plaintiff's copyrighted work — is unquestionably based upon the Rodin sculpture in bronze, which is owned by the Department of Fine Arts of the Carnegie Institute.

Plaintiff claims that defendant Austin infringed plaintiff's copyright by copying its work and marketing products embodying this copying through the retail operations of defendant Winninger. Defendant Austin, however, claims that the piece it marketed was its own original interpretation and representation of the Rodin sculpture which is currently on exhibit at the Metropolitan Museum of Art in New York City.

It is undisputed that the Metropolitan and Carnegie sculptures were in the public domain for some time prior to plaintiff's copyright. Rodin's "Hand of God" was first placed on public exhibit at the New Gallery in London, England, in 1905. The sculptor died on November 17, 1917.

It is hornbook that a new and original plan or combination of existing materials in the public domain is sufficiently original to come within the copyright protection (*Allegrini v. De Angelis*, D.C., 59 F. Supp. 248, at page 250). However, to be entitled to copyright, the work must be original in the sense that the author has created it by his own skill, labor and judgment without directly copying or evasively imitating the work of another (*Hoffman v. Le Traunik*, D.C., 209 F. 375). The plaintiff has the burden of establishing these elements when demanding the preliminary injunction (*ibid.* at page 379).

Plaintiff has sustained this burden. Its copyrighted work embodies and resulted from its skill and originality in producing an accurate scale reproduction of the original. In a work of sculpture, this reduction requires far more than an abridgement of a written classic; great skill and originality is called for when one seeks to produce a scale reduction of a great work with exactitude.

It is undisputed that the original sculpture owned by the Carnegie Institute is 37 inches and that plaintiff's copyrighted work is 18½ inches.

The originality and distinction between the plaintiff's work and the original also lies in the treatment of the rear side of the base. The rear side of the original base is open; that of the plaintiff's work is closed. We find that this difference when coupled with the skilled scaled sculpture is itself creative.

Alfred Wolkenberg, president of the plaintiff corporation, states in his supporting affidavit that:

> The quality of its reproductions are constantly subject to the approval of the curatorial staffs of the museums or the person which owns the original work. Plaintiff alone is granted access to these original works and to make reductions directly from them in spite of their value and on many occasions, their delicacy, because of its reputation, skill, care and unique secret processes which do no harm to such original works.

We find that the granting of approval by the Carnegie Institute's Department of Fine Arts, experts in the field, to be extremely persuasive that the plaintiff's copyrighted work is in itself a work of art which bears the stamp of originality and of skill.

Plaintiff has established that it has a valid copyright in its work.

We have then to determine whether the evidence of infringement is sufficient to support the granting of injunctive relief.

The test as to infringement of copyright is not the test of mere likeness, but the work claimed to constitute the infringement must be a copy, more or less servile, of the copyrighted work, and not an original treatment of a subject open alike to treatment by the copyright holder and others. (*Pellegrini v. Allegrini*, D.C., 2 F.2d 610, at page 612).

Where the principal elements of design of plaintiff's copyrighted work and of defendant's allegedly infringing article are taken, as a common source, from an object in the public domain, mere resemblance will not justify a finding of infringement (*Allegrini v. De Angelis, supra*). Publication of identical works cannot be enjoined if it is the result of independent research (*Aero Sales Co. v. Columbia Steel Co.*, D.C., 119 F.Supp. 693).

One work does not violate the copyright in another simply because there is a similarity between the two, if the similarity between the two results from the fact that both deal with the same subject or have the same source (*Affiliated Enterprises, Inc. v. Gruber*, 1 Cir., 86 F.2d 958, at page 961; *Dorsey v. Old Surety Life Ins. Co.*, 10 Cir., 98 F.2d 872, 119 A.L.R. 1250).

Since both the Carnegie and Metropolitan works are in the public domain (and defendant Austin claims that its piece is based upon the latter), any mere copying from the Carnegie work is not violative of plaintiff's copyright.

The privilege given to plaintiff by its agreement with Carnegie was the complete access to the original and the use of the name of the Institute.

Plaintiff alleges in paragraph 16 of its complaint that:

. . . defendants have made and sold their aforesaid infringing copies of plaintiff's said copyrighted work of art with the intent and purpose of passing off their said copies as and for plaintiff's authorized reproduction, and said passing off has occurred and will continue to occur unless enjoined by this Court.

However, the defendants have been advertising their marketed article as produced from the work on display at the Metropolitan, thereby incurring the disfavor of that institution.

To the underside of the pedestal of its sculpture, the plaintiff has affixed a gold label bearing the following legend:

Authentic copyrighted reproduction made from the original at the
Carnegie Institute
Department of Fine Arts — Detroit, Mich.
By Alva Studios, Inc.   New York

There is no allegation that the defendants have employed such a label. In fact, the specimen of the defendant's article, which was submitted by the plaintiff for our examination, bears no label or authentication of any sort. It is evident that the defendant has not trespassed on the right the plaintiff enjoys to the exclusion of the defendant by the use of the name of the Carnegie Institute.

But, the availability to a defendant of other "common sources" is not a defense to an action for copyright infringement if the defendant actually copied the plaintiff's work (*Caldwell-Clements, Inc. v. Cowan Publishing Corp.*, D.C., 130 F. Supp. 326). Here there is convincing credible evidence to establish actual copying.

We have carefully examined the exhibits presented in this motion and the photographs of the original Rodin sculptures. We are persuaded by this examination and by the affidavit of Hugo Robus, sculptor, submitted by the plaintiff that the defendant's product is a copy of plaintiff's work and that its copyright has been infringed. We are also persuaded that plaintiff's work was copied by sandpapering and smoothing down many of the surfaces of plaintiff's work, slicing off approximately 2 inches at the bottom of the base to reduce it to a 16 inch height, and then etching in several features which had been rendered indistinct because of the sanding and smoothing; exactly as plaintiff alleges.

Defendant's, Austin Productions, Inc., unverified financial statement, as of June 30, 1959, affords no assurance that it will be financially able to respond in damages in the event of plaintiff's probable success in this suit. We have no evidence of the defendant Winninger's worth. We find that unless relief is granted plaintiff until final judgment, it will sustain irreparable harm and damage.

We conclude that plaintiff is entitled to the injunctive relief now sought; let an order so providing be settled on 5 days' notice.

§2.5.2. *Fitzgerald v. Hopkins:* Copying — How Much Can Be Borrowed?

Once it has been decided that a work is original, the next inquiry in an infringement action is whether the alleged infringer "copied" the work. Is awareness of the original work sufficient? Is influence and inspiration adequate? The *Fitzgerald* case, which follows, provides essentially negative answers to these questions. The case also deals with the risk of being sued for defamation when, believing in good faith that his work has been copied, an artist makes libelous remarks about another artist. Not only does the artist risk losing the lawsuit, but he may wind up being responsible for considerably more than might have been recovered if he had prevailed.

FITZGERALD v. HOPKINS
70 Wash. 2d 924, 425 P.2d 920 (1967)

WEAVER, J. At the trial level this case presented a scintillating and intriguing dissertation on the art of sculpturing. It loses much of its glitter on appeal, however, for it presents, basically, a fact question.

Plaintiff, James H. Fitzgerald, 54 years of age, alleges in his complaint and amended complaint that "he has established himself over a period of years, as one of the foremost sculptors in the Northwest." The trial court found, and the evidence supports the finding, that plaintiff "is one of the leading sculptors of the Pacific Northwest." In its oral opinion the trial court stated that plaintiff "by reputation has achieved a position of stature in this community that probably is not matched by many other sculptors in the area." In truth, the record would support the conclusion that plaintiff's eminence in the field of art is even much broader.

In contrast, defendant, Robert Hopkins, 29 years of age, had his bachelor's degree in fine arts and was working and studying for his master's degree in sculpturing in the graduate school of the University of Washington.

Apparently, defendant was a promising student in his chosen field. Mr. George Tsutakawa, professor of sculpturing at the University of Washington and a well-known sculptor, recommended him to a firm of Seattle architects to execute a piece of sculpture for a building they had designed for a Seattle bank.

Defendant executed his commission. Named "Transcending," the work was 8 feet in height. Upon its installation at the bank, the present trouble arose.

In 1959 plaintiff had sculpted a work of art that he named "Rock Totem." It was 13 feet high. We think the name rather significant. "Rock" needs no definition. "Totem" is of Algonquian origin. (Webster's New International Dictionary (2d ed.)). We find no reference to a close relationship between a "totem" and the columns of the Egyptian and Greek temples, or to the abstract art of Picasso, Braque, Cézanne or Brancusi which is discussed so learnedly by the expert witnesses and the trial judge in his oral opinion.

We are impressed with the observation of the trial court: "The use of the vertical form in sculpture, which is one of the issues here, is ancient, possibly dating as far back as 20,000 years ago as asserted by Mr. Fitzgerald [plaintiff], or possibly to 50,000 years ago as asserted by Professor Rader."

Neither plaintiff nor defendant invented vertical statuary, cubism, or abstract art. In fact, both have been exposed to approximately the same artistic influences, except that plaintiff, because of his age and practical knowledge, enjoys a much broader development in the field of sculpturing.

Plaintiff's first "Rock Totem" having been destroyed by fire, his final 13 foot sculpture was completed and exhibited at the Seattle World's Fair in 1962. Defendant saw it during the exhibition.

When plaintiff learned of defendant's "Transcending," he viewed it and then went to the office of the bank's architects. He reported that "Transcending" was a copy of his "Rock Totem." Plaintiff was quite agitated. The person to whom he talked testified:

And he [plaintiff] accused Mr. Hopkins [defendant] of *thievery*, I guess — I think the word was — called him a *thief*, and he became quite hot-tempered within a very few minutes and used *profane language* and a few words I don't recall either. But I remember he became very hot-tempered in a very short time. I didn't expect it myself and I didn't know how to react to it. (Italics ours.)

Prior to the commencement of this action, plaintiff wrote a letter which ultimately came to the attention of counsel for the bank, the architects, and defendant. In it plaintiff wrote:

I know how many years it took me to arrive at this particular art statement and no law of probability would allow *an immature art student* to do it so quickly and in such a like image. *When a thief robs openly from a creative spirit no bit of talk around a legal table can quietly settle the issue. Is it not more important that the art student recognize his desire for money has guided his hand in his path of plagiarism.* . . . I ask this art student to remove his copy and replace it with a work of his own spirit. If this is not done immediately I ask for a suit in damages with the related publicity that will properly expose the time facts to the public. *I am sure no bank wants to be thought of as a thief and no architect wants a design that is not original.* (Italics ours.)

Plaintiff first sued the Seattle bank praying (a) that it be enjoined from using a copy of his statue, and (b) for $50,000 damages. The bank, in turn, joined defendant, Robert Hopkins, and the firm of architects as additional parties defendant. One architect was dismissed by agreement of the parties; the other architect and the bank were dismissed upon their motion for summary judgment.

In his amended complaint, plaintiff prays (a) for judgment of $50,000 against defendant Hopkins and (b) that defendant be enjoined from making "any further copies or imitations" of plaintiff's work. By trial amendment, plaintiff asserts a common-law copyright upon his sculpture "Rock Totem."

Defendant made a general denial and counterclaimed for $25,000 damages (made more specific by trial amendment) based upon alleged libel and slander.

The ultimate decision pivots upon the answer to one question: Is "Transcending" a copy of "Rock Totem"? The superior court is the only court authorized by the constitution to resolve this question of fact. *Gilbert v. Rogers*, 56 Wn. 2d 185, 351 P.2d 535 (1960).

Characteristic of experts testifying in a field other than the exact sciences, there is a diversity of opinion.

After an extended trial and after viewing plaintiff's "Rock Totem" and defendant's "Transcending," the trial court dismissed plaintiff's complaint, based, primarily, upon finding of fact No. 4:

That both pieces of sculpture were similar in that both had a vertical design with angular semihorizontal plane masses to a vertical axis. They were also similar in that they were both abstracts. The plaintiff's "Rock Totem" gave a feeling of rockiness with flowing lines in an upward movement. The texture of the surface material of the plaintiff's sculpture was dripped and brushed for a rough effect and contained little element of anatomy. The defendant's "Transcending" gave a different impression and could not be mistaken for a rock-like quality. This sculpture was squattier and had a semi-smooth surface with a definite feeling of anatomy. These dissimilarities and the testimony pertaining thereto were strong enough to convince the court as the trier of the fact that *there had been no conscious copying done by the defendant.* (Italics ours.)

The thrust of plaintiff's appeal is that the trial court by the italicized portion of finding of fact No. 4, *supra,* placed upon the plaintiff the burden of proving that defendant intentionally copied plaintiff's statue. We do not agree.

On appeal, the negative finding that "there had been no *conscious* copying done by defendant" is not completely satisfactory, but the trial court's oral decision, which we may consider in the circumstances (*Mertens v. Mertens,* 38 Wn. 2d 55, 227 P.2d 724 (1951)), makes it clear that the trial judge found that there had not been *any* copying for he said: "It is the opinion of the Court that the plaintiff has failed to sustain the burden of proving that there was any copying done by the defendant in this case."

There is evidence — although in sharp conflict — to support the trial court's finding that "Transcending" is not a copy of "Rock Totem"; hence, it was not error to dismiss plaintiff's action. . . .

In summary, we affirm the dismissal of plaintiff's action. It is our considered opinion that a reduction of the $15,000 judgment to $7,500 would be fair. If defendant does not accept judgment of $7,500 within 15 days after the remittitur has gone down from this court, a new trial shall be granted, limited to a determination of damages upon defendant's counterclaim.

Each party shall bear his own costs on appeal.

It is so ordered.

DONWORTH, ROSELLINI, HAMILTON, and HALE, JJ., concur.

HUNTER, J. (concurring in part and dissenting in part). I concur with the majority except for its disposition of the issue of damages. I disagree with the majority's reduction of damages awarded the defendant from $15,000 to $7,500 or in the alternative granting the plaintiff a new trial. The sole reason given is that "the amount shocks our sense of justice and sound judgment."

The test to be applied for making such a determination is set forth in *Kramer v. Portland-Seattle Auto Freight,* 43 Wn. 2d 386, 261 P.2d 692 (1953), cited in *Malstrom v. Kalland,* 62 Wn. 2d 732, 384 P.2d 613 (1963):

On the other hand, the balancing factor is the conscience of the appellate court when there is an affirmative showing that passion and prejudice played no part in the jury's determination. Is the amount flagrantly outrageous and extravagant? Is it unjustified in the light of the evidence? Does it disclose circumstances foreign to proper jury deliberations? If it is and does, then it can be said to shock the sense of justice and sound judgment, and the verdict of the jury is excessive.

Applying this test to the trial judge as the fact finder, I find nothing in the record to shock my "sense of justice and sound judgment." To be called a "thief" who "robs openly from a creative spirit . . . in his path of plagiarism" by a man with the standing in the field of sculpturing as that of James H. Fitzgerald is devastating to a novitiate attempting to establish a professional reputation as a sculptor.

In my opinion, the award of $15,000 for damages resulting to the defendant from these libelous and defamatory statements was within the range of the evidence. The judgment of the trial court should be affirmed without modification.

FINLEY, C.J., HILL, J., and LANGENBACH, J. Pro Tem., concur with HUNTER, J.

§2.5.3. *Gracen v. The Bradford Exchange:* **Originality and Derivative Works**

Copyright requires some originality — but how much? Is more creativeness required if the work is derived from some preexisting source rather than from a derivative work? The *Gracen* case, which follows, is one of the most recent decisions on that question. It indicates that indeed there is a more severe test for determining originality if the work is a derivative one. The *L. Batlin & Son, Inc. v. Snyder* case, which is discussed in the opinion, is reproduced at §2.10.3 *infra*.

GRACEN v. THE BRADFORD EXCHANGE
698 F.2d 300 (7th Cir. 1983)

POSNER, C.J. This appeal brings up to us questions of some novelty, at least in this circuit, regarding implied copyright licenses and the required originality for copyrighting a derivative work.

In 1939 MGM produced and copyrighted the movie "The Wizard of Oz." The central character in the movie, Dorothy, was played by Judy Garland. The copyright was renewed by MGM in 1966 and is conceded, at least for purposes of this case, to be valid and in effect today. In 1976 MGM licensed Bradford Exchange to use characters and scenes from the movie in a series of collectors' plates. Bradford invited several artists to submit paintings of Dorothy as played by Judy Garland, with the understanding that the artist who submitted the best painting would be offered a contract for the entire series. Bradford supplied each artist with photographs from the movie and with instructions for the painting that included the following: We do want *your* interpretation of these images, but your interpretation must evoke all the warm feeling the people have for the film and its actors. So, *your* Judy/ Dorothy must be very recognizable as everybody's Judy/Dorothy."

Jorie Gracen, an employee in Bradford's order-processing department, was permitted to join the competition. From photographs and her recollections of the movie (which she had seen several times) she made a painting of Dorothy as played by Judy Garland; Figure 1 [omitted] is a reproduction of a photograph of Miss Gracen's painting (an inadequate one, because the original is in color). Bradford exhibited it along with the other contestants' paintings in a shopping center. The passersby liked Miss Gracen's the best, and Bradford pronounced her the winner of the competition and offered her a contract to do the series, as well as paying her, as apparently it paid each of the other contestants, $200. But she did not like the contract terms and refused to sign, and Bradford turned to another artist, James Auckland, who had not been one of the original contestants. He signed a contract to do the series and Bradford gave him Miss Gracen's painting to help him in doing his painting of Dorothy. The record does not indicate who has her painting now.

Gracen's counsel describes Auckland's painting of Dorothy as a "piratical copy" of her painting. Bradford could easily have refuted this charge, if it is false, by attaching to its motion for summary judgment a photograph of its Dorothy plate, but it did not, and for purposes of this appeal we must assume that the plate is a copy of Miss Gracen's painting. This is not an absurd supposition. Bradford, at least at first, was rapturous about Miss Gracen's painting of Dorothy. It called Miss Gracen "a true prodigy." It said that hers "was the one painting that conveyed the essence of Judy's character in the film . . . the painting that left everybody saying, 'That's Judy in Oz.'"Auckland's deposition states that Bradford gave him her painting with directions to "clean it up," which he understood to mean: do the same thing but make it "a little more professional."

Miss Gracen also made five drawings of other characters in the movie, for example, the Scarecrow as played by Ray Bolger. Auckland's affidavit states without contradiction that he had not seen any of the drawings when he made his paintings of those characters. Pictures of the plates that were made from his paintings are attached to the motion for summary judgment filed by MGM and Bradford, but there is no picture of his Dorothy plate, lending some support to the charge that it is a "piratical copy." But apparently the other plates are not copies at all.

Auckland completed the series, and the plates were manufactured and sold. But Miss Gracen meanwhile had obtained copyright registrations on her painting and drawings, and in 1978 she brought this action for copyright infringement against MGM, Bradford, Auckland, and the manufacturer of the plates. MGM and Bradford counterclaimed, alleging among other things that Miss Gracen had infringed the copyright on the movie by showing her drawings and a photograph of her painting to people whom she was soliciting for artistic commissions.

The district court granted summary judgment against Miss Gracen on both the main claim and the counterclaim. It held that she could not copyright her painting and drawings because they were not original and that she had infringed MGM's copyright. The court entered judgment for $1500 on the counterclaim. Neither the judgment nor the opinion accompanying it refers to the noncopyright claims in the counterclaim, thus inviting the question whether that judgment is final and hence appealable under 28 U.S.C. §1291. But this is not a serious problem, because the judgment purports to dispose of "their [MGM's and Bradford's] counterclaims" and both sides have treated it as disposing of the counterclaim in its entirety. The noncopyright claims must therefore be regarded as having been either dismissed or abandoned.

The briefs and argument in this court follow the district court in treating the principal question as whether Miss Gracen's painting and drawings are sufficiently original to be copyrightable as derivative works under 17 U.S.C. §103. But this emphasis may be misplaced. The question of the copyrightability of a derivative work ("a work based upon one or more preexisting works, such as a[n] . . . art reproduction . . . or any other form in which a work may be recast, transformed, or adapted," 17 U.S.C. §101) usually arises in connection with something either made by the owner (or a licensee) of the copyright on the underlying work, as in *Durham Industries, Inc. v. Tomy Corp.*, 630 F.2d 905, 909 (2d Cir. 1980), or derived from an underlying work that is in the public domain, as in *L. Batlin & Son, Inc. v. Snyder*, 536 F.2d 486, 491-92 (2d Cir. 1976)(en banc). At issue in such a case is not the right to copy the underlying work but whether there is enough difference between the derivative and the underlying work to satisfy the statutory requirement of originality, see 17 U.S.C. §102(a), and thus make the derivative work copyrightable. Since the copyright owner's bundle of exclusive rights includes the right "to prepare derivative works based upon the copyrighted work," 17 U.S.C. §106(2), even if Miss Gracen's painting and drawings had enough originality to be copyrightable as derivative works *she* could not copyright them unless she had authority to use copyrighted materials from the movie. "[P]rotection for a work employing preexisting material in which copyright subsists does not extend to any part of the work in which such material has been used unlawfully." 17 U.S.C. §103(a).

Miss Gracen does not claim that she painted the 16-year-old Judy Garland who appeared in "The Wizard of Oz" in 1939 from life or from photographs taken from the movie, or that her painting is not of Judy Garland but is an imaginative conception of the character Dorothy. The painting was based on the movie, both as independently recollected by Miss Gracen and as frozen in the still photographs that Bradford supplied her. As with any painting there was an admixture of the painter's creativity — how much we shall consider later — but that it is a painting of Judy Garland as she appears in photographs from the movie (such as the photograph [omitted] Figure 2), and is therefore a derivative work, is beyond question. The same is true of the drawings.

Therefore, if Miss Gracen had no authority to make derivative works from the movie, she could not copyright the painting and drawings, and she infringed MGM's copyright by displaying them publicly. But obviously she had *some* authority, having been invited by Bradford to make a painting of Dorothy based on the movie. And although Bradford was not expressly authorized to sublicense the copyright in this way, there can be no serious doubt of its authority to do so. Thus the question is not whether Miss Gracen was licensed to make a derivative work but whether she was also licensed to exhibit the painting and to copyright it.

Bradford made no written agreement with the contestants for the disposition of their paintings. It could have required each contestant to give it full rights as consideration for $200 and a shot at a potentially lucrative contract, but it did not do so, not in writing anyway, and though it argues that it "bought" Miss Gracen's painting of Dorothy for $200 we find no evidence to support this characterization of the transaction. Miss Gracen testified in her deposition that Foster, who was in charge of the contest, said he would return the painting to her; and we must ask what he thought she would do with the painting when she got it back, if they failed to come to terms. Destroy it? Keep it in a closet till MGM's copyright expired? Bradford, in promising Miss Gracen (as for purposes of this appeal we must assume it did) that she could keep the painting, must have known she would exhibit it to advance her career as an artist. And while Bradford's license from MGM may not have authorized it to make any such promise, Bradford may have had apparent authority to do so and that is all that would be necessary to give Miss Gracen (who presumably knew nothing of the terms of the license) the right to exhibit her painting. See Seavey, Handbook of the Law of Agency 125-28 (1964). We do not say she actually had the right, but only that there is a genuine issue of material fact concerning the scope of her implied license to make a derivative work.

It is less likely that Miss Gracen was entitled to exhibit, or even to make, the drawings. Their making was no part of the contest. Yet she testified that Foster told her to make the drawings to improve her chances of winning, and this testimony was not contradicted or inherently incredible. If she was authorized to make the drawings maybe she was also authorized — or reasonably believed she was authorized — to exhibit them, at least if she did not come to terms with Bradford.

The grant of summary judgment on the counterclaim was therefore erroneous — assuming an oral nonexclusive copyright license is enforceable. Nimmer describes this as the law both before and after the Copyright Act was revised in 1976, see 3 Nimmer on Copyright §§10.03[A]-[B] at pp.10-36 to 10-37 and nn.17, 22, 23 (1982), and though support for this conclusion is sparse, and there is some contrary authority, see *Douglas Int'l Corp. v. Baker*, 335 F. Supp. 282, 285 (S.D.N.Y. 1971), we think Nimmer is right. This case shows why. MGM and Bradford do not even argue that Bradford had no authority to permit Miss Gracen to *make* a derivative work, though nothing in the license to Bradford purports to authorize sublicensing. They thus tacitly acknowledge the impracticality of requiring written licenses in all circumstances; and we do not see how it can be argued that only the existence and not the scope of a license can be proved by parol evidence.

This disposes of the counterclaim, but we have still to consider Miss Gracen's claim that she had valid copyrights which the defendants infringed. The initial issue is again the scope of her implied license from Bradford. Even if she was authorized to exhibit her derivative works, she may not have been authorized to copyright them. Bradford was licensed to use MGM's copyright in its series of collectors' plates but not to copyright the derivative works thus created. A copyright owner is naturally reluctant to authorize a licensee to take out copyrights on derivative works — copyrights that might impede him in making his own derivative works or in licensing others to do so. And it would have made no more sense for Bradford, the licensee, to arm Miss Gracen, its sublicensee, with a weapon — the right to copyright her derivative works — that she could use to interfere with Bradford's efforts to get another artist to do the plates if it could not cut a deal with her. The affidavits submitted with the motions for summary judgment deny that Miss Gracen was authorized to copyright derivative works based on the movie and are not contradicted on this point. (In contrast, they do not deny that she was authorized to exhibit her painting of Dorothy.)

We are reluctant to stop here, though, and uphold the dismissal of the complaint on the basis of an issue of fact that the district judge did not address, and that we therefore may have got wrong, so we shall go on and consider his ground for dismissal of the complaint — that Miss Gracen's painting and drawings are not original enough to be copyrightable.

Miss Gracen reminds us that judges can make fools of themselves pronouncing on aesthetic matters. But artistic originality is not the same thing as the legal concept of originality in the Copyright Act. Artistic originality indeed might inhere in a detail, a nuance, a shading too small to be apprehended by a judge. A contemporary school of art known as "Super Realism" attempts with some success to make paintings that are indistinguishable to the eye from color photographs. See *Super Realism: A Critical Anthology* (Battcock ed. 1975). These paintings command high prices; buyers must find something original in them. Much Northern European painting of the Renaissance is meticulously representational, see, e.g., Gombrich, *The Story of Art* 178-80 (13th ed. 1978), and therefore in a sense — but not an aesthetic sense — less "original" than Cubism or Abstract Expressionism. A portrait is not unoriginal for being a good likeness.

But especially as applied to derivative works, the concept of originality in copyright law has as one would expect a legal rather than aesthetic function — to prevent overlapping claims. See *L. Batlin & Son, Inc. v. Snyder, supra,* 536 F.2d at 491-92. Suppose Artist *A* produces a reproduction of the Mona Lisa, a painting in the public domain, which differs slightly from the original. *B* also makes a reproduction of the Mona Lisa. *A*, who has copyrighted his derivative work, sues *B* for infringement. *B's* defense is that he was copying the original, not *A's* reproduction. But if the difference between the original and *A's* reproduction is slight, the difference between *A's* and *B's* reproductions will also be slight, so that if *B* has access to *A's* reproductions the trier of fact will be hard-pressed to decide whether *B* was copying *A* or copying the Mona Lisa itself. Miss Gracen's drawings illustrate the problem. They are very similar both to the photographs from the movie and to the plates designed by Auckland. Auckland's affidavit establishes that he did not copy or even see her drawings. But suppose he had seen them. Then it would be very hard to determine whether he had been copying the movie stills, as he was authorized to do, or copying her drawings.

The painting of Dorothy presents a harder question. A comparison of Figures 1 and 2 [omitted] reveals perceptible differences. A painting (except, perhaps, one by a member of the Super Realist school mentioned earlier) is never identical to the subject painted, whether the subject is a photograph, a still life, a landscape, or a model, because most painters cannot and do not want to achieve a photographic likeness of their subject. Nevertheless, if the differences between Miss Gracen's painting of Dorothy and the photograph of Judy Garland as Dorothy were sufficient to make the painting original in the eyes of the law, then a painting by an Auckland also striving, as per his commission, to produce something "very recognizable as everybody's Judy/Dorothy" would look like the Gracen painting, to which he had access; and it would be difficult for the trier of fact to decide whether Auckland had copied her painting or the original movie stills. True, the background in Miss Gracen's painting differs from that in Figure 2, but it is drawn from the movie set. We do not consider a picture created by superimposing one copyrighted photographic image on another to be "original"— always bearing in mind that the purpose of the term in copyright law is not to guide aesthetic judgments but to assure a sufficiently gross difference between the underlying and the derivation work to avoid entangling subsequent artists depicting the underlying work in copyright problems.

We are speaking, however, only of the requirement of originality in derivative works. If a painter paints from life, no court is going to hold that his painting is not copyrightable because it is an exact photographic likeness. If that were the rule photographs could not be copyrighted — the photographs of Judy Garland in "The Wizard of Oz," for example — but of course they can be, 1 Nimmer on Copyright §2.08[E] (1982). The requirement of originality is significant chiefly in connection with derivative works, where if interpreted too liberally it would paradoxically inhibit rather than promote the creation of such works by giving the first creator a considerable power to interfere with the creation of subsequent derivative works from the same underlying work.

Justice Holmes' famous opinion in *Bleistein v. Donaldson Lithographing Co.*, 188 U.S. 239, 23 S. Ct. 298, 47 L. Ed. 460 (1903), heavily relied on by Miss Gracen, is thus not in point. The issue was whether lithographs of a circus were copyrightable under a statute (no longer in force) that confined copyright to works "connected with the fine arts." Holmes' opinion is a warning against aesthetic criteria to answer the question. If Miss Gracen had painted Judy Garland from life, her painting would be copyrightable even if we thought it *kitsch*; but a derivative work must be substantially different from the underlying work to be copyrightable. This is the test of *L. Batlin & Son, Inc. v. Snyder, supra*, 536 F.2d at 491, a decision of the Second Circuit — the nation's premier copyright court — sitting en banc. Earlier Second Circuit cases discussed in *Batlin* that suggest a more liberal test must be considered superseded.

We agree with the district court that under the test of *Batlin* Miss Gracen's painting, whatever its artistic merit, is not an original derivative work within the meaning of the Copyright Act. Admittedly this is a harder case than *Durham Industries, Inc. v. Tomy Corp., supra*, heavily relied on by the defendants. The underlying works in that case were Mickey Mouse and other Walt Disney cartoon characters, and the derivative works were plastic reproductions of them. Since the cartoon characters are extremely simple drawings, the reproductions were exact, differing only in the medium. The plastic Mickey and its cartoon original look more alike than Judy Garland's Dorothy and Miss Gracen's painting. But we do not think the difference is enough to allow her to copyright her painting even if, as we very much doubt, she was authorized by Bradford to do so.

The judgment dismissing the complaint is therefore affirmed. The judgment on the counterclaim is vacated and the case remanded for further proceedings consistent with this opinion. No costs in this court.

So ordered.

§2.6. PRESERVING COPYRIGHT IN WORKS OF ART: PUBLICATION AND NOTICE

§2.6.1. *Morton v. Raphael:* Publication without Notice and Loss of Copyright

We have included the *Morton* case, which follows, not only for the proposition that a person commissioning a work owns the copyright as against the artist, but also for the concept that under traditional law the act of publication destroys the common law copyright if an adequate notice has not been placed on the work. The case is also of interest for the court's treatment of injury to the artist:

> If the murals were as artistic and effective as all the parties concede, it would seem that plaintiff [the artist] was rather benefitted from the publicity afforded, than damaged thereby and it would be quite strained to hold that her name, reputation and income as an artist had been seriously and permanently damaged.

MORTON v. RAPHAEL

334 Ill. App. 399, 79 N.E.2d 522 (1948)

MR. Presiding Justice FRIEND delivered the opinion of the court.

In the spring of 1946, the plaintiff, Ruth Morton, was commissioned to paint murals on the walls of the Great Lakes Room of the Knickerbocker Hotel in Chicago. After she had completed her work, defendants, interior decorators, were engaged to redecorate the entire room. Thereafter, in the July 1946 issue of the nationally circulated magazine *Hotel Management*, there appeared defendants' advertisement showing several photographic views of the newly decorated room, including plaintiff's murals. After she saw the advertisement she filed suit on the theory that defendants pirated, infringed and published without permission mural paintings, the common-law copyright of which belonged to her, a professional painter-artist, as the result of which "her reputation, name and income as an artist and painter of murals have been seriously and permanently damaged . . . in the sum of fifty thousand dollars." Defendants' motions to strike the original and the amended complaints were both allowed, and an order dismissing the suit was entered, from which plaintiff has taken an appeal.

The principal question presented is whether the amended complaint stated a good cause of action. Plaintiff did not allege nor does she contend that she secured a copyright of the murals. Her cause of action is avowedly based upon an alleged exclusive common-law right in the murals first published by defendants through the advertisement in question. It is apparent, however, from the pleadings, that plaintiff, under hire by the Knickerbocker Hotel, made the first publication of the murals when she painted them on the walls of the Great Lakes Room where they could be seen and were undoubtedly observed by many persons. Under the settled rule in this and other jurisdictions such publication without copyright divests the owner of an exclusive common-law right and the production becomes common property, subject to the free use of the community. In the early case of *Rees v. Peltzer*, 75 Ill. 475, atlases, containing maps of the City of Chicago, were sold to various real estate dealers, and one such atlas was placed in the hands of the city for public use, where any part, or the whole of it, could be copied and used by any citizen who so desired. The court held such act to be voluntary publication, divesting the author of any common-law right in the atlas, saying:

> It may, however, be now considered as established, that when these products are circulated abroad, and published with the author's consent, they become common property, and subject to the free use of the community; or, in other words, that there is no copyright in a *published* work at common law, and such copyright exists only by statute.

In *Van Veen v. Franklin Knitting Mills, Inc.,*145 Misc. 451, 260 N.Y.S. 163, the court posed the question: "When an owner of a common-law copyright publishes his work in a magazine without copyrighting it under the federal statute, can he by an agreement with the publisher which is unknown to the public prevent the public from reproducing the form of the work which is so published?" and stated: "The question is answered in the negative." Again, in *Kipling v. Fenno*, 106 Fed. 692, the court said:

> Baldly stated, the proposition advanced is that an author, whose mental productions, prose, verse, and title, have been given to the world by publication without copyright, so that anyone is free to reprint and sell the whole or any part of them, may nevertheless regulate the manner in which such reprinted matter may be grouped and entitled, and may restrain any application of the title he selected otherwise than as he used or uses it. No authority is cited which supports any such proposition, . . . It would seem that the measure of relief which authors may obtain against unauthorized publication of their works must be found in the copyright statutes, which, when availed of, are an abundant protection against such publication.

See also *Bamforth v. Douglass Post Card & Machine Co.*, 158 Fed. 355, and *Kurfiss v. Cowherd*, 233 Mo. App. 397, 121 S.W.2d 282, wherein a house built in accordance with the plaintiff architect's plans were thereafter open to public inspection with his consent. Although the plans had not been copyrighted the architect sued the defendants for subsequently constructing residences from his plans without his consent and for their own profit. As applicable to these facts the court said:

> Another method [by which publication may be accomplished] is by placing the original on exhibition in a public place . . . where the public may view the same without restriction. . . . But it is universally held that where the work is made available to the public, or any considerable portion thereof, without restriction, there has been a publication.

Plaintiff takes the position that she had a common-law property right in the murals to the exclusion of all except those to whom she might give her permission to publish, and that since defendants did not obtain permission or authority to publish a copy or reproduction of the murals, they were guilty of an infringement of her exclusive right therein, and therefore their conduct was actionable at law. The only two cases cited by plaintiff in support of her contention are *Frohman v. Ferris*, 238 Ill. 430, and *Bleistein v. Donaldson Lithographing Co.*, 188 U.S. 239. In the *Frohman* case the owner of the rights in unpublished manuscript of a play gave a public presentation of it in various theaters. The court held that at common law the author of an intellectual production, including literature, drama, music, art, etc., had an absolute property right in his production of which he could not be deprived so long as it remained unpublished, nor could he be compelled to publish it, and he might permit the use of his production by one or more persons to the exclusion of others, and give a copy of the manuscript to another person without parting with his property in it; but it was also held that presentation of the play was not a publication resulting in the dedication of the play to the public, and that if the play had been printed and circulated there would have been a publication. The difference between the two situations is appropriately stated by the court as follows: "there is a logical distinction to be observed in dealing with the effect upon the author's rights of the public performance of an unprinted drama and the publication of a printed book." In the *Frohman* case the owner of the play had not dedicated the work to the public, whereas in the case at bar the murals were undoubtedly dedicated to the public when they were painted on the walls of the hotel room with plaintiff's name indorsed [sic] on each of the murals, open to the inspection of anyone who visited the hotel. In *Bleistein v. Donaldson Lithographing Co.* the court held that a copyright under the United States statutes will be protected by law. Plaintiff in the case at bar concedes that she had not obtained a copyright, and because her cause of action rests entirely upon a common-law right in the murals, that right was lost upon publication. . . .

In view of these conclusions it becomes unnecessary to discuss other points urged by the respective parties. We are of opinion that the superior court properly sustained defendants' motion to strike the amended complaint and dismiss the cause of action, and the order is therefore affirmed.

§2.6.2. *Coventry Ware, Inc. v. Reliance Picture Frame Co.:* Copyright Notice — Where May It Be Placed?

As has been previously observed, the concept of copyright is based on *notice* and not on registration. A work that is publicly disseminated without the requisite notice has lost its right to be protected against copying. That is basic law. The *Coventry* case, which follows, deals with the placement of the notice. Must it be on the face or front of the work, readily available for the world to see without any further examination? The case traces the history of the relevant statutory provision and holds that under the 1909 Copyright Act (a provision that probably also holds under the present 1976 Act) the notice need not be placed on the front of the work. Regarding a work of art, the statutory form of notice was required to be placed on some "accessible portion of the work itself or of the margin, back, permanent base or pedestal thereof, or of the substance on which the work shall be mounted."[1] As to what was meant by "accessible," however, see the *Scherr v. Universal Match Corp.* case, §2.6.3 *infra*.

The present copyright act requires that the notice be "affixed . . . in such manner and location as to give a reasonable notice of the claim of copyright."[2] Query if this is a more liberal or restrictive standard for the notice requirement.

COVENTRY WARE, INC. v. RELIANCE PICTURE FRAME CO.

288 F.2d 193 (2d Cir. 1961), rev'g 186 F. Supp. 798 (S.D.N.Y. 1960), *cert. denied*, 368 U.S. 818 (1961)

CLARK, C.J. Plaintiff, a corporation engaged in the manufacture and sale of wall plaques, caused certain wall plaques to be designed by an artist and then registered them as "Molded Sculpture" with the Register of Copyrights. The plaques contained a colored, three-dimensional, but relatively flat, design, and were intended as decorative features for walls. The plaques were made by pressing a mold in plastic, and were completed with a rigid backing sheet so that the component parts formed an integral whole which could be attached to a wall and displayed. Defendant admitted copying plaintiff's plaques and selling them at a lower price. In this action for infringement, its only defense is the alleged invalidity of

---

§2.6. [1] Copyright Act of 1909, §19.
[2] Copyright Revision Act of 1976 §401(c).

the copyright notice, which appeared on a small printed label firmly attached to the back of the plaques. Defendant's position is that notice of copyright must appear on the front of the work of art, and that a notice appearing on the back is insufficient. The district court, accepting this contention, granted summary judgment to the defendant, and plaintiff appeals. Judge Dawson's opinion is reported in D.C. S.D.N.Y., 186 F. Supp. 798.

The relevant sections of the Copyright Act, 17 U.S.C. §1 *et seq.*, are section 10, section 19, which deals with the form of notice, and section 20, which prescribes the location of the notice in certain instances. The basic notice requirement is set forth in 17 U.S.C. §10, as follows: "Any person entitled thereto by this title may secure copyright for his work by publication thereof with the notice of copyright required by this title; and such notice shall be affixed to each copy thereof. . . ." The form of the notice required by section 10 is set forth in 17 U.S.C. §19 and "shall consist either of the word 'Copyright,' the abbreviation 'Copr.,' or the symbol ©, accompanied by the name of the copyright proprietor, and if the work be a printed literary, musical, or dramatic work, the notice shall include also the year in which the copyright was secured by publication."

Section 19 then goes on to authorize an optional "short form" of notice which may be used on works of art and other items set forth in 17 U.S.C. §5(f-k) as an alternative to the general form of notice described above. Such "short form" notice "may consist of the letter C enclosed within a circle, thus ©, accompanied by the initials, monogram, mark, or symbol of the copyright proprietor: *Provided,* That on some accessible portion of such copies or of the margin, back, permanent base, or pedestal, or of the substance on which such copies shall be mounted, his name shall appear."

Section 20 prescribes the place where the notice is to appear in the case of books or other printed publications, periodicals, and musical compositions. It places no limitations on the possible location of notice in the case of works of art and kindred items, provided that the notice complies with the general requirement of section 10 that the notice be affixed to each copy. Defendant contends, however, that a limitation on the permissible location of notice for works of art may be found by implication from section 19. Defendant reasons that the shortform notice allowed by section 19 is intended to minimize the disfigurement which would result if the long form were used. In order to prevent the shortform from being mere surplusage, defendant concludes, we must assume that the long form could be used only where it disfigured the work of art — i.e., on the front. Defendant does not explain, however, why Congress would have enacted a copyright law requiring disfiguring notices on the front when a nondisfiguring notice on the back would give equally adequate warning to prospective copyists. Neither does defendant say why, if any limitations on placement were intended with respect to works of art, they were not set forth in section 20, whose specific subject is location of the notice.

It should be noted that section 20 is the culmination of a long history of increasing liberalization of restrictions on the placement of notice. In the case of books and musical compositions, the placement of notice has always been rigidly and narrowly confined. But in the case of other items, a series of revisions have steadily expanded the permissible locations of notice. The acts of 1802, 2 Stat. 171, and of 1831, 4 Stat. 436, 437, both required notice to be "on the face" of nonbook and nonliterary items. This harshly restrictive requirement was abated lightly in the revision of 1870, 16 Stat. 198, 214, which provided that in the case of "a map, chart, musical composition, print, cut, engraving, photograph, painting, drawing, chromo, statue, statuary, or model or design intended to be perfected and completed as a work of the fine arts," the notice must be placed "upon some portion of the face or front thereof, or on the face of the substance on which the same shall be mounted."

The act of 1874, 18 Stat. 78, 79, completely eliminated all references to "face or front," and required instead only that in the case of the items specified above the notice appear "upon some visible portion thereof, or of the substance on which the same shall be mounted." Even this liberalized requirement was apparently thought too restrictive, however, since Congress added a special section in 1882, 22 Stat. 181, permitting "manufacturers of designs for molded decorative articles, tiles, plaques, or articles of pottery or metal subject to copyright" to place the notice "upon the back or bottom of such articles, or in such other place upon them as it has heretofore been usual . . . to employ for the placing of . . . trade marks thereon."

The original House and Senate bills leading to the Copyright Act of 1909 continued the century old practice of prescribing the possible location of notice, but they expanded still further the number of such locations. Section 14 of H.R. 19853 and S. 6330, 59th Cong., 1st Sess. (1906), provided that in the case of maps, works of art, models or designs for works of art, reproductions of a work of art, etc., the notice "shall be applied . . . upon some accessible portion of the work itself or of the margin, back, permanent base or pedestal thereof, or of the substance on which the work shall be mounted." In the act as finally passed, however, 35 Stat. 1075, 1079 (1909), a specific requirement for location of notice was retained only in the case of books or other printed publications, musical compositions, and periodicals. All other items were left subject only to the general requirement, now embodied in 17 U.S.C. §10, that the notice be affixed to each copy.

In the light of this legislative history it is surely incredible that Congress would have intended, by implication in section 19, to revive the requirement of the 1802 and 1831 acts that notice appear on the front. All the copyright legislation of the nineteenth century had prescribed in unambiguous terms the permissible location of notice, and the 1909 revision contained a section dealing specifically with the location of notice and prescribed such location only for three types of items. Thus the failure to limit the placement of notice for other items does not arise from any lack of familiarity with the drafting devices necessary to accomplish that result. Section 19 should not be read to impose a restriction on placement which, had it been intended by Congress, would certainly have been expressly stated.

Defendant's restrictive view of section 19 is also inconsistent with a large body of judicial authority upholding notices which are not on the "front" of the work of art. This court and the District Court for the Southern District of New York have recently rendered a number of decisions upholding copyrighted works of art on dress fabric where the notice appeared on the selvage or margin of the fabric, rather than on the design itself. *Peter Pan Fabrics, Inc. v. Martin Weiner Corp.*, 2 Cir., 274 F.2d 487, *Peter Pan Fabrics, Inc. v. Dixon Textile Corp.*, 2 Cir., 280 F.2d 800, 802; *Peter Pan Fabrics, Inc. v. Candy Frocks, Inc.*, D.C. S.D.N.Y., 187 F. Supp 334; *H. M. Kolbe Co. v. Armgus Textile Co.*, D.C. S.D.N.Y., 184 F. Supp. 423, *affirmed* 2 Cir., 279 F.2d 555. We have also sustained a copyright on a pair of earrings, though the notice was stamped upon only one earring of a pair. *Boucher v. Du Boyes, Inc.*, 2 Cir., 253 F.2d 948, *certiorari denied* 357 U.S. 936, 73 S. Ct. 1384, 2 L. Ed. 2d 1550. In *Scarves by Vera, Inc. v. United Merchants & Mfrs., Inc.*, D.C. S.D.N.Y., 173 F. Supp. 625, works of art contained on ladies' blouses were copyrighted by a notice upon a label sewed into a side seam. Perhaps the best summary of the applicable principle may be found in the decision of Judge Bicks in *Trifari, Krussman & Fishel, Inc. v. Charel Co.*, D.C. S.D.N.Y., 134 F. Supp. 551, 554, enjoining the copying of costume jewelry, copyrighted as a work of art, where the notice appeared on the clasp. He stated: "It is so located, however, as to apprise anyone seeking to copy the article, of the existence of the copyright and is, therefore, sufficient to satisfy the statutory requirements." See also *Shapiro, Bernstein & Co. v. Jerry Vogel Music Co.*, 2 Cir., 161 F.2d 406, *certiorari denied* 331 U.S. 820, 67 S. Ct. 1310, 91 L. Ed. 1837; *Fleischer Studios v. Ralph A. Freundlich, Inc.*, 2 Cir., 73 F.2d 276, *certiorari denied Ralph A. Freundlich, Inc. v. Fleischer Studios*, 294 U.S. 717, 55 S. Ct. 516, 79 L. Ed. 1250.

Defendant also suggests that the notice, having been pasted on by a gummed label, was not "affixed" within the meaning of section 10. We find that it was "affixed." The point does not require discussion.

On remand it would seem appropriate that the court grant the plaintiff's motion for summary judgment, since the defendant has admitted copying plaintiff's plaques. We shall leave to the district court the settling of appropriate remedies.

Judgment reversed and action remanded for proceedings in accordance with this opinion.

§2.6.3. *Scherr v. Universal Match Corp.:* How Visible Must Notice Be?

While a copyright notice need not be on the face or front of a work, the 1909 Copyright Act expressly required that it must be "accessible." The *Scherr* case, which follows, indicates that there are limits to what met this test. Although not an explicit holding (since the court found the work to be a work made for hire), the opinion is instructive for its discussion concerning the placement of the notice on the particular statue, which was 12-feet tall and stood on a 3-foot pile of rocks atop a 12-foot base. The notice had been placed on the uppermost panel, close to the back of the statue, about 22-feet from the ground. The court observed, "it is impossible for anyone standing on the ground to see the notice."

Under the present Copyright Act, would such a notice be "reasonable"? Probably not.

SCHERR v. UNIVERSAL MATCH CORPORATION
297 F. Supp. 107 (S.D.N.Y. 1967)

McGOHEY, D.J. The defendants in this copyright infringement action moved for summary judgment dismissing the complaint on the ground that the subject matter, a statue made at Government expense by soldiers assigned to do so while on active military duty, is a publication of the United States Government and thus is not copyrightable;[1] and that in any event the claimed copyright is invalid for failure of the plaintiffs to affix an adequate notice of copyright to the statue.[2] The latter depicts a charging infantryman in battle dress and is entitled "The Ultimate Weapon."

The action arises from defendant Universal's production and distribution, with the authorization of the Army, of books of matches bearing on the cover a picture of the statue and the legend: "Home of The Ultimate Weapon Fort Dix, N.J." The United States (the Government), not originally named as a defendant, intervened. It asks, additionally, that if the copyright is held valid, it be ordered assigned to the Government as an employer under the "works for hire" rule.[3]

The court finds there is no genuine issue as to any material fact. Summary judgment in favor of the defendants is granted to the extent and for the reasons hereafter stated.

---

[1] 17 U.S.C. §8.

[2] 17 U.S.C. §19.

[3] 17 U.S.C. §26.

The plaintiffs are two ex-servicemen. Goodman served in the Army from April 1957 to April 1959; Scherr from October 1957 to October 1959. Both men, prior to induction, had had education and experience in the fine arts. They were assigned as illustrators to Headquarters Company at Fort Dix, New Jersey, where their duties included the preparation of visual training aids. During his free time, Goodman, using supplies given him by the post hobby shop, began to make a small model of an infantryman which was brought to the attention of the deputy post commander. The latter expressed interest in having constructed a larger statue of an infantryman which would serve as a symbol of Fort Dix. After some preliminary research as to the feasibility of such a project it was agreed that Goodman and Scherr would undertake it. Both men were thereupon relieved of their regular duties as illustrators and they set about to create the proposed statue. With the exception of a few "KP" details and barracks inspections, the plaintiffs devoted all of their regular duty hours, and some of their free time, to the work for a period of nine months.

In the design stage, the plaintiffs used other servicemen, assigned by the Army, as models and photographs of these men taken by Government furnished photographers. The first step in the actual construction of the statue was the making of an "armature" out of scrap metal obtained from various "dumps" located on the base. Sculpt-Metal,[4] which was then applied to the armature, was molded to form the figure of a charging infantryman in battle dress and equipment. The body above the waist is bent forward and on the back, just over the belt, is a field pack. This is boxlike in shape and appears to hang from suspenders which also support a belt. Its front and back panels are of equal size and almost square in dimension. Narrower panels joining the front and back form the other four sides of the box. The completed figure was sprayed with numerous alternate coats of bronze finish and clear lacquer. Most of this work was done in the heavy equipment section of the post engineers' shop at Fort Dix.

The plaintiffs were assisted by two other servicemen who, in addition to the models, had been assigned as part of their regular duty to work on the project.[5] Furthermore, all heavy equipment and the operators there-

---

[4] Sculpt-Metal is a material which can be applied directly to the armature and molded before it hardens, thus saving the time and expense of casting the statue. Goodman had previously worked with this material [Deposition, p.19], although Scherr had not [Deposition, p.60]. During the research phase of the project, both men went to Pittsburgh where they were given technical information and instruction regarding the use of Sculpt-Metal. For this trip, plaintiffs were given the use of a Government truck, and while in Pittsburgh they were billeted overnight at a missile base. When they returned to Fort Dix they were reimbursed for whatever expenses they had incurred.

[5] Plaintiffs were also assisted by soldiers from the stockade. Goodman Deposition, p.41.

for, plus masons, carpenters, blacksmiths and machinists were supplied by the Army. The plaintiffs' only out-of- pocket expenses, estimated to be less than $25 each, were for tools and books. Goodman's car was also used for various errrands around the base. The total estimated cost to the Army was more than $12,000.[6] During the course of the project the plaintiffs prepared and submitted progress reports to their superiors. Although the plaintiffs had complete freedom in the design, at one point the officer in charge of the project, noting what he deemed a similarity between Goodman's face and that on the statue, ordered the latter to be changed, which was done. The statue was unveiled on March 20, 1959, and remains on display at Infantry Park, Fort Dix, a site selected by the Army. The title of the statue was also selected by the Army. The claim of copyright in the names of plaintiffs was registered[7] in June 1959, approximately three months after the unveiling.

The defendants' primary contention is that the statue is a publication of the Government within the meaning of 17 U.S.C. section 8 and is, therefore, not copyrightable. That section provides in pertinent part: "No copyright shall subsist . . . in any publication of the United States Government, or in any reprint, in whole or in part, thereof. . . ." The precise scope of the phrase "publication of the United States Government," has long been a source of conflict and concern, as a result of which many definitions and criteria have been suggested for categorizing various works as within or without the prohibition of the section.[8] The issue presented by this motion does not, however, fall within the ambit of this confusion, since in all discussions of the problem, there seems to be unanimous, albeit tacit, agreement that "publications of the United States Government" refers to printed works.[9] This conclusion is given

---

[6] During the course of the project, Scherr kept a diary [U.S.A. ex. 1 *id.*]. The Army's estimated total cost, $12,367.90, was based in part on the entries in this diary. The Army estimates [U.S.A. ex. 8 *id.*] was conceded by Scherr to be "basically accurate." Scherr Deposition, p.71.

[7] 17 U.S.C. §11.

[8] See, e.g., Berger, Copyright in Government Publications, Study No. 33, in Copyright Law Revision, Report of the Register of Copyrights and Studies Nos. 1-34 (1961); Howell, Copyright Law 47 (rev. ed. 1962); Nimmer, Copyright §66 (1964); 12 ASCAP Copyright Law Symposium 96 (1961); 11 ASCAP Copyright Law Symposium 138 (1960); 8 ASCAP Copyright Law Symposium 3 (1957); Comment, 17 Rutgers L. Rev. 579 (1963). Berger, *supra* at 30 notes:

The confusion may be traceable to the dual meaning of the word "publication"; it may refer to the act of reproducing and distributing copies (printing and distribution by the Government), or it may refer to the work that is being published (a work produced by the Government, i.e., produced for the Government by its employees).

[9] Berger, *supra* note 8 at 35-36 ["In addition to the private use of Government publications for advertising purposes, instances have occurred in which Government publications have been reproduced and sold at high prices without indicat-

added weight by the correspondence of language used to circumscribe the prohibitions found in the Copyright Act and in the Printing Law;[10] and is further buttressed by the fundamental purpose underlying the prohibition which is based on "the necessity of wide public dissemination of the contents of materials produced by and relating to issues and problems of national interest [which] policy is unquestionably a desirable one in a democracy, much of whose success is dependent on a well-informed public." [11] The statue in question, it is concluded, is not a "publication of the United States Government" within the meaning of 17 U.S.C. §8.

The defendants next contend that the copyright notice is inadequate, that the claimed copyright is thus invalid and that "The Ultimate Weapon" is, therefore, in the public domain.[12] The statue is twelve feet tall and stands on a pile of rocks about three feet high which, in turn, stands on a base about twelve feet high. Affixed to this base are two plaques, one of which bears the legend: "The Ultimate Weapon — The only indispensable instrument of war — The fighting man." The smaller plaque bears the names of plaintiffs and of the two men who assisted them. Plaintiffs did not affix their notice of copyright to this base, either as part of one of the plaques or separately, because they feared the repercussions, real or imagined, of the Army. Before the unveiling, the statue, without the pack, was taken from the engineers' shop and placed in position on its base. Scherr, unknown to his superiors, then placed a

---

ing their origin as Government *documents*. . . ." (Emphasis added.)]; Comment, 17 Rutgers L. Rev. 579 at 581 (1960) [The problem is to find criteria for determining "what makes a particular *writing* a Government publication." (Emphasis added.)]. See also, Howell, *supra* note 8 at 47; Nimmer, *supra* note 8 at 267.

[10] See Public Affairs Associates, Inc. v. Rickover, 109 U.S. App. D.C. 128, 284 F.2d 262, 268 (1960), *vacated and remanded*, 369 U.S. 111, 82 S. Ct. 580, 7 L. Ed. 2d 604 (1962). Compare 17 U.S.C. §8 with 44 U.S.C. §58. See Berger, *supra* note 8 at 29-33.

[11] 12 ASCAP Copyright Law Symposium 96 at 105 (1961). Among the other reasons for the prohibition "there is the feeling that if a *literary* product was produced at public expense by a government employee it should be freely available to the public, and the author should not be allowed to impede its free circulation by securing a copyright thereon. . . ." (Emphasis added.) Also, there is

the feeling that the public at large is entitled to make whatever use it desires of materials and publications produced at government expense, inasmuch as the Government is supported by the people. Apparently, Congress felt that this interest of the public outweighs any need to prevent possible abuses which may occur through distortion, misquotation or excessive pricing of government materials which are privately reproduced.

11 ASCAP Copyright Law Symposium 138 at 141 (1960).

[12] Gray v. Eskimo Pie Corp., 244 F. Supp. 785, 788 (D. Del. 1965).

notice of copyright in proper form to the uppermost panel of the pack which he then attached firmly to the back of the soldier. The notice is located close to that back and about twenty-two feet from the ground. It is impossible for anyone standing on the ground to see the notice. In order to do so, one would have to get astride the back of the figure or, in some manner, get positioned above it.[13]

Section 10 of the Copyright Act provides: "Any person entitled thereto by this title may secure copyright for his work by publication thereof with the notice of copyright required by this title. . . ." Section 19 of the Act provides, with respect to *copies* of works of art, that "The notice of copyright required by section 10 . . . may consist of the letter C enclosed within a circle . . . accompanied by the initials, monogram, mark or symbol of the copyright proprietor; *Provided,* That on some accessible portion of such copies or of the margin, back, permanent base, or pedestal, or of the substance on which such copies shall be mounted, his name shall appear." Defendants do not contend that any of the requisite contents of the notice are missing,[14] but rather that the notice is inadequate because it is improperly placed.

The present Act is silent as to where the notice should appear on works of art.[15] However, the unquestioned purpose of the notice requirement is to apprise anyone seeking to copy the article, of the existence of the copyright. . . ."[16] This purpose was clearly frustrated by plaintiffs who, in their own words, sought to make the notice as inconspicuous as possible,[17] an objective they achieved with singular success. Furthermore, although the Certificate of Registration obtained by plaintiffs is prima facie evidence of the validity of the copyright,[18] the defendants have rebutted this presumption by showing that the notice did not fulfill the

---

[13] Goodman Deposition, pp.59-60; Scherr Deposition, p.110.

[14] The notice affixed by plaintiffs contains a letter C enclosed within a circle; the names Stuart Scherr and Steven Goodman; and the date, 1959.

[15] For a thorough discussion of the prior law, see Coventry Ware, Inc. v. Reliance Picture Frame Co., 288 F.2d 193 (2d Cir.), *cert. denied,* 368 U.S. 818, 82 S. Ct. 34, 7 L. Ed. 2d 24 (1961). See also, Nimmer *supra* note 8 at §87.6 to the effect that where the location of the notice is not prescribed it may be placed anywhere so long as it gives reasonable notice of the claim of copyright.

[16] Coventry Ware, Inc. v. Reliance Picture Frame Co., *supra* note 15 at 195, citing Trifari, Krussman & Fishel, Inc. v. Charel Co., 134 F. Supp. 551,554 (S.D.N.Y. 1955). See also Ted Arnold Ltd. v. Silvercraft, Inc., 259 F. Supp. 733 (S.D.N.Y. 1966); Dan Kasoff, Inc. v. Gresco Jewelry Co., 204 F. Supp. 694 (S.D.N.Y.), *aff'd per curiam,* 308 F.2d 806 (2d Cir. 1962).

[17] Goodman Deposition, p.50; Scherr Deposition, p.109. Additionally, Scherr, when questioned by a JAC officer, stated that he had no copyright.

[18] Flick-Reedy Corp. v. Hydro-Line Mfg. Co., 351 F.2d 546 (7th Cir.), *cert. denied,* 383 U.S. 958, 86 S. Ct. 1222, 16 L. Ed. 2d 301 (1965); Manes Fabric Co. v. Miss Celebrity, Inc., 246 F. Supp. 975 (S.D.N.Y. 1965).

statutory purpose — a purpose which plaintiffs had no intention of fulfilling. Since its unveiling, "The Ultimate Weapon" has at all times been, and is today, on view at Infantry Park, a site open to the public. During this time there has never been any restriction, posted or otherwise, on the copying or photographing of the statue.[19] Because the statue was displayed without restriction as to either persons or purpose[20] and without adequate notice, it is concluded that there was divestive publication under an invalid copyright such as to place "The Ultimate Weapon" in the public domain.[21]

However, even if the copyright notice were valid the plaintiffs would not be entitled to any of the benefits of the copyright protection because, as the defendants contend, the statue falls within the "works for hire" rule of 17 U.S.C. §26 and, therefore, any and all copyright interest in the statue belongs to, or inures to the benefit of, the Government.[22]

---

[19] Affidavit of James L. R. Ward, a Civilian Special Services Officer who has been employed at Fort Dix continuously since 1955.

[20] Continental Cas. Co. v. Beardsley, 253 F.2d 702, 706-707 (2d Cir.), *cert. denied*, 358 U.S. 816, 79 S. Ct. 25, 3 L. Ed. 2d 58 (1958).

[21] Ball, Copyright and Literary Property §62 (1944); Cary, The Quiet Revolution in Copyright, 35 Geo. Wash. L. Rev. 652, 659-60 (1967). Compare Carns v. Keefe Bros., 242 F. 745 (D.Mont. 1917) with Werckmeister v. American Lithographic Co., 134 F. 321 (2d Cir. 1904). Compare also Howell, *supra* note 8 at 66 with Nimmer, *supra* note 8 at 212-13.

[22] Section 26 provides in part: "In the interpretation and construction of this title . . . the word 'author' shall include an employer in the case of works made for hire." The initial question to be decided is whether an employment relationship existed. Nimmer, *supra* note 8 at §62.2 states: "The crucial question in determining an employment relationship is whether the alleged employer has the right to direct and supervise the manner in which the writer performs his work. This is, of course, merely a particular application of the general agency doctrine relating to master and servant." (Footnote omitted.) Under this test, there clearly was an employment relationship. Furthermore, "one may be an employee regardless of whether he is paid on the basis of a conventional periodic salary, on a piece work basis, on a fee or royalty basis, or even if the writing is done as an accommodation with no compensation at all." *Id.*

See Sawyer v. Crowell Publishing Co., 142 F.2d 497, 499 (2d Cir.), *cert. denied*, 323 U.S. 735, 65 S. Ct. 74, 89 L. Ed. 589 (1944), *affirming* 46 F. Supp. 471 (S.D.N.Y. 1942): "We conclude therefore that the district court was right in holding that any rights which Mr. Sawyer acquired by copyrighting the map [of Alaska prepared by Mr. Sawyer, the Executive Assistant to the Secretary of the Interior, in connection with an assignment in Alaska] must be held in trust for the United States." See also, United States Ozone Co. v. United States Ozone Co., 62 F.2d 881 (7th Cir. 1932); 7 Ops. Att'y Gen. 656 (1856). Compare, United States v. First Trust Co., 251 F.2d 686 (8th Cir. 1958) with Sherill v. Grieves, 57 Wash. L. Rep. 286, 20 Cpyrt. Off. Bull. 675 (Sup. Ct. D.C. 1929). In Sawyer the Government did not intervene and ask for an assignment of the copyright as was done in the instant case. However, in light of our holding of invalidity we do not reach the question of whether the Government is entitled to an assignment of the copyright

Various criteria have been suggested for determining whether a given work was made for hire, among these being whether the work was produced within the "scope of employment," and, whether the work was produced on the employer's time and using the employer's facilities.[23] Applying these criteria to the instant facts, it appears that the statue was a work made for hire. The plaintiffs were relieved of their regular duties and assigned to designing and constructing what eventually became "The Ultimate Weapon." During this period they were under military supervision, receiving their pay and their instructions from the Government, and, further, being supplied by the Government with all the equipment and materials necessary to complete their work.

The plaintiffs' counterargument is three-pronged: they claim that they were relieved of their "official duties" as opposed to their regular duties; that the work was created in a field outside their official classification as illustrators; and finally, that during the course of the nine months they worked on the statue they expended some of their own time and money and used some of their own materials. The first two contentions are not persuasive. The regular duties assigned to the plaintiffs were their official duties. When they were initially assigned to Headquarters Company their Military Occupational Specialty [MOS] was 814.10 which is that of illustrator. Upon being assigned to work on the statue they were not reclassified or given a new MOS, despite the fact that the MOS most closely corresponding to the sculpting they were performing was 815, that of model builder.[24] However, the fact that they were not reclassified does not alter the nature or character of their work for the purposes here being considered. The Army regulations, in fact provide for the assignment of work outside one's MOS if such an assignment is in the best interests of the Army;[25] and, although reclassification should follow, no

---

or whether its remedy is limited to having a judicial declaration that the copyright is held in trust for it. See Ball, *supra* note 21 §219 at 481; 12 ASCAP Copyright Law Symposium 98 n.8 (1961).

[23] Nimmer, *supra* note 8 §66 at 267; 12 Syracuse L. Rev. 515, 516 (1961). See also Public Affairs Associates, Inc. v. Rickover, 369 U.S. 111, 82 S. Ct. 580, 7 L. Ed. 2d 604 (1962). In Brattleboro Publishing Co. v. Winmill Publishing Corp., 369 F.2d 565 (2nd Cir. 1966) the court stated that the works for hire doctrine "is applicable whenever an employee's work is produced at the instance and expense of his employer." *Id.* at 567.

[24] The work which plaintiffs performed would not fall clearly within the MOS for Model Maker, either. Army Reg. 611-201 at 801 (20 May 1959) defines the duties of a model maker as follows: "Constructs scale models of terrain, bridges, military vehicles and weapons, using materials such as wood, paper maché, plastics and metal."

[25] Army Reg. 611-203 §33(e) (7 March 1955) provided: "When an assignment in the primary advanced MOS is not possible it will be made in the most closely-related MOS."

rights, penalties or other consequences attend failure of reclassification.[26]

The plaintiffs' final contention, that they expended their own time and money carries little weight. For one thing, the Army spent over $12,000, whereas plaintiffs, by their own estimates, spent less than $50 between them. Furthermore, they make no claim that they requested the Army to furnish them with supplies they claim to have purchased with their own funds, nor do they suggest that they requested and were denied reimbursement. Goodman, in fact, testified that although he expended money in the use of his own car, he never requested a Government vehicle. Under the plaintiffs' interpretation, any employee could circumvent the "works for hire" rule by expending a comparatively small amount of his own time and/or money on a project arising out of and performed within the scope of his employment. This contention is rejected.

Summary judgment in favor of the defendants may be entered in accordance herewith.

So ordered.

§2.6.4. *Letter Edged in Black Press, Inc. v. Building Commission:* **Picasso and the Public Domain**

There is no more important name in the history of twentieth-century art than that of Pablo Picasso. He revolutionized every aspect of visual conception and produced images that evoked his unique, overpowering persona. It probably would have seemed to him a cruel, but perhaps harmless, joke that one of his creations — the major sculpture he conceived for the city of Chicago — should have been the subject of a major American copyright case. The *Letter Edged in Black Press* case, which follows, provides fascinating reading concerning the care that must be taken to protect the copyright in a work of art. Publicity and copyright are both techniques to merchandise a unique product; careless handling of the former can unfortunately destroy the latter.

---

[26] Army Reg. 611-203 §35 (16 Sept. 1957) provided that when assignment was not possible within an individual's primary advanced MOS such "individual will be considered misassigned and will be reported for reassignment. . . . Pending reassignment or reclassification, the soldier will be assigned to duty in accordance with the following priorities: (1) MOS in the same entry group (1st two digits of MOS). . . ." The plaintiffs were assigned to work in accordance with this subdivision.

LETTER EDGED IN BLACK PRESS, INC. v. PUBLIC BUILDING COMMISSION
320 F. Supp. 1303 (N.D. Ill. 1970)

NAPOLI, D.J. Plaintiff seeks a declaratory judgment invalidating defendant's copyright to the Pablo Picasso sculpture entitled "The Chicago Picasso." The defendant is the Public Building Commission of Chicago (Commission) and the plaintiff is a publisher who desires to market a copy of the sculpture. Pursuant to Rule 56 of the Federal Rules of Civil Procedure both parties have moved for summary judgment. Succinctly, plaintiff maintains that defendant's copyright is invalid because the sculpture is in the public domain. Defendant asserts that "The Chicago Picasso" has never been in the public domain.

STATEMENT OF FACTS

In 1963 certain of the Civic Center architects, representing the Commission, approached Picasso with a request to design a monumental sculpture for the plaza in front of the proposed Chicago Civic Center. By May, 1965, Picasso completed the maquette (model) of the sculpture. William E. Hartmann, the architect, who had been the chief liaison with Picasso, then had the maquette brought to the basement of the Art Institute of Chicago, without public notice. The design of the maquette was subjected to an engineering analysis to determine the feasibility of constructing the monumental sculpture and three Chicago charitable foundations undertook to finance the actual construction by contributing $300,000 toward the total cost of $351,959.17. An aluminum model of the design with some slight revisions was prepared as a guide to the construction of the sculpture, and Picasso approved a picture of this model on August 9, 1966.

The Commission, through its board, had been given a private viewing of the maquette. Subsequently, the Commission passed a resolution authorizing the payment of $100,000 to Picasso. This sum was intended as the purchase price for the entire right, title and interest in and to the maquette constituting Picasso's design for the monumental sculpture including the copyright, and copyright renewals. Hartmann proffered the $100,000 check to Picasso and asked the artist to sign a document referred to as the "Formal Acknowledgement and Receipt." Picasso refused to accept the money or to sign the document. He stated that he wanted to make a gift of his work. In accordance with Picasso's wish, counsel for Commission and William Hartmann prepared the following "Deed of Gift" which Picasso signed on August 21, 1966:

> The monumental sculpture portrayed by the maquette pictured above has been expressly created by me, Pablo Picasso, for installation on the plaza of the Civic Center in the City of Chicago, State of Illinois, United States of

America. This sculpture was undertaken by me for the Public Building Commission of Chicago at the request of William E. Hartmann, acting on behalf of the Chicago Civic Center architects. I hereby give this work and the right to reproduce it to the Public Building Commission, and I give the maquette to the Art Institute of Chicago, desiring that these gifts shall, through them, belong to the people of Chicago.

In the fall of 1966 the Commission, the public relations department of the City of Chicago, the Art Institute of Chicago and the U.S. Steel Corporation, the latter being the prime contractor for the construction of the sculpture, began a campaign to publicize "The Chicago Picasso." The campaign was directed by Hartmann, with help from Al Weisman head of the public relations department of the advertising firm of Foote, Cone and Belding.

As part of the campaign at least two press showings were conducted. The first was held on September 20, 1966, when the maquette was placed on public exhibition at the Art Institute. No copyright notice was affixed to the maquette. The following notice was however, posted in the Art Institute:

> The rights of reproduction are the property of the Public Building Commission of Chicago. © 1966. All Rights Reserved.

Press photographers attended the showing at the invitation of the Commission and the Art Institute and later published pictures of the maquette and aluminum model in Chicago newspapers and in magazines of national and international circulation. In addition the Commission supplied photographs of the maquette and the uncopyrighted architect's aluminum model to the members of the public who requested them for publication. The second showing took place in December of 1966 when the U.S. Steel Corporation, with the knowledge of the Commission, had completed a twelve-foot six-inch wooden model of the sculpture and invited the press to photograph the model. There was no copyright notice on the model and the pictures were published without copyright notice. U.S. Steel also hired a professional photographer to take pictures of the model and these pictures were used in the publicity drive.

The drive was seemingly successful for pictures of the Picasso design appeared in Business Week Magazine on May 6, 1967, and in Holiday Magazine in March, 1967. Fortune Magazine published three pages of color photographs about "The Chicago Picasso" including pictures of the U.S. Steel wooden model. The Chicago Sun Times, Midwest magazine published a cover story on the sculpture with a drawing of the maquette on the cover of the magazine. And a picture of the maquette was printed in U.S. Steel News, a house organ with a circulation of over 300,000. None of the photographs or drawings that were published in the above named publications bore any copyright notice whatever.

From June, 1967, through August 13, 1967, the maquette was displayed at the Tate Gallery in London, England. In conjunction with the exhibit at the Tate, a catalog was published wherein a picture of the maquette appeared. Neither on the maquette itself nor on the photograph in the catalog did copyright notice appear. The Commission had knowledge of these facts for on July 6, 1967, Hartmann had sent to the Chairman of the Commission the catalog which was placed in the Commission files.

On August 15, 1967, the monumental sculpture, "The Chicago Picasso" was dedicated in ceremonies on the Civic Center Plaza. The sculpture bore the following copyright:

© 1967 PUBLIC BUILDING COM-
MISSION OF CHICAGO ALL
RIGHTS RESERVED

At the dedication, Mr. Hartmann, co-chairman of the event and master of ceremonies said: "Pablo Picasso . . . as you know gave the creation of the sculpture to the people of Chicago and his maquette to the Art Institute of Chicago." The Chairman of the Public Building Commission, in his speech of dedication to the approximately 50,000 persons assembled for the ceremony said: "It's an occasion we've all been anticipating — the dedication of this great gift to our city by the world-renowned artist, Pablo Picasso," and "I dedicate this gift in the name of Chicago and wish it an abiding and happy stay in the City's heart."

In conjunction with the dedication a commemorative souvenir booklet of "The Chicago Picasso" dedication ceremonies was prepared by the Commission. The booklet which contained drawings and photographs of the maquette and the aluminum model were distributed to 96 distinguished men and women from all areas of Chicago life and to honored guests. Neither the booklet itself, nor any of the photographs shown therein bore any copyright notice. Also, on the day of dedication the United States Steel public relations office sent out a press release together with a photo of the monumental sculpture. The photograph bore no copyright notice.

Subsequent to the dedication, the Art Institute published its Annual Report which contained an uncopyrighted picture of the maquette. This publication had a circulation of 40,000 copies, including museums and libraries. The Art Institute also continued selling a photograph of the maquette on a postcard. Between October 1966 and October 1967, 800 copies of this postcard were sold. In 1967, however, the Commission asked the Art Institute to stop selling the postcard and the Art Institute complied with this request.

In October 1967, the Commission caused to be engraved in the granite base of the sculpture the following legend:

CHICAGO PICASSO
THE CREATION OF THE SCULPTURE WAS GIVEN TO THE PEOPLE
OF CHICAGO BY THE ARTIST PABLO PICASSO
THE ERECTION OF THE SCULPTURE WAS MADE POSSIBLE
THROUGH THE GENEROSITY OF WOODS CHARITABLE FUND, INC.
CHAUNCEY AND MARION DEERING McCORMICK FOUNDATION
FIELD FOUNDATION OF ILLINOIS DEDICATED AUGUST 15, 1967
RICHARD J. DALEY, MAYOR.

In November, 1967, the Commission stated its policy that no individuals shall be restricted from "full personal enjoyment of the sculpture, including the right to take photographs and make paintings, etchings and models of the same for personal, non-commercial purposes." The Commission has also had a policy of granting licenses to copy the sculpture for commercial purposes. The Commission requires payment of a nominal fee and a royalty on copies sold. Several such licenses have been granted.

Finally, on January 12, 1968, the Public Building Commission filed its application with the Register of Copyrights asking a copyright in the monumental sculpture entitled "The Chicago Picasso." In due course a certificate of copyright registration was issued to defendant.

STATEMENT OF APPLICABLE LAW

Defendant submits that the attaching of notice to the monumental sculpture on August 4, 1967, and the later registration of the copyright were acts sufficient to obtain a statutory copyright under 17 U.S.C. §10[1] and 17 U.S.C. §11.[2] This attempt to establish a statutory copyright must fail, however, if "The Chicago Picasso" was in the public domain prior to August 4, 1967. Such a conclusion is inescapable given the statutory admonition of 17 U.S.C. §8 that "[n]o copyright shall subsist in the original text of any work which is in the public domain. . . ."

To determine how a work comes to be in the public domain it is necessary to explore the basis of the copyright protection. The common law copyright arises upon the creation of any work of art, be it a first

---

[1] Publication of work with notice:

Any person entitled thereto by this title may secure copyright for his work by publication thereof with the notice of copyright required by this title; and such notice shall be affixed to each copy thereof published or offered for sale in the United States by authority of the copyright proprietor, except in the case of books seeking ad interim protection under section 22 of this title. July 30, 1947, c.391, §1, 61 Stat. 652.

[2] Registration of claim and issuance of certificate:

Such person may obtain registration of his claim to copyright by complying with the provisions of this title, including the deposit of copies, and upon such compliance the Register of Copyrights shall issue to him the certificates provided for in section 209 of this title. July 30, 1947, c.391, §1, 61 Stat. 652.

sketch or the finished product.[3] This common law right protects against unauthorized copying, publishing, vending, performing, and recording.[4] The common law copyright is terminated by publication of the work[5] by the proprietor[6] of the copyright. Upon termination of the common law copyright, the work falls into the public domain if statutory protection is not obtained by the giving of the requisite notice.[7]

In some of the early English decisions there was debate as to whether publication did indeed divest its owner of common law protection.[8] Arguing that divestment should not occur upon publication, because of the seeming irrationality of such a rule, Lord Mansfield observed: " 'The copy is made common, because the law does not protect it: and the law cannot protect it because it is made common.' "[9]

In the United States, however, it has been clear, from the date the question first reached the Supreme Court, that the common law copyright is terminated upon the first publication.[10] And as Judge Learned Hand noted in *National Comics Publications v. Fawcett Publications*,[11] citing *Donaldson v. Becket*,[12] "It is of course true that the publication of a copyrightable 'work' puts that 'work' into the public domain except so far as it may be protected by copyright. That has been unquestioned law since 1774."

One justification for the doctrine, that publication ipso facto divests an author of common law copyright protection, can be found in the copyright clause of the United States Constitution.[13] Protection is granted, but

---

[3] Gold, Protection of the Artist and Sculptor Under the Law of Copyrights, 22 U. Pitt. L. Rev. 710 (1961); Nimmer on Copyright, section 11.2, Matthew Bender Co. (1970).

[4] Nimmer, *ibid*, section 111.

[5] Donaldson v. Becket, *infra*, note 8; Wheaton v. Peters, *infra*, note 10; and National Comics Publications v. Fawcett Publications, *infra*, note 11.

[6] The proprietor may be the original creator or one to whom the copyright has been given or conveyed. Nimmer, *supra*, note 3, section 120.1; Van Cleef and Arpels, Inc. v. Schechter, 308 F. Supp. 674 (S.D.N.Y. 1969).

[7] Donaldson v. Becket, *infra*, note 8; Wheaton v. Peters, *infra*, note 10; and National Comics Publications v. Fawcett Publications, *infra*, note 11.

[8] Millar v. Taylor, 4 Burr. 2303, 98 Eng. rep. 201 (1769 KB); contra, Donaldson v. Becket, 4 Burr. 2408 (1774).

[9] Millar v. Taylor, *ibid*, at 2399.

[10] Wheaton v. Peters, 33 U.S. 591, 8 Pet. 591, 8 L. Ed. 1055 (1834).

[11] National Comics Publications v. Fawcett Publications, 191 F.2d 594, 598 (2nd Cir. 1951).

[12] Donaldson v. Becket, *supra*, note 8.

[13] "To promote the Progress of Science and useful Arts, by securing for limited times to Authors and Inventors the exclusive Right to their respective Writings and Discoveries," U.S. Const. Art. I, sec. 8, cl. 8.

only "for limited times." The inclusion of this caveat in the Constitution makes manifest the right of society to ultimately claim free access to materials which may prove essential to the growth of society. The copyright clause, however, does not impinge on the right of privacy of a creator. An author who refrains from publication and uses his work for his own pleasure may enjoy the common law copyright protection in perpetuity.[14] Once a work is published, however, the Constitution dictates that the time for which the statutory copyright protection is accorded starts to run. An author is not allowed to publish a work and then after a period of time has elapsed choose to invoke statutory copyright protection. If the statutory protection is not acquired at the time of publication by appropriate notice, the work is lost to the public domain. Any other rule would permit avoidance of the "limited times" provision of the Constitution.

An exception to this rule is that a limited publication does not divest the holder of his common law protection.[15] A good definition of limited publication can be found in *White v. Kimmell*[16] wherein the court found that a limited publication "which communicates the contents of a manuscript to a definitely selected group and for a limited purpose, without the right of diffusion, reproduction, distribution or sale." For example, if an artist shows a painting to a selected group of his friends, for the limited purpose of obtaining their criticism, the publication will be said to be limited and thus not divestive of the artist's common law copyright.

Applying these general principles of copyright law to the facts of the case at bar the court is persuaded that the copyright to the work of art known as "The Chicago Picasso" is invalid. General publication occurred without the requisite notice. Accordingly, the common law protection was lost upon publication and the work was thrust into the public domain.

While this suit could have been resolved on any one of several distinct theories[16a] the court has decided to base its opinion on the proposition that "The Chicago Picasso" was placed into the public domain prior to

---

[14] Nimmer, *supra*, note 3, section 112.1.

[15] American Tobacco Co. v. Werckmeister, 207 U.S. 284, 28 S. Ct. 72, 52 L. Ed. 208 (1907).

[16] White v. Kimmell, 193 F.2d 744, 746-747 (9th Cir. 1952).

[16a] The court has found it unnecessary to deal with the following issues: 1) Whether a monumental sculpture of the type at issue can be copyrighted. See Carns et al. v. Keefe Bros. 242 F 745 (D.C. Mont. 1917); 2) Whether the sculpture was dedicated to the public and thus incapable of being copyrighted; 3)Whether a valid copyright can be maintained where the public is totally free to make copies, albeit for non-commercial use; and 4) Whether uncopyrighted copies of the sculpture published after the dedication caused the sculpture to be placed in the public domain.

the attachment of copyright notice on the monumental sculpture. Accordingly, only cursory reference will be paid to the other issues presented in this action. Even limiting the opinion in this fashion, however, multiple and rather sophisticated argument of the defendant must be met in order to sustain the court's opinion.

DEFENDANT'S CLAIM THAT THE MODELS DID NOT NEED COPYRIGHT NOTICE

The defendant's basic contention is that the work of art is the properly copyrighted monumental sculpture not the models. In support of this thesis defendant correctly points out that what was always envisioned by the Civic Center architects and Picasso was a monumental sculpture for the Civic Center Plaza. There can only be one copyright in one work of art it is asserted,[17] and that work allegedly is the sculpture in the Civic Center Plaza; not the various models used in its development. It is therefore concluded that copyright notice on the models was unnecessary before publication of the monumental sculpture.

The court takes a different view of the facts. When Picasso signed the deed of gift on August 21, 1966, there existed but a single copyright. Picasso had a common law copyright in the maquette. He gave the maquette itself to the Art Institute and the right to reproduce it to the defendant. The monumental sculpture did not exist at this point in time and accordingly there could be no copyright in the monumental sculpture, either common law or statutory. It is settled that a copyright can exist only in a perceptible, tangible work.[18] It can not exist in a vision. When Picasso made his deed of gift the monumental sculpture was undeniably but a vision and thus not subject to copyright protection.

The maquette, however, was an original, tangible work of art which would have qualified for statutory copyright protection under 17 U.S.C. §5(g).[19] The court finds that when the maquette was published without statutory notice Picasso's work was forever lost to the public domain. When the monumental sculpture was finally completed it could not be copyrighted for it was a mere copy, albeit on a grand scale, of the maquette, a work already in the public domain.

---

[17] Adventures in Good Eating, Inc. v. Best Places to Eat, Inc., 131 F.2d 809 (7th Cir. 1942).

[18] Baker v. Selden, 101 U.S. 99, 25 L. Ed. 841 (1879); Nimmer, *supra*, note 3, section 8.2; Katz, Copyright Protection of Architectural Plans, Drawings, and Designs, 19 Law and Contemp. Prob., 224, 232 (1954).

[19] Classification of works for registration: "The application for registration shall specify to which of the following classes the work in which copyright is claimed belongs. . . . (g) Works of art; models or designs for works of art."

DEFENDANT'S CLAIM THAT DISPLAY OF THE MAQUETTE DID NOT CONSTITUTE GENERAL PUBLICATION

Three arguments have been submitted to the effect that display of the maquette did not constitute general publication. First, defendant urges that display of the maquette at the Art Institute was a "limited" publication and thus did not place "The Chicago Picasso" in the public domain. In support of this position the defendant's prime authority is *American Tobacco Co. v. Werckmeister.*[20] In the *American Tobacco* case an English artist painted a picture depicting a company of gentlemen with filled glasses, singing in chorus. The artist transferred the copyright in the picture to the Berlin Photographic Company, which Company made copies of the painting bearing appropriate copyright notice. Immediately subsequent to transferring the copyright the artist, who retained ownership of the painting, placed the picture on exhibit at the Royal Academy. The picture as it hung in the gallery bore no notice of copyright. Several years later the Berlin Photographic Company brought an action claiming that the American Tobacco Company had infringed upon its copyright to the painting. As one of its defenses the American Tobacco Company argued that because the painting had been displayed in a public gallery without copyright notice it had been lost to the public domain and accordingly, the copyright was invalid. The court rejected this argument finding that the display in the gallery amounted to a limited publication and thus did not operate to divest the holder of the copyright of its rights. The basis for this decision was the finding that absolutely no copies were permitted to be made by anyone viewing the picture at the gallery. In fact, it was noted that guards were stationed in the gallery to rigidly enforce the rule of the Royal Academy that no copying take place. The court properly decided that the rational basis for the notice requirement would not be transgressed by showing a picture bearing no notice where that picture could not be copied. In closing dicta the Court in *American Tobacco* noted: "We do not mean to say that the public exhibition of a painting or statue, where all might see and freely copy it, might not amount to publication within the statute, regardless of the artist's purpose or notice of reservation of rights which he takes no measure to protect it."[21]

It is this court's finding that the case at bar more closely resembles the situation postulated in the aforementioned dicta than it does the actual facts of the *American Tobacco* case. In the case at bar there were no restrictions on copying and no guards preventing copying. Rather every

---

[20] American Tobacco Co. v. Werckmeister, *supra,* note 15.

[21] American Tobacco Co. v. Werckmeister, *supra,* note 15, 207 U.S. at 300, 28 S. Ct. at 77.

citizen was free to copy the maquette for his own pleasure and camera permits were available to members of the public.[22] At its first public display the press was freely allowed to photograph the maquette and publish these photographs in major newspapers and magazines. Further, officials at this first public showing of the maquette made uncopyrighted pictures of the maquette available upon request. Were this activity classified as limited publication, there would no longer be any meaningful distinction between limited and general publication. The activity in question does not comport with any definition of limited publication. Rather, the display of the maquette constituted general publication.[23]

Defendant's second assertion is that the display of the maquette was inconsequential since an unpublished work, model thereof, or copy thereof does not require a copyright notice.[24] The court has no quarrel with this statement of law. The problem with this argument, however, is that it begs the question of whether or not there was a general publication. Since there was general publication of the maquette, notice was required.

Finally, defendant argues that the Art Institute did not hold the copyright to the maquette and therefore could not have placed notice on the maquette. The answer to this assertion is that the Commission, the alleged holder of the copyright, was required to insure that proper notice was placed on the maquette. The Commission was able to place a proper notice at the showing, i.e., notice in the room, but it did not comply with the statutory requirement that notice be placed on the work itself in order to be effective.[25]

DEFENDANT'S CLAIM THAT UNCOPYRIGHTED PICTURES COULD BE USED IN THE PUBLICITY CAMPAIGN

The defendant's major defense to the use of uncopyrighted pictures of the models in the publicity drive is what appears to be an inverse application of the doctrine of "fair use." Generally it can be stated that certain acts of copying are defensible as "fair use." [26] The doctrine of fair use, however, was meant to be used and has only been used, as a defense in infringement actions.[27] The defendant can not cite a single authority to support its unique claim that the doctrine can be asserted to excuse a

---

[22] The Art Institute camera regulations do, however, require that permission be obtained in order to use photographic copies of works of art commercially.

[23] Morton v. Raphael, 334 Ill. App. 399, 79 N.E.2d 522 (1948).

[24] Nimmer, *supra*, note 3, section 89.1.

[25] 17 U.S.C. §10 *supra*, note 1.

[26] Nimmer, *supra*, note 3, section 145; Copyright Fair Use — Case Law and Legislation, 1969 Duke L.J. 74.

[27] Nimmer, *supra*, note 3, section 149.

failure to put copyright notice on copies of a work of art intended for distribution to the press. The court after diligent research has also failed to find any support for the defendant's position. It seems appropriate to ask why defendant's desire for wide and favorable distribution of copies of the maquette and the other models could not have been fulfilled by distribution of pictures which had copyright notice printed on them?

Defendant has an additional defense to the uncopyrighted printing of pictures of the maquette, the wooden model, and the aluminum model. It is contended that the copies of the work of art that appeared in various newspapers and magazines without notice did not amount to divesting publication because these pictures were protected under the copyright secured by the media in their own publication. It is settled law that if a work is published in the press, without a separate notice in the name of the holder of the copyright of the work in question, that work has been published without valid notice.[28] Defendant contends that the above statement of law has been overruled by *Goodis v. United Artists Television Inc.*[29] and that the *Goodis* case supports its position that the press copyright protects the interests of the work's owner. The issue in the *Goodis* case was "whether a magazine publisher who acquires only the right to serialize a novel before it is published in book form has such an interest in the work that notice of copyright in the publisher's name will protect the copyright of the author of the novel."[30] The court in finding that the publisher's copyright did protect the author, based its opinion on the fact that the magazine had purchased a property interest in the novel, i.e., the right of first publication. Thus, the court found that the publisher's notice was sufficient since the magazine had obtained proprietorship of a portion of the copyright to the novel. The basic issue that the *Goodis* court decided was whether the doctrine of indivisibility of copyright was applicable to the situation presented in that case.

The case at bar is distinguishable from the *Goodis* decision for in the instant case the newspapers and magazines that published the pictures of the work of art did not have as the *Goodis* court said, "such an interest in the work that notice of copyright in the publisher's name will protect the copyright. . . ."[31] The publishers in the case at bar had no interest whatever in the pictures of the work that they published. Accordingly, the court finds that the copyrights of the publishers in their own publications do not serve to rescue the defendant's copyright in this case.

---

[28] Nimmer, *supra*, note 3, section 119.32; McDaniel v. Friedman, 98 F.2d 745 (7th Cir. 1938); Kaplan v. Fox Film Corporation, 19 F. Supp. 780 (S.D.N.Y. 1937).

[29] Goodis v. United Artists Television, Inc., 425 F.2d 397 (2nd Cir. 1970).

[30] *Ibid.*, p.398.

[31] *Ibid.*

DEFENDANT'S CLAIM THAT PUBLICATION OF PICTURES OF THE MODELS CONSTITUTED INFRINGEMENT

The last major defense that the defendant advances in an attempt to excuse the uncopyrighted publication of the work of art is that the publications constituted unauthorized infringement, and therefore they did not place the work in the public domain.[32] In a letter to Hartmann, before the deed of gift was signed, which letter the defendant characterizes as, "instructions to architects," the following directions were set out:

> In order for the PUBLIC BUILDING COMMISSION to preserve all rights in and to this work of art, it is essential that every publication of the work, whether of the maquette, photographs of the maquette, or the ultimate monumental sculpture, bear the following notice:
>
> © 1966 Public Building Commission of Chicago All Rights Reserved
>
> The notice must appear legibly on an exposed surface of the sculpture. Since notice is the essence of protection, we suggest consultation between us before publication of the work in any form.
>
> Would you, or someone at your office, see that the photographs, drawings, and all other reproductions of this work of art are marked with the foregoing copyright notice.

Also, in its contract with the builder of the sculpture the defendant included provisions requiring that notice be placed on the sculpture and on all reproductions and drawings of the design.

Given these instructions the defendant argues that many of the instances of publication were actually acts of infringement because they were unauthorized and accordingly did not defeat defendant's copyright. The court has found no evidence for the period before notice was attached to the monumental sculpture on August 4, 1967, that the Commission intended to have its orders carried out. Rather, the great bulk of the evidence before the Court, shows that the Commission itself disregarded its own instructions. That instead of objecting to uncopyrighted publications, the Commission itself disregarded its own instructions. That instead of objecting to uncopyrighted publications, the Commission passively and in some cases actively engaged in the distribution of uncopyrighted pictures promoting "The Chicago Picasso." The court on the facts before it could not find that any of the publications here in question constituted unauthorized infringing publications. Accordingly, this last defense submitted by the defendant must be rejected.

An analysis of the legal issues presented in this action compels the conclusion that the copyright to the Chicago Picasso is invalid due to the fact that the sculpture has entered the public domain. This decision comports with a strict adherence to copyright law and is also in conso-

---

[32] Nimmer, *supra*, note 3, section 82.

nance with the policy of enriching society which underlies our copyright system. The broadest and most uninhibited reproduction and copying of a provocative piece of public sculpture can only have the end result of benefiting society.

For all of the foregoing reasons this court hereby enters summary judgment in favor of the plaintiff and against the defendant.

§2.6.5. *Goldsmith v. Max:* **Losing a Copyright by Lending a Work**

An artist who permits another person to reproduce his work, even for a limited purpose, runs the risk that the publication will not bear the requisite copyright notice and consequently will not adequately protect the copyright retained by the artist. Under the Copyright Revision Act, any work that entered the public domain in this fashion before January 1, 1978, would not be protected by the 1976 statute. The *Goldsmith* case, which follows, deals with this problem and indicates how easily an artist can either lose or protect a copyright interest.

GOLDSMITH v. MAX
2123 U.S.P.Q. 1008 (S.D.N.Y. 1981)

PIERCE, D.J. This is a copyright infringement action, pursuant to 17 U.S.C. §411, brought by Lynn Goldsmith ("Goldsmith"), a commercial photographer, against Peter Max ("Max"), a well-known artist. The gravamen of plaintiff's complaint is that Max created a collage by painting over and using parts of a poster of rock star Mick Jagger which was enlargement of a Goldsmith photograph.

The matter was heard without a jury in a six day trial on the issue of liability. Having reviewed the evidence presented herein, including the exhibits of the parties and the testimony at trial and having evaluated the credibility of the various witnesses the Court sets forth hereinbelow its findings of fact and conclusions of law. Fed. R. Civ. P.52.

THE PHOTOGRAPH
The photograph of Mick Jagger which forms the basis of this lawsuit was one of several taken by Goldsmith apparently without written permission or a release during a Jagger concert in New York's Madison Square Garden on July 25, 1972. The photograph depicts Jagger from the waist up, hands on hips, face in profile, wearing a black leather jacket open to the waist and a long red neck scarf.

Each party has introduced slides which contain the alleged copyrighted image. The first of these, plaintiff's Exhibit 2, is held in a slide jacket (a white cardboard holder approximately two inches square) which bears a stamped, virtually indistinct legend down the side reading "Photo Lynn Goldsmith, Inc. 16 East 61st St., N.Y.C." together with an unreadable zip code. The defendant has introduced three copies of the same slide contained in similar holders. (Collectively Def. Exh. D). One has been stamped along the side with name "Lynn Goldsmith" and "23 E. 63rd N.Y.C." The address has been changed by hand to "23 E. 74th" and another address has been added by hand, "15 E. 61 St. N.Y. 10021." Along the bottom of the slide jacket is written "Mick Jagger." In the top left corner is written "PP78 Ti" and two letters which cannot be read. The remaining two slides introduced by the defendant merely contain the words "Duggal Color Projects" along the right side. None of the four slides introduced by the parties contains a statutory copyright notice. 17 U.S.C. §401.[1]

The parties stipulated that the slides had been used to produce the Jagger image for at least three commercial ventures — a 26" x 40" poster produced by Personality Posters in 1972, a throw pillow produced by the Now Talent Company sometime after 1973, and an article in Escapade magazine in 1972. It is also agreed that each of these items appeared prior to the time that Goldsmith applied for and received a copyright on the photo.

THE COPYRIGHT

The complaint in this action alleges that Max infringes copyright No. VA 36-881 which Goldsmith holds on the slide. The certificate bearing this registration number (Pl. Exh. 4), dated November 16, 1979, states that the work was first completed in 1972 and lists no information in the box entitled: "Date and Nation of First Publication." From the testimony at trial it appears that the plaintiff sought unsuccessfully to register the poster, the pillow and the Escapade magazine photo. On January 30, 1980 the Copyright Office, apparently acting *sua sponte*, cancelled the aforesaid registration No. VA 36-881 and returned a new registration certificate bearing No. VAU 13-741 (Pl. Exh. 5), a designation used to describe unpublished works. Significantly, neither the slide

---

[1] 17 U.S.C. §401 details the proper form of notice consisting of three elements.

(1) the symbol © (the letter C in a circle), or the word "Copyright," or the abbreviation "Copr."; and

(2) the year of first publication of the work, in the case of complications or derivative works incorporating previously published material, the year date of first publication of the compilation or derivative work is sufficient. The year date may be omitted where a pictorial, graphic, or sculptural work, with accompanying text matter, if any, is reproduced in or on greeting cards, postcards, stationery, jewelry, dolls, toys, or any useful article; and

(3) the name of the owner of copyright in the work, or an abbreviation by which the name can be recognized, or generally known alternative designation of the owner.

nor the slide jacket filed with the Copyright Office (Def. Exh. CC1-2) contains a copyright notice in Goldsmith's name. They merely state her name and address.

The defendant argues that the complaint herein was predicated upon Certificate No. VA 36-881 which has been cancelled, that No. VAU 13-741 covers an unpublished work which is not the image on the slide at issue, and that there is, therefore, no valid registration certificate in effect. . . . Since the statute requires a valid registration §411; *Esquire, Inc. v. Ringer*, 591 F.2d 796, 199 USPQ 1 (D.C. Cir. 1978), *cert. denied*, 440 U.S. 908, 201 USPQ 256 (1979), the defendant argues that the complaint should be dismissed.

While the registration, cancellation and reissuance of the certificates for this work have occurred under wholly unclear circumstances, the failure to allege the proper registration number will not be deemed fatal to the complaint. *Frankel v. Stein & Day, Inc.*, 470 F. Supp. 209, 205 USPQ 51 (S.D.N.Y. 1979). Moreover, since the Court finds, as outlined herein-below, that the alleged copyright on this photograph is invalid, the issue of the validity of the registration certificate is moot.

THE MAX SERIGRAPHS
In early 1973 defendant Max created a series of collages utilizing the Personality Poster copy of the Goldsmith photo. The poster contained a clear, albeit arguably invalid, copyright notice in the name of Personality Poster and a photo credit to Lynn Goldsmith. Nonetheless, without seeking approval from either party the defendant applied acrylic paint and collage materials to the poster. At the time Max did not intend to sell or otherwise reproduce the collage.

Several weeks thereafter Max was solicited to donate one of his works to a relief fund to benefit victims of the Nicaraguan earthquake. He selected one of the Jagger collages from which a limited serigraph edition of 350 prints was prepared. The original collage (Def. Exh. J) was to be auctioned for the benefit of the earthquake fund. Max subsequently withdrew from the Nicaraguan project and, after paying the printer of the serigraph edition, he took title to the prints. Although Max has sold only one of the serigraphs, he has distributed a number of copies as gifts.

To demonstrate copyright infringement the plaintiff must establish her ownership of a valid copyright and that the defendant copied her work. *Mazer v. Stein*, 327 U.S. 201, 217 (1954); *Reyher v. Children's Television Workshop*, 533 F.2d 87, 90 (2d Cir.), *cert. denied*, 424 U.S. 980 (1976).[2]

---

[2] The second element, i.e., copying, is normally established indirectly by circumstantial evidence of defendant's access to the copyrighted work and an ex-

The central issue herein is whether plaintiff has demonstrated the existence and validity of her copyright, "for in the absence of copyright . . . protection, even original creations are in the public domain and may be freely copied." *Durham Industries, Inc. v. Tomy Corporation,* 630 F.2d 905, 908 (2d Cir. 1980). Ownership and validity are generally established by introduction of the certificate of copyright registration which if "obtained within five years after first publication of the work shall constitute prima facie evidence of the validity of the copyright and of the facts stated in the certificate. . . ." 17 U.S.C. §410(c); *Reyher v. Children's Television Workshop, supra,* at 90. Here the Court declines to afford the copyright registration a rebuttable presumption of validity. The initial registration certificate was issued on November 16, 1979 (Pl. Exh. 4). The Personality posters were distributed in 1972 and 1973 more than five years earlier. Moreover, where, as here, the transactions with the Copyright Office "cast serious doubt on the question, validity will not be assumed." *Durham Industries, Inc. v Tomy Corporation, supra,* at 908.

Plaintiff seeks protection under the Copyright Act of 1976, (Pub. L. 94-553, Title I, §101, October 19, 1976, 90 Sta. 2541, effective January 1, 1978). That Act effectively eliminated common law copyright, 1 Nimmer §2.03(G). Because of this limitation on the 1976 Act, the Copyright Act of 1909 and decisions thereunder, including the pre-1978 publication and notice provisions, have continued applicability and are useful in determining whether a work allegedly infringed may have entered the public domain prior to January 1, 1978.

The publication of a copyrightable work with authority from the owner will inject that work into the public domain unless it is protected by the giving of the requisite notice. *National Comics Publications v. Fawcett Publications,* 191 F.2d 594 (2d Cir. 1951); *Letter Edged in Black Press v.Public Bldg. Comm. of Chicago,* 320 F. Supp. 1303, 1308 (N.D. Ill. 1970); *American Fabrics Co. v. Lace Art, Inc.,* 291 F. Supp. 589, 590 (S.D.N.Y. 1968). Thus, under the 1909 Act the proprietor of a copyright would forfeit[3] her rights in a work if she authorized its publication with-

---

amination of the substantial similarity between plaintiff's copyrighted work and defendant's alleged infringing work. *Reyher v. Children's Television Workshop, supra,* at 90; *Arrow Novelty Co., Inc. v. Enco National Corp.,* 393 F. Supp. 157, 160, *aff'd,* 515 F.2d 504 (2d Cir. 1975); 3 Nimmer ¶13.03[A].Here the access is clear; the painting upon the poster depicting plaintiff's photograph is admitted by Max. Notwithstanding that he was creating a new and possibly copyrightable work of art, he was deriving it from an allegedly copyrighted work. He was required to obtain the consent of the publisher of the underlying work prior to distributing his own collage. *H.C. Wainwright & Co. v. Watt St. Transcript Corp.,* 418 F. Supp. 620 (S.D.N.Y. 1976). Since the works are substantially similar and access was conceded, if Goldsmith were to have a valid copyright on the Personality poster, her rights might well have been infringed by the Max serigraphs.

[3] This forfeiture is distinguished from a finding of abandonment which requires an overt act manifesting a purpose to surrender rights in the work and an

out the requisite notice. *Bell v. Combined Registry Company*, 536 F.2d 164, 168 (7th Cir. 1976). Under §26 of the 1909 Act publication occurs when copies are placed on sale, sold, or publicly distributed by the proprietor of the copyright or under her authority. Section 101 of the 1976 Act similarly provides that publication occurs when by consent of the copyright owner, the original or tangible copies of a work are sold, leased, given away or otherwise made available to the general public. 1 Nimmer §4.04. The central issue of this litigation is, therefore, whether Goldsmith's photograph entered the public domain — was published with her consent and without the proper statutory notice — before January 1, 1978. If it had entered the public domain there could be no copyright on the work and accordingly, no infringement.

The Goldsmith photo has been used to create at least three products which were distributed to the public — the Personality poster, the Escapade magazine page and pillow. The Court will consider each of these distributions individually to determine which, if any, injected Goldsmith's work into the public domain.

THE POSTER

The focus of this litigation is clearly the reproduction of Goldsmith's photo on the poster which Max admittedly used to create his collage — the alleged infringing work. Goldsmith testified that in December 1972 she granted a license for her photograph to be reproduced in poster form by Personality Posters, Inc. For this she was to receive royalties and "an appropriate photo credit." She further testified that she entered into a written agreement with Personality (Tr. 146) which included a provision that the copyright notice was to be in the name of Personality Posters "for their line of posters" but that she "maintained [her] copyright to the photograph." Robert Schwartz, a principal of Personality, also testified that Goldsmith had told him she intended to keep her copyright. Significantly, the written agreement between Personality and Goldsmith which purportedly contained this reservation was not introduced.

The poster, widely distributed in 1972 and 1973, contained the following "copyright" notice. "c Personality Posters 641 Sixth Avenue New York, NY 10011 Printed in USA Photo/Lynn Goldsmith." The c was not encircled. Goldsmith testified that she saw the posters almost immediately after they were printed. Although she had immediate

---

acquiescence in the public copying of it. On the other hand, "[a]n author, whose work is 'forfeited', need have had no such purpose, and ordinarily does not; it was indeed long doubtful whether he did 'forfeit' his rights by publication, and when it was settled that he did, the result was a consequence, imposed *invitum* upon him because of his failure to comply with the prescribed formalities." *National Comics Publications v. Fawcett Publications*, 191 F.2d 594, 598 (2d Cir. 1952).

knowledge of the lack of copyright notice in her name, it was not until approximately one year after the posters were initially released that Goldsmith's attorneys drafted a complaint which was to have been filed in Supreme Court, New York County, against Personality (Def. Exh. I) charging failure to render royalty statements and pay royalties. That complaint alleged neither breach of contract nor failure to provide copyright notices. It referred to the royalty agreement which was purportedly annexed as Exhibit A. However, the document produced at trial had no royalty agreement attached. The complaint was apparently never filed and the matter was settled without intervention of the court. Personality agreed to stop distributing the Goldsmith poster and to pay royalties. Although there was testimony that the agreement between plaintiff and Personality was written, it was not introduced into evidence during the trial of the instant action. More importantly, Goldsmith testified that she saw copies of the poster after the agreement was signed but took no action to restrain distribution or to enforce the settlement agreement with respect to the copyright.

Notwithstanding plaintiff's testimony that she intended to safeguard her proprietary rights in the photo, 100,000 posters of the photo bearing no copyright in Goldsmith's name were printed and distributed with Goldsmith's knowledge.[4] There is insufficient credible evidence from which this court can conclude that Goldsmith reserved her copyright in the claimed agreement by which she authorized Personality to use her slide. Moreover, there is nothing from which the Court may conclude that even if the rights were reserved, Goldsmith exercised those rights by promptly halting distribution of the posters.

In examining a similar situation involving the publication of the Superman comic strip, the Second Circuit looked to the language of the contract authorizing use to determine if proprietary rights were protected and forfeiture avoided. In *National Comics, Inc. v. Fawcett Publications,* 191 F.2d 594 (2d Cir. 1951), the defendant sought to defeat a charge of copyright infringement claiming that the plaintiff had forfeited his rights in the work when he authorized the work to be published without the requisite notice. Judge Learned Hand writing for the panel wrote:

> The question is whether the absence or the imperfection of the notices on these "strips" forfeited their copyrights when they were published in the syndicated newspapers. The answer depends on the contract of borrowing. Section 10 [of the 1909 Act] provides that the first publication of a "work" with the "required" notice secures the copyright; but it implies that a failure to

---

[4] The complaint in the action which Goldsmith planned to file in New York State Supreme Court sought recovery of royalties on 100,000 posters. (Def. Exh. I).

affix the notice upon each copy, later published "by authority of the copyright proprietor" will "forfeit" it. . . .

Id. at 601. The Court concluded that if there were an unconditional license to publish the strips, publication without notice would be by authority of the copyright owner thereby forfeiting his proprietary rights in the work. On the other hand, if there were a promise to affix the requisite notice the performance of that promise would be a condition of the license. Under the latter circumstances publication without notice would be without authority of the copyright proprietor and there would be no forfeiture.

Lacking the presumption of copyright validity, the plaintiff must demonstrate that the publication of her work on the Personality poster without copyright notice was unauthorized. The Court finds that the plaintiff has not carried that burden. Schwartz and Goldsmith offered evidence to show that Goldsmith intended to protect her rights in the photo, yet the record is devoid of evidence from which it can be concluded that she in fact protected those rights. From the lack of reference to copyright protection in the plaintiff's state court complaint against Personality it is reasonable to infer, as the Court does, that the unavailable license or royalty agreement with Personality was silent on copyright protection.

Accordingly, the Court finds that the Personality poster of Mick Jagger which was developed from plaintiff's slide was published and distributed with the permission of the copyright proprietor — Goldsmith. Since the poster contained no copyright notice in plaintiff's name, the publication injected the subject work into the public domain and Goldsmith's rights in the work were thereby forfeited.

However, construing the notice requirements liberally it is arguably possible that Personality's defective copyright notice could protect Goldsmith. "[S]ince the purpose of the notice is to advise the public of the 'proprietor's' claim, any notice will serve which does in fact advise it that there is a 'proprietor' who does claim copyright." *National Comics Publications v. Fawcett Publications, supra,* at 602. However, even if Goldsmith protected her proprietary rights in the photograph when it was used by Personality to produce the poster, the credible evidence at trial regarding the publication of the photos on the pillow and in Escapade magazine confirm that the subject work was injected into the public domain at least six years before Goldsmith registered her copyright.

ESCAPADE MAGAZINE

Goldsmith testified that in early 1972 she authorized the slide to appear in photo form in Escapade magazine, a predecessor to Gallery magazine. The record makes clear that Goldsmith received remuneration for this use of her slide. (Tr. 62). The record is silent as to whether the slide casing in which the slide was transmitted to Escapade contained any copyright in Goldsmith's name. In light of all the evidence it is reasonable to infer that it did not.[5] The image in the Escapade photo (Def. Exh. A), introduced as a single 8 x 10¾" page removed from the magazine, is a slightly cropped identical reproduction of the Goldsmith slide at issue. The undated magazine tearsheet contains the words "Mick Jagger: Eros Personified by Mike Jahn" in the upper right corner but this caption does not interfere with the Jagger image portrayed in the photograph. Significantly, the page contains no copyright notice or photocredit of any kind and neither side has introduced the magazine from which the page was removed.

Plaintiff's counsel argues that the magazine's copyright is sufficient to protect the plaintiff's rights in her photograph published therein. In *Goodis v. United Artists Television, Inc.*, 425 F.2d 397, 399, 165 USPQ 3, 4 (2d Cir. 1970) this Circuit endorsed plaintiff's position holding "where a magazine has purchased the right of first publication under circumstances which show that the author has no intention to donate his work to the public, copyright notice in the magazine's name is sufficient to obtain a valid copyright on behalf of the beneficial owner, the author or proprietor." But cf., *Mifflin v. R.H. While Co.*, 190 U.S. 260 (1903); *Moger v. WHDH*, 194 F. Supp. 605, 130 USPQ 441 (D. Mass. 1961). However, plaintiff has failed to satisfy the requisite elements of Goodis. Lacking here is any evidence of an agreement or license wherein plaintiff reserved her proprietary rights in the photograph and manifested her intent not to donate her work to the public. More significantly, there was no evidence that there was even a copyright notice in the magazine's name from which plaintiff could derivatively claim protection. In this instance Goldsmith clearly authorized use of her photograph in a periodical available to the public. Since no evidence was introduced by plaintiff to demonstrate the fact, the Court cannot conclude that the magazine contained a copyright notice. Clearly, this publication injected plaintiff's work into the public domain and deprived it of the potential for copyright protection.

THE PILLOW

In November 1973 plaintiff entered an agreement with Now Talent Co., Ltd. (hereinafter "Now Talent") wherein she granted a license for her photograph of Mick Jagger to be used in the manufacture, sale and distribution of pillows. (Def. Exh. DD). Now Talent agreed to compensate Goldsmith with royalties in the "amount of ten cents for each pillow sold by mail order and two cents for each pillow sold, bar-

---

[5] On the basis of the evidence adduced at trial the Court concludes that at no time when Goldsmith conveyed the slide to licensee did the slide jacket contain a copyright notice of any kind.

tered or distributed in any other manner." (Def. Exh. DD ¶5). In the agreement Now Talent also acknowledge receipt of the Goldsmith photograph and agreed to be responsible for loss or damage to it. (Def. Exh. DD ¶4). While the agreement clearly described Goldsmith as the owner of the photograph, there is no mention of her copyright rights or her proprietary interest in the slide.

Also introduced at trial was an agreement between Sunday Promotions, Inc., described as the owner of "the right to use and to permit others to use the likeness, name and signature of . . . Mick Jagger . . . in connection with commercial ventures." (Pl. Exh. 18) and the Now Talent Co., Ltd. The document grants Now Talent a license to use the Jagger likeness on bed linens, pillow cases, beach towels and throw pillows. This agreement, executed on February 13, 1973, nine months prior to the agreement between Now Talent and Goldsmith provide that Now Talent "shall obtain copyright protection if available in each of the articles in the name of Owner [Sunday Promotions, Inc.] as proprietor and shall execute and deliver any documents reasonably required to confirm Owner's absolute title therein subject only to the rights granted to Licensee hereby." (Pl. Exh. 18 ¶11). On December 11, 1973, Now Talent notified Sunday promotions of their agreement with Goldsmith and conveyed a copy of the photograph to Sunday. (Def. Exh. EE). The notice contained no reference to copyright rights retained by Goldsmith or her proprietary rights in the work.

A pillow containing approximately 50% of Goldsmith's photo was subsequently produced and distributed by Now Talent. (Pl. Exh. 6). The pillow introduced at trial contained no copyright notice in the name Now Talent, Sunday Promotions or Lynn Goldsmith. Goldsmith contends that the requisite notice of copyright was given on a tag attached to the pillow which had subsequently become detached and was unavailable. Her testimony is ambiguous regarding whose name was actually listed on the tag as holder of the copyright.

Were the tag to have existed and contained Goldsmith's name in the copyright notice, it would nonetheless be ineffective in protecting her proprietary rights in the photo. Where "[a] notice is on a detachable tag and will eventually be detached or discarded when the work is put into use" 37 C.F.R. §202.2(b)(9); *Peter Pan Fabrics v. Dixon Title Corp.*, 188 F. Supp. 235, 127 USPQ 329 (S.D.N.Y. 1960); *Scarves by Vera, Inc. v. United Merchants & Mfrs., Inc.*, 173 F. Supp. 625, 121 USPQ 578 (S.D.N.Y. 1959), the Copyright Office will reject an application for copyright registration.

With the introduction of the Now Talent pillow sometime after November 1973, Goldsmith's photo of Jagger was once again injected into the public domain. The item was produced with Goldsmith's permission; she did not protect or reserve her proprietary interest in the photo; the pillow most likely contained no copyright notice in Goldsmith's name and ineffective notice in Sunday or Now Talent's name. To overcome this lack of effective notice plaintiff urges that only 50% of her slide was used to make the pillow and the pillow was distributed after Max's alleged infringement. The Court finds these arguments unpersuasive. The Goldsmith agreement with Now Talent did not restrict the percentage of the image which could be used. Goldsmith authorized unlimited use of her slide without reserving her copyright. When the slide was subsequently used to produce the pillow, the entire slide entered the public domain. Similarly, the fact that the pillow postdates the alleged infringement is of no import. The central issue is not whether the work was in the public domain when Max copied it, but rather whether the work was in the public domain in January 1, 1978, the effective date of the legislation under which plaintiff secured her copyright certificate. (See, pp.6-7 *supra*).

CONCLUSION

Having examined each of the aforesaid published items which utilized the Jagger image produced by Goldsmith, the court concludes that the plaintiff's photograph entered the public domain prior to January 1, 1978. Accordingly, the plaintiff's copyright is invalid and could not be infringed.

The relief sought by plaintiff is denied.[6]

The Clerk shall enter judgment for defendant. Each side shall bear its own costs. So ordered.

§2.6.6. *Yardley v. Houghton Mifflin Co.:* The Significance of the Copyright Notice

The *Yardley* case, which follows, was the first decision to deal with whether a copyright is owned by a party commissioning a work or the artist who executes it. This case held that absent an agreement to the contrary, the commissioning party owned the copyright. Additionally, the *Yardley* case is significant for the conclusion that the placement by an artist of a copyright notice on a work, with his name as the copyright owner, does not by itself reserve the copyright in that artist. For a further discussion of the relative rights of the party commissioning a work and the artist who was commissioned, see the recent cases of *Aldon Accessories Ltd. v. Spiegel* and *Peregrine v. Lauren Corp.* (§§2.7.1 and 2.7.2 *infra*) and the discussions that accompany them.

---

[6] In light of the foregoing opinion the Court need not consider the merits of the affirmative defenses set forth on Max's behalf.

YARDLEY v. HOUGHTON MIFFLIN CO.
108 F. 2d 28 (2d Cir. 1939), *cert. denied,* 309 U.S. 686 (1940)

SWAN, C.J. Before passing to a consideration of the interesting questions presented by this appeal it is desirable to state in outline the facts that give rise to them. The amended complaint seeks damages for infringement of a registered copyright of a mural picture painted by Charles Y. Turner and placed by him on the wall of the auditorium room of the DeWitt Clinton High School. Mr. Turner executed this painting pursuant to a written contract, dated January 14, 1904, between the City of New York and the general contractor for the erection of the school building, by the terms of which the city was to select the artist and the contractor was to pay him upon a certificate issued by the Superintendent of School Buildings, with the approval of the Committee on Buildings of the Board of Education, and to include such payment in the cost of the building. It is conceded that the mural was accepted and the artist received payment. The written contract between the city and the building contractor was silent as to who was to have the copyright of the painting to be made. Nor is there evidence of any agreement on this subject made by Mr. Turner with either the city or the building contractor. But the painting bears an inscription "Copyright, C. Y. Turner, 1905," and there is nothing to suggest that those words were not on it when it was first installed in the building. . . . When an artist accepts a commission to paint a picture for another for pay, he sells not only the picture but also the right to reproduce copies thereof unless the copyright is reserved to the artist by the terms, express or implicit, of the contract; there was no evidence from which such a reservation could be inferred; therefore the copyright registration in Turner's name, if valid at all, was held in trust for the city, and the latter, through its Board of Education, had given consent to the defendant to publish copies of the painting in its histories; hence there was no infringement. Each of the foregoing findings of fact and conclusions of law is disputed by the appellant.

It seems surprising that so little precise authority has been discovered; only one case exactly in point has been turned up. A fairly close analogy, however, may be found in cases discussing the law of copyright with respect to photographers. The rule has been clearly laid down in this circuit that when a photographer takes photographs of a person who goes or is sent to him in the usual course, and is paid for the photographs and for his services in taking them, the right of copyright is in the sitter or in the person sending the sitter to be photographed, and not in the photographer; but the photographer is entitled to copyright where he solicits the sitter to come to his studio and takes the photographs gratuitously for his own purposes and at his own expense. *Lumiere v. Robertson-Cole Distributing Corp.,* 2 Cir., 280 F. 550, 24 A.L.R. 1317, *certiorari denied* 259 U.S. 583, 42 S. Ct. 586, 66 L. Ed. 1075; *Lumiere v. Pathe Exchange,* 2 Cir., 275 F. 428; *Press Pub. Co. v. Falk,* C.C. S.D.N.Y., 59 F. 324; see also *Cory v. Physical Culture Hotel,* 2 Cir., 88 F.2d 411, photograph of inanimate object. We think the rule should be the same when a painting is made by an artist. If he is solicited by a patron to execute a commission for pay, the presumption should be indulged that the patron desires to control the publication of copies and that the artist consents that he may, unless by the terms of the contract, express or implicit, the artist has reserved the copyright to himself. Such a presumption must rest on the supposed intention of the parties, and the appellant argues that when the painting is not a portrait and when the patron who commissioned the artist to paint it is not engaged in publication for profit and apparently desired the painting only for decorative purposes, the presumption is not justified. But we think the distinction is too refined to be accepted. It is not unusual for cities or other municipal bodies to publish postcard copies or other reproductions of publicly owned works of art. The evidence shows that the painting was one of which the city might well be proud and wish to reproduce, as it represented the first attempt of the Board of Education to beautify the walls of city schools. We believe, therefore, that the general rule is applicable and that the right to copyright should be held to have passed with the painting, unless the plaintiff can prove that the parties intended it to be reserved to the artist. *Dielman v. White,* C.C. Mass., 102 F. 892.

The terms of the contract between the city and the contractor show that an artist was to be commissioned to paint a mural for pay. For reasons already discussed this contemplated that the city should get the copyright as well as the painting. There is no evidence as to the precise terms of the agreement made by Turner when he accepted the employment. In the absence of such evidence we must infer that whatever agent of the city negotiated with Turner did his duty and obtained for the city all that its contract for the building required; in other words, that Turner's contract of employment did not reserve the copyright. His subsequent unilateral act in placing on the painting the copyright notice would be ineffective to modify his contract of employment. It was at most an offer to modify it. The acceptance by city officials of the painting bearing the notice would show acceptance of that offer only if the officials observed the notice and had authority to make a contract modifying Turner's original employment. In both respects the proof is insufficient. As to the former, there is no evidence that the Committee on Buildings, whose approval of the painting was required before the Superintendent of School Buildings should issue his certificate for payment, ever had the inscription called to its attention. If it did come to the Committee's attention, it is entirely possible that the Committee protested to Turner and got his consent to waive his claim of reservation of copyright. The subsequent conduct of the parties is entirely consistent with such a possibility. Turner, so far as appears, never made any copies. During Turner's lifetime some school official or teacher whose identity is not clearly proven, caused 30,000 postal card reproductions to be made for sale or free distribution to the students at the school; and after Turner's death, the Board of Education gave permission for publication in the appellee's histories. It is urged that the evidence is insufficient to sustain the court's finding that such permission was given. After so long a lapse of years Mr. Webster could not remember definitely to what official he had applied for permission, but the fact that under the published reproduction the appellee printed the inscription "Copyright, Courtesy New York Board of Education," tends to support an inference that Webster had communicated with the Board and had received its consent. It is urged further that the Board had no legal power to give an effective consent. But whether the consent was effective is immaterial for present purposes. The fact of giving it, regardless of the Board's authority, shows that the Board did not understand that Turner reserved the copyright. But if the opposite view were taken and acceptance of the painting with the copyright notice upon it were held to justify an inference that the accepting officials acceded to Turner's proposal to reserve the copyright, the plaintiff must fail for lack of evidence that such officials had legal power to modify the contract. In this respect the case is precisely like *Dielman v. White*, C.C. Mass., 102 F. 892. There the complainant accepted a commission to design and install a marble mosaic in the reading room of the Congressional Library. The contract of employment was silent as to copyright and the designer placed upon the cartoon and the completed mosaic a notice of copyright in himself. In a well-considered opinion Judge Lowell held that the failure of officials in charge of constructing the building to object to the placing of the copyright notice upon the mosaic panel did not bind the government to a construction of the contract contrary to its legal effect, or entitle the complainant to claim a copyright in the absence of any reservation of such right. We believe the case was correctly decided and should be followed by this court. The principles it announces are conclusive of the case at bar in so far as dismissal of the complaint is concerned. Whether Turner's registration of copyright should be deemed void, because he was not the "proprietor" of the right to apply for it, or should be deemed to be valid but held in trust for the city, we need not decide. On either hypothesis the plaintiff was not entitled to bring the suit. . . .

Judgment affirmed.

It would appear that *Yardley* would have a different result under the Copyright Revision Act of 1976. See, e.g., §§2.1.2 and 2.1.6.

§2.7. WORKS OF ART MADE FOR HIRE

§2.7.1. *Aldon Accessories, Ltd. v. Spiegel:* **Commissions — Who Owns the Work?**

The *Aldon Accessories* and *Peregrine* (see §2.7.2 *infra*) cases represent a recent significant shift in analysis of the work-for-hire provisions of the new Copyright Act. Prior to the decision, it was generally thought by many practitioners that only common law employees were covered by §101 the provision that gave employers a copyright in a work created by an employee. Conversely, it was understood that independent contractors retained copyright unless both the work fell within one of the itemized classes of work set forth in subdivision (2) of the work-made-for-hire definition and there was a separate written instrument stating that the commissioning party owned the copyright. The *Aldon Accessories* and *Peregrine* cases have dealt a blow to this traditional thinking.

As the court concluded in *Aldon Accessories*, the 1976 statute did not change the 1909 Act's stipulation that if an employer supervised and directed the work, an employer-employee relationship could be found, even though the employee was not a regular or formal employee. The case apparently relied on the following language in §201 of the Copyright Revision Act:

> In the case of a work made for hire, the employer *or other person for whom the work was prepared* is considered the author for purposes of this title, and unless the parties have expressly agreed otherwise in a written instrument signed by them owns all of the rights comprised in the copyright. [Emphasis supplied.]

Problematically, however, §201 and the work-for-hire definition in §101 may be read as pointing in opposite directions. Section 201 on its face suggests that any person commissioning a work may be considered the author, and as determined in the *Aldon Accessories* and *Peregrine* cases, such person need not be the traditional common law employer. Section 101 by contrast seems to go the other way.

The *Aldon Accessories* case may have wider implications than might be initially apparent. If a person conceived a graphic design and then gave it to a technician to execute — perhaps as Dürer might have had an engraver execute a woodcut from one of his designs — who would be the artist and who would be the commissioning party? The visual conception is undoubtedly that of Dürer, but the cutting of the wood represented very high technical competence and perhaps added a major contribution to the finished product. Is there not room for both to be considered the artist?

ALDON ACCESSORIES, LTD. v. SPIEGEL

738 F.2d (2d Cir.), *cert. denied,* 105 S. Ct. 387 (1984)

FEINBERG, C.J. Defendant Spiegel, Inc. appeals from a judgment entered in the United States District Court for the Southern District of New York, Pierre N. Leval, J., in favor of plaintiff Aldon Accessories Ltd. for $104,400 and interest at 9.93% for copyright infringement, in violation of 17 U.S.C. §504. Judge Leval denied a motion by Spiegel for a new trial on condition that Aldon agree to remit $20,000 from the jury verdict of $124,400. Spiegel raises numerous arguments before us, all of which are without merit. We find only two that warrant discussion. These concern the scope of the "work made for hire" doctrine under the 1976 Copyright Act and the propriety of the jury instructions on access and similarity.

For reasons given below, we affirm the judgment of the district court.

I

This case arises out of Spiegel's sale, through its widely circulated catalogs, of brass unicorn statuettes that the jury found infringed a valid copyright held by Aldon. There was evidence introduced at the trial from which the jury could, and apparently did, find the following: Aldon is primarily in the business of designing and marketing figurines and other decorative pieces for the home. Most of these are copyrighted by Aldon and represented as exclusively its own. Nationwide sales are made wholesale through catalogs, a showroom in New York City, sales representatives and exhibit booths at trade shows throughout the country. Aldon does not deal directly with consumers.

Aldon has two principals, Arthur Ginsberg, who handles the creative and production side of business, and his brother, Irwin Ginsberg, who handles sales. Some time in 1977, Arthur Ginsberg ("Ginsberg") conceived of a novel line of statuettes depicting mythological creatures, including a unicorn and a Pegasus. In September 1977, Ginsberg wrote a Japanese trading firm, Wado International Corporation, concerning the design and production of the unicorn and Pegasus, ultimately to be done in porcelain. The letter stated in part:

We just got an idea to do several Mythological animal[s], one called UNICORN & the other PEGASUS. Please examine the two clippings attached. Note that they are similar to horses, especially the Pegasus (with eagle-like wings). While the Unicorn has a little beard and split hooves, it still resembles a horse and we do not want to have the beard and the hooves must be like a regular horse.

You remember last year with Okumura that I was trying to design horses but that they were too expensive because they were on their rear legs and had no center support? I'm sure you still have the sketches. Well, we want this pose for both the Unicorn and Pegasus. That is, both should be rearing up on their back legs with the front legs posed as if "kicking out" . . . a feeling of motion or action. The tails should be very full (like on the Unicorn clipping) and touching the base to give additional support. Please make the base as thin & small as possible but make sure the piece stands securely and won't easily fall over.

Shortly thereafter, Ginsberg also sent Wado a very rough sketch of the pose he had in mind for the unicorn and the Pegasus, apparently to remind Wado of the sketches and discussions mentioned in his earlier letter.

In late October or early November, Ginsberg traveled to Japan to work with artists hired by Wado in developing models of the statuettes he had in mind. In describing his participation, Ginsberg testified as follows:

An artist that had worked with me and I sat down together, and we took some of the sketches that we had made on my previous visit . . . and we tried to go over those sketches that we both had done together, to come up with a shape or form that would satisfy me for its acceptability. And finally the artist and I agreed on a certain kind of pose, certain proportions for the horse, the musculature, the way the mane was supposed to be done, the sense of its movement, the way it would be produced [a]nd setting up sketches at that first instance, that would at once be aesthetically pleasing to me and that would have marketability and at the same time as a practical matter could be made economically. . . .

After the sketches were agreed upon we had a model maker who makes models in clay, and interpreting from a two-dimensional sketch to a three-dimensional model takes a lot of work until it is satisfactory. And the model was prepared in front of me, and we spent hours and hours changing shapes, adjusting attitudes and proportions until finally I thought there was a model that I liked.

The process took three days, producing at the end a clay model that was substantially identical to the porcelain unicorn ultimately marketed by Aldon. Ginsberg testified at length as to the precise nature of his interaction with the artists. The gist of his testimony was that while he is not an artist and did not do the sketching or sculpting, he actively supervised and directed the work step by step. For example, Ginsberg testified, "The artist will do it this way, and I will say 'No, put the leg this way, make this proportion, put the head this way, make the hair that way.'"

Aldon first received selling samples of the porcelain unicorn in early 1979 and began advertising by brochures and a general mailing. In July 1980, Ginsberg filed a certificate of copyright registration for the porcelain unicorn in which he identified Aldon as the author and indicated that authorship of the statuette was based on its being a "work made for hire."

Meanwhile, in August 1979, Ginsberg wrote to the Unibright Company in Taiwan to initiate the development of solid brass versions of Aldon's exclusive porcelain unicorn and Pegasus statuettes. Ginsberg expressed interest in producing three sizes: approximately five, seven and ten inches high. He included a color photograph of the porcelain statuettes and sent samples of them separately. In October 1979, Ginsberg visited the Unibright firm during a four-week trip to Taiwan. He testified to working with the Unibright employees in essentially the same manner as he had worked with the Wado artists in developing the porcelain statuettes. Several changes were made from the porcelain design at Ginsberg's direction. Before he left Taiwan, he had final brass models for each of the three sizes he wanted, different in base, tail and head from the porcelain version and each of the sizes slightly different from the others. In July 1980, Ginsberg filed a certificate of copyright registration for the three brass unicorns as works derived from the earlier porcelain unicorn. He listed Aldon as the author and indicated "work made for hire."

Aldon had received the first production samples of the brass unicorns in January 1980. The whole series of brass and porcelain unicorn and Pegasus statuettes was included in Aldon's 1980 and 1981 catalogs and was advertised by a photograph in the January 1981 issue of Gifts & Decorative Accessories magazine, a trade publication. The series was also displayed by Aldon at the Chicago Gift Show in late January 1981. Irwin Ginsberg testified that one of Spiegel's buyers, Jan Vercillo, spent about a half hour at Aldon's booth during this show and examined the entire unicorn collection. Prices were pasted on the bottom of each item, right next to Aldon's copyright notice. Vercillo requested that samples be sent to her, took an Aldon catalog and said she would get in touch with Irwin Ginsberg as soon as she received the samples. The requested samples were sent, but repeated efforts by him to contact Vercillo over the next six to eight weeks were unavailing; Vercillo did not return any of his calls.

Arthur Ginsberg further testified that he first became aware in the middle of 1981 that Spiegel was selling through its catalogs brass unicorns identical to Aldon's unicorns. Attempts to get Spiegel to cease its sales of the brass unicorns were unsuccessful, and this litigation ensued. At trial, the thrust of Spiegel's defense was that the copyright was invalid and that Spiegel had ordered its unicorns from Taiwan before it had access to Aldon's literature and statuettes. Spiegel's buyer, Ms. Vercillo, testified and disputed key aspects of the Ginsbergs' testimony. For example, she claimed her visit to the Aldon booth took place at a show in July and not in January, after Spiegel's catalog containing the brass statuettes had "closed" or gone into production. Such questions of fact, of course, were for the jury, which apparently decided them in favor of Aldon. For the purposes of this appeal, we do not need to describe any more of the proof offered by both Aldon and Spiegel.

II

Spiegel argues that the trial judge gave an erroneous charge on the "work made for hire" provision of the 1976 Copyright Act, 17 U.S.C. §101.[1] Specifically, Spiegel objects to the following instruction:

> A work for hire is a work prepared by what the law calls an employee working within the scope of his employment. What that means is, a person acting under the direction and supervision of the hiring author, at the hiring author's instance and expense. It does not matter whether for-hire creator is an employee in the sense of having a regular job with the hiring author. What matters is whether the hiring author caused the work to be made and exercised the right to direct and supervise the creation.

Spiegel concedes that this may have been a correct instruction under the old copyright law, but maintains that under the express statutory definition of a "work made for hire" of the new Act, see note 1 *supra*, a change was made from the prior work for hire doctrine.[2] Spiegel reasons essentially as follows: Regular employees and independent contractors are treated separately under the new Act, and independent contractors are covered exclusively by subdivision (2) of the definition. Because the artists and artisans of Wado and Unibright were not regular employees of Aldon, the procelain and brass unicorns could be considered works for hire only if they fell within one of the categories of "specially ordered or commissioned" works listed in subdivision (2) and then only if the parties agreed in a signed instrument that they would be considered works for hire. The instruction, however, permitted the jury to find a work for hire by an independent contractor if the work was "at the hiring author's instance and expense" and if "the hiring author . . . exercised the right to direct and supervise the creation," without reference to the categories

---

[1] That section provides the following definition:

A "work made for hire" is —

(1) a work prepared by an employee within the scope of his or her employment; or
(2) a work specially ordered or commissioned for use as a contribution to a collective work, as part of a motion picture or other audiovisual work, as a translation, as a supplementary work, as a compilation, as an instructional text, as a test, as answer material for a test, or as an atlas, if the parties expressly agree in a written instrument signed by them that the work shall be considered a work made for hire. For the purpose of the foregoing sentence, a "supplementary work" is a work prepared for publication as a secondary adjunct to a work by another author for the purpose of introducing, concluding, illustrating, explaining, revising, commenting upon, or assisting in the use of the other work, such as forewords, afterwords, pictorial illustrations, maps, charts, tables, editorial notes, musical arrangements, answer material for tests, bibliographies, appendixes, and indexes, and an "instructional text" is a literary, pictorial, or graphic work prepared for publication and with the purpose of use in systematic instructional activities.

[2] Except when quoting from the statute, we will use the shorter phrase "work for hire," instead of the slightly awkward and cumbersome phrase "work made for hire."

of subdivision (2) or to the requirement of a written instrument. In the instant case, there was no written instrument and the statuettes did not fall within one of the listed categories in subdivision (2).

Spiegel is correct that the statuettes could not be considered works for hire under subdivision (2) of the new statutory definition. But Spiegel gives an overly restrictive interpretation of subdivision (1), "a work prepared by an employee within the scope of his or her employment." We find the judge's instruction to be a proper interpretation of this subdivision. Under the 1909 Act and decisions construing it, if an employer supervised and directed the work, an employer-employee relationship could be found even though the employee was not a regular or formal employee. See *Epoch Producing Corp. v. Killiam Shows, Inc.*, 522 F.2d 737, 744 (2d Cir.1975), *cert. denied*, 424 U.S. 955, 96 S. Ct. 1429, 47 L. Ed. 2d 360 (1976); *Picture Music, Inc. v. Bourne, Inc.*, 457 F.2d 1213, 1216-17 (2d Cir.), *cert. denied*, 409 U.S. 997, 93 S. Ct. 320, 34 L. Ed. 2d 262 (1972); *Donaldson Publishing Co. v. Bregman, Vocco & Conn, Inc.*, 375 F.2d 639, 643 (2d Cir.1967), *cert. denied*, 389 U.S. 1036, 88 S. Ct. 768, 19 L. Ed. 2d 823 (1968). Nothing in the 1976 Act or its legislative history indicates that Congress intended to dispense with this prior law applying the concepts of "employee" and "scope of employment." See *Aitken, Hazen, Hoffman, Miller, P.C. v. Empire Construction Co.*, 542 F. Supp. 252, 257-58 (D. Neb. 1982). The new Act does not define these key terms, thus suggesting that it is necessary to look at the general law of agency as applied by prior copyright cases in applying subdivision (1) under the new Act. 1 M. Nimmer, Nimmer on Copyright §5.03[B][1] at 5-12 to 5-13 (1983). Indeed, the legislative history states that the new Act "adopts one of the basic principles of the present law: that in the case of works made for hire the employer is considered the author of the work." H.R. Rep. No. 1476, 94th Cong., 2d Sess. 121, reprinted in 1976 U.S. Code Cong. & Ad. News 5659, 5736. Had Congress intended, as apparently argued by Spiegel, to narrow the type of employment relationships within the work for hire doctrine to include only "regular" employees, it is unlikely that there would have been no discussion of this change in the legislative history.

The legislative history does indicate that Congress intended to change prior work for hire law dealing with "works prepared on special order or commission," *id.*, 1976 U.S. Code Cong. & Ad. News at 5737. Under prior law, in dealing with *all* works done by an independent contractor, the courts "presume[d] in the absence of contrary proof that the parties expected the employer to own the copyright and that the artist set his price accordingly," *May v. Morganelli-Heumann & Associates*, 618 F.2d 1363, 1368 (9th Cir.1980), *citing Scherr v. Universal Match Corporation*, 417 F.2d 497, 502 (2d Cir.1969) (Friendly, J., dissenting), *cert. denied*, 397 U.S. 936, 90 S. Ct. 945, 25, L. Ed. 2d 116 (1970), and *Brattleboro Publishing Co. v. Winmill Publishing Corp.*, 369 F.2d 565 (2d Cir.1966);

see *Roth v. Pritikin*, 710 F.2d 934, 937 n.3 (2d Cir.), *cert. denied,* — U.S. —, 104 S. Ct. 394, 78 L. Ed. 2d 337 (1983). The presumption applied to all works prepared by an independent contractor, regardless of the presence or absence of direction and supervision by the hiring party. It was apparently felt that this frequently worked an injustice in those situations where the contractor did all of the creative work and the hiring party did little or nothing. H.R. No. 1476, *supra,* at 121, 1976 U.S. Code Cong. & Ad. News at 5737. Subdivision (2) of the work for hire definition in the new Act is a carefully drafted change in this aspect of the prior law. But there is no indication in the legislative history or elsewhere that Congress was focusing on contractors who were actually sufficiently supervised and directed by the hiring party to be considered "employees" acting within "the scope of employment." Rather, as indicated earlier, we believe and hold that Congress intended the prior law in such situations to remain unchanged.

The cases cited by Spiegel are not to the contrary. In *Meltzer v. Zoller,* 520 F. Supp. 847, 854-57 (D.N.J. 1981), the court appeared to conclude that subdivision (2) of the definition under the 1976 Act was the exclusive provision covering independent contractors. But that simply frames the issue: is the contractor "independent" or is the contractor so controlled and supervised in the creation of the particular work by the employing party that an employer-employee relationship exists. The latter is covered by subdivision (1). The *Meltzer* court was not required to consider the range of employer-employee relationships covered by subdivision (1) of the work for hire definition because it found as facts that plaintiff's contribution to the architectural plans at issue was minimal, that the plans differed only slightly from the firm's standard plans and that the firm was an independent contractor.

May v. Morganelli-Heumann & Associates, supra, also involving architectural plans, simply applied the prior work for hire law as to independent contractors because the events at issue antedated January 1, 1978, the effective date of the 1976 Act. The issue was whether the presumption of copyright ownership in the hiring party was rebutted by the proof of a contrary intent evidenced by custom and usage of the architectural profession. In a footnote, *id.* at 1368 n.4, however, the court stated that it viewed the architect as an independent contractor and not an employee and that the work for hire doctrine of the new Act would not apply. This is not inconsistent with our conclusion here, because there is no evidence that the hiring party in *Morganelli-Heumann* actively participated in drafting the plans.[3]

---

[3] Cf. *Childers v. High Society Magazine, Inc.,* 557 F. Supp. 978, 984 (independent photographer; "Defendants cannot possibly assert that plaintiff is an 'employee'."), *aff'd on rehearing,* 561 F. Supp. 1374 (S.D.N.Y. 1983).

Our conclusion that the judge's charge was not incorrect does not produce a result at odds with the Congressional intent. There was evidence in this case that Ginsberg did much more than communicate a general concept or idea to the Japanese and Taiwanese artists and artisans, leaving creation of the expression solely to them. There was evidence that Ginsberg actively supervised and directed the creation of both the porcelain and brass statuettes. While he did not physically wield the sketching pen and sculpting tools, he stood over the artists and artisans at critical stages of the process, telling them exactly what to do. He was, in a very real sense, the artistic creator. Citing *Florabelle Flowers, Inc. v. Joseph Markovits, Inc.*, 296 F. Supp. 304 (S.D.N.Y. 1968), Spiegel argues that, as in that case, Ginsberg had no more than a general conception and the creation was done by the artists and artisans. In *Florabelle*, the judge was acting as fact-finder on a motion for a preliminary injunction and there was virtually no evidence of participation by the plaintiff in the physical creation of the artificial flower in dispute. Here, the question of supervision and direction by Ginsberg was submitted to the jury, and their finding, implicit in the verdict, of an employer-employee relationship is supported by ample evidence.

III

Spiegel also objects to the judge's charge on the relationship between proof of access and proof of similarity in determining whether copying had occurred. One sentence of the charge, quoted selectively by Spiegel, arguably could be interpreted as an instruction that the more convincing the proof of access by the copier the less impressive the similarities have to be to support a conclusion of copying. The sentence at issue is quoted in context in the margin.[4] Spiegel claims that this instruc-

---

Both parties agree that the facts of this case are similar to *Goldman-Morgen, Inc. v. Dan Brechner & Co.*, 411 F. Supp. 382 (S.D.N.Y. 1976), but that case is of no assistance here because the court applied the prior law on independent contractors, now changed by subdivision (2) of the work for hire definition, and had no need to consider whether plaintiff's participation with the Japanese artists in the design of a novel child's bank was sufficient to constitute an employer-employee relationship, *id.* at 385, 391, now covered by subdivision (1) of the definition.

[4] As with all circumstantial evidence, you must use your common sense. That is what circumstantial evidence is all about: common sense. The strength required of any one element or the strength of the proof on any one of those questions depends in a way on the strength of the others. If the degree of similarity between the two works is overwhelming and the similar elements are of such an unusual or distinct nature that it is unlikely that someone else would have dreamed them up on his own or arrived at them in any way other than by copying, and if there is no apparent other source for those similar elements than the plaintiff's work, a strong case of copying would be made by reason of those

tion allowed the jury to find copying without also finding substantial similarity between Aldon's and Spiegel's statuettes. However, we do not think this is so. The judge had just said that "overwhelming" similarity where "the similar elements are of such an unusual or distinct nature that it is unlikely that someone else would have dreamed them up on his own or arrived at them in any way other than by copying" permitted an inference of copying "without very convincing proof" of access. The next sentence, here challenged by Spiegel, simply advised the jury that such an "overwhelming" degree of similarity was not required where proof of access was present. See 3 Nimmer on Copyright, *supra,* §13.03[D] at 13-39. In any event, even if the sentence is interpreted to communicate the meaning attributed by Spiegel, the error was harmless, in view of the statement of Spiegel's counsel to the jury that "I won't tell you that [Aldon's and Spiegel's] products aren't virtually the same." Moreover, a reading of the entire eight-page charge on copying leaves no doubt that the judge properly charged the jury on similarity.

The judgment of the district court is affirmed. The parties' respective requests for award of attorneys' fees are denied.[5]

§2.7.2. *Peregrine v. Lawson Corp.:* "Supervision" and the "Work Made for Hire" Rule

The *Peregrine* case, which follows, adopts the rationale of the *Aldon Accessories* case without citing it in support of its result. The court found that "the longstanding presumption" that the intent of the parties was critical as to whether the work was made for hire was confirmed by §201(b) of the Copyright Revision Act. Accordingly the legislative intent was not to overturn the line of cases that reject the more traditional distinction between an employee and an independent contractor where the supervision was in the hands of the party commissioning the work.

---

similarities, even without very convincing proof of the defendant's access to the plaintiff's work.

On the other hand, the more convincing the proof of access by the copier, the assumed copier [of] the plaintiff's work, the less impressive the similarities have to be to support a conclusion of copying. You should consider these and all other logically relevant circumstances in deciding whether you find that the defendant copied the plaintiff's work. [Emphasis added.]

[5] Aldon challenges the granting of the $20,000 remittitur and requests that the full jury verdict be restored. Aldon accepted the remittitur, and under established law in this circuit could not raise the issue even if it had cross-appealed, which it has not. *Akermanis v. Sea-Land Service, Inc.,* 688 F.2d 898, 903 (2d Cir. 1982), *cert. denied,* — U.S. —, 103 S. Ct. 2087, 77 L. Ed. 2d 298 (1983) and — U.S. —, 104 S. Ct. 700, 79 L. Ed. 2d 165 (1984).

PEREGRINE v. LAWSON CORP.

601 F. Supp. 828 (D. Colo. 1985)

KANE, D.J. Plaintiff, a professional photographer, sues defendant, whose advertising agency commissioned plaintiff's professional services in order to include photographs in an advertising brochure. The photographs taken by Mr. Peregrine were included in the advertising brochure. Defendant, however, believing that plaintiff's October 13, 1983 bill for $4,200 was excessive, refused to pay. Plaintiff, in an attempt to encourage defendant to pay the bill for services, filed for and received a copyright to the unpaid for photographs. This suit was filed upon defendant's continuing refusal to pay the bill. Jurisdiction is invoked under the Copyright Act of 1976, 17 U.S.C. 101 *et seq.*

Although under §401(b) of the Act the plaintiff's certificate of copyright registration for the photographs in question constitutes prima facie evidence of the validity of the copyright and of the facts stated in the certificate, defendant urges that the prima facie presumption has been overcome by the law applicable to the facts of this case.

Section 201(a) of the Copyright Act sets forth the general rule that copyright vests in the author at the moment of creation. However, under section 201(b),

[i]n the case of a work made for hire, the employer or other person for whom the work was prepared is considered the author for purposes of this title, and, unless the parties have expressly agreed otherwise in a written instrument signed by them, owns all of the rights comprised in the copyright.

Section 101(1) defines a "work made for hire"as "a work prepared by an employee in the scope of his or her employment. . . ."

Although the Act does not define "employee" or "scope of employment," according to Professor Nimmer, "the crucial question in determining an employment relationship is whether the alleged employer has the right to direct and supervise the manner in which the writer performs his work." 1 Nimmer on Copyright, 5-12, 5-12.1 (1984). The view that a work for hire relationship exists when an employer has the right to control the party doing the work has received wide judicial acceptance.

Defendant cites *Epoch Producing Corporation v. Killiam Shows, Inc.*, 522 F.2d 737, 744 (2d Cir.1975), *cert. denied*, 424 U.S. 955, 96 S. Ct. 1429, 47 L. Ed. 2d 360 (1976), (in which the requisite power to control or supervise the work was cited as the hallmark of an "employment for hire" relationship sufficient to trigger the "work made for hire" provision of the Copyright Act of 1909) as authority for the finding of a "work made for hire" relationship in the case at bar. Although the *Epoch* opinion contains interesting background information concerning the making of D. W. Griffith's film "The Birth of a Nation," the *Epoch* court declined to find a "work made for hire" relationship. Further, because *Epoch* was decided before the enactment of the Copyright Act of 1976, more recent authority is needed to support a finding that a "work made for hire" relationship existed between Mr. Peregrine and the Lauren Corporation.

In *Murray v. Gelderman*, 566 F.2d 1307 (5th Cir.1978), also decided under the 1909 Act, the court, in deciding whether the "work made for hire" principle governed, looked to whether:

> [T]he motivating factor in producing the work was the employer who induced its creation. . . . Another factor is whether the employer had the *right* to direct and supervise the manner in which the work was being performed. . . . In addition, the nature and amount of compensation may be considered but are of minor importance.

Id. at 1310.

In *Clarkstown v. Reeder*, 566 F. Supp. 137, 141-42 (S.D.N.Y. 1983), the court, construing the 1976 Act, found that a "work made for hire" relationship existed between a writer who had contributed to the writing of the town's "Youth Court" manual and his employer. The *Clarkstown* court reasoned that "[t]he contribution of others included not only ideas and suggestions but also direct control and monitoring of Reeder's expression of his own thoughts. . . ."

There is no question in this case that Mr. Peregrine's work was undertaken at the insistence of the employer and that the employer had the right to supervise Mr. Peregrine's work. Although Mr. Peregrine made suggestions during the course of the shooting sessions which were followed more often than not, it is clear that at any point the employer could have vetoed any of Mr. Peregrine's ideas or otherwise radically changed the course, scope or fact of Mr. Peregrine's photographic exertions on the project.

Given that defendant's method of paying Mr. Peregrine points toward a finding that Mr. Peregrine was an independent contractor rather than an employee, it is instructive to consider the longstanding presumption that the mutual intent of parties to the creation of an artistic work, whether employer/employee or independent contractor, was to vest title to the copyright in the person at whose insistence and expense the work was done. See, e.g., *Lin-Brook Builders Hardware v. Gertler*, 352 F.2d 298 (9th Cir.1965). In this light, it is clear that the section 201(b) statement of this presumption expresses the legislative intent not to overturn the line of cases which, in favor of more rational decisions in the copyright area, eschew the more traditional distinctions between an employee and an independent contractor found in other applications of agency law, such as in the determination of allegations of vicarious liability.

Because I find that the defendant commissioned the plaintiff's services so as to create a "work made for hire," the defendant's motion for summary judgment is granted. The plaintiff's motion for summary judgment is denied. Although Mr. Peregrine undoubtedly filed this suit as a matter of principle as well as a means of compelling payment, the ambiguities which the parties to this creative endeavor failed to resolve before its completion do not resolve in plaintiff's favor. Although a "work made for hire" relationship is premised in part on payment of consideration, neither the federal courts nor the Copyright Act are amenable to the invocation of federal question jurisdiction for the sole purpose of collecting an apparently otherwise legitimate debt. Plaintiff is free to proceed with *quantum meruit* collection efforts in another forum. This order is not to be construed as a res judicata bar to a suit on any issue other than the legitimacy of Mr. Peregrine's claim to a copyright in the photographs taken for defendant.

It is ordered that the defendant's motion for summary judgment is granted. It is further ordered that plaintiff's motion for summary judgment is denied. It is further ordered that each party is to pay its own costs and attorney fees. It is further ordered that the case is dismissed.

Although it is necessary to register a copyright with the Copyright Office before commencing an infringement suit (see 17 U.S.C. §411(a)), such registration may not be required of a commissioning party (an employer) to obtain possession of photographic negatives from the party commissioned (the employee). In *Sykee v. Roulo*,[1] where the defendant had been commissioned to take photographs at a gathering in the plaintiff's home honoring the artist Erte, the court held that the commissioning party owned the negatives since the photographs were taken under a work made for hire arrangement. The court found that since the commissioning party had exercised control over the manner in which the photographer performed the work, the pictures were "done by an employee within the scope of her employment."[2] The plaintiff had not registered her copyright prior to commencing the suit, however.

Also worth noting about this case is that suit was brought in the state court rather than federal court, which generally has exclusive jurisdiction in a copyright infringement action.[3]

We have some reservations about *Sykee*, however. While the court

---

§2.7. [1] 122 Ill. App. 3d 331, 461 N.E.2d 480 (1984).

[2] *Id.* at 335, 461 N.E.2d at 483.

[3] See 28 U.S.C. §1338, which in relevant part provides as follows: "The district courts shall have original jurisdiction of any civil action arising under any Act of Congress relating to . . . copyrights. . . . Such jurisdiction shall be exclusive of the courts of the states in . . . copyright cases."

analyzed the case to involve a question of copyright rather than to be an action for replevin, it failed to draw a distinction between the tangible object and the copyright itself. There is certainly a question as to whether the negatives of a photographer can be regarded as tangible property analogous to a tangible work of art (such as a painting). If so then there would be a distinction between the owner of the object and the owner of the copyright. Most photographers (and collectors), however, would argue that the print rather than the negative is the unique tangible work of art. Compare for example the considerably higher market value of photographs printed by Edward Weston than those printed by his son, Cole Weston, when presumably both father and son printed from the same negatives. Under the Copyright Revision Act of 1976, copyright protection "subsists . . . in original works of authorship fixed in any tangible medium of expression . . . from which [the work] can be perceived, reproduced or otherwise communicated, either directly or with the aid of a machine or device." [4]

§2.8. MAY THE ARTIST REPEAT HIMSELF?

§2.8.1. Introduction

In copyright law, the term artist could be read to include persons who copy others and those who copy themselves. By "copying" we are not referring to the reproduction of original images, but rather to the repetition of subject matter, technique, or vision, either by the original artist or by someone else. Although the vast majority of copyright cases have dealt with a claimed copying by someone other than the original artist, there are cases in which it was alleged that the artist was prohibited from copying himself, either by copyright or by contract. The *Gross v. Seligman, Franklin Mint Corp. v. National Wildlife Art Exchange,* and *Factor v. Stella* cases, all in this section, deal with this issue.

§2.8.2. *Gross v. Seligman: Grace of Youth* versus *Cherry Ripe*

The *Gross* decision, which follows, is probably the earliest American case that deals with the question of to what extent an artist may copy

---

[4] §102(a).

himself by executing a second work similar to an earlier one without violating a copyright interest that may exist in the first work.

GROSS v. SELIGMAN
212 F. 930 (2d Cir. 1914)

Appeal from the District Court of the United States for the Southern District of New York.

This cause comes here upon appeal from an order of the District Court, Southern District of New York, enjoining defendant from publishing a photograph. The suit is brought under the provisions of the Copyright Act. One Rochlitz, an artist, posed a model in the nude, and therefrom produced a photograph, which he named the "Grace of Youth." A copyright was obtained therefor; all the artist's rights being sold and assigned to complainants. Two years later the same artist placed the same model in the identical pose, with the single exception that the young woman now wears a smile and holds a cherry stem between her teeth. He took a photograph of this pose, which he called "Cherry Ripe"; this second photograph is published by defendants, and has been enjoined as an infringement of complainant's copyright.

LACOMBE, C.J. (after stating the facts as above). This is not simply the case of taking two separate photographs of the same young woman.

When the *Grace of Youth* was produced a distinctly artistic conception was formed, and was made permanent as a picture in the very method which the Supreme Court indicated in the Oscar Wilde Case (*Burrow-Giles Company v. Sarony*, 111 U.S. 53, 4 Sup. Ct. 279, 28 L. Ed. 349) would entitle the person producing such a picture to a copyright to protect it. It was there held that the artist who used the camera to produce his picture was entitled to copyright just as he would have been had he produced it with a brush on canvas. If the copyrighted picture were produced with colors on canvas, and were then copyrighted and sold by the artist, he would infringe the purchaser's rights if thereafter the same artist, using the same model, repainted the same picture with only trivial variations of detail and offered it for sale.

Of course when the first picture has been produced and copyrighted every other artist is entirely free to form his own conception of the *Grace of Youth*, or anything else, and to avail of the same young woman's services in making it permanent, whether he works with pigments or a camera. If, by chance, the pose, background, light, and shade, etc., of this new picture were strikingly similar, and if, by reason of the circumstance that the same young woman was the prominent feature in both compositions, it might be very difficult to distinguish the new picture from the old one, the new would still not be an infringement of the old because it is in no true sense a *copy* of the old. This is a risk which the original artist takes when he merely produces a likeness of an existing face and figure, instead of supplementing its features by the exercise of his own imagination.

It seems to us, however, that we have no such new photograph of the same model. The identity of the artist and the many close identities of pose, light, and shade, etc., indicate very strongly that the first picture was used to produce the second. Whether the model in the second case was posed, and light and shade, etc., arranged with a copy of the first photograph physically present before the artist's eyes, or whether his mental reproduction of the exact combination he had already once effected was so clear and vivid that he did not need the physical reproduction of it, seems to us immaterial. The one thing, viz., the exercise of artistic talent, which made the first photographic picture a subject of copyright, has been used not to produce another picture, but to duplicate the original.

The case is quite similar to those where indirect copying, through the use of living pictures, was held to be an infringement of copyright. *Hanfstaengle v. Baines & Co.* (L.R. 1894) A.C. 20, 30; *Turner v. Robinson*, 10 Irish Chancery 121, 510.

The eye of an artist or a connoisseur will, no doubt, find differences between these two photographs. The backgrounds are not identical, the model in one case is sedate, in the other smiling; moreover the young woman was two years older when the later photograph was taken, and some slight changes in the contours of her figure are discoverable. But the identities are much greater than the differences, and it seems to us that the artist was careful to introduce only enough differences to argue about, while undertaking to make what would seem to be a copy to the ordinary purchaser who did not have both photographs before him at the same time. In this undertaking we think he succeeded.

The order is affirmed.

§2.8.3. *Franklin Mint Corp. v. National Wildlife Art Exchange:* Are There Limits to the Artist's Repeating Himself?

It has long been hornbook law that copyright protects the expression and not the idea. The *Franklin Mint Corp.* case, which follows, refused to hold that an artist violated the copyright that he had transferred to another when he created a new expression of his previous idea, particularly where the artist "did not copy" the previous image that he had created.

FRANKLIN MINT CORP. v. NATIONAL WILDLIFE ART EXCHANGE

575 F.2d 62 (3d Cir. 1978)

WEIS C.J. Nearly two centuries ago, Lord Mansfield identified the conflicting interests underlying copyright law in his oft quoted warning:

> [W]e must take care to guard against two extremes equally prejudicial; the one, that men of ability, who have employed their time for the service of the community may not be deprived of their just merits, and the reward of their ingenuity and labour; the other, that the world may not be deprived of improvements, nor the progress of the arts be retarded.

Cary v. Longman, 102 Eng. Rep. 138, 140 (K.B. 1801), *quoting Sayre v. Moore* (Hil. 1785). The necessity of balancing these divergent concepts is illustrated in this case in which we are asked to determine whether an artist infringed a copyright, which he had once owned, by painting another work portraying the same general subject matter. The district court found no infringement and, being in agreement, we affirm.

In a series of suits and cross suits, Albert Earl Gilbert and Franklin Mint Corporation were accused of infringing on the purported copyright of National Wildlife Art Exchange, Inc. to a painting, "Cardinals on Apple Blossom." After a bench trial, the district court found that the copyright was valid, but there had been no copying and, consequently, no infringement. Companion cases of defamation, disparagement, and unfair competition were also decided by the district court but have not been pursued on these appeals, which are confined to the infringement claim.

In late July or early August, 1972, Ralph H. Stewart began to implement a plan of organizing a business enterprise which would publish and market limited edition prints of wildlife. He telephoned Gilbert, a nationally recognized wildlife artist, and asked him to paint a water color of cardinals. Gilbert agreed and in the following months "Cardinals on Apple Blossom," using as source material color slides, photographs, sketches, and two stuffed cardinal specimens. He signed and dated the painting, and placed a copyright notice on it before August 25, 1972, the day when Stewart came to the artist's residence and approved the rendition. While there, Stewart gave Gilbert a check in the amount of $1,500, bearing on the back a notation, "For Cardinal painting, 20 × 24 including all rights — reproduction etc." On the following day, Stewart and Gilbert discussed a proposal to incorporate National Wildlife Exchange, Inc. to market prints of Gilbert's future works. They agreed in general on the plan but it was understood that at a later date both parties would draw up a contract in terms meeting their approval. Gilbert endorsed Stewart's check and cashed it on August 28, 1972.

Early in September, 1972, Gilbert delivered the painting to Stewart. That same month, Stewart incorporated National and transferred the painting to it. In connection with his activities for National, an outline of the design of "Cardinals on Apple Blossom" was embossed on his white business orders for prints of "Cardinals on Apple Blossom," and in the cards. No color was applied to the design and no copyright notice was printed on the cards.

National placed a representation of the painting in the fall 1972 Newsletter to Members of the Cornell University Laboratory of Ornithology. No copyright notice of National was affixed but Gilbert's was visible. National published a brochure encaptioned "Introducing a First," in December, 1972, which sought orders for prints of "Cardinals on Apple Blossom," and in the next month, it distributed an edition limited to 300 prints of the painting. All bore Gilbert's copyright notice. A year later, National filed for copyright registration of "Cardinals on Apple Blossom" which was subsequently granted.

Gilbert and National ultimately were unable to agree upon terms of the business venture discussed in August of 1972, and in January, 1975, Gilbert agreed to paint a series of four water color birdlife pictures, including one of cardinals, for Franklin Mint Corporation. The series was completed in January of 1976, and included a work entitled, "The Cardinal." Franklin made engravings of the four paintings which were sold as a group and not separately.

In painting "The Cardinal," Gilbert used some of the same source material he had utilized for "Cardinals on Apple Blossom," including preliminary sketches from his collection, photographs, slides, and a working drawing. In addition, however, he used other slides of foliage taken after completion of the earlier painting and sketches specifically developed for "The Cardinal," as well as a series of cardinal photographs. He did not use the stuffed bird specimens which had served as models for "Cardinals on Apple Blossom."

After hearing extensive testimony and viewing Gilbert's rendition of a cardinal painted in the courtroom during the trial, the district judge found that the artist had not copied "Cardinals on Apple Blossom" when he painted "The Cardinal." The court also determined that title to the copyright of "Cardinals on Apple Blossom" passed to Stewart when he purchased the painting with the $1,500 check bearing a limited endorsement. In addition, the court ruled that distribution of Stewart's business card did not constitute a publication without notice which would forfeit National's copyright protection. And, since Gilbert's copyright notice appeared on the picture in the Cornell bulletin, the court decided that no forfeiture occurred by such publication.

Unlike a patent, a copyright protects originality rather than novelty or invention — conferring on the owner the sole right to reproduce the work and to "control all the channels through which . . . work or any fragments of . . . work reach the market." Chafee, *Reflections on the Law of Copyright: I*, 45 Colum. L. Rev. 501, 505 (1945). It has been said: "Originality in this context 'means little more than a prohibition of actual copying.' " *Alfred Bell & Co. v. Catalda Fine Arts*, 191 F.2d 99, 103 (2d Cir. 1951) (citations omitted). If there is no copying, there can be no infringement. *Mazer v. Stein*, 347 U.S. 201, 218 (1954); *Universal Athletic Sales Co. v. Salkeld*, 511 F.2d 904 (3d Cir.), *cert. denied sub nom. Universal Athletic Sales Co. v. Pinchock*, 423 U.S. 863 (1975); *Alfred Bell & Co. v. Catalda Fine Arts, supra*, at 103 & n.16. Copying done from memory is as objectionable as that done by tracing or direct view, *Herbert Rosenthal Jewelry Corp. v. Kalpakian*, 446 F.2d 738, 741 (9th Cir. 1971); *Withol v. Wells*, 231 F.2d 550 (7th Cir. 1956). Circumstantial evidence of access to the protected work and substantial similarity between it and the alleged infringing work can be used to infer copying when direct evidence is lacking. See *Reyher v. Children's Television Workshop*, 533 F.2d 87 (2d Cir.), *cert. denied*, 429 U.S. 980 (1976); *Arnstein v. Porter*, 154 F.2d 464, 468 (2d Cir. 1946), *cert. denied*, 330 U.S. 851 (1947).

To reconcile the competing societal interests inherent in the copyright law, copyright protection has been extended only to the particular *expression* of an idea and not to the idea itself. See *Mazer v. Stein, supra* at 217-18; *Baker v. Selden*, 101 U.S. 99, 102-03 (1879). In *Dymow v. Bolton*, 11 F.2d 690, 691 (2d Cir. 1926), the court observed:

> Just as a patent affords protection only to the means of reducing an inventive idea to practice, so the copyright law protects the means of expressing an idea; and it is as near the whole truth as generalization can usually reach that, if the same idea can be expressed in a plurality of totally different manners, a plurality of copyrights may result and no infringement will exist.

See also Comment, *"Expression" and "Originality" in Copyright Law*, 11 Washburn L.J. 440 (1972).

Since copyrights do not protect thematic concepts, the fact that the same subject matter may be present in two paintings does not prove copying or infringement. Indeed, an artist is free to consult the same source for another original painting. As Justice Holmes stated: "Others are free to copy the original [subject matter]. They are not free to copy the copy." *Bleistein v. Donaldson Lithographing Co.*, 188 U.S. 239, 249 (1903).

Precision in marking the boundary between the unprotected idea and the protected expression, however, is rarely possible, see *Peter Pan Fabrics, Inc. v. Martin Weiner Corp.*, 274 F.2d 487, 489 (2d Cir. 1960); *Nichols v. Universal Pictures Corp.*, 45 F.2d 119, 121 (2d Cir. 1930), *cert. denied*, 282 U.S. 902 (1931), and the line between copying and appropriation is often blurred. Troublesome, too, is the fact that the same general principles are applied in claims involving plays, novels, sculpture, maps, directories of information, musical compositions, as well as artistic paintings. Isolating the idea from the expression and determining the extent of copying required for unlawful appropriation necessarily depend to some degree on whether the subject matter is words or symbols written on paper, or paint brushed onto canvas.

Moreover, in the world of fine art, the ease with which a copyright may be delineated may depend on the artist's style. A painter like Monet when dwelling upon impressions created by light on the facade of the Rouen Cathedral is apt to create a work which can make infringement attempts difficult. On the other hand, an artist who produces a rendition with photograph-like clarity and accuracy may be hard pressed to prove unlawful copying by another who uses the same subject matter and the same technique.[1] A copyright in that circumstance may be termed "weak," see *First American Artificial Flowers, Inc. v. Joseph Markovits,* 342 F. Supp. 178, 186 (S.D. N.Y. 1972), since the expression and the subject matter converge. *Sid & Marty Krofft Television Productions, Inc. v. McDonald's Corp.,* 562 F.2d 1157 (9th Cir. 1977); *Herbert Rosenthal Jewelry Corp. v. Kalpakian, supra.* In contrast, in the impressionist's work, the lay observer will be able to differentiate more readily between the reality of subject matter and subjective effect of the artist's work. The limitations imposed upon the artist by convention are also factors which must be considered. A scientific drawing of a bird must necessarily be more similar to another of the same nature than it would be to an abstract version of the creature in flight.

The "copying" proscribed by copyright law, therefore, means more than tracing the original, line by line. To some extent it includes the appropriation of the artist's thought in creating his own form of expression. In *Universal Athletic Sales Co. v. Salkeld, supra* at 907, we observed:

> To establish a copyright infringement, the holder must first prove that the defendant has copied the protected work and, second, that there is a substantial similarity between the two works . . . . Phrased in an alternative fashion, it must be shown that copying went so far as to constitute improper appropriation, the test being the response of the ordinary lay person.

In that case, the district court had found copying but made no specific finding that would meet the second test — "that of substantial similarity in the sense of an appropriation of the original work." Copying which had been determined by dissection of the two works at issue was not sufficient, we said, because:

> substantial similarity to show that the original work has been copied is not the same as substantial similarity to prove infringement. As the *Arnstein* case

---

[1] Compare Esquire, Inc. v. Varga Enterprises, 81 F. Supp. 306, 307-08 (N.D. Ill. 1948), *aff'd in relevant part, rev'd in part,* 185 F.2d 14, 20 (7th Cir. 1950) with Gross v. Seligman, 212 F.930 (2d Cir. 1914).

points out, dissection and expert testimony in the former setting are proper but are irrelevant when the issue turns to unlawful appropriation.

Id.

In the case sub judice, testimony was presented by experts for the respective parties to support and refute substantial similarity. There are indeed obvious similarities. Both versions depict two cardinals in profile, a male and female perched one above the other on apple tree branches in blossom. But there are also readily apparent dissimilarities in the paintings in color, body attitude, position of the birds and linear effect. In one, the male cardinal is perched on a branch in the upper part of the picture and the female is below. In the other, the positions of the male and female are reversed. In one, the attitude of the male is calm; in the other, he is agitated with his beak open. There is a large yellow butterfly in "Cardinals on Apple Blossom," and none in "The Cardinal." Other variances are found in the plumage of the birds, the foliage, and the general composition of the works. Expert testimony described conventions in ornithological art which tend to limit novelty in depictions of the birds. For example, minute attention to detail of plumage and other physical characteristics is required and the stance of the birds must be anatomically correct.

There was also testimony on the tendency of some painters to return to certain basic themes time and time again. Winslow Homer's schoolboys, Monet's facade of Rouen Cathedral, and Bingham's flatboat characters were cited. Franklin Mint relied upon these examples of "variations on a theme" as appropriate examples of the freedom which must be extended to artists to utilize basic subject matter more than once. National vigorously objects to the use of such a concept as being contrary to the theory of copyright. We do not find the phrase objectionable however, because a "variation" probably is not a copy and if a "theme" is equated with an "idea," it may not be monopolized. We conceive of "variation on a theme," therefore, as another way of saying that an "idea" may not be copyrighted and only its "expression" may be protected.

The district court had the opportunity to hear the testimony from the artist and found credible his statement that he did not copy. For further support, Gilbert painted a third picture, "The Cardinal" while in the courtroom and without referring to either of his earlier paintings. The court determined that although some of the same source materials were used in all three paintings, similarity between the works necessarily reflected the common theme or subject and each painting was a separate artistic effort.

It is well settled that credibility determinations are uniquely the province of the fact-finder. *Government of the Virgin Islands v. Gereau,* 502 F.2d 914, 921 (3d Cir. 1974), *cert. denied,* 420 U.S. 909 (1975). Although evidence of access and similarity between the paintings constitute strong circumstantial evidence of copying, they are not conclusive, *Herbert Rosenthal Jewelry Corp. v. Kalpakian, supra,* 2 M. Nimmer on Copyright, §§139.4 at 605, 141.2 at 613-14 (1976). The trial court's finding of no copying based as it is on the testimony of the artist and other evidence of creativity, may be overturned only if it is clearly erroneous. *Rosen v. Loewr's Inc.,* 162 F.2d 785 (2d Cir. 1947). This situation is different from that in *Universal Athletic Sales Co. v. Salkeld, supra,* where we passed on the question of similarity between the copyrighted and accused work *after* copying had been established to determine if there had been appropriation. There, we were in as good a position to make a judgment as the trial court. Here, however, we have not had the opportunity to hear and see the witnesses and, thus, are not in the position to judge credibility as was the district judge. Accordingly, we conclude that the district court did not err in finding that there was no copying.

Even if it be assumed that the trial court's finding was based only on an application of a mechanical standard of copying — a tracing concept — without consideration of the appropriation factor, we would affirm. We have examined the two paintings and based upon our own observations and impressions, we conclude that while the ideas are similar, the expressions are not. A pattern of differences is sufficient to establish a diversity of expression rather than only an echo. *Universal Athletic Sales Co. v. Salkeld, supra; Herbert Rosenthal Jewelry Corp. v. Kalpakian, supra* at 741,42. The similarities here are of a nature not calculated to discourage an artist in the development of a specialty yet sufficiently distinguishable to protect his creativity in that sphere. Just as Justice Holmes would not ban the ballerinas of Degas, we may not excommunicate the Cardinals. See *Bleistein v. Donaldson Lithographing Co., supra* at 251.

We conclude that the district judge did not err in finding that there was no copyright infringement. Consequently, we need not decide whether there was a forfeiture of the copyright by publication of the business cards. Similarly, since there was no infringement established, we do not address ourselves to the issue of whether the district court erred in finding that National had acquired Gilbert's copyright.

The judgment of the district court will be affirmed.

§2.8.4. *Factor v. Stella:* "Duplicates" and the Artist's Duty to Inform

The *Stella* case, which follows, is not strictly a copyright case, but involves rather the obligation of an artist to inform a person to whom he sold a work that he may redo the image in a different medium. The decision, however, is somewhat unsatisfying. Although the court stated that an artist "has a duty to inform a purchaser of his work . . . of the existence of a duplicate work which would materially affect the value or marketability of the purchased work," the court found that the collector could not prove any damages by this lack of disclosure. The decision unfortunately does not throw any light on the nature of proof that would be required to demonstrate damage.

FACTOR v. STELLA
No. C58832 (Sup. Ct. L.A. County, Nov. 2, 1978)

[COURT OPINION REGARDING LIABILITY]

After review of the evidence the court is convinced that defendant Stella painted three "Marquis de Portago's." He initially painted three paintings with ordinary aluminum paint, one of which was titled "Marquis de Portago." He then painted eight paintings in alumichrome paint repeating the first three including the "Marquis de Portago." The eight paintings done in alumichrome make up the aluminum series, and one of them was the "Marquis de Portago" sold to the Factors in 1961. No inquiry was made as to whether there was a duplicate and no disclosure of the "Marquis de Portago" done in ordinary aluminum paint.

In 1964 the Factors' "Marquis de Portago" was damaged and upon inquiry Stella represented that it could not be restored to their satisfaction. Pursuant to agreement between Stella and the Factors Stella repainted the "Marquis de Portago" in 1965 and with their consent and agreement used clear liquitex paint in which aluminum particles were suspended. The use of the liquitex resulted in sharper lines and no bleeding and whiter canvas, and is easily distinguishable from the first and second paintings. The Factors accepted the obviously distinguishable replacement, and did not ask Stella to redo it although he had agreed he would if they were not satisfied.

The Factors' "Marquis de Portago" done in 1965 was sold at auction in 1970. Plaintiff learned just prior to the auction that there was another "Marquis de Portago" by Stella in the Carter Burden collection. Plaintiff was informed that because of the existence of that painting the reserve figure on the painting to be auctioned should be reduced from $35,000 to $15,000. The reserve was reduced and the painting sold for $17,000.

The painting in the Burden collection is the first "Marquis de Portago" painted by Stella with ordinary aluminum paint and traded by Stella to another artist, and it then found its way into the Burden collection.

The damaged "Marquis de Portago" was delivered to Stella at his request in 1969, and pursuant to his instructions is being restored. The Factors were not notified by Stella of his intent to have the painting restored. The state of the art of restoration improved between 1964 and 1967 which increased the possibility of satisfactory restoration. The painting can now be 80 percent restored.

Stella did not intentionally misrepresent the restorability of the damaged painting, nor did he conceal the existence of the first "Marquis de Portago" with intent to defraud. There has been no conspiracy of concealment of the present efforts to restore the damaged painting.

However, Stella's failure to inform the Factors of the existence of another "Marquis de Portago" and his failure to notify them of the possibility that the damaged painting could be restored is a violation of his duty to them.

An artist has a duty to a purchaser of his work to inform the purchaser of the existence of a duplicate work which would materially effect [sic] the value or marketability of the purchased work.

This case will proceed on the issue of damages.

[COURT OPINION REGARDING DAMAGES]

The issue of damages is now called for trial. . . .

The matter having been submitted on the issue of damages, the Court finds:

There is no causal connection between the failure of Stella to notify plaintiff of his intent to restore the damaged painting and any supposed reduction in the value of the auctioned painting.

There is no credible evidence that the auctioned painting would have brought a higher price at auction had not the existence of the other Marquis de Portago been disclosed. The remarks of Castelli must be discounted in view of the facts that the reserve on seven pieces was lowered prior to the auction and many of the auctioned pieces brought less than the Blum appraisal and the anticipated selling price.

Mr. Zachary testified that an unscheduled painting of the same subject would not effect [sic] the value of a painting in a series if there was a discernible difference. The use of different paint made a discernible difference.

The plaintiff has failed to prove any damage caused by this defendant. There is no basis for punitive damages.

Judgment is granted in favor of defendant Stella.

Counsel for defendant Stella is directed to prepare the judgment and forward to the Court.

A copy of this minute order is sent to all counsel, this date. A certificate of mailing is executed and filed.

§2.9. THE FIRST AMENDMENT AND COPYRIGHT

No discussion of copyright law would be complete without recognition of the inherent tension between the provisions of the 1976 Act and the First Amendment. This tension has been manifested most recently in two areas. The first arises when an artist appropriates a part or all of the image of another artist and incorporates it in his own work. The second revolves around the copyrighting of publicly commissioned work.

§2.9.1. Appropriation by One Artist of the Image of Another

The constitutional rights of free speech and the exclusive rights of authorship embodied in the concept of copyright may collide when one artist appropriates a part or all of the image of another in his work. For example, an artist doing a collage might incorporate copyrighted photos of another, or he might include readily discernible images of one or more other artists, as part of an abstract composition. When sued for copyright infringement, the artist might defend on the ground that the First Amendment protects this form of expression and accordingly the copyright benefits, also based on a constitutional clause, must remain subordinate. More specifically, he may argue that two important copyright concepts support his right to use a portion of the otherwise protected material. First, he could point out that the idea-expression dichotomy that exists in the Copyright Act immunizes his expression of the idea first conceived by the copyright holder. This argument is that under standard copyright doctrine no person may appropriate to himself an "idea"; only the expression of that idea can be monopolized. The defendant's expression of that idea is different from its initial expression because of the additional elements he has incorporated into his artwork. Section 102(b) of the Copyright Revision Act provides that "in no case does copyright protection . . . extend to any idea." Second, he could argue that the "fair use" doctrine provides an ample protective cover. Section 107 of the Copyright Revision Act provides that "notwithstanding the provisions of section 106 [the exclusive rights in copyright] the fair use of a copyrighted work . . . is not an infringement of copyright."

A recent note in the Yale Law Journal deals with this subject.[1] After recognizing the tension that exists between the Copyright Act's grant of exclusive rights of authorship and First Amendment interests in wide dissemination of ideas, it argues that courts "should extend First Amendment protection to visual works which use appropriated images to convey original expression, as this is consistent with First Amendment guarantees of free artistic expression. If the art work has significantly

---

§2.9. [1] Note, Copyright, Free Speech and The Visual Arts, 93 Yale L.J. 1565 (1984).

altered or transformed the copyrighted material so that the work as a whole adds meaning beyond that conveyed by the context of the copyrighted image alone, First Amendment protection is warranted."[2] To provide the necessary accommodation for the copyright interest, the writer concludes, "[r]estrictive qualities of copyright are legitimately used to prohibit piracy — copying which contributes no original idea, but merely dilutes the economic worth of the original — but restriction is inappropriate when an infringer incorporates the visual image into a new artistic work that adds to society's cultural legacy."[3]

We share that view, certainly, where one artist utilizes the image of another to produce a new image that is independent of a commercial product. We question, however, whether the First Amendment should be used as a shield to protect a commercial product when the designer has appropriated the essential expression of another, even where some original idea has been added. In the close case, however, we would side with the First Amendment claimant.

§2.9.2. Copyrighting Government-Commissioned Work

A recent note in the Columbia Law Review addresses an appealing constitutional question related to government-commissioned work.[4]Specifically, the note deals with the tension that exists between §105 of the Copyright Act, which prohibits copyrighting a "work of the United States Government," and the judicial doctrine that this section nonetheless permits copyrighting commissioned work. The note contends that "copyrighting commissioned work interferes with the realization of first amendment goals, and that existing copyright doctrines fail to minimize this interference."[5] It recommends the revision of §105 to extend the copyright prohibition to federal contractors, suggesting that such an amendment "would avoid all conflict with the First Amendment, without compromising any legitimate copyright interests."[6]

The note deals extensively — and quite persuasively — with written

---

[2] *Id.* at 1584.

[3] *Id.* at 1583.

[4] Note, A Constitutional Analysis of Copyrighting Government Commissioned Work, 84 Colum. L. Rev. 425 (1984).

[5] *Ibid.*

[6] *Ibid.*

materials funded by the United States government. Its essential point is that permitting federal contractors to copyright their works "impedes public access to these works."[7] The note does not, however, discuss a very significant portion of government commissioned work—public art. Witness the extensive commissioning of public art by the Government Services Administration. Certainly the public has "access" to these works; indeed the essence of the commissions is to display the artworks in public places. It is difficult to see why artists should not retain the copyright, for whatever purpose it may serve them. Experience has indicated that artists who receive public art commissions do not receive an economic windfall. If the copyright is a vehicle to advance an economic right, it should reside in the artist—not in the government—although the government should not be denied a royalty-free license to promote or otherwise publicize the work.

A recent congressional proposal to amend the copyright law with respect to works made for hire[8] would tilt the law further in the direction of the artists. One provision is particularly attractive to those who contribute their work to compilations and other similar works. It provides as follows:

> (f) UNJUST ENRICHMENT.—With respect to those categories of works enumerated in subsection (c) [contributions to collective works, supplementary works, instructional texts, and parts of audiovisual works other than motion pictures] an author may, at any time following the transfer of a copyright or of any rights under such copyright, bring an action to reform or terminate a transfer in which profits received by the transferee or his successors in title are strikingly disproportionate to the compensation, consideration, or share received by the author or his successors. In such action the plaintiff shall have the burden of proving that, taking into consideration all factors including the bargaining position of the parties and their respective contributions to the financial success of the work, the terms of the transfer have proven to be unfair or grossly disadvantageous to the author. The courts shall decide the action in accordance with the principles of equity, and shall have discretion to reform or terminate the transfer on whatever terms it considers just and reasonable.

Query whether this provision was intended to apply to existing works, or was to be prospective only. If it were interpreted to apply to works previously commissioned, it would appear that there would be presented a substantial constitutional question as to whether its provisions impaired the obligation of contracts.

---

[7] *Ibid.*

[8] S. 2138, 98th Cong., 1st Sess. (1983).

C. WORKS OF APPLIED ART

§2.10. THE FEDERAL COPYRIGHT ACT AND WORKS OF APPLIED ART

To this point in the chapter, the discussion has been limited to the application of copyright law to fine arts. In the real world, however, copyright issues have carried over into the much wider realm of applied art.

Art is more than a painting hung on a wall or a sculpture on a free-standing pedestal. Every commercial product sold in the United States has some form of graphic presentation. Is this "art" deserving of protection under the Copyright Act and is the creator an "author" within the constitutional sense?

Although applied art is outside the essential topic of this book, a brief examination of some of these issues further illuminates the general principles (and complexities) of copyright law. This part of the chapter includes the intriguing dissent from *Mazer v. Stein*, as well as four decisions that have wrestled with the applied art problem: *Esquire, Inc. v. Ringer, L. Batlin & Son, Inc. v. Snyder, Kieselstein-Cord v. Accessories By Pearl, Inc.,* and *Carol Barnhart Inc. v. Economy Cover Corp.*

§2.10.1. *Mazer v. Stein:* Copyrighting Useful or Commercial Articles

In the *Mazer* case, the U.S. Supreme Court was presented with the question of whether a lamp manufacturer could copyright his lamp-base. The Court, in reaching its conclusion that the item could be copyrighted, pointed out that as long as one hundred years earlier Congress had eliminated any distinction between "purely aesthetic articles and useful works of art." Because of the wide availability and notoriety of the case, we have limited its reproduction here to the dissent by Justice William Douglas. His opinion succinctly foreshadowed the morass that would be created by the extension of copyright to applied art.

MAZER v. STEIN
    347 U.S. 201, 74 S. Ct. 460, 98 L. Ed. 630 (1954)

[Dissenting] opinion of Mr. Justice DOUGLAS, in which Mr. Justice BLACK concurs.

An important constitutional question underlies this case — a question which was stirred on oral argument but not treated in the briefs. It is whether these statuettes of dancing figures may be copyrighted. Congress has provided that "works of art," "models or designs for works of art," and "reproductions of a work of art" may be copyrighted (17 USC §5); and the Court holds that these statuettes are included in the words "works of art." But may statuettes be granted the monopoly of the copyright?

Article 1, §8 of the Constitution grants Congress the power "To promote the Progress of Science and useful Arts, by securing for limited Times to Authors . . . the exclusive Right to their respective Writings. . . ." The power is thus circumscribed: it allows a monopoly to be granted only to "authors" for their "writings." Is a sculptor an "author" and is his statue a "writing" within the meaning of the Constitution? We have never decided the question.

Burrow-Giles Lithographic Co. v. Sarony, 111 US 53, 28 L ed 349, 4 S Ct 279, held that a photograph could be copyrighted.

Bleistein v. Donaldson Lithographing Co. 188 US 239, 47 L ed 460, 23 S. Ct 298, held that chromolithographs to be used as advertisements for a circus were "pictorial illustrations" within the meaning of the copyright laws. Broad language was used in the latter case, ". . . a very modest grade of art has in it something irreducible, which is one man's alone. That something he may copyright unless there is a restriction in the words of the act." 188 US, at p.250. But the constitutional range of the meaning of "writings" in the field of art was not in issue either in the Bleistein Case nor in *F. W. Woolworth Co. v. Contemporary Arts, Inc.* 344 US 228, 97 L ed 276, 73 S Ct 222, recently here on a writ for certiorari limited to a question of damages.

At times the Court has on its own initiative considered and decided constitutional issues not raised, argued, or briefed by the parties. Such, for example, was the case of *Continental Illinois Nat. Bank & T. Co. v. Chicago,* R. I. & P. R. Co. 294 US 648, 667, 79 L ed 1110, 1120, 55 S Ct 595, in which the Court decided the constitutionality of §77 of the Bankruptcy Act, 11 USC §205 though the question was not noticed by any party. We could do the same here and decide the question here and now. This case, however, is not a pressing one, there being no urgency for a decision. Moreover, the constitutional materials are quite meager (see Fenning, *The Origin of the Patent and Copyright Clause of the Constitution,* 17 Geo LJ 109 (1929); and much research is needed.

The interests involved in the category of "works of art," as used in the copyright law, are considerable. The Copyright Office has supplied us with a long list of such articles which have been copyrighted — statuettes, bookends, clocks, lamps, doorknockers, candlesticks, inkstands, chandeliers, piggy banks, sundials, salt and pepper shakers, fish bowls, and ash trays. Perhaps these are all "writings" in the constitutional sense. But to me, at least, they are not obviously so. It is time that we came to the problem full face. I would accordingly put the case down for reargument.

Reargument was denied, 349 U.S. 949 (1954). The fundamental question raised by Justice Douglas did, however, prompt an extensive law review note. See Note, *Study of the Term "Writings" in the Copyright Clause of The Constitution,* 31 N.Y.U. L. Rev. 1263, 1298, (1956). ("[N]o court has held a painting unprotectable because it was not a writing or a painter not an author.")

§2.10.2. *Esquire, Inc. v. Ringer:* **What Is a "Utilitarian" Article?**

Mazer v. Stein extended copyright law to applied art. To implement that decision, the Copyright Office was required to develop distinctions between useful articles that would be granted copyright protection as "works of art" and those that would not. The *Esquire* case, which follows, indicates the delicacy of the line that the office had to draw. The majority and concurring opinions are also important for their treatment of the procedural question of whether the denial of copyright registration by the Copyright Office may form the basis of a mandamus proceeding to review the office's action.

ESQUIRE, INC. v. RINGER
591 F.2d 796 (D.C. Cir. 1978)

BAZELON, C.J. This case presents the question whether the overall shape of certain outdoor lighting fixtures is eligible for copyright as a "work of art." The Register of Copyrights determined that the overall shape or configuration of such articles is not copyrightable. The district court disagreed, and issued a writ of mandamus directing the Register to enter the claim to copyright. *Esquire, Inc. v. Ringer,* 414 F. Supp. 939 (D.D.C. 1976). For the reasons expressed below, we reverse.

I
Although the issues involved are fairly complex, the facts may be briefly stated. Appellee, Esquire, Inc. (Esquire) submitted three applications to the Copyright Office for registration of what it described as "artistic design[s] for lighting fixture[s]." [1] Photographs accompanying

---

[1] Joint Appendix (J.A.) at 4, 8, 12.

the applications showed stationary outdoor luminaries or floodlights, of contemporary design, with rounded or elliptically-shaped housings.[2] The applications asserted that the designs were eligible for copyright protection as "works of art." 17 U.S.C. §5(g).

The Register of Copyrights (Register) refused to register Esquire's claims to copyright. The principal reason given was that Copyright Office regulations, specifically 37 C.F.R. §202.10(c) (1976), preclude registration of the design of a utilitarian article, such as lighting fixtures, "when all of the design elements . . . are directly related to the useful functions of the article. . . ."[3] The fixtures, according to the Register's analysis, did not contain "elements, either alone or in combination, which are capable of independent existence as a copyrightable pictorial, graphic, or sculptural work apart from the utilitarian aspect."[4] Esquire twice requested reconsideration of its copyright applications,[5] and was twice refused.[6]

Esquire then filed suit in the district court, seeking a writ of mandamus directing the Register to issue a certificate of copyright for its lighting fixture designs. This time, Esquire met with success. The court, per Judge Gesell, concluded that registration was compelled by *Mazer v. Stein*, 347 U.S. 201, 74 S. Ct. 460, 98 L. Ed. 630 (1954), where the Supreme Court upheld the copyright of statuettes intended to be mass-produced for use as table lamp bases. The district court reasoned that to uphold the issuance of the copyrights in *Mazer*, but deny Esquire's applications, would amount to affording certain copyright privileges to traditional works of art, but not to abstract, modern art forms. The court went on to find that "[t]he forms of the articles here in dispute are clearly art" and concluded that they were "entitled to the same recognition afforded more traditional sculpture." 414 F. Supp. at 941. The court also suggested that registration of Esquire's designs was compelled by prior "interpretative precedent." *Id.* This appeal followed.

The heart of the controversy in this case involves, in the district court's words, an "elusive semantic dispute" over the applicable regulation, 37

---

[2] Esquire's more detailed description of its lighting fixtures indicates that:

the lighting fixtures are provided with decorative housings having two different styles of artistic configuration. The ELLIPTRA I and ELLIPTRA II fixtures include oblate housings having a rounded upper portion, a cylindrical band between the upper and lower portions, and a cylindrical lower edge portion. The ELLIPTRA III design utilizes a generally cup-shaped housing having a generally elliptical cross section tapering into a rounded rear portion.

Plaintiff's Brief in Support of Motion for Summary Judgment at 4; Esquire, Inc. v. Ringer, 414 F. Supp. 939 (D.D.C. 1976).

[3] J.A. at 28.

[4] J.A. at 28-29.

[5] J.A. at 30-34 and 37-44.

[6] J.A. at 35-36 and 45-46.

C.F.R. §202.10(c). We have divided our analysis of this dispute into two parts: Part II considers whether the Register adopted a permissible interpretation of the regulation; Part III, whether the regulation, as interpreted, was properly applied to the facts presented by Esquire's applications.[7]

II

A

Section 5(g) of the Copyright Act of 1909, 17 U.S.C. §5(g), indicates that "[w]orks of art; models or designs for works of art" are eligible for copyright.[8] The terse language of the statute is more fully elaborated in regulations drafted by the Register pursuant to Congressional authorization.[9] The provision at issue, 37 C.F.R. §202.10(c), provides as follows:

---

[7] The district court's jurisdiction was based on the mandamus statute, 28 U.S.C. §1361 (1970). Mandamus was clearly an appropriate remedy to compel the Copyright Office to adopt a lawful interpretation of its own regulations. *Workman v. Mitchell*, 502 F.2d 1210, 1215 (9th Cir. 1974); see *Bouve v. Twentieth Century-Fox Film Corp.*, 74 U.S. App. D.C. 271, 122 F.2d 51 (1941). The propriety of mandamus to compel the Copyright Office to apply the regulation differently to the facts is considered in n.28 *infra*.

[8] The Copyright Act of 1976, 17 U.S.C. §§101-810 (1976) does not apply to this case. Section 103 of the Act, 90 Stat. 2599, indicates that "[t]his Act does not provide copyright protection for any work that goes into the public domain before January 1, 1978."

[9] "Subject to the approval of the Librarian of Congress, the Register of Copyrights shall be authorized to make rules and regulations for the registration of claims to copyright as provided by this title." 17 U.S.C. §207 (1970). See also 17 U.S.C. §702 (1976).

The Register has promulgated regulations, codified currently in 37 C.F.R. §202.10, to clarify the parameters of copyrightable "works of art." The general definition of "works of art," §202.10(a), was adopted in 1948. It evidences a concern — pervasive in this area — to distinguish between "works of art" eligible for copyright, and functional or utilitarian articles not so eligible.

WORKS OF ART (CLASS G)
(a) General. This class includes published or unpublished works of artistic craftsmanship, insofar as their form but not their mechanical or utilization aspects are concerned, such as artistic jewelry, enamels, glassware, and tapestries, as well as works belonging to the fine arts, such as paintings, drawings and sculpture.

37 C.F.R. §202.10(a).
Section 202.10(b) was enacted after the Supreme Court's decision in Mazer v. Stein, *supra*. This regulation embodies the principle, affirmed in *Mazer*, that commercial use does not disqualify an otherwise registrable work of art from copyright protection.

(b) In order to be acceptable as a work of art, the work must embody some creative authorship in its delineation or form. The registrability of a work of art is not affected by

(c) If the sole intrinsic function of an article is its utility, the fact that the article is unique and attractively shaped will not qualify it as a work of art. However, if the shape of a utilitarian article incorporates features, such as artistic sculpture, carving, or pictorial representation, which can be identified separately and are capable of existing independently as a work of art, such features will be eligible for registration.

The parties have advanced conflicting interpretations of §202.10(c). The Register interprets §202.10(c) to bar copyright registration of the overall shape or configuration of a utilitarian article, no matter how aesthetically pleasing that shape or configuration may be. As support for this interpretation, the Register notes that the regulation limits copyright protection to features of a utilitarian article that "can be identified separately and capable of existing independently as a work of art." The Register argues that this reading is required to enforce the congressional policy against copyrighting industrial designs, and that it is supported by the continued practice of the Copyright Office and by legislative history.

Esquire on the other hand, interprets §202.10(c) to allow copyright registration for the overall shape or design of utilitarian articles as long as the shape or design satisfies the requirements appurtenant to works of art — originality and creativity.[10] Esquire stresses that the first sentence of §202.10(c) reads in its entirety, "If the *sole* intrinsic function of an article is its utility, the fact that the article is unique and attractively shaped will not qualify it as a work of art." Esquire maintains that it designed its lighting fixtures with the intent of creating "works of modernistic form sculpture,"[11] and therefore that their *sole* intrinsic function is not utility. Esquire also contends that the language of §202.10(c) referring to "features . . . which can be identified separately and are capable of existing independently as a work of art" is not inconsistent with its interpretation. In effect, Esquire asserts that the *shape* of the lighting fixture is the "feature" that makes them eligible for copyright as a work of art. Esquire argues that its reading of §202.10(c) is required by

---

the intention of the author as to the use of the work, the number of copies reproduced, or the fact that it appears on a textile material or textile product. The potential availability of protection under the design patent law will not affect the registrability of a work of art, but a copyright claim in a patented design or in the drawings or photographs in a patent application will not be registered after the patent has been issued.

37 C.F.R. §202.10(b).

[10] "[T]he courts have uniformly inferred the [originality] requirement from the fact that copyright protection may only be claimed by 'authors,' or their successors in interest." 1 M. Nimmer, Copyright §10 at 32 (1976). The requirement of creativity with respect to works of art is embodied in 37 C.F.R. §202.10(b), *supra* n.9: "In order to be acceptable as a work of art, the work must embody some creative authorship in its delineation or form."

[11] Brief for Appellee at 5.

the decisions of the Supreme Court in *Mazer v. Stein*, 347 U.S. 201, 74 S. Ct. 460, 98 L. Ed. 630 (1954) and *Bleisten v. Donaldson Lithographing Co.*, 188 U.S. 239, 23 S. Ct. 298, 47 L. Ed. 460 (1903).

B

We conclude that the Register has adopted a reasonable and well-supported interpretation of §202.10(c).

The Register's interpretation of §202.10(c) derives from the principle that industrial designs are not eligible for copyright. Congress has repeatedly rejected proposed legislation that would make copyright protection available for consumer or industrial products.[12] Most recently, Congress deleted a proposed section from the Copyright Act of 1976 that would have "create[d] a new limited form of copyright protection for 'original' designs which are clearly a part of a useful article, regardless of whether such designs could stand by themselves, separate from the article itself."[13] In rejecting proposed Title II, Congress noted the administration's concern that to make such designs eligible for copyright would be to create a "new monopoly"[14] having obvious and significant anticompetitive effects.[15] The issues raised by Title II were left for further consid-

---

[12] Since 1914, approximately seventy design protection bills have been introduced in Congress, none of which has been enacted into law. Memorandum of Points and Authorities in Support of Defendant's Motion to Dismiss (Appendix A), Esquire, Inc. v. Ringer, 414 F. Supp. 939 (D.D.C. 1976).

[13] H.R. Rep. No. 1476, 94th Cong., 2d Sess. 50 (1976), U.S. Code Cong. & Admin. News 1976, pp.5659, 5663. The report explains that "[t]he Committee chose to delete Title II in part because the new form of design protection provided by Title II could not truly be considered copyright protection and therefore appropriately within the scope of copyright revision." *Id.*

[14] *Id.*

[15] The Register's brief illustrates the problems involved in allowing copyright of the shape of utilitarian articles.

There are several economic considerations that Congress must weigh before deciding whether, for utilitarian articles, shape alone, no matter how aesthetically pleasing, is enough to warrant copyright protection. First, in the case of some utilitarian objects, like scissors or paper clips, shape is mandated by function. If one manufacturer were given the copyright to the design of such an article, it could completely prevent others from producing the same article. Second, consumer preference sometimes demands uniformity of shape for certain utilitarian articles, like stoves for instance. People simply expect and desire certain everyday useful articles to look the same particular way. Thus, to give one manufacturer the monopoly on such a shape would also be anticompetitive [*sic*]. Third, insofar as geometric shapes are concerned, there are only a limited amount of basic shapes, such as circles, squares, rectangles and ellipses. These shapes are obviously in the public domain and accordingly it would be unfair to grant a monopoly on the use of any particular such shape, no matter how aesthetically well it was integrated into a utilitarian article.

Brief for Appellant at 18-19. See also Note, Protection for the Artistic Aspects of Articles of Utility, 72 Harv. L. Rev. 1520, 1532 (1959).

eration in "more complete hearings" to follow the enactment of the 1976 Act.[16]

In the Register's view, registration of the overall shape or configuration of utilitarian articles would lead to widespread copyright protection for industrial designs. The Register reasons that aesthetic considerations enter into the design of most useful objects. Thus, if overall shape or configuration can qualify as a "work of art," "the whole realm of consumer products — garments, toasters, refrigerators, furniture, bathtubs, automobiles, etc. — and industrial products designed to have aesthetic appeal — subway cars, computers, photocopying machines, typewriters, adding machines, etc. — must also qualify as works of art."[17]

Considerable weight is to be given to an agency's interpretation of its regulations. "[T]he ultimate criterion is the administrative interpretation, which becomes of controlling weight unless it is plainly erroneous or inconsistent with the regulation." *Bowles v. Seminole Rock & Sand Co.*, 325 U.S. 410, 414, 65 S. Ct. 1215, 1217, 89 L. Ed. 1700 (1945); accord, *Udall v. Tallman*, 380 U.S. 1, 16-18, 85 S. Ct. 792, 13 L. Ed. 2d 616 (1965); *Stein v. Mazer*, 204 F.2d 472, 477 (4th Cir. 1953), aff'd, 347 U.S. 201, 74 S. Ct. 460, 98 L. Ed. 630 (1954). This is particularly so if an administrative interpretation relates to a matter within the field of administrative expertise and has been consistently followed for a significant period of time. *Southern Mutual Help Ass'n v. Califano*, 187 U.S. App. D.C. 307, 574 F.2d 518, 526 (1977). The Register's interpretation of §202.10(c) reflects both administrative expertise and consistent application.

The regulation in question attempts to define the boundaries between copyrightable "works of art" and noncopyrightable industrial designs. This is an issue of long-standing concern to the Copyright Office, and is clearly a matter in which the Register has considerable expertise.[18]

Whether the Register's interpretation has been consistently followed for a significant period of time is somewhat less clear. Since the Copyright Office does not publish opinions explaining registration decisions, there is little evidence bearing directly on this point. What evidence exists, however, indicates that the Register's construction has been fol-

---

[16] H.R. Rep. No. 1476, *supra* note 13, at 50.

[17] Memorandum of Points and Authorities in Support of Defendant's Motion to Dismiss at 15, Esquire, Inc. v. Ringer, 414 F. Supp. 939 (D.D.C. 1976).

[18] The Register indicates that the concepts of "intrinsic function," "works of art," and separation of features, embodied in 37 C.F.R. §202.10(c), "are the result of a most searching and careful consideration by the Copyright Office of the intendment of the Copyright Act and the substantial economic impact of its decisions in this area. . . . [T]he language of the provision was not casually chosen." Memorandum of Points and Authorities in Support of Defendant's Motion to Dismiss at 20, Esquire, Inc. v. Ringer, 414 F. Supp. 939 (D.D.C. 1976).

lowed consistently.[19] The district court suggested, without elaboration, that prior registration decisions create an "interpretative precedent" favoring Esquire's position. 414 F. Supp. at 941. But we think this confuses the *test* employed by the Copyright Office in evaluating the copyrightability of utilitarian articles with the *results* that obtained after the test was applied. The Register's test requires the application of subjective judgment, and given the large volume of copyright applications that must be processed there may be some results that are difficult to square with the denial of registration here.[20] But this does not mean that the Register has

---

[19] See, e.g., SCOA Industries, Inc. v. Famolare, Inc., 192 U.S.P.Q. 216, 218 (S.D.N.Y. 1976) (affirming denial of registration of shoe sole under §202.10(c) since "the troughs, waves and lines which appear on the shoe sole cannot be identified and do not exist independently as works of art"); Ted Arnold Ltd. v. Silvercraft Co. 259 F. Supp. 733 (S.D.N.Y. 1966) (affirming issuance of copyright under §202.10(c) because the registered article — a simulated antique telephone — could be separated physically and existed independently as a work of art apart from the pencil sharpener housed within the telephone casing). See also Vacheron & Constantin Le Coultre Watches, Inc. v. Benrus Watch Co., 155 F. Supp. 932, 934 (S.D.N.Y. 1957), *rev'd in part on other grounds,* 260 F.2d 637 (2nd Cir. 1958).

The principle that copyright registration is not available for the overall shape or configuration of industrial articles appears to antedate the promulgation of §202.10(c):

> Since 1909, it seems to have been the practice of the Copyright Office to grant copyrights to works of art, and to deny copyrights to purely utilitarian objects. An object of artistic conception in a standard art form — e.g., sculpture or painting — has not been denied registration merely because of its possible utilitarian aspects. It is the work of art that is thus protected, not its utilitarian aspects. Thus copyright registration has been granted for stained glass windows, bas-relief bronze doors, sculptures in book-ends, candlestick holders and statuary lamps.
>
> On the other hand, it has been the practice of the Copyright Office since 1909 to refuse copyright registration *only* to those works of a wholly utilitarian nature, which could not be called works of art although they might possess pleasing design. Rejection has been placed on the ground that protection for such works lay only under the Design Patent Law. Thus, registration has been refused for designs for refrigerators, clocks, stoves, gasoline pumps and oil dispensers.

Stein v. Mazer, 204 F.2d 472, 477 (4th Cir. 1953), *aff'd,* 347 U.S. 201, 74 S. Ct. 460, 98 L. Ed. 630 (1954).

[20] Esquire contends that the Register has copyrighted the shape of useful articles, citing as support Monogram Models, Inc. v. Industro Motive Corp., 492 F.2d 1281 (6th Cir.), *cert denied,* 419 U.S. 843, 95 S. Ct. 76, 42 L. Ed. 2d 71 (1974) (registration of model airplane kit as a kit); S-K Potteries & Mold Co. v. Sipes, 192 U.S.P.Q. 537 (N.D. Ind. 1976) (registration of the designs on master molds for ceramic reproduction); Ted Arnold Ltd. v. Silvercraft Co., 259 F. Supp. 733 (S.D.N.Y. 1966) (registration of simulated antique telephone use as housing of pencil sharpener); Royalty Designs, Inc. v. Thrifticheck Service Corp., 204 F. Supp. 702 (S.D.N.Y. 1962) (registration of plastic molded toy coin banks in the shape of dogs); Copyright Registrations GU 50142 & GU 50143 (registration of candlesticks). The Register maintains with some plausibility that these cases were either [in]correctly decided, see, e.g., Ted Arnold, *supra* n.19, or that they are

employed different standards in reaching these decisions. The available evidence points to a uniform and long-standing interpretation of §202.10(c), and accordingly this interpretation is entitled to great weight.

The Register's interpretation of §202.10(c) finds further support in the legislative history of the recently enacted 1976 Copyright Act.[21] Although not applicable to the case before us,[22] the new Act was designed in part to codify and clarify many of the regulations promulgated under the 1909 Act, including those governing "works of art."[23] Thus, the 1976 Act and its legislative history can be taken as an expression of congressional understanding of the scope of protection for utilitarian articles under the old regulations. "Subsequent legislation which declares the intent of an earlier law is not, of course, conclusive. . . . But the later law is entitled to weight when it comes to the problem of construction." *Federal Housing Administration v. The Darlington, Inc.*, 358 U.S. 84, 90, 79 S. Ct. 141, 145, 3 L. Ed. 2d 132 (1958).

The House Report indicates that the section of the 1976 Act governing "pictorial, graphic and sculptural works" was intended "to draw as clear a line as possible between copyrightable works of applied art and un-

---

distinguishable. For example, the Register asserts that the candlesticks registered in Copyright Registration GU 50142 & GU 50143 belong "to a small special category of articles . . . [whose] utilitarian function . . . has now atrophied." Reply Br. for Appellant at 5.

[21] 17 U.S.C. §§101-810 (1976) (effective January 1, 1978).

[22] See n.8 *supra*.

[23] The former classification "works of art" has been reformulated as "pictorial, graphic, and sculptural works" under the new Act. 17 U.S.C. §102(a)(5) (1976). Section 101 of the Act advises that works encompassed within this category

include two-dimensional and three-dimensional works of fine, graphic, and applied art, photographs, prints and art reproductions, maps, globes, charts, technical drawings, diagrams, and models. Such works shall include *works of artistic craftsmanship insofar as their form but not their mechanical or utilitarian aspects are concerned;* the design of a useful article . . . shall be considered a pictorial, graphic, or sculptural work only if, and only to the extent that such *design incorporates pictorial, graphic or sculptural features that can be identified seperately from, and are capable of existing independently of, the utilitarian aspects of the article.*

17 U.S.C. §101 (1976). The two italicized passages are drawn from 37 C.F.R. §§202.10(a) and (c), respectively. Section 202.10(a) was expressly endorsed by the Supreme Court in Mazer v. Stein, 347 U.S. 201, 74 S. Ct. 460, 98 L. Ed. 630 (1954). The Committee on the Judiciary incorporated its language into "the definition of 'pictorial, graphic, and sculptural works' in an effort to make clearer the distinction between works of applied art protectable under the bill and industrial designs not subject to copyright protection." H.R. Rep. No. 1476, *supra* n.13, at 54, U.S. Code Cong. & Admin. News 1976, p.5667. The second italicized passage "is an adaption of [§202.10(c)], added to the Copyright Office Regulations in the mid-1950's in an effort to implement the Supreme Court's decision in the *Mazer* case." *Id.* at 54-55, U.S. Code Cong. & Admin. News 1976, p.5668.

copyrighted works of industrial design." [24] The Report illustrates the distinction in the following terms:

> [A]lthough the shape of an industrial product may be aesthetically satisfying and valuable, the Committee's intention is not to offer it copyright protection under the bill. Unless the shape of an automobile, airplane, ladies' dress, food processor, television set, or any other industrial product contains some element that, physically or conceptually, can be identified as separable from the utilitarian aspects of that article, the design would not be copyrighted under the bill. The test of separability and independence from "the utilitarian aspects of the article" does not depend upon the nature of the design — that is, *even if the appearance of an article is determined by esthetic (as opposed to functional) considerations, only elements, if any, which can be identified separately from the useful article as such are copyrightable.* And even if the three dimensional design contains some such element (for example, a carving on the back of a chair or a floral relief design on silver flatware), *copyright protection would extend only to that element, and would not cover the over-all configuration of the utilitarian article as such.*

H. Rep. No. 1476, 94th Cong., 2d Sess. 55 (1976), U.S. Code Cong. & Admin. News 1976, p.5668 (emphasis added).

This excerpt is not entirely free from ambiguity. Esquire could arguably draw some support from the statement that a protectable element of a utilitarian article must be separable "physically *or conceptually*" from the utilitarian aspects of the design. But any possible ambiguity raised by this isolated reference disappears when the excerpt is considered in its entirety. The underscored passages indicate unequivocally that the overall design or configuration of a utilitarian object, even if it is determined by aesthetic as well as functional considerations, is not eligible for copyright. Thus the legislative history, taken as congressional understanding of existing law, reinforces the Register's position.

The legislative history of the 1976 Act also supports the Register's practice of ascribing little weight to the phrase "sole intrinsic function." As noted above, see TAN 11 *supra*, Esquire contends that as long as the overall shape of a utilitarian article embodies *dual* intrinsic functions — aesthetic and utilitarian — that shape may qualify for registration. But the new Act includes a definition of "useful article," referred to by the House Report as "an adaptation" of the language of §202.10(c), H.R. Rep. No. 1476, *supra* n.13, at 54, U.S. Code Cong. & Admin. News 1976, p.5668, which provides: "A 'useful article' is an article having *an* intrinsic utilitarian function that is not merely to portray the appearance of the article or to convey information." 17 U.S.C. §101 (1976) (emphasis added). In deleting the modifier "sole" from the language taken from §202.10(c), the draftsmen of the 1976 Act must have concluded that the

---

[24] H.R. Rep. No. 1476, *supra* n.13, at 55.

definition of "useful article" would be more precise without this term. Moreover, Congress may have concluded that literal application of the phrase "sole intrinsic function" would create an unworkable standard. For as one commentator has observed, "[t]here are no two-dimensional works and few three-dimensional objects whose design is absolutely dictated by utilitarian considerations."[25]

C

The district court basically ignored the foregoing considerations. Instead, it advanced two reasons for rejecting the Register's interpretation of §202.10(c) as a matter of law. It concluded, first, that the Register's construction was inconsistent with the Supreme Court's decision in *Mazer v. Stein,* 347 U.S. 201, 79 S. Ct. 141, 3 L. Ed. 2d 132 (1954). Second, it found that the Register's interpretation amounted to impermissible discrimination against abstract modern art. We respectfully disagree on both counts.

We are unable to join in the district court's broad reading of *Mazer v. Stein, supra.*[26] The principal issue in *Mazer* was whether objects that are concededly "works of art" can be copyrighted if incorporated into mass-produced utilitarian articles. The Register had issued copyright certificates for the statuettes of Balinese dancing figures created with the intent to reproduce and sell them as bases for table lamps. The Court noted that the "long-continued construction of the statutes" by the Copyright Office permitted registration of the statuettes as "works of art." 347 U.S. at 213, 74 S. Ct. at 468. It then concluded that there was "nothing in the copyright statute to support the argument that the intended use or use in industry of *an article eligible for copyright* bars or invalidates its registration." *Id.* at 218, 74 S. Ct. at 471 (emphasis added).

The issue here — whether the overall shape of a utilitarian object is "an article eligible for copyright" — was not addressed in *Mazer.* In fact, under the Register's interpretation of §202.10(c), the dancing figures considered in *Mazer* would clearly be copyrightable. The statuettes were undeniably capable of existing as a work of art independent of the utilitarian article into which they were incorporated. And they were clearly a "feature" segregable from the overall shape of the table lamps. There is

---

[25] Comment, Copyright Protection for Mass-Produced, Commercial Products: A Review of the Developments Following Mazer v. Stein, 38 U. Chi. L. Rev. 807, 812 (1971).

[26] A number of authorities are in agreement that *Mazer* should not be read as opening the door to the inclusion of industrial designs under copyright law. See B. Kaplan, An Unhurried View of Copyright 55 (1968); 38 U. Chi. L. Rev. *supra* note 25, at 823; 72 Harv. L. Rev., *supra*, n.15 at 1526.

thus no inconsistency between the copyright upheld in *Mazer* and the Register's interpretation of §202.10(c) here.

The district court's second conclusion is somewhat more problematical. The court found, in effect, that that Register's interpretation of §202.10(c) amounted to impermissible discrimination against designs that "emphasize line and shape rather than the realistic or the ornate. . . ." 414 F. Supp. at 941.

We agree with the district court that the Copyright Act does not enshrine a particular conception of what constitutes "art." *Id.*[27] As Justice Holmes noted in *Bleistein v. Donaldson Lithographing Co.*, 188 U.S. 239, 251, 23 S. Ct. 298, 300, 47 L. Ed. 460 (1903), "[i]t would be a dangerous undertaking for persons trained only to the law to constitute themselves final judges of the worth of pictorial illustrations. . . ." Neither the Constitution nor the Copyright Act authorizes the Copyright Office or the federal judiciary to serve as arbiters of national taste. These officials have no particular competence to assess the merits of one genre of art relative to another. And to allow them to assume such authority would be to risk stultifying the creativity and originality the copyright laws were expressly designed to encourage. *Id.* at 251-52, 23 S. Ct. 298; accord, *Mazer v. Stein, supra* at 214, 79 S. Ct. 141.

But in our view the present case does not offend the nondiscrimination principle recognized in *Bleistein*. *Bleistein* was concerned only with conscious bias against one form of art — in that case the popular art reflected in circus posters. Esquire's complaint, in effect, is that the Register's interpretation of §202.10(c) places an inadvertent burden on a particular form of art, namely modern abstract sculpture. We may concede, for present purposes, that an interpretation of §202.10(c) that bars copyright for the overall design or configuration of a utilitarian object will have a disproportionate impact on designs that exhibit the characteristics of abstract sculpture. But we can see no justification, at least in the circumstances of this case, for extending the nondiscrimination principle of *Bleistein* to include action having an unintentional, disproportionate impact on one style of artistic expression. Such an extension of the nondiscrimination principle would undermine other plainly legitimate goals of copyright law — in this case the congressional directive that copyright protection should not be afforded to industrial designs.

At oral argument, Esquire proposed for the first time a test which it claimed would respect the principle disfavoring the copyright of in-

---

[27] The House Report accompanying the 1976 Copyright Act reaffirms this principle. "[T]he definition of 'pictorial, graphic, and sculptural works' carries with it no implied criterion of artistic taste, aesthetic value, or intrinsic quality." H.R. Rep. No. 1476, *supra* n.13, at 54, U.S. Code Cong. & Admin. News 1976, p.5667.

dustrial designs, and yet would not impose a differential burden on modernistic art forms. Esquire suggested that the overall design or configuration of a utilitarian article should be copyrightable as a work of art if its shape is original and creative, and it exhibits "a sufficient quantity of intellectual labor" to distinguish it from everyday industrial designs. However, Esquire was unable to cite any authority in support of this proposed test. Moreover, such a test would pose obvious administrative difficulties, and would appear to thrust the Copyright Office and the courts into the very role Esquire argues so forcefully against — as overseers of the relative "worth" or value of different forms of art. Accordingly, we find no basis for requiring the Register to consider Esquire's belated suggestion.

III

Given that the Register adopted an appropriate interpretation of §202.10(c), the question remains whether the regulation was properly applied to the materials presented by Esquire's copyright claims. In general, the Copyright Act "establishes a wide range of selection within which discretion must be exercised by the Register in determining what he has no power to accept." *Bouve v. Twentieth Century-Fox Film Corp.*, *supra* 74 U.S. App. D.C. at 273, 122 F.2d at 53; accord, Op. Att'y, Gen., 183 U.S.P.Q. 624, 628 (1974); 30 Op. Att'y Gen. 422, 424 (1915). Here, the application of the regulation to the facts presented by Esquire's copyright applications unquestionably involved the exercise of administrative discretion.[28]

---

[28] Traditionally, of course, the writ of mandamus is not available to review nonministerial, discretionary decisions. See, e.g., Panama Canal Co. v. Grace Line, Inc., 356 U.S. 309, 318, 78 S. Ct. 752, 2 L. Ed. 2d 788 (1958). Recently, however, a number of courts have indicated that even discretionary decisions may be set aside under the mandamus statute, 28 U.S.C. §1361, if they fall outside the bounds of "any rational exercise of discretion." United States v. Commanding Office, Armed Forces, 403 F.2d 371, 374 (2d Cir. 1968), *cert. denied*, 394 U.S. 929, 89 S. Ct. 1195, 22 L. Ed. 2d 460 (1969); accord, Miller v. Ackerman, 488 F.2d 920, 922 (8th Cir. 1973); Lovallo v. Froehlke, 468 F.2d 340, 346 (2d Cir. 1972). The interpretation of 28 U.S.C.§1361 supported by the concurrence would extend mandamus jurisdiction one step further, and implies that mandamus is appropriate whenever, under §10 of the Administrative Procedure Act, 5 U.S.C. §706, a discretionary decision is "arbitrary, carpricious, an abuse of discretion, or otherwise not in accordance with law." See Peoples v. United States Dept. of Agriculture, 138 U.S. App. D.C. 291, 295, 427 F.2d 561, 565 (1970). The possible distinctions between these standards, and the considerations relevant to which should apply, were neither briefed nor argued. Nor is it necessary to resolve these questions here, for it is abundantly clear that under any standard the Register's application of §202.10(c) did not constitute an abuse of discretion.

When the question of the application of the regulation was raised at oral argument, Esquire took the position that its copyright applications should be read as requesting registration for only *part* of a utilitarian object. Specifically, Esquire maintained that it sought registration for the *housing* of each fixture, not for the design of the entire lighting assembly — including base, housing, electrical fixture, and light bulb. But Esquire's applications were not so limited. Each characterized the work for which registration was sought as an "artistic design for lighting fixtures." [29] The photographs accompanying the applications portrayed both housings and bases for the lighting fixtures. No lesser feature was singled out as being that for which registration was sought. On the basis of these submissions, the Register could quite reasonably conclude that Esquire was claiming a copyright for the overall design of its outdoor lighting fixtures. The denial of registration in these circumstances did not amount to an abuse of discretion.

For the aforesaid reasons, the decision of the district court is

Reversed.

LEVENTHAL, C.J., concurring. I concur in the judgment of reversal. I also concur in Judge Bazelon's opinion which I understand to hold that the provision of the Copyright Act limiting design copyright protection to "works of art," 17 U.S.C. §5(g) (1976), authorizes the issuance of the pertinent Copyright Office regulations, 37 C.F.R. §202.10(c) (1977), and that both statute and regulations may be interpreted to preclude registration (a) of the design of a useful article, however aesthetically valuable, and (b) of any elements of the design unless they can be identified

---

We do not question that in appropriate circumstances, the denial of registration may be reviewed in the district court in an action in the nature of mandamus. Indeed, as noted earlier, (see n.7 *supra*) mandamus would be an appropriate remedy where federal officials are acting contrary to their own regulations. Other copyright cases have presented situations where jurisdiction was found to lie under mandamus. See, e.g., Bouve v. Twentieth Century-Fox Film Corp., 74 U.S. App. D.C. 271, 122 F.2d 51 (1941); Hoffenberg v. Kaminstein, 130 U.S. App. D.C. 35, 396 F.2d 684, *cert. denied*, 393 U.S. 913, 89 S. Ct. 235, 21 L. Ed. 2d 199 (1968). But cf. Public Affairs Associates, Inc. v. Rickover, 268 F. Supp. 444 (D.D.C. 1967).

We note that the new Copyright Act provides a jurisdictional basis other than mandamus to challenge the denial of copyright registration. Under the old Act, an infringement suit could not be brought until registration had been obtained. Vacheron & Constantin-Le Coultre Watches, Inc. v. Benrus Watch Co., 260 F.2d 637 (2d Cir. 1958). Under the 1976 Copyright Act, however, an infringement action may be brought after applying for registration, even if registration has been denied. 17 U.S.C. §411 (1976). In such an infringement suit the court would then review the denial of registration. *Id.* See H.R. Rep. No. 1476, *supra* note 13, at 157.

[29] J.A. at 4, 8, 12.

separately from the utilitarian aspects of the design. Esquire contends that the restrictive passage of section 202.10(c), which refers to situations where "the sole intrinsic function of an article is its utility," must be read narrowly, so as to make the prohibition on registration inapplicable where an article possesses from the outset not only utility but an aesthetically original and pleasing design form. I join in the rejection of that contention. Form follows function, in the credo of one school of art. Yet the overall legislative policy against monopoly for industrial design sustains the Copyright Office in its effort to distinguish between the instances where the aesthetic element is conceptually severable and the instances where the aesthetic element is inextricably interwoven with the utilitarian aspect of the article.

I add a word to note that Judge Bazelon's opinion reflects the court's premise that the district court had jurisdiction of this action even though Esquire requested issuance of a writ of mandamus to the Register of Copyrights.

The courts have issued mandatory instructions to federal officials notwithstanding the wording of Federal Rule of Civil Procedure 81(b), which by its terms abolishes the writ of mandamus in the federal district courts.[1] The rule permits equivalent relief, and the courts have issued orders that "for brevity, we may still speak of as . . . 'mandamus.' "[2]

The Mandamus and Venue Act of 1962, 28 U.S.C. §1361 (1970), authorizes district courts generally to issue writs of mandamus to federal officials and "to issue appropriate corrective orders where Federal officials are not acting within the zone of their permissible discretion but are abusing their discretion or otherwise acting contrary to law."[3] Although 28 U.S.C. §1361 applies only in case of a "duty owed to plaintiff," it is not bounded by the hoary strictures of old mandamus law.

Apart from an action in mandamus, which may retain residual rigidity, there is jurisdiction to provide declaratory relief under the 1976 amendment to 28 U.S.C. §1331. That eliminated the jurisdictional amount requirement for any federal question in an "action brought

---

[1] See K. Davis, Administrative Law Treatise §23.10 (1958).

[2] Vacheron & Constantin-Le Coultre Watches, Inc. v. Benrus Watch Co., 260 F.2d 637, 640 (2d Cir. 1958) (L. Hand, J.).

[3] People v. United States Dept. of Agriculture, 138 U.S. App. D.C. 291, 295,427 F.2d 561, 565 (1970); Haneke v. Secretary of HEW, 175 U.S. App. D.C. 329, 333-34, 535 F.2d 1291, 1295-96 (1976). Prior to 1962 the District Court of District of Columbia was the only federal court that had authority, by virtue of its general equity jurisdiction, to issue a writ against a federal official. See Kendall v. United States, 37 U.S. (12 Pet.) 524, 9 L. Ed. 1181 (1838); McIntire v. Wood, 11 U.S. (7 Cranch) 504, 3 L. Ed. 420 (1813). See generally Byse & Fiocca, Section 1361 of the Mandamus and Venue Act of 1962 and "Nonstatutory" Judicial Review of Federal Administrative Action, 81 Harv. L. Rev. 308, 310-13 (1967).

against the United States, any agency thereof, or any officer or employee thereof in his official capacity." Now section 1331 broadly confers jurisdiction on federal courts to review agency action "subject only to preclusion-of-review statutes created or retained by Congress." *Califano v. Sanders,* 430 U.S. 99, 105, 97 S. Ct. 980, 984, 51 L. Ed. 2d 192 (1977). Regulations implementing federal statutes have the "force and effect of law"[4] and cases arising under them are cases arising "under . . . laws . . . of the United States." 28 U.S.C. §1331(a) (1970).[5]

As Judge Bazelon's opinion notes (fn. 28) the 1976 revision of the Copyright Act permits a copyright claimant to bring an infringement action even though the copyright has not been registered. 17 U.S.C. §411 (1976). That statutory provision permits review of the Register's negative decision, and gives the Register an option to intervene. But the Copyright Act requires an infringement, and the claimant may wish to seek prior relief, i.e., to obtain the copyright registration, precisely in order to avoid the infringement and its disastrous business consequences.[6]

---

[4] Batterton v. Francis, 432 U.S. 416, 425 n.9, 97 S. Ct. 2399,53 L. Ed. 2d 448 (1977); Foti v. Immigration and Naturalization Serv., 375 U.S. 217, 222, 84 S. Ct. 306, 11 L. Ed. 2d 281 (1963); see Service v. Dulles, 354 U.S. 363, 77 S. Ct. 1152, 1 L. Ed. 2d 1403 (1957).

As to the "force of law" given to administrative regulations, a striking instance is Paul v. United States, 371 U.S. 245, 83 S. Ct. 426, 9 L. Ed. 2d 292 (1963), holding that Armed Services Procurement Regulation requiring competitive bidding has "the force of law" and overrides California's minimum price regulation of milk insofar as it purported to regulate sales of milk to military installations. Thus regulations were federal law for purposes of the Supremacy Clause. In 1963 the Court of Claims held that although the standard termination-for-convenience clause had been omitted from a contract, it would be deemed part of the procurement agreement since its inclusion was required by regulation, which had the "force of law." G. L. Christian and Associates v. United States, 312 F.2d 418, 160 Ct. Cl. 1, *cert. denied,* 375 U.S. 954, 84 S. Ct. 444, 11 L. Ed. 2d 314 (1963). See generally Leventhal, Public Contracts and Administrative Law, 52 A.B.A.J. 35 (1966).

The foregoing does not preclude an attack, for reasons of procedure or substance, on the regulations or any provision of the regulations.

[5] Compare Judge Friendly's opinion in Empresa Hondurena De Vapores v. McLeod, 300 F.2d 222 (2d Cir. 1962,) *vacated on other grounds sub nom.* McCulloch v. Sociedad Nacional de Marineros de Honduras, 372 U.S. 10, 83 S. Ct. 671, 9 L. Ed. 2d 547 (1963). That case involved an attempt by a Honduran corporation to enjoin a Regional Director of the NLRB from conducting a representation election on a Honduran registered vessel. In holding that the controversy was one "arising under" federal law, Judge Friendly observed: "it would run counter both to the language and to the policy underlying [28 U.S.C. §1337] to hold that the jurisdictional grant did not include an action whose sole purpose is to challenge an order of a Federal agency sought to be justified by a Federal statute." 300 F.2d at 226-27.

[6] Whether the Copyright Act remedy is exclusive in the event of infringement is a separate question.

As for litigation involving details of application of a regulation, the Register of Copyrights has broad discretion. In this case, as Judge Bazelon points out, the application of the regulation to the facts involved the exercise of administrative discretion, and the denial of registration in the circumstances did not amount to an abuse of discretion. The subject-matter of copyrights is such as to suggest that rarely if ever will a ruling denying an application for copyright on the basis of the application of a regulation be considered a contravention of a duty owed to the applicant. There is jurisdiction but no large likelihood of sucessful invocation.

§2.10.3. L. Batlin & Son, Inc. v. Snyder: How Original Is a Mass-Produced Product?

The *Batlin* case, which follows, is presented at this point in the chapter, but could just as well have been inserted earlier following the *Alva Studios, Inc. v. Winninger* case, reproduced at §2.5.1 *supra*. One of the key issues in the case is the extent to which a work, in order to be granted copyright protection, must contain originality. The test under the decision is that it must contain "some substantial," "not merely a trivial" originality. This test should be contrasted with the result — but not the rationale — reached in the *Alva Studios* case. Indeed, the *Batlin* court specifically distinguished the facts in *Alva Studios*. *Batlin* can also be read as disclosing the extent to which a party can obtain a copyright in a mass-produced commercial item — in this case, a mechanical toy savings bank. It further indicates that the issue of copyright can arise in a proceeding other than a straight infringement action. The plaintiff instituted suit to compel the cancellation of a recordation with the U.S. Custom Service of a copyright that would have prevented the plaintiff from importing the product into the United States.

L. BATLIN & SON, INC. v. SNYDER
536 F.2d 486 (2d Cir. 1976)

OAKES, C.J. Appellants Jeffrey Snyder and Etna Products Co., Inc., his licensee, appeal from a preliminary injunction granted L. Batlin & Son, Inc. (Batlin), compelling appellants to cancel a recordation of a copyright with the United States Customs Service and restraining them from enforcing that copyright. The district court held, 394 F. Supp. 1389 (S.D.N.Y. 1975), as it had previously in *Etna Products Co. v. E. Mishan & Sons*, 75 Civ. 428 (S.D.N.Y. Feb. 13, 1975), that there was "little probability" that appellants' copyright "will be found valid in the trial on the merits" on the basis that any variations between appellants' copyrighted plastic bank and a cast iron bank in the public domain were merely "trivial," and hence appellants' bank insufficiently "original" to support a copyright. 394 F. Supp. at 1390, *citing Alfred Bell & Co. v. Catalda Fine Arts, Inc.*, 191 F.2d 99 (2d Cir. 1951). We agree with the district court and therefore affirm the judgment granting the preliminary injunction.

Uncle Sam mechanical banks have been on the American scene at least since June 8, 1886, when Design Patent No. 16,728, issued on a toy savings bank of its type. The basic delightful design has long since been in the public domain. The banks are well documented in collectors' books and known to the average person interested in Americana. A description of the bank is that Uncle Sam, dressed in his usual stove pipe hat, blue full dress coat, starred vest and red and white striped trousers, and leaning on his umbrella, stands on a four- or five-inch wide base, on which sits his carpetbag. A coin may be placed in Uncle Sam's extended hand. When a lever is pressed, the arm lowers, and the coin falls into the bag, while Uncle Sam's whiskers move up and down. The base has an embossed American eagle on it with the words "Uncle Sam" on streamers above it, as well as the word "Bank" on each side. Such a bank is listed in a number of collectors' books, the most recent of which may be F. H. Griffith, Mechanical Banks (1972 ed.) where it was listed as No. 280, and is said to be not particularly rare.

Appellant Jeffrey Snyder doing business as "J.S.N.Y." obtained a registration of copyright on a plastic "Uncle Sam bank" in Class G ("Works of Art") as "sculpture" on January 23, 1975. According to Snyder's affidavit, in January, 1974, he had seen a cast metal antique Uncle Sam bank with an overall height of the figure and base of 11 inches.[1] In April, 1974, he flew to Hong Kong to arrange for the design and eventual manufacture of replicas of the bank as Bicentennial items, taking the cast metal Uncle Sam bank with him. His Hong Kong buying agent selected a firm, "Unitoy," to make the plastic "prototype" because of its price and the quality of its work. Snyder wanted his bank to be made of plastic and to be shorter than the cast metal sample "in order to fit into the required price range and quality and quantity of material to be used." The figure of Uncle Sam was thus shortened from 11 to nine inches, and the base shortened and narrowed. It was also decided, Snyder averred, to change the shape of the carpetbag and to include the umbrella in a one-piece mold for the Uncle Sam figure, "so as not to have a problem with a loose umbrella or a separate molding process." The

---

[1] No cast iron *antique* bank was introduced in evidence below. A cast metal *replica* bank was, and the court below, the parties, the witnesses, and this court have treated the case as if the appellants' plastic bank were to be compared to the cast metal replica.

Unitoy representative made his sketches while looking at the cast metal bank. After a "clay model" was made, a plastic "prototype" was approved by Snyder and his order placed in May, 1974. The plastic bank carried the legend "© Copyright J.S.N.Y." and was assertedly first "published" on October 15, 1974, before being filed with the Register of Copyrights in January, 1975.

Appellee Batlin is also in the novelty business and as early as August 9, 1974, ordered 30 cartons of cast iron Uncle Sam mechanical banks from Taiwan where its president had seen the bank made. When he became aware of the existence of a plastic bank, which he considered "an almost identical copy" of the cast iron bank, Batlin's trading company in Hong Kong procured a manufacturer and the president of Batlin ordered plastic copies also. Beginning in April, 1975, Batlin was notified by the United States Customs Service that the plastic banks it was receiving were covered by appellants copyright. In addition the Customs Service was also refusing entry to cast iron banks previously ordered, according to the Batlin affidavit. Thus Batlin instituted suit for a judgment declaring appellants' copyright void and for damages for unfair competition and restraint of trade. The sole question on this appeal is whether Judge Metzner abused his discretion in granting Batlin a preliminary injunction. We find that he did not.

This court has examined both the appellants' plastic Uncle Sam bank made under Snyder's copyright and the uncopyrighted model cast iron mechanical bank which is itself a reproduction of the original public domain Uncle Sam bank. Appellant Snyder claims differences not only of size but also in a number of other very minute details: the carpetbag shape of the plastic bank is smooth, the iron bank rough; the metal bank bag is fatter at its base; the eagle on the front of the platform in the metal bank is holding arrows in his talons while in the plastic bank he clutches leaves, this change concededly having been made, however, because "the arrows did not reproduce well in plastic on a smaller size." The shape of Uncle Sam's face is supposedly different, as is the shape and texture of the hats, according to the Snyder affidavit. In the metal version the umbrella is hanging loose while in the plastic item it is included in the single mold. The texture of the clothing, the hairline, shape of the bow ties and of the shirt collar and left arm as well as the flag carrying the name on the base of the statue are all claimed to be different, along with the shape and texture of the eagles on the side. Many of these differences are not perceptible to the casual observer. Appellants make no claim for any difference based on the plastic mold lines in the Uncle Sam figure which are perceptible.

Our examination of the banks results in the same conclusion as that of Judge Metzner in *Etna Products*, the earlier case enjoining Snyder's copyright, that the Snyder bank is "extremely similar to the cast iron bank, save in size and material" with the only other differences, such as the shape of the satchel and the leaves in the eagle's talons being "by all appearances, minor." Similarities include, more importantly, the appearance and number of stripes on the trousers, buttons on the coat, and stars on the vest and hat, the attire and pose of Uncle Sam, the decor on his base and bag, the overall color scheme, the method of carpetbag opening, to name but a few. After seeing the banks and hearing conflicting testimony from opposing expert witnesses as to the substantiality or triviality of the variations and as to the skill necessary to make the plastic model, the court below stated:

> I am making a finding of fact that as far as I'm concerned, it is practically an exact copy and whatever you point to in this [sic] differences are so infinitesimal they make no difference. All you have proved here by the testimony today is that if you give a man a seven-inch model and you say I want this to come out in a five-inch model, and he copies it, the fact that he has to have some artistic ability to make a model by reducing the seven to the five adds something to it. That is the only issue in this case.
>
> Mr. Faber: No, sir.
>
> The Court: That is the only issue. I have given you my finding of fact.

As Judge Metzner went on to say in his opinion, the appellants' plastic version "reproduces" the cast iron bank "except that it proportionately reduces the height from approximately eleven inches to approximately nine inches with trivial variations." 394 F. Supp. at 1390. The court noted that appellants "went to great pains on the hearing to prove that there were substantial differences between the iron and the plastic articles," *id.* at 1391, and found that there had been no "level of input" such as in *Alva Studios, Inc. v. Winninger*, 177 F. Supp. 265, 267 (S.D.N.Y. 1959) ("great skill and originality" called for in producing an exact scale reduction of Rodin's famous "Hand of God," to museum specifications). The substance of appellee's expert's testimony on which the district judge evidently relied was that the variations found in appellants' plastic bank were merely "trivial" and that it was a reproduction of the metal bank made as simply as possible for the purposes of manufacture. In other words, there were no elements of difference that amounted to significant alteration or that had any purpose other than the functional one of making a more suitable (and probably less expensive) figure in the plastic medium.

What the leading authority has called "the one pervading element prerequisite to copyright protection regardless of the form of the work" is the requirement of originality — that the work be the original product of the claimant. 1 M. Nimmer, The Law of Copyright §10, at 32 (1975). This derives from the fact that, constitutionally, copyright protection may be claimed only by "authors." U.S. Const., art. I, §8; *Burrow-Giles Lithographic Co. v. Sarony*, 111 U.S. 53, 58, 4 S. Ct. 279, 281, 28 L. Ed. 349, 351

(1884). Thus, "[o]ne who has slavishly or mechanically copied from others may not claim to be an author." 1 M. Nimmer, *supra*, §6, at 10.2. Since the constitutional requirement must be read into the Copyright Act, 17 U.S.C. §1 *et seq.*, the requirement of originality is also a statutory one. *Chamberlin v. Uris Sales Corp.*, 150 F.2d 512 (2d Cir. 1945). It has been the law of this circuit for at least 30 years that in order to obtain a copyright upon a reproduction of a work of art under 17 U.S.C. §5(h)[2] that the work "contain some substantial, not merely trivial original-ity. . . ." *Chamberlin v. Uris Sales Corp.*, *supra*, 150 F2d at 513.

Originality is, however, distinguished from novelty; there must be independent creation, but it need not be invention in the sense of striking uniqueness, ingeniousness, or novelty, since the Constitution differen-tiates "authors" and their "writings" from "inventors" and their "dis-coveries." *Alfred Bell & Co. v. Catalda Fine Arts, Inc.*, *supra*, 191 F.2d at 100; *Runge v. Lee*, 441 F.2d 579, 581 (9th Cir.), *cert. denied*, 404 U.S. 887, 92 S. Ct. 197, 30 L. Ed. 2d 169 (1971). Originality means that the work owes its creation to the author and this in turn means that the work must not consist of actual copying. *Alfred Bell & Co. v. Catalda Fine Arts, Inc.*, *supra*, 191 F.2d at 102-03; *Sheldon v. Metro-Goldwyn Pictures Corp.*, 81 F.2d 49, 54 (2d Cir. 1936), *aff'd*, 309 U.S. 390, 60 S. Ct. 681, 84 L. Ed. 825 (1940).[3]

The test of originality is concededly one with a low threshold in that "[a]ll that is needed . . . is that the 'author' contributed something more than a 'merely trivial' variation, something recognizably 'his own.'" *Alfred Bell & Co. v. Catalda Fine Arts, Inc.*, 191 F.2d at 103. But as this court said many years ago, "[w]hile a copy of something in the public domain will not, if it be merely a copy, support a copyright, a distinguish-able variation will. . . ." *Gerlach-Barklow Co. v. Morris & Bendien, Inc.*, 23 F.2d 159, 161 (2d Cir. 1927).

Necessarily, none of these underlying principles is different in the case of "[r]eproductions of a work of art," 17 U.S.C. §5(h), from the case of "[w]orks of art . . . ," 17 U.S.C. §5(g). The requirement of substantial as opposed to trivial variation and the prohibition of mechanical copy-ing, both of which are inherent in and subsumed by the concept of

---

[2] While appellant Snyder's copyright was obtained for a "Work of Art," it may be treated as one obtained for "reproductions of a work of art," Soptra Fabrics Corp. v. Stafford Knitting Mills, Inc., 490 F.2d 1092, 1094 (2d Cir. 1974), since errors in classification do not invalidate or impair copyright protection under this express language of 17 U.S.C. §5.

[3] The only case that appears to be an exception to this rule is the "Hand of God" case. Alva Studios, Inc. v. Winninger, 177 F. Supp. 265 (S.D.N.Y. 1959) (exact scale artistic reproduction of highly complicated statue made with great precision was "orginal" as requiring "great skill and originality"). This case is discussed in the text *infra*.

originality, apply to both statutory categories. There is implicit in that concept a "minimal element of creativity over and above the requirement of independent effort." 1 M. Nimmer, *supra*, §10.2 at 36. While the quantum of originality that is required may be modest indeed, *Herbert Rosenthal Jewelry Corp. v. Grossbardt*, 436 F.2d 315, 316 (2d Cir. 1970), we are not inclined to abandon that requirement, even if in the light of the constitutional and statutory bases therefor and our precedents we could do so.

A reproduction of a work of art obviously presupposes an underlying work of art. Since *Mazer v. Stein*, 347 U.S. 201, 218, 74 S. Ct. 460, 470, 98 L. Ed. 630, 642 (1954) (statuette of Balinese dancer copyrightable despite intended use as lamp base), it has been established that mass-produced commercial objects with a minimal element of artistic craftsmanship may satisfy the statutory requirement of such a work. See also *Puddu v. Buonamici Statuary, Inc.*, 450 F.2d 401, 402 (2d Cir. 1971). So, too, a toy which qualifies as a work of art such as the original Uncle Sam mechanical bank may qualify as a "work of art" under Section 5(g). See *Rushton v. Vitale*, 218 F.2d 434, 435-36 (2d Cir. 1955); *Ideal Toy Corp. v. Sayco Doll Corp.*,302 F.2d 623, 624 (2d Cir. 1962). The underlying work of art may as here be in the public domain. But even to claim the more limited protection given to a reproduction of a work of art (that to the distinctive features contributed by the reproducer), the reproduction must contain "an original contribution not present in the underlying work of art" and be "more than a mere copy." 1 M. Nimmer, *supra*, §20.2, at 93.

According to Professor Nimmer, moreover, "the mere reproduction of a work of art in a different medium should not constitute the required originality for the reason that no one can claim to have independently evolved any particular medium." *Id.* at 94. See *Millworth Converting Corp. v. Slifka*, 276 F.2d 443, 444-45 (2d Cir. 1960). Cf. *Gardenia Flowers, Inc. v. Joseph Markovitz, Inc.*, 280 F. Supp. 776, 781 (S.D.N.Y. 1968). Professor Nimmer refers to *Doran v. Sunset House Distributing Corp.*, 197 F. Supp. 940 (S.D. Cal. 1961)., *aff'd*, 304 F.2d 251 (9th Cir. 1962), as suggesting "the ludicrous result that the first person to execute a public domain work of art in a different medium thereafter obtains a monopoly on such work in such medium, at least as to those persons aware of the first such effort." 1 M. Nimmer, *supra*, §20.2, at 94. We do not follow the *Doran* case. We do follow the school of cases in this circuit and elsewhere supporting the proposition that to support a copyright there must be at least some substantial variation, not merely a trivial variation such as might occur in the translation to a different medium.

Nor can the requirement of originality be satisfied simply by the demonstration of "physical skill" or "special training" which, to be sure, Judge Metzner found was required for the production of the plastic molds that furnished the basis for appellants' plastic bank. A considerably *higher* degree of skill is required, true artistic skill, to make the reproduction copyrightable. Thus in *Alfred Bell & Co. v. Catalda Fine Arts, Inc., supra*, 191 F.2d at 104-05 n.22, Judge Frank pointed out that the mezzotint engraver's art there concerned required "great labour and talent" to effectuate the "management of light and shade . . . produced by different lines and dots . . . ," means "very different from those employed by the painter or draughtsman from whom he copies. . . ." See also *Millworth Converting Corp. v. Slifka, supra* (fabric designer required one month of work to give three-dimensional color effect to flat surface). Here on the basis of appellants' own expert's tesimony it took the Unitoy representative "[a]bout a day and a half, two days work" to produce the plastic mold sculpture from the metal Uncle Sam bank. If there be a point in the copyright law pertaining to reproductions at which sheer artistic skill and effort can act as a substitute for the requirement of substantial variation, it was not reached here.

Appellants rely heavily upon *Alva Studios, Inc. v. Winninger, supra*, the "Hand of God" case, where the court held that "great skill and originality [were required] to produce a scale reduction of a great work with exactitude." 177 F. Supp. at 267. There, the original sculpture was, "one of the most intricate pieces of sculpture ever created" with "[i]nnumerable planes, lines and geometric patterns . . . interdependent in [a] multidimensional work." *Id.* Originality was found by the district court to consist primarily in the fact that "[i]t takes 'an extremely skilled sculptor' many hours working directly in front of the original" to effectuate a scale reduction. *Id.* at 266. The court, indeed, found the exact replica to be so original, distinct, and creative as to constitute a work of art in itself. The complexity and exactitude there involved distinguishes that case amply from the one at bar. As appellants themselves have pointed out, there are a number of trivial differences or deviations from the original public domain cast iron bank in their plastic reproduction. Thus concededly the plastic version is not, and was scarcely meticulously produced to be, an exactly faithful reproduction. Nor is the creativity in the underlying work of art of the same order of magnitude as in the case of the "Hand of God." Rodin's sculpture is, furthermore, so unique and rare, and adequate public access to it such a problem that a significant public benefit accrues from its precise, artistic reproduction. No such benefit can be imagined to accrue here from the "knock-off" reproduction of the cast iron Uncle Sam bank. Thus appellants' plastic bank is neither in the category of exactitude required by *Alva Studios* nor in a category of substantial originality; it falls within what has been suggested by the amicus curiae is a copyright no-man's land.

Absent a genuine difference between the underlying work of art and the copy of it for which protection is sought, the public interest in promoting progress in the arts — indeed, the constitutional demand, *Cham-*

berlin v. Uris Sales Corp., supra— could hardly be served. To extend copyrightability to minuscule variations would simply put a weapon for harassment in the hands of mischievous copiers intent on appropriating and monopolizing public domain work. Even in *Mazer v. Stein, supra,* which held that the statutory terms "works of art" and "reproduction of works of art" (terms which are clearly broader than the earlier term "works of fine arts") permit copyright of quite ordinary mass-produced items, the Court expressly held that the objects to be copyrightable, "must be original, that is, the author's tangible expression of his ideas." 347 U.S. at 214, 74 S. Ct. at 468, 98 L. Ed. at 640. No such originality, no such expressions, no such ideas here appear.

To be sure, the test of "originality" may leave a lot to be desired, although it is the only one we have, in that as one scholar has said, the originality requirement does not perform the function of excluding commonplace matters in the public domain from copyright status very effectively. See Comment, *Copyright Protection for Mass Produced Commercial Products: A Review of the Developments Following Mazer v. Stein,* 38 U. Chi. L. Rev. 807 (1971). In any event, however, the articles should be judged on their own merits, *id.* at 823, and on these merits appellants' claim must fail. Here as elsewhere in the copyright law there are lines that must be drawn even though reasonable men may differ where.

Judgment affirmed.

§2.10.4. *Kieselstein-Cord v. Accessories By Pearl, Inc.:* No Ordinary Buckle

Congress, never having enacted a comprehensive statute dealing with the design protection of utilitarian objects, has left this copyright question to the courts. The *Kieselstein-Cord* case, which follows, states that protection of useful objects is on "a razor's edge of copyright law." It would seem likely that many similar cases will be on that same edge and only articles that are marketed at prices in substantial excess of what the usefulness of the article would warrant will meet the test of copyrightability. The dissenting opinion of Judge Weinstein is particularly informative as to the legislative history surrounding the distinction made by the Copyright Revision Act between "copyrightable works of applied art" and "uncopyrightable works of industrial design." In his view, by denying protection to low-priced reproductions of artistically designed articles, the majority opinion reduces the ability of the less affluent "to afford beautiful artifacts." He sees that decision as involving important public policies that extend beyond the definition of art. Obviously, defining art is itself an art that may involve social policy as well as aesthetics.

Kieselstein-Cord should be contrasted with the more recent case of *Carol Barnhart Inc. v. Economy Cover Corp.* (reproduced in §2.10.5 *infra*), also decided by the Second Circuit Court of Appeals.

KIESELSTEIN-CORD v. ACCESSORIES BY PEARL, INC.
632 F.2d 989 (2d Cir. 1980)

OAKES, C.J. This case is on a razor's edge of copyright law. It involves belt buckles, utilitarian objects which as such are not copyrightable. But these are not ordinary buckles; they are sculptured designs cast in precious metals — decorative in nature and used as jewelry is, principally for ornamentation. We say "on a razor's edge" because the case requires us to draw a fine line under applicable copyright law and regulations. Drawing the line in favor of the appellant designer, we uphold the copyrights granted to him by the Copyright Office and reverse the district court's grant of summary judgment, 489 F. Supp. 732, in favor of the appellee, the copier of appellant's designs.

FACTS
Appellant Barry Kieselstein-Cord designs, manufactures exclusively by handcraftsmanship, and sells fashion accessories. To produce the two buckles in issue here, the "Winchester" and the "Vaquero," he worked from original renderings which he had conceived and sketched. He then carved by hand a waxen prototype of each of the works from which molds were made for casting the objects in gold and silver. Difficult to describe, the buckles are solid sculptured designs, in the words of district court Judge Goettel, "with rounded corners, a sculpted surface, . . . a rectangular cutout at one end for the belt attachment," and "several surface levels." The Vaquero gives the appearance of two curved grooves running diagonally across one corner of a modified rectangle and a third groove running across the opposite corner. On the Winchester buckle two parallel grooves cut horizontally across the center of a more tapered form, making a curving ridge which is completed by the tongue of the buckle. A smaller single curved groove flows diagonally across the corner above the tongue.

The Vaquero buckle, created in 1978, was part of a series of works that the designer testified was inspired by a book on design of the art nouveau school and the subsequent viewing of related architecture on a trip to Spain. The buckle was registered with the Copyright Office by appellant's counsel on March 3, 1980, with a publication date of June 1, 1978, as "jewelry," although the appellant's contribution was listed on the certificate as "original sculpture and design." Explaining why he named the earlier buckle design "Winchester," the designer said that he saw "in [his] mind's eye a correlation between the art nouveau period and the butt of an antique Winchester rifle" and then "pulled these elements together graphically." The registration, which is recorded on a form used for works of art, or models or designs for works of art, specifically describes the nature of the work as "sculpture."

The Winchester buckle in particular has had great success in the marketplace: more than 4,000 belts with Winchester buckles were sold from 1976 to early 1980, and in 1979 sales of the belts amounted to 95% of appellant's more than $300,000 in jewelry sales. A small women's size in silver with "double truncated triangle belt loops" sold, at the time this lawsuit commenced, at wholesale for $147.50 and a larger silver version for men sold at wholesale with loops for $662 and without loops for $465. Lighter-weight men's versions in silver wholesaled for $450 and $295, with and without loops respectively. The gold versions sold at wholesale from $1,200 to $6,000. A shortened version of the belt with the small Winchester buckle is sometimes worn around the neck or elsewhere on the body rather than around the waist. Sales of both buckles were made primarily in high fashion stores and jewelry stores, bringing recognition to appellant as a "designer." This recognition included a 1979 Coty American Fashion Critics' Award for his work in jewelry design as well as election in 1978 to the Council of Fashion Designers of America. Both the Winchester and the Vaquero buckles, donated by appellant after this lawsuit was commenced, have been accepted by the Metropolitan Museum of Art for its permanent collection.

As the court below found, appellee's buckles "appear to be line-for-line copies but are made of common metal rather than" precious metal. Appellee admitted to copying the Vaquero and selling its imitations, and to selling copies of the Winchester. Indeed some of the order blanks of appellee's customers specifically referred to "Barry K Copy," "BK copy," and even "Barry Kieselstein Knock-off." Thus the only legal questions for the court below were whether the articles may be protected under the copyright statutes and, if so, whether the copyrights were adequate under the laws. Having found that the copyrights were invalid—the Winchester under the Copyright Act of 1909, and the Vaquero under the 1976 Act[1]—because they "fail[ed] to satisfy the test of separability and independent existence of the artistic features, which is required under both statutes," Judge Goettel did not go on to make a conclusive determination on the further question whether the notice requirements of the acts had been met by appellant. Instead, he found that the Winchester buckle "probably" satisfies the 1909 Act notice requirements, and he

---

[1] The Winchester buckle was registered before the January 1, 1978, effective date of the Copyright Act of 1976.

reserved the question whether, with respect to the Vaquero buckle, appellant met the notice requirements of the 1976 Act by way of a saving clause that preserves a copyright despite publication without adequate notice, 17 U.S.C. §405. We therefore only reach the question whether the buckles may be copyrighted.

DISCUSSION

We commence our discussion by noting that no claim has been made that the appellant's work here in question lacks originality or creativity, elements necessary for copyrighting works of art. See *L. Batlin & Son, Inc. v. Snyder*, 536 F.2d 486 (2d Cir.), *cert. denied*, 429 U.S. 857, 97 S. Ct. 156, 50 L. Ed. 2d 135 (1976); *Alfred Bell & Co. v. Catalda Fine Arts, Inc.*, 191 F.2d 99 (2d Cir. 1951); 1 *Nimmer on Copyright* §§2.01, 2.08[B] (1980). The thrust of appellee's argument, as well as of the court's decision below, is that appellant's buckles are not copyrightable because they are "useful articles" with no "pictorial, graphic, or sculptural features that can be identified separately from, and are capable of existing independently of, the utilitarian aspects" of the buckles. The 1976 copyright statute does not provide for the copyrighting of useful articles except to the extent that their designs incorporate artistic features that can be identified separately from the functional elements of the articles. See 17 U.S.C. §§101, 102.[2] With respect to this question, the law adopts the language of the longstanding Copyright Office regulations, 37 C.F.R. §202.10(c) (1977)[3] (revoked Jan. 5, 1978, 43 Fed. Reg. 965, 966 (1978)).

---

[2] 17 U.S.C. §101 provides in relevant part:

As used in this title, the following terms and their variant forms mean the following . . .

Pictorial, graphic and sculptural works include two-dimensional and three dimensional works of fine, graphic, and applied art, photographs, prints and art reproductions, maps, globes, charts, technical drawings, diagrams, and models. Such works shall include works of artistic craftsmanship insofar as their form but not their mechanical or utilitarian aspects are concerned; the design of a useful article, as defined in this section, shall be considered a pictorial, graphic, or sculptural work only if, and only to the extent that, such design incorporates pictorial, graphic, or sculptural features that can be identified separately from, and are capable of existing independently of, the utilitarian aspects of the article. . . .

A "useful article" is an article having an intrinsic utilitarian function that is not merely to portray the appearance of the article or to convey information. An article that is normally a part of a useful article is considered a "useful article."

17 U.S.C. §102 provides generally for copyright protection of "pictorial, graphic, and sculptural works."

[3] 37 C.F.R. §202.10, reprinted in 4 Nimmer on Copyright, App. 11, at 11-13 to 11-14 (1980), provided as follows:

WORKS OF ART (CLASS G)

(a) General[.] This class includes published or unpublished works of artistic craftsmanship, insofar as their form but not their mechanical or utilitarian aspects are concerned, such as artistic jewelry, enamels, glassware, and tapestries, as well as works

The regulations in turn were adopted in the mid-1950's, under the 1909 Act, in an effort to implement the Supreme Court's decision in *Mazer v. Stein*, 347 U.S. 201, 74 S. Ct. 460, 98 L. Ed. 630 (1954). See H.R. Rep. No. 1476, 94th Cong., 2d Sess. 54-55 (1976), *reprinted in* [1976] U.S. Code Cong. & Admin. News, pp.5659, 5668 [hereinafter cited as *House Report*]. The Court in *Mazer*, it will be recalled, upheld the validity of copyrights obtained for statuettes of male and female dancing figures despite the fact that they were intended for use and used as bases for table lamps, with electric wiring, sockets, and lampshades attached. *Mazer* itself followed a "contemporaneous and long-continued construction" by the Copyright Office of the 1870 and 1874 Acts as well as of the 1909 Act, under which the case was decided. 347 U.S. at 211-13, 74 S. Ct. at 467. As Professor Nimmer points out, however, the Copyright Office's regulations in the mid-1950's that purported to "implement" this decision actually limited the Court's apparent open-ended extension of copyright protection to all aesthetically pleasing useful articles. See 1 Nimmer, *supra*, §2.08[B], at 2-88 to 2-89.

Ultimately, as Professor Nimmer concludes, none of the authorities — the *Mazer* opinion, the old regulations, or the statute — offer any "ready answer to the line-drawing problem inherent in delineating the extent of copyright protection available for works of applied art." *Id.* at 2-89. Congress in the 1976 Act may have somewhat narrowed the sweep of the former regulations by defining a "useful article" as one with "*an* intrinsic utilitarian function," 17 U.S.C. §101 (emphasis added), instead of one, in the words of the old regulations, with utility as its "*sole* intrinsic function," 37 C.F.R. §202.10(c) (1977) (revoked Jan. 5, 1978, 43 Fed. Reg. 965, 966 (1978)) (emphasis added).

We are left nevertheless with the problem of determining when a pictorial, graphic, or sculptural feature "can be identified separately from, and [is] capable of existing independently of, the utilitarian aspects

---

belonging to the fine arts, such as paintings, drawings and sculpture. [Revoked Jan. 1, 1978, 43 Fed. Reg. 965, 966 (1978).]

(b) In order to be acceptable as a work of art, the work must embody some creative authorship in its delineation or form. The registrability of a work of art is not affected by the intention of the author as to the use of the work, the number of copies reproduced, or the fact that it appears on a textile material or textile product. The potential availability of protection under the design patent law will not affect the registrability of a work of art, but a copyright claim in a patented design or in the drawings or photographs in a patent application will not be registered after the patent has been issued. [Current version at 37 C.F.R. §202.10(b) (1979).]

(c) If the sole intrinsic function of an article is its utility, the fact that the article is unique and attractively shaped will not qualify it as a work of art. However, if the shape of a utilitarian article incorporates features, such as artistic sculpture, carving, or pictorial representation, which can be identified separately and are capable of existing independently as a work of art, such features will be eligible for registration. [Revoked Jan. 1, 1978, 43 Fed. Reg. 965, 966 (1978).]

of the article," 17 U.S.C. §101. This problem is particularly difficult because, according to the legislative history explored by the court below, such separability may occur either "physically or conceptually," House Report at 55, [1976] U.S. Code Cong. & Admin. News at 5668. As the late Judge Harold Leventhal observed in his concurrence in *Esquire, Inc. v. Ringer*, 591 F.2d 796, 807 (D.C. Cir. 1978), *cert. denied*, 440 U.S. 908, 99 S. Ct. 1217, 59 L. Ed. 2d 456 (1979), legislative policy supports the Copyright Office's "effort to distinguish between the instances where the aesthetic element is conceptually severable and the instances where the aesthetic element is inextricably interwoven with the utilitarian aspect of the article." [4] Examples of conceptual separateness as an artistic notion may be found in many museums today and even in the great outdoors. Professor Nimmer cites Christo's "Running Fence" as an example of today's "conceptual art": it "did not contain sculptural features that were physically separable from the utilitarian aspects of the fence, but the whole point of the work was that the artistic aspects of the work were conceptually separable." 1 Nimmer, *supra*, §2.08[B] at 2-94.

Appellee argues that the belt buckles are merely useful objects, which include decorative features that serve an aesthetic as well as a utilitarian purpose. And the copyright laws, appellee points out, were never intended to nor would the Constitution permit them to protect monopolies on useful articles. But appellee goes too far by further arguing that "copyrightability cannot adhere in the 'conceptual' separation of an artistic element." Brief for Defendant-Appellee at 17. This assertion flies in the face of the legislative intent as expressed in the House Report, which specifically refers to elements that "physically or conceptually, can be identified as separable from the utilitarian aspects of" a useful article. House Report at 55, [1976] U.S. Code Cong. & Admin. News at 5668.

We see in appellant's belt buckles conceptually separable sculptural elements, as apparently have the buckles' wearers who have used them as ornamentation for parts of the body other than the waist. The primary ornamental aspect of the Vaquero and Winchester buckles is conceptually separable from their subsidiary utilitarian function. This conclusion is not at variance with the expressed congressional intent to distinguish copyrightable applied art and uncopyrightable industrial design, House Report at 55, [1976] U.S. Code Cong. & Admin. News at 5668. Pieces of applied art, these buckles may be considered jewelry, the form of which is subject to copyright protection, *Boucher v. Du Boyes, Inc.*, 253 F.2d 948, 949 (2d Cir.), *cert. denied*, 357 U.S. 936, 78 S. Ct. 1384, 2 L.

---

[4] The court of appeals in the *Esquire* case reversed Judge Gesell's finding of conceptual separateness in the overall artistic design of an outdoor lighting fixture, 414 F. Supp. 939 (D.D.C. 1976). See 591 F.2d 796, 800 (D.C. Cir. 1978), *cert. denied*, 440 U.S. 908, 99 S. Ct. 1217, 59 L. Ed. 2d 456 (1979).

Ed. 2d 1550 (1958); *Cynthia Designs, Inc. v. Robert Zentall, Inc.*, 416 F. Supp. 510, 511-12 (S.D.N.Y. 1976); *Trifari, Krussman & Fishel, Inc. v. Charel Co.*, 134 F. Supp. 551, 552-53 (S.D.N.Y. 1955).[5]

Appellant's designs are not, as the appellee suggests in an affidavit, mere variations of "the well-known western buckle." As both the expert witnesses for appellant testified and the Copyright Office's action implied, the buckles rise to the level of creative art. Indeed, body ornamentation has been an art form since the earliest days, as anyone who has seen the Tutankhamen or Scythian gold exhibits at the Metropolitan Museum will readily attest. The basic requirements of originality and creativity, which the two buckles satisfy and which all works of art must meet to be copyrighted, would take the vast majority of belt buckles wholly out of copyrightability. The Copyright Office continually engages in the drawing of lines between that which may be and that which may not be copyrighted. It will, so long as the statute remains in its present form, always be necessary to determine whether in a given case there is a physically or conceptually separable artistic sculpture or carving capable of existing independently as a work of art.

We reverse the grant of summary judgment to the appellee and remand the case for consideration of whether appellant has satisfied the copyright notice requirements.

WEINSTEIN, D.J. (dissenting). The trial judge was correct on both the law and the facts for the reasons given in his excellent opinion holding that plaintiff was not entitled to copyright protection. *Kieselstein-Cord v. Accessories By Pearl, Inc.*, 489 F. Supp. 732 (S.D.N.Y. 1980). The works sued on are, while admirable aesthetically pleasing examples of modern design, indubitably belt buckles and nothing else; their innovations of form are inseparable from the important function they serve — helping to keep the tops of trousers at waist level.

---

[5] These cases were decided under the old Copyright Act of 1909, which protected "all the writings of an author."17 U.S.C. §4 (1976), and which included as one of the classes to which copyrighted work might belong "works of art; models or designs for works of art," *id*. §5. Regulations promulgated under the 1909 Act listed "artistic jewelry" as an example of "works of art." 37 C.F.R. §202.10(a) (1977), see note 3 *supra*.

The current statute extends copyright protection to "pictorial, graphic, and sculptural works," 17 U.S.C. §102(a)(5), and notes that, in the words of the old regulation, 37 C.F.R. §202.10(a) (1977), see note 3 *supra*, "[s]uch works shall include works of artistic craftsmanship insofar as their form but not their mechanical or utilitarian aspects are concerned." 17 U.S.C. §101, see note 2 *supra*. The new statute, while incorporating this regulatory definition, omits the specific examples, such as "artistic jewelry," listed in the old regulations. This omission does not suggest that jewelry may not be copyrighted. In fact, the explicit congressional adoption of the Copyright Office's definition indicates that jewelry remains within the scope of copyright protection.

The conclusion that affirmance is required is reached reluctantly. The result does deny protection to designers who use modern three-dimensional abstract works artfully incorporated into a functional object as an inseparable aspect of the article while granting it to those who attach their independent representational art, or even their trite gimmickry, to a useful object for purposes of enhancement. Moreover, this result enables the commercial pirates of the marketplace to appropriate for their own profit, without any cost to themselves, the works of talented designers who enrich our lives with their intuition and skill. The crass are rewarded, the artist who creates beauty is not. All of us are offended by the flagrant copying of another's work. This is regrettable, but it is not for this court to twist the law in order to achieve a result Congress has denied.

Both of appellant's designs may be described as rough geometric shapes with uneven surfaces, one of them having two wavy lines in the corner. These arrangements are embodied within a useful article — a belt buckle. They transform the ordinary square buckle — with each of its sides of equal width, and a narrow tongue attached to one side — into a four sided structure with sides of unequal thickness and the usual narrow tongue. The artist has enhanced the appearance of the buckles by rendering their shape aesthetically pleasing without interfering with function. It is the originator's success in completely integrating the artistic designs and the functional aspects of the buckles that preclude copyright.

[Photographs of "Winchester" and "Vaquero" belt buckles omitted.]

The 1976 Copyright Act protects only those portions of useful articles, such as belt buckles, consisting of "sculptural features that can be identified separately from, and are capable of existing independently of the utilitarian aspects of the article." In relevant portions, the copyright law, title 17 of the United States Code, reads:

§101. DEFINITIONS. . . .

"Pictorial, graphic, and sculptural works" include two-dimensional and three-dimensional works of fine, graphic, and applied art, photographs, prints and art reproductions, maps, globes, charts, technical drawings, diagrams, and models. Such works shall include works of artistic craftsmanship insofar as their form but not their mechanical or utilitarian aspects are concerned; *the design of a useful article,* as defined in this section, shall be considered a pictorial, graphic, or sculptural work only if, *and only to the extent that, such design incorporates pictorial, graphic, or sculptural features that can be identified separately from, and are capable of existing independently of, the utilitarian aspects of the article.* . . .

A "useful article" is an article having an intrinsic utilitarian function that is not merely to portray the appearance of the article or to convey information. *An article that is normally a part of a useful article is considered a "useful article."*

§102. SUBJECT MATTER OF COPYRIGHT: IN GENERAL.

(a) Copyright protection subsists, in accordance with this title, in original works of authorship fixed in any tangible medium of expression, now known or later developed, from which they can be perceived, reproduced, or otherwise communicated, either directly or with the aid of a machine or device. *Works of authorship* include the following categories: . . .

　　(5) *pictorial, graphic, and sculptural works;*

　(b) In no case does copyright protection for an original work of authorship extend to any idea, procedure, process, system, method of operation, concept, principle, or discovery, regardless of the form in which it is described, explained, illustrated, or embodied in such work.

(Emphasis supplied.)

The statute follows the decision of the Supreme Court in *Mazer v. Stein,* 347 U.S. 201, 74 S. Ct. 460, 98 L. Ed. 630, *rehearing denied,* 347 U.S. 949, 74 S. Ct. 637, 98 L. Ed. 1096 (1954). In *Mazer,* the Court held that independent works of art may be copyrighted even if they are incorporated into useful articles — "nothing in the copyright statute . . . support[s] the argument that the intended use or use in industry of an article eligible for copyright bars or invalidates its registration." *Id.* at 218, 74 S. Ct. at 471. But the copyright protection covered only that aspect of the article that was a separately identifiable work of art independent of the useful article, in that instance a statuette used as part of a lamp.

Among recent decisions making this same distinction is *Esquire v. Ringer,* 591 F.2d 796 (D.C. Cir.), *cert. denied,* 440 U.S. 908, 99 S. Ct. 1217, 59 L. Ed. 2d 456, *rehearing denied,* 441 U.S. 917, 99 S. Ct. 2019, 60 L. Ed. 2d 389 (1979). *Esquire* denied copyright protection to the overall shape of a lighting fixture because of its integration of the functional aspects of the entire lighting assembly. The "overall design or configuration of a utilitarian object, even if it is determined by aesthetic as well as functional considerations, is not eligible for copyright." *Id.* at 804.

While the distinction is not precise, the courts, both before and after *Mazer,* have tried to follow the principle of the copyright act permitting copyright to extend only to ornamental or superfluous designs contained within useful objects while denying it to artistically designed functional components of useful objects. Generally they have favored representational art as opposed to non-representation artistic forms which are embodied in, and part of the structure of, a useful article. Compare, e.g., *Ted Arnold Ltd. v. Silvercraft Co.,* 259 F. Supp. 733 (S.D.N.Y. 1966) (antique telephone used to encase a pencil sharpener copyrightable); *Royalty Designs Inc. v. Thrifticheck Service Corp.,* 204 F. Supp. 702 (S.D.N.Y. 1962) (toy banks in shape of dogs copyrightable); *Scarves by Vera, Inc. v. United Merchants and Mfrs., Inc.,* 173 F. Supp. 625 (S.D.N.Y. 1959) (designs printed upon scarves copyrightable); *Syracuse China Corp. v. Stanley Roberts, Inc.,* 180 F. Supp. 527 (S.D.N.Y. 1960) (designs on dinnerware copyrightable) *with Esquire v. Ringer*, 591 F.2d 796 (D.C. Cir.), *cert. denied*, 440 U.S. 908, 99 S. Ct. 1217, 59 L. Ed. 2d 456, *rehearing denied*, 441 U.S. 917, 99 S. Ct. 2019, 60 L. Ed. 2d 389 (1979) (copyright denied to overall design of lighting fixture); *SCOA Industries, Inc. v. Famolare, Inc.*, 192 U.S.P.Q. 216 (S.D.N.Y. 1976) (wavy lines on soles of shoes not copyrightable); *Vacheron & Constantin-Le Coultre Watches, Inc. v. Benrus Watch Co.*, 155 F. Supp. 932 (S.D.N.Y. 1957), *affirmed in part, reversed on other grounds*, 260 F.2d 637 (2d Cir. 1958) (artistically designed non-representational watchface not copyrightable); *Russell v. Trimfit, Inc.*, 428 F. Supp. 91 (E.D. Pa. 1977), *affirmed*, 568 F.2d 770 (3d Cir. 1978) (designs of "toe socks" not copyrightable); *Jack Adelman, Inc. v. Sonners & Gordon, Inc.*, 112 F. Supp. 187 (S.D.N.Y. 1934) (picture of a dress may be copyrighted but the dress itself may not be). The relative certainty that has developed in this area of the law should not be disturbed absent some compelling development — and none has thus far been presented.

Interpretation and application of the copyright statute is facilitated by House Report No. 94-1476, U.S. Code Cong. & Admin. News 1976, p.5658, by the Committee on the Judiciary. It explicitly indicated that the rule of *Mazer* was incorporated.

In accordance with the Supreme Court's decision in *Mazer v. Stein*, 347 U.S. 201, 74 S. Ct. 460, 98 L. Ed. 630 (1954), works of "applied art" encompass all original pictorial, graphic, and sculptural works that are intended to be or have been embodied in useful articles, regardless of factors such as mass production, commercial exploitation, and the potential availability of design patent protection. . . .

The Committee has added language to the definition of "pictorial, graphic, and sculptural works" in an effort to make clearer the distinction between works of applied art protectable under the bill and industrial designs not subject to copyright protection. The declaration that "pictorial, graphic, and sculptural works" include "works of artistic craftsmanship insofar as their form but not their mechanical or utilitarian aspects are concerned" is classic language. it is drawn from Copyright Office regulations promulgated in the 1940's and expressly endorsed by the Supreme Court in the *Mazer* case. . . .

In adopting this amendatory language, the Committee is seeking to draw as clear a line as possible between copyrightable works of applied art and uncopyrighted works of industrial design. A two-dimensional painting, drawing, or graphic work is still capable of being identified as such when it is printed on or applied to utilitarian articles such as textile fabrics, wallpaper, containers, and the like. The same is true when a statue or carving is used to embellish an industrial product or, as in the *Mazer* case, is incorporated into a product without losing its ability to exist independently as a work of art. On the other hand, *although the shape of an industrial product may be aesthetically satisfying and valuable, the Committee's intention is not to offer it copyright protection under the bill.* Unless the shape of an automobile, airplane, ladies' dress, food processor, television set, or any other industrial product contains some element that, physically or conceptually, can be identified as separable from the utilitarian aspects of that article, the design would not be copyrighted under the bill. The test of separability and independence from "the utilitarian aspects of the article" does not depend upon the nature of the design — that is, even if the appearance of an article is determined by aesthetic (as opposed to functional) considerations, only elements, if any, which can be identified separately from the useful article as such are copyrightable. *And, even if the three-dimensional design contains some such element (for example, a carving on the back of a chair or a floral relief design on silver flatware), copyright protection would extend only to that element, and would not cover the overall configuration of the utilitarian article as such.*

1976 U.S. Code Cong. & Admin. News, pp.5667-5668. (Emphasis supplied.)

Congress considered and declined to enact legislation that would have extended copyright protection to "[t]he 'design of a useful article' . . . including its two-dimensional or three-dimensional features of shape and surface, which make up the appearance of the article." H.R. 2223, Title II, §201(b)(2), 94th Cong., 1st Sess. (January 28, 1975). Passage of this provision was recommended by the Register of Copyrights, Hearings on H.R. 2223 Before the Subcomm. on Courts, Civil Liberties, and the Administration of Justice of the House Comm. on the Judiciary (Oct. 30, 1975) (testimony of Barbara Ringer), Reprinted in 16 Omnibus Copyright Revision Legislative History, 1855-59 (1975), and the United States Department of Commerce, Hearings on H.R. 2223 Before the Subcomm. on Courts, Civil Liberties and the Administration of Justice of the House Comm. on the Judiciary (May 8, 1975) (testimony and statement of Rene Tegtmeyer), Reprinted in 14 Omnibus Copyright Revision Legislative History, 161-162, 166-169. It was opposed by the Department of Justice on policy grounds. Hearings on H.R. 2223 Before the Subcomm. on Courts, Civil Liberties and the Administration of Justice of the House Comm. on the Judiciary (May 8, 1975) (testimony of Irwin Goldbloom), Reprinted in 14 Omnibus Copyright Revision Legislative History, 127-130, 139-141. The Justice Department noted the important substantive objections to the proposal — primarily it would charge the public a fee for the use of improved and pleasing new designs and styles in useful articles.

Of particular concern to this Department is the new form of copyright protection provided by title II of the bill.

This new form of protection is a hybrid between design patents, 35 U.S.C. 171-173, issued for a period of up to 14 years by the Patent Office for new, original and ornamental designs of articles of manufacture and the copyright laws which provide for registration and issuance of certificates of copyrights for the writings of authors. The new protection that is provided under the bill is not presently available under the copyright laws and can only be obtained through a design patent after an examination procedure which determines whether the ornamental design meets the criteria of patentability, including unobviousness in view of the prior art, as provided by 35 U.S.C. 102, 103.

While the protection period as proposed for the new type of ornamental design protection is only a maximum of 10 years as compared with the maximum of 14 years available for a design patent, it is granted without the need of meeting the novelty and unobviousness requirements of the patent statute.

A *threshold consideration* before finding that the needs are such that this new type of protection should be available *is whether the benefits to the public of such protection outweigh the burdens. We believe that insufficient need has been shown to date to justify removing from the public domain and possible use by others of the rights and benefits proposed under the present bill for such ornamental designs.* We believe that design patents, as are granted today, are as far as the public should go to grant exclusive rights for ornamental designs of useful articles in the absence of an adequate showing that the new protection will provide substantial benefits to the general public which outweigh removing such designs from free public use.

While it has been said that the examination procedure in the Patent Office results in serious delays in the issuance of a design patent so as to be a significant problem and damaging to "inventors" of ornamental designs of useful articles, *the desirable free use of designs which do not rise to patentable invention of ornamental designs of useful articles are believed to be paramount.*

If the contribution made to the public by the creation of an ornamental design of a useful article is insufficient to rise to patentable novelty, the design should not be protected by the law. The Department of Justice has consistently opposed legislation of this character.

To omit Federal statutory protection for the form of a useful object is not to deny the originator of that form any remedy whatsoever. If he can prove that competitors are passing their goods as the originator's by copying the product's design, he may bring an unfair competition action against such copyists.

Id. at 139-140. (Emphasis supplied).

No additional testimony was received with respect to this aspect of the House bill. The Joint Senate-House Conference Committee deleted the design protection section to give further consideration to its administrative difficulties and to the benefits and burdens created by limiting the free public domain. 1976 U.S. Code Cong. & Admin. News, pp.5663, 5832. The attempt to gain protection was again mounted when Representative Thomas F. Railsback introduced H.R. 4530 on June 19, 1979 to amend the Copyright Act of 1976. H.R. 4530's section 902 contains protections for the design of useful objects identical to those omitted from the 1976 Copyright Act. It was not adopted by Congress.

Interestingly, even if the design protection section proposed by the Department of Commerce and Representative Railsback had been passed, appellant's buckles might still have been excluded under the following subsection excluding three-dimensional features of apparel:

DESIGNS NOT SUBJECT TO
PROTECTION
§202. PROTECTION UNDER THIS TITLE SHALL
NOT BE AVAILABLE FOR A DESIGN THAT IS
(e) *composed of three-dimensional features of shape and surface with respect to
men's, women's and children's apparel,* including undergarments and outer-
wear.

(Emphasis supplied.) See also proposed §202(b) (shape which has become common); §202(c) (variants).

The distinctions between copyrightable "pictorial, graphic and sculptural works" and noncopyrightable industrial "designs" reflect serious
concerns about the promotion of competition, the widespread availability of quality products and the advancement of technology through
copying and modification. See, e.g., G. Nelson, *Design,* 170 (1979) (experience suggests that free copying results in more rapid development);
Comment, *Copyright Protection for Mass Produced, Commercial Products:
A Review of the Developments Following* Mazer v. Stein, 38 U. Chi. L. Rev.
807, 819-22 (1971); Note, *Protection for the Artistic Aspects of Articles of
Utility,* 72 Harv. L. Rev. 1520, 1532-4 (1959). A similar need to balance
societal interest in the availability of literary and dramatic works against
the copyright holders' interest in their exclusive enjoyment is reflected in
the fair use provisions of the Copyright Act of 1976. 17 U.S.C. §§107-
112. See also, e.g., Note, *Copyright Infringement and the First Amendment,*
79 Col. L. Rev. 320 (1979); Ramos, *The Betamax Case: Accommodating
Public Access and Economic Incentive in Copyright Law,* 11 Intellectual
Property L. Rev. 221, 230-1 (1979).

Important policies are obviously at stake. Should we encourage the
artist and increase the compensation to the creative? Or should we allow
cheap reproductions which will permit our less affluent to afford beautiful artifacts? Appellant sold the original for $600.00 and up. Defendant's
version went for one-fiftieth of that sum.

Thus far Congress and the Supreme Court have answered in favor of
commerce and the masses rather than the artists, designers and the
well-to-do. Any change must be left to those higher authorities. The
choices are legislative not judicial.

§2.10.5. *Carol Barnhart Inc. v. Economy Cover Corp.:* **The Elusive Test of "Conceptual Separability"**

The *Carol Barnhart* case, which follows, relied heavily on the
authority of the *Kieselstein-Cord* case, yet with it the Second Circuit Court
of Appeals pointed in a different direction. In *Carol Barnhart* the majority

opinion perceived that the test of "conceptual separability" under the Copyright Act required a result that denied copyright protection to the creator of a model of a human torso mannequin. In his dissent Judge Jon Newman argued that "conceptual separability" must be distinguished from "physical separability." The test of separability, in his view, would rest on whether the "non-utilitarian concept can be entertained in the mind of the ordinary observer without at the same time contemplating the utilitarian function." Query whether this question — purportedly to be answered by the "ordinary observer" — is for the judge and jury alone or is to be based on the perception of an "art expert," a person not generally thought of as an ordinary observer. The majority opinion indicates that Judge Newman's test would amount to a "non-test" that would be extremely difficult, if not impossible, to apply.

CAROL BARNHART INC. v. ECONOMY COVER CORP.
773 F.2d 411 (2d Cir. 1985)

MANSFIELD, C.J.: Carol Barnhart Inc. ("Barnhart"), which sells display forms to department stores, distributors, and small retail stores, appeals from a judgment of the Eastern District of New York, Leonard D. Wexler, *Judge,* granting a motion for summary judgment made by defendant Economy Cover Corporation ("Economy"), which sells a wide variety of display products primarily to jobbers and distributors. Barnhart's complaint alleges that Economy has infringed its copyright and engaged in unfair competition by offering for sale display forms copied from four original "sculptural forms" to which Barnhart holds the copyright. Judge Wexler granted Economy's motion for summary judgment on the ground that plaintiff's mannequins of partial human torsos used to display articles of clothing are utilitarian articles not containing separable works of art, and thus are not copyrightable. We affirm.

The bones of contention are four human torso forms designed by Barnhart, each of which is life-size, without neck, arms, or a back, and made of expandable white styrene. Plaintiff's president created the forms in 1982 by using clay, buttons, and fabric to develop an initial mold, which she then used to build an aluminum mold into which the poly-styrene is poured to manufacture the sculptural display form. There are two male and two female upper torsos. One each of the male and female torsos is unclad for the purpose of displaying shirts and sweaters, while the other two are sculpted with shirts for displaying sweaters and jackets. All the forms, which are otherwise life-like and anatomically accurate, have hollow backs designed to hold excess fabric when the garment is fitted onto the form. Barnhart's advertising stresses the forms' uses to display items such as sweaters, blouses, and dress shirts, and states that they come "[p]ackaged in UPS-size boxes for easy shipping and [are] sold in multiples of twelve."

Plaintiff created the first of the forms, Men's Shirt, shortly after its founding in March, 1982, and by the end of July it had attracted $18,000 worth of orders. By December 1982, plaintiff had designed all four forms, and during the first morning of the twice-yearly trade show sponsored by the National Association of the Display Industry ("NADI"), customers had placed $35,000 in orders for the forms. Plaintiff's president maintains that the favorable response from visual merchandisers, Barnhart's primary customers, "convinced me that my forms were being purchased not only for their function but for their artistically sculptured features."

Economy, which sells its wide range of products primarily to jobbers, distributors, and national chain stores, not to retail stores, first learned in early 1983 that Barnhart was selling its display forms directly to retailers. After observing that no copyright notice apeared either on Barnhart's forms or in its promotional literature, Economy contracted to have produced for it four forms which it has conceded, for purposes of its summary judgment motion, were "copied from Barnhart's display forms" and are "substantially similar to Barnhart's display forms." Economy began marketing its product, "Easy Pin Shell Forms," in September 1983. Later in the same month, Barnhart wrote to NADI to complain that Economy was selling exact duplicates of Barnhart's sculptural forms at a lower price and asked it to stop the duplication and underselling. Economy responded with a letter from its counsel dated October 17, 1983 to the Chairman of NADI's Ethics Committee stating that Economy was not guilty of any "underhanded" business practices since Barnhart's forms were not protected by "patent, copyright, trademark, or otherwise."

On the same date (October 17, 1983) Barnhart applied for copyright registration for a number of products, including the four forms at issue here. It identified each of the forms as "sculpture" and sought expedited examination of its applications because of the possibility of litigation over copyright infringement. Copyright registration was granted the same day. Then, on October 18, Barnhart informed Economy that its Easy Pin Shell Forms violated Barnhart's rights and demanded that it discontinue its advertising and sale of the forms. In November 1983, more than 18 months after selling its first form, Barnhart advised its customers that copyright notice had "inadvertently [been] omitted" from the display forms previously distributed and enclosed adhesive stickers bearing a copyright notice, which it asked the customers to affix to unmarked products in inventory.

Barnhart filed this suit in December 1983. Count I charges Economy with violating Barnhart's rights under the Copyright Act, 17 U.S.C. §§101-810 (1982), by copying and selling Barnhart's four display forms.

Count II alleges that Economy has engaged in unfair competition under the common law of the State of New York. The complaint seeks an adjudication that Economy has infringed Barnhart's copyrights, a preliminary and permanent injunction against Economy's producing, advertising, or selling its forms, damages (consequential, statutory, and punitive), and attorney's fees. Economy moved for summary judgment on the issue of the copyrightability of Barnhart's display forms (and the issue of statutory damages and attorney's fees).

After a hearing on February 3, 1984, Judge Wexler issued an order and opinion on September 12, 1984, granting defendant's motion for summary judgment on the issue of copyrightability. 594 F. Supp. 364 (E.D.N.Y. 1984). The district court rejected plaintiff's arguments that the issue of copyrightability was an improper subject for summary judgment and that the Copyright Office's issuance of certificates of registration for Barnhart's four forms created an insurmountable presumption of the validity of the copyrights. On the central issue of copyrightability, it reviewed the statutory language, legislative history, and recent case authority, concluding that they all speak with "a single voice," i.e., that a useful article may be copyrighted only to the extent that "there is a physically or conceptually separable work of art embellishing it. . . ." *Id.* at 370. Applying this test, the district court determined that since the Barnhart forms possessed no aesthetic features that could exist, either physically or conceptually, separate from the forms as utilitarian articles, they were not copyrightable.

On March 6, 1985, 603 F. Supp. 432, Judge Wexler denied Barnhart's motion for reargument. The present appeal followed.

DISCUSSION

Appellant's threshold argument, that the district court erred in ignoring the statutory presumption of validity accorded to a certificate of copyright registration and to the line-drawing expertise of the Copyright Office, can be disposed of briefly. With respect to the prima facie validity of Copyright Office determinations, 17 U.S.C. §410(c) states:

> In any judicial proceedings the certificate of a registration made before or within five years after first publication of the work shall constitute prima facie evidence of the validity of the copyright and of the facts stated in the certificate. The evidentiary weight to be accorded the certificate of a registration made thereafter shall be within the discretion of the court.

However, "a certificate of registration creates no irrebuttable presumption of copyright validity." *Durham Industries, Inc. v. Tomy Corp.*, 630 F.2d 905, 908 (2d Cir. 1980). Extending a presumption of validity to a certificate of copyright registration merely orders the burdens of proof. The plaintiff should not ordinarily be forced in the first instance to prove all of the multitude of facts that underline the validity of the copyright unless the defendant, by effectively challenging them, shifts the burden of doing so to the plaintiff.

H. Rep. No. 1476, 94th Cong., 2d Sess. 157, *reprinted in* 1976 U.S. Code Cong. & Ad. News 5659, 5773. See also *Oboler v. Goldin*, 714 F.2d 211, 212 (2d Cir. 1983); 3 M. Nimmer, Nimmer on Copyright §12.11[B], at 12-79 to 12-80 (1985).

Judge Wexler properly exercised the discretion conferred on him by 17 U.S.C. §410(c). Once defendant's response to plaintiff's claim put in issue whether the four Barnhart forms were copyrightable, he correctly reasoned that the "mute testimony" of the forms put him in as good a position as the Copyright Office to decide the issue. While the expertise of the Copyright Office is in "interpretation of the law and its application to the facts presented by the copyright application," *Norris Industries, Inc. v. I.T. & T.*, 696 F.2d 918, 922 (11th Cir.), *cert. denied*, — U.S. —, 104 S. Ct. 78, 78 L. Ed. 2d 89 (1983), it is permissible for the district court itself to consider how the copyright law applies to the articles under consideration.[1]

Since the four Barnhart forms are concededly useful articles, the crucial issue in determining their copyrightability is whether they possess artistic or aesthetic features that are physically or conceptually separable from their utilitarian dimension. A "useful article" is defined in 17 U.S.C. §101 as "an article having an intrinsic utilitarian function that is not merely to portray the appearance of the article or to convey information." Although 17 U.S.C. §102(a)(5) extends copyright protection to "pictorial, graphic, and sculptural works," the definition of "pictorial, graphic, and sculptural works," at 17 U.S.C. §101, provides that the design of a useful article "shall be considered a pictorial, graphic, or sculptural work only if, and only to the extent that, such design incorporates pictorial, graphic, or sculptural features that can be identified separately from, and

---

[1] Appellant's failure to provide copyright notice until 18 months after initial distribution of its forms is not fatal to its claim. 17 U.S.C. §405(a)(2) provides:

The omission of the copyright notice prescribed by sections 401 through 403 from copies of phonorecords publicly distributed by authority of the copyright in a work if —
(2) registration for the work has been made before or is made within five years after the publication without notice, and a reasonable effort is made to add notice to all copies or phonorecords that are distributed to the public in the United States after the omission has been discovered; or. . . .

At oral argument counsel for appellant maintained that Barnhart's president had made no affirmative decision not to copyright her forms from the very beginning; rather, she later discovered this omission and took steps to remedy it by corresponding with previous purchasers of the forms.

are capable of existing independently of, the utilitarian aspects of the article." To interpret the scope and applicability of this language, and the extent to which it may protect useful articles such as the four Barnhart forms, we must turn to the legislative history of the 1976 Copyright Act, which is informative.

Congress, acting under the authority of Art. I, §8, cl. 8 of the Constitution, extended copyright protection to three-dimensional works of art in the Copyright Act of 1870, which defined copyrightable subject matter as: "any book, map chart, dramatic or musical composition, engraving, cut, print, or photograph or negative thereof, or of a painting, drawing, chromo, statue, statuary, and of models or designs intended to be perfected as works of the fine arts. . . ." Act. of July 8, 1870, ch. 230, §86, 16 Stat. 198, 212 (repealed 1916). The Supreme Court upheld an expansive reading of "authors" and "writings" in *Burrow-Giles Lithographic Co. v. Sarony*, 111 U.S. 53, 60, 4 S. Ct. 279, 282, 28 L. Ed. 349 (1884), rejecting the claim that Congress lacked the constitutional authority to extend copyright protection to photographs and negatives thereof. The Court further contributed to the liberalization of copyright law in *Bleistein v. Donaldson Lithographing Co.*, 188 U.S. 239, 23 S. Ct. 298, 47 L. Ed. 460 (1903) (Holmes, J.), in which it held that chromo-lithographs used on a circus poster were not barred from protection under the copyright laws. In *Bleistein*, Justice Holmes stated his famous "anti-discrimination" principle:

> It would be a dangerous undertaking for persons trained only to the law to constitute themselves final judges of the worth of pictorial illustrations, outside of the narrowest and most obvious limits. At the one extreme some works of genius would be sure to miss appreciation. Their very novelty would make them repulsive until the public had learned the new language in which their author spoke. It may be more than doubted, for instance, whether the etchings of Goya or the paintings of Manet would have been sure of protection when seen for the first time. At the other end, copyright would be denied to pictures which appealed to a public less educated than the judge.

Id. at 251-52, 23 S. Ct. at 300-01.

The Copyright Act of 1909 expanded the scope of the copyright statute to protect not only traditional fine arts, but also "[w]orks of art; models or designs for works of art." Copyright Act of 1909, ch. 320, §5(g), 35 Stat. 1075, 1077 (codified at 17 U.S.C. §§1-216 (1976)), *reprinted in* 4 M. Nimmer, *supra*, App. 6, at 6-5. However, this language was narrowly interpreted by Copyright Office regulations issued in 1910, which stated in part:

> *Works of art.* — This term includes all works belonging fairly to the so-called fine arts. (Paintings, drawings, and sculpture).

> Productions of the industrial arts utilitarian in purpose and character are not subject to copyright registration, even if artistically made or ornamented.

Copyright Office, Rules and Regulations for the Registration of Claims to Copyright, Bulletin No. 15 (1910), 8; *reprinted in Mazer v. Stein,*347 U.S. 201, 212 n.23, 74 S. Ct. 460, 467 n.23, 98 L. Ed. 630 (1954).

The prospects for a work of applied art obtaining a copyright were enhanced in December 1948, when the Copyright Office changed the definition of a "work of art" in its Regulation §202.8:

> *Works of art (Class G) — (a) In General* This class included works of artistic craftsmanship, in so far as their form but not their mechanical or utilitarian aspects are concerned, such as artistic jewelry, enamels, glassware, and tapestries, as well as all works belonging to the fine arts, such as paintings, drawings and sculpture.

37 C.F.R. §202.8 (1949), *reprinted in Mazer v. Stein, supra,* 347 U.S. at 212-13, 74 S. Ct. at 467-68. While this regulation seemed to expand coverage for works of applied art, it did not explicitly extend copyright protection to industrial design objects.

The next significant historical step was taken not by Congress but by the Supreme Court in its 1954 decision in *Mazer v. Stein, supra,* where it upheld §202.8 as a proper standard for determining when a work of applied art is entitled to copyright protection, in the context of deciding whether lamps which used statuettes of male and female dancing figures made of semivitreous china as bases were copyrightable. The narrow question faced was whether the addition of the lamp attachments deprived the statuettes of the copyright protection to which they were separately entitled. The Court answered that question in the negative, holding that an ornamental design does not necessarily cease to be artistic when embodied in a useful article and may therefore be entitled to copyright protection. *Id.* at 214, 74 S. Ct. at 468.

The Copyright Office implemented *Mazer v. Stein* by promulgating new regulations interpreting §5(g) of the 1909 Act, which stated in part:

> (c) If the sole intrinsic function of an article is its utility, the fact that the article is unique and attractively shaped will not qualify it as a work of art. However, if the shape of a utilitarian article incorporates features, such as artistic sculpture, carving, or pictorial representation, which can be identified separately and are capable of existing independently as a work of art, such features will be eligible for registration.

37 C.F.R. § 202.10(c)((1959), as amended June 18, 1959)(revoked 1978), *reprinted in* 4 M. Nimmer, *supra,* App. 11, at 11-13, to 11-14 (1985).

In an effort to provide some form of protection to "three-dimensional designs of utilitarian articles as such," a number of separate design bills were introduced into Congress. See, e.g., H.R. 8873 (Willis Bill), 85th Cong., 1st Sess. July 23, 1957, and S. 2075 (O'Mahoney-Wiley-Hart Bill), 86th Cong., 1st Sess. May 28, 1959. Finally, Title II of a bill passed by the Senate in 1975, S.22 (The Design Protection Act of 1975), proposed to offer legal protection to the creators of ornamental designs of useful articles.[2] It defined "pictorial, graphic, and sculptural works" to "include two-dimensional works of fine, graphic, and applied art, photographs, prints and art reproductions, maps, globes, charts, plans, diagrams, and models."

The House, however, responded by passing a strikingly different version. To the text passed by the Senate it added the following:

> Such works shall include works of artistic craftsmanship insofar as their form but not their mechanical or utilitarian aspects are concerned; the design of a useful article, as defined in this section, shall be considered a pictorial, graphic, or sculptural work only if, and only to the extent that such design incorporates pictorial, graphic, or sculptural features that can be identified separately from, and are capable of existing independently of, the utilitarian aspects of the article.

Both of the added clauses were from work of the Copyright Office: the first from its 1948 Regulation §202.8, approved by the Supreme Court in

---

[2] The Senate Report offered this description of Title II's purpose:

> The purpose of the proposed legislation, as amended, is to encourage the creation of original ornamental designs of useful articles by protecting the authors of such designs for a limited time against unauthorized copying. The title is intended to offer the creator of ornamental designs of useful articles a new form of protection directed toward the special problems arising in the design field, and is intended to avoid the defects of the existing copyright and design patent statutes by providing simple, easily secured, and effective design protection for the period of 5 years, or, if renewed, a period of 10 years, under appropriate safeguards and conditions.
>
> Such designs are presently protected by design patents issued under title 35, United States Code, if they meet the requirements of title 35. A design patent may not be issued until a search has been made to determine that such design possesses novelty. The design patent law, while affording protection to some designs, has proved adequate to protect those whose designs have only a short life expectancy.
>
> The present copyright statute is equally inappropriate for the protection of such designs. The term of copyright protection is too long for the majority of designs. The scope of copyright protection is too broad, while the notice and registration requirements do not fit the needs of design protection. Also, the copyright law protects only those designs which can be separately identified as "works of art."
>
> Because of the limitations of both the design patent and copyright laws, this legislation proposes to establish a new form of protection for "original ornamental designs of useful articles." The subject matter of the bill is limited to designs of useful articles, the term "design" referring to those features of the useful article intended to give it an ornamental appearance. The protection provided by this legislation would begin when a useful article, bearing the design, is made public, and would last for 5 or, if renewed, 10 years."

S. Rep. No. 473, 94th Cong., 1st Sess. 161-62 (1975).

Mazer v. Stein; the second from its post-*Mazer* §202.10(c).³ The bill as finally enacted omitted entirely the proposed Title II.⁴

---

³ The House Report offered this explanation for the change in definition:

In adopting this amendatory language, the Committee is seeking to draw as clear a line as possible between copyrightable works of applied art and uncopyrighted works of industrial design. A two-dimensional painting, drawing, or graphic work is still capable of being identified as such when it is printed on or applied to utilitarian articles such as textile fabrics, wallpaper, containers, and the like. The same is true when a statue or carving is used to embellish an industrial product or, as in the *Mazer* case, is incorporated into a product without losing its ability to exist independently as a work of art. On the other hand, although the shape of an industrial product may be aesthetically satisfying and valuable, the Committee's intention is not to offer it copyright protection under the bill. Unless the shape of an automobile, airplane, ladies' dress, food processor, television set, or any other industrial product contains some element that, physically or conceptually, can be identified as separable from the utilitarian aspects of that article, the design would not be copyrighted under the bill. The test of separability and independence from "the utilitarian aspects of the article" does not depend upon the nature of the design — that is, even if the appearance of an article is determined by esthetic (as opposed to functional) considerations, only elements, if any, which can be identified separately from the useful article as such are copyrightable. And, even if the three-dimensional design contains some such element (for example, a carving on the back of a chair or a floral relief design on silver flatware), copyright protection would extend only to that element, and would not cover the over-all configuration of the utilitarian article as such."

H. R. Rep. No. 1476, *supra*, at 55, 1976 U.S. Code Cong. & Ad. News at 5668. One commentator has stated:

The amended text thus subjected virtually all industrial art seeking copyright protection under Title I to the separability criterion of sections 101 and 102(a)(5). . . . This doctrine of separability could then authorize the denial of copyrightability to modern, functional designs. . . .

Reichman, Design Protection in Domestic and Foreign Copyright Law: From the Berne Revision of 1948 to the Copyright Act of 1976, 1983 Duke L.J. 1143, 1261.

⁴ The House Report explained this deletion as follows:

In reporting S. 22, the House Judiciary Committee has deleted Title II. Until 1954, designs for useful articles were not generally subject of copyright protection. The primary protection available was the design patent, which requires that the design be not only 'original', the standard applied in copyright law, but also 'novel', meaning that it has never before existed anywhere.

However, in 1954 the Supreme Court decided the case of Mazer v. Stein, 347 U.S. 201 [74 S. Ct. 460, 98 L. Ed. 630], in which it held that works of art which are incorporated into the design of useful articles, but which are capable of standing by themselves as art works separate from the useful article, are copyrightable. The example used in the *Mazer* case was an ornamental lamp base.

Title II of S. 22 as passed by the Senate would create a new limited form of copyright protection for "original" designs which are clearly a part of useful article, regardless of whether such designs could stand by themselves, separate from the article itself. Thus designs of useful articles which do not meet the design patent standard of "novelty" would for the first time be protected.

S.22 is a copyright revision bill. The Committee chose to delete Title II in part because the new form of design protection provided by Title II could not truly be considered copyright protection and therefore appropriately within the scope of copyright revision.

The legislative history thus confirms that, while copyright protection has increasingly been extended to cover articles having a utilitarian dimension, Congress has explicitly refused copyright protection for works of applied art or industrial design which have aesthetic or artistic features that cannot be identified separately from the useful article. Such works are not copyrightable regardless of the fact that they may be "aesthetically satisfying and valuable." H.R. Rep. No. 1476, *supra*, at 55, 1976 U.S. Code Cong. & Ad. News at 5668.

Applying these principles, we are persuaded that since the aesthetic and artistic features of the Barnhart forms are inseparable from the forms' use as utilitarian articles the forms are not copyrightable. Appellant emphasizes that clay sculpting, often used in traditional sculpture, was used in making the molds for the forms. It also stresses that the forms have been responded to as sculptural forms, and have been used for purposes other than modeling clothes, e.g., as decorating props and signs without any clothing or accessories. While this may indicate that the forms are "aesthetically satisfying and valuable," it is insufficient to show that the forms possess aesthetic or artistic features that are physically or conceptually separable from the forms' use as utilitarian objects to display clothes. On the contrary, to the extent the forms possess aesthetically pleasing features, even when these features are considered in the aggregate, they cannot be conceptualized as existing independently of their utilitarian function.

Appellant seeks to rebut this conclusion by arguing that the four forms represent a concrete expression of a particular idea, e.g., the idea of a woman's blouse, and that the form involved, a human torso, is traditionally copyrightable. Appellant suggests that since the Barnhart forms fall within the traditional category of sculpture of the human body, they should be subjected to a lower level of scrutiny in determining its copyrightability. We disagree. We find no support in the statutory language or

---

In addition, Title II left unanswered at least two fundamental issues which will require further study by the Congress. These are: first, what agency should administer this new design protection system and, second, should typeface designs be given the protections of the title?

Finally, the Committee will have to examine further the assertion of the Department of Justice, which testified in opposition to the Title, that Title II would create a new monopoly which has not been justified by a showing that its benefits will outweigh the disadvantage of removing such designs from free public use.

The issues raised by Title II have not been resolved by its deletion from the Copyright Revision Bill. Therefore, the Committee believes that it will be necessary to reconsider the question of design protection in new legislation during the first session 95th Congress. At that time more complete hearings on the subject may be held and, without the encumbrance of a general copyright revision bill, the issues raised in Title II of S. 22 may be resolved.

H.R. Rep. No. 1476, *supra*, at 50, 1976 U.S. Code Cong. & Ad. News at 5663.

legislative history for the claim that merely because a utilitarian article falls within a traditional art form it is entitled to a lower level of scrutiny in determining its copyrightability. Recognition of such a claim would in any event conflict with the antidiscrimination principle Justice Holmes enunciated in *Bleistein v. Donaldson Lithographing Co., supra,* 188 U.S. at 251-52, 23 S. Ct. at 30.

Nor do we agree that copyrightability here is dictated by our decision in *Kieselstein-Cord v. Accessories by Pearl, Inc.,* 632 F.2d 989 (2d Cir.1980), a case we described as being "on a razor's edge of copyright law." There we were called on to determine whether two belt buckles bearing sculptured designs cast in precious metals and principally used for decoration were copyrightable. Various versions of these buckles in silver and gold sold wholesale at prices ranging from $147.50 to $6,000 and were offered by high fashion and jewelry stores. Some had also been accepted by the Metropolitan Museum of Art for its permanent collection.

In concluding that the two buckles were copyrightable we relied on the fact that "[t]he primary ornamental aspect of the Vaquero and Winchester buckles is conceptually separable from their subsidiary utilitarian function." *Id.* at 993. A glance at the pictures of the two buckles, reproduced at *id.* 995, coupled with the description in the text, confirms their highly ornamental dimensions and separability. What distinguishes those buckles from the Barnhart forms is that the ornamented surfaces of the buckles were not in any respect required by their utilitarian functions; the artistic and aesthetic features could thus be conceived of as having been added to, or superimposed upon, an otherwise utilitarian article. The unique artistic design was wholly unnecessary to performance of the utilitarian function. In the case of the Barnhart forms, on the other hand, the features claimed to be aesthetic or artistic, e.g., the life-size configuration of the breasts and the width of the shoulders, are inextricably intertwined with the utilitarian feature, the display of clothes. Whereas a model of a human torso, in order to serve its utilitarian function, must have some configuration of the chest and some width of shoulders, a belt buckle can serve its function satisfactorily without any ornamentation of the type that renders the *Kieselstein-Cord* buckles distinctive.[5]

The judgment of the district court is affirmed.

---

[5] Our learned colleague, Judge Newman, would have copyrightability of a utilitarian article turn on "whether visual inspection of the article and consideration of all pertinent evidence would engender in the [ordinary] observer's mind a separate non-utilitarian concept that can displace, at least temporarily, the utilitarian aspect." (Dissenting Op. p.423). The difficulty with this proposal is that it uses as its yardstick a standard so ethereal as to amount to a "non-test" that would be extremely difficult, if not impossible, to administer or apply. Whether a

NEWMAN, C.J., dissenting: This case concerns the interesting though esoteric issue of "conceptual separability" under the Copyright Act of 1976. Because I believe the majority has either misunderstood the nature of this issue or applied an incorrect standard in resolving the issue in this case, I respectfully dissent from the judgment affirming the District Court's grant of summary judgment for the defendant. I would grant summary judgment to the plaintiff as to two of the objects in question and remand for trial of disputed issues of fact as to the other two objects in question.

The ultimate issue in this case is whether four objects are eligible for copyright protection. The objects are molded forms of styrene. Each is a life-size, three-dimensional representation of the front of the human chest. Two are chests of males, and two are chests of females. For each gender, one form represents a nude chest, and one form represents a chest clad with a shirt or a blouse.

Section 102(a)(5) of the Act extends copyright protection to "sculptural works," which are defined to include "three-dimensional works of fine, graphic, and applied art" and "works of artistic craftsmanship

---

utilitarian object could temporarily be conceived of as a work of art would require a judicial investigation into the ways in which it might on occasion have been displayed and the extent of the displays. It might involve expert testimony and some kind of survey evidence, as distinguished from reliance upon the judge as an ordinary observer.

Almost any utilitarian article may be viewed by some separately as art, depending on how it is displayed (e.g., a can of Campbell Soup or a pair of ornate scissors affixed to the wall of a museum of modern art). But it is the object, not the form of display, for which copyright protection is sought. Congress has made it reasonably clear that copyrightability of the object should turn on its ordinary use as viewed by the average observer, not by a temporary flight of fancy that could attach to any utilitarian object, including an automobile engine, depending on how it is displayed.

The illusory nature of the standard suggested by Judge Newman is confirmed by his suggestion that under it some mannequins might qualify as copyrightable sculptures whereas others might not, depending on numerous factors, including the material used, the angular configuration of the limbs, the facial figures and the hair. Indeed, his uncertainty as to whether the styrene mannequin chests clothed with a shirt or blouse could be viewed by the ordinary observer as art only serves to underscore the bottomless pit that would be created by such a vague test. However, regardless of which standard is applied we disagree with the proposition that the mannequins here, when viewed as hollowed-out three dimensional forms (as presented for copyright) as distinguished from two-dimensional photographs, could be viewed by the ordinary observer as anything other than objects having a utilitarian function as mannequins. It would be by concealing the open, hollowed-out rear half of the object, which is obviously designed to facilitate pinning or tucking in of garments, that an illusion of a sculpture can be created. In that case (as with the photos relied on by the dissent) the subject would not be the same as that presented for copyright.

insofar as their form but not their mechanical or utilitarian aspects are concerned." 17 U.S.C. §101 (1982). The definition of "sculptural works" contains a special limiting provision for "useful articles":

> the design of a useful article, as defined in this section, shall be considered a . . . sculptural work only if, and only to the extent that, such design incorporates . . . sculptural features that can be identified separately from, and are capable of existing independently of, the utilitarian aspects of the article.

Id. Each of the four forms in this case is indisputably a "useful article" as that term is defined in section 101 of the Act, 17 U.S.C §101 (1982), since each has the "intrinsic utilitarian function" of serving as a means of displaying clothing and accessories to customers of retail stores. Thus, the issue becomes whether the designs of these useful articles have "sculptural features that can be identified separately from, and are capable of existing independently of, the utilitarian aspects" of the forms.

This elusive standard was somewhat clarified by the House Report accompanying the bill that became the 1976 Act. The Report states that the article must contain "some element that, *physically or conceptually*, can be identified as separable from the utilitarian aspects of that article." H.R. Rep. No. 1476, 94th Cong., 2d Sess. 55, *reprinted in* 1976 U.S. Code Cong. & Ad. News 5668 (emphasis added). In this Circuit it is settled, and the majority does not dispute, that "conceptual separability" is distinct from "physical separability" and, when present, entitles the creator of a useful article to a copyright on its design. See *Kieselstein-Cord v. Accessories by Pearl, Inc.,* 632 F.2d 989, 993 (2d Cir.1980); see also *Trans-World Manufacturing Corp. v. Al Nyman & Sons, Inc.,* 95 F.R.D. 95, 98-99 (D. Del. 1982); but see *Esquire, Inc. v. Ringer,* 591 F.2d 796, 803-04 (D.C. Cir. 1978), *cert. denied,* 440 U.S. 908, 99 S. Ct. 1217, 59 L. Ed. 2d 456 (1979) (arguably rejecting the independent force of "conceptual separability").

What must be carefully considered is the meaning and application of the principle of "conceptual separability." [1] Initially, it may be helpful to

---

[1] The principle of "conceptual separability" of functional design elements in copyright law should be distinguished from the somewhat similar principle of "functionality" as developed in trademark law. A design feature may not serve as a trademark protected by section 43(a) of the Lanham Act, 15 U.S.C. §1125(a) (1982), if it is functional. Inwood Laboratories, Inc. v. Ives Laboratories, Inc., 456 U.S. 844, 102, S. Ct. 2182, 72 L. Ed. 2d 606 (1982); LeSportsac, Inc. v. K Mart Corp., 754 F.2d 71 (2d Cir.1985); Warner Bros., Inc. v. Gay Toys, Inc. 724 F.2d 327 (2d Cir. 1983). For trademark purposes, a design feature has been said to be functional if it is "essential to the use or purpose of the article" or "affects the cost or quality of the article." Inwood Laboratories, *supra,* 456 U.S. at 850 n.10, 102 S. Ct. at 2187 n.10. Copyright law, however, does not deny copyright protection to a design simply because the design features are functional. If the design engenders a concept that is separable from the concept of the utilitarian function, the

make the obvious point that this principle must mean something other than "physical separability." That latter principle is illustrated by the numerous familiar examples of useful objects ornamented by a drawing, a carving, a sculpted figure, or any other decorative embellishment that could physically appear apart from the useful article. Professor Nimmer offers the example of the sculptured [*sic*] jaguar that adorns the hood of and provides the name for the well-known British automobile. See 1 *Nimmer on Copyright* §2.08[B] at 2-96.1 (1985). With all of the utilitarian elements of the automobile physically removed, the concept, indeed the embodiment, of the artistic creation of the jaguar would remain. Since "conceptual separability" is not the same as "physical separability," it should also be obvious that a design feature can be "conceptually separable" from the utilitarian aspect of a useful article even if it cannot be separated physically.[2]

There are several possible ways in which "conceptual separability"

---

design is copyrightable. That is a reward for the special creativity shown by the designer of such an article. No comparable protection is warranted under trademark law since the marketer of the product with functional design features has available innumerable ways, other than these design features, to identify the source of his goods. He may use a distinctive trade name or trade dress or add distinctive non-functional design features. Any concern that copyright protection may accord a monopoly to advances in functional design, see Warner Bros., *supra*, 724 F.2d at 331 (explaining rationale for functionality defense in trademark law), is adequately met by confining the scope of copyright protection to the precise expression of the proprietor's design. Appellant is not seeking a copyright on the general form of a molded chest serving the function of displaying clothes, only on the precise designs of the four forms in this lawsuit.

[2] Professor Nimmer contends that the principle of "conceptual separability" is illustrated by the work deemed entitled to copyright in Mazer v. Stein, 347 U.S. 201, 74 S. Ct. 460, 98 L. Ed. 630 (1954). In that well-known decision, the Supreme Court upheld a copyright for the design of dancing figures used as the base of a lamp. This cannot be a case of "physical separability," Professor Nimmer maintains, because "[p]hysical removal of all utilitarian features of the lamp must include removal of its base," which would "hardly leave the sculptured dancer intact since the dancer *is* the base." 1 Nimmer, *supra*, §2.08[B] at 2-96.1 (emphasis in original). This may be so, but it is also arguable that the dancing figure, though functioning as the base, is not really essential to the utilitarian functioning of the lamp; only the wiring, the hollow metal stem enclosing the wiring (which was presumably encased in the figurine), the bulb socket, the bulb, and the switch were necessary to enable the object to function as a lamp. The dancing figure, though described in the opinion as a base, may really have been no more than a decorative enclosure for the stem, capable of physical separation from the functional elements of the lamp. Since Mazer v. Stein was decided before the principle of "conceptual separability" was explicitly identified as a criterion of copyrightability of the design of a useful article, it is not surprising that the Court's opinion does not illuminate the distinction between "physical" and "conceptual" separability.

might be understood. One concerns usage. An article used primarily to serve its utilitarian function might be regarded as lacking "conceptually separable" design elements even though those design elements rendered it usable secondarily solely as an artistic work. There is danger in this approach in that it would deny copyright protection to designs of works of art displayed by a minority because they are also used by a majority as useful articles. The copyrightable design of a life-size sculpture of the human body should not lose its copyright protection simply because mannequin manufacturers copy it, replicate it in cheap materials, and sell it in large quantities to department stores to display clothing.

A somewhat related approach, suggested by a sentence in Judge Oakes' opinion in *Kieselstein-Cord*, is to uphold the copyright whenever the decorative or aesthetically pleasing aspect of the article can be said to be "primary" and the utilitarian function can be said to be "subsidiary." 632 F.2d at 993. This approach apparently does not focus on frequency of utilitarian and non-utilitarian usage since the belt buckles in that case were frequently used to fasten belts and less frequently used as pieces of ornamental jewelry displayed at various locations other than the waist. The difficulty with this approach is that it offers little guidance to the trier of fact, or the judge endeavoring to determine whether a triable issue of fact exists, as to what is being measured by the classifications "primary" and "subsidiary."

Another approach, also related to the first, is suggested by Professor Nimmer, who argues that "conceptual separability exists where there is any substantial likelihood that even if the article had no utilitarian use it would still be marketable to some significant segment of the community simply because of its aesthetic qualities." 1 *Nimmer, supra*, §2.08[B] at 2-96.2 (footnote omitted). This "market" approach risks allowing a copyright only to designs of forms within the domain of popular art, a hazard Professor Nimmer acknowledges. See *id.* at 2-96.3. However, various sculptured forms would be recognized as works of art by many, even though those willing to purchase them for display in their homes might be few in number and not a "significant segment of the community."

Some might suggest that "conceptual separability" exists whenever the design of a form has sufficient aesthetic appeal to be appreciated for its artistic qualities. That approach has plainly been rejected by Congress. The House Report makes clear that, if the artistic features cannot be identified separately, the work is not copyrightable even though such features are "aesthetically satisfying and valuable." H.R. Rep. No. 1476, *supra*, at 55, 1976 U.S. Code Cong. & Ad. News at 5668. A chair may be so artistically designed as to merit display in a museum, but that fact alone cannot satisfy the test of "conceptual separateness." The viewer in the museum sees and apprehends a well-designed chair, not a work of art with a design that is conceptually separate from the functional purposes of an object on which people sit.

How, then, is "conceptual separateness" to be determined? In my view, the answer derives from the word "conceptual." For the design features to be "conceptually separate" from the utilitarian aspects of the useful article that embodies the design, the article must stimulate in the mind of the beholder a concept that is separate from the concept evoked by its utilitarian function. The test turns on what may reasonably be understood to be occurring in the mind of the beholder or, as some might say, in the "mind's eye" of the beholder. This formulation requires consideration of who the beholder is and when a concept may be considered "separate."

I think the relevant beholder must be that most useful legal personage — the ordinary, reasonable observer. This is the same person the law enlists to decide other conceptual issues in copyright law, such as whether an allegedly infringing work bears a substantial similarity to a copyrighted work. See, e.g., *Herbert Rosenthal Jewelry Corp. v. Honora Jewelry Co.*, 509 F.2d 64 (2d Cir. 1974); 3 *Nimmer, supra*, §13.03[E]. Of course, the ordinary observer does not actually decide the issue; the trier of fact determines the issue in light of the impressions reasonably expected to be made upon the hypothetical ordinary observer. And, as with other issues decided by reference to the reactions of an ordinary observer, a particular case may present undisputed facts from which a reasonable trier could reach only one conclusion, in which event the side favored by that conclusion is entitled to prevail as a matter of law and have summary judgment entered in its favor. See, e.g., *Kieselstein-Cord v. Accessories by Pearl, Inc., supra* (copyright proprietor prevails on issue of "conceptual separability" as a matter of law).

The "separateness" of the utilitarian and non-utilitarian concepts engendered by an article's design is itself a perplexing concept. I think the requisite "separateness" exists whenever the design creates in the mind of the ordinary observer two different concepts that are not inevitably entertained simultaneously. Again, the example of the artistically designed chair displayed in a museum may be helpful. The ordinary observer can be expected to apprehend the design of a chair whenever the object is viewed. He may, in addition, entertain the concept of a work of art, but, if this second concept is engendered in the observer's mind simultaneously with the concept of the article's utilitarian function, the requisite "separateness" does not exist. The test is not whether the observer fails to recognize the object as a chair but only whether the concept of the utilitarian function can be displaced in the mind by some other concept. That does not occur, at least for the ordinary observer, when viewing even the most artistically designed chair. It may occur, however, when viewing some other object if the utilitarian function of the object is not perceived at all; it may also occur, even when the utilitarian function is perceived by observation, perhaps aided by explanation, if the concept of the utilitarian function can be displaced in the observer's mind while he entertains the separate concept of some non-utilitarian function. The separate concept will normally be that of a work of art.

Some might think that the requisite separability of concepts exists whenever the design of a form engenders in the mind of the ordinary observer any concept that is distinct from the concept of the form's utilitarian function. Under this approach, the design of an artistically designed chair would receive copyright protection if the ordinary observer viewing it would entertain the concept of a work of art in addition to the concept of a chair. That approach, I fear, would subvert the Congressional effort to deny copyright protection to designs of useful articles that are aesthetically pleasing. The impression of an aesthetically pleasing design would be characterized by many as the impression of a work of art, thereby blurring the line Congress has sought to maintain. I believe we would be more faithful to the Congressional scheme if we insisted that a concept, such as that of a work of art, is "separate" from the concept of an article's utilitarian function only when the non-utilitarian concept can be entertained in the mind of the ordinary observer without at the same time contemplating the utilitarian function. This temporal sense of separateness permits the designs of some useful articles to enjoy copyright protection, as provided by the 1976 Act, but avoids according protection to every design that can be appreciated as a work of art, a result Congress rejected. The utilitarian function is not truly a separate concept for purposes of "conceptual separateness" unless the design engenders a non-utilitarian concept without at the same time engendering the concept of a utilitarian function.

In endeavoring to draw the line between the design of an aesthetically pleasing useful article, which is not copyrightable, and the copyrightable design of a useful article that engenders a concept separate from the concept of its utilitarian function, courts will inevitably be drawn into some minimal inquiry as to the nature of art. The need for the inquiry is regrettable, since courts must not become the arbiters of taste in art or any other aspect of aesthetics. However, as long as "conceptual separability" determines whether the design of a useful article is copyrightable, some threshold assessment of art is inevitable since the separate concept that will satisfy the test of "conceptual separability" will often be the concept of a work of art. Of course, courts must not assess the *quality* of art, but a determination of whether a design engenders the concept of a work of art, separate from the concept of an article's utilitarian function, necessarily requires some consideration of whether the object *is* a work of art.

Both the trier determining the factual issue of "conceptual separability" and the judge deciding whether the undisputed facts permit a reasonable trier to reach only one conclusion on the issue are entitled to consider whatever evidence might be helpful on the issue, in addition to the visual impressions gained from the article in question. Thus, the fact that an object has been displayed or used apart from its utilitarian function, the extent of such display or use, and whether such display or use resulted from purchases would all be relevant in determining whether the design of the object engenders a separable concept of a work of art. In addition, expert opinion and survey evidence ought generally to be received. The issue need not turn on the immediate reaction of the ordinary observer but on whether visual inspection of the article and consideration of all pertinent evidence would engender in the observer's mind a separate non-utilitarian concept that can displace, at least temporarily, the utilitarian concept.

This approach seems consistent with and may even explain the few cases to have considered the issue, although the language in all of the decisions may not be entirely reconcilable. In *Kieselstein-Cord*, we upheld the copyrightability of the artistic design of two belt buckles. This holding was based upon a conclusion that the design of the buckles was conceptually separate from the utilitarian function of fastening a belt. That view, in turn, was based in part on the undisputed fact that consumers with some frequency wore the buckles as ornamental jewelry at locations other than the waist. The Court apparently concluded that the buckles had created in the minds of those consumers a conception of the design as ornamental jewelry separate from the functional aspect of a belt buckle. Expert testimony supported the view that the buckles "rise to the level of creative art." 632 F.2d at 994. The case was characterized by Judge Oakes as "on a razor's edge of copyright law," *id*. at 990, as indeed it was; some might have thought that even though some consumers wore the buckle as ornamental jewelry, they still thought of the article as a belt buckle, albeit one so artistically designed as to be appropriate for wearing elsewhere than at the waist. Whether the concept in the mind of the ordinary observer was of a piece of ornamental jewelry separate from the concept of a belt buckle, or only the concept of a belt buckle that could be used either to fasten a belt or decorate clothing at any location was undoubtedly a close question.

In *Trans-World Manufacturing Corp.*, *supra*, the interesting design of a display case for eyeglasses was deemed to create for the trier of fact a fair question as to whether a concept separable from the utilitarian function existed. By contrast, the designs of the wheel cover in *Norris Industries v. I.T. & T.*, 696 F.2d 918 (11th Cir.), *cert. denied*, 464 U.S. 818, 104 S. Ct. 78, 78 L. Ed. 2d 89 (1983), and the outdoor lighting fixture in *Esquire, Inc. v. Ringer*, *supra*, were each deemed, as a matter of law, to engender no concept that was separable from the utilitarian function of each article. It evidently was thought that an ordinary observer viewing the articles would have in mind no conception separate from that of a wheel cover (*Norris*) or a lighting fixture (*Esquire*).

Our case involving the four styrene chest forms seems to me a much easier case than *Kieselstein-Cord*. An ordinary observer, indeed, an ordinary reader of this opinion who views the two unclothed forms depicted in figures 1 and 2 [omitted], would be most unlikely even to entertain, from visual inspection alone, the concept of a mannequin with the utilitarian function of displaying a shirt or a blouse. The initial concept in the observer's mind, I believe, would be of an art object, an entirely understandable mental impression based on previous viewing of unclad torsos displayed as artistic sculptures. Even after learning that these two forms are used to display clothing in retail stores, the only reasonable conclusion that an ordinary viewer would reach is that the forms have both a utilitarian function and an entirely separate function of serving as a work of art. I am confident that the ordinary observer could reasonably conclude only that these two forms are not simply mannequins that happen to have sufficient aesthetic appeal to qualify as works of art, but that the conception in the mind is that of a work of art *in addition to and capable of being entertained separately from* the concept of a mannequin, if the latter concept is entertained at all. As appellant contends, with pardonable hyperbole, the design of Michaelangelo's "David" would not cease to be copyrightable simply because cheap copies of it were used by a retail store to display clothing.

This is not to suggest that the design of every form intended for use as a mannequin automatically qualifies for copyright protection whenever it is deemed to have artistic merit. Many mannequins, perhaps most, by virtue of the combination of the material used, the angular configuration of the limbs, the facial features, and the representation of hair create the visual impression that they are mannequins and not anything else. The fact that in some instances a mannequin of that sort is displayed in a store as an eye-catching item apart from its function of enhancing the appearance of clothes, in a living room as a conversation piece, or even in a museum as an interesting example of contemporary industrial design does not mean that it engenders a concept separate from the concept of a mannequin. The two forms depicted in figures 1 and 2 [omitted], however, if perceived as mannequins at all, clearly engender an entirely separable concept of an art object, one that can be entertained in the mind without simultaneously perceiving the forms as mannequins at all.

The majority appears to resist this conclusion for two reasons. First, the majority asserts that the appellant is seeking application of a lower level of scrutiny on the issue of copyrightability because the forms depict a portion of the human body. I do not find this argument anywhere in the appellant's briefs. In any event, I agree with the majority that no lower level of scrutiny is appropriate. But to reject a lower level is not to explain why appellant does not prevail under the normal level. Second, the majority contends that the design features of the forms are "inextricably intertwined" with their utilitarian function. This intertwining is said to result from the fact that a form must have "some configuration of the chest and some width of shoulders" in order to serve its utilitarian function. With deference, I believe this approach misapplies, if it does not ignore, the principle of "conceptual separability." Of course, the design features of these forms render them suitable for their utilitarian function. But that fact only creates the issue of "conceptual separability"; it does not resolve it. The question to be decided is whether the design features of these forms create in the mind of an ordinary viewer a concept that is entirely separable from the utilitarian function. Unlike a form that always creates in the observer's mind the concept of a mannequin, each of these unclothed forms creates the separate concept of an object of art—not just an aesthetically pleasing mannequin, but an object of art that in the mind's eye can be appreciated as something other than a mannequin.

Of course, appellant's entitlement to a copyright on the design of the unclothed forms would give it only limited, though apparently valuable, protection. The copyright would not bar imitators from designing human chests. It would only bar them from copying the precise design embodied in appellant's forms.

As for the two forms, depicted in figures 3 and 4 [omitted], of chests clothed with a shirt or a blouse, I am uncertain what concept or concepts would be engendered in the mind of an ordinary observer. I think it is likely that these forms too would engender the separately entertained concept of an art object whether or not they also engendered the concept of a mannequin. But this is not the only conclusion a reasonable trier could reach as to the perception of an ordinary observer. That observer might always perceive them as mannequins or perhaps as devices advertising for sale the particular style of shirt or blouse sculpted on each form.[3] I think a reasonable trier could conclude either way on the issue of "conceptual separability" as to the clothed forms. That issue is therefore not amenable to summary judgment and should, in my view, be remanded for trial. In any event, I do not agree that the only reasonable conclusion a trier of fact could reach is that the clothed forms create no concept separable from the concept of their utilitarian function.

I would grant summary judgment to the copyright proprietor as to the design of the two nude forms and remand for trial with respect to the two clothed forms.

---

[3] If the concepts always engendered in the mind of an ordinary observer were that of a mannequin to display sweaters or accessories on top of the shirt or blouse, or of a form to advertise the style of the sculpted shirt or blouse itself, these utilitarian functions would not, in the absence of some separable concept, support a copyright in the design of the clothed forms.

D. PATENTS: ADDITIONAL PROTECTION FOR THE ARTIST

§2.11. PROS AND CONS OF PATENTS

Artists have not generally concerned themselves with patents; coping with copyright has been enough of a problem. In an appropriate situation, however, a patent is available to an artist and should not be overlooked. If the artist is involved in the frontiers of conceptual art, for instance, the possibility of obtaining a utility patent should be explored. Indeed, a number of artists have done so.[1]

A patent may be acquired for either the utility or the design of a work. Utility patent protection requires that the invention be useful, new, and unobvious to those skilled in the particular art. For a work to qualify for a design patent, it must be an article of manufacture with a design that is ornamental, new, and unobvious. A utility patent is valid for 17 years, while a design patent is valid for 14; neither is renewable.

Although both copyright and patent protection stem from the same provision in the Constitution, they are essentially different, having developed along dissimilar lines. A patent is based on the concept of "invention" (subject to a very severe test) that represents a significant advance over the "prior art"; whereas to be copyrightable material need only be "original," not necessarily creative, with the particular author or artist. For example, one could obtain a design patent on the shape of a pair of flared pants. In contrast, a copyright would only be available for the print used on the fabric from which the pants were to be manufactured (e.g., a floral print), not for the shape of the pants. In short, the useful aspect of the item is not copyrightable.

The test for copyright protection is whether the original work was copied. Thus, it is generally necessary in a copyright infringement suit to show that the alleged infringer had "access" to the original work. Theoretically, it is possible for two people working miles apart to create identical artwork independently of each other; therefore, neither could successfully sue the other for infringement, since neither copied the work. Not so in patent law. Patent protection gives the owner of a patent (whether utility or design) the right to prevent others from making, using, or selling the patented article or design.

The Copyright Revision Act provides that copyright protection does not extend to "any idea, procedure, process, system, method of opera-

---

§2.11. [1] But cf. Greenewalt v. Stanley Co. of America, 54 F.2d 1985 (3rd Cir. 1931).

tion, concept, principle, or discovery, regardless of the form in which it is described, explained, illustrated, or embodied in such work."[2] The purpose of this provision is to preserve the distinction between copyrights and patents. Further, the decision of the U.S. Supreme Court in *Goldstein v. California*[3] indicates that the landmark *Sears, Roebuck & Co. v. Stiffel Co.*[4] and *Compco Corp. v. Day-Brite Lighting, Inc.*[5] decisions were limited to patent or invention cases and did not extend to copyright or "writings" cases.

Types of articles to which design patent protection has been accorded include airplanes, pliers, common nasal inhalers, and "other useful objects of streamlined or extremely simple lines of which the sales appeal is based on a 'choice' dictated by appearance rather than function."[6] Although there is an overlap in the copyright and design patent fields, the latter's approach to modern industrial ornamental designs is more liberal. There is, however, very little law on the subject of design patents; what exists is often too confused to be instructive.[7] An early draft of the copyright revision bill attempted to clarify the confusion.[8] Title II of the bill, which was to be known as the Design Protection Act, was drafted to protect the author of "an original ornamental design of a useful article." It stated that a design has to be "ornamental" if it is "intended" to make the article attractive or distinct in appearance. The bill's definition of "useful article" is critical, and came to mark the dividing line between works eligible for copyright and those eligible for design protection. The definition reads:

A "useful article" is an article which in normal use has an intrinsic utilitarian function that is not merely to portray the appearance of the article or to convey information. An article which normally is part of a useful article shall be deemed to be a useful article.[9]

This approach was taken in light of the Copyright Office's experience following *Mazer v. Stein* (reproduced at §2.10.1 *infra*), which demon-

---

[2] Copyright Revision Act of 1976, §102(b).

[3] 412 U.S. 546, 93 S. Ct. 2303, 37 L. Ed. 2d 163 (1973).

[4] 376 U.S. 225, 84 S. Ct. 784, 11 L. Ed. 2d 661 (1964).

[5] 376 U.S. 234, 84 S. Ct. 779, 11 L. Ed. 2d 669 (1964).

[6] See Mott, Analysis of the "Unity of Art" Concept in European Legal Sytems, 11 Bull. Copyright L. Symp. 242, 260 (ASCAP 1964).

[7] Application of Richard Q. Yardley, 493 F. 2d 1389 (C.C.P.A. 1974), held that an author-inventor may receive both a copyright and design patent in the overlap area.

[8] S. 1361, 93rd Cong., 1st Sess. (1973).

[9] *Ibid.*

strated the difficulty of ascertaining what constitutes a "work of art." Thus the traditional patent test of "novelty" and "invention" was discarded by the bill in favor of copyright's concept of "originality."

The obtaining of a patent is usually expensive and time consuming, often entailing a protracted period of correspondence with the Patent Office and many years of waiting for a patent to issue. Conversely, copyright protection is available from the point of creation. Under the bill, patent protection would commence when the design "is first made public." This was defined as occurring when "an existing useful article embodying the design is anywhere publicly exhibited, publicly distributed, or offered for sale or sold to the public." [10] These provisions, however, were not included in the 1976 Copyright Act as adopted. Although Title II (the Design Protection Act) passed the Senate as separate legislation on three occasions, the House Judiciary Committee deleted it from the bill for the reasons stated in the final House report:

> In reporting S. 22, the House Judiciary Committee has deleted Title II. Until 1954, designs for useful articles were not generally subject to copyright protection. The primary protection available was the design patent, which requires that the design be not only "original," the standard applied in copyright law, but also "novel," meaning that it has never before existed anywhere.
>
> However, in 1954 the Supreme Court decided the case of *Mazer v. Stein*, 347 U.S. 201, in which it held that works of art which are incorporated into the design of useful articles, but which are capable of standing by themselves as art works separate from the useful article, are copyrightable. The example used in the *Mazer* case was an ornamental lamp base.
>
> Title II of S. 22 as passed by the Senate would create a new limited form of copyright protection for "original" designs which are clearly a part of a useful article, regardless of whether such designs could stand by themselves, separate from the article itself. Thus designs of useful articles which do not meet the design patent standard of "novelty" would for the first time be protected.
>
> S. 22 is a copyright revision bill. The Committee chose to delete Title II in part because the new form of design protection provided by Title II could not truly be considered and therefore appropriately within the scope of copyright revision.
>
> In addition, Title II left unanswered at least two fundamental issues which will require further study by the Congress. These are: first, what agency should administer this new design protection system and, second, should typeface designs be given the protections of the Title?
>
> Finally, the Committee will have to examine further the assertion of the Department of Justice, which testified in opposition to the Title, that Title II would create a new monopoly which has not been justified by a showing that

---

[10] *Ibid.*

its benefits will outweigh the disadvantage of removing such designs from free public use.

The issues raised by Title II have not been resolved by its deletion from the Copyright Revision Bill. Therefore, the Committee believes that it will be necessary to reconsider the question of design protection in new legislation during the first session 95th Congress. At that time more complete hearings on the subject may be held and, without the encumbrance of a general copyright revision bill, the issues raised in Title II of S. 22 may be resolved.[11]

As with patent protection, the copyright laws do not grant any immunity from antitrust violation. In *United States v. Chicago Tribune-New York News Syndicate, Inc.*,[12] the Tribune argued that by reason of the copyright it owned, an exclusive territorial license may be granted, no matter how "arbitrary" or "unreasonably broad" the territory may be.[13] The court assumed for purposes of its decision that as a matter of copyright law a license may be made exclusive within a specified territory. It went on to point out, however, that this proposition is not firmly established in the law. In patent law, there is a specific provision for conveyance of an exclusive right "to the whole or any specified part of the United States."[14] As the court indicated, there is no similar provision in the Copyright Act. The fact that the copyright law may permit a geographically exclusive license did not, however, remove the license from the antitrust laws; the copyright monopoly provides no blanket exemption from these laws.

---

[11] H.R. Rep. No. 1476, 94th Cong., 2d Sess. 50 (1976), *reprinted in* 1976 U.S. Code Cong. & Ad. News, vol. 5 at 5663. For an instructive discussion of the public policy issues involved in balancing the interests of the artists against those of the consumer, see the *Kieselstein-Cord* case, reproduced at §2.10.4 *supra*.

[12] 309 F. Supp. 1301 (S.D.N.Y. 1970).

[13] *Id.* at 1302.

[14] 26 U.S.C. §261.

CHAPTER THREE

Relationships with Art Dealers

•

§3.1. **Contractual Rights**

§3.1. CONTRACTUAL RIGHTS

§3.1.1. Checklist of Points to Be Considered in Consignment Agreements between Artist and Gallery

Many artists and some gallery owners believe that their relationship with each other is, like marriage, too special to be bound by a formal, written agreement. "If we're getting along, it won't add any-thing; if we're not, it won't help."

Overlooked by this view is that the primary requirement — "getting along" — may itself depend on the existence of some prior, clear-cut, formal arrangement. Experience suggests that the negotiation of an agreement between an artist and a gallery offers a thoughtful opportunity to anticipate and resolve in advance many of the problems that most typically arise in the course of such a relationship. If they cannot agree on how their relationship is to be conducted, both may be far better off finding that out at the negotiating stage than after misinterpretations and disagreements have pushed them along the path of bitterness, estrangement, accusation, and, not infrequently, litigation.

Among those opposed to such agreements — the authors of this book not among them — are the artists Robert Rauschenberg and Robert Motherwell. According to Rauschenberg, "a written contract indicates a strange relationship — a lack of trust." Said Motherwell, "In the end, the function of a contract is to guard one party against the other's being crooked, and I don't deal with people who I think are crooked."[1] Needless to say, other things a contract can guard against are one party's confusion as to details, a mutual misunderstanding of what was agreed upon, and the impairment of memory due to the passage of time, accident, illness, or death. We all perforce must deal with people who are subject to at least some of these.

The checklist that follows is intended to apply only to consignment agreements. Specifically excluded are two areas that generally require separate and altogether different kinds of agreements:

(a) commissions to be executed by the artist that have been obtained through the gallery's efforts — it is generally best simply to indicate that, if and when necessary, these will be negotiated separately; and

(b) prints and other multiples that are more often dealt with by service contracts or through outright sale or by some form of joint venture.

The systematic outright sale to the gallery of unique works of painting or sculpture is rare in the United States, although traditionally more common in Europe. Here, consignment arrangements have seemed the more desirable: They permit the gallery to do more with less capital and allow the artist to move to another gallery without leaving his unsold past production in what may have become hostile hands.

---

§3.1. [1] Art Letter, Feb. 1977, at 2. This issue contains a summary of some arguments for and against written agreements between artists and galleries, along with a useful bibliography.

Included on this checklist are those points that will most frequently arise between the artist and the gallery. It is not intended to be either exhaustive — anyone who has worked in this area could add another several dozen — or used in its entirety in every instance. Only in the cases of the most successful artists, where the largest amounts of money or the most complex arrangements as to subdealerships are involved, is it likely that anyone would negotiate an agreement covering all of these points.

In the common situation, the parties should concentrate their efforts on the points most relevant to their particular situation. If the artist is a painter who makes small canvases and lives near the gallery, the question of shipping costs to and from may be irrelevant. If he is a sculptor resident in Europe, making two-ton constructions and dealing with a Chicago gallery, the question of shipping costs to and from the gallery may be, economically, the most important single item to be negotiated.

To the negotiation of most of the points on the checklist, the artist and the gallery will bring conflicting interests. For example, their positions as to 1(a)(ii) — continuity of personnel — might be as follows:

The Artist: In joining the Harry Blackacre Gallery, Inc., I want it understood that it's really Harry Blackacre himself that I'm counting on. Harry understands how to present my work and knows how to sell it. If Harry gets rid of the gallery or moves away or dies, I may want to go too. I don't want to be saddled with a bunch of strangers for five years.

Harry Blackacre: Don't be silly. I can't run a business that way. Your contract is one of the gallery's assets, and how can I invest money — or even raise it — to promote you if you can just walk out the moment I get sick or circumstances change.

And so on. As in any negotiation involving multiple issues, the negotiation of artist-gallery consignment agreements involves tradeoffs of one point for another, compromises where they can be made, and foresight as to what the real problems may be. Hopefully, this checklist will prove helpful toward these ends.

Checklist: Consignment Agreements between Artist and Gallery

1. Contracting Parties
   (a) Gallery
      (i) Legal form
      (ii) Continuity of personnel

    (iii) Continuity of location

    (iv) Assignability

  (b) Artist

    (i) Extension to donees (wife, children, etc.)

    (ii) Estate

2. Duration

  (a) Fixed term

  (b) Term contingent on sales or productivity

  (c) Options to extend term

  (d) Special treatment of sales at beginning and end of term

3. Scope

  (a) Media covered

  (b) Availability of past and future work

  (c) Gallery's right to visit studio

  (d) Commissions

  (e) Exclusivity

    (i) Territorial (point of sale and/or domicile of purchaser)

    (ii) Studio sales

    (iii) Barter or exchange

    (iv) Charitable gifts

    (v) Other gifts

    (vi) If non-exclusive, priority of gallery in choosing work

    (vii) Courtesy credit to gallery on loans by artist

4. Shipping

  (a) Expense to and from gallery

    (i) Location of studio

    (ii) Works at other locations

    (iii) Limitation on scale

  (b) Carriers

  (c) Crating

  (d) Initiative for shipments

5. Storage

  (a) Expense

  (b) Volume

  (c) Location

  (d) Storage of crates

  (e) Access by artist

6. INSURANCE
   (a) Expenses
   (b) Transit and location
   (c) Valuation
   (d) Risks protected
   (e) Interests protected and disposition of proceeds
   (f) Product liability (kinetic, light works, etc.)

7. FRAMING
   (a) Initial expense
   (b) Amount to be framed
   (c) Specifications
   (d) Treatment of framing expense on works sold
   (e) Ownership at end of term

8. PHOTOGRAPHS
   (a) Expense
   (b) Amount required, black and white and color
   (c) Ownership of negatives and transparencies
   (d) Control of negatives and transparencies

9. ARTISTIC CONTROL
   (a) Permissions for book and magazine reproductions
   (b) Inclusion in gallery group exhibitions
   (c) Inclusion in other group exhibitions
   (d) Artist's veto over purchasers

10. GALLERY EXHIBITIONS
    (a) Dates
    (b) Space
    (c) Choice of works to be shown
    (d) Control over installation
    (e) Expenses of partitions, painting, pedestals, etc.
    (f) Scope and expense of advertising
    (g) Scope and expense of catalogue
        (i) Format
        (ii) Quantity
        (iii) Reproductions
        (iv) Disposition of proceeds from sale
    (h) Scope and expense of opening
    (i) Scope and expense of announcement and other mailings
    (j) Benefit exhibitions

11. OTHER FORMS OF PROMOTION
    (a) Subsidies for museum exhibitions
    (b) Subsidies for color reproductions
    (c) Printing and updating of resumes
    (d) General publicity

12. REPRODUCTION RIGHTS
    (a) Control prior to sale of work
    (b) Retention on transfer or sale of work
    (c) Copyrights

13. INVENTORY RECORDS
    (a) Separate transit record for artist
    (b) Records of illustrations and exhibitions
    (c) Right to inspect

14. DAMAGE TO, OR DETERIORATION OF, WORKS CONSIGNED TO THE GALLERY
    (a) Choice of restorer
    (b) Expense of outside restoration
    (c) Compensation to artist for restoration performed by him
    (d) Right to inspect
    (e) Defective workmanship or materials
        (including claims after sales)
    (f) Financial treatment of partial or total losses

15. PROTECTION OF THE MARKET
    (a) Right of gallery to sell at auction
    (b) Protection of works at auction
    (c) Works for sale by collectors or other galleries or dealers
    (d) Pricing of works independently acquired by gallery
    (e) Pricing of works offered by the artist through other galleries

16. SELLING PRICES
    (a) Initial scale
    (b) Periodic review
    (c) Permission discounts
    (d) Negotiation of commissioned works
    (e) Right of gallery to rent in lieu of right to sell

17. BILLING AND TERMS OF SALE
    (a) Extended payment
        (i)   Credit risk
        (ii) Allocation of monies as received
        (iii) Division of interest charges

(iv) Qualified installment sales for tax purposes

(v) Filing of financing statement under U.C.C.

(b) Valuation of works by other artists accepted by the gallery in partial payment

(c) Exchanges ("trading up")

(d) Returns

(e) Separate statements of framing, packing, shipping, or other charges

18. Compensation of the Gallery; Net Price Method

   (a) Right of gallery to purchase for its own account

   (b) Accelerated review of net prices in case of rapidly changing market

19. Compensation of the Gallery; Commission Method

   (a) Uniform and sliding scales

   (b) Special cases

     (i) Graphics

     (ii) Sculpture in which cost of fabrication is material

     (iii) Commissioned works

   (c) Calculating the net proceeds on the basis of which artist and gallery will receive their respective shares

     (i) Framing

     (ii) Discounts

     (iii) Shipment to client

     (iv) Commissions to agents or other galleries

   (d) Global invoices

   (e) Sales to dummies

20. Income from Other Than Sales

   (a) Rentals

   (b) Lecture and similar fees

   (c) Prizes and purchase awards

   (d) Reproduction rights

21. Accounting and Payment

   (a) Periodicity

   (b) Degree of completeness required

   (c) Time in which payments must be made

   (d) Right to inspect financial records

   (e) Currency to be used for payment

22. STATUS OF ART WORKS AND/OR FUNDS IN HANDS OF GALLERY
    (a) Filing of financing statement under U.C.C.
    (b) Sales proceeds as trust funds
    (c) Waiver of rights under applicable artist-art dealer consignment statutes[2]

23. ADVANCES AND GUARANTEES
    (a) Amounts and intervals at which available
    (b) Effects of monies due from sales on amounts to be advanced
    (c) Time of repayment
    (d) If repayable by the artist with work
        (i) Selection of work
        (ii) Time of selection
        (iii) Valuation for purposes of repayment
        (iv) Relationship of gallery's owned inventory to consigned inventory

24. MISCELLANEOUS
    (a) Confidentiality of artist's personal mailing list
    (b) Resale agreements with purchasers (use of the artist's reserved rights transfer and sale agreement)
    (c) Right of gallery to use artist's name and image for promotional purposes

25. GENERAL CONTRACT PROVISIONS
    (a) Representations and warranties
    (b) Entire agreement and amendment procedure
    (c) Applicable law
    (d) Arbitration

§3.1.2. What Is an "Exclusive" Arrangement? — Studio Sales and Barter

Perhaps the most troublesome and least understood facet of the artist-art dealer relationship involves a sale by an artist, from his studio, without the involvement of the artist's dealer. At times the purchaser is either a friend of the artist or knows where he can be located and deals directly with him; at other times the purchaser has visited the dealer's

---

[2] See §3.2 *infra* for a discussion and an example of this statute.

premises, takes note of the retail prices, and then seeks out the artist to obtain a better deal.

The issue is particularly sensitive when the art dealer has an "exclusive" consignment arrangement. But what does "exclusive" mean? As a purely legal matter, the law in the analogous field of real estate brokerage may provide an answer. In real estate law there are two types of exclusivity vis-à-vis the broker: (a) an exclusive agency or (b) an exclusive power to sell.[3] It is now fairly well settled that if the broker is simply the exclusive agent, the principal can sell the property directly without incurring any liability to the exclusive broker-agent. Conversely, if the broker has an "exclusive power to sell," the principal would be responsible for the commission if he were to effect the sale without the use of the agent.[4]

These principles should be applicable to the artist-art dealer relationship. Most art dealers, however, believe that their exclusivity gives them broader rights, i.e., that the artist may never sell independently without incurring the obligation of a commission for the dealer. This may be the expectation of the dealer, but this view does not accord with the principles that undoubtedly would be applicable.

Of course, there is an additional element present in the artist-art dealer relationship that adds a different and significant perspective to the arrangement. The real estate broker engaged to sell property rarely occupies the same position as the art dealer engaged to promote a reputation from which sales will flow. Despite legal principles, an artist who fears that his dealer will turn his back on him may well think twice before incurring his wrath.

A related and equally troublesome question concerns barter arrangements. Imagine an artist's astonishment upon learning that his dealer (not to mention his tax collector) feels entitled to compensation following the artist's exchange of three paintings for a Porsche, the use of a Florida condominium or dental work. From the dealer's perspective, this sort of transaction is extremely difficult to control, unfailingly leads to ill will, and in many cases may actually divert a substantial portion of the artist's saleable production. Swaps between artists are a variation on the theme. Some of these are executed in contemplation of tax evasion, others out of mutual admiration. Whether they violate a dealer's exclusivity would again depend on the intention of the parties. Enforcing this exclusive power to sell, however, would require a Scrooge, let alone a mini FBI.

---

[3] See E. Biskind & C. Barasch, The Law of Real Estate Brokers §67.03 (1969).
[4] *Id.* at 171.

§3.1.3. *O'Keeffe v. Bry:* Confirming the Importance of a Writing

In his 1937 biography, *The Great Goldwyn*, Alva Johnston quotes Samuel Goldwyn as having said a "verbal contract isn't worth the paper it's written on." As the *O'Keeffe* case, which follows, suggests, that observation may be as applicable to the relationship between artists and dealers as to that between film stars and movie studios.

Operative here was the New York Statute of Frauds, the direct lineal descendant — together with the comparable Statute of Frauds adopted by either the legislature or judiciary of virtually every other state — of a law first enacted by the British Parliament in 1677. This provided that certain kinds of agreements should be unenforceable unless they were evidenced by a writing signed by the party against whom their enforcement was sought.[5] In the instant case, the party against whom enforcement was sought was the artist Georgia O'Keeffe. The inability of her long-term agent, Doris Bry, to produce any documents signed by O'Keeffe granting her the right to act as the artist's exclusive agent proved fatal to various counterclaims she introduced in the law suit that attended the parting of their ways. Here, under even the most liberal interpretation of the Statute of Frauds, the "confluence of memoranda" approach referred to by Judge Lasker, Ms. Bry's case still failed without some "core document evidencing a promise."

As concerns artists and art dealers alike, it should be clear that — for anything more than a deliberately casual and transient relationship — a *written* agreement signed by both parties is the only basis upon which any pattern of ongoing expectations can reliably be built.

O'KEEFFE v. BRY
456 F. Supp. 822 (S.D.N.Y. 1978)

LASKER, D.J. For many years during her remarkable and long artistic career, Georgia O'Keeffe employed the services of a commissioned sales agent, Doris Bry.[1] Bry was authorized to sell not only O'Keeffe's works of art, which include paintings , watercolors, drawings

---

[5] The Statute of Frauds is also discussed in National Historic Shrines Foundation, Inc. v. Dali and its accompanying commentary in Chapter 4.

[1] Exhibit A to Affidavit of Maurice Nessen, July 19, 1977; Exhibit A to Affidavit of James Downey, annexed to the motion for preliminary injunction, May 13, 1977.

and pastels, but also the photographic works of Alfred Stieglitz, O'Keeffe's late husband.

After an apparent falling out between the artist and her agent, O'Keeffe terminated the agency (see Exhibit F, Downey Affidavit) and demanded the return of all her works of art, as well as the works of Stieglitz. When Bry refused to honor O'Keeffe's demand, this action was commenced, in May, 1977. O'Keeffe prays for the return of all of her and Stieglitz's works and seeks an accounting by Bry for moneys due on the sale of those works.

Shortly after the filing of the complaint, O'Keeffe moved for a preliminary injunction, requiring that all the relevant artworks (as well as certain ancillary items belonging to her) in Bry's custody be transferred to a safe place. Upon finding, inter alia, that "Miss O'Keeffe is the owner of the properties for which she seeks replevin or recovery," (Transcript of proceedings of June 10, 1977 at 33), the motion was granted. No order was entered because counsel for Bry represented that his client would comply voluntarily.

After preliminary relief had been granted, Bry then filed an answer, later superseded by an amended answer, which asserted five counterclaims, for breach of contract and for recovery in quantum meruit. O'Keeffe moved to dismiss the counterclaims on the grounds that: (1) the contract claims were barred by the statute of frauds and (2) the quantum meruit claim was precluded by the existence of an express contract covering the services for which equitable restitution was sought. In opposition, Bry argued that with regard to the contract claims, discovery might yield documents satisfying the statute of frauds requirement. As for the allegedly preemptive express contract, Bry contended that examination of the contract alone gave no indication whether the services underlying the quantum meruit claim were within the ambit of the express agreement. It was claimed that resolution of the quantum meruit claim involved a question of interpretation, a matter of fact that could not be decided on the motion to dismiss. On August 12, 1977, the motion to dismiss the counterclaims was denied, without prejudice to renewal after completion of the following discovery: (1) the taking of depositions of Bry and Downey (O'Keeffe's personal attorney), and (2) the delivery to the court for in camera inspection of O'Keeffe's wills and trusts (which documents Bry believed would contain the written terms of the oral agreements asserted in her counterclaims).

Now, after completion of that discovery, as well as production of the wills and trusts for inspection by Bry's counsel, O'Keeffe renews her motion to dismiss the counterclaims pursuant to 12(b)(6), Federal Rules of Civil Procedure, or, in the alternative, to dispose of them by summary judgment. Because Bry has failed to raise a genuine issue of fact that there is any writing sufficient to satisfy the statute of frauds, judgment is granted in O'Keeffe's favor with respect to the first three counterclaims. As for the fourth counterclaim, in quantum meruit, although it presently appears that it may be barred by the express contract governing the O'Keeffe/Bry business relationship, the question whether services for which Bry seeks additional compensation are covered by the contract raises a genuine issue of material fact that cannot be resolved on the present state of the record.[2]

I

Before analyzing the impact of the statute of frauds on the counterclaims, two preliminary issues, of discovery and choice of law, must be resolved.

(A)

First, Bry's counsel contends that until O'Keeffe is deposed, it will be impossible to know whether there exists some document sufficient to satisfy the writing requirement. Against the history of this case, this contention appears to be disingenuous.

At the outset of this litigation, Bry submitted a sworn statement (Bry Affidavit, June 6, 1977) in which she unequivocally identified the documents said to contain the alleged oral agreements: these were the "Harvard Agreement" and O'Keeffe's wills and trusts (*id.*, at ¶¶12, 13, 16, quoted *infra* . . . ; and ¶27). Upon our view that production of these extremely personal documents would constitute a possibly unwarranted invasion of O'Keeffe's privacy, we declined to order their immediate transmittal to Bry. Instead, they were submitted for in camera inspection. Review quickly revealed that the documents did not contain the claimed agreements, and this was communicated to Bry's counsel.

All agreed that the documentation issue ought to be expeditiously resolved, and to this end, Bry's deposition testimony was crucial. However, months passed without any word from Bry's corner how, in light of the court's negative findings with regard to the wills and trusts, Bry expected to establish her contractual counterclaims. (Apparently, substantial delays were experienced in the attempt to depose Bry.) In March, 1978, a conference was called and the court requested that Bry demonstrate how she planned to eliminate the apparent bar of the statute of frauds. At the court's request, and on the basis of Bry's deposition testi-

---

[2] The fifth counterclaim is for (1) an order placing all O'Keeffe paintings that have been in Bry's possession into court custody and (2) specific performance of the promises alleged in the first three counterclaims. The first branch of the counterclaim was mooted by the court's ruling of June 10, 1977 (see *supra*, at 824). The request for specific relief must be denied pursuant to the conclusion that enforcement of the alleged promises is barred by the statute of frauds (see *infra*, at 828-830).

mony, her counsel submitted a letter with a "list of documents upon which we rely to fulfill the Statute's requirements."[3] The list mentions: (1) seventeen documents that were marked at the depositions of Bry and Downey, (2) drafts — including the final one — of the Harvard Agreement, (3) O'Keeffe's wills and trusts, and (4) ten letters from the correspondence between Downey and O'Keeffe, as to which O'Keeffe asserted the attorney client privilege.[4] (The deposition documents and the drafts of the Harvard Agreement, all of which papers Bry's counsel had seen at the time the letter was written, were merely listed. No explanation was offered how they satisfied the statute of frauds.) The newly denominated items were submitted for inspection by the court. Again, it was plain that none of them contained a contractual commitment by Bry to O'Keeffe.

Nevertheless, disposition of the contractual counterclaims was deferred. A pre-trial conference was held in May, 1978, and at the urging of Bry's counsel, the court agreed to make the wills and trusts available under a protective order. Bry's counsel was instructed to complete their inspection of the documents and to identify those portions of the wills, trusts, and any other writings that, in their view, established compliance with the statute of frauds.

In response to this straightforward request, Bry's counsel two months later submitted a lengthy affidavit.[5] Most of it is unresponsive, but to the extent that the affidavit does not analyze the wills and trusts, it confirms the court's earlier conclusion that those documents do not embody a contractual commitment. Bry's counsel now urges inspection of 82 fur-

---

[3] See Bry's counsel's letter of March 10, 1978. The letter indicated that in addition to the listed documents, deposition of O'Keeffe might lead to relevant writings, although there was no suggestion of Bry's inability to identify the documents on which she relied. To the contrary: for her part, Bry, testifying on deposition, clearly identified the writings on which her contract claims are based. As she had done previously (by her June, 1977 affidavit) she mentioned the Harvard Agreement and the wills, as well as incidental items of correspondence that were marked at her and Downey's deposition (Transcript of Bry Deposition at 442-52, 572).

[4] The O'Keeffe-Downey letters have been submitted to the court for the purpose of determining the propriety of the claim of privilege. Having reviewed the letters in camera, we find that all of them either give or seek legal advice and, as such, are clearly privileged communications between attorney and client. Stix Products, Inc. v. United Merchants & Manufacturers, Inc., 47 F.R.D. 334, 339 (S.D.N.Y. 1969); United States v. United Shoe Machinery Corp., 89 F. Supp. 357, 358-59 (D. Mass. 1950). Letters by Downey — eight of the ten that are mentioned — do not qualify. At the very least, the statute of frauds requires a writing signed by the party to be charged. Crabtree v. Elizabeth Arden Sales Corp., 305 N.Y. 48, 55, 110 N.E.2d 551 (1953).

[5] Nessen Affidavit of July 14, 1978.

ther documents, which have been withheld under a claim of attorney client privilege,[6] and he repeats the need to depose O'Keeffe. As for the requested deposition, no offer of proof is made. Indeed, we can conceive of no purpose that such deposition would serve, except to ask O'Keeffe if she ever executed a writing containing any of the promises alleged by Bry. This question could long since have been resolved by written interrogatory.

In sum, Bry's position on the identity of the alleged writings has evolved from one of specificity to one of undefined generality.

(B)

Bry suggests that enforceability of the alleged contracts is controlled by New Mexico law, whose statute of frauds is said to present "no possible bar to the contracts pleaded" (Bry Memorandum of July 20, 1977, at 20). New Mexico law might permit the enforcement of some of the contracts alleged by Bry, notwithstanding the absence of a writing.[7]

---

[6] None of the documents mentioned in the current affidavit was mentioned in the March 10th letter from Bry's counsel, which was supposed to contain a list of all the documents upon which Bry was relying. Although the request is untimely, we have considered it, and find that none of the documents advances Bry's position.

Of the 82 documents, only eight are signed by O'Keeffe, and therefore, are the only ones that could conceivably satisfy the statute of frauds.

Moreover, upon our in camera inspection of all the requested documents — letters and memoranda — we find that all but six of them are clearly privileged and that the six others may perhaps be privileged. The letters either seek or give legal advice. The memoranda either record confidential communications between attorney and client or else fall within the classic definition of attorney work product.

The six letters as to which there is a question of privilege are from O'Keeffe's attorney to a trustee of O'Keeffe's estate. Counsel for O'Keeffe has been instructed by the Court to make them available to counsel for Bry (without prejudice to O'Keeffe's claim of privilege). Having received Bry's counsel's arguments with respect to these letters, we find that the letters are irrelevant to Bry's contract claims: they are not signed by O'Keeffe, and in any event, they contain no promises.

[7] New Mexico has no codified version of the statute of frauds. It has, by court ruling, adopted the English version of the statute, 29 Charles II, c.3. Childers v. Talbott, 4 N.M. 336, 16 P. 275, 276 (1888); accord, Skarda v. Skarda, 87 N.M. 497, 536 P.2d 257, 269 (1975); Jennings v. Ruidoso Racing Association, 79 N.M. 144, 441 P.2d 42, 44 (1968); Pitek v. McGuire, 51 N.M. 364, 184 P.2d 647, 651 (1947). Though the English Statute of Frauds might bar the promise to create a $50,000, per annum trust, 72 Am. Jr. 2d §77 at 630 ("An agreement to bequeath personality is in the nature of a contract for its sale and is under the provision of the statute of frauds relating to contracts for the sale of personality when the value exceeds the statutory amount"), it would not preclude the promise of a lifetime and continuing agency or the promise to make Bry the executor of the O'Keeffe estate. See 72 Am. Jur. 2d §§28, 42.

Because this is a diversity action, New York's choice of law rules govern, *Klaxon v. Stentor Electric Manufacturing Co., Inc.*, 313 U.S. 487, 61 S. Ct. 1020, 85 L. Ed. 1477 (1941), and under those rules, "controlling effect [is given] to the law of the jurisdiction which, because of its relationship or contact with the occurrence or the parties, has the greatest concern with the specific issue in the litigation." *Babcock v. Jackson*, 12 N.Y.2d 473, 481, 240 N.Y.S.2d 743, 749, 191 N.E.2d 279, 283 (1963). The "specific issue" involved here might be characterized as the applicability of the statute of frauds to a contract, or contracts, involving promises by O'Keeffe to establish a trust and to make various testamentary provisions and a promise by Bry to render a performance that cannot be completed before a lifetime. Under this characterization, New York State's interest would be determined by analyzing the purposes of §5-701(a)(1) of the General Obligations Law ("G.O.L.") (McKinney's 1978) and §13-2.1 of the Estates, Powers & Trusts Law ("E.P.T.L.") (McKinney's 1967), which specifically require written memoranda of contracts containing such categories of promise. *Miller v. Miller*, 22 N.Y.2d 12, 15-16, 290 N.Y.S.2d 734, 737, 237 N.E.2d 877, 879 (1968) (". . . the facts or contacts which obtain significance in defining State interests are those which relate to the purpose of the particular law in conflict"). However, a compartmentalized analysis would be artificial in this case. The various promises alleged to have been made by O'Keeffe constituted the consideration in an overarching agency agreement, one that was allegedly to last a lifetime, so that in deciding whether the specific provisions of New York law apply, we are guided not by the policies underlying the individual statutes, but by more general considerations having to do with New York's interest in policing agents. Put another way, the decision whether New York law applies depends on the nature of the alleged contract viewed as a whole.

New York's interest in the enforcement issue involved here was plainly described in *Intercontinental Planning Limited v. Daystrom, Incorporated*, 24 N.Y.2d 372, 300 N.Y.S.2d 817, 248 N.E.2d 576 (1969). There, a New York agent sought recovery from a foreign principal on an oral contract for finder's fees in connection with having arranged the purchase of a business. Although the New York Court of Appeals was construing a different provision of the statute of frauds, §5-701(a)(10) of the G.O.L. (covering contracts for broker's fees), its remarks apply to the present case, and its observations about the role of New York State in the business world equally describe the State's role in the art world:

It is common knowledge that New York is a national and international center for the purchase and sale of businesses. . . . We conclude therefore [that enactment of §5-701(a)(10) was] intended to protect not only [New York] residents, but also those who come into New York and take advantage of our position as an international clearing house and market place. This is true because of all the jurisdictions involved, New York Law affords the foreign principals the greatest degree of protection against the unfounded claims of brokers and finders. This encourages the use of New York brokers and finders by foreign principals and contributes to the economic development of our State.

Intercontinental Planning Limited v. Daystrom, Incorporated, supra, 24 N.Y.2d at 383-4, 300 N.Y.S.2d at 826-7, 248 N.E.2d at 582. In light of the facts of this case, the policies described in *Daystrom* would be furthered by application of the relevant provisions of New York's statute of frauds. O'Keeffe is a resident of New Mexico. She has employed the services of a New York agent, Bry, and has entrusted her with numerous, valuable works of art. Having brought her art and her business here, she is entitled to the protection which New York provides in such circumstances. Moreover, since Bry is a New Yorker and since a substantial part, if not all, of her agency work was conducted in New York, application of New York law cannot be said to disappoint her reasonable expectations.

Against New York's substantial interest, Bry has suggested no stake that New Mexico might have in applying its statute of frauds (thereby affording less protection to one of its residents than New York State offers). We conclude, therefore, that New York law applies.[8]

II
First Counterclaim
In her first counterclaim, Bry alleges

. . . Miss O'Keeffe contracted with Miss Bry to make her the exclusive agent and market-maker for Miss O'Keeffe's artwork during Miss O'Keeffe's lifetime in consideration for Miss Bry agreeing to act as exclusive agent to market her artworks and to perform curatorial and public relations work for Miss O'Keeffe and her artwork. . . .

(¶21, Amended Answer). A more detailed description of this claim is provided in Bry's affidavit of June 7, 1977, submitted in opposition to the motion for a preliminary injunction. There, Bry asserts that

In 1972, Miss O'Keeffe and I, with our joint lawyer, James F. Downey, began discussions with representatives of Harvard University about Miss O'Keeffe leaving a gift of her works to the University. At this time, Miss O'Keeffe, at my insistence, abandoned the notion that she could discharge me at will: she told me that I was her "exclusive agent" and said that the agency would continue for her life [She also gave other assurances] At her request, the Harvard University agreement was to be worded to reflect and ensure all of that.

---

[8] Statutes of frauds also serve the general purpose of protecting the integrity of the judicial process in the courts of the enacting state. *Daystrom,* 24 N.Y.2d at 385, 300 N.Y.S.2d at 828, 248 N.E.2d at 583. In this regard, only the forum state, New York, has an interest in applying its statutes.

The Harvard Agreement was signed in October, 1972. . . . I was told by Mr. Downey . . . that it . . . reflected necessarily the commitment that I would be the exclusive agent for Miss O'Keeffe during her life.

. . . Thus, by 1973, with the commitments made by Miss O'Keeffe— embodied, I believed, in her will and in the provisions of the Harvard Agreement—I thought that I had finally achieved the security I needed. . . ."

(¶¶12, 13, 16, Bry Affidavit).

Applying New York's statute of frauds to the first counterclaim, the relevant provision of New York law is §5-701(a)(1) of the G.O.L., which requires a writing in cases of an agreement which, like this one, cannot be fully performed before the conclusion of a (O'Keeffe's) lifetime. *Meltzer v. Koenigsberg*, 302 N.Y. 523, 99 N.E.2d 679 (1951); *Bayreuther v. Reinisch*, 264 App. Div. 138, 34 N.Y.S.2d 674 (1st Dept. 1942), *aff'd*, 290 N.Y. 553, 47 N.E.2d 959 (1943).

Bry argues that §5-701(a)(1) is satisfied by the Harvard Agreement and the wills and trusts, that these documents, either in and of themselves or in conjunction with "contemporaneous memoranda and all the surrounding circumstances, clearly evidence . . . the existence of a contractual relationship between Miss Bry and Miss O'Keeffe." (Bry Memorandum of May 9, 1978 at 14; see also, Bry's counsel's letter of March 10, 1978.) Specifically, Bry relies on paragraph "Sixth" of the Harvard Agreement, which provides that:

Doris Bry has been associated with O'Keeffe for over twenty-five . . . years, and has been the exclusive agent for the sale of her paintings for more than seven . . . years, . . . and O'Keeffe anticipates and is arranging her affairs in such a way that Doris Bry will supervise the disposition of all or most of the paintings owned by O'Keeffe at the time of her death. To the extent that the pictures are not disposed of by Doris Bry, and Harvard is charged with the responsibility of disposing of them. . . . O'Keeffe expresses the wish but does not direct that Harvard will employ such agent for the sale of the paintings and give heed to such other requests and advice as Doris Bry may have specified from time to time during her lifetime.

However, this passage is not concerned with the matter of a lifetime agency (to continue throughout O'Keeffe's life), but rather with distribution of O'Keeffe's work after her death. More to the point, the language of this clause is plainly insufficient to constitute a binding commitment, since it is expressly precatory.

In an attempt to overcome the fundamental deficiency of the quoted writing, Bry argues that "[u]nder New York Law, . . . a 'confluence of memoranda' may be used to avert the impact of the statute of frauds. Almost any kind of writing is sufficient. . . . A number of writings, both signed and unsigned, may be pieced together to satisfy the statute's requirements." (Memorandum of July 20, 1977 at 16) This casual theory of the statute of frauds is said to be founded upon *Crabtree v. Elizabeth Arden Sales Corp.*, 305 N.Y. 48, 110 N.E. 551 (1953) and Bry's counsel have merely submitted a lengthy list of documents which are claimed to "connect up" so as to satisfy the writing requirement. (See Bry's counsel's letter of March 10, 1978. As indicated above, the letter offers a list without any explanation; for example: "Letter dated December 11, 1969, O'Keeffe to Bry (PX 34); Letter dated August 4, 1971, Bry to Downey (BX 38) . . .").

There is no need for extensive discussion of Bry's counsel's interpretation of New York law. To the extent that Crabtree permits the use of a "confluence of memoranda," the minimum condition for such use is the existence of one document establishing the basic, underlying contractual commitment. *Crabtree, supra*, 305 N.Y. at 55, 110 N.E.2d 551. In every case cited by Bry in support of the "connective" theory, a core document evidencing a promise was present, and additional memoranda were permitted only to supply essential terms of the agreement (provided that the additional documents referred on their face to the transaction covered by the core document), not to piece together the existence of the agreement itself. See *Bruce Realty Company of Florida v. Berger*, 327 F. Supp. 507 (S.D.N.Y. 1971); *Crabtree v. Elizabeth Arden Sales Corp., supra*, 305 N.Y. 48, 110 N.E.2d 551; *Stulsaft v. Mercer Tube & Mfg. Co.*, 288 N.Y. 255, 43 N.E.2d 31 (1942); *Marks v. Cowdin*, 226 N.Y. 138, 123 N.E. 139 (1919); *Papaioannou v. Britz*, 285 App. Div. 596, 139 N.Y.S.2d 658 (1st Dept. 1955). It has never been held that the fundamental assent to contractual status may be read out of a collage of documents. *Oswald v. Allen*, 417 F.2d 43 (2d Cir. 1969). Moreover, even if the law permitted a party to "add up" documents in order to show the basic promise, the documents in this case do not, when so added, come to a promise.

The contract alleged in the first counterclaim is not evidenced by a writing signed by O'Keeffe. Therefore, its enforcement is barred by the statute of frauds, and the counterclaim is dismissed.

Second Counterclaim

Bry's second counterclaim alleges that in return for the promise to act as "agent, market-maker, publicist and 'in-house' curator . . . during . . . O'Keeffe's lifetime," O'Keeffe agreed to create a trust "and did, in fact, create a trust in one or more wills" that would guarantee Bry "an income of at least $50,000 a year should she outlive Miss O'Keeffe." (¶25, Amended Answer)

Either as a contract that cannot be performed before the end of O'Keeffe's lifetime or as one to establish a trust, this agreement is unenforceable under New York law absent a writing meeting the requirements of G.O.L. §5-701(a)(1); E.P. T.L. §13-2.1(a)(1).

The Harvard Agreement, one of the documents on which Bry relies in her attempt to satisfy the requirement of a writing, does not contain a promise to create a trust; neither do the wills or trusts. The fact that an early version of an O'Keeffe trust agreement provided for an annuity (though not as described by Bry) does not surmount the statute of frauds problem. First, the early trust was revocable and was in fact revoked (see ¶23, Nessen Affidavit of July 14, 1978). Moreover, it is evident that a provision in a revocable trust cannot be invoked as proof of a binding contract to make such a provision, since otherwise the power of revocation would be utterly lost. When a trust agreement itself is offered as proof of compliance with the statute of frauds it must contain more than a beneficial provision such as is alleged to have been agreed to orally: it must clearly recite the contract, including words of promise or agreement.[9] No such recitation appearing in the wills, the trust agreement, or in any other document, Bry's claim based on the alleged promise to create a trust fails under the statute of frauds.

Third Counterclaim

The third counterclaim is based on alleged promises to make Bry the executor of O'Keeffe's estate and to empower Bry to act as a sales agent after O'Keeffe's death. In return, Bry alleges, she agreed to "perform as Miss O'Keeffe's agent, market-maker, publicist and 'in-house' curator for Miss O'Keeffe's artworks during her life and for her estate . . ." (¶29, Amended Answer). These promises were oral (¶12, Bry Affidavit) although Bry swears that she was told that the Harvard Agreement would reflect the promised sales agency and that O'Keeffe's wills would contain the commitment to make Bry the executor (*Id.*, at ¶13).

The alleged promises are unenforceable. Bry's falls within §5-701(a)(1) of the G.O.L. since her performance cannot be completed before O'Keeffe's lifetime. O'Keeffe's promises are governed by E.P.T.L. §13-2.1, as promises to make a testamentary disposition. Because the promises are not evidenced in the Harvard Agreement, the wills, the trust agreement, or in any other document, they are unenforceable, and the third counterclaim must be dismissed.

III

In addition to her contract claims, Bry seeks recovery in quantum meruit for services that she has rendered on behalf of O'Keeffe (Fourth Counterclaim):

---

[9] Pershall v. Elliot, 249 N.Y. 183, 163 N.E. 554 (1928); Hunt v. Hunt, 55 App. Div. 430, 66 N.Y.S. 957 (4th Dept. 1900), *aff'd*, 171 N.Y. 396, 64 N.E. 159 (1902); In the Matter of Estate of Thoens, 88 Misc. 2d 1006, 392 N.Y.S.2d 774 (Surr. Ct. 1975), *aff'd*, 41 N.Y.2d 823, 393 N.Y.S.2d 398, 361 N.E.2d 1046 (1977). The rationale of these cases, involving agreements to make testamentary dispositions, applies with equal force to agreements to create trusts.

From 1971 to date, Miss Bry has performed services for Miss O'Keeffe as an agent, market-maker, publicist and 'in-house' curator for her artworks. She has foregone other opportunities and large sums of money to perform these services properly and has devoted virtually her full working hours in order to perform the services.

Miss O'Keeffe was aware that Miss Bry expected to be paid compensation in excess of commissions actually earned and was prepared to compensate Miss Bry adequately for her services.

(¶¶33, 34, Amended Answer) O'Keeffe asserts that Bry's work for her was covered by an express contract, which fixed Bry's rate of commission at 25% of the amount received for sales of O'Keeffe's or Stieglitz' works of art:

Dear Miss O'Keeffe:

I am writing you with reference to your letters to me of September 15 and 23, which authorize me to sell your paintings, drawings, and Stieglitz material at a commission of 25%. I confirm that this is our agreement.

(Exhibit A to Downey Affidavit)

O'Keeffe is correct in her argument that quantum meruit recovery is unavailable when the services for which it is sought are covered by an express contract. *Miller v. Schloss*, 218 N.Y. 400, 406-7, 113 N.E. 337 (1916); accord, *Altman v. Curtiss-Wright Corporation*, 124 F.2d 177, 180 (2d Cir. 1941); *Robinson v. Munn*, 238 N.Y. 40, 43, 143 N.E. 784 (1924); *Levi v. Power Conversion, Inc.*, 47 A.D.2d 543, 363 N.Y.S.2d 103, 104 (2d Dept. 1975); *Jontow v. Jontow*, 34 A.D.2d 744, 310 N.Y.S.2d 145 (1st Dept. 1970); *Abinet v. Mediavilla*, 5 A.D.2d 679, 169 N.Y.S.2d 231, 232 (2d Dept. 1957); *Moore v. Mason & Hanger Co.*, 35 N.Y.S.2d 687 (Sup. Ct. N.Y. Co. 1942). Were the rule otherwise, written compensation terms would be meaningless.

However, the coverage of the express contract here involves issues of fact, which cannot be resolved as the record stands. In particular, when quantum meruit recovery is sought by a salaried employee for "services rendered which fall outside the scope of duties of [the expressly agreed to] employment," entitlement to recovery turns on the question whether the "additional services" are "so distinct from the duties of [the] employment that it would be unreasonable for the employer to assume that they were rendered without expectation of further pay." *Robinson v. Munn*, *supra*, 238 N.Y. at 43, 143 N.E. 784, 785. The question of reasonable expectations is one of fact which remains for determination.[10]

_____

[10] It should be emphasized that if Bry prevails on her quantum meruit counterclaim, she will not be entitled to recover anything more than the fair value of her "additional services." In particular, she cannot use the device of quantum meruit to enforce the alleged promises — barred by the statute of frauds — for a lifetime and continuing agency, a trust income, and executorship. Dung v.

In sum, plaintiff's motion for summary judgment is granted with respect to counterclaims "First," "Second," "Third," and "Fifth." The motion is denied with respect to counterclaim "Fourth."

It is so ordered.

§3.2. STATUTORY RIGHTS

§3.2.1. Artist-Art Dealer Consignment Statutes in General

In the first half of this chapter we considered the contractual relationship between artist and dealer: those elements that ought be included, the ambiguity of the exclusive arrangement, and the importance of the written document detailing and clarifying the intent of the parties. In this section we go beyond agreements voluntarily made between artist and dealer; we now turn to those terms of the relationship believed important enough to be stipulated by legislative mandate.

As of this writing, 20 states have adopted artist-art dealer consignment statutes.[1] Lurking behind the presumed necessity of adopting these laws was the vision of a villainous dealer with infernal intent, ever ready to pounce on the deprived and defenseless artist. The occasional materialization of this vision in New York City during the early 1960s led to the passage of such a law in New York in 1966.

At the heart of the consignment statute is the fiduciary relationship it

---

Parker, 52 N.Y. 494 (1873); Hausen v. Academy Printing & Specialty Co., 34 A.D. 2d 792, 311 N.Y.S.2d 613, 614 (2d Dept. 1970); Potter v. Emerol Mfg. Co., 275 A.D. 265, 89 N.Y.S.2d 68, 71 (1st Dept. 1949).

§3.2. [1] Ariz. Rev. Stat. Ann. §44-1771 to 44-1778 (Supp. 1984); Ark. Stat. Ann. §§68-1806 to 68-1811 (Supp. 1983); Cal. Civ. Code §§1738 & 1738.5 to 1738.9 (1985); Colo. Rev. Stat. §§6-15-101 to 6-15-104 (Supp. 1984); Conn. Gen. Stat. Ann. §§42-116k to 42-116m (West Supp. 1985); Md. Com. Law Code Ann. §§11-8A-01 to 11-8A-04 (1983) & §11-8A-03 (Supp. 1984); Mass. Ann. Laws ch. 104A, §§1 to 6 (Law. Co-op. Supp. 1985); Mich. Comp. Laws Ann. §§442.311 to 442.315 (West Supp. 1985); Minn. Stat. Ann. §§324.01 to 324.10 (West Supp. 1985); Mo. Rev. Stat. §§407.900 to 407.910 (Vernon Supp. 1985); Mont. Code Ann. tit. 22 §§2-501 to 2-505 (1985); N.M. Stat. Ann. §§56-11-1 to 56-11-3 (Supp. 1984); N.Y. Arts & Cultural Affairs Law art. 12 (McKinney Supp. 1986); N.C. Gen. Stat. §§25C-1 to 25C-5 (Supp. 1983); Ohio Rev. Code Ann. §§1339.71 to 1339.78 (Page Supp. 1984); Or. Rev. Stat. §§359.200 to 359.240 (1983); Tenn. Code Ann. §§47-25-1001 to 47-25-1007 (1984); Tex. Occ. & Bus. Code Ann. art. 9018 (Vernon Supp. 1985); Wash. Rev. Code Ann. §§18.110.010 to 18.110.905 (Supp. 1985); and Wis. Stat. Ann. §§129.01 to 129.08 (West Supp. 1984).

establishes between artist and dealer. The statutes generally provide that the delivered artworks, and their proceeds, are "trust property . . . for the benefit of the consigner", i.e., the artist. Most states follow New York's lead and specifically reverse or exempt the relationship from U.C.C. §2-326 (or its equivalent in the state), thereby making it perfectly clear that the creditors may not reach these assets.

Of equal importance is the issue of who bears the risk for works damaged or stolen while in the possession of the dealer. Several states specifically place the burden on the dealer (either through negligence or strict liability), while other statutes are silent on this matter. Query who, in the instance of such a silent statute, bears the risk, particularly if the jurisdiction in question follows the usual laws of principal and agency? (See also the *Colburn* and *Gardini* cases in Chapter 12 concerning how the issue of risk is handled when the museum acts as bailee.)

What of the nonartist consigning work to the dealer? Is he covered by a similar trust relationship? Several states would seemingly go this far; see, for example, Michigan's and Connecticut's[2] statutes, which extend the relationship to a "consignor" who may or may not be the "artist delivering a work of fine art of his own creation" to the dealer.

Can the dealer assert that he is a purchaser and therefore not subject to the statute's mandate of fiduciary obligation? Most statutes again follow New York's lead by anticipating this; they specifically state that any arrangement that was one "on consignment" from its inception cannot be transformed into anything else before the artist has been paid in full. (See also in this regard, the cases of *Estate of Franz Kline, In the Matter of Wilhelmina Friedman*, and accompanying commentaries in Chapter 8.)

What of the arrangement whereby dealer and artist have agreed to deferred payments from a purchaser — who bears the risk? Is the dealer obligated to pass along to the artist all first monies received and wait for his share? Some states permit limited waivers on behalf of the artist; the waivers might, presumably, be thus employed. Others, however, permit no waiver, in addition to requiring that the artist-art dealer relationship be in writing, which document would probably include the usual covenant that the writing contain the entire agreement between the parties. What then?

§3.2.2. A Legislative Model

New York's artist-art dealer consignment statute has served as a model for nearly half the states in the country. The law creates a trust

---

[2] *Ibid.*

relationship between the artist and the art merchant unlike and beyond the usual consignment arrangement by virtue of the fiduciary obligation placed on the merchant. (See also in this regard *In the Matter of Wilhelmina Friedman* and accompanying commentary in Chapter 8.)

Starting in 1966 this area of the law developed gradually in New York; the statutes were scattered throughout the state's General Business Law. In 1983, however, the state legislature pulled these diffuse laws together by enacting the Arts and Cultural Affairs Law, Chapter 876 of the Laws of 1983. While the new law achieved the purpose of consolidation, it brought together some contradictory provisions — there were, for example, four separate definitions of "artist," three of "fine art," and three of "art merchant."

In order to reconcile these inconsistencies, the legislature enacted another version of the law, Chapter 849 of the Laws of 1984.[3] (This newest statute replaced the former Title C.) The first article of this legislation contains a single set of definitions that are applicable to the entire statute, in keeping with the intention of the lawmakers' "to clear up the present confusing and often contradictory sections of law in this area."[4]

DEFINITIONS

N.Y. Arts and Cultural Affairs Law, Art. 11 (McKinney Supp. 1986)

§11.01 DEFINITIONS

As used in this title:

1. "Artist" means the creator of a work of fine art or, in the case of multiples, the person who conceived or created the image which is contained in or which constitutes the master from which the individual print was made.

2. "Art merchant" means a person who is in the business of dealing, exclusively or non-exclusively, in works of fine art or multiples, or a person who by his occupation holds himself out as having knowledge or skill peculiar to such works, or to whom such knowledge or skill may be attributed by his employment of an agent or other intermediary who by his occupation holds himself out as having such knowledge or skill. The term "art merchant" includes an auctioneer who sells such works at public auction, and except in the case of multiples, includes persons, not otherwise defined or treated as art merchants herein, who are consignors or principals of auctioneers.

3. "Author" or "authorship" refers to the creator of a work of fine art

---

[3] See Memorandum of Sen. Tarky L. Lombardi, Jr., N.Y. 1984 Legis. Ann. 277.

[4] *Ibid.*

or multiple or to the period, culture, source or origin, as the case may be, with which the creation of such work is identified in the description of the work.

4. "Creditors" means "creditor" as defined in subdivision twelve of section 1-201 of the uniform commercial code.

5. "Counterfeit" means a work of fine art or multiple made, altered or copied, with or without intent to deceive, in such manner that it appears or is claimed to have an authorship which it does not in fact possess.

6. "Certificate of authenticity" means a written statement by an art merchant confirming, approving or attesting to the authorship of a work of fine art or multiple, which is capable of being used to the advantage or disadvantage of some person.

7. "Conservation" means acts taken to correct deterioration and alteration and acts taken to prevent, stop or retard deterioration.

8. "Craft" means a functional or non-functional work individually designed, and crafted by hand, in any medium including but not limited to textile, tile, paper, clay, glass, fiber, wood, metal or plastic; provided; however, that if produced in multiples, craft shall not include works mass produced or produced in other than a limited edition.

9. "Fine art" means a painting, sculpture, drawing, or work of graphic art, and print, but not multiples.

10. "Limited edition" means works of art produced from a master, all of which are the same image and bear numbers or other markings to denote the limited production thereof to a stated maximum number of multiples, or are otherwise held out as limited to a maximum number of multiples.

11. "Master" when used alone is used in lieu of and means the same as such things as printing plate, stone, block, screen, photographic negative or other like material which contains an image used to produce visual art objects in multiples.

12. "On consignment" means that no title to, estate in, or right to possession of, the work of fine art or multiple that is superior to that of the consignor vests in the consignee, notwithstanding the consignee's power or authority to transfer or convey all the right, title and interest of the consignor, in and to such work, to a third person.

13. "Person" means an individual, partnership, corporation, association or other group, however organized.

14. "Print" in addition to meaning a multiple produced by, but not limited to, such processes as engraving, etching, woodcutting, lithography and serigraphy, also means multiples produced or developed from photographic negatives, or any combination thereof.

15. "Proofs" means multiples which are the same as, and which are produced from the same masters as, the multiples in a limited edition, but

which, whether so designated or not, are set aside from and are in addition to the limited edition to which they relate.

16. "Reproduction" means a copy, in any medium, of a work of fine art, that is displayed or published under circumstances that, reasonably construed, evinces an intent that it be taken as a representation of a work of fine art created by the artist.

17. "Reproduction right" means a right to reproduce, prepare derivative works of, distribute copies of, publicly perform or publicly display a work of fine art.

18. "Signed" means autographed by the artist's own hand, and not by mechanical means of reproduction, after the multiple was produced, whether or not the master was signed or unsigned.

19. "Visual art multiples" or "multiples" means prints, photographs, positive or negative, and similar art objects produced in more than one copy and sold, offered for sale or consigned in, into or from this state for an amount in excess of one hundred dollars exclusive of any frame. Pages or sheets taken from books and magazines and offered for sale or sold as visual art objects shall be included, but books and magazines are excluded.

20. "Written instrument" means a written or printed agreement, bill of sale, invoice, certificate of authenticity, catalogue or any other written or printed note or memorandum or label describing the work of fine art or multiple which is to be sold, exchanged or consigned by an art merchant.

ARTIST-ART MERCHANT RELATIONSHIPS
N.Y. Arts and Cultural Affairs Law, Art. 12 (McKinney Supp. 1986)

§12.01. ARTIST-ART MERCHANT RELATIONSHIPS

1. Notwithstanding any custom, practice or usage of the trade, any provision of the uniform commercial code or any other law, statute, requirement or rule, or any agreement, note, memorandum or writing to the contrary:

(a) Whenever an artist or craftsperson, his heirs or personal representatives, delivers or causes to be delivered a work of fine art, craft or a print of his own creation to an art merchant for the purpose of exhibition and/or sale on a commission, fee or other basis of compensation, the delivery to and acceptance thereof by the art merchant establishes a consignor/consignee relationship as between such artist or craftsperson and such art merchant with respect to the said work, and:

(i) such consignee shall thereafter be deemed to be the agent of such consignor with respect to the said work;

(ii) such work is trust property in the hands of the consignee for the benefit of the consignor;

(iii) any proceeds from the sale of such work are trust funds in the hands of the consignee for the benefit of the consignor;

(iv) such work shall remain trust property notwithstanding its purchase by the consignee for his own account until the price is paid in full to the consignor; provided that, if such work is resold to a bona fide third party before the consignor has been paid in full, the resale proceeds are trust funds in the hands of the consignee for the benefit of the consignor to the extent necessary to pay any balance still due to the consignor and such trusteeship shall continue until the fiduciary obligation of the consignee with respect to such transaction is discharged in full; and

(v) no such trust property or trust funds shall be subject or subordinate to any claims, liens or security interest of any kind or nature whatsoever.

(b) Waiver of any provision of this section is absolutely void except that a consignor may lawfully waive the provisions of clause (iii) of paragraph (a) of this subdivision, if such waiver is clear, conspicuous, in writing and subscribed by the consignor, provided:

(i)   no such waiver shall be valid with respect to the first two thousand five hundred dollars of gross proceeds of sales received in any twelve month period commencing with the date of the execution of such waiver;

(ii) no such waiver shall be valid with respect to the proceeds of a work initially received on consignment but subsequently purchased by the consignee directly or indirectly for his own account; and

(iii) no such waiver shall inure to the benefit of the consignee's creditors in any manner which might be inconsistent with the consignor's rights under this subdivision.

2. Nothing in this section shall be construed to have any effect upon any written or oral contract or arrangement in existence prior to September first, nineteen hundred sixty-nine or to any extensions or renewals thereof except by the mutual written consent of the parties thereto.

§3.2.3. What Does the Fiduciary Relationship Cover?

Recognizing that the original 1966 New York statute was not clear as to whether proceeds from sales enjoyed the same protection as the artworks themselves, the legislature amended the statute in 1969 specifically to place proceeds in the same position. The attorney general's legislative memorandum issued at that time, and reprinted below, was intended to clarify the language of the amendment, but it also gives insight into the breadth of the protection envisioned by the lawmakers.

MEMORANDUM OF THE ATTORNEY GENERAL OF NEW YORK CONCERNING ARTICLE 12*

N.Y. 1969 Legis. Ann. 92

ART CONSIGNMENT, MISAPPROPRIATION

General Business Law, §§219, 202. This bill, recommended by the Attorney General amends sections which comprise Article 12-C of the General Business Law enacted in 1966. As enacted, §220 provides in substance that a consignment of a work of fine art by the creator thereof to an art dealer for the purpose of exhibition and/or sale on a commission basis (known in the trade as a "consignment arrangement," as distinguished from the practice of purchasing an artist's output in return for a guaranteed annual income or other analogous arrangement) creates a principal-agent relationship with respect to the property and further provides a dealer who unlawfully withholds or appropriates such property is guilty of larceny. Article 12-C also renders void any waiver of any provisions thereof by the artist-consignor.

Under the law of agency a selling agent is not relieved of his fiduciary responsibilities with respect to property entrusted to him for sale until the final completion of the transaction, which includes the delivery of the proceeds of the sale to his principal, (*Britton v. Ferrin*, 171 N.Y. 235, 244). Article 12-C as enacted did not specifically provide that the proceeds of sale were also subject to a fiduciary obligation. Some prosecutors have accordingly been reluctant to entertain complaints against dealers for wrongfully withholding or appropriating proceeds of sale while acknowledging that similar conduct with respect to unsold works of art would constitute larceny under this statute. This bill amends Article 12-C by specifically providing that proceeds of sales are trust funds in the hands of the consignee for the benefit of the consignor.

It is to be noted that the original aim of Article 12-C was merely to clarify the inherently fiduciary character of the "consignment arrangement" in the artist-art dealer relationship (not to be confused with "*sales on consignment*" where the resulting relationship resembles that of debtor and creditor rather than that of principal and agent).

---

* Article 12-C, the predecessor to Article 11 of the N.Y. Arts and Cultural Affairs Law, was in the N.Y. General Business Law. In the recent re-enactment of the Arts and Cultural Affairs Law, Article 11 was renumbered as Article 12.

Although there was never any doubt as to an agent's *civil* liability for a tortious conversion of his principal's property (*Britton v. Ferrin, supra,* and *Hudson v. Yonkers Fruit Co.,* 258, N.Y. 168), some District Attorneys were reluctant to prosecute such tortfeasors for embezzlement (now denominated as larceny) because art dealers had for many years beclouded the issue by unilaterally assuming to treat the relationship as a mere creditor-debtor, rather than principal-agent, relationship. The abuses resulting from such unilateral assumption necessitated legislation which would remove any residue of doubt as to the fiduciary nature of the consignment arrangement in the artist-art dealer relationship and lay the legal foundation for the application of criminal sanctions against embezzlement (larceny) of the principal's property as set forth in subsection 2 of §220 of Article 12-C.

The Office of the District Attorney of New York County, in which most of the art galleries are situated, has taken the position that subsection 2 of §220 serves no useful purpose since the larceny statutes as contained in the revised Penal Law would necessarily be applicable because subsection 1 clearly spells out the fiduciary nature of the consignment arrangement between an artist and his dealer. Accordingly, this bill further amends Article 12-C by repealing subsection 2 as enacted in 1966. *Such repeal is not to be misconstrued as abolishing prosecution of wrongdoers in this area: such prosecutions will hereafter be pursued under the larceny statutes contained in the Penal Law. . . .*

This bill also relaxes the prohibition against an artist's voluntary waiver of the protection of this article with respect only to the treatment of proceeds of sale provided that (a) such waiver is in writing and (b) such waiver will in no event be operative as to the first $2,500.00 of annual gross proceeds of sale. Subject to the aforesaid conditions, the parties may agree that proceeds of sale in the hands of a dealer may be treated as an ordinary debt; it goes without saying that a dealer's failure to pay over such proceeds would not subject him to any tort or criminal liability.

The bill provides that existing contracts are not affected by these changes except by mutual agreement between the parties.

This bill is part of the legislative program of the Attorney General.

§3.2.4. Can the Code Be the Foil?

Of equal concern to the legislators was that no provision of the U.C.C. be construed as capable of undoing the work of the artist-art dealer consignment statute. Another amendment was introduced for this purpose. What follows are the remarks of New York State Senator, Roy Goodman, explaining that the amendment was needed so that the artists' rights in artworks consigned to dealers might be "strengthened." Goodman was concerned that U.C.C. §2-326 (which follows his memorandum *infra*) or some other section of the Code would be available to third-party creditors — i.e., those of art dealers — seeking to avoid the New York legislature's intent of precluding the attachment of artworks or the proceeds from their sale. In those jurisdictions without an artist-art dealer consignment statute where U.C.C. §2-326 (or its equivalent) has been adopted, it presumably would be controlling.

MEMORANDUM OF NEW YORK STATE SENATOR ROY GOODMAN CONCERNING ARTICLE 12*

N.Y. 1975 Legis. Ann. 96

General Business Law: §§219, 219-a. The purpose of this bill is to strengthen artists' rights in art works consigned to art dealers.

The bill would clarify and continue the trust relationship between artist and art dealer by specifically providing that creditors of art dealers may not avail themselves of the rights under Section [2-326] of the Uniform Commercial Code or any other provision of said code to assert claims against such consigned art works or the trust funds arising out of the sale of said works of art.

Article 12-C creates a trust relationship between artists and art dealers that is different than the relationship between other consignors and consignees.

However, it is not now clear that Article 12-C is the exclusive governing statute. An apparent conflict exists with the Uniform Commercial Code.

The large number of marginal art dealers in this State makes this industry susceptible to declines in the economy. The current economic climate requires immediate consideration of this proposed bill to prevent a potential loss to an increasing number of artists should the ambiguity between the Uniform Commercial Code and the General Business Law be construed adverse to the interests of such artists. This bill would cure the ambiguity.

This bill was introduced as S. 10,145 in 1974 and passed in Senate. It was not acted upon in the Assembly. The bill was an Attorney General program bill in 1974.

---

* Article 12-C, the predecessor to Article 11 of the N.Y. Arts and Cultural Affairs Law, was in the N.Y. General Business Law. In the recent re-enactment of the Arts and Cultural Affairs Law, Article 11 was renumbered as Article 12.

UNIFORM COMMERCIAL CODE §2-326

SALE ON APPROVAL AND SALE OR RETURN;
CONSIGNMENT SALES AND RIGHTS OF CREDITORS

(1) Unless otherwise agreed, if delivered goods may be returned by the buyer even though they conform to the contract, the transaction is

(a) a "sale on approval" if the goods are delivered primarily for use, and

(b) a "sale or return" if the goods are delivered primarily for resale.

(2) Except as provided in subsection (3), goods held on approval are not subject to the claims of the buyer's creditors until acceptance; goods held on sale or return are subject to such claims while in the buyer's possession.

(3) Where goods are delivered to a person for sale and such person maintains a place of business at which he deals in goods of the kind involved, under a name other than the name of the person making delivery, then with respect to claims of creditors of the person conducting the business the goods are deemed to be on sale or return. The provisions of this subsection are applicable even though an agreement purports to reserve title to the person making delivery until payment or resale or uses such words as "on consignment" or "on memorandum." However, this subsection is not applicable if the person making delivery

(a) complies with an applicable law providing for a consignor's interest or the like to be evidenced by a sign, or

(b) establishes that the person conducting the business is generally known by his creditors to be substantially engaged in selling the goods of others, or

(c) complies with the filing provisions of the Article on Secured Transactions (Article 9).

(4) Any "or return" term of a contract for sale is to be treated as a separate contract for sale within the statute of frauds section of this Article (Section 2-201) and as contradicting the sale aspect of the contract within the provisions of this Article on parol or extrinsic evidence (Section 2-202).

CHAPTER FOUR

Commissioned Works

•

§4.1. Private Commissions

§4.2. Public Commissions

§4.1. PRIVATE COMMISSIONS

§4.1.1. Introduction

Compared with purchasing an already existing painting or sculpture, commissioning an artist to create a work of art is a risky business. The artist may decide not to complete the commission, he may become ill, he may die, or he may just be dilatory. If he does complete the work (possibly even on time), it may not satisfy the commissioning party. This type of arrangement, probably more than any other, rests not only on the good faith of the parties (which is probably an objective test), but also on the satisfaction of both parties (which undoubtedly is a very subjective test). In this chapter, we examine commissioned works, both private and public, and the various problems that may arise.

§4.1.2. *Estate of Saint-Gaudens v. Emmet:* **What Is the Nature of a Commission?**

The unpublished 1911 decision in *Saint-Gaudens*, which follows, raises an intriguing title question regarding a portrait for which a sitter had posed. The crux of the dispute, decided by a referee in the United States Circuit Court for the Southern District of New York, was the following issue: Is a portrait for which a sitter has posed at the sole request of the artist the property of the artist? Or, conversely, is it always the property of the sitter, regardless of whether it has been commissioned? The referee in *Saint-Gaudens* faced this quandry with an additional, intriguing wrinkle — the sitter was an artist as well, whose very prominence was recognized by the portrait in question having been purchased by the Metropolitan Museum of Art. It should also be noted that the defendant painter, Miss Emmet (later to be known as Ellen Emmet Rand), was to become a very important painter of portraits — her portrait of Franklin Delano Roosevelt was initially acquired by the White House and later returned in 1947 to the FDR Library in Hyde Park, New York.

ESTATE OF SAINT-GAUDENS v. EMMET
C.C.S.D.N.Y. (May 26, 1911)

BROWN, Ref. In my opinion the testimony in this action does not show that the title to the portrait was ever vested in Mr. Saint-Gaudens.

The testimony discloses nothing as to the agreement or arrangement between Mr. Saint-Gaudens and the defendant under which the portrait was painted.

Mrs. Hunter, the defendant's mother testifies that when the defendant was an art student in Paris between 1896 and 1900 she met Mr. Saint-Gaudens frequently; and on some of these occasions the defendant asked Mr. Saint-Gaudens "if he would sit for her." The witness testifies that Mr. Saint-Gaudens used to say: "Bay, some day I am going to have you paint my portrait and will sit for you; some day I am going to sit for you."

In November or December 1904 the defendant and her mother met Mr. Saint-Gaudens on Fifth Avenue in the City of New York and had some conversation with him. He was then residing at Cornish, New Hampshire. One of the ladies said to him: "Why Mr. Saint-Gaudens are you in New York, what brings you here?" He replied that he was under the care of a doctor. The defendant then said to him: "Why wouldn't this be a good time; why can't you sit for me?" He replied: "Why I can. I am busy with the doctor part of the day but we can arrange some time so I can sit for you."

After that the witness testifies that she saw him at the defendant's studio, and on one occasion his son Homer accompanied him to the studio.

The portrait was painted during December 1904 and January 1905, and finished probably about February 1st, as it was in the possession of D. B. Butler & Co. to be framed on February 13th.

This meagre testimony is all that I know about the conversations between the parties in reference to the painting of the portrait or the circumstances surrounding the painting. It is not sufficient to sustain the finding that the portrait was painted under a contract which vested the title to it in Mr. Saint-Gaudens.

The portrait was not painted at Mr. Saint-Gaudens' request but at the request of the defendant, and the testimony quoted is entirely consistent with the theory that Mr. Saint-Gaudens gave the privilege to the defendant of painting his portrait. If such was the case the title vested in the defendant.

This conclusion is corroborated by the undisputed fact that from the time the portrait was completed until it was sold to the Metropolitan Museum it remained in the possession of the defendant. She caused it to be framed at her own expense. She exhibited it in New York and in Boston and at two exhibitions of Saint-Gaudens' work one in New York and one in Washington. Upon the return of the portrait from Washington she placed it in a private residence in New York City where it remained until it was sold by her to the Metropolitan Museum.

It does not appear that Mr. Saint-Gaudens or any member of his family ever saw the portrait after it was finished, and his consent was not asked by the defendant in reference to the exhibitions I have referred to.

The learned counsel for the plaintiff to prove title in Mr. Saint-Gaudens relies mainly upon certain letters which have been introduced in evidence. These letters relate to a proposal made by Mr. Charles F. McKim that he and other friends of Mr. Saint-Gaudens should be permitted to present the portrait to the Metropolitan Museum. In my opinion two only of these letters are important.

The letter of June 6th, 1907 written by Homer Saint-Gaudens to the defendant and which was discussed by him with his father and which his father saw before it was mailed contains self-serving declarations which are not admissible to prove title in Mr. Saint-Gaudens.

The defendant was under no obligation to reply to that letter, and her failure to do so cannot be treated as an admission on her part of the truth of the statements contained in the letter.

The same must be said of the letters of Mr. Saint-Gaudens to Mr. McKim under date of April 16th, 1906, and Mrs. Saint-Gaudens to Mr. McKim the same date, if such letters are susceptible of the construction of asserting title to the portrait; I do not think they bear such a construction.

They are entirely consistent with the theory that Mr. and Mrs. Saint-Gaudens expected that the portrait would ultimately be given to them. This I think is clear from Mrs. Saint-Gaudens' remark: "When she gets through exhibiting it and is kind enough to send it to us, we shall welcome it with joy."

This is hardly the expression which one would use if the portrait was her own or her husband's property. At the most, however, these letters are equivocal and the mere expression in them of ownership not admitted by the defendant is insufficient to overcome the conclusion drawn from the fact that the portrait was the product of the defendant's skill, labor and materials and always remained in her possession.

The more important letters are Mr. McKim's letter to Mr. Saint-Gaudens of April 13th, 1906 and the defendant's letter to Mr. Saint-Gaudens of May 28th, 1907.

In Mr. McKim's letter he proposed to pay Mr. Saint-Gaudens for the value of the portrait. In other words he proposed to purchase it from him.

The learned counsel for the plaintiff argues that the defendant knew of this letter before it was sent and of this offer, and that it is strong evidence that the portrait belonged to Mr. Saint-Gaudens.

If the defendant saw this letter or knew of Mr. McKim's proposal, I should be inclined to agree with the learned counsel's argument, but the testimony of Miss Emmet, as I understand it, does not permit the inference that she was aware of this offer to Mr. McKim.

Miss Emmet testified that when Mr. McKim spoke to her about giving the portrait to the Museum she said to him: "I can give you no answer until you have written to Mr. Saint-Gaudens and found out about how he feels having his portrait in the Museum."

On her direct examination she was shown a copy of Mr. McKim's letter and asked if it was the original of the letter enclosed to her in the letter of April 20th, 1906, and she answered: "Yes, that is *his* all right."

Concededly no copy of this letter was enclosed to her in Mr. McKim's letter of April 20th, 1906.

She was then asked and answered the following questions:

Q: Did you know Miss Emmet that Mr. McKim was corresponding with Mr. Saint-Gaudens on the subject of putting his portrait in the Metropolitan Museum?

A: Yes.

Q: And did you request him to communicate with Mr. Saint-Gaudens?

A: I did.

Q: Now did Mr. McKim ever show you the letter that he wrote to Mr. Saint-Gaudens to which the letter I have just read is a reply?

A: Yes, the letter from Mr. Saint-Gaudens.

Q: No, the letter from himself, Mr. McKim to Saint-Gaudens?

A: No, he did not show me that, not before; he showed it to me after.

Q: (exhibiting paper) Please look at the letter I now show you and tell me if that is the letter of which he showed you either the original or a copy — a copy I suppose?

A: Yes; but not before he sent it.

Mr. Macfarlane: I offer it in evidence.

The letter offered in evidence was Mr. McKim's letter of April 13th, 1906.

Upon her cross-examination Miss Emmet testified.

Q: Now Miss Emmet I think you stated on your direct examination that this letter was shown you but not before it was sent by Mr. McKim, do you remember that?

A: Yes sir.

Q: Do you remember as a fact when it was shown to you?

A. I stated the other day that it had been shown to me by Mr. McKim, but since then I have investigated into it and thought it up, and to the best of my recollection now I didn't see the letter until it was sent to me by Mr. Homer Saint-Gaudens with all the other letters. I think I made a mistake the other day. I didn't know the facts and I think I made an incorrect statement.

The letter sent by Mr. Homer Saint-Gaudens was after the death of his father.

On the redirect examination she testified as follows:

Q: I understand you to say now that you were mistaken in your testimony the other day when you said that Mr. McKim had shown you his letter to Mr. Saint-Gaudens after he had written it?

A: Yes, sir.

Q: You were not mistaken, however, in saying that you received Mr. McKim's letter of April 20th, enclosing the two Saint-Gaudens' letters?

A: Yes.

Q: You were not mistaken about that?

A: No.

Q: Now when you got that letter of April 20th from Mr. McKim with the letters from Mr. and Mrs. Saint-Gaudens didn't you ask him then what he had written?

A: I knew what he had written. I may have asked him, I do not remember if I did, but I knew the gist of what he had written.

Q: You may have asked him, you are not sure whether you did or not?

A: I do not remember the circumstances of that particular case, but I had asked him to write as I told you here.

Q: I understand that, but I want you to tell me now, refreshing your recollection on the basis of this letter from Mr. McKim enclosing the letters of Mr. and Mrs. Saint-Gaudens, about a week after he had written to Saint-Gaudens, didn't you ask him then what he had written?

A: No, I don't think I did.

Q: You did not ask him to show you his letter?

A: No.

Q: You are sure he did not show you his letter at or about that time?

A: Well, as I recall it now, no he did not.

The result of this testimony is that the defendant did not see Mr. McKim's letter until after Mr. Saint-Gaudens' death. She knew, however, the gist of the letter.

I cannot infer from this that she knew that Mr. McKim proposed to purchase the portrait from Mr. Saint-Gaudens. The gist of Mr. McKim's letter was not in that proposal but in the proposition that Mr. Saint-Gaudens should permit Mr. McKim and his friends to present the portrait to the Museum, and it was in reference to that proposal that the defendant said she could give no answer until Mr. McKim had written to Mr. Saint-Gaudens and ascertained how he felt about having his portrait in the Museum.

Moreover, if the portrait belonged to Mr. Saint-Gaudens there was no occasion to consult the defendant about it at all. It is only upon the theory that she was the owner or had some interest in it that it was necessary to consult her.

Yet in connection with the offer to purchase the portrait Mr. McKim wrote to Mr. Saint-Gaudens: "If this should appeal to you will you let me know after consulting with Miss Emmet on the subject."

On August 21st, 1906, Mr. Saint-Gaudens wrote to the defendant in reference to her making a copy of the portrait to be sent to the Roman Academy of S. Luca of which Mr. Saint-Gaudens was a member. The defendant replied to this letter on September 6th, 1906, saying a copy could be made by her sister and that the price would be $250 and on September 13th, 1906 Mr. Saint-Gaudens wrote her by his son accepting the proposal.

Prior to May 28th, 1907, this copy was made, and on the latter date the defendant wrote to Mr. Saint-Gaudens a letter advising him of that fact. In this letter she wrote:

> I have a suggestion to make. You know of Mr. McKim's great desire to have your portrait in the Metropolitan Museum of Art. It seems to me that we have found a solution. Mrs. Saint-Gaudens being unwilling to part with the only portrait which exists of you, she could not fail to be satisfied with this perfect fac-simile. I will make an equally good one for her, etc.

It is contended by the learned counsel for the plaintiff that the expression, "Mrs. Saint-Gaudens being unwilling to part with the only portrait which exists of you" should be construed as an admission by the defendant that the portrait belonged to Mr. Saint-Gaudens.

In my opinion it is not entitled to have any such meaning given to it. This expression must be interpreted in connection with all the other facts surrounding the painting of the portrait and its possession by the defendant. It would be manifestly unjust to the defendant in the view of these other facts to hold that in thus writing she admitted the portrait was not her property.

The letter was not written with reference to any dispute as to the title to the portrait. It is the communication of one friend to another suggesting a way in which the original portrait could be placed in the Metropolitan Museum and Mrs. Saint-Gaudens' desire complied with by sending her a copy equally as good as the original.

The letter is entirely consistent with the idea that the defendant believed that the portrait belonged to her and that she could do as she pleased with it and that in painting it she had intended at some time to present it to Mr. and Mrs. Saint-Gaudens. In this view it recognizes the wish of Mrs. Saint-Gaudens expressed in her letter of April 16th, 1906, that when she (the defendant) was through exhibiting it, if she (the defendant) would send it to her it would be welcomed with joy.

If the expression is to be interpreted as a recognition of ownership in a person other than the writer such other person was Mrs. Saint-Gaudens and not Mr. Saint-Gaudens, and so construed it would not sustain the allegations of the complaint.

Undoubtedly the testimony has not disclosed the whole truth about the painting of the portrait. The defendant cannot testify as to the arrangement or agreement between herself and Mr. Saint-Gaudens if there was any. It is not unlikely that some arrangement was made as to the permanent disposition of the portrait which the testimony does not disclose. It is also not improbable that no arrangement was made at all. The parties were intimate friends. One was a great artist of international fame desiring to aid a young lady to establish her reputation as a portrait painter, and in my opinion it was not improbable that Mr. Saint-Gaudens relied upon her to make no final disposition of the portrait that would not be approved by him.

It is evident from his letter of April 16th, 1906 that he personally had no objection to the portrait going to the Metropolitan Museum as a gift to that institution by Mr. McKim, and if the fire had not occurred which consumed, as Mrs. Saint-Gaudens expresses it, "nearly all our most cherished possessions," it is quite likely that Mrs. Saint-Gaudens would have probably acquiesced in the gift of the portrait to the Museum.

But however this may be, I cannot assume the existence of a contract by which Mr. Saint-Gaudens was vested with the title to the portrait of which there is no proof, and there is no basis in the testimony for the claim that the title to the portrait was in Mr. Saint-Gaudens.

It was the work of the defendant. The materials which were used and the skill and labor which produced it were hers. These are the controlling facts in the case and the legal conclusions necessarily find that the completed picture belonged to her.

The few facts and circumstances which are relied on to prove a contrary result are consistent with the theory that the defendant intended ultimately to present the portrait to Mr. and Mrs. Saint-Gaudens. If such was the fact the gift was never consummated.

There must be judgment for the defendant.

Requests to find may be presented to me by either party within ten days.

§4.1.3. *National Historic Shrines Foundation, Inc. v. Dali:* When Must an Artist Create?

When is the understanding between an artist and a patron sufficiently fixed so as to become a legally binding contract whereby the artist must create a certain work of art? *Dali,* which follows, addresses this issue in an action involving the surrealist artist Salvador Dali. The court took up the question of whether the artist's alleged agreement to paint a picture on a television show was, as a matter of law, one for the sale of services or the sale of goods, the legal distinction dictating whether a binding obligation existed.

Query whether the commission of a portrait, or any artwork, for that matter, is one for the sale of services or the sale of goods? If all such contracts were deemed to be service contracts (and therefore not within the sale of goods provision of the Statute of Frauds), what would be the result when the work was not required by its contract to be completed within the year, even though a statute in the jurisdiction required contracts to be capable of performance within a year if they were to be enforceable without a writing?

For an interesting view of the Statute of Frauds in another context, see *O'Keeffe v. Bry* and the commentary that precedes it in Chapter 3.

NATIONAL HISTORIC SHRINES FOUNDATION, INC. v. DALI
4 U.C.C. Rep. Serv. (Callaghan) 71 (N.Y. Sup. Ct. 1967)

GELLER, J. Defendant, Dali, an artist, moves for an order granting summary judgment dismissing the complaint or, in the alternative, determining that the plaintiff's maximum damages recoverable are its out-of-pocket expenses of $264.91.

In this action plaintiff, a non-profit corporation, sues Dali for breach of an oral agreement whereby, allegedly, Dali agreed to appear on a television program designed to raise funds for plaintiff. As part of the program Dali was to paint before the cameras a picture of the Statue of Liberty (the location of a museum to be completed by the National Park Service of the United States Department of the Interior with funds to be raised by plaintiff) and present the completed painting at the end of the program to plaintiff, to be sold for its charitable purposes. The value of such a painting, estimated by Dali, according to plaintiff, would have been $25,000. Dali is alleged to have at the last moment refused to go through with the planned arrangements, and the program was not held.

The facts claimed by plaintiff to support its theory that a binding oral contract was entered into are vigorously disputed by Dali. Accordingly, a trial would appear to be necessary to resolve the factual issues. But Dali urges that no cognizable or enforceable cause of action is asserted against him on the basis of any credible evidence presented by plaintiff at an inquest for a pleading default subsequently opened or which could be adduced by plaintiff

Plaintiff's theory is that under the special circumstances of this case a contract supported by consideration was made with Dali for his appearance and rendition of services on a television program, time for which, plaintiff claims, had been given for a certain date by a named station. Plaintiff claims to have received definite promises as the result of conversations with Dali and a person referred to as his agent, allegedly confirmed in part by correspondence. The consideration to Dali is claimed to be his own stated acceptance of plaintiff's offer on the ground of his obtaining appropriate publicity out of the idea. This publicity aspect was actually carried out in a preliminary public wreath-laying ceremony by Dali at the foot of the Washington statue in Wall Street and at a party in a hotel, sponsored with expenses of $264.91 paid by plaintiff; Dali then announcing to the press that he intended to participate in plaintiff's television program in the manner outlined.

It will be noted that the nature of the understanding and arrange-ments, as here claimed by plaintiff, may conceivably spell out a contrac-tual obligation, as distinguished from the usual practice whereby celebrities and performers voluntarily and without any contractual obli-gation contribute their talents and names to various public and charitable functions.

On this motion Dali urges that the agreement, as alleged, is too indefi-nite to be binding; founded upon insufficient consideration; void for lack of mutuality; and unenforceable under the statute of frauds.

With respect to the contention of indefiniteness, there is sufficient shown in the testimony offered by plaintiff on the inquest and in the present supporting papers, if believed, to indicate a binding commitment to the extent that plaintiff relied thereon in making its arrangements. As to consideration, that is sufficiently shown, for the purpose of entitling plaintiff to a trial of the issues, by plaintiff's testimony, if believed, regarding Dali's acceptance on the ground of the publicity inuring to him and by the two preliminary promotional events. Concerning lack of mutuality, there appears to be no reason under these particular circum-stances why Dali could not have recovered damages had he in reliance upon plaintiff's final and definite arrangements suffered actual damages if plaintiff had thereafter unjustifiably cancelled the program.

Regarding the statute of frauds, Dali's argument is that this is an alleged agreement for the sale of goods, consisting of the painting he was to make, of the value of $500 or more, which must be in writing signed by the party against whom enforcement is sought (Uniform Commercial Code, §2-201). Plaintiff's theory and offer of proof on this submission shows, however, an alleged agreement for rendition of services by Dali during an appearance before the cameras with resultant contribution of the painting then made and subsequent hope of sale thereof by plaintiff to the public. This is not viewed as a sale of goods within the terms of the statute of frauds.

Defendant's motion for summary judgment is denied. While plain-tiff's theory of a binding oral contract may be difficult to establish in the context of this type of transaction, the special circumstances here shown entitle it to a trial at which it may present proof of its alleged cause of action.

§4.1.4. *Zaleski v. Clark:* **Whom Must the Artist Satisfy?**

Although decided more than a century ago, *Zaleski*, which fol-lows, still carries the clear, fresh scent of New England practicality. If the terms of a commission are that the patron must be satisfied, then the fact that her dissatisfaction is wholly unreasonable is totally beside the point.

ZALESKI v. CLARK
44 Conn. 218 (1876)

Assumpsit, to recover the price of a bust made for the defendant; brought to the Court of Common Pleas of New Haven County, and tried to the court on the general issue, before Robinson, J. The court made the following finding of facts:

The plaintiff in March, 1875, was a sculptor by profession, and particularly devoted himself to modeling in plaster, from photographs, the busts of deceased persons. A certain Mrs. Johnson formed his acquaintance, saw his work and was much pleased with it, and endeavored to procure him some orders. Mrs. Johnson was herself an artist, and it had been agreed between her and the plaintiff that they would together occupy a certain store in New Haven and pay the rent therefor, and that Mrs. Johnson should get orders for the plaintiff, if she could, and was to receive a commission therefor, and that the plaintiff should assist her in her business in a similar way and for similar remuneration. Among others she went to Mrs. Clark, the defendant, an old friend of hers, a widow, told her of the plaintiff, and asked her if she would not like a bust of her deceased husband. Mrs. Clark said she would very much. Mrs. Johnson said that she believed the plaintiff would give perfect satisfaction, and that Mrs. Clark would run no risk in ordering it as she need not take it unless she was satisfied with it. These representations of Mrs. Johnson as to Mrs. Clark's not being liable to take the bust unless it satisfied her were made without any authority to make them from the plaintiff.

Mrs. Clark thereupon gave Mrs. Johnson a photograph, which was a good likeness of the deceased, to be used by the plaintiff in preparing the bust, and Mrs. Johnson gave it to the plaintiff. The plaintiff made the bust, and while at work on it was visited by the defendant, who made some suggestions regarding it which were followed by the plaintiff. When the bust was completed the defendant notified the plaintiff that she should not accept it or pay the price for it, which it had been agreed should be £150.

The bust was a fine piece of work, was a correct copy of the photograph, and accurately represented and portrayed the features of the deceased. The only fault found with it was that it did not have the expression of the deceased during his life, and this the court found from the evidence to have resulted not from any imperfection in the workmanship, but from the nature of a bust as a dead white model, and necessarily destitute of the expression of color and life. The defendant was not satisfied with it, but her dissatisfaction was caused by reasons which would have applied to any bust whatever, and not to this as distinguished from any other.

Upon these facts the plaintiff claimed that he was entitled to recover, that the defendant in ordering a bust was supposed to know the character of the object ordered, and was bound to receive and pay for it, unless there was some objections to this particular bust which did not arise out of the inherent character of busts in general. The defendant claimed that the plaintiff was bound to satisfy her at all events, and that unless she was satisfied she was not bound to take the bust, no matter what was the reason of her dissatisfaction.

The court overruled the claim of the defendant and rendered judgment for the plaintiff to recover £150, with interest from May 1st, 1875.

The defendant moved for a new trial for error in the above ruling of the court.

CARPENTER, J.: Courts of law must allow parties to make their own contracts, and can enforce only such as they actually make. Whether the contract is wise or unwise, reasonable or unreasonable, is ordinarily an immaterial inquiry. The simple inquiry is, what is the contract? and has the plaintiff undertook to make a bust which should be satisfactory to the defendant. The case shows that she was not satisfied with it. The plaintiff has not yet then fulfilled his contract. It is not enough to say that she ought to be satisfied with it, and that her dissatisfaction is unreasonable. She, and not the court, is entitled to judge of that. The contract was not to make one that she ought to be satisfied with, but to make one that she would be satisfied with. Nor is it sufficient to say that the bust was the very best thing of the kind that could possibly be produced. Such an article might not be satisfactory to the defendant, while one of inferior workmanship might be entirely satisfactory. A contract to produce a bust perfect in every respect, and one with which the defendant ought to be satisfied is one thing; an undertaking to make one with which she will be satisfied is quite another thing. The former can only be determined by experts, or those whose education and habits of life qualify them to judge of such matters. The latter can only be determined by the defendant herself. It may have been unwise in the plaintiff to make such a contract, but having made it, he is bound by it. *McCarren v. McNulty*, 7 Gray 139; *Brown v. Foster*, 113 Mass. 136.

It further appears that the plaintiff did not make this contract personally, but it was made through the agency of a Mrs. Johnson; and the court below has found that her representations as to the defendant's "not being liable to take the bust unless it satisfied her, were made without any authority to make them from the plaintiff."

It appears that she had a general authority to procure orders for the plaintiff. In the absence of any limitation of her power it would seem that she would be authorized to agree upon the terms of the contract: but conceding that she had no power to make such a contract as this is, we do not see how that circumstance will aid the plaintiff's case. There was no other contract; and if this was unauthorized and not binding upon the plaintiff, then there was no special contract. If none, then, inasmuch as the defendant never accepted the bust, there was no sale and she is not liable.

A new trial is advised.

In this opinion the other judges concurred.

A new trial was ordered; plaintiff's counsel tried the case de novo and prevailed. Defendant's further attempt to upset the verdict was unavailing.[1]

§4.1.5. *Pennington v. Howland:* Confirming the "Personal Taste" Standard

In *Pennington,* which follows, the court distinguished commissions for works of art from contracts under which a party's performance might be measured against some objective standard. While workmanship that is "reasonably satisfactory" may be sufficient to satisfy an obligation under the latter type of agreement, it is not enough for an agreement such as an art commission. There, the measure may be "personal taste and judgment" and a court will not substitute its own taste or judgment for that of the dissatisfied party.

PENNINGTON v. HOWLAND
21 R.I. 65, 41 A. 891 (1898)

STINESS, J.; The plaintiff was employed to paint a pastel portrait of the defendant's wife for the sum of five hundred dollars, under a contract by correspondence which only provided for the price. The plaintiff went to the defendant's house in Washington, D.C., and began his work. The defendant testified that he at once objected to the proposed portrait, in street dress and hat, but the plaintiff said it was an artistic idea which he wished to carry out and that if it was not satisfactory he would paint the defendant one "until satisfied." He also testified that the plaintiff undertook the commission with the understanding that he would paint a satisfactory portrait.

The plaintiff denies this, and says that upon the completion of his work Mrs. Howland said that she wanted another portrait, taken in different style of dress, to show a pearl necklace which had belonged to her mother. He then painted a second portrait and went away, leaving his implements, as he says, to be sent to him, or, as the defendant says,

---

§4.1. [1] See 45 Conn. 397 (1877).

because the portrait was not finished and because he was to return to complete it.

The defendant says that he received a letter from the plaintiff stating that the pictures should be framed to keep the pastel from brushing off, and that he would give instructions to a man whom he usually employed, to do it. The frames came, the pictures were put into them, and after some correspondence the defendant paid for the frames, and the pictures are still in his possession.

Upon this general statement of testimony the plaintiff's claim was that he painted one portrait at an agreed price, and then another upon request, for which he has charged the same price, and that both were not only without conditions but were said to be satisfactory.

The defendant claims that the plaintiff agreed, upon starting his work, that if the picture was not satisfactory he would paint another; that after expressing his dissatisfaction the plaintiff immediately started another which he did not finish; that the pictures were framed simply to preserve them until the last one should be finished, and that they have since remained with him in that way.

These conflicting claims present obvious questions of fact for a jury. Numerous exceptions were taken at the trial which can be better considered generally than in detail. According to the defendant's statement that the work was to be satisfactory to him, he asked the court to instruct the jury that he had the right to reject the first portrait if he was not satisfied with it.

(1) The judge instructed the jury that "satisfactory" means "reasonably satisfactory"; but in response to another request he also instructed the jury that "an artist, if he agreed to paint a picture to one's satisfaction, has no cause of action for the price unless the buyer is satisfied, however good the picture is," adding, "But unless the man returns the picture he is conclusively held to be satisfied." This last instruction, without the added sentence, states the law correctly, according to the current of authority, and in giving the preceding instruction, that a portrait must be "reasonably satisfactory," the judge doubtless had in mind another class of cases to which that limitation may apply.

When the subject of the contract is one which involves personal taste or feeling, an agreement that it shall be satisfactory to the buyer necessarily makes him the sole judge whether it answers that condition. He cannot be required to take it because other people might be satisfied with it; for that is not what he agreed to do. Personal tastes differ widely, and if one has agreed to submit his work to such a test he must abide by the result. A large number of witnesses might be brought to testify that the work was satisfactory to them; that they considered it perfect, and that they could see no reasonable ground for objecting to it. But that would not be the test of the contract, nor should a jury be allowed to say in such a case that a defendant must pay because by the preponderance of evidence he ought to have been satisfied with the work— or, in other words, that it was "reasonably satisfactory." Upon this principle numerous cases have been decided.

In *McCarren v. McNulty*, 7 Gray 139, an action to recover the price of a book-case, the court said:

> It may be that the plaintiff was injudicious or indiscreet in undertaking to labor and furnish material for a compensation, the payment of which was made dependent upon a contingency so hazardous or doubtful as the approval or satisfaction of a party particularly in interest. But of that he was the sole judge. Against the consequences resulting from his own bargain the law can afford him no relief. Having voluntarily assumed the obligations and risk of the contract, his legal rights are to be ascertained and determined solely according to its provisions.

Gibson v. Cranage, 39 Mich. 49, was to the same effect, where the subject of the action was a portrait.

In *Zaleski v. Clark*, 44 Conn. 218, the plaintiff was to make a bust of the defendant's deceased husband satisfactory to her. The court held that it was for her alone to determine whether it was so, and that it was not enough to show that her dissatisfaction was unreasonable.

Brown v. Foster, 113 Mass. 136, was for a suit of clothes. Devens, J., said: "It is not for any one else to decide whether a refusal to accept is or is not reasonable, when the contract permits the defendant to decide himself whether the articles furnished are to his satisfaction."

The doctrine was carried to very great length in *Singerly v. Thayer*, 108 Pa. St. 291, where an elevator had been erected in a building and "warranted satisfactory in every respect." It was held that, if it had been substantially completed so that the owner of the building could understand how it would operate, it could be rejected if it was not satisfactory.

In *Duplex Boiler v. Garden*, 101 N.Y. 387, the opinion sets out the two classes of cases, with reference to which a distinction has been made. One class is that which involves personal taste and judgment, examples of which we have shown, and the other class is that where the subject-matter of the contract is such that the satisfaction stipulated for must be held to apply to quality, workmanship, salability, and other like considerations, rather than to personal satisfaction. For example, if one agrees to sell land with a satisfactory title, and shows a title valid and complete, the parties must have intended such a title to be satisfactory, rather than to leave an absolute right in the purchaser to say: "I am not satisfied," when no reason could be shown why he should not be satisfied. So if one agrees to do work in a satisfactory manner it must mean a workmanlike manner— as well as it would be expected to be done —rather than a merely personal or whimsical rejection. It is this class of cases to which the term "reasonably satisfactory" applies. Hence in the boiler case, last cited, it was held that a simple allegation of dissatisfaction, without some good reason assigned for it, might be a mere pretext, and would not be regarded.

In *Wood Reaping Co. v. Smith*, 50 Mich. 565, the court says:

> In the one class the right of decision is completely reserved to the promisor, without being liable to disclose reasons or account for his course, and a right to inquire into the grounds of his action and overhaul his determination is absolutely excluded from the promisee and from all other tribunals.
>
> In the other class the promisor is supposed to undertake that he will act reasonably and fairly, and found his determination upon grounds which are just and sensible, and from thence springs a necessary implication that his decision in point of correctness and the adequacy of the grounds of it is open to consideration and subject to the judgment of judicial triers.

See also *McClure v. Briggs*, 58 Vt. 82; *Daggett v. Johnson*, 49 Vt. 345; *Hartford Sorghum Co. v. Brush*, 43 Vt. 528; 1 Beach Mod. Law Contr. §104.

Even in cases of the latter class, where a rejection is made in good faith, the dissatisfaction of the purchaser is held in many decisions to be sufficient. See note to *Duplex Co. v. Garden*, 54 Am. Rep. 709 (711).

The instruction to the jury in the present case that "satisfactory" means "reasonably satisfactory" was erroneous as applied to the subject-matter of the alleged contract.

(2) Evidently the trial judge thought that the definition of the term was of little weight, because the defendant had not returned the pictures, or either of them, and hence he added the words: "But unless the man returns the pictures he is conclusively held to be satisfied." The same instruction appears so clearly in other parts of the charge that the jury must have understood that the retention of the pictures made the defendant liable for the price of both.

Taken generally the instruction would be quite correct, upon the ground that one cannot retain the property of another and still refuse to pay for it. But the instruction as given ignores the defense set up in this case, which is that the first picture was not accepted and the second not completed.

The demand relied on by the plaintiff is contained in his letter of January 7, 1896, in which he asks the defendant to send him both pictures for exhibition. To this the defendant replied that he wanted one and objected to the other being shown as a likeness of his wife. He also testified that he had not objected to the removal of this one, but only to its exhibition. Now whether, under the circumstances of this case, there was a refusal to return the pictures, or an excuse for the retention of the other because it was not completed, were questions of fact for the jury. The question whether the contract was as claimed by the defendant also raised a question of fact. If the jury had found that the contract was for a satisfactory portrait; that the second was satisfactory but not completed, and that the other was not returned because of the suggestion of its exhibition, they might have found for the defendant. The facts that the pictures were on the walls of the defendant's home and that he had paid for the frames are such as would naturally be considered in determining an acceptance, but they do not conclude such determination nor remove the questions from the jury. The instruction, therefore, that by the mere retention of the pictures, under the circumstances of the case, the defendant was conclusively held to be satisfied and liable for both, was erroneous.

New trial granted.

§4.1.6. *The Walrus Corporation v. Stein:* **A Recent Twist**

In 1983, the name of the artist David Stein — the central figure in *New York v. Wright Hepburn Webster Gallery, Ltd.* (reproduced at §9.4.9 *infra*) — again emerged in a court proceeding. This time it was in a suit brought against him in the U.S. District Court for the Southern District of New York by The Walrus Corporation, the owner of the Old Ebbitt Grill, a popular restaurant in downtown Washington, D.C.

In December 1982, the plaintiff had commissioned Stein to create an enormous (15' x 34') painting to be installed on the restaurant's ceiling. Several months later, he was also commissioned to execute five additional and smaller paints for the walls. Taking advantage of Stein's notorious ability to paint "in the style of," the corporation made it understood that the ceiling painting was to be "in the style of" the nineteenth-century French salon painter William Bouguereau. While neither agreement specifically required that the artist work in any particular manner, both contained the strongest provisions imaginable reserving to the plaintiff the right to reject Stein's paintings if it thought them unsatisfactory. Thus, ¶3 of the December, 1982 agreement provided:

> This Agreement is expressly made contingent upon and is subject to continuous inspection and approval by WALRUS of all preliminary drawings of the proposed Art Work and approval by WALRUS, in its sole and absolute discretion, of the completed Art Work. The parties hereto recognize that payment of the contract price for the Art Work contemplates that WALRUS will be completely satisfied with each part of the Art Work and, if any part of the Art Work is not satisfactory, in the sole and absolute discretion of WALRUS, then, in that event, the Art Work will not be deemed completed under the terms of this Agreement.

Coupled with this was the stipulation in ¶10: "If the ARTIST fails to deliver the satisfactorily completed Art Work within the specified time,

WALRUS may decline to accept the Art Work and recover any and all amounts which may have been advanced to the ARTIST."

Seeking to recover its advances, the plaintiff alleged in its complaint that the artist had failed to deliver satisfactorily completed works of art within the time specified. Under the principles of *Zaleski v. Clark* and *Pennington v. Howland* (both reproduced in this section *supra*), it would have been no defense for the artist to answer that the plaintiff was unreasonable in rejecting his work as unsatisfactory. Instead he argued that there had in fact been an actual delivery of the paintings to, and an acceptance by, the plaintiff. He also counterclaimed for the unpaid balance of the purchase price. The case was still pending as of this writing.

§4.2. PUBLIC COMMISSIONS

§4.2.1. Introduction: Public Commissions and "Site-Specific" Art

In *Probing the Earth: Contemporary Land Projects*,[1] John Beardsley provides the following description of *Double Negative*, a 1969-1970 "earthwork" by Michael Heizer dug into the eastern rim of the Mormon Mesa, some five miles east of Overton, Nevada:

> Two cuts in the surface of the mesa, each 30 feet wide and 50 feet deep, facing each other across a scallop in the escarpment which separates the mesa from the river valley below. The work, including the two cuts and the space between them, measures about 1,500 feet in total length, and displaces 240,000 tons of earth.[2]

In the same publication, Robert Morris' 1973-1974 *Grand Rapids Project*, constructed on the side of a hill in Belknap Park, a recreation area in Grand Rapids, Michigan, is described as

> Two crossing ramps paved in asphalt, forming an "X" on the side of a hill. The ramps level out at the point of their crossing; this occurs more than half way up the hill, as the upper arms of the "X," each 200 feet long, are somewhat shorter than the lower arms, which are 278 feet long. The ramps are 18 feet 6 inches wide and cover a vertical distance of 78 feet over a horizontal distance of 260 feet.[3]

Works such as these differ from conventional art objects not only in their scale and complexity but also in the sorts of legal arrangements that

---

§4.2. [1] J. Beardsley, Probing the Earth: Contemporary Land Projects (1977).
[2] *Id.* at 40.
[3] *Id.* at 61.

surround them. Unlike the easel paintings and generally portable sculpture that commercial galleries customarily buy and sell, these earthworks and similar site-specific objects such as works of public art are most often executed on commission. Except for temporary "installation pieces" (discussed in §4.2.6 *infra*), they are also most often envisioned as being permanently installed, or at least intended to remain in place for a very long time. In a curious way, the arrangements that attend the creation of such works of art—including the fact that they are produced mostly under patronage rather than on speculation—are reminiscent of those of the late Middle Ages when painting generally took the form of commissioned frescos and sculpture of architectural embellishment.[4]

Reproduced in the following pages are some typical contracts for public commissions.[5] What should be understood by anyone undertaking such a commission is that the pertinent legal considerations will often be paralleled by a series of political, administrative and/or funding considerations that must be dealt with as well. The Robert Morris *Grand Rapids Project*, for example, required approval at the local level from not only the city manager but also the city commission and the parks and recreation department. At the state level it had to be cleared by the Michigan Department of Natural Resources. Funding was provided by a combination of the National Endowment for the Arts, the Michigan Council for the Arts, the Women's Committee of the Grand Rapids Art Museum, and the Grand Rapids Parks and Recreation Department. Christo is the contemporary artist who has best mastered such complex arrangements, employing them on the grandest imaginable scale for such temporary installation projects as *Running Fence, Wrapped Reichstag,* and *Surrounded Islands.* (For a discussion of Christo's unsuccessful attempts to mount a work in New York City entitled *The Gates,* and how he might

---

[4] On December 12, 1985, the N.Y. Times reported that Heizer's *Double Negative* had been given to the Museum of Contemporary Art in Los Angeles. See §13.2 *infra*, n.1, concerning the gift. Commenting several weeks later on the gift of this unconventional art object, John Russell wrote in the N.Y. Times, "But a new era may have begun with the recent acquisition by the Museum of Contemporary Art in Los Angeles of Michael Heizer's 'Double Negative,' a deep two-fold cut in the Nevada Desert that cannot be moved to Los Angeles or duplicated, but has to be visited in situ. The role of the museum, in this case, is to record it, to publish it (in art-historical terms) and to make it possible and relatively easy to go and see it through periodic air trips to the site. (Maintenance is minimal, since Heizer wishes the piece to take its chances in nature.)" Russell, An Earthwork Looks to the Sky, N.Y. Times, Jan. 5, 1986, §2, at 1, 29.

[5] See also the annotated model agreement commissioning a work of public art, prepared in 1985 by the Committee on Art Law of the Association of the Bar of the City of New York, reproduced in 10 Colum. J.L. & Arts 1 (1985).

claim that his right to create had been restricted by the approval process, see Chapter 1.)

Also, the initial installation of a site-specific work of art may not be the end of the legal complexities that surround it. Judging from the tempest raised in 1985 by the proposed relocation of Richard Serra's sculpture *Tilted Arc* from the plaza in front of the Jacob Javits Federal Building in New York City, it may be that the removal of such a work involves considerations wholly different from those that would attend the removal to a different site of a conventional painting or sculpture. The dispute over *Tilted Arc* is discussed further in §4.2.3 *infra*.

§4.2.2. General Services Administration's Art-in-Architecture Program

Among the most ambitious programs of public art yet undertaken in the United States is the Art-in-Architecture program of the federal government's General Services Administration (G.S.A.). Under this program, major works of art are commissioned for incorporation into federal buildings.[6] Some of the best-known works created under the Art-in-Architecture program include Claes Oldenburg's monumental *Baseball Bat* and Alexander Calder's stabile *Flamingo*, both in Chicago; Jack Beal's murals depicting the history of the American working man, at the Department of Labor Building in Washington; and George Segal's sculptural tableau, *The Restaurant*, in Buffalo, New York. Richard Serra's *Tilted Arc* (discussed in §4.2.3 *infra*) was also a G.S.A. commission.

Originally initiated in 1963, suspended in 1966 following a public dispute over Robert Motherwell's mural for the John F. Kennedy Federal Building in Boston, and reinstituted in 1972, the program had commissioned more than two hundred and fifty works of art by the mid-1980s. Most of these were produced under the same (or substantially the same) form of agreement that follows. For reasons presumably relevant to the federal government's procurement procedures, this agreement is cast as a contract for services rather than an agreement for the purchase of a work of art. Article 6, captioned "Ownership," nonetheless makes it clear that the work, when finished, becomes the property of the United States. Regarding the second sentence of Article 6, which appears to provide that this finished work will be "conveyed . . . to the National Museum of American Art-Smithsonian Institution," an individual long familiar with

---

[6] For a sympathetic history of the program, see D. W. Thalacker, The Place of Art in the World of Architecture (1980).

the G.S.A. program has suggested that this was improperly drafted and that only the "designs, sketches [and] models" for the finished work were intended to be so conveyed. The finished work itself is presumably to remain at the site for which it was created. Notwithstanding the arguments of Richard Serra and his sympathizers, however, this may be no more than a presumption. At bottom it can be argued that the G.S.A., as the sole owner of the work, can do with it whatever it wants. The agreement is certainly bare of any language that would indicate otherwise.

Article 6 also attempts to provide a substitute for the copyright, which §105 of the Copyright Revision Act of 1976 precludes the federal government from obtaining. By prohibiting the artist from making "exact reproductions or reductions of the finished work," the agreement virtually ousts the artist from whatever reproduction rights he might otherwise have retained in a simple and straightforward sale. Can the artist nevertheless prevent G.S.A. or a third party from reproducing the work?[7] For a starkly contrasting approach to this copyright question, see ¶18 of the Seattle Arts Commission form of agreement, reproduced in this section *infra*.

Most important for the artist contracting with G.S.A.'s Art-in-Architecture program is that he begin with a solid understanding of what material, fabrication, shipping, installation, travel, insurance, and other expenses will need to be covered. This is a fixed-price agreement, not one for cost plus. The only circumstances under which the price may be renegotiated are when changes are recommended by the contracting officer (Article 3), or when the contracting officer orders a suspension of work (Article 10). It is also important that the artist be assured that the cash flow generated under Article 7 will be adequate to meet the interim bills to be incurred in the course of creating, transporting, and installing the finished work.

Interestingly, no provision is made for any settlement if the commissioned artist dies or becomes incapacitated before the work is completed. In the event of the artist's death, the contracting officer would presumably terminate the contract under Article 11 (omitted). Thereafter,

---

[7] Probably so, if we assume that the artist has the copyright. Any other assumption, however, leads to a no-win situation for G.S.A. If it argues that this is a work for hire, then §105 of the Copyright Revision Act of 1976 would push the commissioned work into the public domain, the ludicrous result of which would be to permit everybody *but* the artist to make "exact reproductions." G.S.A. is thus better off maintaining that the artist retains the copyright, but that his exploitation of such copyright is limited by contract.

G.S.A. would return all "sketches, designs, models or other documents or materials" previously delivered, and the artist's estate, in turn, would be required to remit a sum equal to whatever payments had theretofore been received. If death is not a stipulated excuse for noncompletion, strikes, acts of war, or similar events beyond the artist's control are no more acceptable. The agreement makes no explicit provision for *force majeur.*

The larger part of the G.S.A. contract, however, consists of federal procurement boilerplate — also omitted from the contract that follows. Except for those who regularly negotiate construction and other agreements with the United States Government, no attorney — never mind an artist — should reasonably be expected to understand fully the host of other federal laws and regulations that are incorporated by reference. Some seem all but a burlesque of bureaucracy. Article 14(b), for example, covers the contingency that the specifications for a work of art may be marked "top secret," while Article 23 limits the artist's right to employ convict labor. Others may be real hazards of which an artist could unknowingly run afoul. Among these are the requirement that the Buy American Act and several related Executive Orders be observed (Article 26), and, in the case of contracts that exceed $100,000, that the artist follow the Clean Air Act and the Federal Water Pollution Control Act (Article 25). There are also equal opportunity and affirmative action provisions (Articles 19-21) of such a complexity that it is inherently unbelievable that any artist has ever or could ever actually comply with all of them. Also, unlikely as the event may be, the G.S.A. does retain the unilateral right to terminate the agreement for the "convenience of the Government" (Article 11).

No doubt G.S.A.'s general counsel has advised the Art-in-Architecture program that all of this is necessary. If so, then it may be pointless for an attorney representing an artist who has been given the desirable opportunity to carry out a G.S.A. commission to attempt any modification of these terms. It may simply be an instance of take it or leave it, and an artist might well be advised to "take it" — providing he makes a careful calculation of the expenses, figures the cash flow correctly, and tries not to die.

G.S.A. CONTRACT FOR FINE ARTS SERVICES*

On this _____ day of _____, _____ the United States of America (hereinafter referred to as the Government), acting by and

---

* Provisions that contain federal procurement boilerplate have been omitted.

through the General Services Administration, and _____ (hereinafter referred to as the Artist), an individual whose address is _____ do hereby mutually agree as follows:

Article 1. *Definitions*

(a) The term "head of the agency" as used herein means the Administrator of General Services, and the term "his duly authorized representative" means any person or persons or board (other than the Contracting Officer) authorized to act for the head of the agency.

(b) The term "Contracting Officer" as used herein means the person executing this contract on behalf of the Government and includes a duly appointed successor or authorized representative.

Article 2. *Scope of Services*

(a) The Artist shall perform all services and furnish all supplies, material and equipment as necessary for the design and execution of _____ (hereinafter referred to as "the work") to be placed in _____ at the location shown on Contract Drawing No. _____ attached hereto. The Artist shall execute the work in an artistic, professional manner and in strict compliance with all terms and conditions of this contract.

(b) The Artist shall determine the artistic expression, subject to its being acceptable to the Government. The Artist shall submit to the Government a sketch or other document which conveys a meaningful presentation of the work which he/she proposes to furnish in fulfillment of this contract; he/she shall allow _____ calendar days for the Government to determine acceptability of the proposed artistic expression.

(c) The work shall be of a material and size mutually acceptable to the Government and to the Artist.

(d) The Artist shall install the work, in the location shown on the attached drawings.

(e) The Artist shall be responsible for prepayment of all mailing or shipping charges on sketches, models or other submissions to the Government.

(f) Upon installation the artist is to provide written instructions to the contracting officer for appropriate maintenance and preservation of the artwork. The Government is responsible for the proper care and maintenance of the work.

(g) The Artist shall furnish the Government with the following photographs of the finished work as installed:

(1) One black and white negative 4" x 5"
(2) One color negative 4" x 5"
(3) Two black and white prints 8" x 10"

(4) Two color prints 8" x 10"
(5) One color transparency 4" x 5"
(6) Five representative 35mm color slides

ARTICLE 3. *Changes*

(a) The Artist shall make any revision necessary to comply with such recommendations as the Contracting Officer may make for practical (non-aesthetic) reasons.

(b) If the Contracting Officer makes any recommendations within the scope of paragraph (a) above, after approval of any submission by the Artist, the Artist's fee shall be equitably adjusted for any increase or decrease in the Artist's cost of, or time required for, performance of any services under this contract; the contract shall be modified in writing to reflect any such adjustment. Any claim of the Artist for adjustment under this clause must be asserted in writing within 30 days from the date of receipt by the Artist of the recommendation, unless the Contracting Officer grants a further period of time before the date of final payment under the contract.

(c) If the Contracting Officer makes any recommendations within the scope of paragraph (a) above, prior to approval of any submission by the Artist, the Artist shall make the revisions necessary to comply with these recommendations, at no additional cost to the Government.

(d) No services for which an additional cost or fee will be charged by the Artist shall be furnished without the prior written authorization of the Contracting Officer.

ARTICLE 4. *Inspection and Care*

(a) The Artist shall furnish facilities for inspection of the work in progress by authorized representatives of the Contracting Officer. The Government will contact the Artist in advance of any inspection to arrange a mutually convenient time.

(b) The Artist shall be responsible for the care and protection of all work performed by him/her until completion of the installed work and acceptance by the Contracting Officer and shall repair or restore any damaged work; provided, however, that the Artist shall not be responsible for any damage which occurs after installation is complete and before acceptance by the Contracting Officer which is not caused by any acts or omissions of the Artist or any of his/her agents or employees.

(c) The Artist shall give the Contracting Officer at least 10 days advance written notice of the date the work will be fully completed and ready for final inspection. Final inspection will be started within 10 days from the date specified in the aforesaid notice unless the Contracting

Officer determines that the work is not ready for final inspection and so informs the Artist.

ARTICLE 5. *Time for Completion*

The Artist shall complete all work as follows:
(a) The preliminary submittal as required by Article 2.(b): _____ calendar days after the receipt of notice to proceed.
(b) The completed work in place: _____ calendar days after receipt of notice to proceed.

ARTICLE 6. *Ownership*

All designs, sketches, models, and the work produced under this Agreement for which payment is made under the provisions of this contract shall be the property of the UNITED STATES OF AMERICA. All such items will be conveyed by the Contracting Officer to the National Museum of American Art-Smithsonian Institution for exhibiting purposes and permanent safekeeping.

The Artist shall neither publicly exhibit the final work, nor shall he/she make exact reproductions or reductions of the finished work except by written permission of the Contracting Officer.

ARTICLE 7. *Fee and Payment*

In consideration of the Artist's performance of the services required by this contract, the Government shall pay the Artist a fixed-fee not to exceed _____. The fee shall be paid in installments as follows:
(a) $_____ upon approval of the proposed artistic expression as required by Article 2.(b).
(b) $_____ when the work is completed, approved, and ready for installation.
(c) $_____ upon completion, and acceptance by the Government, of all services required under this contract.

The Contracting Officer shall advise the Artist in writing of the approval or reasons for disapproval within 30 days after (i) receipt of the document(s) showing the artistic expression, (ii) receipt of the notice that the work is completed and ready for installation, or (iii) after inspection of the installed work.

Upon approval and/or acceptance (whichever is applicable) of the work performed under this contract, the amount due the Artist shall be paid as soon as practicable after receipt of a correct billing from the Artist. Prior to the final payment the Artist shall furnish the Government with a release of all claims against the Government under this Agreement, other than such claims as the Artist may except. The Artist shall describe and state amount of each excepted claim.

ARTICLE 8. *Travel*

All travel by the Artist and his/her agents or employees as may be necessary for proper performance of the services required under this contract is included in the fee amount set out in Article 7, above, and shall be at no additional cost to the Government.

ARTICLE 9. *Responsibility of the Artist*

(a) Neither the Government's review, approval or acceptance of, nor payment for, any of the services required under this contract shall be construed to operate as a waiver of any rights under this contract or of any cause of action arising out of the performance of this contract, and the Artist shall be and remain liable to the Government in accordance with applicable law for all damages to the Government caused by the Artist's negligent performance of any of the services furnished under this contract.

(b) The rights and remedies of the Government provided for under this contract are in addition to any other rights and remedies provided by law.

(c) The artist guarantees all work to be free from defective or inferior materials and workmanship for one year after the date of final acceptance by the government. If within one year the contracting officer finds the work in need of repair because of defective materials or workmanship, the artist shall, without additional expense to the government, promptly and satisfactorily make the necessary repairs. . . .

§4.2.3. Richard Serra's *Tilted Arc:* Notoriety in the G.S.A. Program

Among the most notorious of the works commissioned by the G.S.A.'s Art-in-Architecture program is Richard Serra's *Tilted Arc*, created for the plaza in front of the Jacob Javits Federal Building in New York City. The work has been a source of controversy since its placement at 26 Federal Plaza in 1981. On May 31, 1985, Dwight Ink, the acting administrator of the G.S.A., determined that the regional administrator should consider a new location for the piece and, further, requested that the National Endowment for the Arts establish a relocation panel to "review whether a specific alternative location would be an appropriate site."[8] The regional administrator is to consult with the NEA relocation panel before seeking possible alternative sites. Ink further stated that the artist and the Federal Plaza architects "should be consulted" by the panel.[9]

Substantial controversy has been engendered by the Serra sculpture. One commentator believes that the G.S.A., having acknowledged that a mistake was made in selecting the Serra piece, should have it removed and be done with it. In his view the work was a mistake, the selection was a mistake, and it would be an even greater mistake not to recognize these poor judgments. He feels that it is a case of the emperor's new clothes, and that most of the editorial comment was naive and would unwittingly destroy the Art-in-Architecture program. In one editorial it was argued that the public should be drawn into the decision as to whether a work should be selected and then erected: "The G.S.A. must be committed not only to community representation but [also] to establishing a dialogue between newly commissioned work and the public that lives with them."[10] Another called for a "fair procedure" for resolving controversial commissions.[11] In the above commentator's view, however, this would mean the end of the program. Art cannot be determined by voice votes, majority rule, or democratic dialogues. By its very nature, the selection of art is subjective and, for better or worse, elitist. If these approaches were taken up, in the opinion of this commentator, Richard Serra's work would have done more to destroy the Art-in-Architecture program than any other single event.

Another commentator has a slightly different view. His concern is not so much with how the selection was made as with what he considers an unwise attempt to extend the concept of moral right beyond the boundaries of the artwork itself. (For a discussion of moral right, see Chapter 5.) His view of the issue follows.

In urging that there is some legally cognizable relationship between the work of art and its site, Serra and his supporters cannot simply stop at the proposition that this work—because of this relationship—cannot be moved to some other location. Ultimately they must argue that the site itself cannot be substantially altered. If the sculpture is integral to the site,

---

[8] Ink, Acting Administrator of G.S.A., decision on the *Tilted Arc*, May 31, 1985 (summary at iii, ¶2).

[9] *Ibid.*

[10] N.Y. Times, May 19, 1985, §2, at 1.

[11] Tomkins, The New Yorker, May 20, 1985, at 95.

then the site must be equally integral to the sculpture. As Serra himself has testified: "site-specificity and permanence are inseparable."[12] In other words, the site is the ground on which the artist has projected the figure of the sculpture; change that ground and you alter the sculpture. How far does this ground extend? To the facades of the surrounding buildings? To the sky above? To the adjacent streets?

Imagine that the G.S.A. elects to fill the rest of Federal Plaza with 30-foot tall marble likenesses of Civil War generals, or to install the plumbing necessary to create a streaming canopy of water above the sculpture, or to radically alter the shape and size of the plaza, or even all the above. In each instance, the artist could legitimately make the same complaint as Serra has made about the removal of *Tilted Arc:* The bond between his work and its setting will be broken and his aesthetic intentions will have been perverted.

According to the commentator's view, this is the difficulty. Once we acknowledge an artist's right to assure not only the integrity of his work but also the way in which it relates to its environment, then in effect we have permitted him to expropriate that environment. By according to works of art and their authors a status so radically privileged in comparison to other objects and their makers, we would throw into question their continued desirability as public goods. If that should ever happen, then the commentator would likely concur with others who believe that the Art-in-Architecture program (and for that matter, every other public art program) will have been dealt a serious blow. Artworks that expropriate their sites might prove a luxury beyond our means.

§4.2.4. Seattle Arts Commission Program: A Simpler Approach

Through a variety of means (including a 1%-for-art ordinance adopted in 1973), the city of Seattle has long maintained one of the most vigorous public art programs of any municipality in the United States. The works created under this program range from monumental sculptures to artist-designed street furniture. At one extreme are Ronald Bladen's 60-foot construction *Black Lightning* and Stephen Antonakos's neon sculpture for the facade of the Bagley Wright Theatre. At the other are cast-iron manhole covers modeled by Anne Knight (a "map" of the city) and Nathan Jackson (a Tlinget whale). The city has also acquired a

---

[12] R. Serra, Statement at G.S.A. Public Hearing on *Tilted Arc* (March 6, 1985).

large collection of portable works of art — it numbered some 700 objects by the end of 1983 — which is rotated among various public sites (the Citizens Service Bureau and the Licenses Department, for instance) throughout the year.

For the larger "permanently" installed works, the Seattle Arts Commission uses the form of agreement that follows. In at least two particulars (and in both instances, to the artist's advantage) it differs sharply from the preceding G.S.A. contract. Paragraph 12 is a built-in moral right clause that assures that the work cannot be destroyed or altered during the artist's lifetime without the artist's written consent. It is unclear whether the removal of the work to another site would constitute "destruction or alteration." (The answer might perhaps depend on the nature of the work, with an arguably different outcome for a sculpture modeled in the round than for a neon sculpture applied to a facade.) Paragraph 18 clearly reserves the copyright to the artist while granting the city a license (nonexclusive, presumably, although this is not explicit) to reproduce the work for noncommercial purposes. Note also that ¶10 specifically gives the artist the right to have his name associated with the work in a public notice. This is another aspect of the moral right.

Like the G.S.A. contract, the Seattle agreement provides for a fixed fee and requires a careful advance estimate of what the artist's actual costs will be. In other respects, though, its economic terms are gentler. There is no provision for unilateral termination, and there is a broad *force majeur* provision that protects both parties.

SEATTLE ARTS COMMISSION AGREEMENT

This Agreement is entered into by The City of Seattle (hereinafter referred to as "The City"), acting by and through the Seattle Arts Commission and the Executive Secretary thereof, and _____ (hereinafter referred to as the "Artist").

Whereas, the City is implementing a public art program pursuant to Ordinance 102210, as amended, by allocating certain funds for the establishment of artworks in public places and authorizing the making of payments for the design, execution and placement of works of art and the support of an artist-selection process; and

Whereas, Seattle _____ Department 1% for Art funds have been allocated for the selection, purchase and placement of artwork (hereinafter referred to as the " _____ Project"); and

WHEREAS, the Artist was selected by the City through procedures duly adopted by the Seattle Arts Commission; and

WHEREAS, both parties wish the integrity and clarity of the Artist's ideas and statements in the artwork to be maintained;

NOW THEREFORE, in consideration of the mutual covenants hereinafter contained, the parties hereto agree as follows:

1. *Description of Work.* The Artist shall design, fabricate and install the following work of art:

The above work of art hereinafter referred to as the "Work."

2. *Scope of Work.* The Artist shall accomplish the following:

3. *Price and Payment Schedule.* As payment for the services of the Artist and for the completed Work, and subject to the conditions herein, the City shall pay the Artist the total sum of _____ ($ _____) upon invoice from the Artist as follows:

   a) 30 percent upon presentation and acceptance by the Arts Commission of the artwork proposal;
   b) 30 percent upon commencement of fabrication;
   c) 30 percent upon commencement of installation;
   d) 10 percent upon completion and acceptance of the Work by the Arts Commission.

4. *Taxes.*

   a) Sales taxes shall be payable by the City in addition to the actual final cost set forth above.
   b) The Artist is solely responsible for complying with all relevant Federal, State and City laws, including laws related to business tax and license responsibilities.

5. *Non-Discrimination.* In carrying out the performance of the services designated, the Artist shall not discriminate as to race, creed, religion, sex, age, national origin or the presence of any physical, mental or sensory handicap, and the Artist shall comply with the equality of employment opportunity provisions of Seattle Ordinance 101432 as presently existing or hereafter amended.

6. *Review.* The City shall have the right at reasonable times to review the Work while in the process of execution and to receive progress reports.

7. *Protection of Premises.* The Artist must take all reasonable precautions to protect City property adjacent to the installation site of the Work. The Artist will be responsible for securing adequate protection of the public during installation.

8. *Liability.* The Artist shall indemnify and hold the City harmless from any and all loss, claims, actions, or damages suffered by any person or persons not a party to this Agreement by reason of, or resulting from, performance or alleged lack of performance under this Agreement. In the event that any suit based upon such loss, claims, actions, or damages is brought against the City, the Artist shall, upon notice of the commencement thereof, defend the same at its sole cost and expense; and if final judgment be adverse to the City, or the City and the Artist jointly, the Artist shall promptly satisfy the same. The liability described in this Section shall not be diminished by the fact, if it be a fact, that any such death, injury, damage, loss, cost or expense may have been contributed to, or may be alleged to have been contributed to in part by the negligence of the City, its officers, employees or agents; Provided that nothing contained in this Section shall be construed as requiring the Artist to indemnify the City against liability for damages arising out of bodily injury to persons or damage to property caused by or resulting from the sole negligence of the City, its officers, employees or agents.

9. *Compliance with Laws.* The Artist shall comply with all applicable federal and state laws, the Charter and ordinances of the City of Seattle, and rules and regulations of the administrative agencies of all such governmental units.

10. *Notice.* A public notice, including the Artist's name and mention of the City's ownership shall be publicly displayed and identified with the Work, and shall be designed, fabricated, installed and paid for by the Artist.

11. *Guarantee.* The Artist shall guarantee to repair or replace any defects of material or workmanship in the Work for a period of up to one year from date of final payment.

12. *Non-Destruction/Alteration.* The City shall not intentionally destroy the Work during the Artist's lifetime, without the Artist's written consent. Alteration of the Work other than restoration or maintenance shall not be done during the Artist's lifetime without the Artist's written consent. The City has the right to restore and maintain the work as it deems necessary.

13. *No Waiver.* No waiver of full performance by either party shall be construed, or operate, as a waiver of any subsequent default of any of the terms, covenants and conditions of this Agreement. The payment or acceptance of fees for any period after a default shall not be deemed a waiver of any right or acceptance of defective performance.

14. *No Assignment or Transfer.* The rights and privileges granted by this Agreement are not subject to assignment, or transfer in any manner whatsoever without the prior written consent of the City. The giving of a consent to an assignment or transfer shall not authorize a further assignment of lease or transfer without further prior written consent by the City.

15. *Excuse and Suspension of Contractual Obligations.* The parties hereto shall be excused from their affected contractual obligations when their performance is prevented by acts of God, war, war-like operations, civil commotion, riots, labor disputes including strikes, lock-outs and walk-outs, sabotage, governmental regulations or controls, fire, or other casualty. Failure to fulfill contract obligations due to conditions beyond either party's reasonable control will not be considered a breach of contract; *Provided*, those obligations affected shall be suspended only for the duration of such conditions. During the existence of any such condition, both parties shall use a reasonable effort to protect each other's property, equipment and inventory.

16. *Documentation.* As documentation of the Work, the Artist shall provide one unmarked 35 mm. color slide, accurate in color and detail, and the information to complete the catalogue worksheet (Attachment A).

17. *Records.* The City shall maintain on permanent file a record of this Agreement and of the condition and location of the Work as long as the City is the owner of the Work.

18. *Reproduction.* The Artist shall retain the copyright and all other rights in and to the Work except ownership and possession; Provided that the Artist grants to the City an irrevocable license to reproduce the Work in any manner whatsoever, for non-commercial purposes.

19. *Amendments.* No modification or amendment of the terms hereof shall be effective unless written and signed by authorized representatives of the parties hereto. The parties hereto expressly reserve the right to modify this Agreement from time to time by mutual agreement.

20. *Entire Agreement.* This Agreement is all of the covenants, promises, agreements, and conditions, either oral or written, between the parties.

§4.2.5. San Francisco International Airport's Approach to Site-Specific Artworks

Since the end of World War II, municipally owned airports have become increasingly important sites for public art commissions.[13] Among the cities with the most richly developed programs for such commissions is San Francisco. There, 1½% of its International Airport's construction budget was set aside to procure works of art; this amounted to nearly $2 million. The documents that follow illustrate the multi-step approach that San Francisco has at times used to commission these site-specific

---

[13] For an overview of this development, see D. P. Bowman, Design Art and Architecture — A Study of Airports (F.A.A. 1981).

works. We have reproduced the agreement with the Northwest coast artist Larry Kirkland.

The initial step involves the selection of an artist by the San Francisco Art Commission, the body officially authorized to act for the city. This is done through a recommendation made by a joint committee, Airport Art Enrichment. Once a selection is made, the artist is asked to enter into what in essence are two different agreements. The first requires that he submit a formal proposal and prepare a full-scale maquette which remains the artist's property. In addition (see ¶2), the artist must provide extensive technical information relative to the fabrication and maintenance of the proposed final work. For this effort, the artist is paid a fee — in the agreement that follows, $5,000.

The key section is ¶5. This gives the city the option — if the commission approves the maquette and the attendant arrangements for transportation and installation — to trigger a prenegotiated *second agreement* under which the artist is to fabricate and install the final work. This second agreement is incorporated into the first as an appendix. The scheme is eminently practical. Before either the city invests its money in the project or the artist his time in creating a maquette, both parties are assured that there are agreeable terms on which they will be able to proceed if the maquette and attending arrangements prove acceptable. The city, at the same time, remains wholly free to reject the proposal if any part of it proves unacceptable. Under ¶6, it may even recover the fee if the artist sells the maquette within seven years of the date of the agreement. This is apparently the case whether or not the maquette has been accepted and whether or not the selling price equals the fee. The artist is not, however, under any obligation to offer the maquette for sale and may even destroy it without liability to the city.

The second agreement in the example that follows is an elaborate one. It reflects, as it must, the complexities of installing a 67-foot long metal sculpture in an airport, while portions of the facility were still under construction. There is a strong emphasis on structural integrity and the need to meet building code requirements (see ¶¶2(a) and 3(b)). There are also provisions for the contingency that the site may not be ready to receive the sculpture on schedule (see ¶¶3(d), 4(e)(i), and 4(f)). There are also extensive insurance requirements set forth in ¶9, including one that the artist maintain life and disability insurance in an amount of not less than $168,600 (his fee of $149,600 plus the ¶4(i) supplements of $19,000 for lighting and ceiling modifications). The city is at all times to be named as beneficiary for such amounts as the artist may theretofore have received as advances against his fee or as supplementary payments. Fine arts insurance, with the city as a beneficiary, is also to be maintained.

While the agreement ostensibly permits the artist to retain the copyright (¶10(a)), this is to a degree undercut by another provision (in ¶6(d)) that precludes either him or, for 50 years after his death, his heirs from making any further copies of the sculpture on a scale exceeding 75% of the dimensions of the commissioned work. This may be subject to the 35-year termination provision of the Copyright Revision Act of 1976. Paragraph 10(b) concerning the right of display appears to be superfluous and possibly based on a misreading of the federal Copyright Act. As the owner of the work, the city does not require a license from the copyright holder to display the work. (See §109(b) of the Copyright Revision Act of 1976.) Paragraph 10(d) is a curiously elaborate provision providing for royalties on poster sales.

With respect to moral right, in ¶14 the parties acknowledge that the California Art Preservation Act (reproduced in Chapter 5) is controlling. This is strengthened by additional provisions favorable to the artist that concern label credits (¶¶11(a) and 11(b)), repairs and restoration (¶13), and reputation (¶15(a)). Also beneficial to the artist (albeit at a price) is ¶16, which permits him to buy the work back if the city gives him notice, within three years after the date of the agreement, that it intends to remove the work. After such period, the city is presumably free to do whatever it wants with the work, subject, of course, to the continuing restraints on defacement, mutilation, alteration, or destruction set forth in the Art Preservation Act.

SAN FRANCISCO INTERNATIONAL AIRPORT AGREEMENTS*

AGREEMENT

FOR

PROPOSAL FOR WORK OF ART

AND

OPTION ON AGREEMENT TO FABRICATE AND INSTALL WORK
AT SAN FRANCISCO INTERNATIONAL AIRPORT
BOARDING AREA B
HANGING SCULPTURE

The parties to this agreement are the City and County of San Francisco, acting by and through its Art Commission ["Commission"] and

---

* These agreements are between the San Francisco International Airport and artist Larry Kirkland. Signatures have been omitted.

LARRY KIRKLAND ["Artist"]. For the convenience of the parties, this agreement is dated August 1, 1984.

RECITALS

A. Pursuant to Section 3.13 of the San Francisco Administrative Code, the City has allocated funds for acquisition of works of art to adorn the South Terminal at San Francisco International Airport and authorized the Commission to supervise and control the expenditures for these works.

B. The Commission has appointed a Joint Committee, Airport Art Enrichment, ["Committee"] to evaluate and recommend artists to produce works of art for the Airport.

C. Charter Section 3.601 requires that the Commission approve a design or model of a work of art for a specific location before letting a contract for the work.

D. The Committee has recommended that the Commission obtain a proposal from the Artist for a work of art for a specific location in the Airport with an option to enter into another agreement for fabrication, transportation and installation of the work.

E. The Commission, by resolution number 1984-<u>184</u>, approved the Committee's recommendation and authorized its Director to enter into an agreement with the Artist on the terms which follow.

TERMS OF AGREEMENT

1. *Submission of Proposal.* The Artist shall submit to the Commission no later than August 15, 1984 a proposal for a work of art suitable for installation in the South Terminal of the San Francisco International Airport. A description and sketch of the location for which the work is to be proposed, and the specifications for the proposed work are set forth as Appendix A [omitted]. Site plans have already been provided the Artist.

2. *Contents of Proposal.* The Artist's proposal shall consist of:

a. One maquette of the proposed work, to-scale and illustrating the relationship of the work to the site. Because of the materials in which the Artist works, the to-scale maquette will be too large to transport from the Artist's studio in Portland, Ore., the Artist will supply the Commission with color slides or prints of the maquette illustrating it from all points from which it may be viewed when installed. The Artist and Committee agree that approval of the proposed work shall be based on slides, photographs or other illustrations of the maquette. If requested to do so by the Committee, the Artist will allow studio visits for review and/or approval of the proposed work.

b. A section or cross-section of the proposed work which represents the full thickness of the materials to be used, the surface treatment of the materials and any edges, welds or transitions which will appear in the finished work.

c. A description of all materials to be used, their durability, and the degree to which they are weather and fire resistent; the manner in which the edges of the work and base will be finished; the total height, diameter and the estimated weight of the work, including any base and structural support; and any unusual maintenance or conservation requirements.

d. A description of a recommended routine maintenance program.

e. A description of the method of fabrication and installation.

f. An estimate of the time required for installation of the proposed work and a description of any large equipment which will be used.

g. A description of any barriers which may be necessary for protection of the public or the proposed work.

h. The fee for fabrication, transportation and installation of the work on the terms set forth in the agreement which appears as Appendix B and is incorporated herein by reference. The fee shall not be in excess of $170,000.

3. *Consultation.* It is anticipated that the Artist will consult with the Committee and the architects for the Airport in order to prepare the proposal. The Commission will be responsible for scheduling these consultations. The cost of engineering or other drawings and travel to the site in connection with preparation of the proposal is the responsibility of the Artist.

4. *Viewing Maquette.* The Artist agrees that the Commission may have access to his studio during reasonable hours to view the maquette, if so desired.

5. *City's Option.* The Artist agrees that, if requested to do so in writing by the Commission, the Artist will enter into an agreement for the fabrication, transportation and installation of the work proposed by the Artist on the terms set forth in the agreement to fabricate, transport and install work of art, which is attached hereto as Appendix B and incorporated herein. This right of the City is hereinafter referred to as the "City's option." The City's option right runs for 180 days from the date the Artist's proposal is submitted to the Commission. Nothing in this agreement, or in the relationship of the parties hereto, shall be construed as obligating the City to exercise the City's option.

6. *Fee.* For the proposal including the Artist's time, materials and all shipping costs, and the City's option, the City shall pay the Artist the sum of $5,000. If the Artist sells the maquette within 7 years of the date of this agreement, the Artist agrees to refund the fee to the City. If the Artist destroys the maquette, he will notify the City that this has been done.

7. *Reproduction of Maquette Photographs.* The Artist hereby authorizes the City to make, and to authorize the making of, reproductions of the photographs of the maquette for publicity and program purposes.

8. *Employment Nondiscrimination.* The Artist shall not discriminate against any employee or applicant for employment because of race, creed, ancestry, sexual preference, disability, sex, marital status, age, religion, or national origin.

9. *Notices.* Submittals, requests, notices and reports required under this agreement shall be delivered as follows:

For the Artist: Larry Kirkland. . . .

cc: Louise Allrich
Allrich Gallery
251 Post Street
San Francisco, CA 94108

For the Commission: San Francisco Arts Commission
45 Hyde Street, Room 319
San Francisco, CA 94102
Attn: Regina Almaguer

A change in the designation of the person or address to which submittals, requests, notices and reports shall be delivered is effective when the other party has received notice of the change by certified mail.

APPENDIX B

AGREEMENT
TO
FABRICATE, TRANSPORT AND INSTALL A WORK OF ART
AT SAN FRANCISCO INTERNATIONAL AIRPORT
BOARDING AREA B
HANGING SCULPTURE

The parties to this agreement are the City and County of San Francisco, acting by and through its Art Commission ["Commission"] and LARRY KIRKLAND ["Artist"]. For the convenience of the parties, this agreement is dated September 1, 1984.

RECITALS

A. Pursuant to Section 3.13 of the San Francisco Administrative Code, the City has allocated funds for acquisition of works of art to adorn the South Terminal at the San Francisco International Airport and authorized the Commission to supervise and control the expenditures for these works.

B. The Commission has appointed a Joint Committee, Airport Art Enrichment, ["Committee"] to research and recommend artists to produce works of art for the Airport.

C. Charter Section 3.601 requires that the Commission approve a design or model of a work of art for a specific location before a contract is let for the work.

D. Pursuant to an agreement between the City and the Artist dated August 1, 1984, the Artist submitted a proposal for a work of art for a specific location at the Airport to the Committee.

E. The Committee approved the Artist's maquette and recommended that the Commission enter into an agreement with the Artist for the work if the work as described in the remaining components of the proposal to be submitted to the Commission by the Artist pursuant to the terms of the August 1, 1984 agreement ["Proposal"] are first approved by the Committee.

F. The Commission, by resolution number _____; accepted the Committee's recommendation and authorized its Director to enter into this agreement with the Artist for fabrication, transportation and installation of the work in the proposed location at the Airport on the terms which follow if the Proposal is approved by the Committee.

G. On _____, the Committee approved the Artist's Proposal.

Terms of Agreement

1. *Scope of Artist's Services.*

(a) *Fabrication, Transportation and Installation.* The Artist shall fabricate the work of art, or cause it to be fabricated, under the artist's personal supervision, in conformity with the Proposal approved by the Committee and the following specifications:

Dimensions 19' high × 67' long × 24' wide (approx.)
Materials aluminum, sheet metal, stainless steel, paint
Support or Base
Estimated Weight of Work with Base 2,000 estimated
This work shall be entitled

_____.

The work shall not deviate in size, design or material from the Proposal and the foregoing specifications unless the change is approved by resolution of the Commission. The Artist is also responsible for transportation of the work to, and installation of the work at the site specified in Paragraph 2 and for all of the expenses associated with fabrication, transportation and installation of the work.

(b) *Consultation and Deviations from Proposal.* The goal of the parties is a work which represents the creative talents of the Artist and satisfies the specifications set forth in Appendix A to the agreement for the Proposal, [omitted]. [See Paragraph 1 of the agreement for the Proposal]. The parties recognize that they must consult closely during fabrication and installation of the work in order to accomplish these goals and that changes in the design may become desirable as the work is fabricated. However, the work may not deviate from the Proposal and the specifications set forth in subparagraph (a) unless the deviation is approved by resolution of the Commission. Conformance of the work with the terms set forth in subparagraph (a) is an essential element of this agreement.

2. *Plans for Installation and Identification of Subcontractor.*

(a) *Plans for Installation.* No later than August 1, 1985, the Artist shall submit to the Commission plans for installation of the work prepared by a structural engineer licensed by the State of California and conforming to Uniform Building Code requirements.

(b) *Fabrication by Subcontractor.* If the work will be fabricated by a subcontractor, the Artist shall provide the Commission with the name, address and telephone number of the subcontractor no later than October 15, 1984.

3. *Fabrication and Installation.*

(a) *Schedule for Fabrication and Installation.* The Artist shall complete fabrication of the work no later than July 15, 1985; provided, however, if the Artist returns an executed original of this agreement to the Commission by September 15, 1984, but does not receive his first interim payment under the agreement by October 15, 1984, the date for completing fabrication of the work shall be extended automatically by one day for every day between October 15, 1984 and the date he receives the first interim payment. No later than October 1, 1985, the Commission shall designate a two week period in which the work shall be installed. The Artist shall give the Commission no less than 15 days notice of the day installation of the work is to begin. Timely fabrication and installation of the work is an essential element of this agreement.

(b) *Review of Work.* The Committee and the Commission shall be given access to the work during reasonable business hours in order to review the work and the Artist's progress with fabrication of it.

(c) *Reports on Fabrication and Installation.* The Artist shall submit written reports to the Commission no later than August 1, 1985, describing (1) the fabrication process and (2) the details involved in installation of the work. The report on fabrication shall include the names of any assistants who are responsible for major portions of the fabrication process. The report shall be accompanied by photographs or slides showing the fabrication process and substantiating that the fabrication process has been completed. The report on installation shall include plans for installation and a description of any activities which will have to be coordinated with either the Artist's subcontractors or City personnel or contractors.

(d) *Storage and Insurance.* If the period designated by the Commission for installation of the work begins later than April 1, 1986, the City will be responsible for the reasonable cost of storing and insuring the work until the period for installation.

(e) *Site, Site Preparation, and Access.* The Artist shall install the completed work at the San Francisco International Airport South Terminal location described in Appendix A [omitted] to the agreement for a Proposal [site]. The City shall provide the site broom clean and free of obstructions. Any other preparation of the site is the responsibility of the Artist.

(f) *Alteration of Site.* If the site as constructed differs substantially from the site plans provided the Artist and such differences would significantly affect the cost of installing the work, the City shall be deemed to have waived its right to require the Artist to install the work unless the City agrees to pay for the increased costs of installation directly attributable to the differences in the site.

(g) *Arrangements for Access.* Arrangements for access to the site for installation must be made through the Commission and access shall not be scheduled until the Commission has received a certificate evidencing liability insurance as required by paragraph 9. Access to the site may be scheduled for night or early morning hours to avoid interference with passenger flow, airline use, and construction activities. The Artist shall provide the Commission with a written list of the workers, vehicles and equipment which will be involved in the installation of the work at least 15 days in advance of installation so that permits can be issued and security and unloading arrangements made. Cost for vehicle parking shall be the responsibility of the Artist.

(h) *Structural Requirements.* The Artist shall consult with the project architects to determine as early as possible whether a base or footing, or any other type of structural support, is required for installation of the work. Unless the Commission agrees in writing to the contrary, the Artist is responsible for the cost and installation of any structural support required especially for the work.

4. *Fee, Interim Payments and Additional Services.*

(a) *Fee.* The Artist's fee for fabrication, transportation and installation of the work, including all expenses relating thereto, whether or not identified in the itemization of expenses included in the Proposal, is $149,600. (U.S.) The fee is due and payable by the City when the work is finally accepted by the Commission and an invoice submitted by the Artist. The commission will make a good faith effort to process the final payment so that it reaches the Artist within 30 days of the date the

Commission adopts a resolution finally accepting the work pursuant to subsection 3(c).

(b) *Interim Payments.* The City is not obligated to pay any part of the Artist's fee unless and until the work is finally accepted by the Commission. The City will, however, make payments to the Artist against the fee to assist the Artist with financing the execution, transportation and installation of the work. The amount of the payments is based on the Artist's documented need and shall be made as follows:

(i) Upon contract certification and submission of a request for payment: $52,360.00. [Unless specifically approved by resolution of the Commission, this amount may not exceed 35% of the fee.]

(ii) Following (A) the Commission's determination that fabrication of the work in studio has been ⅔ completed, (B) submission of the Artist's reports on fabrication as ⅔ completed and (C) review and approval of the work as ⅔ completed by authorized representatives of the Commission and (D) request for an interim payment: $29,920.00. [Unless specifically approved by resolution of the Commission, this amount may not exceed 20% of the fee.]

(iii) Following (A) the Commission's determination that fabrication of the work in studio has been completed, (B) submission of the Artist's reports on fabrication and installation of the work, (C) review and approval of the work by authorized representatives of the Commission, (D) submission of a certificate evidencing liability insurance coverage as set forth in paragraph 9, and (E) a request for an interim payment: $22,440.00. [Unless specifically approved by resolution of the Commission, this amount may not exceed 15% of the fee.]

(c) *Effect of Approval for Interim Payment.* Approval of the work to permit an interim payment is solely for the benefit of the Artist. Unless the approval of the work is in the form of a resolution by the Commission, the approval does not constitute acceptance or approval of the work by the City nor shall it be construed as a waiver of the City's right to require that the work conform strictly to the Proposal and to the specifications set forth in subparagraph 1(a).

(d) *Final Acceptance by the City.* The work shall be finally accepted by the City when the Commission adopts a resolution finding:

(i) that the work conform to the Proposal and specifications set forth in subparagraph 1(a) hereof, or to any modifications thereof approved by resolution of the Commission;

(ii) that the Artist transported the work to and installed the work at the site on a timely basis, or that the Commission for good cause waived the City's right to so require; and

(iii) that the Artist is in substantial compliance with the other terms of this agreement which the Commission has not waived.

(iv) that the Commission will make a good faith effort to complete the review process and adopt the foregoing resolution within 45 days of the Artist notifying the Commission that he has completed the installation of the work.

(e) *Waiver of Final Acceptance.* If the Artist is in all other respects in compliance with the terms of this agreement, the City shall be deemed to have waived:

(i) the Artist's obligation to transport and install the work at the site, if the Artist is not given access to the site for installation by April 1, 1986; or

(ii) the right to reject the work as not conforming to the Proposal or the specifications set forth in paragraph 1(a), if the work is accessible within 20 miles of San Francisco for review by the Commission and the Commission fails to determine by September 15, 1985 whether or not the work conforms to the Proposal and specifications as provided for in subparagraph 4(d)(i).

The Artist may relinquish the right to enforce the foregoing waivers in a dated, signed writing.

(f) *Waiver of Installation.* If for any reason the Commission waives the Artist's obligation to transport and install the work at the site, [an amount] to be determined, which represents the anticipated savings to the Artist, shall be deducted from the fee otherwise payable pursuant to subparagraph 4(a).

(g) *Refund of Interim Payments.* If the City terminates this agreement pursuant to paragraph 24, the Artist must refund the interim payments.

(h) *Sales Tax.* The Commission will be responsible for any sales tax which may be due on the fees.

(i) *Additional Services.* In addition to fabricating, transporting and installing the work, the artist will design and install special lighting for the work and a modification to the ceiling in order that the structural attachments of the work may be recessed. Upon receipt of documentation of incurred expenses, the City will reimburse the artist for his out-of-pocket costs of these items, not to exceed $12,000 for lighting and $7,000 for modification of the ceiling.

5. *Indemnification.* The Artist agrees to defend, indemnify and hold harmless the City and County of San Francisco, its members, officers, agents and employees, from and against all claims, costs and damages arising out of the Artist's activities under this agreement.

6. *Artist's Warranties.*

(a) *Defects in Material or Workmanship and Inherent Vice.* The Artist warrants that the work will be free of defects in workmanship or materials, including inherent vice, and that the Artist will, at the Artist's own expense, remedy any defects due to faulty workmanship or materials, or to inherent vice, which appear within a period of three years of the date the work is finally accepted by the City. If the work should deteriorate because of an inherent vice between three and fifteen years from the date the work is finally accepted by the City, the Artist will repair or replace the work for the cost of materials and supplies. "Inherent vice" refers to a quality within the material or materials which comprise the work which, either alone or in combination, results in the tendency of the work to destroy itself. "Inherent vice" does not include any tendency to deteriorate which is specifically identified in the Proposal submitted by the Artist.

(b) *Public Safety.* The Artist warrants that the work will not contain sharp points or edges which the Commission deems a danger to the public and agrees to cooperate in making or permitting adjustments to the work if necessary to eliminate other hazards which become apparent within one year of the date the work is finally accepted by the City.

(c) *Title.* The Artist warrants that the work is the result of the artistic efforts of the Artist and that it will be installed free and clear of any liens, claims or other encumbrances of any type.

(d) *Unique.* The Artist warrants that the work is unique and an edition of one, and that the Artist will not execute or authorize another to execute another work of the same design, dimensions and materials as the work commissioned pursuant to this agreement. For the purposes of this warranty, if the dimensions of another work exceed 75% of the dimensions of the commissioned work, the other work shall be deemed to be of the same dimensions as the commissioned work. This warranty shall continue in effect for a period consisting of the life of the Artist plus 50 years and shall be binding on the Artist's heirs and assigns.

7. *Excuse or Suspension of Contractual Obligations.* The parties shall be excused from performing an obligation under this agreement if performance of that obligation is prevented by a condition beyond the control of the parties, such as acts of God, war, public emergency, or strike or other labor disturbance. An obligation affected by a condition beyond the control of the parties shall be suspended only for the duration of the condition. Both parties shall take all reasonable steps during the existence of the condition to assure performance of their contractual obligations when the condition no longer exists.

8. *Claims, Mediation and Arbitration.*

(a) *Claims.* Each claim against the City arising out of this Agreement shall be submitted to the Controller of the City and County of San Francisco or to the Clerk of the Board of Supervisors within 100 days of the time that the cause of action arises. This requirement is in accordance with California Government Code Sections 910 and following. Any claim expressly denied or deemed denied by the City and County of San Francisco may be submitted to mediation or arbitration as provided in subsection (b).

(b) *Mediation and Arbitration.* The parties may submit disputes or claims arising under this agreement to mediation or nonbinding arbitration. For this purpose, the parties may utilize the services of the Arts Arbitration and Mediation Services, a program of Bay Area Lawyers for the Arts, or some other service acceptable to the parties.

9. *Insurance.*

(a) *Type, Amount, and Duration.* The Artist shall:

(i) Procure and maintain until the work is finally accepted by the City life and disability insurance in an amount not less than $168,600 with the City named as the beneficiary of an amount equal to the total of the Proposal fee and any interim payments made pursuant to this agreement.

(ii) Procure and maintain throughout the fabrication, transportation and installation phases of this agreement, worker's compensation, with employer's liability insurance, with limits of no less than $1 million each accident. If the Artist has no employees as defined by California Labor Code Sections 3350-3371, and the Artist submits a letter so stating, this requirement may be waived in writing by the Commission.

(iii) Procure and maintain until the work is installed by the artist and custody relinquished to the City, fine arts insurance on all-risk form with limits not less than $168,600 and deductible not to exceed $1,000 each loss, with any loss payable to the City as its interests may appear.

(iv) Procure prior to requesting the second interim payment, or entering the Airport premises for the purpose of installing the work, whichever occurs earlier, and maintain until the work is accepted by the City:

(A) General liability insurance, with limits of not less than $1 million each occurrence, combined single limit bodily injury and property damage, including coverage for contractual liability, broad form property damage, completed operations and, if any subcontracted work, independent contractors.

(B) Automobile liability insurance with limits not less than $1 million each occurrence combined single limit for bodily injury and property damage, including coverages for owned, non-owned and hired vehicles, as applicable.

(b) *Endorsements.* Automobile and general liability insurance shall be endorsed to:

(i) Name as additional insureds the City and County of San Francisco and the Joint Committee, Airport Art Enrichment, and their officers, agents and employees.

(ii) Provide that the policies are primary insurance to any other insurance available to the additional insureds, with respect to claims arising out of this agreement, and that the insurance applies separately to each insured against whom claim is made or suit is brought.

(iii) Provide 45 days advance written notice of cancellation, non-renewal or reduction in coverage mailed to:

Claire Isaacs, Director
San Francisco Art Commission
45 Hyde Street, Room 319
San Francisco, 94102

(c) *Certificate.* Certificates of insurance evidencing worker's compensation and fine arts coverages and endorsements set forth above shall be furnished to the City prior to certification of this agreement by the Controller. Certificates of insurance evidencing the liability coverages and endorsements set forth above shall be furnished to the City at the time of the Artist's request for the second interim payment, or of the Artist's request for access to the site for installation of the work, whichever may occur earlier. Upon request certified copies of all policies shall be furnished to the City.

(d) *Fine Arts After Installation.* The City shall procure and maintain fine arts insurance on the work on an all-risk form with limits not less than $168,600.00, and deductible not to exceed $1000 each loss, from the time the work is installed at the site and the Artist relinquishes custody to the City, until the work is finally accepted by the City and the fee is paid to the Artist. The Artist shall be named as an additional insured on the policy. A certificate of insurance evidencing such coverage shall be furnished to the Artist upon request. The Commission will prepare a condition report on the work as installed. The City will accept custody of the work when the condition report has been approved by the Artist or a person authorized in writing by the Artist to act on behalf of the Artist.

10. *Copyright.*

(a) *General.* The Artist shall place a copyright notice on the work in the form and manner required to protect copyrights in the work under United States copyright law. If the copyright is registered with the U.S. Copyright Office, the artist shall provide the City with a copy of the application for registration, the registration number and the effective date of registration. Except as provided in this agreement, the Artist retains all copyrights in the work.

(b) *Display.* The Artist hereby grants the City the exclusive right to display the work and to loan the work to other persons or institutions with authority to display it publicly.

(c) *Reproductions.* The Artist hereby authorizes the City to make, and to authorize the making of, photographs and other two-dimensional reproductions of the work for educational, public relations, arts promotional and other noncommercial purposes. For the purposes of this agreement, the following are deemed to be reproductions for noncommercial purposes: reproduction in exhibition catalogues, books, slides, photographs, postcards, posters, and calendars; in art magazines, art books and art and news sections of newspapers; in general books and magazines not primarily devoted to art but of an educational, historical or critical nature; slides and film strips not intended for a mass audience; and television from stations operated for educational purposes or on programs for educational purposes from all stations. On any and all such reproductions, the City shall place a copyright notice in the form and manner required to protect the copyrights in the works under the United States copyright law.

(d) *Royalties on Posters.* The City shall pay to the Artist 50% of any royalty which the City receives from the sale of poster reproductions of the work in excess of 7500 copies. If the City makes poster reproductions itself, it shall pay to the Artist a royalty of 15% on the net wholesale price from the sale of reproductions in excess of 7500 copies. For the purposes of this section, the "net wholesale price" is the wholesale billing price to customers or distributors less customary discounts and allowances actually allowed and less any returns and transportation charges allowed on returns. The Artist is responsible for keeping the Commission informed of his or her current address, and the City shall mail notice of any amount due hereunder to the Artist annually at his or her last known address. The right to any royalty not claimed within three years from the date of the annual notice to the Artist reverts to the City.

11. *Credits.*

(a) *Label.* A label identifying the Artist, the title of the work and the year it is completed shall be publicly displayed in the area adjacent to the work.

(b) *Artist's Credit.* The City agrees that unless the Artist requests to the contrary in writing, all references to the work and all reproductions of the work shall credit the work to the Artist.

(c) *City's Credit.* The Artist agrees that all formal references to the work shall include the following credit line: "From the Collection of the City and County of San Francisco, San Francisco International Airport Commissioned through the Joint Committee of the San Francisco Arts Commission and San Francisco Airports Commission."

12. *Documentation.* The Artist shall provide information on the work requested by the Commission for its registration files and two copies of any slides or photographs the Artist takes to document the work after it is installed. The City shall provide the Artist with one 35-mm color slide of the work, accurate in color and detail, after the work has been installed.

13. *Repair and Restoration.* It is the policy of the Commission to consult with an Artist regarding repairs and restoration which are undertaken during the Artist's lifetime when that is practicable. To facilitate consul-

tation, Artist will, to the extent feasible, notify the Commission of any change in permanent address.

14. *California Art Preservation Act.* A copy of the California Art Preservation Act, Section 987 of the California Civil Code, which generally prohibits the physical defacement, mutilation, alteration or destruction of a work of fine art by anyone other than the Artist, appears as Exhibit A [omitted] hereto for reference by the parties.

15. *Reputation.*

(a) *City's Commitment.* The City agrees that it will not use the work or the Artist's name in a way which reflects discredit on the work or on the name of the Artist or on the reputation of the Artist as an artist.

(b) *Artist's Commitment.* The Artist agrees that Artist will not make reference to the work or reproduce the work, or any portion thereof, in a way which reflects discredit on the City or the work.

16. *Return of Work.* If the Commission removes the work permanently from the site within three years of the date of this agreement, the Commission shall give the Artist prompt notice of the removal. The work will be returned to the Artist and the City will waive its right to make additional reproductions of the work if the Artist refunds to the City the fee paid pursuant to this agreement within 60 days of receiving notice of the removal and pays all of the expenses related to the return.

17. *Title and Risk of Loss.* Title to the work passes to the City when the fee is paid to the Artist. The Artist bears the risk of damage to or loss of the work until title passes to the City.

18. *No Assignment or Transfer.* The personal skill, judgment and creativity of the Artist is an essential element of this Agreement. Therefore, although the parties recognize that the Artist may employ qualified personnel to work under Artist's supervision, the Artist shall not assign, transfer or subcontract the creative and artistic portions of the work to another party without the prior written consent of the City.

19. *Artist as Independent Contractor.* The Artist shall perform all work under this agreement as an independent contractor and not as an agent or an employee of the City.

20. *Employment Non-Discrimination.* The provisions of Section 12.B.2 of the San Francisco Administrative Code are attached hereto as Exhibit B and incorporated herein.

21. *Amendments.* No modification or amendment of the terms of this agreement shall be effective unless written and signed by authorized representatives of the parties hereto.

22. *Governing Law.* This agreement and all matters pertaining thereto shall be construed according to the laws of the State of California.

23. *Budget and Fiscal Provisions of Charter.* This agreement is subject to the budget and fiscal provisions of the City's Charter. Charges will accrue only after the City's Controller certifies that funds are available for

the City's obligation under the agreement. The amount of the City's obligation under this agreement shall not exceed the amount certified as available for the purposes stated in the agreement. This section shall control against any and all other provisions of this agreement.

24. *Remedies for Violation of Terms of Agreement.*

(a) The remedy described in subparagraph (b) is in addition to all other remedies available to either party under the laws of the State of California should the other party fail to comply with the terms of this agreement.

(b) The City may terminate this agreement if the work as fabricated does not conform to the Proposal and the specifications as provided in paragraph 1(a) hereof. The agreement shall be deemed terminated 60 days after the Commission delivers to the Artist a notice of intent to terminate. The notice shall specify the grounds for termination. The Commission may rescind the notice or extend the date for termination, but no rescission or extension is valid unless it is in writing and approved by resolution of the Commission. If the agreement is terminated pursuant to this paragraph, the Artist shall refund any interim payments which have been made.

25. *Notices.* Submittals, requests, notices and reports required under this agreement shall be delivered as follows:

For the Artist: Larry Kirkland. . . .

cc: Louise Allrich
     Allrich Gallery
     251 Post Street
     San Francisco, CA 94108
For the Commission: San Francisco Art Commission
     45 Hyde Street, Room 319
     San Francisco, Calif. 94102
     Attn: Regina Almaguer

A change in the designation of the person or address to which submittals, requests, notices and reports shall be delivered is effective when the other party has received notice of the change by certified mail.

§4.2.6. Temporary Installation Pieces: *Sic Transit*

A phenomenon of recent years has been the creation by visual artists of installation pieces or projects designed for particular spaces in museums, commercial art galleries, or outdoor sites. Often constructed of disposable and even mundane materials, such pieces are frequently (but by no means always — consider Red Grooms' *Ruckus Manhattan*) intended to have only a transient existence. In many instances they resemble stage sets into which the viewer is invited. In others, like Bernini's

Ecstasy of St. Theresa, they are intended to be seen from a discrete dis-tance.[14]

Installation pieces strongly resemble public commissions in that gen-erally they are created under a patronage agreement of some sort. Where they differ most importantly is in the necessity that such an agreement clearly set forth what is to happen at the expiration of the limited period for which their existence is scheduled. Any vagueness, either as to the length of this period or as to the actions expected or permitted at its conclusion, can have damaging consequences. Consider, for example, the case of a museum that is unable to locate an artist at the close of an exhibition and undertakes to remove such a piece itself. Unless there has been a clear, prior understanding, it may thereafter be perceived that the museum has "destroyed" or "thrown into the trash" what an artist can publicly claim was still existing as a viable work of art.

The agreement that follows is a relatively simple one used by the Walker Art Center in Minneapolis for an exhibition entitled *Scale and Environment: 10 Sculptors,* which it mounted in the autumn of 1977. In form, the agreement provided for the artist to perform a residency at the center, the purpose being the creation of an installation piece. (A contract such as this, instead of the customary museum loan agreement, was necessary since, apart from the "idea" for such a piece, there was gener-ally nothing that existed to be borrowed.) Cast as an agreement for services, it provided for the artist to receive a fee, a living stipend, and travel reimbursement.

From the center's point of view, some of the more important provi-sions of the agreement were ¶3, which puts a cap on the expenses that could be charged to it, the last sentence of ¶7, which gave it the right to remove and dispose of the work if the artist failed to do so, and ¶8, which freed it from any liability concerning damage to the work. This last would presumably bar any claim by the artist for damages resulting from the center's total destruction of the piece — a contingency that the agree-ment contemplated.

The first sentence of ¶7 is particularly worth noting. It gave the center the right to remove the piece before the scheduled end of the exhibition, or even to remove it before the exhibition actually opened. Such a provi-sion is of the utmost importance. A temporary installation piece may initially be no more than a general plan in an artist's mind. As the piece

---

[14] For a useful outline of a number of the problems that an organization should consider when planning to commission such an installation piece, see Fox, The Thorny Issues of Temporary Art, Museum News, July-Aug. 1979.

proceeds towards realization — a process that the artist Paul Thek has likened to that of improvisation in jazz — the museum or other patron may not be in a position to play any ongoing role as either a critic or a censor. Its only choice may be to allow the artist to complete the piece and then, having paid the fee in full, make a decision as to whether it should be exhibited. In the overwhelming number of instances it will be. There may, however, be instances in which the patron would prefer not to exhibit the work (for example, if it turned out to be pornographic, or subversive, or defamatory). Under this sort of provision, the patron retains that choice. For the artist to whom this sort of arrangement is unacceptable, the alternative is to plan such a piece in sufficient detail that the patron can make a final decision before the installation begins. What can happen in the absence of either a flexible contract provision or such detailed advance planning can be seen in the case of *Wong v. Vancouver Art Gallery*, discussed at the end of this chapter.

WALKER ART CENTER AGREEMENT FOR TEMPORARY INSTALLATION PIECES

[TITLE OF WORK AND/OR EXHIBITION]

ARTIST IN RESIDENCE AGREEMENT

This agreement is made this _____ day of _____ 19 ____, by and between WALKER ART CENTER, a Minnesota nonprofit corporation, with offices at Vineland Place, Minneapolis, Minnesota 55403 (hereinafter referred to as "Walker"), and _____ (hereinafter referred to as the "Artist"), for the purpose of defining the terms of the Artist's residency at Walker.

RECITALS

For valuable consideration Walker and Artist agree as follows:

1. The Artist shall perform a residency at Walker including appearances at Walker in accordance with the scope of services (the "Services") set forth on Schedule A attached hereto.

2. As full compensation to the Artist for the performance of the Services pursuant to this Agreement, Walker shall pay to the Artist the following: Fee: $_____

      Living Stipend: $_____ a week for no more than ____ weeks

       Travel: $_____ for roundtrip auto and subsistence expenses from _____ to Minneapolis

The fee will be paid to the Artist upon completion of the Services and other payments will be made promptly after receipt by Walker of Artist's itemized invoices.

3. The materials, services, labor and essential equipment specified on Schedule B attached hereto shall be provided by Walker up to a maximum cost of $_____.

4. The Artist agrees to permit Walker to photograph the Artist's work (the "Work") for incorporation into the record describing the artist residency program at Walker and for such purposes that Walker shall determine. Such photographs shall be the property of Walker.

5. Any plans, diagrams, drawings and models received from Artist for purpose of planning and/or exhibition shall remain the property of the Artist.

6. The Artist shall receive from Walker at no cost five (5) copies of the exhibition catalogue and the following photographic documentation of the Work: 10 color slides of installation of Work, 5 color slides of completed Work, 5 black and white 8 x 10" photographs of completed Work. Additional slides and photographs will be provided to the Artist at the standard Walker photographic services fee.

7. The Work shall remain on its site from the date of completion until _____ subject to earlier removal at the option, sole discretion and expense of Walker. At such time, the Artist shall remove all the work at Artist's own expense. Should the Artist fail to remove all the Work by _____, it shall become the property of Walker which may utilize or dispose of the Work.

8. Walker will provide on site inspection of the Work twice daily. Walker agents and employees shall not be responsible or liable for any damage or destruction whatsoever to the Work or any artwork or equipment of Artist regardless of the cause of such destruction or damage. If Artist desires insurance, Artist shall provide insurance for the Work and equipment.

9. Artist shall be an independent contractor during the period of performance under this Agreement and not an employee of Walker. Artist shall be required to carry whatever insurance is deemed necessary for purposes of performance hereunder. Artist agrees to defend, indemnify and hold harmless Walker from any and all claims and liabilities arising directly or indirectly out of the Artist's activities hereunder.

10. Any reproduction or exhibition of any artwork produced as a result of this Agreement shall carry the credit line "Installation, Walker Art Center, Minneapolis."

11. This Agreement is intended to secure the personal Services of the Artist and shall not be transferred or assigned in any manner whatsoever without the prior written consent of the Walker.

IN WITNESS WHEREOF, the parties hereto have executed this Agreement as of the day and year first above written.

SCHEDULE A

1. Construction of the Work on a site designated by Walker and the Artist.
2. The Artist shall perform in residency at Walker for not less than three weeks and no more than four weeks.

SCHEDULE B

1. Material for construction of the Work: steel, lumber, concrete and miscellaneous hardware.
2. Equipment for construction of the Work: arc welder, oxygen and acetylene tanks, cement mixer and sand blaster.
3. Services to be provided for construction of the Work: excavation of land.

§4.2.7. *Wong v. Vancouver Art Gallery:* **An Example of What Can Go Wrong**

Wong v. Vancouver Art Gallery is a suit still pending before the Canadian courts. Involving a temporary installation piece that was commissioned but never put on exhibit (or not, in any event, by its patron), the case vividly illustrates what can go wrong when neither the artist nor his patron gives sufficient consideration in advance as to how their relationship will be structured.

The plaintiff is Paul Wong, a young Canadian video artist. In November, 1983, Wong—whose work had been shown at the Vancouver Art Gallery on several previous occasions—was approached by a member of the Vancouver Art Gallery curatorial staff and asked to prepare a video piece to serve as the opening presentation in a new exhibition space that the gallery was then constructing. Working under a grant from the Canada Council, Wong created a piece entitled *Confused: Sexual Views*. It consisted of 27 interviews, each in a straight-on, head-and-shoulders view, of different individuals responding to an off-camera interviewer about their sexual interests, fantasies, experiences, and opinions. In all, there were some nine hours of tape intended to be played in a variety of combinations through four video monitors. After one postponement, the piece was scheduled to "open" on February 24, 1984.

That the gallery had advance notice of the contents is not disputed. In the February/March calendar sent to its members, *Confused: Sexual Views* was described as ". . . provocative, entertaining, humorous and moving. Because the subject matter may be offensive to some people, entry is restricted to those 18 years and over." Similar language was used in a press release. Nonetheless, just three days before the scheduled opening, the museum's director— after viewing several hours of the tapes — ordered the exhibition cancelled.

Justifying his action to the press, the director said, "The material that I looked at dealt with social-sexual investigations of some sort. These tapes are simply the faces of people being interviewed. This in itself does not constitute a creative act. There is no connection with visual art." He also acknowledged that he had been concerned about alienating the gallery's membership (some fifteen thousand new members had been recruited when the gallery relocated to a renovated courthouse the previous year) and the hostile public reception given to some of the works of art shown in the new building's inaugural exhibition. "Press coverage of the controversial pieces was relentless," he said. "My feeling is that at this moment I will not get intelligent treatment of [the Wong piece]." He added that the decision to cancel was "the most difficult one I have had to make in my professional career. . . . I realize I am in a no-win situation." [15]

The artist almost immediately commenced an action against both the Vancouver Art Gallery and its director claiming a breach of contract and demanding immediate injunctive relief. In the alternative, he asked for damages. In support of his claim for damages were the allegations that, as a result of the cancellation of his exhibition, he would suffer "loss of reputation, mental anguish and the loss of the opportunity for his work to be viewed in a major Canadian Gallery." [16] The demand for an injunction was denied.

The defendants have offered a number of defenses: The plaintiff's potential losses were too remote to serve as a basis for damages, the arrangements made by the curator did not constitute an enforceable agreement (Was the curator not an agent empowered to bind the Gallery? Were the terms too vague?), and, if indeed there *had* been an enforceable agreement, it was an implied term of that agreement that the Gallery retained the right not to exhibit the work if, in the Gallery's opinion, the work was not suitable for exhibition. [17]

---

[15] Globe and Mail, Feb. 23, 1984, at E1.

[16] Plaintiff's Statement of Claim at 3, c841083 Vancouver Registry (S.C. of B.C., Feb. 23, 1984).

[17] See Defendants' Statements of Defense, c841083 Vancouver Registry (S.C. of B.C., Feb 27, 1984).

Such a policy would certainly seem to be a reasonable or even an essential one for the gallery to follow—museum loan agreements, in fact, generally provide the borrower with the option *not* to exhibit a borrowed work of art; a well-drafted agreement for a temporary installation piece may include a comparable provision (see the discussion in §4.2.6 *supra*). It is difficult to see, however, how this could be deemed part of the gallery's arrangements with the artist through nothing more than implication. Where the artist, as here, was apparently to receive no fee, there would have been little reason for him to invest several months of work *except* in the belief that the gallery had guaranteed a showing for his work. To the gallery's — or any museum's — response that it must always be the final arbiter of what can or cannot be shown on its premises, the proper reply might be that it accordingly had the obligation to make sure that everybody it dealt with knew of this policy. If it failed to make policy clear, then it would have to bear the consequences.

What about damages? If assessed at all, ought these be limited to the artist's out-of-pocket expenses for video tape and equipment rentals in making *Confused: Sexual Views?* Or should the investment of his time and his talent count as well? On the other hand, since he still owns the work, can it be argued that he has suffered no loss at all (or, at least, no loss measurable by what went into creating the work)? Does the fact that the work was produced under a grant mean that he is not the injured party at all? The notoriety of the case has given Wong the opportunity to install and show this piece at other sites in Canada. Might this in fact bear on (and mitigate) damages stemming from his claim of "loss of the opportunity for his work to be viewed in a major Canadian Gallery?" But assume all of these other losses may to a degree have been ameliorated by subsequent events: Are there not other damages? For a young artist whose work is scheduled to be shown at a major museum and who finds the exhibition summarily cancelled at the last moment, is not the mental anguish very real? And can that anguish be measured in dollars?

For artists, art galleries and museums alike, temporary installation pieces are a bold and often exciting extension of the traditional forms of the visual arts. What must be understood, however, is that engaging an artist to create a complex, ephemeral, and site-specific work involves a very different set of rules from those that govern the loan of a painting or sculpture. This difference requires reflection in new forms of agreement. Those who proceed without heeding this difference can find themselves enmeshed in the same unhappy (and by no means inexpensive) tangle as the plaintiff and defendants in the instant case.

CHAPTER FIVE

Moral Right

●

§5.1. Introduction
§5.1.1. Overview and Discussion

§5.2. European Background and the Berne Convention
§5.2.1. The French Perspective: A Broad Concept
DaSilva, *Droit Moral and the Amoral Copyright: A Comparison of Artists' Rights in France and the United States*
§5.2.2. *Snow v. The Eaton Centre Ltd.*: Red Ribbons, Geese, and the Berne-Convention Approach
§5.2.3. Two Recent European Cases: Public and Private Sculpture by Dubuffet and Serrano

§5.3. American Backgrour.d
§5.3.1. *Crimi v. Rutgers Presbyterian Church*: An Early Rejection of Moral Right
§5.3.2. *Gilliam v. American Broadcasting Cos.*: Monty Python Goes to Court
§5.3.3. A Comparison of *Crimi* and *Gilliam*: No Clear Path
§5.3.4. *Stella v. Mazoh*: Does the Moral Right Cover Discarded Works?

§5.4. American Legislation and Case Law
§5.4.1. California Art Preservation Acts (§§987 and 989): Private and Public Interest Provisions
§5.4.2. New York Arts and Cultural Affairs Law §14.03: Artists' Authorship Rights
§5.4.3. The United States Perspective: A Narrower Concept
Damich, *The New York Artists' Authorship Rights Act: A Comparative Critique*
§5.4.4. *Newmann v. Delmar Realty Co.*: First Test of the New York Statute

§5.5. Final Observations on the California and New York Moral Right Statutes

§5.1. INTRODUCTION

§5.1.1. Overview and Discussion

The development in Europe of those elements of the law that are generally clustered together as the "moral right" has proceeded chiefly on a theoretical and intellectual basis. (For a useful review of this development, see the article by DaSilva, *Droit Moral and the Amoral Copyright: A Comparison of Artists' Rights in France and the United States,* reproduced in the next section.) In sharp contrast, the movement to establish some form of moral right in the United States — a movement that can thus far claim credit for the passage of legislation in California, New York, Massachusetts, and, on a minor note, Maine — has been spurred largely by the various and well-publicized indignities inflicted on specific works of art and the general public response that "there oughtta be a law" to prevent such abuses.

Perhaps the best-known American incident was the obliteration in 1946 of a mural that Alfred D. Crimi had painted some eight years earlier for the Rutgers Presbyterian Church in New York City. The litigation that followed posed the property-right-versus-moral-right issue in terms so clear and dramatic that it has since become a textbook case in the evolution of American art law.[1] The *Crimi* decision is reproduced in this chapter.

---

§5.1. [1] See also Meliodon v. School Dist. of Philadelphia, 195 A. 905 (Sup. Ct. Pa. 1938), in which the court dismissed the plaintiff's bill in equity for $500,000 in damages for injury to artistic reputation due to altered construction of sculptural works based on models prepared by plaintiff. The court held that plaintiff's action was not the subject for equitable relief as against the school district, but rather one of tort as against the superintendent employed by defendant who had interfered with the construction. The court also denied plaintiff's prayer for an injunction directing defendant to tear down the sculptural units and

Other examples frequently cited (none of which, however, was the subject of a subsequent legal action) involved a large mobile sculpture by Alexander Calder installed at the Greater Pittsburgh International Airport, a stainless steel construction by Isamu Noguchi fabricated especially for the New York offices of the Bank of Tokyo Trust Company, and several painted sculptures by David Smith from which the surface color was either removed by a collector or allowed to weather away by the executors of the artist's estate.[2]

Concerning the first of the David Smith episodes, the late Thomas B. Hess asked in a 1960 ARTnews[3] editorial whether the time had not come "to press for legislation that would give the American artist at least a part of the legal protection and proprietary rights that are enjoyed by his colleagues in civilized countries?" Such legislation, however, was to be nearly two decades in coming. In the interval, interest centered on two possible alternatives. The first involved tracing out the bits and pieces of the existing American law that might provide some equivalents to various elements of moral right.[4] *Gilliam v. American Broadcasting Cos.,*

---

to permit plaintiff to replace said units to his own satisfaction at defendant's expense. See also Nathan Wasserberger v. Sotheby Parke Bernet, Inc. No. 77 Civ. 17536 (N.Y. County Sup. 1977) in which the court granted summary judgment to defendant, dismissing the complaint and finding that "plaintiff has . . . shown only that his feelings were hurt by defendant's . . . treatment of him." Plaintiff, an artist, claimed that a painting for sale by defendant was not his and publicly stated this, at an auction, in response to questioning by defendant. The defendant auctioneer then stated, allegedly in such a way as to give the impression that plaintiff was prevaricating, that the work be sold "as not a Nathan Wasserberger."

[2] Another example resulted from the unfortunate demolition of two stone Art Deco bas-relief sculptures embedded in the facade of Bonwit Teller building in New York City, torn down for development of The Trump Tower. Similarly, alterations of portraits abound throughout history. One such poignant example is the tale of William Holman Hunt's *Miss Flamborough*, a painting for which the artist's then four-year-old daughter posed between 1881 and 1882; some fifty years later she ruined the painting after she had inherited it from her mother. Consider also, for example, the following incident, as told in Winzola McLendon's Martha: A Biography of Martha Mitchell (1979):

> The oil painting, by artist Gloria Schumann, was in a frame so heavy it took two men to hang it. But Martha, alone, removed it from the wall. Then with turpentine and such kitchen supplies as SOS pads, Ajax, Clorox, mayonnaise and Heinz catsup, Martha erased John Mitchell's face from the canvas.

[3] ARTnews, May 1960, at 23.

[4] See Meliodon v. School Dist. of Philadelphia, 195 A. 905 (Sup. Ct. Pa. 1938), where the court, in dicta, suggested an action in tort, and not in equity, for damages to artistic reputation.

For a description of these efforts, see Treece, American Law Analogues of the Author's "Moral Right," 16 Am. J. Comp. L. 487 (1968).

reproduced in this chapter, is an illuminating example of how a statute adopted with an ostensibly different purpose might, in a proper fact situation, furnish an artist-plaintiff with a remedy comparable to that which might be provided by one of the elements of the moral right, in this case the right of integrity.[5]

The second alternative lay in trying to establish certain elements of the moral right through purchase agreements between artists and collectors. This was well exemplified in 1971 by Robert Projansky's draft of a model agreement, *Artist's Reserved Rights Transfer and Sale Agreement*, discussed at §6.1.1. *infra* and its sequel, Charles Jurrist's draft agreement (reprinted at §6.3.1 *infra*). These agreements were directed principally at obtaining resale royalties. The explanatory preface to the Projansky agreement, in fact, barely mentions the right of integrity that the agreement would have also secured for the artist. Nonetheless, together with other contract forms that were then in circulation — a number of these drafted by artists for their own use — they evidence the degree to which the art community had by the 1970s become sensitive to the question of moral right and the possibility that it might, in whole or in part, be replicated in American law.[6]

The big breakthrough, however, came in 1979 when California enacted its Civil Code §987, the California Art Preservation Act (reproduced in this chapter). While the Act provides for a right of paternity — i.e., "the right to claim authorship, or, for just and valid reason, to disclaim authorship" in a work of art — its chief focus is on the right of integrity. (The same is true of the Massachusetts statute, enacted in 1984 and modeled on the California Act.) Unlike the California Resale Royalties Act of 1976 (reproduced in Chapter 6), which many observers felt had been rushed through the legislature in virtual secrecy, the Art

---

[5] See also Latin American Advisory Council v. Withers, (reproduced in Chapter 1) in which attempts to block the creation of a mural, under a zoning ordinance regulating the size and placement of signs, were unsuccessful. The court found that the zoning ordinance was inapplicable and that the mural was a form of expression protected by the First Amendment.

[6] The art community was not alone in this effort. In 1982, the court in Mirella Belshe v. Charles Fairchild, C.A. 16988-80 (D.C. Super. Ct., Aug. 13, 1982), enjoined the altering and mutilating of a work that a real estate developer had commissioned the plaintiff to create for the lobby of a building he was constructing. The *Belshe* dispute suggests how a court itself, some thirty years after *Crimi*, might be more inclined than it would have been in 1949 to search for an implied contractual or other basis to prevent the deliberate mutilation of a commissioned work of art.

Preservation Act was widely circulated in draft for more than a year. Its final form reflected a number of changes that were of considerable help in securing broad support for its ultimate passage. Typical of these were the limitation of the Act's coverage to works of "recognized quality" — a limitation intended to reduce the frivolous litigation the Act might otherwise have been expected to engender — and the requirement that (except in the case of a framer or conservator) the acts of defacement, mutilation, alteration, or destruction that would trigger the Act be intentional and not merely the result of negligence. While framers and conservators were to be held to a higher standard of care — in their cases "gross negligence" as well as intentional injury could be the basis for a cause of action — this was strictly defined to mean "the exercise of so slight a degree of care as to justify the belief that there was an indifference to the particular work of fine art."

The California Art Preservation Act has yet, at this writing, to receive any substantive interpretation in the courts of that state. While most of its provisions seem clear, there is nonetheless some question as to the measure of damages — and particularly of "actual damages" — it provides. If vandal X destroys a painting by artist Y belonging to collecter Z, which painting has a then current fair market value of $5,000, it seems clear that collector Z has suffered "actual damages" of $5,000 and would have a claim in that amount against vandal X under the normal rules of tort law. The Act, however, gives artist Y a separate cause of action against vandal X. And what are *his* damages? Would they be related to the time and effort he had originally expended to create the subject work of art? Might they be calculated instead by the possible diminution of his future earnings attributable to the loss of that particular example of his work? Could damages be awarded simply for his psychic pain and suffering? Or would the potential loss of reputation also be a factor? And what if he argued that the loss had so distressed him that he had not been able to paint for a year?

Also unanswered is whether artist Y's claim for actual damages would be greater or less if collector Z's painting had simply been mutilated rather than wholly destroyed. The prevailing interpretation of France's Law of March 11, 1957[7] — the most frequently cited statute in this field — is that it more severely restricts acts of alteration than total destruction

---

[7] Loi du 11 mars 1977 Sur La Propriété Littéraire Artistique, [1957] J.O., translated in UNESCO, Copyright Laws and Treaties of the World (1976).

on the grounds that a mutilated work of art is potentially more damaging to an artist's reputation than one that no longer exists.

This focus on reputation is central to the very different moral right legislation that was subsequently adopted in New York. This is the Artists' Authorship Rights Act of 1983 reproduced at §5.4.2 *infra*. With a slight variation, the New York and California laws are similar in their grants of a right of paternity. Beyond that, however, in their effort to establish a right of integrity, they approach the problem from wholly opposite poles. Whereas the California statute proscribes certain conduct — i.e., the defacement, mutilation, alteration, or destruction of a work of fine art — the New York enactment looks solely to the "knowing" public display, publication, or reproduction of a work of fine art in "an altered, defaced, mutilated, or modified form." Even then such conduct is only actionable if damage to the artist's reputation might be a consequence.

The difference between these two statutes was highlighted by Judith L. Teichman, a deputy city attorney of San Francisco, at a museum law conference.[8] She observed that somebody could deliberately deface a painting in New York and subsequently exhibit it in California without incurring liability under either law. The converse is also true. A deliberate defacement in California followed by a "knowing" public display in New York would create causes of action under *both* statutes.

In the end, however, a successful action under the New York statute would still require something more: evidence that the artist's reputation had been damaged. Given this, the Artists' Authorship Rights Act appears to be — from one point of view, at least — less a moral right statute than an extension of the law of defamation. As such its application may yet run up against some constitutional boundaries. This is particularly likely since — unlike the California law, which deals solely with original works of art — the New York law covers reproductions (including, presumably, newspaper and magazine reproductions in which works of art might appear in altered form as an expression of opinion). This remains to be explored, however.

Among those who followed the three-year development of the New York Act with special interest (and some apprehension) were the professional conservators. What they feared was the inclusion of language under which conservation and/or restoration might per se constitute a form of alteration and serve as the basis for a cause of action. The

---

[8] Course of Study in Legal Problems of Museum Administration, at The High Museum of Art, Atlanta, Ga. (March 1984).

penultimate version of the Act attempted to deal with this through the curiously worded provision that "[n]othing contained in this article shall abridge the right of a person to frame or restore a work of fine art." In the final version, this provision was substituted by the present §14.03.3(c). This provides that "[c]onservation shall not constitute an alteration, defacement, mutilation or modification . . . unless the conservation work can be shown to be negligent." While not as favorable to conservators as the California provision, which limits a conservator's liability to instances of *gross* negligence, this change — together with the inclusion in the Act's definitional sections of language adopted from the code of ethics of the American Institute of Conservation — was sufficient for the conservators to withdraw their objections.

For art museums, this conservation issue was complicated by its link to a more fundamental problem: display. Under the Act as drafted, it was not so much the potentially negligent conservation of a work of art that might give rise to a cause of action, but, rather, the public display, publication, or reproduction of a work of art that the artist *claimed* had been improperly conserved. The allegedly improper conservation (or, for that matter, any other alteration, deliberate or otherwise) could have occurred many years earlier, even before the work came into the museum's possession and even in another place. Once the museum was on notice that the artist claimed the work to have been altered, then institutional liability might attach to its further public display.

Further, even with respect to processes that were wholly within the museum's own control, there were ongoing and deep divisions among professional conservators as to what procedures were most suitable for particular kinds of art. As Ashton Hawkins, the secretary and counsel to the Metropolitan Museum of Art, pointed out in a letter to New York Governor Mario Cuomo:

> even the experts disagree as to the techniques that should be used to protect works of art. To create a cause of action as a remedy against the use of one or another such technique would not only have a chilling effect on the development and improvement of this very important field but would run the risk of generating much fruitless litigation.

While similar and other objections were presented to the governor by the Museum of Modern Art and the Whitney Museum of American Art, these came only at the last minute and too late to persuade the governor to veto the Act.

While other states such as Connecticut, Iowa, Texas, and Washington have expressed an interest in pursuing moral right legislation, there seems little prospect for a more comprehensive approach; namely, the adoption of a federal moral right statute, most likely by an amendment to the Copyright Act. In the late 1970s and early 1980s, Representative Robert Drinan of Massachusetts and his successor, Representative Barney Frank, introduced a series of three bills that through just such an amendment would have established in principle — but without providing a mechanism for enforcing — the rights of paternity and integrity with respect to "pictorial, graphic or sculptural work." Following the language of the Berne Convention,[9] these provided that "independently of the author's copyright . . . the author or the author's legal representative shall have the right, during the life of the author and fifty years after the author's death, to claim authorship of such work [of visual art] and to object to any distortion, mutilation or other alteration thereof."

All three bills died in committee, without even being the subject of hearings. That the bills were all so narrowly proscribed to the visual arts — carefully avoiding the legislatively powerful realms of literature and music, not to mention the still more powerful ones of film and television — suggests the magnitude of the forces that would have been summoned to oppose any sweeping federal legislation that threatened to alter the existing property relationships in the arts. For the moment, at least, the prospect of establishing moral right on a state-by-state basis appears by far the more promising approach. A statute adopted by Massachusetts, which is based on the California enactment, is discussed at §5.4.5 and §5.4.6 *infra*. Maine has thus far adopted only a resolution urging that artists and their patrons employ a form of agreement incorporating certain aspects of the moral right (see §5.4.7 *infra*).

The right of integrity provides artists with a means of protecting their works of art from corruption. Closely related are the questions of whether the general public might also be provided with some means

---

[9] The Berne Convention, to which the United States is not a signatory, reads (Art. 6 bis) as follows:

(1) Independently of the author's economic rights, and even after the transfer of the said rights, the author shall have the right to claim authorship of the work and to object to any distortion, mutilation or other modification of, or other derogatory action in relation to, the said work, which would be prejudicial to his honor or reputation.

(2) The rights granted to the author in accordance with the preceding paragraph shall, after his death, be maintained, at least until the expiry of the economic rights, and shall be exercisable by the persons or institutions authorized by the legislation of the country where protection is claimed. However, those countries whose legislations, at the moment of their ratification of or accession to this Act, does not provide for the protection after the death of the author of all the rights set out in the preceding paragraph may provide that some of these rights may, after his death, cease to be maintained.

(3) The means of redress for safeguarding the rights granted by this Article shall be governed by the legislation for the country where protection is claimed.

of protecting the integrity of works of art (and particularly older works of art) whose preservation is considered to be in the common interest, and how such a right might be exercised. In their original versions, both the California and New York moral right statutes addressed this topic by including broad provisions for such "public preservation." In each case, these provisions ultimately had to be dropped. The original California approach was particularly sweeping. It would have conferred standing to sue on virtually anybody within the state prepared to charge a person or institution — e.g., a neighbor, a prominent collector, a museum, or even a church — with caring improperly for any work of art in his or its posses- sion. The potential for mischief seemed unlimited.[10]

In 1982, with its moral right law safely on the books, the California legislature returned to this theme by adopting new Civil Code §989 (see §5.4.1 *infra*). This created a considerably more limited right of public preservation, one that could only be exercised by established nonprofit arts organizations and only with respect to artworks of "substantial pub- lic interest." Unlike California's moral right legislation, which provides for either injunctive relief or damages, §989 provides for injunctive relief only.

Beyond California, however, the ability to extend legal protection to older works of art depends almost entirely on the circumstances of their ownership. For works in public ownership — especially those held in the collections of museums — there recently has been a rapid development in both the willingness and the ability of local authorities (and most particularly of the states' attorneys general) to intervene and salvage such collections when threatened by mismanagement or neglect. Two causes seem to lie behind this development. First, with the increase in direct public funding for museums since the middle 1960s, there has been a correspondingly increased interest in seeing to it that museums operate for the public benefit. This includes taking proper care of their collections. And second, in striving (as it has in recent years) for greater professionalism, the museum community — without, perhaps, alto- gether meaning to do so — has provided those responsible for its over- sight with the standards necessary to bring its occasional lapses under control.

Not so well protected, however — in fact, not protected at all except, perhaps, by the self-interest of its owner — is the older work of art in private ownership. In the predecessor to this book, it was written that

---

[10] Such a broad class of potential plaintiffs might, however, have been a great assistance in avoiding the destruction of the Bonwit Teller Art Deco bas-relief sculptures referred to in note 2 *supra*.

"[a]n eccentric American collector who, for a Saturday evening's amuse-ment, invited his friends to play darts using his Rembrandt portrait as the target would neither violate any public law nor be subject to any private restraint."[11] The law remains the same, and the question of how to change it is a perplexing one. Any new public preservation right could only be established at the sacrifice of some deeply founded concept of private rights. The situation might be analogous to the imposition of landmark status on the unwilling owner of an historic building. Enforce-ment, however, would be immeasurably more difficult. Unlike build-ings, works of art are portable and susceptible to transport across state boundaries and even national borders. Beyond that, they are most often kept within the private space of a home or office, not in full public view along the street. The development of some reasonable means for protect-ing the integrity of privately owned works of public significance remains among the most challenging tasks in the field of art law.

§5.2. EUROPEAN BACKGROUND AND THE BERNE CONVENTION

§5.2.1. The French Perspective: A Broad Concept

A number of articles have been published in the last years on the subject of moral right. The first substantial ones were written by Ray-mond Sarraute and James M. Treece and appeared in 1968 in the Ameri-can Journal of Comparative Law.[1] Since then, many academicians, lawyers, and law students have been attracted to the topic. What could be more appealing than introducing into American law principles that have existed only under a foreign legal system? Individual artists and various groups that lobby on their behalf have also been taken up with the concept. From their point of view, the introduction of moral right would be a bargain — a grant of additional rights to artists with no correspond-ing increase in duties.

Russell J. DaSilva's fairly recent article, which follows, deals with the subject in a most comprehensive way. His emphasis on the historical basis for moral right is particularly useful since the concept still has not

---

[11] F. Feldman & S. Weil, Art Works: Law, Policy, Practice 15 (1974).

§5.2. [1] See Sarraute, Current Theory of the Moral Right of Authors and Art-ists Under French Law, 16 Am. J. Comp. L. 465 (1968); Treece, American Law Analogues of the Author's "Moral Rights," 16 Am. J. Comp. L. 487 (1968).

been effectively introduced into American law. In order to understand the full import of the doctrine, it is important to determine which, if any, of its many facets merits recognition in a society as economically oriented as the United States. While we do not believe that the introduction of moral right legislation would change in any significant way either the quality of work or the financial rewards of working artists, we think it useful to understand the extensive background and efforts of others in developing the concept.

DaSILVA, DROIT MORAL AND THE AMORAL COPYRIGHT: A COMPARISON OF ARTISTS' RIGHTS IN FRANCE AND THE UNITED STATES
28 Bull. Copyright Socy. U.S.A. 1 (1980)*

In the 1940's, Twentieth Century-Fox released a film entitled "The Iron Curtain." The movie depicted Soviet espionage in Canada, and for its background used selections from the uncopyrighted music of Dmitri Shostakovich and three other eminent Soviet composers. One might suppose that "The Iron Curtain" was not a highly favorable documentary of Soviet foreign policy, for in 1948, the four Russian composers brought suit in New York State against Twentieth Century-Fox, seeking damages and a permanent injunction against the exhibition of the film.[1] They contended, *inter alia*, that the use of their music in a film which was so politically objectionable cast upon them "a false imputation of disloyalty to their country."[2] This, they claimed, constituted defamation, and violated something called their "moral right."

Moral right? The New York court paused to consider that issue, but was at a loss to find any standard by which to test such a claim.[3] In the end, the court dismissed the complaint, and as for moral right, stated: "In

---

* [DaSilva, Russell J., Droit Moral and the Amoral Copyright: A Comparison of Artists' Rights in France and the United States, 28 Bull. Copyright Socy. U.S.A. 1 (1980). Copyright © by Russell J. DaSilva. Mr. DaSilva received his J.D. in 1979 from the Harvard Law School and is associated with the law firm of Milbank, Tweed, Hadley & McCloy in New York City. Reprinted with permission. This article was written prior to the passage of legislation in New York and Massachusetts and a resolution in Maine dealing with the subject of moral right. — Eds.]

[1] Shostakovich v. Twentieth Century-Fox Film Corp., 196 Misc. 67, 80 N.Y.S.2d 575 (Sup. Ct. 1948), *aff'd*, 275 App. Div. 695, 87 N.Y.S.2d 430 (1st Dept. 1949).

[2] 196 Misc. at 70.

[3] "Is the standard to be good taste, artistic worth, political beliefs, moral concepts, or what is it to be?" *Id.* at 71.

the present state of our law, the very existence of such a right is not clear."[4]

The four composers also brought the suit in a French court — and won.[5]

The *Shostakovich* case illustrates the common contention that American law has not evolved doctrines which adequately protect the artist's rights of personality in his or her own work.[6] For while France is considered to be in the vanguard of protection of the artist's rights of personality,[7] American law has only grudgingly begun to recognize the non-pecuniary interests of artists. Today, however, the attention of American lawmakers is being drawn to the long-neglected area of artists' rights. For example, the California Art Preservation Act[8] (the "Preservation Act"), while it does not speak of "moral rights," is the first significant state legislation to attempt to rectify the disparity between French and American law.

Enacted in 1979, the Preservation Act affords to the creator of a painting, sculpture or drawing[9] the right, with several limitations, to prevent the intentional "physical defacement, mutilation, alteration or destruction"[10] of his created work, and secures the right of the artist to claim or disclaim its authorship.[11] These rights subsist until fifty years after the author's death,[12] and may be waived only by the artist himself in a signed, written instrument. Thus, although Shostakovich could not have availed himself of the Preservation Act to protect against misuse of his music, still California has taken an important step in recognizing the author's rights of personality.

---

[4] *Id.*

[5] Soc. Le Chant de Monde v. Soc. Fox Europe et Soc. Fox Americaine Twentieth Century, Judgment of Jan. 13, 1953 [1953] 1 Gaz. Pal. 191 [1954] D.A. 16, 80 (Cour d'Appel Paris). For a discussion of moral rights protection in the Soviet Union, see S. Strömholm, 1 Droit de L'Auteur 423-24 (1966).

[6] Roeder, The Doctrine of Moral Right: A Study in the Law of Artists, Authors and Creators, 53 Harv. L. Rev. 554, 557 (1940); Strauss, The Moral Right of the Author, 4 Am. J. Comp. L. 506 (1955). See generally Comment, Toward Artistic Integrity: Implementing Moral Right Through Extension of Existing American Legal Doctrines, 60 Geo. L.J. 1539 (1972) [hereinafter cited as *Georgetown Comment*]; Comment, Moral Rights for Artists Under the Lanham Act: Gilliam v. American Broadcasting Cos., 18 Wm. & Mary L. Rev. 595 (1977) [hereinafter cited as *William and Mary Comment*].

[7] Giocanti, Moral Rights: Author's Protection and Business Needs, 10 J. Int'l L. & Econ. 627, 627 n.1 (1975).

[8] Cal. Civ. Code §987 (West) [hereinafter cited as Preservation Act].

[9] *Id.* §(b)(2)

[10] *Id.* §(c)(1)

[11] *Id.* §(d)

[12] *Id.*§(g)(1)

This article does not purport to examine the applicability or enforcement of the Preservation Act under California law. It does, however, seek to illustrate the significance of the Preservation Act in light of the development of artists' rights in the United States and in civil law countries, and further, to assess, on the basis of French law, which rights of authors deserve to be further developed in the United States.

The French *droit d'auteur* is a concept far broader than American copyright, so broad, in fact, that French scholars dispute whether it really can be called a property right at all.[13] While United States copyright seeks to protect primarily the author's pecuniary and exploitative interests,[14] French law purports to protect the author's intellectual and moral interests, as well.[15] The French law of *droit d'auteur*, therefore, protects not only the artist's pecuniary rights *(droits patrimoniaux)*, but also his moral right *(droit moral)*.[16]

The *droits patrimoniaux* are analogous to the American federal copyright.[17] They include a statutory monopoly over the exploitation of the work until fifty years after the author's death, including the right of reproduction, and in the case of dramatic works, the right of representation.[18] *Droit moral*, on the other hand, is by nature non-pecuniary. It is a "collection of prerogatives, all of which proceed from the necessity of preserving the integrity of intellectual works and the personality of the author."[19]

The unitary concept of moral right traditionally is divided into four

---

[13] See, e.g., H. Desbois, Cours de Propriété Littéraire, Artistique et Industrielle 4 (1961); P. Recht, Le Droit d'Auteur, Une Nouvelle Forme de Propriété. For convenience, however, this paper will at times refer to the *droits patrimoniaux* in terms of "property" interests.

French law describes *droit d'auteur* as a right of "incorporeal property," the precise meaning of which still is disputed by French scholars. See G. Gavin, Le Droit Moral de l'Auteur Dans la Jurisprudence et la Legislation Françaises 15 (1960); H. Desbois, *supra* note 13, at 4; P. Recht, *supra* note 13, at 11.

[14] See, e.g., Comment, An Artist's Personal Rights in His Creative Works; Beyond the Human Cannonball and the Flying Circus, 9 Pac. L.J. 885 (1978) [hereinafter cited as *Pacific Comment*].

[15] Loi du 11 mars 1957 Sur La Propriété Littéraire Artistique, [1957] J.O., *translated in* UNESCO, Copyright Laws and Treaties of the World (1976) [hereinafter cited as 1957 Law]. Article 1, clause 2, provides: "This right bears attributes of a moral and intellectual order, as well as attributes of a patrimonial order, which are determined by the present law."

[16] *Id.* Article 6 describes *droit d'auteur* as a *"droit de propriété incorporelle."* See author's comment, note 13 *supra*.

[17] Sarraute, Current Theory on the Moral Right of Authors and Artists Under French Law, 16 Am. J. Comp. L. 465 (1968).

[18] *Id.* Also see 1957 Law, *supra* note 15, art. 21, 26-42.

[19] A. LeTarnec, Manuel de la Propriété Littéraire et Artistique 25 (1966).

overlapping categories: first, the *droit de divulgation*, the right of the author to determine the publication or non-publication of his work; second, the *droit de retrait ou de repentir*, the right of the author to withdraw or modify a work which already has been made public; third, the *droit à la paternité*, the right of an author to be acknowledged as the creator of his work, and to disclaim authorship of works falsely attributed to him; and most important, the *droit au respect de l'oeuvre*, the right of the author to preserve his work from alteration, mutilation, or even from excessive criticism.[20]

There also exists under French law the *droit de suite*,[21] which is the right of an artist to receive a royalty on future resales of his work.[22] Since this right is pecuniary and lasts only until fifty years after the author's death, some French scholars consider *droit de suite* simply to be one of the *droits patrimoniaux*.[23] Other scholars, recognizing the essentially "moral" origin of this right, prefer to treat it as a third category of *droit d'auteur*.[24] In the United States, *droit de suite* is not recognized by federal copyright law, although at least one state, California, has estalished the right by statute.[25] It is no longer uncommon in this country, moreover, to find similar rights secured for artists by contract.[26]

In the view of French jurists, moral rights are not trifling interests which merely are appended to the law of copyright. On the contrary, they derive from the same natural law principles which established the *droits patrimoniaux*; indeed, moral rights are independent from and superior to any pecuniary interest in a work of art.[27] *Droits patrimoniaux*, after all, may be transferred, sold, or made the subject of contracts or com-

---

[20] See discussion in section II *infra*.

[21] 1957 Law, *supra* note 15, art. 42.

[22] The most comprehensive discussion of *droit de suite* is in M. Nimmer, Legal Rights of the Artist (1971) (unpublished), which contains essays on *droit de suite* by legal scholars throughout the world. For a classic study of the subject, see J.-L. Duchemin, Le Droit de Suite des Artistes (1948). For a discussion of *droit de suite* in relation to the United States, see 1 J. Merryman and A. Elsen, Law, Ethics and the Visual Arts 4-102 – 4-141 (1979).

[23] See H. Desbois, *supra* note 13, at 207; C. Colombet, Propriété Littéraire et Artistique 173 (1976).

[24] See *Pacific Comment, supra* note 14, at 857.

[25] Cal. Civ. Code. §986 ("Artist's Resale Royalty Act"). Morseburg v. Baylon, et al., No. 78-2129 (9th Cir. June 17, 1980) held that the Artist's Resale Royalty Act did not violate the pre-emption clause of the United States copyright statute, 17 U.S.C. §301 (1976); also see *Pacific Comment, supra* note 14, at 858.

[26] 1 J. Merryman and A. Elsen, *supra* note 22, at 4-141 – 4-166.

[27] H. Desbois, *supra* note 13, at 23-26, 58. In West Germany, however, moral rights and patrimonial rights are not wholly separable.

merce. *Droit moral*, on the other hand, is deemed by statute to be "personal, perpetual, inalienable, and unassignable,"[28] and at least in theory, it cannot be abandoned by the author by contract or will.[29] Moreover, the moral right survives both the *droits patrimoniaux* and the author's own life; it may be asserted after the work has fallen into the public domain, and it may be enforced, with some limitations, by the author's heirs even after the author's death.[30] Violations of moral right may give rise to civil or penal sanctions.[31]

In short, *droit moral* is the very core of the French *droit d'auteur*, for it is by virtue of the moral right that an author may secure and assert his pecuniary interests.[32]

Although the concept of moral right may seem anomalous to the American lawyer, it has been incorporated into the copyright laws of at least sixty-three countries of the world.[33] The Berne Convention,[34] to which the United States does not subscribe, affords some international protection to moral rights, expecially to *droit à la paternité* and *droit au respect*.[35]

The moral right doctrine originated in France, and as a child of the civil law, it is not recognized in the United Kingdom, although many of the

---

[28] 1957 Law, *supra* note 15, art. 6. West German law also provides that moral rights are inalienable. Law of Sept. 9, 1965, [1965] Bundesgesetzblatt [BGB1] I 1924, §29 [hereinafter cited as German Law]. The term which this author prefers to translate as "unassignable" also can be translated "imprescriptible." See, e.g., Giocanti, *supra* note 7, at 631.

[29] See W. Goldbaum, Derecho de Autor Panamericano 42 (1943).

[30] See, e.g., 1957 Law, *supra* note 15, art. 6.

[31] A discussion of penal and civil sanctions for violations of *droit moral* is beyond the scope of this paper. Sanctions and procedures are codified in articles 64-76 of the 1957 Law. For a discussion of sanctions and procedures, see G. Gavin, *supra* note 13, 225-48.

[32] H. Desbois, *supra* note 13, at 299.

[33] *Pacific Comment*, *supra* note 14, at 859.

[34] The Berne Convention for the Protection of Literary and Artistic Works [hereinafter cited as Berne Convention] was first convened in 1886 to develop rules for multinational protection of authors' rights. The Convention has been revised in 1908, 1928, 1948, 1967 and in 1971. For a brief statement of the Berne Convention, see Copyright L. Rep. (CCH) ¶6025 (1979).

[35] See Berne Convention, June 26, 1948 (Brussels) art. 6(2), *reprinted in* UNESCO, *supra* note 11 and in *Georgetown Comment*, *supra* note 7, at 1540 n.7. The Universal Copyright Convention, of which the United States is a member, contains only limited recognition of moral rights. For a discussion of moral rights under the Berne Convention and the Universal Copyright Convention, see Diamond, Legal Protection for the "Moral Rights" of Authors and Other Creators, 68 Trademark Rep. 244, 245-248 (1978).

rights included in *droit moral* do receive protection under British law.[36] United States copyright law[37] makes no mention of moral rights, and American courts, both state and federal, traditionally have rejected the doctrine, at least in name, calling it "meta-legal" and "the law of least effort." [38]

At least one federal court, however, has shown itself a bit more receptive to the moral right doctrine.[39] Moreover, legal scholars have argued quite persuasively[40] that the major principles of moral right — especially *droit à la paternité* and *droit au respect* — have been protected by American law when claims have been brought under doctrines of breach of contract, defamation, invasion of privacy, unfair competition, right of publicity, and more recently, under section 43(a) of the Lanham Act on trademarks.[41] The California Preservation Act, although far more limited than *droit moral*, is the closest American equivalent to a "moral right," at least for paintings, sculptures and drawings of recognized quality.

Still, it cannot be maintained that artists' rights are protected as fully in the United States as they are in those countries which have adopted the unitary concept of moral right.[42] After all, even where state law does afford artists remedies for violations of their rights of personality, the law has "grown up in an unprincipled way," [43] and has reached inconsistent results from state to state. Moreover, as illustrated in the *Shostakovich* case, there do exist some important aspects of *droit moral* which are not yet protected in any state, and which may indeed prove to be irreconcilable with American law. Above all, one may argue that no matter how diligently a state may try to protect moral rights, the failure of the federal copyright law even to address the issue creates a national standard of indifference toward artists' rights, and firmly establishes a legal notion of

---

[36] For a discussion of moral rights in the United Kingdom, see Marvin, The Author's Status in the United Kingdom and France; Common Law and the Moral Right Doctrine, 20 Int'l & Comp. L.Q. 675 (1971); also see Diamond, *supra* note 35, at 276-277.

[37] 17 U.S.C.§101 (1976).

[38] Granz v. Harris, 198 F.2d 585, 590 (2d Cir. 1952) (Frank, J. concurring). See discussion in *Georgetown Comment, supra* note 6, at 1545; Streibich, The Moral Right of Ownership to Intellectual Property: Part II — From the Age of Printing to the Future, 7 Mem. St. U. L. Rev. 45, 78 (1976) [hereinafter cited as *Streibich Part II*].

[39] Gilliam v. American Broadcasting Cos., 538 F.2d 14 (2d Cir. 1976).

[40] See generally Roeder, *supra* note 6; Strauss, *supra* note 6; Treece, American Law Analogues of the Authors' "Moral Right," 16 Am. J. Comp. L. 487 (1968).

[41] See discussion at text accompanying note 333, *infra*.

[42] Roeder, *supra* note 6, at 557; *William and Mary Comment, supra* note 6, at 595. But see Strauss, *supra* note 6, at 538.

[43] Treece, *supra* note 40, at 487.

intellectual property which puts the rights of the copyright proprietor above the rights of the artistic creator. By ignoring moral rights, federal law creates a fundamentally "amoral" copyright.

Scholarly interest in *droit moral* has increased in recent years, and a few writers have advocated legislative, or at least judicial, recognition of the moral right doctrine.[44] Legislators — even outside of California — have shown interest in the doctrine, and have gone so far as to propose an amendment to the federal Copyright Act, which would secure the moral rights of authors, artists, and musicians.[45] This scholarly and political attention has served to underscore the pressing need for American law to recognize artists' rights beyond the present notion of copyright, and to take note of developments in continental jurisprudence regarding intellectual property.

However, those who suggest that the unitary doctrine of moral right be adopted in this country may fail to observe the complexity of the doctrine in theory, the difficulty which civil law countries have faced in applying it, and the many limitations which courts in those countries have found it necessary to establish. American scholars also pay too little attention to the precise historical and cultural context in which *droit moral* arose, and to the significant differences which have emerged even among those countries which have adopted the doctrine. Finally, scholars too often fail to consider the practical and theoretical difficulties which would attend the wholesale introduction of the doctrine into the United States, and the undesirable consequences which it might have.

After an exploration of these issues, we may find that the goal of protecting the artist's rights of personality cannot be solved, as one scholar has suggested, simply by legislative or judicial recognition of the words "moral right."[46] Indeed, the challenge is far more enticing.

I. THE MORAL RIGHT DOCTRINE IN FRANCE
A. Origins
One can hardly begin a study of *droit moral* without pausing to observe the inexhaustible reverence with which French jurists approach the subject of authors' rights.[47] Pierre Recht accurately has observed, "When *droit moral* fanatics discuss moral rights, they take the attitude of a religious zealot talking of sacred things, or a Girondin reading the

---

[44] See, e.g., *Streibich Part II, supra* note 38, at 76, 83-84.

[45] H. R. 8261, 95th Cong., 1st Sess. (1977); H.R. 288, 96th Cong., 1st Sess. (1979).

[46] *Streibich Part II, supra* note 38, at 84.

[47] See, e.g., statements in F. Wey. La Propriété Littéraire Sous le Régime du Domaine Public Payant 16 (1862); G. Gavin, Strömholm, *supra* note 5, at 113.

Declaration of the Rights of Man."[48] Perhaps one reason for this sentiment is that French scholars regard the *droit d'auteur* as a natural right,
deeply rooted in the principles of the French Revolution from which
modern French jurisprudence emerged.

Scholars have sought the origins of *droit moral* in the earliest periods
of recorded history.[49] Until the end of the Middle Ages, however, recognition of authors' rights generally was limited to a ban on plagiarism,[50]
and it was not until the eighteenth century that the notion of *droit d'auteur*, as it is now known, came into being.[51] During the *Ancien Régime*,
virtually all rights in an intellectual work were conferred by the sovereign, and generally were bestowed upon printers.[52] Rights in books went
scarcely beyond a monopoly on the reproduction of the work for a fixed
term, and did not even include a right to sell the work.[53] Voltaire, in 1769,
grumbled that druggists, by comparison, at least could sell their own
concoctions freely.[54]

Yet, even before the French Revolution and its emergent "natural
right" concept of *droit d'auteur*, important principles of modern civil law
regarding authors' rights were debated in France. As early as 1725, it was
argued that an author had a perpetual property interest in his unpublished manuscript.[55] Consequently, in the two decades preceding the

---

[48] P. Recht, *supra* note 13, at 281.

[49] See, e.g., Streibich, The Moral Right of Ownership to Intellectual Property:
Part I — From the Beginning to the Age of Printing, 6 Mem. St. U. L. Rev. 1 (1975)
[hereinafter cited as *Streibich Part I*].

[50] F. Wey, *supra* note 47, at 46. For a discussion of antiplagiarism laws in
ancient Rome and the Middle Ages, see *Streibich Part I, supra* note 49, at 407; V.
Segrelles-Chillida, La Nueva Ley Francesa Sobre Derechos De Autor 5 (1959)
[hereinafter cited as *Chillida*]. Interestingly, ancient China, unlike Europe, did
not outlaw plagiarism. *Id.*

[51] The issue of authors' rights gained prominence in the age of printing. 1 S.
Strömholm, *supra* note 5, at 67. *Chillida, supra* note 50, at 5, speaks of "the
transcendental apparition of printing." The earliest traces of a copyright system
are said to be found in the Guild of Printers and Publishers of Venice, which was
founded in 1548. See *Streibich Part II, supra* note 38, at 57; P. Recht, *supra* note
13, at 44-45.

[52] Monta, The Concept of "Copyright" Versus the Droit D'Auteur, 32 S. Cal.
L. Rev. 177, 178 (1959); *Chillida, supra* note 50, at 5; Pottinger, Protection of
Literary Property in France During the Ancien Régime, 2 Romanic Rev. 81-108
(1951). P. Recht, *supra* note 13, at 43-44, points out that during the 17th and 18th
centuries in Germany, protection of books was by local ordinance. Authors'
rights appeared late in Spain — not until the law of Don Carlos de Bourbon in
1762. *Id.*

[53] P. Recht, *supra* note 13, at 27.

[54] Letter of Oct. 21, 1769, to Luneau de Boisgermain, *quoted in* P. Recht, *supra*
note 13, at 27.

[55] In 1725, l'avocat d'Hericourt argued:

French Revolution, various ordinances and decrees were published, which defined more explicitly the prerogatives of editors and publishers,[56] and affirmed the existence of perpetual interests of writers "emanating from the creative activity of the author."[57]

During and after the French Revolution, jurists sought to abolish any notion that *droit d'auteur* was a royal privilege.[58] Early legislation eased the freedom to perform plays in public, and confirmed the authors' exploitative rights, based on the notion that these rights were inherent in the artist.[59] The *droits patrimoniaux* at last were enunciated in the law of 19-24 juillet 1793.[60] Although they—like American copyright—were primarily pecuniary rights, they expressed the principle that *droit d'auteur* was not merely a privilege of the sovereign, as in the *Ancien Régime*, but it was, rather, a natural right, arising simply from the author's act of creation.[61]

Droit moral, on the other hand, emerged not from statute, but from judicially created doctrines, which developed slowly in the nineteenth century, and more rapidly in the twentieth. But *droit moral*, too, arose from the spirit of these laws, and from the philosophy of individualism which accompanied the French Revolution.[62]

Scholars divide the history of *droit moral* into three periods: the first from 1793 to 1878; the second from 1878 to 1902; and the third from 1902 to 1957.[63] During the first period, French scholars began to debate the "property" nature of an author's rights.[64] Gastambide and his fol-

---

A manuscript is the property of the author, and he cannot be deprived of it any more than he can be deprived of his money, his personal property or his land, for it is the fruit of his labor and is personal to him, and he should have the liberty to dispose of it at will. . . .

Quoted in 1 S. Stromholm, *supra* note 5, at 112, *quoted and discussed in* P. Recht, *supra* note 13, at 29-30.

[56] See P. Recht, *supra* note 13, at 46.

[57] The most notable were les arrêts de 1771 et de 1777. See discussion in *id*. at 33-38.

[58] Monta, *supra* note 52, at 178.

[59] Decrét de 13-19 janvier 1791, and decrét de 19-24 juillet 1793, *discussed in* Sarraute, *supra* note 17, at 465; Monta, *supra* note 52, at 178; P. Recht, *supra* note 13, at 8, 38-40.

[60] J. Labaurie, L'Usurpation en Matière Littéraire et Artistique 9 (1919); 1 S. Strömholm, *supra* note 5, at 113.

[61] See Monta, *supra* note 52, at 178.

[62] Sarraute, *supra* note 17, at 465; P. Recht, *supra* note 13, at 48; 1 S. Strömholm, *supra* note 5, at 114.

[63] See generally P. Recht, *supra* note 13, at 49-93. But Strömholm extends the second period to 1928.

[64] See generally *id*. 48-60.

lowers in the 1830's held to the traditional notion that *droit d'auteur* was a property right, albeit a temporary one.[65] On the other hand, Renouard and his school, influenced by Kant,[66] preferred to dislodge authors' rights from the notion of property, and considered them instead to derive from a more abstract "right of personality."[67] Recht observes that opposition to the "property" characterization of *droit d'auteur* grew even stronger with the early influence of Marx in the 1840's and 1850's,[68] and by the 1860's, a generation of "personalist" writers emerged, who strongly discredited the idea that *droit d'auteur* was a form of property.[69]

It should come as no suprise, then, that during this first period, the notion that there may exist non-property "moral" rights easily could gain acceptance in French courts. By 1880, the foundations had been laid in French jurisprudence for *droit de divulgation, droit à la paternité,* and *droit au respect de l'oeuvre.*[70]

The doctrine of *droit moral* received even greater development in the second period, from 1878 to 1902. In this period, the application of traditional notions of property to *droit d'auteur* was virtually abandoned,[71] and scholars continued to search for a more precise characterization of *droit moral,* and of its place in the larger *droit d'auteur.* Some French scholars, led by Pouillet,[72] tended to hold onto fragments of the property notion of *droit d'auteur,* and developed a theory of "intellectual property," by which *droit d'auteur* combined certain elements of property with elements of purely personal or intellectual rights.

However, the central debate over the nature of authors' rights arose in Germany. Joseph Kohler[73] developed a theory of *"Doppelrecht,"* which considered an intellectual work to be a *"bien immatériel "*[74] from which various rights of personality arose. These personal prerogatives could be separated into two distinct categories of either a patrimonial or a moral

---

[65] For a discussion of Gastambide and his followers, see 1 S. Strömholm, *supra* note 5, at 150-53.

[66] Kant's writings had an even stronger influence over the development of moral rights in Germany. For a discussion of Kant's influence, see *id.* at 182-95.

[67] *Id.* at 154-56. This view was even more popular in Germany. *Id.* at 237-52.

[68] P. Recht, *supra* note 13, at 54.

[69] *Id.* at 58-60. For a discussion of the rise of the "personalists" in Germany, see 1 S. Strömholm, *supra* note 5, at 197-204.

[70] 1 S. Strömholm, *supra* note 5, at 150.

[71] P. Recht, *supra* note 13, at 67-69. Recht discusses the significance of the first Berne Convention in 1886 with regard to the abandonment of the term "property" as applied to intellectual works.

[72] See discussion in *id.* at 62-64.

[73] For a discussion of Kohler's theory, see 1 S. Strömholm, *supra* note 5, at 327-29; P. Recht, *supra* note 13, at 75-82.

[74] P. Recht, *supra* note 13, at 78.

nature.[75] The other principal view, advocated by Alfred Gierke,[76] considered both personal and patrimonial rights to be inseparable parts of a single *"Persönlichkeitsrecht."* [77]

It was in the third period, from 1902 to 1957, that the debate over these two views became resolved.[78] Kohler's "dualist" view triumphed in France, where to this day, *droit d'auteur* is considered to be a right of *"propriété incorporelle"* separable into moral and partrimonial rights.[79] In Germany, the monist school prevailed, and as a result, moral rights *("Urheberpersönlichkeitsrecht")* and exploitative interests form a single right, which expires seventy years after the author's death.[80]

We see, then, that *droit d'auteur* is part of a larger debate over the meaning of "property" and "personality" rights in the civil law system. The debate, in fact, engendered two systems of authors' rights with different characterizations of *droit moral* — each purporting to be as vigilant of the authors' well-being as the other.[81]

B. Characteristics

In France today, both the *droits patrimoniaux* and *droit moral* are enshrined in a single statute, the law of 11 March 1957 ("1957 Law"), whose opening sentence reflects the "natural right" origins of *droit d'auteur:* "The author of a work of the spirit enjoys in that work, by sole virtue of its creation, a right of incorporeal property, exclusive and opposable against all." [82]

This "natural right" character of author's rights is linked to a particular characterization of the artist and his work. *Droit d'auteur* arises from the assumption that an artist infuses into his work something of his own creative personality,[83] and further, that the interests of society fundamentally are opposed to that artistic presence. "When an artist creates, he does more than bring into the world a unique object having only exploi-

---

[75] 1 S. Strömholm, *supra* note 5, at 327; P. Recht, *supra* note 13, at 80-81, comments that Kohler's theory created a right too analogous to the old idea of property.

[76] See discussion in 1 S. Strömholm, *supra* note 5, at 316-18, 329-30; P. Recht, *supra* note 13, at 83-87.

[77] P. Recht, *supra* note 13, at 84.

[78] *Id.* at 90-93.

[79] H. Desbois, *supra* note 13, at 175. But see P. Recht, *supra* note 13, at 274-75.

[80] German Law, *supra* note 28, art. 64(1).

[81] See Pakuscher, Recent Trends in German Copyright Law, 23 Bull. Copr. Soc'y 65, 75 (1976).

[82] 1957 Law, *supra* note 15, art. 1, ¶1 (emphasis added).

[83] *Pacific Comment, supra* note 14, at 860; Giocanti, *supra* note 7, at 628. Also see statement of Poinsard, *quoted in Chillida, supra* note 50, at 12-13.

tive possibilities; he projects into the world part of his personality and subjects it to the ravages of public use.[84]

This is a romantic characterization of the artist, perhaps conjuring up visions of poets in garrets, burning their lyric masterpieces for heat in the icy Parisian winter, or of Walt Whitman, crying out to the corporeal world, "I celebrate myself, and sing myself." [85] Yet, it is because of this characterization of the author and his art that French law feels a need to protect the honor of the author's personality and the integrity of his work. The author has, in a sense, made a gift of his creative genius to the world; in return, he has a right — a moral right — to expect that society respect his creative genius.

With this in mind, French law recognizes a personal, perpetual, inalienable and unassignable moral right in "works of the spirit." Yet as idealistic as the statute may seem, in practice these characteristics have proved to be far more limited.

1. PERSONAL

Even before *droit moral* was codified, French jurists recognized that *droit moral* is attached not to the work, but to the person who created it, and thus, it remains vested in the artist even after the object itself has been transferred.[86] This principle has been codified in article 1 of the 1957 Law,[87] and it holds true even in the case of a work made for hire.[88] French law, however, imposes two conditions in order for moral rights to attach: the person must be (1) a natural person (2) who is in fact the creator of the work.[89] These two conditions have posed practical difficulties, especially in cases of collective or collaborative works, and they have proved to be particularly cumbersome when applied to newer art forms, such as film and television.

The "natural person" requirement means that an organization, such as a private corporation, cannot claim moral rights. Thus, ironically, the requirement can end up restricting the ability of artists' guilds or societies to defend the rights of their members.[90] More important, the requirement

---

[84] Roeder, *supra* note 6, at 557.

[85] Whitman, Song of Myself, in Leaves of Grass. It is interesting to observe that the emergence of *droit moral* in the early 19th century parallels the rise of romanticism in French literature.

[86] "The *droit moral* is inherent in the person, and, according to us, it cannot be conceded by the author to the editor." J. Labaurie, *supra* note 60, at 14.

[87] 1957 Law, *supra* note 15, art. 1, ¶3: "The existence or the conclusion of a contract for licensing of an artist's work or services regarding a work of the spirit does not carry with it any derogation of his enjoyment [of his rights]."

[88] Giocanti, *supra* note 7, at 629.

[89] *Id.* at 628.

[90] See discussion in Sarraute, *supra* note 17, at 483.

seems uniquely inapplicable to collective works, such as newspapers and magazines, where no one natural person has complete responsibility for the work's creation. The 1957 Law, therefore, found it neccessary to create a statutory exception for collective works,[91] so that the rights of authorship may vest in a legal entity.[92]

The "personal" character of *droit moral* is even more cumbersome in the case of collaborative works,[93] for each collaborator could assert his own moral right to detriment of all the others — for example, by enjoining publication of the entire work. Article 10 of the 1957 Law attempted to solve this problem by providing that a collaborative work is the joint property of the co-authors, and that the co-authors may exercise their rights only in unanimity.[94] The unanimity rule itself, however, may have harsh results in the case of a serious disagreement among the authors. Thus, article 10 provides that in such cases, a court, at its own discretion, may choose to ignore the rule.[95]

Finally, the two requirements of being a natural person and having been the creator of the work are most troublesome in the case of cinematographic works,[96] where the contributors are so numerous; indeed, film seems to be the exception to almost everything under the 1957 Law. The statute says that in films, authorship is reserved to "the physical persons who realize the intellectual creation of the work," and creates five categories of persons who qualify as authors: the author of the script, the author of the adaptation, the author of the dialogue, the composer of the

---

[91] 1957 Law, *supra* note 15, art. 9, ¶3, defines a "collective" work as:

a work created under the initiative of a natural or legal person, who edits, publishes, and discloses it under his direction and name, and in which the personal contribution of the various authors who participate in its creation blend into the whole, in view of which such contribution was created, to the extent that it is not possible to attribute to each of them a distinct right over the collectively realized work.

[92] *Id.* art. 13. Portuguese law contains an interesting provision, by which the *droit moral* of a work which falls into the public domain attaches to the state, which exercises it by means of "adequate cultural institutions." Kerever, Le Droit d'Auteur en Europe Occidentale, in Hommage a Henri Desbois: Etudes de Propriete Intellectuelle 35, 50 (1974).

[93] 1957 Law, *supra* note 15, art. 9, ¶1, defines a "collaborative" work as "a work in whose creation several physical persons have concurred." Unlike a collective work, the contribution of each collaborator is less readily separable from the whole.

[94] *Id.* art. 10, ¶2. Paragraph 4 adds, however, that each author may exploit his own contribution separately provided that such exploitation does not prejudice the exploitation of the larger collaborative work.

[95] *Id.* art. 10, ¶3. Also see Giocanti, *supra* note 7, at 629.

[96] The problems of cinematographic works are equally applicable to broadcasting and television. Article 18 of the 1957 Law resolves them in a similar fashion.

music, and the director.[97] Moreover, if the film is adapted from a pre-existing work which is still protected by copyright, the authors of the original work are "assimilated" into the authorship of the film.[98] Thus, actors, camera crew, lighting designers, and other "creators" are excluded from authorship, although their rights may be protected through other doctrines.[99]

2. PERPETUAL

Article 6 unequivocally deems *droit moral* to be perpetual, for it survives both the *droits patrimoniaux* and the author's life.[100] In order for this principle to be of any utility, there must be some way for future generations to assert the right. Thus, even before *droit moral* was codified, it was held that the moral right could be transmitted by will to the author's heirs "under the conditions of applicable law,"[101] and today, the inheritability of the right is set forth in article 6, paragraph 4.

At first glance, the inheritability of *droit moral* would seem to contradict, at least in theory, the principle that *droit moral* attaches only to the person of the creator of the work. French law may have resolved this issue by distinguishing between the moral right itself and the right to exercise it.[102] Thus, if the *droit moral* is transferred by will, the artist's heirs get only the right to exercise the right, not the right itself. One may question the practical wisdom of this distinction, for the heir, while not possessing the moral right, still is entitled to damages for its violation.

We should observe, moreover, that certain moral rights in a work do indeed expire upon the author's death. It generally held that *droit à la paternité* and *droit au respect* survive the author, once again with the limitation that the heirs inherit only the right to exercise the right, not the right itself.[103] On the other extreme, those aspects of *droit moral* which depend on the exercise of the author's volition are said to expire with the death of the author.[104] Accordingly, *droit de retrait* and *droit de repentir* may not be exercised by the author's successors.

A more difficult issue arises with the *post mortem* exercise of *droit de*

---

[97] 1957 Law, *supra* note 15, art. 14.

[98] *Id.* art. 14.

[99] In many European countries, rights of performers and technical crews are protected under the doctrine of *"droits voisins"* or *"neighboring rights."* For a discussion of neighboring rights in West Germany, see Pakuscher, *supra* note 81, at 73-74.

[100] 1957 Law, *supra* note 15, art. 6 ¶3. See discussion in Sarraute, *supra* note 17, at 483; Giocanti, *supra* note 7, at 631.

[101] J. Labaurie, *supra* note 60, at 14.

[102] *Chillida, supra* note 50, at 17.

[103] LeTarnec, *supra* note 19, at 74.

[104] *Id.*, at 72-73.

divulgation. First, there is the problem of who may assert the right. Article 19 provides that the right of disclosure is to be exercised by the artist's executors during their lives, and afterwards by the author's descendants, spouse, heirs, or legatees, in that order.[105]

A second problem with the right of disclosure is the manifest possibility that the heirs will abuse the right. Article 20 provides that in a case of serious abuse, the courts have the power "to order any appropriate measures." The courts also may take charge of administering the right of disclosure in case of serious conflict among the artist's successors in interest, or in case there is no heir, or in case of disinheritance.[106]

It is not yet settled whether the power of the courts to administer the *droit de divulgation* under article 20 may be extended to include *droit à la paternité* and *droit au respect*, as well.[107] French courts have, however, recognized the possible abuses which may result from the exercise of these rights *post mortem*, and have held that "an heir must exercise the moral right, insofar as he is vested with it, for the sole purpose of effectuating the wishes of the deceased and not to serve his own interests."[108]

A final complication arises if the artist believes that his heirs will not adequately safeguard his moral interests. French law resolved this issue by allowing an artist to transfer his rights by will to a third party.[109]

Even with these limitations, the perpetual nature of *droit moral* has evoked criticism. Pierre Recht declares article 6 to be "juridical heresy,"[110] for nowhere else in French law does a personal right exist in perpetuity.

3. Inalienable and Unassignable

Article 6 declares the moral right to be inalienable, and the strongest proponents of *droit d'auteur* have emphasized the transcen-

---

[105] 1957 Law, *supra* note 15, art. 19.

[106] *Id.* art. 20, ¶1:

In a case of manifest abuse of the right to exercise or not to exercise the droit de divulgation on the part of the deceased author's representatives, as provided for in the preceding article, the civil court may order any appropriate measure. The same shall apply if there is a conflict among said representatives, if they have no knowledge of the right, or in case of absence or disinheritance of said representatives.

[107] Giocanti, *supra* note 7, at 643, citing Françon, says that article 20 probably does include *droit à la paternité and droit au respect.* LeTarnec, *supra* note 19, at 72-73, is less certain.

[108] Sarraute, *supra* note 17, at 484. For a brief discussion of *abus de droit,* see *Chillida, supra* note 50, at 17. It should be noted that in France, the National Literary Fund is entrusted with the task of securing respect for art works in the public domain. Sarraute, *supra* note 17, at 486.

[109] "The author can, if he judges his heirs to be unworthy, withhold from them the custody of his moral right, and vest it in a third party." J. Labaurie, *supra* note 60, at 19. Article 6 of the 1957 Law codifies this principle.

[110] P. Recht, *supra* note 13, at 292 (agreeing with Savarier).

dent importance of this principle. "Renouncing [one's] moral right," says Desbois, "would be equivalent to moral suicide."[111] And if an author may not renounce his *droit moral*, neither may he, during his life, contract it away to a third-party, even when the third-party has been assigned the material object and the exploitative rights in it.[112] Thus, if a contract contains a clause requiring transfer of the moral right as a condition of employment, some writers assert that the clause is unenforceable.[113]

As a matter of practice, however, such clauses often are found in contracts, and courts do enforce them in many situations.[114] Pierre Recht, the strongest critic of the inalienability principle, states that the courts are correct to do so, for any other decision would render meaningless the force of contracts.[115]

The statutory declaration of inalienability, moreover, is riddled with exceptions.[116] We already have seen that in a collaborative work, each co-author is deemed to have relinquished most of his own moral preroga-tives, and to have accepted his position in a commonly held moral right. Articles 15 and 16 establish a comparable exception for films. As we shall see later, an assignment of the right to adapt a work to another medium necessarily requires the abandonment of at least part of the right of integrity.[117] Furthermore, the *droit de repentir* ordinarily may be exercised only over a work that is not yet made public; thus, publication of a book or performance of a play may constitute an implicit waiver of that right.[118]

Recht points out, finally, that the German Law of 1965 is more lenient than French law on the issue of assignment of authors' rights, and the Berne Convention ignores the inalienability rule altogether. Thus, he concludes, "One will discover in its application the unreality of the formula; the imperatives of practicality must survive."[119]

We see from its application that the basic formulation of the charac-teristics of *droit moral* gives rise to practical difficulties, which French law has only begun to resolve through statutory and judge-made exceptions. And yet, if United States legislators or judges decide to adopt the princi-ple of moral right by name, these are but the first of the problems which ought to be addressed.

---

[111] Giocanti, *supra* note 7, at 630 (discussing Desbois).

[112] 1957 Law, *supra* note 15, art 6, ¶3. See Giocanti, *supra* note 7, at 630.

[113] See, e.g., statements of Françon, *cited in* Giocanti, *supra* note 7, at 630.

[114] See, e.g., Bernstein v. Matador et Pathé Cinéma, [1933] D.H. 1933, 533, D.A. 1933, 104, *discussed in* Strauss, *supra* note 6, at 516 n.48.

[115] P. Recht, *supra* note 13, at 281-86.

[116] Treece, *supra* note 40, at 505-06.

[117] P. Recht, *supra* note 13, at 283, and discussion *infra*.

[118] P. Recht, *supra* note 13, at 282, and discussion *infra*.

[119] P. Recht, *supra* note 13, at 285.

C. Categories

During the author's life, a work of art is protected both during the period of creation and after it has been disclosed to the public. "These are two distinct periods, separated by the artist's act of disengaging himself from his work and submitting it to the judgment of the public."[120]

The "pre-disengagement" period affords the artist absolute sovereignty over his work; even if the artist is under contract, he has a right to alter or destroy his work, and to decide whether and when to make it public. "No one [else] can claim any right to it whatsoever."[121] After disengagement, the work may become the subject of contracts or commercial transactions, and property or exploitative rights in it may be transferred.[122] The author, however, retains certain moral prerogatives.

1. DROIT DE DIVULGATION

The *droit de divulgation*, or "right of disclosure,"[123] involves the very moment of "disengagement." It is the right of the author to have complete authority over the decision to publish, sell, unveil, or by any other means make his work public. The right undoubtedly stems from a belief that only the artist himself can determine when a work is completed, and also from a recognition of the fact that public disclosure of a work has a direct impact on the artist's reputation.

Droit de divulgation was codified in Italy as early as 1941,[124] and is recognized in France in article 19 of the 1957 law. "The author alone has the right to disclose his work. . . . He determines the process of disclosure and fixes the conditions thereof."[125] In order to appreciate the full significance of this provision, it is important to review briefly the judicial doctrine which engendered it.

Droit de divulgation received its most celebrated endorsement in the landmark case of *Whistler v. Eden*[126] in 1898. James McNeill Whistler had

---

[120] Sarraute, *supra* note 17, at 466.

[121] *Id.* at 466.

[122] *Id.* at 466.

[123] "*Droit de divulgation*" sometimes has been translated as "right of publication." That translation, however, may cause some confusion with the common law "publication" doctrine. Moreover, in the case of graphic arts, "publication" might become confused with the right of "reproduction," which is one of the *droits patrimoniaux*.

[124] Italian Law of April 22, 1941 (Law No. 633), UNESCO, *supra* note 15, art. 12 [hereinafter cited as Italian Law], *also cited in* Giocanti, *supra* note 7, at 631. Also see the Japanese Law of May 6, 1970 (Law No. 48 of 1970), art. 18, *translated in* UNESCO, Copyright Laws and Treaties of the World [hereinafter cited as Japanese Law].

[125] 1957 Law, *supra* note 11, art. 19 ¶1.

[126] Judgment of Mar. 20, 1895, Trib. civ. Seine, [1898] D.P.2 465; Judgment of Dec. 2, 1897, Cour d'Appel Paris; Judgment of May 14, 1900, Cass. Civ., [1900]

been commissioned to paint a portrait of the wife of Lord Eden. When the time came for delivery, a dispute arose as to payment. Whistler then claimed to be dissatisfied with the work, painted out the face of the subject, and refused to deliver the portrait. Lord Eden sued for breach of contract, and a trial court ordered that the portrait be delivered. The Paris Court of Appeals, however, reversed the decision holding that so long as the artist was dissatisfied with his work, he could not be compelled to deliver it. The artist, while excused from specific performance, was required to pay damages to Lord Eden for his failure to perform under the contract.

The *Whistler* case reflects the French view that an artist is the absolute master of the decision to disclose his work, even when the right of disclosure would seem to impair contractual obligations. "Thus, the artist's lack of inspiration is not a breach of contract. . . . [I]t is a 'normal risk,' foreseeable by all parties." [127] The exercise of the *droit de divulgation*, however, requires good faith on the part of the artist; he could not, for example, claim to be dissatisfied with a work and then sell it unaltered to another buyer for a higher price.[128]

An American lawyer may find it anomalous that a contract which does not call for either party's satisfaction as a condition for delivery could be held unenforceable simply because one contracting party is dissatisfied with his own performance. Yet critics have observed that an American or English court of equity also would refuse to grant specific performance for a contract to create.[129]

The second leading case, *L'Affaire Camoin*,[130] upheld the artist's *droit de divulgation* not at the expense of another party's contractual right, but rather at the expense of another party's property right. An artist, dissatisfied with some of his own paintings, slashed and discarded them. The defendant found the mutilated paintings, restored them, and put them up for auction. The Paris Court of Appeals, holding for the artist, ordered that the works be destroyed according to the artist's wishes, and said: "[A]lthough whoever gathers up the pieces becomes the indisputable owner of them through possession, the ownership is limited to the physical quality of the fragments, and does not deprive the painter of the moral right which he always retains over his work." [131]

D.P.1. 5000, *discussed in* 1 S. Strömholm, *supra* note 5, at 282-83; Sarraute, *supra* note 17, at 467-68; Roeder, *supra* note 6, at 559.

[127] Sarraute, *supra* note 17, at 468.

[128] *Id.* at 468. The issue also is discussed in Roeder, *supra* note 6, at 559.

[129] Roeder, *supra* note 6, at 558-59. It may even be argued that, in English and American Law, equity is a form of "moral right."

[130] Judgment of Mar. 6, 1931, Cour d'Appel Paris, [1931] D.P.2. 88, *discussed in* Sarraute, *supra* note 17, at 468-69.

[131] Sarraute, *supra* note 17, at 468.

Camoin illustrates dramatically the extent of an artist's *droit moral*, but it has not gone without criticism. Writers have asked what is the meaning of "ownership of a material object" if the artist's *droit de divulgation* can require the material object to be destroyed;[132] indeed, French law does not adequately resolve this paradox. One also might question whether courts ought to be in the business of fulfilling artists' wishes so literally. After all, if *droit moral* arises from a notion that art works somehow are more sacred than fungible property, it would be ironic for the doctrine to justify court-ordered art-burnings.

Droit de divulgation was again at issue in *L'Affaire Rouault*.[133] In that case, Vollard, an art dealer, kept locked in his room over 800 paintings, which the artist Rouault would visit from time to time, to apply finishing touches. Upon Vollard's death, the art dealer's heirs claimed ownership of the works, but Rouault claimed that since the works were unfinished, only he "could decide their final delivery." [134] The court held that ownership in the paintings had never passed to Vollard, and ordered the works returned to Rouault, upon repayment to the heirs of the advances which Vollard had paid Rouault on the paintings.

An artist retains absolute sovereignty over a work until he chooses to disclose it, but the *Rouault* case illustrates the great difficulty of determining what constitutes disclosure. After all, here the artist accepted advances and kept the virtually completed works in the custody of an art dealer; one might well ask how many more incidents of disclosure must be present before a work is deemed to have been "made public," and, therefore, to have become transferable. Moreover, the *Rouault* court decided the issue of disclosure on the basis of whether or not the work was finished, and we might question, once again, whether such issues are appropriate for judicial inquiry.[135] Indeed, the court's failure to separate the issue of "disclosure" from the issue of "completion" has been a source of criticism.[136]

Although one may well question the wisdom of the decisions in these cases, it was these principles which shaped the development of *droit de*

---

[132] *Id.* at 469.

[133] Judgment of Mar. 19, 1947, Cour d'Appel Paris, [1949] D.P. 20, *discussed in* Sarraute, *supra* note 17, at 469-70.

[134] Sarraute, *supra* note 17, at 469.

[135] "It is hardly necessary to point out that the court's assumption of power to decide on the completeness [of a work of art] is a negation of the most obvious aspect of the artist's moral right." *Id.* at 471 (discussing l'Affaire Bonnard, Judgment of Oct. 10, 1951, Trib. Civ. Seine, [1951] Gaz. Pal. 2. 290; Judgment of Jan. 19, 1953, Cour d'Appel Paris, [1953] Gaz. Pal. 1.99; [1953] J.C.P. 7427).

[136] In *Bonnard, supra* note 135, the court insisted that the issue of *droit de divulgation* is not whether or not the work has been completed, but, rather, whether or not it has been made public. See Sarraute, *supra* note 17, at 470-71.

divulgation, and which the French legislature sought to enshrine in the 1957 Law. Today, the right has even broader scope, which article 19 only begins to reflect.

Under the modern formulation, first, the *droit de divulgation* is considered a "personal" right, which means that the author alone can decide when and how the work will be publicly disclosed, even when the work and all pecuniary rights in it are owned by the transferee.[137] Thus, if an artist wants one of his paintings reproduced, the owner of the painting cannot, without compelling reasons, refuse to cooperate.[138] The right is not absolute, however, for the subject of a portrait may validly refuse to allow reproduction of the portrait if the reproduction would endanger the subject's privacy.[139]

Secondly, *droit de divulgation* is considered to be "discretionary," for the artist has sole discretion over the decision to disclose. An important application of this principle would be a case where a creditor seizes a manuscript against the author's wishes. Such seizure, while arguably legal in Great Britain or the United States,[140] could violate the artist's *droit de divulgation* in France.

Another important application of the right's discretionary character is in cases where, as a result of the artist's marriage, an art work has become community property.[141] The extent of the spouse's rights, unsettled before 1957,[142] was resolved by article 25 of the 1957 Law, which declares that the author alone retains discretion over the decision to publish.[143]

Finally, the statutory scheme deems the *droit de divulgation* to be

---

[137] 1957 Law, *supra* note 15, art. 19, ¶1, art. 29, ¶1. Also see discussion in Giocanti, *supra* note 7, at 632.

The scheme is somewhat different under the Japanese Law, *supra* note 124, art. 18, §2 (Right to Make Public), which provides that if the copyright in an unpublished work is assigned, the author is deemed to have consented to having his work made public. See Iijima, Musical Copyrights in Japan, 23 Bull. Copr. Soc'y 371, 395 (1976).

[138] 1957 Law, *supra* note 15, art. 29, ¶3; Giocanti, *supra* note 7, at 632.

[139] S. Strömholm, La Concurrence Entre L'Auteur d'Une Oeuvre de l'Esprit et le Cessionnaire d'Un Droit d'Exploitation 17-18 (1969) [hereinafter cited as *Concurrence*]; Giocanti, *supra* note 7, at 632 n.37.

[140] The issue of whether or not a manuscript under common law copyright could be seized and published was unsettled. See Treece, *supra* note 40, at 490. Giocanti, *supra* note 7, at 632; Roeder, *supra* note 6, at 559.

[141] A discussion of *droit moral* in relation to marital rights is beyond the scope of this paper. For a discussion, see G. Gavin, *supra* note 13, at 185-223.

[142] See, e.g., *Bonnard, supra* note 135.

[143] "Article 25 provides, moreover, that in all matrimonial arrangements, and with the penalty of rendering void all contrary clauses in the marriage contract, the *droit de divulgation* remains vested solely in the author. This confirms the discretionary character of this right." A. LeTarnec, *supra* note 19, at 28-29.

"exclusive."[144] This means that a work which is transferred may be exploited only within the limitations prescribed by the author.[145] The impact of this principle falls most heavily on the interpretation of contracts. An artist who contracts for a gallery to display his work cannot be held to have authorized its reproduction, as well, even if the language of the contract is ambiguous. Thus, "[a]ny method of disclosure that is not accepted unequivocally by the author shall be excluded from the exploitation."[146]

Armed with this personal, discretionary, and exclusive right, an artist who desires not to complete a work may refuse to create under contract, so long as he is willing to pay damages to the injured party.[147] Even if the artist has completed the work, he still may refuse to deliver it, again, if he is willing to pay damages.[148] Once the artist has paid damages as ordered by the court, the parties are free of all obligations to one another, and the author is free to exhibit, sell, or otherwise exploit the work,[149] subject to requirements of good faith.

Despite the apparent breadth of the right of disclosure, French law has found it necessary to limit its application in certain cases.[150] We already have seen the unanimity rule for the exercise of moral rights over collaborative works. This principle is especially important in the exercise of *droit de divulgation*, for it is here that the assertion of the right by one author — for example, in demanding the destruction of the work — could most readily prejudice the rights of the other co-authors. French law also has held that if one collaborator fails to complete his part of the work, "the author who is unable to complete his contribution shall not be entitled to oppose the use of the part of his contribution already in existence."[151]

---

[144] 1957 Law, *supra* note 15, art. 30, ¶¶2-3.

[145] Giocanti, *supra* note 7, at 632 (citing Desbois).

[146] *Id.* at 632.

[147] A. LeTarnec, *supra* note 19, at 30, G. Gavin, *supra* note 13, at 11. For a detailed discussion of the validity of contracts to create under French, German, and Scandinavian legal systems, see 2, 1 S. Strömholm, *supra* note 5, at 121-262.

[148] "The result of this principle is that the refusal of the author to deliver the work invokes the responsibility of the author, to the extent he is at fault, and that the sanction for such refusal may be translated into an assessment of damages to be paid to the creditor." A. LeTarnec, *supra* note 19, at 36. Also see G. Gavin, *supra* note 13, at 47.

[149] A. LeTarnec, *supra* note 19, at 37.

[150] Giocanti, *supra* note 7, at 633-36, suggests that limitations on *droit de divulgation* may be classified either as those which arise from the contract (i.e., where the exercise of the right is limited by the author's duty to pay damages) or as those which arise from the nature of the work itself.

[151] *Id.* at 635. But see l'Affaire Léo Ferré, Judgment of Dec. 2, 1963, Cour d'Appel Paris, *cited in* Sarraute, *supra* note 17, at 474, in which the court refused to follow the unanimity rule.

Droit de divulgation is especially cumbersome when applied to cinematographic works, because the detailed process of film editing and distribution makes it difficult to determine when a film has been "made public." Thus, the French legislature found it necessary to create detailed provisions for films. First, article 16 states that co-authors of a film may exercise their rights only over the *completed work*, and it defines completion as the time when "the first master-print has been made by common consent of the co-authors and the producer." [152] Then, article 17 and 19 together allow the producer by himself to exercise the *droit de divulgation*. [153]

Droit de divulgation is a useful doctrine, but it functions best when the artist works alone. The exceptions for film and collaborative works demonstrate the impracticality of the right when it is applied to works with many creators. At present, we cannot even imagine the problems which will arise as new art forms — such as electronically realized music — emerge, requiring numerous "technical," as well as "artistic," authors for their creation. [154]

Furthermore, even in the case of a single artist, *droit de divulgation* seldom can be asserted without indemnifying another party's contract or property rights, for even French law has recognized the inequities which the right of disclosure creates. This means that, ultimately, the right of disclosure depends on the artist's ability and willingness to purchase it.

2. DROIT DE RETRAIT OU DE REPENTIR

As a corollary to *droit de divulgation*, there exists a second category of moral rights: even after the work has been disengaged and made public, the artist has a right to withdraw the work from publication (*droit de retrait*) or to make modifications in it (*droit de repentir*).

These two rights are recognized in Italian and German law. [155] In France, they are codified in article 32 of the 1957 Law, which states that even if the rights of exploitation in a work have been transferred, and even after the work has been published, the author enjoys the right to withdraw or modify the work, so long as the artist indemnifies the

---

[152] 1957 Law, *supra* note 15, art. 16. For an excellent discussion of this issue, see Giocanti, *supra* note 7, at 635.

[153] In the United States, ordinarily the producer of the film holds the copyright over the entire film, and exercises all rights of distribution.

[154] A related issue arises with regard to "random" music, for it is arguable that the work is different every time it is performed, and therefore is never really "disclosed" to the public.

[155] Giocanti, *supra* note 7, at 638. See, e.g., Italian Law, *supra* note 124, arts. 142-143.

transferee in advance of the exercise of the right.[156] Scholars add that the withdrawal or modification requires no justification other than the author's "change of conviction,"[157] and that French courts will not pass judgment on the artist's motives for assertion of the right[158] — a kind of artistic "act of state" doctrine.

It is difficult to evaluate *droit de retrait* and *droit de repentir*, for both their existence and their application in the courts are disputable. Before 1957, the rights had been discussed by French jurists, but virtually never applied in the courts.[159] Since 1957, few French cases have even addressed the issue, and those scholars who do support *droit de retrait ou de repentir* still differ as to the nature of the right and the parameters of its application.[160]

The French statute on its face would seem to indicate that *droit de*

---

[156] 1957 Law, *supra* note 15, art. 32, ¶1:

Notwithstanding the transfer of his right of exploitation, the author, even subsequent to the publication of his work, enjoys a right of modification or withdrawal vis-à-vis the transferee. Nonetheless, he may not exercise the right unless he agrees to indemnify the transferee in advance for any prejudice which such modification or withdrawal may cause him.

[157] In German law, *droit de repentir* actually is called "right of revocation for change of conviction." Kerever, *supra* note 92, at 49.

[158] "The author's decision presents an absolute unilateral and discretionary right. The author does not need to justify himself before the court. French law does not submit the author's decision to judicial authority, because the court would be forced to take into consideration 'the motives of an intellectual and moral nature' that prompted the retraction." Giocanti, *supra* note 7, at 637. Note, however, that Italian courts will review the artist's motives for withdrawal. *Id.* at 638.

[159] In 1953, Tager wrote:

This right often is spoken of, but it has not yet fully manifested itself in French law. Not one judicial decision has recognized it. Few authors have seriously mantained its existence, and yet it exists, even if only as a myth; an advantage — a bit fictitious and indeterminate — attached to his status as artist.

Quoted in G. Gavin, *supra* note 13, at 64. Also see Sarraute, *supra* note 17, at 476-77.

It is arguable, however, that the case of Anatole France v. Lemerre, Judgment of Dec. 4, 1911, Pataille 1912. 1. 98, represents an early recognition of *droit de retrait*. In 1882, Anatole France had sold a manuscript to a publisher for 3000 francs. The publisher delayed publication for 25 years, at which point the author, now a famous writer, claimed that the manuscript no longer represented his work, and sought to enjoin publication. The court upheld France's claim, but ordered him to return the 3000 francs. See Roeder, *supra* note 6, at 560.

[160] For a discussion of the positions of various French jurists on *droit de retrait ou de repentir*, see P. Recht, *supra* note 13, at 304. Also see G. Gavin, *supra* note 13, at 63-74.

retrait allows a writer to interrupt the publication of his book,[161] or even attempt to remove a published work from circulation; *droit de repentir* could even mean that an artist may make changes in a work already disseminated to the public. Both situations give rise to tremendous practical difficulties, and readily could place an unrealistic burden on publishers and distributors of literary and artistic works.

It is no wonder, then, that French law has seen fit to impose limitations on the right, even this early in the right's development. Article 32, for example, states that the artist must be prepared to indemnify the transferee in advance for any losses which the retraction or modification may cause.[162] While this provision does attempt to rectify the inequities which could result from an exercise of moral rights, it also renders it difficult for the artist to assert his right. As in *droit de divulgation*, the exercise of *droit de retrait ou de repentir* often depends simply on the artist's ability to pay for it.

As a second restriction on *droit de retrait*, article 32 adds that in the case of a withdrawal, "if the author does publish the retracted work, he must first offer it to the original transferee on the same terms as the original contract." [163] This provision attempts to protect the publishers from bad faith exercise of moral rights, but one may question whether the publisher's interests are adequately protected. The statute, after all, does not specify whether an author who retracts a work and then makes changes so significant as to constitute a new work still can be compelled to offer it to original transferee for publication.

The *droit de repentir* also is limited. It is said, for example, that a writer may not make changes in a manuscript after the exploitative rights have been transferred, unless the changes are insignificant and do not substantially alter the work.[164] Moreover, the editor needs only accept those changes which were "normally foreseeable when the contract was signed." [165]

---

[161] Indeed, LeTarnec refers to *droit de retrait* as the "right to interrupt publication." A. LeTarnec, *supra* note 19, at 43.

[162] 1957 Law, *supra* note 15, art. 32, ¶1. Note, also, that German law has created the same limitation. Kerever, *supra* note 92, at 49.

[163] 1957 Law, *supra* note 15, art. 32, ¶2. (Translation in Giocanti, *supra* note 7, at 638).

[164] "The editor cannot be forced to accept changes of such nature as to alter the work in a substantial manner, for the object of the contract cannot be changed, even in part, without the agreement of both parties." *Id.* at 639.

G. Gavin, *supra* note 13, at 72, also writes: "The modifications which the author may be required to accept can only be secondary modifications which tend to give to the work a more elevated degree of completion, in conformity with an already established literary or artistic reputation."

[165] Giocanti, *supra* note 7, at 639. Also see G. Gavin, *supra* note 13 (citing Michaelidis-Nouaros).

Most important, although article 32 applies even after a contract of exploitation has been signed, French courts eventually may hold that *droit de retrait* and *droit de repentir* exist only as long as the artist retains all property rights in the work, for leading scholars believe that as soon as the property rights are alienated, the *droit de retrait* and *droit de repentir* cease to exist.[166] This means that an artist who sells a painting or sculpture "cannot unilaterally cancel the contract of sale or donation."[167] It also means that the *droit de repentir* may not be exercised without the consent of the owner of the art work, for the artist has no right to repossess his creation in order to make the desired modifications.[168]

This limitation did receive some judicial recognition by the Paris Court of Appeals in 1961, when it assessed damages against the artist Vlaminck.[169] Vlaminck had erased his signature from a painting, claiming it to be a forgery. The court's reasoning was twofold: "If the painter was correct in his estimate, he still had no right to alter another person's property. If, on the contrary, the painting was not a forgery, Vlaminck's moral right did not permit him to exercise a right of withdrawal after having sold the canvas."[170]

These limitations may constitute the only equitable way of administering such an unorthodox area of *droit moral*. Indeed, without them, *droit de retrait* and *droit de repentir* could prove to be an invitation for injustice and impracticality. Yet, the limitations also should serve to illustrate that the two rights not only are commercially impracticable, but also are fundamentally inapplicable to many art forms, most notably, the plastic arts. Moreover, when we observe the extensive limitations on the two rights, we can only wonder what is left of them at all.

3. DROIT À LA PATERNITÉ

Since the artist injects his own creative personality into his work, French law vests him with the right to claim authorship of it. Thus, article 6 of the 1957 Law states: "The author enjoys the right to have his name, his status as author, and his work respected."[171] Although this clause also embodies the right of integrity, it is considered to be the statutory source of the *droit à la paternité*, the right of authorship.

The deceptively simple concept of *droit à la paternité* was first recog-

---

[166] See, e.g., statements of Savatier and Desbois, *cited in* G. Gavin, *supra* note 13, at 70.

[167] Giocanti, *supra* note 7, at 638.

[168] Sarraute, *supra* note 17, at 477.

[169] Judgment of Apr. 19, 1961, Cour d'Appel Paris, [1961] Gaz. Pal. 2.218, *discussed in* Sarraute, *supra* note 17, at 477.

[170] Sarraute, *supra* note 17, at 477.

[171] 1957 Law, *supra* note 15, art. 6, ¶1.

nized in 1837, when the Paris Court of Appeals declared: "The collaborator whose name has been omitted without his knowledge from the title of a work may obtain recognition of his authorship and his rights through the courts."[172]

Today, *droit à la paternité* has blossomed into three rights. First, an author has a right to be recognized by name as the author of his work,[173] and by the same reasoning, he has a right to publish anonymously or under a pseudonym.[174] Second, the author has a right to prevent his work from being attributed to someone else.[175] And, third, the artist has a right to prevent his name from being used on works which he did not in fact create.[176]

The first category of *droit à la paternité* has been applied broadly in a multitude of situations. First, it has been held to mean that the author's name must appear not only on his work but also on all copies of the work,[177] as well as on all publicity materials which precede or accompany its sale,[178] even if the author has contracted otherwise.[179] If an author is quoted or cited in another work, he has a right to have his name appear with the quote or citation.[180] A reproduction of a painting, sculpture, or architectural model must bear the name of the original artist.[181] All co-

---

[172] Jurisprudence Général Dalloz, 1857, under the heading "Propriété littéraire et artistique," N° 194, cited in G. Gavin, *supra* note 13, at 50-51. (Translation in Sarraute, *supra* note 17, at 478.)

[173] Strauss, *supra* note 6, at 508; *William and Mary Comment, supra* note 6, at 597; *Georgetown Comment, supra* note 6, at 1540; Comment, The Monty Python Litigation — Of Moral Right and the Lanham Act, 125 U. Pa. L. Rev. 611, 615 (1977) [hereinafter cited as *Pennsylvania Comment*].

[174] Judgment of Dec. 7, 1955, Trib. civ. Seine, 1 Ch., [1956] Gaz. Pal. I. 195, *cited in* A. LeTarnec, *supra* note 19, at 39. Anonymous or pseudonymous publication may give rise to practical difficulties, especially the problem of determining the duration of copyright. These matters are addressed in article 22 of the 1957 Law. For a discussion, see G. Gavin, *supra* note 13, at 58-59.

[175] See sources cited in note 173 *supra*.

[176] *Id.* Also see Giocanti, *supra* note 7, at 637.

[177] G. Gavin, *supra* note 13, at 53.

[178] Judgment of Feb. 20, 1922, Trib. civ. Seine, [1922] Gaz. Pal. 2.282, cited in A. LeTarnec, *supra* note 19, at 39. Also see Strauss, *supra* note 6, at 506.

[179] Sarraute, *supra* note 17, at 485.

[180] Judgment of July 24, 1924, Trib. civ. Seine, [1925] Gaz. Pal.II.463; Judgment of Mar. 19, 1926, Cass. crim. [1927] D.P.25, *cited in* A. LeTarnec, *supra* note 19, at 39.

[181] A. LeTarnec, *supra* note 19, at 39. In 1954, a lower French court held that an artist, whose signature on a war monument had been defaced, had a right to have the monument repaired and his signature restored. Judgment of July 8, 1954, Trib. civ. Confolens, discussed in G. Gavin, *supra* note 13, at 51.

authors have a right to be identified as the creators of a collaborative work, as do authors of films.[182] Interestingly, a photographer has a right to be named the "author" of his photograph,[183] even though the film camera-man need not be included among the "authors" of a film.[184] And in a collective work, such as newspaper or magazine, each contributor has a moral right to sign his own article.[185]

The artist's right to sign his own paintings was dramatically upheld in the 1966 case of *Guille c. Colmant.*[186] In that case, a contract between an artist and an art dealer required the artist to sign with a designated pseudonym all works commissioned by the dealer, and to leave all of his other works unsigned. The Paris Court of Appeals declared the contract void, as a violation of the artist's *droit à la paternité.*

Oddly enough, examples of the second category under *droit à la paternité* are difficult to find in French court decisions.[187] The third category, however, has been applied in at least two kinds of cases. First, an author or his heir has the right to remove the author's name from distorted or mutilated editions of his work.[188] And, secondly, the right to prevent wrongful attribution of authorship allows the author to protest the use of his name without his permission in advertisements.[189] For example, *Pangrazi e Silvestri c. Comitato,*[190] an Italian case in 1974, held that an artist's *diritto alla paternità* was violated when his picture was used, without his permission, to advertise a political issue.

Droit à la paternité may well be the least controversial of all the moral rights. It suffers from few, if any, restrictions, and its exercise appears to have the least tendency to prejudice the contract or property rights of

---

[182] Sarraute, *supra* note 17, at 478.

[183] *Id.*

[184] 1957 Law, *supra* note 15, art. 14.

[185] Giocanti, *supra* note 7, at 636.

[186] Cour d'Appel, Paris, [1967] Gaz. Pal. 1.17, discussed in Sarraute, *supra* note 17, at 478-79.

[187] P. Recht, *supra* note 13, at 288. An example of the second category, however, may be the Judgment of May 30, 1955, Trib. civ. Clermont, [1951] D. 780, discussed in G. Gavin, *supra* note 13, at 51. In that case, a tombstone had been signed by the marble cutter and not by the artist. The artist was held to have a right to have his authorship take precedence over that of the marble cutter.

[188] J. Labaurie, *supra* note 60, at 15; *William and Mary Comment, supra* note 6, at 597. It is here that *droit à la paternité* and *droit au respect de l'oeuvre* overlap.

[189] See, e.g., Bernard-Rousseau c. Société des Galéries Lafayette, Judgment of Mar. 13, 1973, Trib. gr. inst. Paris, 3 Ch. (unpublished), cited in 1 J. Merryman and A. Elsen, *supra* note 22, at 4-25, and discussion *infra.*

[190] Judgment of May 6, 1974, Pret. Roma, *cited and discussed in* 1975 Il Diritto di Autore 119-22.

others. It comes as no surprise, then, that the right is recognized by the Berne Convention,[191] and it even receives some protection in the People's Republic of China.[192]

Yet, the *droit à la paternité* poses problems which too often are overlooked by American observers. First, there is the question of abandonment, waiver, or assignment of the right. Early in the development of *droit moral*, French jurists differed as to whether the author could by contract divest himself of his *droit à la paternité*,[193] to the extent that one observer, in 1940, declared the question to be "one of the most difficult in the entire realm of moral right."[194] The possibility that an artist could assign or waive the right gained further support from early court decisions holding that a work done at the command of an editor could be considered the unrestricted property of the editor.[195]

The 1957 Law presumably answered the question by declaring the artist's rights to be personal, perpetual, inalienable, and unassignable,[196] but even today, French scholars continue to debate the wisdom of that rule and the scope of its applicability.[197] Desbois, at one extreme, writes that an author "can no more abandon his authorship than a father can abdicate his status as father." [198] Recht, on the other hand, asks why the law should forbid an author to promise — in return for compensation — that he will not announce himself to be the true author of his work:

> Must we always consider authors to be nursery school children? I ask, like Monsieur Lyon-Caen: "Why should we treat authors like minors, and defend

---

[191] 1971 Paris Revision to the Berne Convention, *supra* note 34, art. 6 bis, *reprinted in* UNESCO, *supra* note 15.

[192] For a discussion of authors' rights in China, see Loeber, Copyright Law and Publishing in the People's Republic of China, 24 U.C.L.A. L. Rev. 907 (1977).

[193] See A. LeTarnec, *supra* note 19, at 40-41.

[194] Roeder, *supra* note 6, at 564. G. Gavin, *supra* note 13, at note 28, at 59-62, discusses the traditional debate over the inalienability of *droit à la paternité*. Of particular interest is the attitude of Pouillet, *id.* at 60:

> There are today, and there always will be, obscure writers, working for a pittance, and valuing glory less than money. Such people license their industry away, and cannot reclaim a single property right over the work which they themselves conceived and wrote under the employ and for the account of a third party.

[195] See, e.g., Judgment of Mar. 27, 1905, Trib. civ. Nantes, [1907] D. II.297, *cited in* G. Gavin, *supra* note 13, at 60. This issue was settled by the 1957 Law, *supra* note 15, art. 1, ¶3. See note 87, *supra*. In the United States, copyright in works made for hire is presumed to be vested in the employer. 17 U.S.C. §201(b)(1976).

[196] 1957 Law, *supra* note 15, art. 6.

[197] But see A. LeTarnec, *supra* note 19, at 40-41, who says that the 1957 Law definitively settled the issue.

[198] H. Desbois, *cited in* G. Gavin, *supra* note 13, at 58.

them against acts permitted to every other person, regarding every other type of property and every type of rights?" [199]

The result, as Giocanti observes, is that while artists in Great Britain and the United States may waive their right to authorship by contract, "in France, agreements for anonymity or concealed collaboration are 'legal but revocable *ad nutum*. The author may at any time disclose his authorship.'" [200]

French scholars have criticized the third category of *droit à la paternité* on the ground that the right would be better protected under other legal doctrines. Even Desbois, the most emphatic proponent of *droit moral*, believes that the right to prevent false attribution of authorship "is inherent in any person and has nothing to do with a copyright in [the work of art]." [201]

A still more serious point of scholarly disagreement has been the extension of *droit à la paternité* to include protection of the author's reputation.[202] The source of this dilemma may be the 1957 Law itself, for article 6, instead of speaking specifically of *droit à la paternité*, joins the right of authorship with the right of integrity in one broadly worded clause which includes respect "for one's name." [203] Yet, under its most precise formulation, an author's right to be recognized as the creator of his work is not the same as his right to safeguard his reputation.

In reality, the status which the law protects is the author's status under the law, not his reputation. Any other view is excluded by the principles which underlie the law of March 11, 1957, since legal protection is granted "solely for the performance of the creative act" (Article 1), regardless of the artistic merit of the work produced (Article 2).[204]

Sarraute points out the danger of extending *droit à la paternité* too far in this direction.[205] For example, if an artist's works were to be sold by a gallery at low prices for the purpose of raising money quickly, the artist could claim that the sale is an assault on his reputation as an artist. *Droit moral*, Sarraute warns, was never intended to be a doctrine by which

---

[199] P. Recht, *supra* note 13, at 291.

[200] Giocanti, *supra* note 7, at 636.

[201] Strauss, *supra* note 6, at 508 n.5. G. Gavin, *supra* note 13, at 55, also admits that the right to prevent usurpation of one's name by another author does not proceed from the *droit à la paternité*, and quotes Michaelidis-Nouaros: "This protection derives more appropriately from the general right of each individual over his honor and his personality, and has nothing to do with *droit moral*."

[202] See cases discussed in Sarraute, *supra* note 17, at 478-80.

[203] See text accompanying note 171, *supra*.

[204] Sarraute, *supra* note 17, at 479.

[205] *Id.* at 479-80.

artists can be guaranteed court-ordered inflation of market prices in works of art.

Thus, despite the utility of the doctrine, *droit à la paternité* at times may prove to be an unnecessary exercise of paternalism, which achieves no more for artists than could be secured by other, less restrictive legal principles.[206]

4. Droit au Respect de l'Oeuvre

Finally, we come to the *droit au respect de l'oeuvre*, the right of an author to demand respect for his work. We save it for last because it arises only after a work has been completed, published, performed, or transferred.[207] In France, *droit au respect* is codified in the same clause of article 6 which established the *droit à la paternité*, and it is considered by virtually all scholars to be the most essential part of *droit moral*.[208] Simply stated, *droit au respect* or "right of integrity" means that the artist has a right to preserve his work from any alteration or mutilation whatsoever.[209]

The right of integrity was recognized as early as 1874,[210] and had developed in the twentieth century at a startling pace. As early as 1919,[211] it had been recognized in France that if an editor made significant changes or omissions in a manuscript, the author or his heirs had a right to suppress the work.

The right of integrity was illustrated vividly in the now classic case of

---

[206] P. Recht, *supra* note 13, at 288, in fact, ridicules the second category of *droit à la paternité* for duplicating that which already is protected under plagiarism laws. "Why do jurists, who study *droit moral*, feel the need to waste their time inventing a 'moral' right of paternity, to designate that which simple common sense would call 'highway robbery'. . . ?"

[207] Sarraute, *supra* note 17, at 480.

[208] P. Recht, *supra* note 13, at 291: "The doctrine is considered to be the essential element of the so-called moral right." G. Gavin, *supra* note 13, at 75; Roeder, *supra* note 6, at 565.

[209] P. Recht, *supra* note 13, at 291: "The *droit au respect* is the right of the author to prohibit any modification whatsoever, made in his work, without his express consent. It guarantees the integrity of the work." Also see *Pacific Comment, supra* note 14, at 859; Sarraute, *supra* note 17, at 480.

[210] See discussion in G. Gavin, *supra* note 13, at 75.

[211] In 1919, for example, Labaurie, observing the trend in court decisions, analyzed the following hypothetical situation:

Let us imagine a literary work which has fallen into the public domain. A third party reproduces it, making additions or cuts to such an extent as to alter the meaning of the work. The deceased author has direct descendents who are living. They may bring suit on the basis of *droit moral* and obtain the suppression of the offending publication.

J. Labaurie, *supra* note 60, at 13.

Bernard Buffet in 1965.[212] Buffet had painted designs on all sides of a refrigerator. The owner of the refrigerator proposed to dismantle it and sell its individual panels as separate art works. Buffet opposed the sale, claiming that the refrigerator was "an indivisible artistic unit."[213] The Paris Court of Appeals, affirmed by the Cour de Cassation, held that the sale constituted a violation of the artist's right of integrity.[214]

The same principle received even broader application in a German case in 1975.[215] An opera conductor ordered the alteration of certain stage directions in a production of Wagner's *Götterdämmerung*, claiming that the staging has created a scandal on opening night. Peter Mussbach, the director, argued that by modifying the stage directions, the conductor had offended the integrity of his work. The district court of Frankfurt-on-Main agreed with Mussbach, and issued an injunction against performance of the opera with the conductor's alterations.

In the *Buffet* case, the transferee's inability to sell the refrigerator in pieces seems to be a minor sacrifice in comparison to the artist's interest in preserving his art work. In the *Mussbach* case, however, the interests of the two parties appear more equal. The argument is inescapable that the public's response to the staging was a risk which the producer assumed when he hired Mussbach and allowed the production to open, and yet it also appears unjust to require a controversial production to complete its run, when it may jeopardize the reputation and financial status of the entire opera company and of the other artists involved.

The right of integrity, like *droit à la paternité*, has been asserted on the grounds of injury to the artist's reputation, as in the *Shostakovitch* case[216] Another case arose in 1973, when the granddaughter of Henry Rousseau sued to enjoin a Paris department store from using reproductions of her grandfather's paintings as window displays.[217] The court agreed that the use of the paintings damaged the deceased artist's reputation and violated his moral right.[218]

---

[212] Fersing v. Buffet, Judgment of May 30, 1962, Cour d'Appel Paris, [1962] D. 570; Judgment of July 6, 1965, Cour de Cassation, [1965] Gaz. Pal. 2.126, *cited in* Sarraute, *supra* note 17, at 480, *discussed in* 1 J. Merryman and A. Elsen, *supra* note 22, at 4-2; P. Recht, *supra* note 13, at 287-97. Also see Merryman, The Refrigerator of Bernard Buffet, 27 Hastings L.J. 2023 (1976).

[213] Sarraute, *supra* note 17, at 480.

[214] P. Recht, *supra* note 13, at 296, writes that the same result might have been reached through the doctrine of *abus de droit*.

[215] Judgment of Aug. 14, 1975, LGE Frankfurt-on-Main, *discussed in* Pakuscher, *supra* note 81, at 68-69.

[216] See discussion, *supra*, in text accompanying notes 1-5.

[217] Trib. gr. inst. Paris, 3 ch., note 189 *supra*.

[218] Italian courts, it should be noted, have been particularly generous in recognizing damage to reputation as a basis for finding violation of the right of integ-

It can hardly be disputed that in cases like *Shostakovitch*, an artist should have some means for vindication of his reputation. But in France the broad extension of *droit au respect* to achieve that purpose is of questionable legal basis, for as we have seen, scholars still question whether protection of the artist's reputation — as opposed to protection of the work itself — is an appropriate application of article 6.

The supposed right of an artist to defend his reputation in court has even allowed artists a right of action against excessive criticism. In France a successful claim of excessive criticism gives the artist at least a right to have his reply published.[219] In practice, however, the right against excessive criticism seldom has been successfully asserted, for the general rule is that only criticism of the work — not criticism of the artist — is actionable, and the criticism must be extreme.[220] Furthermore, we may well challenge the advisability of enforcing such a right, for its exercise could manifestly restrict the freedom of others to criticize, a right which arguably is just as valuable to the flourishing of the arts as is *droit moral*.

Even apart from such theoretical difficulties, French courts have found the need to impose restrictions on the exercise of the right in certain situations. For example, the right of integrity is more limited in the case of collaborative works or film, where the artist's only remedy may be to remove his name from the work.[221] In some cases, courts have required the artist to indemnify a publisher for expenses incurred due to the author's exercise of his right.[222]

Interestingly, the right to prevent alteration or mutilation of a work has at times been held not to include a right to prevent complete demolition of it.[223] Roeder discusses the rationale for this distinction:

> The doctrine of moral right finds one social basis in the need of the creator for protection of his honor and reputation. To deform his work is to present him to the public as the creator of a work not his own, and thus make him subject

---

rity. See, e.g., Ente autonomo "La Biennale di Venezia" c. De Chirico. Judgment of Mar. 25, 1955; Foro. it. 1955. I. 177, *discussed in* 1 J. Merryman and A. Elsen, *supra* note 22, at 4-26; see discussion *infra*.

[219] See discussion in Roeder, *supra* note 6, at 572.

[220] *Streibich Part II, supra* note 38, at 77.

[221] Giocanti, *supra* note 7, at 640.

[222] Roeder, *supra* note 6, at 565.

[223] See, e.g., Judgment of June 23, 1922, Trib. civ. Versailles, [1932] D.H. 487, *discussed in* P. Recht, *supra* note 13, at 297. See also Lacasse c. Abbé Quenard, Judgment of Apr. 27, 1934, Cour d'Appel Paris, [1934] D.H. 385, *discussed in* Roeder, *supra* note 6, at 569, and in 1 J. Merryman and A. Elsen, *supra* note 22, at 4-26, where the Paris Court of Appeals denied relief to an artist whose murals, owned by a church, were destroyed by the abbé.

to criticism for a work he has not done; the destruction of the work does not have this result.[224]

The law on this issue, however, does not appear to be settled, and some French courts do hold that a transferee of an art work has no right to destroy it.[225]

Giocanti points out that French courts give broadest protection to the right of integrity when the artist has transferred only the exploitative rights, and has retained his property interests in the work.[226] Such transfers only of rights of exploitation are quite common, for example, in contracts for presentation of a play.[227] Accordingly, in a Belgian case, the author of *The Merry Widow* successfully enjoined a performance of his play, on the sole basis that the staging violated the "spirit" of the work.[228] It should be noted that in France, article 47 of the 1957 Law creates a special right of integrity with regard to dramatic works.[229]

Even when the property rights in an art work have been transferred, many courts limit the exercise of *droit au respect* to protection of "the material integrity of the work,"[230] as in the case of Buffet's refrigerator. By this principle, a court denied relief to Salvador Dali, who claimed that the addition of another artist's sets and costumes to those which Dali had designed for a ballet gave an "imprecise idea of his work."[231] The court said that since Dali's creations had not been physically mutilated, no moral right had been violated.[232] By similar reasoning, an Italian court of appeals denied relief to the artist De Chirico, who sued to prohibit an exhibition of his paintings on the ground that it disproportionately repre-

---

[224] Roeder, *supra* note 6, at 569.

[225] See, e.g., Judgment of Dec. 9, 1937, [1937] G.P. 347, discussed in P. Recht, *supra* note 13, at 297.

[226] Giocanti, *supra* note 7, at 640. Giocanti suggests that the opposite may be true in the United States.

[227] A. LeTarnec, *supra* note 19, at 50, also points out that the impact of the right of integrity falls most heavily on the assignee of the right of reproduction of an art work, or of the right of presentation of a play.

[228] Judgment of Sept. 29, 1965, Cour d'Appel, 2 Chambre, Bruxelles, [1966] J.C.P. Ed. G. 14, 820, *cited in* Giocanti, *supra* note 7, at 641.

[229] 1957 Law, *supra* note 15, art. 47: "The producer of a play shall make sure that the staging and public performance shall be undertaken with the proper technical conditions necessary to guarantee observance of the intellectual and moral rights of the author."

[230] Giocanti, *supra* note 7, at 640. But it is not clear whether "material integrity" means physical integrity of the work, or "material" in the sense of avoiding significant or extreme alteration.

[231] See discussion in P. Recht, *supra* note 13, at 297.

[232] Arguably, if Dali had wanted no costumes or sets other than his own to be used in the ballet, he should have secured that right by contract.

sented his early works and thereby damaged his reputation.[233] The "material integrity" limitation, although it provides no precise criteria for its application, is a fortunate one, not only because it helps avoid frivolous claims, but also because it may serve to spare courts the need to decide issues which do not lend themselves well to adjudication.

An artist's *droit au respect* has proved to be uniquely cumbersome in cases of adaptations or derivative works.[234] When a work is transferred to another medium — for example, when a novel is made into a film — certain organic changes are inevitable, and yet paradoxically, the original artist's right of integrity protects the original work from any alterations whatsoever. The question becomes, then, at what point does the adapter violate the original artist's moral right? This problem gains further complexity when we bear in mind that the adapter himself is an independent artist, who enjoys moral rights in his own work, and who, just like the original artist, must be guaranteed absolute sovereignty over the creative process by which his work comes into being.[235]

As a partial solution to this problem, French courts have adopted what we may term the "transfer of medium" rule. The author of the original must accept all changes which are necessitated by the transfer to another medium.[236] The adapter, on the other hand, is expected to "transpose, with honesty, the spirit, character and substance of the work."[237] As a matter of practice, the rights of the adapter are given greater weight in French courts.[238]

The discretion of an adapter to alter the original work commonly is defined by contract, and French courts have been called upon to determine the enforceability of various types of contract clauses. First, clauses which unconditionally authorize the adaptation of the work generally

---

[233] [1955] Foro, it. I. 177, *supra* note 218.

[234] Sarraute, *supra* note 17, at 481.

[235] 1957 Law, *supra* note 15, art. 4: "Authors of translations, adaptations, transformations or arrangements of works of the spirit enjoy the protection afforded by this law, without prejudice to the rights of the author of the original work."

[236] G. Gavin, *supra* note 13, at 84:

The *Tribunal de Bordeaux* . . . has affirmed [the principle] that, when transferring the right to adapt his work, the author implicitly consents to all modifications which are necessitated by the technical conditions and applicable rules of an art which is essentially different from that of the preexisting work.

[237] Giocanti, *supra* note 7, at 642, discussing Bernanos v. Bruckberger, Cour d'Appel Paris, [1964] Gaz. Pal. 2.286, *aff'd*, Cass. civ. 1re,[1967] D.S. Jur. 485, which involved the film adaptation of *Dialogues des Carmelites*. Also see discussion in G. Gavin, *supra* note 13, at 82-83.

[238] *Pennsylvania Comment, supra* note 173, at 633.

are held valid,[239] but the adapter is required to act in good faith and to refrain from distorting the spirit of the original work. In unconditional contracts, the standard for judging distortion of the spirit of the original was first pronounced in the landmark case of *l'Affaire Bernstein*.[240]

> Even though the characters may be the same, and they evolve in the same milieu and participate in a plot whose general theme remains basically intact, one does not find in the film that which constitutes the *genuine originality of the piece*, that which bears the mark of the author's own genius.[241]

The standard, however, is vague, and Giocanti points out that as a matter of practice, lower courts in France "rarely decide that an adapter has modified the preexisting work."[242]

A second type of contract clause is one which simply "authorizes all changes which do not distort the spirit and character of the original."[243] Courts generally uphold these contracts, too, and many of the considerations which apply to unconditional authorizations apply here as well. In this context, a case arose in Italy in 1974, where an author, granting the film rights to his autobiography, gave the adapter and actors "liberal latitude" to interpret the original.[244] The film, however, distorted the author's personality to such an extent as to jeopardize his reputation. The court concluded that in the case of autobiographies, "modifications in the personality of the character require, as their only limitation, respect for the propriety and reputation of the author."[245]

Finally, the third type of contract clause is one where all modifications of the original require the approval of the original artist. These clauses have been held valid, but courts do require that the artist of the original may not unreasonably withhold his consent.[246]

These principles may for the time being solve the problem of applying *droit au respect* to adaptions, but they raise an important theoretical question. In virtually all cases of adaptations, courts are called upon to decide whether an adaptation had violated the spirit of the original work,

---

[239] Giocanti, *supra* note 7, at 642.

[240] Judgment of July 23, 1933, Trib. civ. Seine, [1933] D.H. Jur. 5, 33, *cited in* Giocanti, *supra* note 7, at 642, *discussed in* G. Gavin, *supra* note 13, at 87.

[241] G. Gavin, *supra* note 13, at 87.

[242] Giocanti, *supra* note 7, at 641-42. For example, in Judgment of Mar. 8, 1968. Trib. gr. inst. Paris, [1968] D.S. Jur. 742, *discussed in id.* at 642 n.117, a court held that changing the locale of a story did not violate the spirit of the original work.

[243] Sarraute, *supra* note 17, at 481-82.

[244] Anastasio c. Documento Film, Judgment of Jan. 7, 1974, Pret. Roma, *discussed in* 1974 It. Diritto di Autore 459-61.

[245] *Id.* at 459.

[246] Giocanti, *supra* note 7, at 642; Sarraute, *supra* note 17, at 482.

and not a few French scholars have challenged the appropriateness of judicial inquiry into such matters. Sarraute, discussing the case of the film adaptation of *Dialogues des Carmélites*,[247] writes:

> The court found it necessary to determine whether the adaptation respected the spirit of the adapted work, and proceeded to analyze and compare the basic elements and the spirit of the original work with the film version. This dangerous undertaking is difficult to justify on theoretical grounds. In fact, it is disquieting to see the courts take on such powers.[248]

Sarraute's objection, however, also serves to underscore more fundamental problems of *droit au respect*, indeed, of all of *droit moral*. The right of intregrity is bold in its ideals, and plays an essential role in the defense of artists' rights. But like all other categories of *droit moral*, it is a self-serving right, which, formulated in the abstract, refuses to balance itself against the interests of contracting parties or even against the interests of other artists, unless the courts impose equitable limitations. Moreover, the right of integrity, in the end, is based on artistically subjective judgments which are inappropriate to judicial examination, for French courts, like American courts, are reluctant to pass the judgment on literary or artistic merit.[249] These considerations force us to question whether vesting the artist with a "moral right of integrity" is necessarily the fairest and most effective way to ensure that artists' interests are protected.

II. PROTECTION OF MORAL RIGHTS IN THE UNITED STATES
A. Origins

The development of authors' rights in Britain and the United States bears little resemblance to the history of *droit d'auteur*. Prior to 1710, England, like France, afforded few rights to authors. The Stationers' Company of London, chartered in 1557,[250] had complete control over the publication of books, and held all rights in them. The Stationers' Company also had rules which frequently were enforced by acts of Parliament or by decrees of the Star Chamber, and it thereby served as an arm of censorship by the sovereign.[251]

England established the world's first modern copyright system with the Statute of Anne in 1710,[252] whose stated purpose was "the encouragement of learning" by vesting authors with the right of publication for

---

[247] [1964] Gaz. Pal. 2.286, *supra* note 237.

[248] Sarraute, *supra* note 17, at 482.

[249] This reluctance derives in part from the 1957 Law, *supra* note 15, art. 2, which provides: "The dispositions of this law protect the rights of authors in all works of the spirit irrespective of the genre, the form of expression, the merit or the intended purpose of the work."

[250] For a brief history of the Stationers' Company, see *Streibich Part II, supra* note 38, at 57.

[251] *Id.*

[252] 8 Anne, ch. 19 (1710).

a period to be limited by Parliament.[253] The Statute of Anne, however, did not derive from principles of natural law, as we have observed in early French legislation. The Statute was regarded as a three-way compromise between interests of publishers, interests of censorship, and the interests of authors.[254] The author had only those property rights which were conferred by statute, and the question of whether there existed any perpetual "common law" interests in an unpublished manuscript would only be determined many years later by the courts;[255] indeed, both in Britain and in the United States, the common law traditionally has been reluctant to recognize authors' rights outside of copyright.[256] As a result, the Statute of Anne has been called "an owner's statute, and not an author's statute." [257]

It was from these principles that the American law of author's rights was born in 1790, when Congress passed the first American copyright act,[258] and much of that tradition has persisted, even as copyright protection has been expanded to include art forms other than writing.[259] As in Britain, the subject of statutory copyright protection in the United States has been limited to the property interests bestowed upon the copyright owner,[260] who may not necessarily be the author.[261] Unlike the French system, American law has required that formalities be met if the work becomes published;[262] even today, federal copyright accidentally may be lost for failure to comply with formalities.[263] Interests of the author beyond copyright, when they have existed at all, traditionally have been the concern only of the common law as recognized by the courts, and of the state legislatures.

---

[253] See discussion of the Statute of Anne in Wheaton v. Peters, 33 U.S. (8 Peters) 590, 656 (1834).

[254] See B. Kaplan, An Unhurried View of Copyright 6-12 (1967); *Georgetown Comment, supra* note 6, at 1542.

[255] See Millar v. Taylor, 4 Burr. 2303, 98 Eng. Rep. 201 (K.B. 1769); Donaldson v. Beckett, 4 Burr. 2408, 1 Eng. Rep. 837 (H.L. 1774); B. Kaplan, *supra* note 254, at 12-17.

[256] *Pennsylvania Comment, supra* note 173, at 616-17 & n.27.

[257] *Georgetown Comment, supra* note 6, at 1542.

[258] 1 Stat. 124; 1st Cong., 2d Sess., c. 15, *reprinted in* B. Kaplan & R. Brown, Cases on Copyright, Unfair Competition, and Other Topics Bearing on the Protection of Literary, Musical, and Artistic Works 981-983 (1974).

[259] See discussion in 1 M. Nimmer on Copyright §1.08 (1978).

[260] 17 U.S.C. §106 (1976) grants copyright protection to "the owner of copyright under this title."

[261] For example, copyright in works made for hire vests initially in the employer unless the parties provide otherwise. *Id.* §201(b).

[262] *Id.* §§401-404.

[263] The 1976 statute, however, makes it difficult to lose copyright protection by failure to comply with formalities. See *id.* §§405-406. See, e.g., California's *droit de suite* statute, Cal. Civ. Code §986, and Preservation Act, *supra* note 8.

Today, the 1976 copyright statute[264] secures an author's property interest in his work, and protects the work from unauthorized exploitation.[265] The statute does not purport to protect the author's rights of personality; a code of moral rights, in fact, has been introduced in Congress at least twice, and both times was defeated.[266] Most American courts, too, have rejected the moral right doctrine in name.[267]

This does not mean that American law ignores completely the issue of artists' rights, for American courts have upheld rights analogous to at least some of the prerogatives of *droit moral*. It does mean, however, that those rights which have been recognized in this country have been vindicated not through copyright law, but through familiar doctrines of tort, contract, property or trademark law.[268] Moreover, the American judiciary has not felt the need to unify the different judge-made principles of artists' rights into a unitary doctrine, as have continental jurists.

Recently, American analogues for *droit moral* have been the subject of exhaustive scholarly attention,[269] and so a restatement of that research here would be unnecessary. It is useful, however, to observe the framework of moral right protection in the United States, the gaps in that framework, and the overall posture with which American law approaches the subject of authors' rights.

B. Categories
1. DROIT DE DIVULGATION

Before the 1976 copyright statute went into effect, American law offered both "common law" and "statutory" copyright protection.[270]

---

[264] 17 U.S.C. §101 *et seq.* (1976).

[265] *William and Mary Comment, supra* note 6, at 578; *Georgetown Comment, supra* note 6, at 1542; *Pacific Comment, supra* note 14, at 858.

[266] See note 45 *supra.*

[267] See, e.g., Granz v. Harris, *supra* note 38, at 590 (Frank, J. concurring); Vargas v. Esquire Inc., 164 F.2d 522, 526 (7th Cir. 1947), *cert. denied,* 335 U.S. 813 (1948); Crimi v. Rutgers Presbyterian Church, 194 Misc. 570, 575, 89 N.Y.S.2d 813, 818 (Sup. Ct. 1949), *cited in* Giocanti, *supra* note 7, at 627. But see Gilliam v. American Broadcastings Cos., *supra* note 39, at 24.

[268] *William and Mary Comment, supra* note 6, at 599; Giocanti, *supra* note 7, at 625; *Pacific Comment, supra* note 14, at 879.

[269] Generally, *see* sources cited notes 6-7, 38 & 40; Katz, The Doctrine of Moral Right and American Copyright Law—A Proposal, 24 S. Cal. L. Rev. 375 (1951); Stevenson, Moral Right and the Common Law: a Proposal, 6 ASCAP Copyright L. Symp. 89 (1953); Comment, The Moral Rights of the Author: A Comparative Study, 71 Dickinson L. Rev. 93 (1966); Diamond, *supra* note 35; Comment, Copyright: Moral Right—A Proposal, 43 Fordham L. Rev. 793 (1975); Note, Monty Python and the Lanham Act: In Search of the Moral Right, 30 Rutgers L. Rev. 452 (1977); Comment, An Author's Artistic Reputation Under the Copyright Act of 1976, 92 Harv. L. Rev. 1490 (1979).

[270] See 1 Nimmer, *supra* note 259, §2.02.

First, as long as an art work was unpublished,[271] it generally was protected by each state's "common law" copyright.[272] Under "common
law" copyright, the author was considered to be the original owner of the
work, and he and his heirs enjoyed the perpetual right to determine the
work's first publication. Then, if the work became published,[273] it shed
its state law protection, and either gained a federal "statutory"
monopoly — which was limited in duration — or lost all protection entirely.[274]

It has been argued persuasively that before the 1976 statute, much of
the French *droit de divulgation* was protected in the United States by
"common law" copyright.[275] Indeed, we may observe a touch of the
"natural right" character of *droit d' auteur* in the perpetual right of disclosure offered by the common law.

The 1976 statute effectively abolished "common law" copyright for
all works created on or after January 1, 1978. Now, federal statutory
protection begins not at publication, but rather at the time of creation,
and endures until fifty years after the author's death.[276] The result is that
the right of first publication still belongs to the author, so long as he has
not transferred his copyright, [277] but the right no longer is perpetual, and
it is a matter of federal, not state, law. Thus, the right of first disclosure
still is protected in the United States, but the elimination of any perpetual
right removes the American concept even farther from the French. Moreover, the federalization of the right seems to undermine whatever "natural right" character the prerogative may have had under the common
law.

In addition to protection afforded by copyright, *droit de divulgation*
has analogues in other aspects of United States law. We already have

---

[271] Standards for determining whether or not "publication" of an art work
had occurred was a central issue of the pre-1976 copyright system. Generally, see
id. §2.02.

[272] §12 of the 1909 Copyright Act, however, provided for optional registration
of unpublished works. Copyright Law of the United States of America §12
(1909), *reprinted in* B. Kaplan & R. Brown, *supra* note 258, 828-853.

[273] Standards for determining whether or not "publication" of an art work had
occurred were a central issue of the pre-1976 copyright system. Generally, see *id.*
§2.02.

[274] To gain statutory monopoly, the author had to comply with certain formalities. See 2 *id.* §7.04. The 1976 statute still requires compliance with formalities.
17 U.S.C. §401 (1976).

[275] For an excellent comparison of common law copyright and *droit de divulgation*, see Treece, *supra* note 40, at 488-94.

[276] 17 U.S.C. §302 (1976). The duration of copyright for works created before
January 1, 1978, is covered by 17 U.S.C. §§303-304 (1976). §101 specifies that a
work is "created" for purposes of federal copyright protection when it is "fixed"
in a "tangible medium of expression."

[277] 17 U.S.C. §201(a)(1976).

observed that courts of equity ordinarily will not grant specific performance for a contract to create,[278] although a negative injunction against
performance for another party may be available.[279] A practical difference
between French and American law, however, may be that in the United
States, courts will more readily assess damages against an artist for his
failure to perform without reason.[280]

Treece points out that the right of disclosure is protected by "unfair
competition," for an author in the United States may sell all rights to his
work, and yet be deemed to have retained the right to continue developing and publishing individual elements of it.[281] For example, in *Warner
Brothers Pictures, Inc. v. Columbia Broadcasting System, Inc.*,[282] Dashiell
Hammett had transferred all rights in the "Maltese Falcon," but the court
held that Hammett could continue to exploit the character of Sam Spade
in other works.[283] Moreover, in appropriate situations, the right to prevent unauthorized dissemination of one's likeness has been upheld on
the basis of right of publicity.[284]

California, finally, has enacted a limited statutory *droit de divulgation*,
which provides that an artist is deemed to have retained the right to
reproduce his art work unless that right is expressly transferred by written instrument signed by the artist or his agent.[285]

There are several differences between American and French law regarding the right of disclosure. First, and most important, in the United
States, the right readily may be waived, transferred, or sold, especially
when the author no longer holds the copyright in his work. Secondly, in
community property states, the rights of a surviving spouse to control

---

[278] See discussion at text accompanying note 129, *supra*. Also see Sarraute,
supra note 17, at 485; Roeder, *supra* note 6, at 558-59.

[279] Roeder, *supra* note 6, at 559 n.28.

[280] Sarraute, *supra* note 17, at 485.

[281] Treece, *supra* note 40, at 491-92.

[282] 216 F.2d 945 (9th Cir. 1954); *cert. denied*, 348 U.S. 971 (1955), *discussed in*
Treece, *supra* note 40, at 491-92.

[283] An earlier case which utilized the "unfair competition" argument was
Fisher v. Star Company, 231 N.Y. 414, 132 N.E. 133 (1918), which involved the
cartoon characters of "Mutt" and "Jeff". A case involving the character of Dracula has affirmed this principle. See Lugosi v. Universal Pictures Co., 172
U.S.P.Q. 541 (Cal. Super. 1972); 70 C.A. 3d 552 (Cal App. 1977); 25 Cal. 3d 813,
160 Cal. Rptr. 323, 603 P.2d 425 (Sup. Ct. Cal. 1979). See discussion of unfair
competition in Diamond, *supra* note 35, at 266.

[284] Price v. Hall Roach Studios, Inc., 400 F. Supp 1032 (S.D.N.Y. 1973), *aff'd*,
508 F.2d 909 (2d Cir. 1974), *cited and discussed in Streibich Part II, supra* note 38,
at 79. See discussion of right of publicity, *infra* notes 313-316, and accompanying
text.

[285] Cal. Civ. Code §982 (West).

publication of an art work are broader in the United States than in France. Third, the federal copyright statute contains provisions for compulsory licensing of cable television transmissions and phonorecords,[286] and it has been argued that the very concept of compulsory license runs counter to *droit de divulgation*.[287]

2. DROIT DE RETRAIT OU DE REPENTIR

The principal difference between American and continental jurisprudence lies in *droit de retrait* and *droit de repentir*. In general, the United States recognizes no right of withdrawal, and at least one writer considers this a fortunate policy.[288] Similarly, the right of an artist to modify a work already made public has never been recognized in this country.[289]

Nevertheless, it should be observed that the common law infrequently has recognized a right to withdraw a work from publication upon some showing of fault on the part of the publisher.[290] Although one writer believes that this rarely used principle could be expanded,[291] no trend in that direction is discernible.[292] Moreover, the federal copyright law does contain provision for termination of licenses, which in some situations could prove to be analogous to *droit de retrait*.[293]

3. DROIT À LA PATERNITÉ

American law does pay some attention to the right of authorship, and of the three categories of the French *droit à la paternité*, the second and third are quite well protected in the United States. The second category — the right of an author to prevent others from taking credit for

---

[286] See, e.g., 17 U.S.C. §§111(d), 115.

[287] "May I add that no such compulsory mechanical license is conceivable under the droit d'auteur system; it does not exist in French statute and statutes related thereto." Monta, *supra* note 52, at 180-81. However, the Japanese law, *supra* note 124, art. 69, does provide for compulsory licenses. See discussion in Iijima, *supra* note 137, at 399.

[288] Sarraute, *supra* note 17, at 485.

[289] Roeder, *supra* note 6, at 565.

[290] See, e.g., Gale v. Leckie, 2 Starkie 107 (1817), discussed in Roeder, *supra* note 6, at 560.

[291] Roeder, *supra* note 6, at 560.

[292] See, e.g., Autrey v. Republic Products, Inc., 213 F.2d 667 (9th Cir. 1954), *discussed in* Treece, *supra* note 40, at 500. But see Fairbanks v. Winik, 206 App. Div. 449, 201 N.Y.S. 487 (1923), *cited in* Treece, *supra* note 40, at 500 n.51.

[293] 17 U.S.C. §203 (1976).

his work — has been upheld not only in suits for copyright infringement, but also in suits based upon unfair competition.[294] In those cases, factors such as lost sales and loss of business reputation have been the basis for awarding damages.[295] The third category of *droit à la paternité*, the right of an author to prevent use of his name on a work he did not create, has been protected under tort theories of libel,[296] right of publicity,[297] and invasion of privacy.[298] In such cases, even damages for mental anguish have been awarded.[299]

However, the first category of *droit à la paternité* — the right to claim authorship — generally has been neglected by American law.[300] The general rule in the United States is that unless an author secures the right by contract, he has no right to claim authorship of his own work, after it has been transferred.[301] This is true especially in cases of works made for hire,[302] where the copyright statute states affirmatively that, unless otherwise established by contract, the employer is deemed to be the author of the work.[303]

Case law illustrates the American principle. In the leading case of *Vargas v. Esquire, Inc.*,[304] Vargas sold his drawings to the defendant *Esquire* magazine, and the defendant published them without attributing authorship to Vargas. The court held that without a contractual provision requiring that plaintiff's name be used, Vargas had no right to claim authorship.[305]

An early New York case,[306] however, did uphold the right of an author to enjoin publication of a work under his real name, when the stories previously had been published under a *nom de plume*. The court based its decision on the plaintiff's right to privacy.[307] Moreover, a few artists have won the right to claim authorship of their own works by using a contract

---

[294] For a discussion and cases, see *Pacific Comment, supra* note 14, at 867-71.

[295] *Id.* at 870-71.

[296] See discussion in Diamond, *supra* note 35, at 264-265.

[297] See cases discussed *supra*, notes 284 and 285, and accompanying text.

[298] See discussion in *Diamond, supra* note 35, at 266; *Pacific Comment, supra* note 14, at 871-73.

[299] *Pacific Comment, supra* note 14, at 873.

[300] Treece, *supra* note 40, at 494; Diamond, *supra* note 35, at 255.

[301] *Pacific Comment, supra* note 14, at 856, 863.

[302] The statutory definition of "works made for hire" appears in 17 U.S.C. §101 (1976).

[303] 17 U.S.C. §201(b)(1976).

[304] 164 F.2d 522 (7th Cir. 1947), *cert. denied*, 335 U.S. 813 (1948).

[305] *Id.* at 526.

[306] Ellis v. Hurst, 66 Misc. 235, 121 N.Y.S. 438 (Sup. Ct. 1910).

[307] 66 Misc. at 236.

theory to show that the intent of the parties was to give credit.[308] But for the most part, such cases seldom succeed.[309]

From the precedents, it should come as no surprise that American law, unlike French law, liberally allows an author to waive whatever rights of authorship he may have, and indeed courts have implied such a waiver in cases where the contract involved was silent on the question.[310] While this policy undeniably is harsh on artists' rights, at least one leading American proponent of moral rights feels that the presumption of waiver is consistent with the general policies of tort law.[311]

Interestingly, the right of an author to protect his artistic reputation, while only a questionable component of the right of authorship in France, has received judicial support in the United States under the doctrine of "right of publicity."[312] This right is defined as "the individual's right to take advantage of his existing name and reputation,"[313] and has been recognized as early as 1917.[314] Some writers believe that expansion of this doctrine may be the key to developing an American *droit à la paternité*.[315] Indeed, courts have been quite receptive to arguments based on right of publicity, although jurisdictions are divided on the question of whether or not the right survives the death of the author.[316]

---

[308] See e.g., Clemens v. Press Publishing Co., 67 Misc. 183, 122 N.Y.S. 206 (Sup. Ct. App. Term 1910): "Even the matter-of-fact attitude of the law does not require us to consider the sale of the rights to a literary production in the same way that we would consider the sale of a barrel of pork." 67 Misc. at 183. Also see discussion in *William and Mary Comment, supra* note 6, at 599-600.

[309] See *William and Mary Comment, supra* note 6, at 600.

[310] See, e.g., Vargas, *supra* note 267. Also see discussion in *Georgetown Comment, supra* note 6, at 1543.

[311] Moral rights are akin to those rights in tort which protect the individual against injury. They may not, therefore, be assigned; in general, however, they may be effectively waived before or after violation just as a blood donor, or boxer, waives his right against bodily injury. Waiver may, moreover, be implied from the nature of work or the type of publication for which it was written.

Roeder, *supra* note 6, at 564.

[312] For an excellent discussion, see *Georgetown Comment, supra* note 6, at 1545-47.

[313] *Id.* at 1546.

[314] Wood v. Lucy, Lady Duff-Gordon, 222 N.Y. 88, 118 N.E. 214 (1917). See also Uhlaender v. Henricksen, 316 F. Supp. 277 (D. Minn. 1970); discussion in *Georgetown Comment, supra* note 6, at 1546.

[315] *Georgetown Comment, supra* note 6, at 1546-47; *Pacific Comment, supra* note 14, at 883-86.

[316] See e.g., *Factors Etc., Inc. and Boxcar Enterprises, Inc. v. Pro Arts, Inc. and Stop and Shop Companies, Inc.*, 579 F.2d 215 (2d Cir. 1978) [Elvis Presley's right of publicity held to have survived his death]; Memphis Development Foundation v. Factors Etc., Inc., 616 F.2d 956, U.S.P.Q. 784 (6th Cir. 1980) [Elvis Presley's right to exploit his likeness was not an inheritable property right].

4. Droit au Respect de l'Oeuvre

In France, a publisher or producer who obtains the right to exploit a work has an implied duty to preserve its material integrity. Apart from California's new Preservation Act, however, the general rule in the United States is that the publisher or producer has no such duty, unless the author has secured the right of integrity by contract.[317] This principle was most clearly enunciated in *Preminger v. Columbia Pictures Corp.*[318] In that case, Otto Preminger unsuccessfully sought to enjoin a distribution of his film, "Anatomy of a Murder," claiming that the distribution contracts, which allowed television broadcasters to make cuts or commercial interruptions in the film, would amount to mutilation of his work.[319]

Although there is no judicially recognized right of integrity in the United States, artists have brought suit successfully for mutilation of their works, under various tort theories. Most notably, alteration of art works occasionally has been actionable as a tort of defamation.[320] This theory, however, has been of limited utility, because courts generally will not grant an injunction against personal libel, and thus, the artist is unable to *prevent* the mutilation of his work.[321]

The right of integrity also has been vindicated on the theory that mutilation of an art work constitutes misappropriation of the author's name, which in some states is actionable under privacy laws.[322] On this theory, John Lennon was able to enjoin distribution of a recording of his music, on the grounds that poor editing and an inartistic cover design amounted to mutilation of his work.[323]

---

[317] *Georgetown Comment, supra* note 6, at 1541; *Streibich Part II, supra* note 38, at 80.

[318] 148 U.S.P.Q. 398 (N.Y. Sup. Ct.), *aff'd*, 149 U.S.P.Q. 872 (App. Div.), *aff'd* 150 U.S.P.Q. 829 (Ct. App. 1966), *discussed in* Treece, *supra* note 40, at 496. Also see Melodion v. Philadelphia School District, 328 Pa. 457, 195 A. 905 (1938).

[319] But dictum in *Preminger,* 148 U.S.P.Q. at 402, indicated that if a 161-minute feature were cut to 100 minutes, it would constitute mutilation and entitle the author to an injunction. Note also that *Preminger* was limited in *Gilliam, supra* note 39, at 23; see *Pennsylvania Comment, supra* note 173, at 633.

[320] *William and Mary Comment, supra* note 6, at 601; see dictum in Seroff v. Simon & Schuster, Inc., 6 Misc. 2d 383, 383, 389, 162 N.Y.S.2d 770, 778 (1957).

[321] *William and Mary Comment, supra* note 6, at 601.

[322] *Pacific Comment, supra* note 14, at 875; see N.Y. Civ. Rights Law §§50-51 (McKinney 1976).

[323] Big Seven Music v. Lennon, 554 F.2d 504 (2d Cir. 1977), *discussed in Pacific Comment, supra* note 14, at 875. Also see *Georgetown Comment, supra* note 6, at 1548-49.

The right to privacy also has been asserted in terms of the "false light" theory, where the activities of the defendant are shown to shed a "false light" on the plaintiff. *Georgetown Comment, supra* note 6, at 1549. This theory has served better to protect the artist's reputation than to protect the material integrity of his work.

Finally, if the author or artist has retained the property rights in his work, or at least a future residuary interest, some courts have upheld the right to prevent mutilation under the doctrine of waste, which forbids a lessee or licensee to damage permanently the leased or licensed property.[324] At least one author believes that this doctrine could be expanded in the search for judge-made right of integrity.[325]

Whatever right of integrity does exist in the United States has not been carried so far as to protect an artist against complete destruction of his work.[326] Moreover, unlike France, the United States has not recognized a right to be protected against excessive criticism, short of defamation, or even a right to such criticism.[327] In view of the First Amendment considerations which would arise, it is unlikely that such a right will be advocated strongly in this country.[328]

As in France, the United States has found that the artist's interest in preserving the integrity of his work is even more limited in the case of adaptations of the work to another medium. In 1938, for example, a court denied relief to Theodore Dreiser, who claimed that a film adaptation of *An American Tragedy* grossly distorted the character of his work.[329] However, if a copyrighted work is licensed for adaptation with a contract

---

[324] For an excellent discussion of the doctrine of waste and case law in which artists' rights were upheld, see *Georgetown Comment, supra* note 6, at 1550-54.

[325] *Id.* at 1554.

[326] See, e.g., Crimi v. Rutgers Presbyterian Church, *supra* note 267; Roeder, *supra* note 6, at 569.

[327] Under the common law the right to criticize is protected and great liberality is shown the critic. . . . The only protection accorded the creator is under the law of libel which does not condemn the libel of a product as much as it does a libel of a person; criticism of a created work, if libelous at all, is regarded as libel of a product, and the plaintiff must prove falsity, malice and damages.

Roeder, *supra* note 6, at 572.

[328] *Pacific Comment, supra* note 14, at 860-61 & n.51.

[329] Dreiser v. Paramount Publix Corp., 22 Copyright Off. Bull., 106 (N.Y. Sup. Ct. 1938), discussed in *Georgetown Comment, supra* note 6, at 1544.

The callous tone of the *Dreiser* court's opinion may well be the low-watermark of American judicial attitudes toward artists' rights:

[T]he producer [will be permitted to] give consideration to the fact that the great majority of . . . the audience . . . will be more interested that justice prevail over wrongdoing, than that the inevitability of Clyde's end clearly appear.

22 Copyright Off. Bull., 106, 107, *quoted in Georgetown Comment, supra* note 6, at 1544.

In another case, Chamberlain v. Columbia Pictures Corp., 186 F.2d 923 (9th Cir. 1951), *cited in* Treece, *supra* note 40, at 500 n.51, another court refused to enjoin the use of the name of Mark Twain on a film version of "The Celebrated Jumping Frog of Calaveras County," even when the author's heirs claimed that the film had garbled the original work.

provision against excessive editing, courts generally will require that the adaptation be faithful to the original.[330]

Thus, despite the traditional failure of American law to protect the right of integrity as it is known in France, there is little question that at least a right to protect art works from mutilation is emerging in this country.[331] Case law upholds the right under tort and contract theories, and scholars agree that there is ample room for expansion of those doctrines.[332]

The most heralded judicial development in the emerging American right of integrity is the case of *Gilliam v. American Broadcasting System* in 1977.[333] The authors of Monty Python, the British comedy group, sought to enjoin a television broadcast of their film, claiming that the defendants had excessively edited their work. In a landmark decision, the Second Circuit issued the injunction, holding that the distortion of the work had been extreme,[334] and would be actionable both under copyright law[335] and under section 43(a) of the Lanham Act on trademarks,[336] which prohibits misleading labeling.

Gilliam is significant not only because of its broad application of the Lanham Act,[337] but also because of its implicit recognition that an artist has legally enforceable personal rights which are at least coincident with

---

[330] *Pennsylvania Comment, supra* note 173, at 631.

[331] See Treece, *supra* note 40, at 505. But precise remedies for violation may differ between the two countries. The right of integrity also is evolving in British law. Roeder, *supra* note 6, at 565.

[332] *Pacific Comment, supra* note 14, at 886-88, for example, suggests the expansion of the right of privacy and the right of publicity as a basis for an American *droit au respect; Georgetown Comment, supra* note 6, at 1561, says that the right of integrity may be best achieved through development of presumptions of non-waiver under contract law.

[333] 538 F.2d 14 (2d Cir. 1976).

[334] *Id.* at 19.

[335] *Id.* at 21.

[336] *Id.* at 24-25. See Lanham Trade-Mark Act of 1946, ch. 540, 60 Stat. 427 (codified in scattered sections of 15 U.S.C.). Lanham Act. §43(a), 15 U.S.C. §1125(a), provides in part:

Any person who shall affix, apply, or annex, or use in connection with any goods or services, . . . a false designation of origin, or any false description or representation . . . and shall cause such goods or services to enter into commerce . . . shall be liable to a civil action by any person . . . who believes that he is or is likely to be damaged by the use of any such false description or representation.

[337] This was not the first time that a federal court applied the Lanham Act to cases of mutilation of art works. See Rich v. RCA Corp., 390 F. Supp. 530 (S.D.N.Y. 175); Geisel v. Poynter Prod. Inc., 283 F. Supp. 261, 266-68 (S.D.N.Y. 1968); Yameta Co. v. Capitol Records, Inc., 279 F. Supp. 582, 586-87 (S.D.N.Y. 1968). Also see discussion in *William and Mary Comment, supra* note 6, at 609-10.

economic interests in his created work.[338] This, we should recall, is a rudimentary concept of *droit moral*, and interestingly, the court alluded to the French doctrine in support of its reasoning.[339] While this is not the first case in which an American court has discussed *droit moral*,[340] it demonstrates a new respect for the civil law doctrine.[341]

The holding in *Gilliam*, however, should not be oversimplified, nor should its significance be overstated. The decision was based more on the copyright claim than on the Lanham Act argument, and it rested in part on the fact that the contract between Monty Python and the original British licensee had expressly prohibited unauthorized editing of the script.[342] We can only question whether a *droit moral* claim, in the absence of such a contractual provision, would be upheld. Furthermore, writers have observed that the decision was based on assumptions that were not wholly precedented, and on broad interpretations of previous cases.[343] The court also emphasized the excessive nature of ABC's editing, and we must question, again, whether a claim or more moderate editing would have yielded the same result. Finally, we should observe that the court, while it did allude to the French doctrine of moral right, did not in any way indicate that a claim of violation of *droit moral*, without more, would be actionable under the copyright statute or under the Lanham Act.

Still, *Gilliam* should reveal the extent to which courts now may go to expand the right of integrity in the United States.

C. The California Art Preservation Act

The California Art Preservation Act[344] creates, for the first time in American law, a statutory right of integrity and right of paternity for

---

[338] *William and Mary Comment, supra* note 6, at 610.

[339] 538 F.2d at 24.

[340] See, e.g., *Granz v. Harris, supra* note 38, at 590 (Frank, J. concurring).

[341] Our resolution of these technical arguments serves to reinforce our initial inclination that the copyright law should be used to recognize the important role of the artist in our society and the need to encourage production and dissemination of artistic works by providing adequate legal protection for one who submits his work to the public.

538 F.2d at 23.

[342] See *id.* at 17.

[343] The larger holding on unauthorized editing can be viewed as grounded in a presumption that, when the contract is silent, the artist did not intend to permit editing by the licensee.

. . . Although [this] qualification appears to be sound as a matter of policy, its relation to the prior case law is troublesome.

Pennsylvania Comment, supra note 173, at 631. See discussion *id.* at 631-33.

[344] California Art Preservation Act, *supra* note 8.

California artists. It provides that no person other than the creator of a work of fine art[345] may alter or destroy such work,[346] and further, that the artist retains the right to claim or disclaim authorship of it.[347]

At first glance, one would think that the Preservation Act is the genuine Gallic concept of *droit moral*, emerging unruffled and triumphant on the Pacific coast of America. Indeed, although its title could be mistaken for an environmental protection statute, the Art Preservation Act contains a preamble which bears a striking resemblance to the French 1957 Law:

> The Legislature hereby finds and declares that the physical alteration or destruction of fine art, which is an expression of the artist's personality, is detrimental to the artist's reputation, and artists therefore have an interest in protecting their works of fine art against such alteration or destruction; and that there is also a public interest in preserving the integrity of cultural and artistic creations.[348]

It seems, at last, that the artist's right of personality has been recognized by legislation, at least for works of painting, sculpture or drawing that are not attached to a building.[349]

The Preservation Act, however, differs widely from the unitary concept of *droit moral*, and significantly, the California legislature chose not to call the artist's new prerogatives a "moral right."

The most prominent difference is that the California law applies only to works of fine art, which are defined as "original painting, sculpture or drawing of recognized quality."[350] This is far more limited than the French law, which applies to virtually all art forms, and which contains no restrictions based on the prominence of the artist or the work.

Then, although the preamble demonstrates concern for the artist's reputation and for the public expression of his personality, the artist's rights under the Preservation Act are not of the "natural right" character which we have observed in French law. While *droit d'auteur* exists solely by virtue of the act of creation, the artist's rights under California law exist because the legislature has declared them to exist.[351] Furthermore, the preamble makes sure to point out that the interest in preserving artworks belongs not only to the artist, but also to the public.[352] The

---

[345] The Preservation Act defines "fine art" as "an original painting, sculpture or drawing of recognized quality" but excludes any "work prepared under contract for commercial use by its purchaser."*Id.*, at §(b)(2).

[346] *Id.* §(c)(1).

[347] *Id.* §(d).

[348] *Id.* §(a).

[349] *Id.* §(h).

[350] *Id.* §(b)(2).

[351] *Id.* §(a).

[352] *Id.* §(a).

method which the legislature has chosen for protecting the artist's and the public's statutorily defined interests is to vest the artist with a right to seek legal and equitable relief — including punitive damages — for mutilation of his created work, or for violation of his right to claim authorship.

Unlike *droit moral*, which is perpetual and unassignable, the California artist's rights expire fifty years after his death,[353] and may be transferred to another party in writing.[354] Moreover, the Act contains a statute of limitations,[355] which further restricts the duration of the artist's prerogatives.

The Preservation Act, like federal copyright law,[356] vests no rights in the artist when the work is made for hire,[357] an exception which proved to be unacceptable to the French system.[358]

It should be observed, finally, that the phrasing of the statute contains a kind of *droit de repentir*, for the Act states that "no person, except an artist who owns and possesses a work of fine art which the artist has created"[359] may alter a work of art. This would imply that an artist who owns his work does possess the right to alter it, perhaps even if the copyright or other exploitative interest has been transferred to another party. If this does constitute a *droit de repentir*, however, it is more limited than the similar right secured by French law, for the California artist has the right only as long as he retains ownership and possession of the work, and he has no apparent right to repossess, reacquire, or otherwise withdraw a work the property interests in which have been transferred.

Although the California statute is more limited than *droit moral*, it also is less problematic. By restricting the scope of the statute to works of visual art, by limiting the duration of the rights and the period for their enforcement, and by making the rights transferable, California has avoided some of the troublesome aspects of *droit moral*, and at the same time, has created a scheme of rights that is compatible with the scope and duration of federal copyright protection.[360]

---

[353] *Id.* §(g)(1).

[354] *Id.* §(g)(3).

[355] *Id.* §(h)(3)(i)

[356] 17 U.S.C. §201(b).

[357] Preservation Act, *supra* note 8, §(b)(2). In federal copyright law, the copyright in a work made for hire vests in the employer. 17 U.S.C. §201 (b). Observe, however, that by excluding works for hire from the definition of "fine art," the Preservation Act effectively creates no right of integrity for such works, not even a right that vests in the employer or purchaser of the work.

[358] See text accompanying notes 193-196, *supra*.

[359] Preservation Act, *supra* note 8, §(c)(1).

[360] For example, rights secured under the Preservation Act, like federal copyright, subsist only until fifty years after the artist's death, and do not vest in the artist when the work is made for hire. See text accompanying notes 253 and 257, *supra*.

This does not mean that the California law is without ambiguity. Like the French 1957 Law, the Preservation Act has joined into a single statute the *droit au respect* and *droit à la paternité,* leaving unanswered the question of whether the Act exists principally to protect artists (as the preamble proclaims) or art works (as the title would have us believe). The Act does not address the problems which we observed in French law, of exercise of moral rights when there is more than one author of a work of art.

Still, the Preservation Act recognizes a rudimentary right of personality, creates a basis for securing the interests of artists beyond copyright, and should serve as a model for the emergence of other, more comprehensive statutory schemes for protecting authors' and artists' rights. And further, the Preservation Act remains mindful of the competing interests of transferees, employers, contracting parties, and real estate proprietors.

Droit moral, at last, has a distinct cousin in America.

III. COMPARISON OF ARTISTS' RIGHTS IN FRANCE AND THE UNITED STATES

United States copyright law focuses on economic rather than personal rights in art works,[361] but courts and, recently, legislatures increasingly acknowledge the need to protect the artist's moral prerogatives.[362] As a result, American law does afford rights which are analogous to at least parts of *droit moral;* in the defense of the artist's reputation, American law may at times provide even broader protection.[363]

On the whole, however, artists' rights receive less respect under the American system than they do in France.[364] *Droit de retrait* and *droit de repentir,* although their value is at best questionable, barely exist at all in the United States. The first category of *droit à la paternité* — the right to claim authorship of one's own creation is underdeveloped in this country, and *droit au respect,* which is considered by the French to be the very essence of an artist's prerogative, is only in its infancy.

Furthermore, whatever moral rights do exist in the United States have far less weight than they do in France. Although this difference ulti-

---

[361] *Pacific Comment, supra* note 14, at 855.

[362] *Id.* at 862.

[363] See discussion at text accompanying notes 312-316 *supra.*

[364] Although some scholars suggest that these tort remedies provide authors and artists with protection equivalent to the moral right of paternity and integrity, a comparison of French and American case law indicates otherwise.

Georgetown Comment, supra note 6, at 1543. But see Strauss, *supra* note 6, at 537-38; Treece, *supra* note 40, at 505-06; Monta, *supra* note 52, at 185, all of whom believe that protection of artists' rights in the United States is just as broad as in France.

mately may reflect only a discrepancy in social status between French and American artists,[365] it also is rooted in legal realities. In the United States, authors' rights may more readily be waived, and they generally cease to exist upon the author's death.[366] This contrasts markedly with the "personal, perpetual, inalienable and unassignable" character of *droit moral*.[367] And in the United States, a contract between the artist and the transferee of his rights is presumed to be the repository of all the artist's remaining rights in his work; French law will more readily look beyond contractual obligations in order to assert the artist's moral rights.[368]

The question remains whether fuller protection of artists' rights in this country may be best achieved by importing the French system or by expansion of existing American theories. The American system has the advantage of being of native vintage, but even if it continues to evolve, its full potential may be limited, and its application may be cumbersome: "The application of so many different doctrines to a subject matter which is so intrinsically homogeneous produces confusion; choice of theory depends on a fortuitous combination of factors, rather than on the basic needs of the problem."[369] The French system, on the other hand, has the advantages of unity, tradition, and world recognition, and at least one observer believes that it is more adaptable to the invention of new art forms and new methods of exploitation.[370] Yet, as we have seen, the French system, too, can be problematic, unpredictable, and frequently impractical, especially when it is applied to collective or collaborative works or to film.

The more difficult question is how readily the French system could be transported to the United States. A few scholars have written that Congress, or at least the courts, could adopt *droit moral* virtually intact.[371] That view, however, overlooks the fundamentally different attitudes with which the two systems approach authors' rights.

---

[365] "We have not that respect for art that is one of the glories of France." Tyson & Brothers v. Banton, 273 U.S. 418, 447 (1927) (Holmes, C.J., dissenting).

[366] Giocanti, *supra* note 7, at 643. But see *Streibich Part II, supra* note 38, at 79. Recall that at least one Federal Court of Appeals holds that the right of publicity survives the death of the author. See note 316 *supra*.

[367] Sarraute, *supra* note 17, at 485.

[368] *Id.*

[369] Roeder, *supra* note 6, at 575. Also see *Streibich Part II, supra* note 38, at 486.

[370] *Streibich Part II, supra* note 38, at 76-77, 83-84; *Pacific Comment, supra* note 14, at 861. But perhaps the American system, because it is not tied to any one particular statute or doctrine, may be more flexible in accommodating new art forms and new methods of exploitation. See *Concurrence, supra* note 139, at 12-13.

[371] See, e.g., *Streibich Part II, supra* note 38, at 82-83.

French law regards *droit moral* as a natural right, stemming from the special nature of artistic creation and from the mystical presence of the author's personality in his work. In the United States, the same "moral" prerogatives, when they exist at all, are merely applications of principles of tort, contract, property, and equity — principles which apply equally to other professions, other forms of property, other commercial transactions. It is questionable, in fact, whether American law — other than the Preservation Act — even conceives of these prerogatives as protection of the artist's personality.[372]

Thus, the French concept of *droit moral*, indeed all of *droit d'auteur*, is far more idealistic than any American notion of authors' rights.[373] It proceeds, as we have observed, from a romantic idea of the artist and his work; it treats artists as a special class of laborers, and art works as a special category of property; and at least in theory, it defends artists' rights even against the contract or property interests of third parties. Within the conception of *droit d'auteur*, *droit moral* takes on a transcendent, even spiritual quality,[374] which even its own name reveals.

In the United States, on the other hand, the protection of artists' rights beyond copyright has developed on a more pragmatic and democratic basis. American law refuses to recognize artists as a special class, and insists on a more equitable balance between the interests of artists and the interests of others who are involved in the exploitation, publication or

---

[372] The question of whether United States law — apart from the Preservation Act — recognizes the right of personality is disputed. *Streibich Part II, supra* note 38, at 73, says that American courts:

. . . have steadfastly refused to accept the [moral right] appellation or the doctrine's underlying concept, which is basically concerned with the protection of an author's interests of personality in his own creation.

Pacific Comment, supra note 14, at 857, on the other hand, says that American courts do speak of an artist's right of personality, and quotes the Supreme Court of California in Desny v. Wilder, 299 P.2d, 257, 272 (1956):

Writing — portraying characters and events and emotions with words, no less than with brush and oils — may be an art which expresses personality. . . . "The [work] is the personal reaction of an individual upon nature. Personality always contains something unique. It expresses singularity even in handwriting, and a very modest grade of art has in it something irreducible, which is one man's alone."

[373] Observe Monta's amusing statement, *supra* note 52, at 185: "[W]e, as Anglo-Saxons tend to be rational and logical, and more concerned with practical considerations; the French are revolutionary, emotional, and irremediably attached to idealistic principles."

[374] *Chillida, supra* note 50, at 17:

Let us observe the spiritual primacy of the moral right and its decisive influence not only on the law of contract, but also on the laws of inheritance and of the economic ordering of marriage, more or less altering the classic rules of customary law.

See also *id.* at 13-14.

adaptation of works of art. Furthermore, American law characterizes the artist's work more as an object of commerce than as a product of the spirit, and the artist's rights of personality in his work generally must be protected by the same legal language which would be applied to any commercial venture.

The argument that *droit moral*, as it is known in France, could be adopted intact in the United States also overlooks the significant differences which we have observed in the historical origins of the two systems, and in the issues which have been the fulcrum of each system's development. In particular, as American copyright has evolved, its principal issues have focused on such questions as whether or not publication has occurred;[375] whether or not copyright formalities have been observed;[376] whether or not statutory definitions can be expanded to include new art forms and technological advances;[377] and whether or not infringement has taken place.[378] Although American law regards copyright as a right separate from the material object itself,[379] the question of the attention of continental scholars — has not been a significant issue in the United States.[380] It goes without saying that British and American the United States.[380] It goes without saying that British and American scholars have been able to ignore the controversy between the monist and dualist views of *droit d'auteur*.[381]

In comparison to the civil law system, the American tradition seems mechanical and uncompassionate. But it is important to observe that federal copyright derives from the Constitution, which not only creates the federal power to grant copyright protection, but also recites the basic philosophy on which the American system is based: "To promote the Progress of Science and the Useful Arts by securing for limited Times to Authors and Inventors the exclusive Right to their Respective Writings and Discoveries."[382] The constitutional mandate reveals that American copyright arises not from a perpetual, natural right of *propriété incorporelle*, as in France, nor even from a "right of personality," as in Germany,

---

[375] For a discussion and cases, see B. Kaplan & R. Brown, *supra* note 258, at 24-106.

[376] See discussion in *id*. at 107-59.

[377] See discussion in *id*. at 160-276. See M. Nimmer, *supra* note 259, §1.08.

[378] See discussion in B. Kaplan & R. Brown, *supra* note 258, at 276-375, 454-68.

[379] U.S.C. §202 (1976): "Ownership of a copyright, or any of the exclusive rights under a copyright, is distinct from ownership of any material object in which the work is embodied."

[380] P. Recht, *supra* note 13, at 25-26.

[381] *Id*. at 90.

[382] U.S. Const. art. 1, §8, cl. 8.

but rather from the people's interest in promoting a socially desirable end.[383]

This may, in fact, illustrate the most significant difference between the European and American systems. Under the civil law, the source of an author's rights is the author himself, and positive law exists to clarify, codify, and guarantee a right which presumably already exists when the author has performed the creative act.[384] In the United States, while copyright cannot be called a mere privilege of the sovereign, it does exist primarily to the extent that positive law creates it,[385] and that law springs not from the author's act of creation, but from a constitutionally recognized social purpose. Then, as we have seen, any further protection of the artist beyond copyright — the American "moral" rights — also must reflect social needs, for those rights may be asserted only by application of legal and equitable principles, which balance the prerogatives of the artist with competing public or private interests.

We see, then, that the "amoral" American copyright actually embodies a system which aims more at social balancing than at unilaterally vindicating the artist's personal interests. This "social balancing" policy is clearly reflected in the 1976 copyright statute, which codifies the doctrine of fair use,[386] expands the use of compulsory licenses,[387] and eliminates perpetual common law copyright,[388] at the same time as it extends the scope and duration of federal copyright protection.[389] The same policy resounds in the California Art Preservation Act, which balances the artist's rights of personality against the competing interests of the artist's employer,[390] the transferee of the work,[391] and the proprietor of the building to which the work has been attached.[392] In this sense, the Preservation Act is not at all a *droit moral* statute, but rather a uniquely American legislation.

Thus, even as American law begins to recognize artists' rights beyond

---

[383] P. Recht, *supra* note 13, at 25-26.

[384] Whereas in our [Anglo-American] system it is the statute that creates these rights, in the French system it is not the law that gives birth to these rights, because by the very act of creation of the work the *droit d'auteur* is born in the very person of the author and the author has the exclusive enjoyment thereof. Hence no need that the work have a body, no formality, no deposit. Monta, *supra* note 52, at 178.

[385] *See* note 377, *supra*.

[386] 17 U.S.C. §§107-112 (1976).

[387] *Id.* §§ 111(a), 115.

[388] *Id.* §§ 302-305.

[389] See *id.*

[390] Preservation Act, *supra* note 8, at §(b)(2).

[391] *Id.* §§(b)(2), (c)(1).

[392] *Id.* §(h).

copyright, it does so within a tradition that is concerned for the interests of many parties; the American artist may indeed "sing" his own personality, but his copyright celebrates more than just himself. To adopt *droit moral* in the United States might require us to abandon that notion, and to subscribe to a tradition which our country does not share.[393]

IV. CONCLUSION

In the United States, as in Europe, artists frequently suffer from an inferior bargaining position in the commercial arena, and only the most well-known artists are able to procure by contract those rights which the law has not yet seen fit to protect.[394] Civil law countries have chosen to ensure artists' rights through the moral right doctrine, and despite its complexities and inconsistencies, *droit moral* may prove to be successful in achieving that purpose.

The United States also needs to expand artists' rights, and to raise, in the eyes of the law, the dignity of professions in the arts.[395] But, as we have seen, *droit moral* has arisen in a specific legal and cultural context, and it may not be transportable into the Anglo-American system without a complete overhaul of our copyright law and its implicit conception of the relationship between artists and society. We may find, too, that the moral right doctrine is not worth the ideological transformation which it might require.

A traditional dilemma of the world of arts and letters has been the conflict between the interests of publishers, producers, and exhibitors of

---

[393] But see *Streibich Part II, supra* note 38, at 76-77:

> While the French and other continental legal systems have explicitly relied on natural law or moral right theory, American courts have traditionally considered themselves limited to notions of property, contract or tort. This is indeed curious when one recalls that the American republic's whole theoretical justification is "to secure these rights."

[394] *Streibich Part II, supra* note 38, at 77; *Georgetown Comment, supra* note 6, at 1539, 1560; *William and Mary Comment, supra* note 6, at 595 n.6.

Even Mark Twain, a successful writer, observed the plight of American authors in the face of an uncompassionate copyright system:

> The charming absurdity of restricting property-rights in books to forty-two years sticks prominently out in the fact that hardly any man's books ever *live* forty-two years, or even half of it; and so, for the sake of getting a shabby advantage of the heirs of about one Scott or Burns or Milton in a hundred years, the lawmakers of the "Great" Republic are content to leave that poor little pilfering edict upon the statute-books. It is like an emperor lying in wait to rob a phoenix's nest, and waiting the necessary century to get the chance.

Mark Twain, "Petition Concerning Copyright" (1875). The Complete Humorous Sketches and Tales of Mark Twain (1961).

[395] See statement of the court in *Gilliam, supra* note 39, at 23.

intellectual works, and the freedom of the creator.[396] *Droit moral*, as it now is formulated in France, poses formidable challenges to the force of contracts between the artist and the exploiters of his work, but has not yet found a way to protect adequately the interests of the exploiter. Indeed, even zealous proponents of *droit moral* have criticized the failure of the French system to reconcile the interests of the business community with those of the artist under contract.[397] Thus, while *droit moral* achieves certain rights for artists, in practice it also may serve to aggravate the tension between artistic and commercial interests.[398]

The French system also poses theoretical difficulties. It has been criticized for being based on the troublesome assumption that "moral" and "economic" interests even can be separated.[399] The separation does appear somewhat artificial when we consider that an artist's name, reputation, and personality — like the goodwill of a business — are economic assests, and their violation gives rise to injuries which are at least analogous to business losses.[400] Moreover, the civil law doctrine has not yet resolved the question of whether *droit moral* exists primarily to protect the artist or to protect his work, and how far it legitimately may go to protect either.[401]

Finally, *droit moral* seeks to broaden the rights of the artist, but it ignores the fact that society, too, has legitimate interests in a work of art. While the artist may wish to withhold his work from public view or to preserve his creations from alteration or even from criticism, society has an interest in promoting education, in facilitating the diffusion of culture, and in stimulating new ideas, new art forms, and even new methods of

---

[396] *Chillida, supra* note 50, at 8; Concurrence, *supra* note 139, at 12-16.

[397] *Chillida, supra* note 50, at 8.

[398] E.g., Pakuscher, *supra* note 81, at 71, speaking of a recent German case, writes:

> The reported decision of the Federal Supreme Court will promote the tendency of radio and film corporations to double their contract forms in size because of a desire to cover all conceivable means of exploitation and to have them spelled out in writing or printing.

[399] This division of the right into two — one pecuniary, the other moral — is a false notion, since experience has shown us that moral rights can be pecuniary, and vice versa. In brief, the need has been felt to impose an order on this subject by making a division and arbitrarily separating the pecuniary prerogatives from the moral prerogatives.

P. Recht, *supra* note 13, at 276. See also Diamond, *supra* note 35, at 249.

[400] See Concurrence, *supra* note 139, at 13.

[401] See Sarraute, *supra* note 17, at 478-79.

exploitation,[402] especially after an author or artist has been deceased for many years.[403] The Anglo-American system, it has been argued,[404] more effectively accounts for these interests.

This author advocates the conscientious legislative and judicial evolution of artists' rights through the expansion of existing American legal doctrines. As California has demonstrated, American legislation can accomodate many of the legal and equitable prerogatives enjoyed by French artists, without unfurling the banner of *droit moral*. As for the courts, what is needed is not a unification of the various doctrines into a single theory of "moral right," but simply a clarification of the special factors to be considered as tort, contract, property and trademark theories continue to be applied to cases involving authors and artists. Such factors may best be studied by giving careful attention to the time-honored experience of the civil law.

§5.2.2. *Snow v. The Eaton Centre Ltd.*: Red Ribbons, Geese, and the Berne-Convention Approach

Section 12(7) of Canada's federal Copyright Act provides:

Independently of the author's copyright, and even after the assignment, either wholly or partially, of the said copyright, the author has the right to claim authorship of the work, as well as the right to restrain any distortion, mutilation or other modification of the work that would be prejudicial to his honour or reputation.[2]

This language basically traces the moral right provision of the Berne Convention (reproduced in §5.1.1, n.9 *supra*) to which Canada, unlike the United States, is a signatory.

In 1982, the artist Michael Snow sucessfully relied on §12(7) to restrain a large shopping center in Toronto from draping Christmas ribbons over the necks of the 60 geese that constituted *Flight Stop*, a sculpture by Snow that belonged to the center. The court's opinion follows. Interest-

---

[402] See generally Giacobbe, *Interesse Pubblico e Interesse Privato Nella Tutela del Diritto di Autore*, 1975 Il Diritto di Autore 520. *See also Chillida, supra* note 50, at 8; F. Wey, *supra* note 47, at 11; Roeder, *supra* note 6, at 575.

[403] By analogy, the Rule Against Perpetuities forbids a trust to exist in perpetuity, in part because we believe that people who have been deceased for a great number of years no longer should have firm control over the alienation of uses of property.

[404] P. Recht, *supra* note 13, at 245.

[2] Can. Rev. Stat. 1970, c. C-30(7).

ingly, although the distortion or modification about which Snow complained was temporary and wholly reversible, the court nonetheless treated it as a sufficient encroachment on his rights to sustain injunctive relief.

SNOW v. THE EATON CENTRE LTD.
70 C.P.R.2d 105 (1982)

O'BRIEN, J. The Applicant in this motion relies solely on section 12(7) of the Copyright Act and in particular that part which gives the author the right to restrain any distortion, mutilation or other modification of his work that would be prejudicial to his honour or reputation.

The distortion or modification complained of is that of attaching ribbons to the necks of the 60 geese forming a sculpture known as 'Flight Stop,' a work of the plaintiff sold to the defendants and paid for by them and by a Wintario Grant.

The geese were be-ribboned by the defendants without the knowledge or consent of the plaintiff.

The plaintiff, an artist of international reputation takes the position that the work as presently displayed is prejudicial to his honour and reputation. Counsel advise there are no cases which interpret s. 12(7) of the Copyright Act.

The defendants argue that the plaintiff's complaint is not one which comes within s. 12(7) but if it does, that section is unconstitutional. The Attorney Generals of Canada and Ontario have been notified of this Application and hearing but are not intervening at this stage of proceedings.

The defendants further submit s. 12(7) should be looked (at) in a manner similar to a libel or slander action. I am not persuaded the section of the Act is unconstitutional. In my view the use of the word "independently" in s. 12(7) merely indicates the rights conferred by that section are in addition to the author's right of copyright. I reject the argument that I interpret 12(7) as suggested; in my view, the section gives rights broader than those based on libel or slander.

It is conceded that the sculpture is a "work" within the meaning of the Copyright Act.

I believe the words "prejudicial to his honour or reputation" in s. 12(7) involve a certain subjective element or judgment on the part of the author so long as it is reasonably arrived at.

The plaintiff is adamant in his belief that his naturalistic composition has been made to look ridiculous by the addition of ribbons and suggests it is not unlike dangling earrings from the Venus de Milo. While the matter is not undisputed, the plaintiff's opinion is shared by a number of other well respected artists and people knowledgeable in his field.

The plaintiff does not seek to interfere with the Christmas advertising campaign of the defendants other than to have the ribbons removed from the necks of the geese.

I am satisfied the ribbons do distort or modify the plaintiff's work and the plaintiff's concern this will be prejudicial to his honor or reputation is reasonable under the circumstances.

Application granted. Ribbons to be removed by Monday, December 6th at 9 A.M. If the matter goes no further, costs to the plaintiff in any event. If the matter proceeds, costs at discretion of trial judge.

§5.2.3. Two Recent European Cases: Public and Private Sculpture by Dubuffet and Serrano

In the past few years, two European jurisdictions have been faced with a similar question: To what extent can the "moral right" prevent the party who has commissioned a major sculpture from dismantling the piece or electing not to complete it in its contemplated enlarged format? While the issues presented to courts in France and Spain had a striking similarity, the results of the litigations varied.

The French action involved the artist Jean Dubuffet and automobile manufacturer Renault (Régie Nationale des Usines Renault). Dubuffet had signed an agreement with Renault to design a "monumental work" for the grounds of its main office. The artist was to supply the maquette, plans, and instructions for the work's construction; Renault was to bear all construction costs and select the materials and colors as suggested by Dubuffet. Half of Dubuffet's commission was paid at the signing of the agreement; the balance was paid at the time the maquette was delivered.

Renault had commenced construction of the piece, but then a year later decided to halt further work and dismantle the portion it had completed. Dubuffet subsequently brought an action in the French Court, arguing that he was the "author" of the work and that Renault had an obligation to complete the project, and did not have the right to destroy the portion that had been constructed.

The Court of Cassation, the highest French tribunal, ruled in favor of Dubuffet. It held that although under the contract Renault had no obligation to construct the work in the first place, once the company had started the project it had to complete it to satisfy the moral right of the artist.[3]

The Spanish decision involved a somewhat different set of facts.

---

[3] La Régie Nationale des Usines Renault v. Dubuffet, Court of Cassation, No. 229 (March 16, 1983). See Françon & Ginsburg, Authors' Rights in France: The Moral Right of the Creator of a Commissioned Work to Compel the Commissioning Party to Complete the Work, 9 Art. & L. 381 (1985).

There, the Spanish sculptor Pablo Serrano brought suit against the Intusa Hotel chain, which owns the Tres Carabelas Hotel in Torremolinos, for having disassembled a work it had bought from the sculptor more than twenty years previously in 1962. The courts held against the sculptor in a succession of determinations and appeals. Eventually Serrano based his claim on the proposition that the Spanish Constitution, enacted in 1978, provided for "fundamental rights." He further argued that, based on a recent Supreme Court decision, "the rights of the author are both patrimonial and moral." The defendant countered that the issue had been previously decided under the law that then existed, and argued further that the artist's rights had not been violated since the work was being disassembled and not destroyed. The hotel chain contended that having paid for the work, it had the right to disassemble it. The Regional Tribunal of Madrid held for the defendant.[4]

The United States has recently faced a similar controversy involving the proposed removal of the public sculpture *Tilted Arc*, commissioned by the General Services Administration from Richard Serra for the plaza adjacent to the Jacob Javits Federal Office Building in Manhattan. For a discussion of the Serra dispute, see Chapter 4.

§5.3. AMERICAN BACKGROUND

§5.3.1. *Crimi v. Rutgers Presbyterian Church:* An Early Rejection of Moral Right

Crimi, which follows, is one of those rare cases in which the issue is so sharply drawn as to leave no ambiguity as to the meaning of the court's decision. Did the sale by an artist of a work of art leave him with any cognizable interest concerning its threatened destruction? The clear answer given at that place and time — New York in 1949 — was that absent some contractual arrangement, the artist retained no interest. What is significant about *Crimi* is that the court was fully briefed about moral right but flatly rejected the contention that it had any application within the United States.

CRIMI v. RUTGERS PRESBYTERIAN CHURCH
194 Misc. 570, 89 N.Y.S.2d 813 (Sup. Ct. 1949)

LOCKWOOD, Official Ref. In 1937 the Rutgers Presbyterian Church invited members of the National Society of Mural Painters to

---

[4] See El Pais, Jan. 16 & 20, 1985.

enter a competition to design and execute a mural to be placed on the rear chancel wall of its edifice on West Seventy-third street, Manhattan.

Some twenty artists competed, and after study the committee in charge unanimously selected the plans and sketches of the well-known Alfred D. Crimi for a fresco mural painting twenty-six feet wide by thirty-five feet high. A contract in which the church is designated as "Owner" and Mr. Crimi as "Artist" was prepared by the attorney for the church and the attorney for Mr. Crimi, and signed by the chairman of the board of trustees of the church and by the artist on February 4, 1938.

The work was completed in time, as per contract, and the agreed price of $6,800 paid in full.

The manner in which the work was done is described by Mr. Crimi as follows:

> [T]he fresco had to be built over the existing wall which had a metal lath base suspended four inches over the brick structure on steel channels running perpendicularly. Holes were cut through the wall and the existing channels were re-inforced in order that they could carry the weight of the new structure. New channels were then fastened horizontally over the existing ones and in turn were furred with metal lath over which the plaster was laid. To avoid contact between the new and existing wall, after the holes were replastered, a heavy coat of asphalt was applied over the old. This also served as water-proofing, eliminating the possibility of dampness penetrating through the brick structure.
>
> Fresco painting is done on wet plaster. The color adheres to the plaster through chemical action—the union of carbonic acid gas and lime oxide producing carbonate of lime as the water evaporates on the surface of the plaster. In fresco no binding agent need be mixed with the pigment as in other painting processes; the pigments are simply well ground in water and applied to the wet surface. As the plaster dries, *the color is actually incorporated in the plaster* and—if the work is properly executed—the painting is assured a permanence surpassing that achieved in any other method of wall decoration. (Emphasis supplied.)

The contract provides that the executed fresco mural, as soon as affixed to the chancel wall, would become a part of the church building. Also that the work of the artist was to be copyrighted and such copyright duly and properly assigned to the owner—the church. This was done.

The mural, signed by the artist, was dedicated November 20, 1938. At the service a leaflet was distributed to the congregation, reading in part:

> Thus the desires and hopes and the thoughtful study, over a period of twelve years, of a difficult aesthetic and deeply religious problem comes to consummation on this twentieth day of November, 1938. Whether the committee and the artist have done well is not for them to say. They have done their best. The verdict must be left to the present congregation, to the successive generations of worshippers who will look upon the fresco, and to Him whose glory is all in all. . . . With the passage of time the mural will grow less brilliant but richer in color.

Plaintiff says that the Reverend Ralph W. Key, former pastor of the church, told him that some parishioners objected to the mural, feeling that a portrayal of Christ with so much of His chest bare placed more emphasis on His physical attributes than on His spiritual qualities.

The number of those objecting evidently increased, for in 1946, when the church was redecorated, the mural was painted over without first giving notice to plaintiff.

Upon learning what had been done, plaintiff brought this proceeding, alleging three causes of action for equitable relief:

1. To compel the defendant to remove the obliterating paints on the fresco mural.
2. In the alternative, to permit the plaintiff to take the fresco mural from the defendant's church at the cost and expense of the defendant.
3. In the event that the fresco mural cannot be thus removed, for judgment against the defendant for $50,000 on each of the three alleged causes of action.

Defendant has denied plaintiff's requests that the obliterations be removed or that he be given right to take away the mural.

Plaintiff contends that "Defendant's obliteration of the mural constituted a breach of the custom and usage considered part of the contract of commission; violates plaintiff's continued, albeit limited, proprietary interest therein; constitutes irreparable damage to plaintiff; and constitutes an anti-social act and one against public policy."

Defendant asserts:

a. That the mural, under the terms of the contract, became part of the building owned by the church.
b. That the church is not a public or semipublic building.
c. That the contract between an artist and his patron is basically and essentially a service contract.
d. That when the artistic work has been completed and delivered to the patron and accepted and paid for by the patron there is no right whatever in and to the subject matter of the painting reserved to the artist in the absence of a specific agreement providing therefor.
e. That the contract here contains no such reservation.

Thus, the question presented is whether the sale by an artist of a work of art wipes out any interest he might have therein.

Certain general customs and usages are claimed between artists and those who contract with them for the creation of a work to which the artists' name and reputation will be attached — more specifically between mural artists and public or semipublic institutions open to the public. The gist of this claimed custom is that the work, if accepted as being of high artistic standard, will not be altered, mutilated, obliterated or destroyed.

The existence of these customs and usages, their universality, and their acceptance by the public was testified to by leading artists, art critics and art experts.

Plaintiff also pleads that, aside from the question of custom and usage, the artist has a continued limited proprietary interest in his work after its sale, to the extent reasonably necessary to the protection of his honor and reputation as an artist, and that within this limited ambit of protection was the right to have the work continue without destruction, mutilation, obliteration or alteration.

The fact that artists, as distinguished from artisans and mechanics, have peculiar and distinctive rights in their work has been accepted in some countries of the Continent of Europe, where it has been given the appellation "droit moral" (see "The International Protection of Literary and Artistic Property," by Stephen P. Ladas, 1938 Ed.).

The extent to which such doctrine has been adopted in common-law jurisdictions is considered by Martin A. Roeder in 53 Harvard Law Review, p.554, "The Doctrine of Moral Right: A study in the Law of Artists, Authors and Creators," in which (p.557) the author distinguishes the protection provided by the copyright laws from that provided by the "droit moral."

> When an artist creates, be he an author, a painter, a sculptor, an architect or a musician, he does more than bring into the world a unique object having only exploitive possibilities; he projects into the world part of his personality and subjects it to the ravages of public use. There are possibilities of injury to the creator other than merely economic ones. . . . Nor is the interest of society in the integrity of its cultural heritage protected by the copyright statute.

However, this author, discussing the Bern Convention as revised at Rome in 1928, says, at page 569 of his article:

> The right to prevent deformation does not include the right to prevent destruction of a created work. The doctrine of moral right finds one social basis in the need of the creator for protection of his honor and reputation. To deform his work is to present him to the public as the creator of a work not his own, and thus make him subject to criticism for work he has not done; the destruction of his work does not have this result. Thus even in France, in *Lacasse et Welcome c. Abbé Quénard* (Cour de Paris, April 27, 1934, D. H. 1934 p.385), it was held that the artist could not recover when murals painted by him on the walls of a church were destroyed, without notice, by the abbe.

The Bern Convention, the International Copyright Union, article 6 reads:

> 1. Independently of the patrimonial rights of the author, and even after the assignment of the said rights, the author retains the right to claim the paternity of the work, as well as the right to object to every deformation, mutilation or other modification of the said work, which may be prejudicial to his honor or to his reputation.

2. It is left to the national legislation of each of the countries of the Union to establish the conditions for the exercise of these rights. The means for safeguarding them shall be regulated by the legislation of the country where protection is claimed.

The United States of America was not a signatory to these conventions held at Bern and Rome.

Plaintiff concedes "there is a decided paucity of legal authority" on the question in this country. He quotes from Stephen P. Ladas' work (International Protection of Literary and Artistic Property, vol. 1, §287 p.603):

> The author may demand respect for the integrity of his work. This applies only to cases in which his work has been presented to the public. It does not extend to the personal or private use of a reproduction of his work by the purchaser thereof, but it does when the original work of the author is involved. This is particularly the case with works of art, the nature of which calls for exhibition by the purchaser. The latter is not permitted to violate its integrity but is he permitted to destroy the work of art? A decision of the Court of Appeals in Paris has recognized the right of a purchaser of a work of art to destroy it. While this may be justified on a strict interpretation of the legal position based on the general law of property, it is questionable whether it should be admitted in the case of works of art. *Modern legislation and court decisions have admitted several limitations of the property right in cases where public or social interests are involved. The maintenance and preservation of a work of art is invested with the public interest in culture and the development of the arts.*

(Italics supplied.)

In a footnote Ladas cites *Lacasse et Welcome c. Abbé Guénard*, "reported in Dalloz, 1934, p.385," where "the Court reversed the decision of the Tribunal Civil de Versailles and held that the proprietor of a church containing wall paintings may destroy the latter without advising the artist and permitting him to remove them." The author severely criticizes this holding in the language italicized above.

Ladas cites Nicola Stolfi and Hermann Otavsky (foreign authors) for the proposition that the owner may not destroy a work of art because of the "intention of the parties at the time of purchase, and . . . claim that such intention is limited to the transfer of the work for the purpose of its being used according to its nature, and not for the purpose of destruction" (Ladas, *op. cit. supra*, p.604). Thus Ladas, Stolfi and Otavsky are all in agreement that the owner should not have the right to destroy the work of art, Ladas on the ground of public policy and Stolfi and Otavsky on the ground of original intent of the parties.

Counsel overlooked the statement at page 802, section 363, Volume II, where Ladas writes:

> The conception of "moral right" of authors, so fully recognized and developed in the civil countries, has *not yet received acceptance in the law of the*

United States. No such right is referred to by legislation, court decisions or writers.
(Italics supplied.)

This comment is supported by Vargas v. Esquire, Inc., 7 Cir., 164 F.2d 522, at page 526, where the court said:

> The conception of "moral rights" of authors so fully recognized and developed in the civil law countries has not yet received acceptance in the law of the United States. No such right is referred to by legislation, court decisions or writers.
>
> What plaintiff in reality seeks is a change in the law in this country to conform to that of certain other countries. We need not stop to inquire whether such a change, if desirable, is a matter for the legislative or judicial branch of the government; in any event, we are not disposed to make any new law in this respect.

And by Yardley v. Houghton Mifflin Co., 25 F. Supp. 361, 364 *affirmed* 2 Cir., 108 F.2d 28:

> When a man, hereinafter referred to as a patron, contracts with an artist to paint a picture for him, of whatever nature it may be, the contract is essentially a service contract, and when the picture has been painted and delivered to the patron and paid for by him, the artist has no right whatever left in it.
>
> Whilst the artist in such a case may by contract reserve the right of reproduction, and so reserve his right of copyright, *Werckmeister v. Springer Lithographing Co.*, C.C., 63 F. 808, 809, if the sale is not shown to have been thus limited, the patron becomes the sole owner and has all the rights in the picture, including the right to reproduce it, and the artist employed to make the picture cannot derogate from his patron's rights by taking out a copyright thereon without his patron's permission.

In *Pushman v. New York Graphic Society*, Sup., 25 N.Y.S.2d 32, page 34, Mr. Justice O'Brien, at Special Term, said:

> In this case the absolute sale and delivery of the painting without any condition, reservation or qualification of any kind, to a state-owned public institution where it has been displayed for a long period of time, constitute an abandonment of all the plaintiff's rights and a publication and dedication to public use free for enjoyment and reproduction by anybody.

Our Court of Appeals, *affirming*, 287 N.Y. 302, 308, 39 N.E.2d 249, 251, in a unanimous decision by Desmond, J., stated in part:

> Our conclusion is that under the cases and the texts, this unconditional sale carried with it the transfer of the common law copyright and right to reproduce. Plaintiff took no steps to withold or control that right. "The courts cannot read words of limitation into a transfer which the parties do not choose to use." *Dam v. Kirk La Shelle Co.*, 2 Cir., 175 F. 902, 904. . . .

Thus, the claim of this plaintiff that an artist retains rights in his work after it has been unconditionally sold, where such rights are related to the protection of his artistic reputation, is not supported by the decisions of our courts.

This court does not agree with the contention that the destruction of the mural to which plaintiff's name had been publicly attached constitutes a "body blow" to plaintiff's artistic reputation. It merely shows that those representing the 1938 congregation of this church thought highly of the fresco mural, while those representing the 1946 congregation did not like it.

The case cited involving literary productions — authors of plays, attempts to restrain modifications of paintings in public or semi-public buildings, and the maintenance and preservation of works of art presented to public authorities, are not in point.

In *Trustees of First Baptist Church of Ithaca v. Bigelow*, 16 Wend. 28, the court held that the interest of a party in a pew in a church, although a limited and qualified interest, is an interest in real estate and the sale thereof necessitates a writing.

Plaintiff designed and executed this fresco mural as part and parcel of the wall of the church building — on part of the real estate.

Thus, any interest, proprietary or otherwise, claimed to have arisen by custom and usage as part of the contract of commission, or in any manner, would have to be in writing, or it would violate section 242 of the Real Property Law.

The time for the artist to have reserved any rights was when he and his attorney participated in the drawing of the contract with the church. No rights in the fresco mural were reserved, and, by the terms of the written agreement between the parties, signed February 4, 1938, the artist plaintiff sold and transferred to defendant all his right, title and interest in the mural.

Judgment for defendant. Submit proposed judgment on five day's notice.

§5.3.2. *Gilliam v. American Broadcasting Cos.:* Monty Python Goes to Court

While *Gilliam*, which follows, dealt with the alleged "mutilation" of a television program created by the group known as Monty Python, there is no reason to believe that its logic is not equally applicable to protecting the integrity of a work of art. Here, a federal court used a federal trademark statute as a vehicle to prevent the broadcast of a work that had been altered without the consent of the authors. Particularly valuable is Circuit Judge Lumbard's discussion of how American law, while generally refusing to acknowledge the existence of the moral right, has found alternative ways to protect artists against having their work misrepresented to the public.

GILLIAM v. AMERICAN BROADCASTING COS.
538 F.2d 14 (2d Cir. 1976)

Before LUMBARD, HAYS AND GURFEIN, Circuit Judges.

LUMBARD, C.J. Plaintiffs, a group of British writers and performers known as "Monty Python,"[1] appeal from a denial by Judge Lasker in the Southern District of a preliminary injunction to restrain the American Broadcasting Company (ABC) from broadcasting edited versions of three separate programs originally written and performed by Monty Python for broadcast by the British Broadcasting Corporation(BBC). We agree with Judge Lasker that the appellants have demonstrated that the excising done for ABC impairs the integrity of the original work. We further find that the countervailing injuries that Judge Lasker found might have accrued to ABC as a result of an injunction at a prior date no longer exist. We therefore direct the issuance of a preliminary injunction by the district court.

Since its formation in 1969, the Monty Python group has gained popularity primarily through its thirty-minute television programs created for BBC as part of a comedy series entitled "Monty Python's Flying Circus." In accordance with an agreement between Monty Python and BBC, the group writes and delivers to BBC scripts for use in the television series. This scriptwriters' agreement recites in great detail the procedure to be followed when any alterations are to be made in the script prior to recording of the program.[2] The essence of this section of the agreement is that, while BBC retains final authority to make changes, appellants or

---

[1] Appellant Gilliam is an American citizen residing in England.

[2] The Agreement provides:

V. When script alterations are necessary it is the intention of the BBC to make every effort to inform and to reach agreement with the Writer. Whenever practicable any necessary alterations (others than minor alterations) shall be made by the Writer. Nevertheless the BBC shall at all times have the right to make (a) minor alterations and (b) such other alterations as in its opinion are necessary in order to avoid involving the BBC in legal action or bringing the BBC into disrepute. Any decision under (b) shall be made at a level not below that of Head of Department. It is however agreed that after a script has been accepted by the BBC alterations will not be made by the BBC under (b) above unless (i) the Writer, if available when the BBC requires the alterations to be made, has been asked to agree to them but is not willing to do so and (ii) the Writer has had, if he so requests and if the BBC agrees that time permits if rehearsals and recording are to proceed as planned, an opportunity to be represented by the Writers' Guild of Great Britain (or if he is not a member of the Guild by his agent) at a meeting with the BBC to be held within at most 48 hours of the request (excluding weekends). If in such circumstances there is no agreement about the alterations then the final decision shall rest with the BBC. Apart from the right to make alterations under (a) and (b) above the BBC shall not without the consent of the Writer or his agent (which consent shall not be unreasonably withheld) make any structural alterations as opposed to minor alterations to the script, provided that such consent shall not be necessary in any case where the Writer is for any reason not immediately available for consultation at the time which in the BBC's opinion is the deadline from the production point of view for such alterations to be made if rehearsals and recording are to proceed as planned.

their representatives exercise optimum control over the scripts consistent with BBC's authority and only minor changes may be made without prior consultation with the writers. Nothing in the scriptwriters' agreement entitles BBC to alter a program once it has been recorded. The agreement further provides that, subject to the terms therein, the group retains all rights in the script.

Under the agreement, BBC may license the transmission of recordings of the television programs in any overseas territory. The series has been broadcast in this country primarily on non-commercial public broadcasting television stations, although several of the programs have been broadcast on commercial stations in Texas and Nevada. In each instance, the thirty-minute programs have been broadcast as originally recorded and broadcast in England in their entirety and without commercial interruption.

In October 1973, Time-Life Films acquired the right to distribute in the United States certain BBC television programs, including the Monty Python series. Time-Life was permitted to edit the programs only "for insertion of commercials, applicable censorship or governmental . . . rules and regulations, and National Association of Broadcasters and time segment requirements." No similar clause was included in the scriptwriters' agreement between appellants and BBC. Prior to this time, ABC had sought to acquire the right to broadcast excerpts from various Monty Python programs in the spring of 1975, but the group rejected the proposal for such a disjoined format. Thereafter, in July 1975, ABC agreed with Time-Life to broadcast two ninety-minute specials each comprising three thirty-minute Monty Python programs that had not previously been shown in this country.

Correspondence between representatives of BBC and Monty Python reveals that these parties assumed that ABC would broadcast each of the Monty Python programs "in its entirety." On September 5, 1975, however, the group's British representative inquired of BBC how ABC planned to show the programs in their entirety if approximately 24 minutes of each 90 minute program were to be devoted to commercials. BBC replied on September 12, "we can only reassure you that ABC have decided to run the programmes 'back to back,' and that there is a firm undertaking not to segment them."

ABC broadcast the first of the specials on October 3, 1975. Appellants did not see a tape of the program until late November and were allegedly "appalled" at the discontinuity and "mutilation" that had resulted from the editing done by Time-Life for ABC. Twenty-four minutes of the original 90 minutes of recording had been omitted. Some of the editing had been done in order to make time for commercials; other material had been edited, according to ABC, because the original programs contained offensive or obscene matter.

In early December, Monty Python learned that ABC planned to

broadcast the second special on December 26, 1975. The parties began negotiations concerning editing of that program and a delay of the broadcast until Monty Python could view it. These negotiations were futile, however, and on December 15 the group filed this action to enjoin the broadcast and for damages. Following an evidentiary hearing, Judge Lasker found that "the plaintiffs have established an impairment of the integrity of their work" which "caused the film or program . . . to lose its iconoclastic verve." According to Judge Lasker, "the damage that has been caused to the plaintiffs is irreparable by its nature." Nevertheless, the judge denied the motion for the preliminary injunction on the grounds that it was unclear who owned the copyright in the programs produced by BBC from the scripts written by Monty Python; that there was a question of whether Time-Life and BBC were indispensable parties to the litigation; that ABC would suffer significant financial loss if it were enjoined a week before the scheduled broadcast; and that Monty Python had displayed a "somewhat disturbing casualness" in their pursuance of the matter.

Judge Lasker granted Monty Python's request for more limited relief by requiring ABC to broadcast a disclaimer during the December 26 special to the effect that the group dissociated itself from the program because of the editing. A panel of this court, however, granted a stay of that order until this appeal could be heard and permitted ABC to broadcast, at the beginning of the special, only the legend that the program had been edited by ABC. We heard argument on April 13 and, at that time, enjoined ABC from any further broadcast of edited Monty Python programs pending the decision of the court. . . .

It also seems likely that appellants will succeed on the theory that, regardless of the right ABC had to broadcast an edited program, the cuts made constituted an actionable mutilation of Monty Python's work. This cause of action, which seeks redress for deformation of an artist's work, finds its roots in the continental concept of droit moral, or moral right, which may generally be summarized as including the right of the artist to have his work attributed to him in the form in which he created it. See 1 M. Nimmer, *supra*, at §110.1.

American copyright law, as presently written, does not recognize moral rights or provide a cause of action for their violation, since the law seeks to vindicate the economic, rather than the personal, rights of authors. Nevertheless, the economic incentive for artistic and intellectual creation that serves as the fondation for American copyright law, *Goldstein v. California*, 412 U.S. 546, 93 S. Ct. 2303, 37 L. Ed. 2d 163 (1973), *Mazer v. Stein*, 347 U.S. 201, 74 S. Ct. 460, 98 L. Ed. 630 (1954), cannot be reconciled with the inability of artists to obtain relief for mutilation or misrepresentation of their work to the public on which the artists are financially dependent. Thus courts have long granted relief for misrepresentation of an artist's work by relying on theories outside the statutory law of copyright, such as contract law, *Granz v. Harris,* 198 F.2d 585 (2d Cir. 1952) (substantial cutting of original work constitutes misrepresentation), or the tort of unfair competition, *Prouty v. National Broadcasting Co.,* 26 F. Supp. 265 (D. Mass. 1939). See Strauss, The Moral Right of the Author 128-138, in Studies on Copyright (1963). Although such decisions are clothed in terms of proprietary right in one's creation, they also properly vindicate the author's personal right to prevent the presentation of his work to the public in a distorted form. See *Gardella v. Log Cabin Products Co.,* 89 F.2d 891, 895-96 (2d Cir. 1937); Roeder, The Doctrine of Moral Right, 53 Harv. L. Rev. 554, 568 (1940).

Here, the appellants claim that the editing done for ABC mutilated the original work and that consequently the broadcast of those programs as the creation of Monty Python violated the Lanham Act §43(a), 15 U.S.C. §1125(a).[10] This statute, the federal counterpart to state unfair competition laws, has been invoked to prevent misrepresentations that may injure plaintiff's business or personal reputation, even where no registered trademark is concerned. See *Mortellito v. Nina of California,* 335 F. Supp. 1288, 1294 (S.D.N.Y. 1972). It is sufficient to violate the Act that a representation of a product, although technically true, creates a false impression of the product's origin. See *Rich v. RCA Corp.,* 390 F. Supp. 530 (S.D.N.Y. 1975) (recent picture of plaintiff on cover of album containing songs recorded in distant past held to be a false representation that the songs were new); *Geisel v. Poynter Products, Inc.,* 283 F. Supp. 261, 267 (S.D.N.Y. 1968).

These cases cannot be distinguished from the situation in which a television network broadcasts a program properly designated as having been written and performed by a group, but which has been edited, without the writer's consent, into a form that departs substantially from the original work. "To deform his work is to present him to the public as the creator of a work not his own, and thus makes him subject to criticism for work he has not done." Roeder, *supra,* at 569. In such a case, it is the writer or performer, rather than the network, who suffers the consequences of the mutilation, for the public will have only the final product by which to evaluate the work.[11] Thus, an allegation that a defendant has presented to the public a "garbled," *Granz v. Harris, supra* (Frank, J., concurring), distorted version of plaintiff's work seeks to redress the very rights sought to be protected by the Lanham Act, 15 U.S.C. §1125(a), and

---

[10] That statute provides in part:

Any person who shall affix, apply, or annex, or use in connection with any goods or services, . . . a false designation of origin, or any false description or representation . . . and shall cause such goods or services to enter into commerce . . . shall be liable to a civil action by any person . . . who believes that he is or is likely to be damaged by the use of any such false description or representation.

[11] This result is not changed by the fact that the network, as here, takes public responsibility for editing. See Rich v. RCA Corp., *supra.*

should be recognized as stating a cause of action under that statute. See *Autry v. Republic Productions, Inc.*, 213 F.2d 667 (9th Cir. 1954); *Jaeger v. American Intn'l Pictures, Inc.*, 330 F. Supp. 274 (S.D.N.Y. 1971), which suggest the violation of such a right if mutilation could be proven.

During the hearing on the preliminary injunction, Judge Lasker viewed the edited version of the Monty Python program broadcast on December 26 and the original, unedited version. After hearing argument of this appeal, this panel also viewed and compared the two versions. We find that the truncated version at times omitted the climax of the skits to which appellants' rare brand of humor was leading and at other times deleted essential elements in the schematic development of a story line.[12] We therefore agree with Judge Lasker's conclusion that the edited version broadcast by ABC impaired the integrity of appellants' work and represented to the public as the product of appellants what was actually a mere caricature of their talents. We believe that a valid cause of action for such distortion exists and that therefore a preliminary injunction may issue to prevent repetition of the broadcast prior to final determination of the issues.[13] . . .

For these reasons we direct that the district court issue the preliminary injunction sought by the appellants.

Gurfein, C.J. (concurring): I concur in my brother Lumbard's scholarly opinion, but I wish to comment on the application of Section 43(a) of the Lanham Act, 15 U.S.C. §1125(a).

I believe that this is the first case in which a federal appellate court has held that there may be a violation of Section 43(a) of the Lanham Act

---

[12] A single example will illustrate the extent of distortion engendered by the editing. In one skit, an upper class English family is engaged in a discussion of the tonal quality of certain words as "woody" or "tinny." The father soon begins to suggest certain words with sexual connotations as either "woody" or "tinny," whereupon the mother fetches a bucket of water and pours it over his head. The skit continues from this point. The ABC edit eliminates this middle sequence so that the father is comfortably dressed at one moment and, in the next moment, is shown in a soaked condition without any explanation for the change in his appearance.

[13] Judge Gurfein's concurring opinion suggests that since the gravamen of a complaint under the Lanham Act is that the origin of goods has been falsely described, a legend disclaiming Monty Python's approval of the edited version would preclude violation of that Act. We are doubtful that a few words could erase the indelible impression that is made by a television broadcast, especially since the viewer has no means of comparing the truncated version with the complete work in order to determine for himself the talents of plaintiffs. Furthermore, a disclaimer such as the one originally suggested by Judge Lasker in the exigencies of an impending broadcast last December would go unnoticed by viewers who tuned into the broadcast a few minutes after it began. We therefore conclude that Judge Gurfein's proposal that the district court could find some form of disclaimer would be sufficient might not provide appropriate relief.

with respect to a common-law copyright. The Lanham Act is a trademark statute, not a copyright statute. Nevertheless, we must recognize that the language of Section 43(a) is broad. It speaks of the affixation or use of false designations of origin or false descriptions or representations, but proscribes such use "in connection with any goods or services." It is easy enough to incorporate trade names as well as trademarks into Section 43(a) and the statute specifically applies to common law trademarks, as well as registered trademarks. Lanham Act §45, 15 U.S.C. §1127.

In the present case, we are holding that the deletion of portions of the recorded tape constitutes a breach of contract, as well as an infringement of a common-law copyright of the original work. There is literally no need to discuss whether plaintiffs also have a claim for relief under the Lanham Act or for unfair competition under New York law. I agree with Judge Lumbard, however, that it may be an exercise of judicial economy to express our view on the Lanham Act claim, and I do not dissent therefrom. I simply wish to leave it open for the District Court to fashion the remedy.

The Copyright Act provides no recognition of the so-called *droit moral*, or moral right of authors. Nor are such rights recognized in the field of copyright law in the United States. See 1 *Nimmer on Copyright*, §110.2 (1975 ed.). If a distortion or truncation in connection with a use constitutes an infringement of copyright, there is no need for an additional cause of action beyond copyright infringement. *Id*. at §110.3. An obligation to mention the name of the author carries the implied duty, however, as a matter of contract, not to make such changes in the work as would render the credit line a false attribution of authorship, *Granz v. Harris*, 198 F.2d 585 (2 Cir. 1952).

So far as the Lanham Act is concerned, it is not a substitute for *droit moral* which authors in Europe enjoy. If the licensee may, by contract, distort the recorded work, the Lanham Act does not come into play. If the licensee has no such right by contract, there will be a violation in breach of contract. The Lanham Act can hardly apply literally when the credit line correctly states the work to be that of the plaintiffs which, indeed it is, so far as it goes. The vice complained of is that the truncated version is not what the plaintiffs wrote. But the Lanham Act does not deal with artistic integrity. It only goes to misdescription of origin and the like. See *Societe Comptoir De L'Industrie Cotonniere Etablissements Boussac v. Alexander's Dept. Stores, Inc.*, 299 F.2d 33, 36 (2 Cir. 1962).

The misdescription of origin can be dealt with, as Judge Lasker did below, by devising an appropriate legend to indicate that the plaintiffs had not approved the editing of the ABC version.[1] With such a legend,

---

[1] I do not imply that the appropriate legend be shown only at the beginning of the broadcast. That is a matter for the District Court.

there is no conceivable violation of the Lanham Act. If plaintiffs complain that their artistic integrity is still compromised by the distorted version, their claim does not lie under the Lanham Act, which does not protect the copyrighted work itself but protects only against the misdescription or mislabelling.

So long as it is made clear that the ABC version is not approved by the Monty Python group, there is no misdescription of origin. So far as the content of the broadcast itself is concerned, that is not within the proscription of the Lanham Act when there is no misdescription of the authorship.

I add this brief explanation because I do not believe that the Lanham Act claim necessarily requires the drastic remedy of permanent injunction. That form of ultimate relief must be found in some other fountainhead of equity jurisprudence.

§5.3.3. A Comparison of *Crimi* and *Gilliam:* No Clear Path

The *Crimi* and *Gilliam* cases represent in some ways divergent approaches in facing a potential area of protected rights. In *Crimi*, the court was faced with the prospect of introducing into the American system a concept that had concededly existed for a number of years in Europe. The court took notice of the fact that the concept of moral right had been established in a number of foreign countries, but concluded that the law had not sufficiently developed in the Unied States to warrant its imposition in the case. *Gilliam* pointed in an opposite direction. The Lanham Act, which is essentially a trademark statute and had little to do with the rights of visual artists, was used by the federal court as a lever to expand the concept of distortion of creative effort. There is little doubt that the results in the cases could have been the reverse. In *Crimi* the court could have blazed a trail of moral right. In the very least, it might have stated that, although the concept existed, for one reason or another its application should be limited to the precise factual situation, perhaps by permitting the artist to have the mural returned to him upon the payment of its value at that time. A statute need not have been necessary. Often a state will adopt a legal concept, such as a right of privacy, without establishing a statutory basis. Similarly, in *Gilliam*, the court need not have stretched the statutory language to protect the distortion of the creator's rights, particularly where the creator was compensated for the commercial exploitation of the product that formed the basis for its suit. In *Crimi* the product was destroyed; in *Gilliam*, despite the plaintiff's opinion that the integrity of its product was impaired, it broadcast extensively with substantial promotion of the authors' name. In *Gilliam* there was no evidence that the public was left with a negative reaction to the Monty Python creation. The gist of the creators' claim was that the product as exhibited was not essentially theirs. If the broadcaster had so concluded prior to the suit and accordingly had eliminated the Monty Python name from the program, would not the plaintiff have felt more aggrieved? Should the *Gilliam* suit be treated as little more than a contract action? If *A* agrees with *B* that *B* cannot change its creative efforts to any extent without *A*'s permission, is not the claim based on a consensual breach? Perhaps the court in *Gilliam* felt that it was time to introduce the concept of moral right into American jurisprudence, and if the Lanham Act was to be the handle, then so be it.

§5.3.4. *Stella v. Mazoh:* Does the Moral Right Cover Discarded Works?

Even as late as 1982, an artist in New York could not use a violation of moral right as the basis of a cause of action to disclaim authorship, even when such a violation was the crux of his complaint. Technically, another route had to be found. Thus, in 1982, Frank Stella resorted to a "stolen property" action in a suit—*Stella v. Mazoh*[1]—to enjoin the defendant gallery from (1) selling two paintings claimed to be Stella's and (2) representing them as his work. The two paintings in question, Stella claimed, were rain-damaged canvasses that sometime in 1966 he had placed on the landing outside his loft-studio, fully intending to dispose of them. The canvases disappeared, only to turn up during the Spring of 1982 in the defendant's gallery.

In his moving papers, Stella set forth a complaint that virtually anticipated the moral right statute adopted in New York the following year. He said his reputation would be damaged if these incomplete works were sold as paintings by him. He made the following claim in an affidavit:

> I verily believe that as an artist and as a creator, I am entitled to pick and choose and select those items which are to be sold, distributed and more important, to be known to the general public and the world as a painting or work of Frank Stella. [N]o one is entitled to cause another to have his reputation demeaned, diminished or tarnished by taking his rejected paintings *from within or without his premises* and then offer them to the public and to the world as the artist's works and representative of his abilities, talents and creativity.[2]

Stella sought to regain control of the works.

---

§5.3. [1] Stella v. Mazoh, No. 07585-82 (N.Y. Sup. Ct. April 1, 1982)

[2] *Id.* Affidavit of Frank Stella at 6-7.

A temporary restraining order was granted, pending a hearing by the court. The hearing, however, and Stella's claim to a right of reputation was never pursued. The parties settled out of court; Stella recovered the works and destroyed them.

Query what would have been Stella's plight if no settlement had occurred? Would a *Crimi* result have ensued?

§5.4. AMERICAN LEGISLATION AND CASE LAW

§5.4.1. California Art Preservation Acts (§§987and 989): Private and Public Interest Provisions

Moral right legislation in the United States was pioneered by California when in 1979 it enacted the California Art Preservation Act (§987), which follows. Its companion legislation, protecting art of "substantial public interest" (§989), was adopted in 1982 and also appears in this section.[1]

CALIFORNIA ART PRESERVATION ACT
Cal. Civ. Code §987 (West Supp. 1985)

§987. PRESERVATION OF WORKS OF ART
(a) Legislative findings and declaration. The Legislature hereby finds and declares that the physical alteration or destruction of fine art, which is an expression of the artist's personality, is detrimental to the artist's reputation, and artists therefore have an interest in protecting their works of fine art against such alteration or destruction; and that there is also a public interest in preserving the integrity of cultural and artistic creations.

(b) Definitions. As used in this section:

(1) "Artist" means the individual or individuals who create a work of fine art.

(2) "Fine art" means an original painting, sculpture, or drawing, or an original work of art in glass, of recognized quality, but shall not include work prepared under contract for commercial use by its purchaser.

(3) "Person" means an individual, partnership, corporation, association or other group, however organized.

(4) "Frame" means to prepare, or cause to be prepared, a work of fine

---

§5.4. [1] For an in-depth analysis of the California statutes, see Karlen, Moral Rights in California, 19 San Diego L. Rev. 675 (1982).

art for display in a manner customarily considered to be appropriate for a work of fine art in the particular medium.

(5)"Restore" means to return, or cause to be returned, a deteriorated or damaged work of fine art as nearly as is feasible to its original state or condition, in accordance with prevailing standards.

(6) "Conserve" means to preserve, or cause to be preserved, a work of fine art by retarding or preventing deterioration or damage through appropriate treatment in accordance with prevailing standards in order to maintain the structural integrity to the fullest extent possible in an unchanging state.

(7) "Commercial use" means fine art created under a work-for-hire arrangement for use in advertising, magazines, newspapers, or other print and electronic media.

(c) Mutilation, alteration or destruction of a work. (1) No person, except an artist who owns and possesses a work of fine art which the artist has created, shall intentionally commit, or authorize the intentional commission of, any physical defacement, mutilation, alteration, or destruction of a work of fine art.

(2) In addition to the prohibitions contained in paragraph (1), no person who frames, conserves, or restores a work of fine art shall commit, or authorize the commission of, any physical defacement, mutilation, alteration, or destruction of a work of fine art by any act constituting gross negligence. For purposes of this section, the term "gross negligence" shall mean the exercise of so slight a degree of care as to justify the belief that there was an indifference to the particular work of fine art.

(d) Authorship. The artist shall retain at all times the right to claim authorship, or, for just and valid reason, to disclaim authorship of his or her work of fine art.

(e) Remedies. To effectuate the rights created by this section, the artist may commence an action to recover or obtain any of the following:

(1) Injuctive relief.

(2) Actual damages.

(3) Punitive damages. In the event that punitive damages are awarded, the court shall, in its discretion, select an organization or organizations engaged in charitable or educational activities involving the fine arts in California to receive such damages.

(4) Reasonable attorneys' and expert witness fees.

(5) Any other relief which the court deems proper.

(f) Determination of recognized quality. In determining whether a work of fine art is of recognized quality, the trier of fact shall rely on the opinions of artists, art dealers, collectors of fine art, curators of art museums, and other persons involved with the creation or marketing of fine art.

(g) Rights and duties. The rights and duties created under this section:

(1) Shall, with respect to the artist, or if any artist is deceased, his heir, legatee, or personal representative, exist until the 50th anniversary of the death of such artist.

(2) Shall exist in addition to any other rights and duties which may now or in the future be applicable.

(3) Except as provided in paragraph (1) of subdivision (h), may not be waived except by an instrument in writing expressly so providing which is signed by the artist.

(h) Removal from building; waiver. (1) If a work of fine art cannot be removed from a building without substantial physical defacement, mutilation, alteration, or destruction of such work, the rights and duties created under this section, unless expressly reserved by an instrument in writing signed by the owner of such building and properly recorded, shall be deemed waived. Such instrument, if properly recorded, shall be binding on subsequent owners of such building.

(2) If the owner of a building wishes to remove a work of fine art which is a part of such building but which can be removed from the building without a substantial harm to such fine art, *and in the course of or after removal, the owner intends to cause or allow the fine art to suffer physical defacement, mutilation, alteration, or destruction,* the rights and duties created under this section shall apply unless the owner has diligently attempted without success to notify the artist, or, if the artist is deceased, his heir, legatee, or personal representative, in writing of his intended action affecting the work of fine art, or unless he did provide notice and that person failed within 90 days either to remove the work or to pay for its removal. If such work is removed at the expense of the artist, his heir, legatee, or personal representative, title to such fine art shall pass to that person.

(3) Nothing in this subdivision shall affect the rights of authorship created in subdivision (d) of this section.

(i) Limitation of actions. No action may be maintained to enforce any liability under this section unless brought within three years of the act complained of or one year after discovery of such act, whichever is longer.

(j) Operative date. This section became operative on January 1, 1980, and shall apply to claims based on proscribed acts occurring on or after that date to works of fine art whenever created.

(k) Severability. If any provision of this section or the application thereof to any person or circumstance is held invalid for any reason, such invalidity shall not affect any other provisions or applications of this section which can be effected without the invalid provision or application, and to this end the provisions of this section are severable.

CALIFORNIA ART PRESERVATION ACT
Cal. Civ. Code §989 (West Supp. 1985)

§989. PRESERVATION OF CULTURAL AND ARTISTIC CREATIONS

(a) Legislative findings and declaration. The Legislature hereby finds and declares that there is a public interest in preserving the integrity of cultural and artistic creations.

(b) Definitions. As used in this section:

(1) "Fine art" means an original painting, sculpture, or drawing, or an original work of art in glass, of recognized quality, and of substantial public interest.

(2) "Organization" means a public or private not-for-profit entity or association, in existence at least three years at the time an action is filed pursuant to this section, a major purpose of which is to stage, display, or otherwise present works of art to the public or to promote the interests of the arts or artists.

(3) "Cost of removal" includes reasonable costs, if any, for the repair of damage to the real property caused by the removal of the work of fine art.

(c) Injunctive relief. An organization acting in the public interest may commence an action for injunctive relief to preserve or restore the integrity of a work of fine art from acts prohibited by subdivision (c) of Section 987.

(d) Determination of recognized quality and substantial public interest. In determining whether a work of fine art is of recognized quality and of substantial public interest the trier of fact shall rely on the opinions of those described in subdivision (f) of Section 987.

(e) Removal from real property. (1) If a work of fine art cannot be removed from real property without substantial physical defacement, mutilation, alteration, or destruction of such work, no action to preserve the integrity of the work of fine art may be brought under this section. However, if an organization offers some evidence giving rise to a reasonable likelihood that a work of art can be removed from the real property without substantial physical defacement, mutilation, alteration, or destruction of the work, and is prepared to pay the cost of removal of the work, it may bring a legal action for a determination of this issue. In that action the organization shall be entitled to injunctive relief to preserve the integrity of the work of fine art, but shall also have the burden of proof. The action shall commence within 30 days after filing. No action may be brought under this paragraph if the organization's interest in preserving the work of art is in conflict with an instrument described in paragraph (1) of subdivision (h) of Section 987.

(2) If the owner of the real property wishes to remove a work of fine art which is part of the real property, but which can be removed from the real property without substantial harm to such fine art, and in the course of or after removal, the owner intends to cause or allow the fine art to suffer physical defacement, mutilation, alteration, or destruction the owner shall do the following:

(A) If the artist or artist's heir, legatee, or personal representative fails to take action to remove the work of fine art after the notice provided by paragraph (2) of subdivision (h) of Section 987, the owner shall provide 30 days' notice of his or her intended action affecting the work of art. The written notice shall be a display advertisement in a newspaper of general circulation in the area where the fine art is located. The notice required by this paragraph may run concurrently with the notice required by subdivision (h) of Section 987.

(i) If within the 30-day period an organization agrees to remove the work of fine art and pay the cost of removal of the work, the payment and removal shall occur within 90 days of the first day of the 30-day notice.

(ii) If the work is removed at the expense of an organization, title to the fine art shall pass to that organization.

(B) If an organization does not agree to remove the work of fine art within the 30-day period or fails to remove and pay the cost of removal of the work of fine art within the 90-day period the owner may take the intended action affecting the work of fine art.

(f) Attorney's and expert witness fees. To effectuate the rights created by this section, the court may do the following:

(1) Award reasonable attorney's and expert witness fees to the prevailing party, in an amount as determined by the court.

(2) Require the organization to post a bond in a reasonable amount as determined by the court.

(g) Limitation of actions. No action may be maintained under this section unless brought within three years of the act complained of or one year after discovery of such act, whichever is longer.

(h) Operative date. This section shall become operative on January 1, 1983, and shall apply to claims based on acts occurring on or after that date to works of fine art, whenever created.

(i) Severability. If any provision of this section or the application thereof to any person or circumstances is held invalid, such invalidity shall not affect other provisions or applications of this section which can be given effect without the invalid provision or application, and to this end the provisions of this section are severable.

§5.4.2. New York Arts and Cultural Affairs Law §14.03: Artists' Authorship Rights

New York was the second state to enact moral right legislation. Whereas the California statute is focused on maintaining the integrity of the artwork, the emphasis in New York is on keeping the artist's reputation free from damage that might result from displaying his work in an altered, defaced, mutilated, or modified form. Like the California law, New York's moral statute, which follows, also includes the right of paternity.

For definitions that pertain to the following statute, see article 11 of the New York Arts and Cultural Affairs Law reproduced at §3.2.2 *supra*.

ARTISTS' AUTHORSHIP RIGHTS
New York Arts and Cultural Affairs Law §14.03 (McKinney Supp. 1986)

1. Except as limited by subdivision three of this section, on and after January first, nineteen hundred eighty-five,* no person other than the artist or a person acting with the artist's consent shall knowingly display in a place accessible to the public or publish a work of fine art or limited edition multiple of not more than three hundred copies by that artist or a reproduction thereof in an altered, defaced, mutilated or modified form if the work is displayed, published or reproduced as being the work of the artist, or under circumstances under which it would reasonably be regarded as being the work of the artist, and damage to the artist's reputation is reasonably likely to result therefrom, except that this section shall not apply to sequential imagery such as that in motion pictures.

2. (a) Except as limited by subdivision three of this section, the artist shall retain at all times the right to claim authorship, or, for just and valid reason, to disclaim authorship of such work. The right to claim authorship shall include the right of the artist to have his or her name appear on or in connection with such work as the artist. The right to disclaim authorship shall include the right of the artist to prevent his or her name from appearing on or in connection with such work as the artist. Just and valid reason for disclaiming authorship shall include that the work has been altered, defaced, mutilated or modified other than by the artist, without the artist's consent, and damage to the artist's reputation is reasonably likely to result or has resulted therefrom.

(b) The rights created by this subdivision shall exist in addition to any other rights and duties which may now or in the future be applicable.

3. (a) Alteration, defacement, mutilation or modification of such work

---

*[The original 1983 statute was effective January 1, 1984. In the 1984 recodification, the date was changed to January, 1985.—Eds.]

resulting from the passage of time or the inherent nature of the materials will not by itself create a violation of subdivision one of this section or a right to disclaim authorship under subdivision two of this section; provided such alteration, defacement, mutilation or modification was not the result of gross negligence in maintaining or protecting the work of fine art.

(b) In the case of a reproduction, a change that is an ordinary result of the medium of reproduction does not by itself create a violation of subdivision one of this section or a right to disclaim authorship under subdivision two of this section.

(c) Conservation shall not constitute an alteration, defacement, mutilation or modification within the meaning of this section, unless the conservation work can be shown to be negligent.

(d) This section shall not apply to work prepared under contract for advertising or trade use unless the contract so provides.

(e) The provisions of this section shall apply only to works of fine art or limited edition multiples of not more than three hundred copies knowingly displayed in a place accessible to the public, published or reproduced in this state.

4. (a) An artist aggrieved under subdivision one or subdivision two of this section shall have a cause of action for legal and injunctive relief.

(b) No action may be maintained to enforce any liability under this section unless brought within three years of the act complained of or one year after the constructive discovery of such act, whichever is longer.

§5.4.3. The United States Perspective: A Narrower Concept

Is the purpose of the moral right to protect the work of art, the artist's personality, or the artist's reputation? In the following article, written by Edward J. Damich, the author distinguishes among these purposes and shows how various moral right statutes are each based on a different premise.

DAMICH,* THE NEW YORK ARTISTS' AUTHORSHIP RIGHTS ACT: A COMPARATIVE CRITIQUE
84 Colum. L. Rev. 1733 (1984)

In 1980, the Bank of Tokyo decided to remove from the lobby of its Wall Street branch a massive sculpture by the renowned Japanese

* Associate Professor of Law, George Mason University School of Law; J.D. 1976 Catholic University; L.L.M. 1983, Columbia University. The author wishes to thank Professor John M. Kernochan, Columbia University, and Professor John Henry Merryman, Stanford Law School, for their helpful comments and sugges-

artist, Noguchi. To do so, the Bank had to cut the sculpture into pieces, thus effectively destroying it.[1] Noguchi termed the bank's action "vandalism"[2] and many in the New York arts community were similarly indignant. Contemporary law, however, provided him with no relief, since he had transferred all of his rights in the sculpture to the bank which was simply exercising a traditional property right—the right to injure or destroy.[3] Such conflicts between artist and owner inspired the New York Artists' Authorship Rights Act (effective January 1, 1984),[4] which gives some measure of protection to the artist even after all property rights have been transferred. The New York statute, however, might have given Noguchi little solace even if it had existed in 1980, as it does not clearly address the problem of destruction.[5] In general, the Act provides a cause of action for damage to reputation due to public display of a work of fine art in an altered state. Nevertheless, insofar as it accords

---

tions. The author also wishes to recognize the research assistance of Gerald C. Montella, Delaware Law School '84, and Matthew I. Hirsch, Delaware Law School '85.

[1] Glueck, Bank Cuts Up Noguchi Sculpture and Stores It, N.Y. Times, Apr. 19, 1980, §1, at 1, col. 4.

[2] Id.

[3] See Pound, The Law of Property and Recent Juristic Thought, 25 A.B.A. J. 993, 997 (1939).

The bank felt that is was merely exercising its property rights, as evidenced by its response when asked why the sculptor was not notified: "We didn't feel it was necessary, since the sculpture is the property of the bank." Glueck, *supra* note 1, §1, at 12, col.6 (quoting an unidentified bank spokesman).

[4] N.Y. Arts & Cultural Affairs Law §§14.51-14.59 (McKinney 1984).

[5] Newmann v. Delmar Realty Co., No. 2955/84 (N.Y. Sup. Ct. Mar. 2, 1984), illustrates the uncertainty surrounding this aspect of the New York statute. In *Newmann*, plaintiff, an artist, sought to enjoin the owner of a building from destroying his partially completed mural and from preventing him from finishing it. Judge Wilk granted a preliminary injunction based on the plaintiff-artist's agreement with defendant's lessor and on the New York statute. The opinion, however, does not clearly focus on whether the New York statute provides a right against destruction. Instead, it states that "[d]efendants' continued denial . . . of access to the [mural] results in a public display of [plaintiff's] work in an unfinished and modified form to the probable detriment of plaintiff's reputation. . . ." *Id.*, slip op. at 9. The opinion does not state that the statute prevents the destruction of the partially-completed work nor does it suggest that the statute would prevent its destruction once completed. In fact, Judge Wilk wrote: "Whether plaintiff will choose to complete the work at the risk of its subsequent obliteration is for him to decide." *Id.* The "subsequent obliteration" referred to is related to the plaintiff's agreement with defendant's lessor which provided for display until March 3, 1988. By negative implication it would seem that the mural could be obliterated after that date. *Id.*; see also Margolick, Manhattan Wall Spurs a Test Case over Art, N.Y. Times, Mar. 3, 1984, §1, at 1, col. 4 (*Newmann* is a "test case" under the recently enacted statute).

some legal recourse to the artist after transfer of property rights, it reflects the broader concept of the personal rights of authors that finds a more comprehensive recognition in California,[6] in sixty-three countries,[7] and in The Berne Convention.[8]

The personal rights of authors were first legally recognized in France under the name of droit moral, and that country remains their foremost exponent.[9] In France, the law covering works of the mind is divided into two categories: economic rights (*droits patrimoniaux*) and personal rights (*droit moral*). The former resemble the kind of rights recognized in the United States under the Copyright Act of 1976,[10] while the latter are founded on a legal recognition of the bond between an author and his work based on the fact that the artwork is an expression of the author's personality.[11] From the time of its creation, the artwork continuously embodies the creative personality of the author; consequently, the transfer of the material object — or the economic rights — is irrelevant to the existence of personal rights, although it may affect their exercise.[12] First legally recognized in 1902,[13] the French concept of droit moral has been elaborated by statute[14] so that there is now general agreement as to

---

[6] Cal. Civ. Code §§987-989 (West Supp. 1984).

[7] DaSilva, Droit Moral and the Amoral Copyright, 28 Bull. Copyright Soc'y 1, 5 (1980).

[8] See The Berne Convention for the Protection of Literary and Artistic Works (Paris Revision; July 24, 1971) [hereinafter cited as Berne Convention], reprinted in World Intellectual Property Organization, Guide to the Berne Convention (1978). The complete text of The Berne Convention may be found also in N. Boorstyn, Copyright Law 715-37 (1981), and 4 M. Nimmer, Nimmer on Copyright, app. 27-1 (1984). Article 6 *bis* (1) of the 1971 Revision provides:

Independently of the author's economic rights, and even after the transfer of the said rights, the author shall have the right to claim authorship of the work and to object to any distortion, mutilation, or other modification of, or other derogatory action in relation to, the said work, which would be prejudicial to his honor and reputation.

[9] DaSilva, *supra* note 7, at 2.

[10] 17 U.S.C. §§101-810 (1982).

[11] See generally H. Desbois, Le Droit d'Auteur en France 260-86 (3d ed. 1978)(contrasting this "dualistic conception" adopted by the Law of Mar. 11, 1957, see *infra* note 14, with the "unitary conception").

[12] For example, according to French law the author has no absolute right to compel the owner of the material object that embodies the work of art to place it at the disposal of the author for the exercise of his droit moral. See Code civil [C. civ.] art. 543(29) (82e ed. Petits Code Dalloz 1983).

[13] The first judicial recognition of the concept took place in the 1902 case of Cinquin v. Lecocq. See Judgment of June 25, 1902, Cour de cassation première section civile [Cass. civ. 1re],Fr.; see also 1 S. Stromholm, Le Droit Moral D'Auteur, (1966) 285 (noting that the court's broad discussion of artistry as a "faculty inherent to [the author's] personality" transcends the facts of this divorce case).

[14] See Loi du 11 Mars 1957 sur la propriété littéraire et artistique, 1957 Journal

its components. They include the rights of disclosure, retraction, integrity, and attribution.[15]

Some of the components of the French concept of droit moral find expression in American law. For example, federal copyright law protects an author's right to divulge his work to the public.[16] Copyright protection roughly corresponds to the right of disclosure, although it embodies an economic rights perspective. With the passage of the California and New York statutes,[17] the right of an artist to insist on attribution of authorship (or anonymity) and the concept of protecting the integrity of a work of fine art despite alienation have become part of the American statutory scene; at least one federal circuit has explicitly recognized the personal rights of artists as providing a legal basis for relief.[18] One commentator, in fact, has gone so far to make the highly disputed claim that American law already provides protection equivalent to the French concept of droit moral.[19]

Despite increased American interest in protection comparable to that of French law, however, a closer comparison reveals striking descrepancies, wide gaps, and theoretical conflicts. The federal copyright law remains the only significant national legislation dealing with authors' rights; in forty-eight states only one component of droit moral, the right of disclosure, is recognized, and that in an economic rights context. Case law treatment of the personal rights of authors has also been scant and piecemeal. Even in California and New York, the legislation protective of the personal rights of authors is in many respects inadequate by droit moral standards. The California Art Preservation Act, for example, despite its broad protection against alteration, destruction, and nonattribution, allows the artist's rights to be waived completely, thereby rendering nugatory its protection for artists in necessitous circumstances.[20] The

---

Officiel de la Republique Francaise [J.O.] 2723, 1957 Recueil Dalloz Législation [D.L.] 102 (codified as C. civ. art. 543, Code pénal [C. pén.] arts. 425-429)(Law of Mar. 11, 1957, on literary and artistic property).

[15] The right of disclosure is the right of the author to decide when and if a work is to be divulged to the public. The right of retraction is the right of the author to withdraw from the public a work which is no longer faithful to his thought. The right of integrity is the right of the author to protect the integrity of his work even after transfer of all property rights in it. The right of attribution is the right of the author to be recognized (or not) as the creator of the work. See generally H. Desbois, supra note 11, at 472-561 (discussing these four rights in detail).

[16] Section 106(3) of the Copyright Act of 1976 recognizes the right to "distribute copies . . . to the public." 17 U.S.C. §106(3) (1983).

[17] See supra notes 4, 6.

[18] Gilliam v. ABC, 538 F.2d 14 (2d Cir. 1976).

[19] Strauss, The Moral Right of the Author, in 1 Omnibus Copyright Revision Legislative History, Study No. 4 at 128-29 (1960 & photo. reprint 1976).

[20] Cal. Civ. Code, §987(g)(3) (West Supp. 1984).

New York statute confines its protection of the integrity of an artwork to circumstances damaging to the artist's reputation, leaving the statute susceptible to the interpretation that it does not prohibit complete destruction of art works.[21] Finally, traditional American attitudes regarding property rights may not include sympathy for the artist's plight and sensitivity to mutilation and destruction of works of art.[22]

It is significant, nontheless, that the two states often considered the art centers of the United States have addressed the protection of the personal rights of artists. In so doing, they have raised important issues regarding a state's authority to enact such legislation and the form such statutes should take. The threshold question, of course, is whether the preemption doctrine allows states to legislate in this sphere, since the concept of the personal rights of authors seems to find its natural place in the domain of federal copyright law.[23] Once this question is answered in the affirmative, broad policy decisions must be made. Do we seek to protect art as the embodiment of the author's personality, or for the benefit of the public? Or do we seek to guard the artist's reputation, so that protection of the work is necessary only to protect the reputation of the author? Next, we must clarify the details. Will all authors be entitled to the benefits of the statute? Will all works be protected? Will the rights by waivable? How long will statutory protection last? Should special consid eration be given to public service organizations such as museums? What remedies will be available? The purposes underlying any statute protecting the rights of authors will be reflected in these particulars.

The statutes of France, California, and New York represent three ways of answering these questions. The French Law of March 11, 1957 (1957 Law),[24] the prototypical personal rights statute, is aimed at protecting the author's personality, not at preserving art. It provides that the personal rights of authors are "perpetual, inalienable and imprescriptible,"[25] It applies to all works of the mind and therefore accords its benefits broadly to all "authors."[26] The California Art Preservation Act[27] aims, in general,

---

[21] N.Y. Arts & Cultural Affairs Law §14.57.4 (McKinney 1984).

See N.Y. Times, *supra* note 5, §1, at 1, col. 6 (according to one of its sponsors, the statute "balance[s] the property rights of owners against the creative rights of artists")(quoting Assemblyman Richard N. Gottfried).

[22] In France, by contrast, the economic rights roughly corresponding to American copyright are included with the droit moral in the same law. C. civ. art. 543(26)-543(28) (82e ed. Petits Codes Dalloz 1983).

[23] See 17 U.S.C. §§101-810 (1982).

[24] C. civ. art. 543 (82e ed. Petits Code Dalloz); see *supra* note 14.

[25] C. civ. art. 543(6) (82e ed. Petits Codes Dalloz 1983) (author's translation).

[26] See generally H. Desbois, supra note 11, at 3-254 (noting that the 1957 Law provides no positive definition of the works within its scope, and investigating the type of works to which authors' rights attach).

[27] Cal. Civ. Code §§987-989 (West Supp. 1984).

at protection of the artist's personality and preservation of artwork. It protects only the rights of integrity and attribution, and these rights are susceptible to a blanket waiver. The statute's purpose is reflected in the fact that only certain "artists" are benefited and only works of "fine art of recognized quality" are protected. The New York Artists' Authorship Rights Act[28] focuses on protecting the reputation of the artist. Like the California statute, it addresses itself to the rights of attribution and integrity. It provides a stronger argument against waiver than the California statute, but seems to afford protection only for the life of the artist.[29]

This article first addresses preemption objections frequently voiced against state authors' rights legislation. It then compares the New York statute with those of France and California. Such a comparison seems desirable given the great dissimilarity between its underlying rationale and that of the French and California enactments. The Article goes on to apply the New York statute to three representative cases. It concludes that the New York statute's focus on protecting the reputation of artists significantly weakens the statute's effectiveness.

I. PREEMPTION

The initial question is whether state authors' rights statutes have been preempted by federal copyright legislation. The Copyright Act of 1976 contains a preemption section,[30] designed by Congress to establish a uniform preemption analysis.[31] In 1973, the United States Supreme

---

[28] N.Y. Acts & Cultural Affairs Law §§14.51-.59 (McKinney 1984).

[29] Although the operative language of the New York and California statutes provides a basis for differentiating the two statutes (personality protection and art preservation in the case of California, and reputation protection in the case of New York), their preambles reflect ambivalence about which interest each statute seeks to protect. The California statute, for example, in addition to clear references to destruction, personality protection, and art preservation, also mentions reputation in its section on "legislative findings and declaration." Cal. Civ. Code §987(a)(West Supp. 1984). Similarly, the New York statute, in most of its preamble references to the artist's reputation, uses the phrase, "to the *artist* and the artist's reputation," suggesting that protection of the artist's personality may also have been a consideration. 1983 N.Y. Laws ch. 994 §1 (emphasis added), reprinted in N.Y. Arts & Cultural Law §14.55 historical note (McKinney 1984). The California statute's reference to reputation protection is not as troublesome as New York's allusion to an interest beyond that of reputation. The former does not expand the scope of the statute, since personality protection includes reputation protection. The latter, however, provides an argument (although a weak one) that the New York statute is not aimed exclusively at reputation protection. Furthermore, the California statute's preamble reference to personality protection and its effect makes it more akin to the French statute.

[30] 17 U.S.C. §301 (1982).

[31] Note, Copyright Preemption: Effecting the Analysis Prescribed by Section 301, 24 B.C.L. Rev. 963, 963 (1983).

Court had held in *Goldstein v. California*[32] that the Copyright Act of 1909 did not preempt a California statute prohibiting the copying of sound recordings with intent to sell the copies. The Court found that the copyright clause of the Constitution[33] did not grant the federal government exclusive control over copyrights;[34] the states retain concurrent power to afford copyright protection as long as state provisions do not conflict with federal law.[35] The Copyright Act of 1976 did not invalidate the *Goldstein* holding;[36] it merely provided a more precise analysis with a view toward more consistent results.[37] The Act provides that a state law will be preempted if it deals with works subject to federal copyright law and provides rights equivalent to those found in federal legislation.[38] In order for preemption to occur, both elements must be present.[39]

The California and New York statutes appear to meet the first element of federal preemption: similar coverage. Although they limit protection to works of "fine art" (and, in the case of California, also to works "of recognized quality"), it is clear from the statutes' respective definitions[40] of covered artworks that those works fall within the comprehensive definition of the subject matter of copyright protection found in the Copyright Act.[41] Thus, whether the New York and California statutes are preempted by federal law depends on whether they create rights different from those embodied in federal law.

The federal statute recognizes four fundamental rights: the rights to reproduce a work, to prepare derivative works, to distribute copies of a

---

[32] 412 U.S. 546, 571 (1973); see Compco v. Day-Bright, 376 U.S. 234 (1964); Sears v. Stiffel, 376 U.S. 225 (1964).

[33] The Constitution grants power to Congress "to promote the Progress of Science and useful Arts, by securing for limited Times to Authors and Inventors the exclusive Right to their respective Writings and Discoveries. . . ." U.S. Const. art I, §8, cl. 8.

[34] Goldstein v. California, 412 U.S. at 560.

[35] 1 M. Nimmer, *supra* note 8, §1.01, at 1-3 to 1-4 (1984), see Goldstein v. California, 412 U.S. at 561.

[36] H.R. Rep. No. 1476, 94th Cong., 2d Sess. 131, reprinted in 1976 U.S. Code Cong. & Ad. News 5747; accord 1 M. Nimmer, *supra* note 8, §1.01[B] n.22; Gantz, Protecting Artist's Moral Rights: A Critique of the California Art Preservation Act as a Model for Statutory Reform, 49 Geo. Wash. L. Rev. 873 (1981).

[37] See H. R. Rep. No. 1476, 94th Cong., 2d Sess. 129, 130, reprinted in 1976 U.S. Code Cong. & Ad. News 5659, 5746.

[38] See 17 U.S.C. §301 (1982).

[39] 1 M. Nimmer, *supra* note 8, §1.01 (B) at 1-9; Note, *supra* note 31.

[40] See Cal. Civ. Code §987(b)(2) (West Supp. 1984); N.Y. Arts & Cultural Affairs Law §14.51.5 (McKinney 1984).

[41] See 17 U.S.C. §102 (1982) ("[w]orks of authorship include . . . pictorial, graphic, and sculptural works . . .").

work, and to publicly perform or display a work.[42] The right of attribution found in both the California and New york statutes would appear sufficiently distinct to escape preemption. The right of integrity created by the California statute, on the other hand, conceivably overlaps with the right to prepare derivative works,[43] although it has been argued that the California statute, inspired as it is by the French concept of droit moral, creates rights qualitatively different[44] from the purely economic protection that the Copyright Act affords.[45] The New York statute's protection of the right of integrity presents a more difficult question since it expressly raises the elements of reproduction and public display. Here, too, it may be argued that there is a qualitative difference between New York and federal law, since the state statute aims at protecting the artist's reputation, a species of tort law traditionally reserved to the states.[46]

This thumbnail sketch of the preemption doctrine is intended merely to suggest some of the problems that may arise when states turn to legislative protection of the personal rights of authors; a more detailed presentation is beyond the scope of this Article. The ambiguities present in the scope of the California and New York statutes suggest, however, that state personal rights legislation should carefully and expressly distinguish its objectives from those of the Copyright Act in order to avoid preemption.

II. ATTRIBUTES OF THE STATUTES
To compare the effects and underlying rationales of the French, California, and New York statutes, it is necessary to look to the particulars of those statutes.

A. Works and Persons Protected
The 1957 Law covers "all works of the mind, whatever the type, form of expression, artistic merit, or purpose."[47] Both American statutes,

---

[42] 17 U.S.C. §106 (1982).

[43] 2 M. Nimmer, *supra* note 8, §8.21(c), at 8-261 (1984).

[44] Francione, The California Art Preservation Act and Federal Preemption by the 1976 Copyright Act—Equivalence and Actual Conflict, 18 Cal. W.L. Rev. 189, 214 (1982).

[45] Katz, Copyright Preemption Under the Copyright Act of 1976: The Case of Droit de Suite, 47 Geo. Wash. L. Rev. 200, 218 (1978).

[46] What precisely is meant by a reproduction and whether the New York statute protects against the public display of unfaithful reproductions is not clear. See *infra* notes 51-57 and accompanying text.

[47] C. civ. art. 543(2) (82e ed. Petits Codes Dalloz 1983) (author's translation). Curiously, the 1957 Law does not cover all photographs, but only those "of an artistic or documentary character." *Id.* art. 543(3) (author's translation). In contrast, United States copyright law protection is broader. See N. Boorstyn, *supra* note 8, §2:15, at 51-52 (only a photograph which is a copy of another photograph lacks sufficient originality to be protected under United States law).

by contrast, strictly limit protection to works of *fine* art, and, in the case of California, the class of works protected is further limited to works "of recognized quality."[48] Although the American statutes lack the majestic sweep of the French statute, they perhaps gain in specificity, thereby avoiding overbreadth, irresolvable controversies, and opposition to legislative enactment.[49] The California criterion of "recognized quality," for example, deftly avoids a lawsuit stemming from a teacher's destruction of a student's doodling.[50] Furthermore, both the New York and California statutes recognize the special demands of commercial art and the motion picture industry.[51]

The New York statute, however, engenders a controversy of its own with regard to whether it protects against unfaithful reproductions. In general, it defines "reproduction" to be a "copy" intended to be a representation of a preexisting work of fine art,[52] and section 14.53 prohibits public display or publication of "a work of fine art . . . or a reproduction thereof" in an altered state.[53] Thus, the statute seems to contemplate damage to the artist's reputation from the public display of an *imitation* of his work in an altered state. But this literal reading of the statute would create a right of little significance, since the author of the original normally would not care as much if the imitation of his work were altered

---

[48] Cal. Civ. Code §987 (b)(2) (West Supp. 1984); N.Y. Arts & Cultural Affairs Law §14.51.5 (McKinney 1984).

[49] J. Merryman has stated that many European legal scholars admire the California statute because it is more precise than the statements of general principles commonly found in European statutes, such as the 1957 Law. J. Merryman, Comment made at the meeting of the AALS Section of Law and the Arts (Jan. 7, 1984).

[50] "Recognized quality" is to be determined by relying on the opinions of "artists, art dealers, collectors of fine art, curators of art museums, and other persons involved with the creation or marketing of fine art." Cal. Civ. Code §987(f) (West Supp. 1984).

[51] The California statute excludes "work prepared under contract for commercial use," and limits protection to "painting, sculpture, or [sic] drawing, or an original work of art in glass." Id. §987(b)(2). The New York statute excludes "work prepared under contract for advertising or trade use unless the contract so provides" and "sequential imagery such as that in motion pictures." See N.Y. Arts & Cultural Affairs Law §§14.57.4, 14.51.5 (McKinney 1984). The California statute defines "work prepared . . . for commercial use" as "fine art created under a work-for-hire arrangement for use in advertising, magazines, newspapers, or other print and electronic media." See Cal. Civ. Code §987(b)(7) (West Supp. 1984). The New York statute does not define "advertising or trade use."

[52] " 'Reproduction' means a copy, in any medium, of a work of fine art, that is displayed or published under circumstances that, reasonably construed, evince an intent that it be taken as a representation of a work of fine art as created by the artist." N.Y. Arts & Cultural Affairs Law §14.51.4 (McKinney 1984).

[53] Id. §14.53. The main clause contains only the verbs "display" and "publish"; the subordinate clause adds the predicate adjective "reproduced."

and then displayed, as he would if a poor reproduction of his work were displayed and attributed to him. The author of the imitation might conceivably care if his reproduction were altered and then displayed, especially if he felt his representation of the original was itself a work of art due to the skill involved. In that case, however, the "imitation" arguably would be a work of fine art in its own right and the statute would protect the author of the imitation.

A more plausible interpretation of the reproduction provision — and one supported by statutory language — is that unfaithful reproductions activate the protection of the statute if publicly displayed so as to damage the reputation of the author of the original. Section 14.53, for example, prohibits display of any work "if the work is displayed, published or *reproduced*" as being the work of the artist, and is altered, defaced, mutilated, or modified.[54] Section 14.57 — by which section 14.53 is expressly limited[55] — states that "[i]n the case of reproduction, a change that is an ordinary result of the medium of reproduction does not by itself create a violation. . . ."[56] The two phrases read together suggest that changes which occur as a result of the reproduction process, that ordinarily do not result from that process, could constitute violations.

This frustrating ambiguity is created by the asymmetrical language of section 14.53 and the failure to distinguish, as federal copyright law does, between reproductions that are mere "copies" and those that, although derived from a preexisting work, are nevertheless original works of art in themselves.[57] Moreover, when examined in this light, the New York statute raises serious preemption problems, since it deals with "derivative works."[58]

The California statute does not specifically deal with the question of reproductions, and it would seem that the prohibition of alteration cannot be convincingly stretched to cover reproductions.[59] French law, however, is clear. In *Bernard-Rousseau v. Galeries Lafayette*,[60] a granddaughter

---

[54] *Id.*

[55] *Id.*

[56] *Id.* §14.57.2.

[57] A "reproduction" is a form of derivative work and is copyrightable insofar as it represents an additional original element. A "copy," however, since it lacks any original element, will not support a copyright. See N. Boorstyn, *supra* note 8, §2:13, at 50. Thus, a "reproduction" for federal copyright purposes can be more than a "copy."

[58] See generally Part I. A "reproduction" is a form of derivative work.

[59] The argument that a photograph of an artwork could be construed under the Copyright Act of 1976 to be an "alteration" seems a bit strained. Such an argument is made in Francione, *supra* note 44, at 211.

[60] Judgment of March 13, 1973, Tribunaux de grand instance [Trib. gr. inst.], Paris, 1974 Juris-Classeur périodique, la semaine juridique [J.C.P. IV] 224.

of Henri Rousseau successfully sued a Paris department store that had used unfaithful reproductions of the painter's work in its window decorations. The case indicated that in France the right of integrity forbids not only alterations of the work itself, but also reproductions not faithful to the original.

B. Acts Prohibited

1. *The Right of Integrity.* — The operative words of the New York statute prohibit the public display or publication of "a work of fine art . . . or a reproduction thereof in an altered, defaced, mutilated or modified form" without the artist's consent where "damage to the artist's reputation is reasonably likely to result therefrom."[61] Furthermore, the work must be (1) knowingly displayed or published, and (2) identified as the work of the artist or reasonably identifiable as the work of the artist from the circumstances. Clearly, the thrust of the New York statute is more toward the protection of the artist's reputation than toward protection of the work. In order to recover, an artist has to prove at least that the display or publication *could* damage his reputation. The statute does not mention total destruction of the work, presumably because, to show damage to reputation, the work must exist to provide public linkage of the work and its creator.[62] One might argue, however, that the destruction of the only work, best work, or a representative work of the artist could damage his reputation.[63]

The California statute, by contrast, prohibits not only the "physical defacement, mutilation, [or] alteration" of a work of fine art, but also its "destruction." Moreover, the California statute does not require that the work be displayed or published. Damage to the artist's reputation need not be proved; the simple intentional commission or authorization of the prohibited acts makes out the prima facie case.[64] The failure to include

---

[61] See N.Y. Arts & Cultural Affairs Law §14.53 (McKinney 1984).

[62] Martin Roeder notes the link between reputation and nonliability for complete destruction:

> The right to prevent deformation does not include the right to prevent destruction of a created work. The doctrine of moral right finds one social basis in the need of the creator for protection of his honor and reputation. To deform his work is to present him to the public as the creator of a work not his own, and thus make him subject to criticism for work he has not done; the destruction of his work does not have this result.

Roeder, The Doctrine of Moral Right: A Study in the Law of Artists, Authors and Creators, 53 Harv. L. Rev. 554, 569 (1940). But see Newmann v. Delmar Realty, No. 2955/84 (N.Y. Sup. Ct. Mar. 2, 1984).

[63] Merryman, The Refrigerator of Bernard Buffet, 27 Hastings L.J. 1035 (1976). Since this article was published, the French Court of Cassation has recognized that the droit moral protects against complete destruction. See *infra* note 71.

[64] See Cal. Civ. Code §987(c)(1) (West Supp. 1984).

reproduction, however, weakens the California statute vis-a-vis its New York counterpart since the former does not cover unfaithful copying.[65]

Under French law the right of integrity gives the author the right "to forbid any modification whatsoever of his work without his consent."[66] Although not identified as such, the right of integrity is embodied in article 6 of the 1957 Law: "The author enjoys the right of respect for his name, his professional standing, and *his work*."[67] According to the prevailing view, the right of integrity is not aimed at protecting the author's reputation, but instead is based on a theory that views the work as an extension of the author's personality.[68] Any act that modifies the work, whether public or not, is an injury to the author's personality and thus his dignity as a human being.[69] The right of integrity also includes a prohibition against unfaithful reproduction[70] and complete destruction.[71]

2. *The Right of Attribution.* — Although at least one recent case decided

---

[65] There is some question as to whether the New York statute provides a remedy for faithless copying or merely for the display of a copy (no matter what its quality) in an altered or defaced state that can be reasonably identified with the work of an artist. See *supra* notes 52-58 and accompanying text.

[66] P. Recht, Le Droit D'Auteur: Une Nouvelle Forme de Propriété 291 (1969) (author's translation).

[67] See C. civ. art. 543(6) (82e ed. Petits Code Dalloz 1983) (author's translation; emphasis added).

[68] See H. Desbois, supra note 11, at 469 ("The work bears the expression of a personality, of an ideal, of sentiments and of thoughts of the one who strove to put the best of himself into it.") (author's translation); Sarraute, Current Theory on the Moral Right of Authors and Artists Under French Law, 16 Am. J. Comp. L. 465, 479 (1968) ("In reality, the status which the law protects is the author's status under the law, not his reputation. Any other view is excluded by the principles which underlie the law of March 11, 1957."). But see DaSilva, Droit Moral and the Amoral Copyright, 28 Bull. Copyright Soc'y 1, 38 (1980) ("[S]cholars still question whether the protection of the artist's reputation — as opposed to protection of the work itself — is an appropriate application of article 6 [of the 1957 Law].").

[69] See H. Desbois, *supra* note 11, at 549. In Buffet v. Fersing, however, the Court of Paris allowed the owner to keep the artwork in a dismantled state in the privacy of his own home. See Judgment of May 30, 1962, Cour d'appel, Paris, 1962 Recueil Jurisprudence [D. Jur.] 570, aff'd, Judgment of July 6, 1965, Cass. civ. 1re, Fr., 1965 No. 644 (available on LEXIS, Prive library, Cass file); see also text accompanying notes 156-158.

[70] In Bernard-Rousseau v. Galeries Lafayette, the court held a Paris department store could not display unfaithful reproductions of the work of Henri Rousseau. Judgment of March 13, 1973, Trib. gr. inst., Paris, 1974 J.C.P. IV 224.

[71] The Court of Cassation, the highest French court for private law matters, recently affirmed that the personal rights of authors include the right to prevent destruction. Judgment of Mar. 16, 1983, Cass. civ. 1re, Fr. (available on LEXIS, Prive library, Cass file); see Le Salon d'Été de Jean Dubuffet, S. Padem: Propriété Artistique, June-Oct. 1983, at 1.

under the Lanham Act suggests otherwise,[72] the prevailing view of American law is that an author does not have the right to be identified as the creator of a work unless he has secured it by contract.[73] It is also difficult to find cases recognizing a right to remain anonymous or to display a work under a pseudonym.[74] This deficiency in the protection of authors is remedied somewhat in the case of fine art by section 14.55 of the New York statute which gives the artist the right "at all times" to claim or disclaim authorship of a work. His right to *disclaim* is limited to circumstances in which there is "just and valid reason."[75] The refusal to have one's name associated with an "altered, defaced, mutilated or modified" work is a just and valid reason, so long as attribution of authorship of the altered work has resulted or is reasonably likely to result in damage to the artist's reputation.[76] The California statute is similar except that it fails to specify that modification of a work is a "just and valid reason"[77] to disclaim. Article 6 of the 1957 Law provides a right of attribution, while article 11 safeguards anonymous and pseudonymous authorship.[78] The "just and valid reason" qualification does not exist in French law, although it is a fundamental part of French law that one cannot exercise one's own right so as to impair another's.[79]

---

[72] In Smith v. Montoro, 648 F.2d 602 (9th Cir. 1981), the court said: "'Implied' reverse passing off occurs when the wrongdoer simply removes or otherwise obliterates the name of the manufacturer or source and sells the product in an unbranded state." *Id.* at 605. The case, however, involved express reverse passing off. Contra PIC Design Corp. v. Sterling Precision Corp., 231 F. Supp. 106, 115 (S.D.N.Y. 1964).

[73] Note, An Artist's Personal Rights in His Creative Work: Beyond the Human Cannonball and the Flying Circus, 9 Pac. L.J. 855, 863-67 (1978).

[74] In Ellis v. Hurst, 66 Misc. 235, 121 N.Y.S. 438 (Sup. Ct. 1910), the court enjoined the publication of two stories under the plaintiff's real name when he had previously published under a pseudonym. The case, however, was based on a New York privacy statute that prohibited the appropriation of a person's name for purposes of trade. *Id.* at 236-37, 121 N.Y.S. at 239.

[75] N.Y. Arts & Cultural Affairs Law §14.55 (McKinney 1984).

[76] *Id.* The New York statute is susceptible to the argument that the right of attribution is also limited by the public display requirement. Section 14.57, by which §14.55 is expressly limited, provides: "The provisions of this article shall apply only to works of fine art knowingly dislplayed in a place accessible to the public, published or reproduced in this state." *Id.* §14.57.5. It would seem, however, that this provision relates exclusively to §14.53, since this section covers display, publication, and reproduction.

[77] Cal. Civ Code, §987(d) (West Supp. 1984).

[78] Article 11 provides: "The authors of works done under pseudonyms or anonymously enjoy in those works the same rights recognized by the first article." See C. civ. art. 543(11) (82e ed. Petits Codes Dalloz 1983) (author's translation); H. Desbois, *supra* note 11, at 510, 519.

[79] It is a fundamental tenet of French law, however, that one cannot exercise one's own right so as to impair unreasonably another's. This concept is known as

Both the New York and the California statutes are deficient in that they do not specifically provide for the case of pseudonymous authorship, especially when it is not clear that the right to disclaim authorship includes that situation. Furthermore, the requirement of a "just and valid reason" to demand nonattribution is too imprecise to effectively prevent litigation by predetermining whether in a particular case a disclaimer is arbitrary and capricious. A clearer standard such as "substantial economic harm to the copyright holder" would seem more advisable.[80]

C. Waiver

The 1957 Law declares that the personal rights of authors are "inalienable"[81]; consequently, an author's waiver of his personal rights is probably unenforceable.[82] The California statute, by contrast, expressly provides for waiver. Section 987(g)(3) is a blanket waiver provision that is effective as long as the artist employs a signed writing.[83] The New York statute, again, is less clear. Section 14.55, the right of attribution section, states that "at all times" the artist retains the right to claim or disclaim authorship, thereby suggesting that the right of attribution, at least, cannot be waived.[84] Section 14.53, the right of integrity section, states that one may publicly display an artwork in an altered state with the

---

"abuse of rights." See C. civ. art. 1382 (82e ed. Petits Codes Dalloz 1983); Amos & Walton, Introduction to French Law, 219-20 (2d ed. 1963). Disclaimer without a just and valid reason could thus be prohibited if it unreasonably impaired the rights of another.

[80] For example, is it just and valid to forbid attribution of an earlier work to an author whose views have matured so that the earlier work is now unrepresentative, perhaps an embarrassment? This is part of the right of withdrawal recognized in French law. Although article 32 of the 1957 Law explicitly recognizes this right, it also compels the author to indemnify the copyright holder for any damage caused by its exercise. This requirement has effectively prevented arbitrary and capricious exercise. Sarraute maintains that "it has never, to our knowledge, been exercised since the 1957 law was promulgated." Sarraute, *supra* note 68, at 477.

[81] See C. civ. art. 543(6) (82e ed. Petits Codes Dalloz 1983).

[82] They may be specified to some extent, as in the case of adaptations from one medium to another. See Sarraute, *supra* note 68, at 481-83.

[83] See Cal. Civ. Code §987(g)(3) (West Supp. 1984). Section 987(h) also provides for an implied waiver in the case of removal of artworks from buildings. If an artwork cannot be removed from a building without substantial physical damage to the artwork, the artist is deemed to have waived his right of integrity unless it has been reserved in a writing signed *by the owner of the building* and recorded. Where the artwork can be removed without substantial harm, there is no implied waiver unless the owner has given written notice, or unsuccessfully attempted to do so, of the intended removal, and the artist has not within 90 days removed the artwork. See *id.* §987(h).

[84] See N.Y. Arts & Cultural Affairs Law §14.55.1 (McKinney 1984).

artist's consent, thereby suggesting that one could insulate oneself from liability by obtaining that consent prior to display.[85] *Consent,* however, may be distinguished from binding *waiver.* It is possible that the artist may be able to consent and at the same time retain his right to withdraw that consent. In any event, it is also arguable that a statute which does not expressly forbid waiver ipso facto allows it — especially when the statute contains a provision permitting an owner to alter the work after obtaining the consent of the artist.

A blanket waiver provision such as California's defeats one of the major purposes of personal rights. Although an artist of high stature may be able to resist pressure to waive his rights, many artists without established reputations may not. As a result, the artists most in need of the law's protection may be deprived rather easily of its benefit.[86] Even if allowing waiver of the rights of integrity and attribution is justifiable because of the need for maximum flexibility in the commercial use of art, such as in advertising, the California and New York statutes already serve that policy by excluding such work from protection.[87] Thus, the California waiver provision has the potential to deprive artists — and the public — of the protection of the statute. To the extent that the New York statute is unclear concerning waiver, it should be construed to prohibit it.

D. Conservation

One of the reasons major New York museums opposed the Artists, Authorship Rights Act was a fear that they could be held liable for damage done to an artwork through improper conservation techniques or even for failure to protect an artwork from the ravages of time.[88] The Act attempts to assuage their fears by clarifying the grounds for liability without providing a complete exemption. It provides that no liability will

---

[85] See *id.* §14.53.

[86] "In the United States, as in Europe, artists frequently suffer from an inferior bargaining position in the commercial arena, and only the most well-known artists are able to procure by contract those rights which the law has not yet seen fit to protect." DaSilva, *supra* note 68, at 56.

[87] See *supra* note 51 and accompanying text. Allowing limited waivers in particular situations would avoid some of the difficulties encountered in applying the French statute. In the case of adaptations from one medium to another, for example, French courts are often called upon to decide whether the adaptation is faithful to the original. The existence of a waiver or of specified author's rights, in the underlying contract, supplies the court with a useful standard with which to reach its decision. See Sarraute, *supra* note 68, at 481-83. Dreiser v. Paramount Publix Corp., 22 Copyright Dec. 106 (N.Y. Sup. Ct. 1938), is an interesting American case in which the court considered whether or not a film adaptation of Theodore Dreiser's play, *An American Tragedy,* was a distortion of the original.

[88] See Barbanel, New York State Law Gives Artists Right to Sue to Protect Work, N.Y. Times, Aug. 14, 1983, §1, at 1, col. 5.

ensue for changes resulting merely from "the passage of time or the inherent nature of the materials," provided that the changes are not the result of "gross negligence in maintaining or protecting the work of fine art";[89] that there will be no liability in the case of a reproduction when the change "is an ordinary result of the medium of reproduction";[90] and that there is no liability for conservation "unless the conservation work can be shown to be negligent."[91] "Conservation" is defined as "acts taken to correct deterioration and alteration[,] and acts taken to prevent, stop or retard deterioration."[92] The New York statute, however, does not exclude from liability someone who merely possesses an artwork; it imposes a duty to take measures to maintain and protect an artwork, although liability will be imposed on the possessor only for gross negligence. Under this standard, a museum or a private collector might be held liable for causing the colors of an oil painting to fade by hanging it in direct sunlight. If the owner were to go beyond maintenance and protection and take more active measures to preserve the artwork from deterioration or to restore it to its original condition, then the standard of ordinary negligence would be imposed.[93]

The liability for improper maintenance and conservation imposed by the statute must be understood in the context of the statute's concern with protecting the artist's reputation. For example, a museum would not be liable — even in the case of gross negligence — for deterioration of an artwork if it were not publicly displayed.[94] It is a well-known fact that in most museums only a portion of the entire collection is on display. Damage to a painting under circumstances constituting gross negligence — perhaps through storage in a basement where water was known to collect — would not occasion liability if the painting were never hung in a gallery. Thus, the New York statute is not as effective in encouraging museums or private collectors to take measures to maintain and protect artwork as are statutes that do not tie liability to public exposure.

By contrast, the California statute appears to impose no affirmative

---

[89] N.Y. Arts & Cultural Affairs Law §14.57.1 (McKinney 1984).

[90] *Id.* §14.57.2.

[91] *Id.* §14.57.3.

[92] *Id.* §14.51.2. "Conservation" in the New York statute thus includes the concept of restoration. But see Cal. Civ. Code §987(b)(5)-(6) (West Supp. 1984) ("restore" and "conserve" defined separately).

[93] This distinction is somewhat blurred by the definition of "conservation," which includes "acts taken to prevent . . . or retard deterioration." N.Y. Arts & Cultural Affairs Law §14.51.2 (McKinney 1984). It is difficult to distinguish these acts from the "maintaining or protecting" of §14.57.1 and the slighter duty of care those demand. *Id.* §14.57.1.

[94] While §14.57.1 sets gross negligence as the standard of care, it does so only in reference to the prohibited acts of §14.53. And §14.53 links liability solely to public display. See *id.* §§14.53, 14.57.

duty to maintain and protect artwork in one's possession, even if it is on public display. The statute imposes liability for alteration or destruction due to gross negligence on the part of one who "frames, conserves, or restores" a work of fine art.[95] Since the statute declares that "no person who . . . *conserves* . . . a work of fine art" shall alter or destroy it "by any act constituting gross negligence,"[96] the statute implies that one must embark upon the activity of conservation for liability to be imposed. Put another way, one must begin "appropriate treatment,"[97] under the definition of conservation, in order for the possibility of liability to arise. Hence no statutory duty to conserve or maintain derives from mere possession of an artwork.[98] A museum that placed an oil painting in direct sunlight would escape any liability under California law; it would be irrelevant whether a museum that merely possessed a work were grossly negligent. The policy of preservation behind the California statute would be thwarted significantly if museums had no duty to maintain and protect artworks in their possession, especially when the standard of care is so slight.[99]

The 1957 Law does not distinguish between intentional and negligent injury, or among the various owners or activities that may affect a work. Injury occurring through negligent conservation has been addressed hypothetically;[100] and, in an actual case, no liability was imposed upon a municipality for failing to reerect an outdoor sculpture that had collapsed because of lengthy exposure to the elements.[101] This case, however, cannot be interpreted to mean that French courts will not impose liability

---

[95] See Cal. Civ. Code §987(c)(2) (West Supp. 1984). Under the California Act, "restore" means "to return . . . a deteriorated or damaged work of fine art . . . to its original state." *Id.* §987(b)(5). "Conserve" means "to preserve . . . a work of fine art by retarding or preventing deterioration or damage through appropriate treatment . . . in order to maintain the structural integrity in an unchanging state." *Id.* §987(b)(6).

[96] *Id.* §987(c)(2) (emphasis added).

[97] *Id.* §987(b)(6).

[98] This argument finds further support in the fact that subsection (c) of §987 — which imposes liability for alteration or destruction — is divided into two subdivisions, (1) dealing with one who "owns and possesses" the artwork, and (2) dealing with one who "frames, conserves, or restores" it. *Id.* §987(c).

[99] "Gross negligence" is defined as "the exercise of so slight a degree of care as to justify the belief that there was an indifference to the particular work of fine art." *Id.* §987(c)(2).

[100] Desbois writes: "The owner does not destroy the work of art, but he lets the changes in the weather, the persistent humidity of a gallery, day after day tarnish the coloring, then indeed, the canvas itself. Could not the painter complain about his indifference, his negligence?" H. Desbois, *supra* note 11, at 545 (author's translation).

[101] Judgment of Feb. 18, 1976, Tribunal administratif [Trib. admin.], Grenoble, 1977 Rev. trim. de Droit comm. 120.

for negligent mutilation or destruction. The court emphasized that the author knew he had built the sculpture out of perishable materials — railroad ties — and that it was destined for exposure to the elements. Moreover, the court noted that his work in fact had been visible to the public in an intact state for a substantial period of time.[102]

Both the New York and California statutes concern themselves with imposition of liability for negligent as well as intentional acts. The New York statute, however, more clearly imposes a duty of care on the art owner by specifically providing for maintenance and protection. Furthermore, it reduces to ordinary negligence the level of culpability needed to impose liability in the case of acts beyond mere maintenance, such as conservation and restoration. The California statute uses the more demanding standard of gross negligence in those cases.[103]

E. Duration

Article 6 of the 1957 Law declares that the personal rights of authors are "perpetual, inalienable, and imprescriptible," and that they are "transferable at death to the heirs or legatees of the author."[104]

---

[102] The Administrative Tribunal noted:

[T]he removal was motivated by the danger, established by expert testimony, that the work presented to the public; [the authorities] only intervened at the end of four years, at which time the totem made of assembled railroad ties remained exposed to the view of admirers; in maintaining this work exposed to the view of passers-by as long as their safety was not threatened, the mayor of Grenoble reconciled the requirements of public security with the respect which is due to the creative genius of the artist and to his work.

Id. (author's translation).

[103] The California statute, despite its seemingly more narrow scope and its lesser standard of care, is aimed at preventing damage and destruction while the New York statute looks to reputation protection even when it addresses safekeeping of artwork. See *supra* text accompanying notes 88-99. Given its reputation protection rationale, the New York statute's distinction between acts of gross and ordinary negligence is puzzling. If the display of an altered artwork damages an artist's reputation, what difference does it make whether the injury to the artwork was grossly negligent, ordinarily negligent, or intentional? The tort of defamation, which protects reputation, does not require a distinction between negligence and intent, much less gross versus ordinary negligence. Unless a public figure is involved, a person is liable for defamation if he passes on false information injurious to someone's reputation whether he has acquired it through sloppy research or whether he has engaged in sheer invention. See generally W. Keeton, D. Dobbs, R. Keeton & D. Owen, Prosser and Keeton on the Law of Torts, §§111-116A (5th ed. 1984) (hornbook anaylsis of defamation law) [hereinafter cited as Prosser & Keeton.] Where injury to property is concerned, however, tort law preserves the distinction between intent and negligence. Thus, it is more logical for a statute aimed at protection of the work to contain a variation in the standard of care. See *id.,* §113 at 802. Compare Cal. Civ. Code §987(c)(2) (West Supp. 1984), with *id.* §987(c)(1) (standard of gross negligence as opposed to standard of intentional damage).

[104] C. civ. art. 543(6) (82e ed. Petits Codes Dalloz 1983) (author's translation).

Although the New York statute does not expressly address the duration of its protections, it is reasonable to conclude that at least the right of integrity does not survive the artist, given that the statute is aimed at protecting the artist's reputation.[105] Some question arises, however, regarding the right of attribution, since the statute states that "the artist shall retain *at all times* the right to claim authorship."[106] The fact that the *artist* retains the right, however, renders this clause susceptible to a similar limitation.[107]

The California statute that the rights and duties created "[s]hall, with respect to the artist, or if any artist is deceased, his heir, legatee, or personal representative, exist until the fiftieth anniversary of the death of such artist."[108] This is identical to the copyright term provided by the 1976 federal Copyright Act[109] and is also the limitation found in The Berne Convention.[110] This policy, also, is consistent with the California statute's concern with protecting artwork rather than reputation.

F. The Public Interest

One of the primary misconceptions regarding the French concept of droit moral is the assumption that it seeks to protect the public interest by preserving artworks for posterity. In fact, the 1957 Law is aimed at protecting the *personal* rights of the *author* in his creation.[111] The theoretical basis for this protection is that the artwork is seen as an extension or expression of the author's personality.[112] The author and his heirs or legatees can exercise these rights.[113] Moreover, the very recognition of a right of withdrawal as part of droit moral is proof that it is the author's — not the public's — wishes that are being protected. The right of withdrawal allows the author to withdraw his work from public scru-

---

[105] See *supra* notes 61 62 and accompanying text. Ordinarily, only a living person can be defamed. See Prosser & Keeton, *supra* note 103, at 778-80.

[106] See N.Y. Arts & Cultural Affairs Law §14.55.1 (McKinney 1984) (emphasis added).

[107] There is also a three-year statute of limitations. See *id*. §14.59.2

[108] Cal. Civ. Code §987(g)(1) (West Supp. 1984). The statute of limitations is three years. *Id*. §987(i).

[109] 17 U.S.C. §302(a) (1982).

[110] See Berne Convention, *supra* note 8, art. 7.3.

[111] "The legislature has revealed the *raison d'etre*, the mission and the nature of the *droit moral* in declaring (art. 6, §2) that *it is attached to the person of the author*. Without a doubt, it has as its point of application the work, but only insofar as it bears the imprint of the sensibility and the intelligence of him who conceived and created it." H. Desbois, *supra* note 11, at 470 (author's translation).

[112] See *supra* note 68 and accompanying text.

[113] "It is transferable at death to the heirs or legatees of the author." C. civ. art. 543(6) (82e ed. Petits Codes Dalloz 1983) (author's translation).

tiny,[114] provided that he indemnify the parties affected.[115] Once in his hands, he is free to destroy the artwork, despite public sentiment to the contrary.[116] French law provides for the protection of certain works of art considered national treasures through other legislation, not through droit moral.[117]

The New York statute, based as it is on the protection of the artist's reputation, also fails to mention the public interest. The preamble, for example, states that the physical state of a work of fine art is of enduring and crucial importance "to the artist and the artist's reputation."[118] The violation of the integrity of an artwork causes a loss "to the artist and the artist's reputation."[119] Indeed, the very title of the statute concerns itself with the *artist's* rights, not those of the *public*. The section of the statute dealing with relief begins: "[A]n *artist* aggrieved."[120] Finally, the New York statute permits the display of a work of fine art in an altered state if the alteration was done by the artist or with the artist's consent.[121] Thus, the artist could alter the work even if it had charmed the public in its original state for years.

In contrast, the California Art Preservation Act, as its title suggests, aims at protecting artwork in the public interest as well as protecting the artist's personality. The preamble explicitly states that there is "a public interest in preserving the integrity of cultural and artistic creations."[122]

---

[114] See *supra* note 15. Sarraute maintains that the right of retraction only applies to written works because article 29 of the 1957 Law states that the creator cannot require that the owner of the material object return it to him for the exercise of his personal rights. See Sarraute, *supra* note 68, at 477.

[115] See C. civ. art. 543(32) (82e ed. Petits Codes Dalloz 1983).

[116] Sarraute, *supra* note 68, at 476. Such a fact situation was presented in the French case of Camoin v. Carco. The painter Camoin had slashed and thrown away some canvasses which were retrieved, restored and offered for public sale by Carco. Camoin sued to have the canvasses seized and destroyed. The Paris Court of Appeals held for Camoin, saying:

> [A]lthough whoever gathers up the pieces becomes the indisputable owner of them through possession, this ownership is limited to the physical quality of the fragments, and does not deprive the painter of the moral right which he always retains over his work. If the artist continues to believe that his paintings should not be put into circulation, he is within his rights to oppose any restoring of the canvas [sic] and to demand, if necessary, that it be destroyed.

Judgment of Mar. 6, 1931, Cour d'appel, Paris, 1931 Recueil Périodique et Critique [D.P.] II 88 (author's translation), reprinted in Sarraute, *supra* note 68, at 468. The basis for the decision, however, was the right of disclosure, not the right of retraction.

[117] See A. Francon, La Propriété Littéraire Et Artistique (2d ed. 1979).

[118] N.Y. Arts & Cultural Affairs Law §14.55 historical note (McKinney 1984).

[119] See *id.*

[120] N.Y. Arts & Cultural Affairs Law §14.59.1 (McKinney 1984).

[121] Id. §14.53.

[122] Cal. Civ. Code §987(a) (West Supp. 1984).

Although the section dealing with remedies declares that "[t]o effectuate the rights created by this section, the *artist* may commence an action," [123] the recently added section 989(c) grants "standing to an organization acting in the public interest" to seek injunctive relief "to preserve or restore the integrity of a work of fine art." [124] The statute expressly defines "organization," [125] and to the criterion, "fine art of recognized quality," it adds a requirement that the artwork be "of substantial public interest," [126] in order for an "organization" to bring suit. A public interest organization can also bring legal action to determine whether a work of fine art can be removed from real property without substantial injury to the work, but the organization must be prepared to pay for the cost of removal.[127] The California statute thus seeks to serve the public interest as well as to safeguard artists' personal rights.[128]

Of course, a statute may have the incidental effect of preserving artwork, despite the fact that preservation is not its primary goal. In the majority of cases, the artist will attempt to preserve the original integrity of his work rather than attempting to alter it himself.[129] Nevertheless, the 1957 Law and the New York statute were directed toward creation of rights for exercise by the artist; any benefit to the public in the preservation of artwork is incidental.

G. Remedies

The French, New York, and California statutes all have provisions for injunctive relief as well as monetary damages.[130] In addition,

---

[123] *Id.* §987(e) (emphasis added).

[124] *Id.* §989(c).

[125] Section 989(b)(2) defines "[o]rganization" as

a public or private not-for-profit entity or association, in existence at least three years at the time an action is filed pursuant to this section, a major purpose of which is to stage, display, or otherwise present works of art to the public or to promote the interest of the arts or artists.

Id. §989(b)(2).

[126] *Id.* §§989(b)(1), 989(c).

[127] *Id.* §989(e)(1).

[128] The blending of the two policies is not always successful. For example, §987(c)(1) permits the artist-creator to alter his work, but a public interest organization could arguably prevent the artist from doing so under §987(c), which gives §987(c) rights to organizations. However, since §987(c)(1) provides an exception for the artist, it is arguable that an organization could not prevail over the artist.

[129] Indeed, the California statute recognized the interrelationship between the artist's wishes and the public interest in the usual case by inserting public interest considerations into the preamble even before the 1982 amendments provided for actions by public interest organizations. See Cal. Civ. Code §987(a) (West 1982 & Supp. 1984).

[130] Loi du 11 Mars 1957 arts. 70-76, 1957 J.O. 2729, 1957 D.L. 106; N.Y. Arts

the California statute provides for punitive damages and the recovery of attorneys' and expert witness' fees.[131] The punitive damages, however, are not payable to the artist, but to "organizations engaged in charitable or educational activities involving the fine arts."[132] Furthermore, the organizations given standing by section 989(c) are limited to injunctive relief.[133]

Because the New York statute is aimed at protecting the artist's reputation, a problem may arise regarding injunctive relief, given that virtually all courts have refused to enjoin a personal libel.[134] Were an art dealer to display a work in modified form, the aggrieved artist seemingly could not secure an injunction to have the work removed from display. However, a reward of monetary damages that accounted for continued display might serve the same purpose. The law of defamation presents artists with other problems as well — for example, the distinction between general and special damages, and the issues of proof associated with that distinction.[135]

The California statute attempts to avoid these problems by concentrating on injury to the work itself rather than to the artist's reputation. Yet this scheme raises its own questions. For example, destruction of an artwork may be an unmitigated disaster for the artist, but the statute may confine recovery to the fair market value of the work at the time of the destruction.[136] On the other hand, one could argue that the destruction of a single example of an artist's work actually may benefit the artist by increasing the value of remaining works. In that case, the recovery of fair market value may be a windfall.[137]

III. REPRESENTATIVE CASES

The preceding section compared the New York statute with the California and French statutes in a number of significant areas. To understand better the effect of the New York statute, this Part will consider the result that would be reached under the statute in three representative cases adjudicated before its enactment. In *Vargas v. Esquire*,[138] an artist

---

& Cultural Affairs Law §14.59.1 (McKinney 1984); Cal. Civ. Code §§987(c)(1), 989(c) (West Supp. 1984).

[131] Cal. Civ. Code §§987(e)(3)-987(e)(4) (West Supp. 1984).

[132] *Id.* §987(e)(3).

[133] *Id.* §989(c).

[134] See D. Dobbs, Handbook on the Law of Remedies 523-24 (1973).

[135] See generally *id.* at 513-22 (a survey of the law of general and special damages in defamation cases).

[136] Gantz, Artists Benefit from State "Moral Rights" Statute, Legal Times, Nov. 21, 1983, 16, 19.

[137] *Id.*

[138] 164 F.2d 522 (7th Cir. 1947), *cert. denied*, 335 U.S. 813 (1948).

sued *Esquire* magazine for publishing his drawings without attribution; thus, *Vargas* is representative of a claim based on the right of attribution. In *Crimi v. Rutgers Presbyterian Church*,[139] an artist sued a church for painting over a mural he had done; thus, *Crimi* is representative of a claim based on the right of integrity where destruction is involved. In *Buffet v. Fersing*,[140] a French case, an artist sued the owner of an artwork for altering it; thus, *Buffet* is representative of a claim based on the right of integrity where alteration rather than destruction is involved.

In the first of these cases, Alberto Vargas was employed under contract to provide drawings for *Esquire* magazine. Vargas supplied several pictures that were published in the magazine and identified (by mutual consent) as the work of "Varga"; the drawings themselves were known as "Varga Girls."[141] As a result of a contract dispute, Vargas refused to furnish *Esquire* with further drawings. *Esquire* nevertheless published drawings that Vargas had already made pursuant to the agreement, but did so without attribution. The Seventh Circuit held that Vargas had "by plain and unambiguous language completely divested himself of every vestige of title and ownership of the pictures"[142] and of the name "Varga Girls."[143] Thus, *Esquire* had no implied contractual obligation to attribute the drawings to him. The court went on to hold that there was also no obligation based on the "moral rights" of authors because American law did not recognize such a concept.[144]

It seems that Vargas would have had a cause of action if his case had been decided under the New York statute. The statute specifically covers "drawing[s],"[145] and section 14.55 clearly gives him the right "at all times . . . to claim authorship."[146] Section 14.57, however, exempts work "prepared under contract for advertising or trade use unless the contract so provides."[147] Since the contract contained a sweeping provision by which Vargas yielded "all rights with respect to"[148] the drawings and the name, it would seem that the contract did not provide for the right of attribution. Thus, it becomes crucial to determine whether the drawings were prepared for "advertising or trade use." Insufficient facts

---

[139] 194 Misc. 570, 89 N.Y.S.2d 813 (Sup. Ct. 1949).

[140] Judgment of May 30, 1962 Cour d'appel, Paris, 1962 D. Jur. 570, *rev'g*, Judgment of June 7, 1960, Trib. gr. inst., Paris, *aff'd* Judgment of July 6, 1965, Cass. civ. 1re, Fr., No. 644 (available on LEXIS, Prive library, Cass file).

[141] *Vargas*, 164 F.2d at 524.

[142] *Id.* at 525.

[143] *Id.* at 526.

[144] *Id.*

[145] N.Y. Arts & Cultural Affairs Law §14.51.5 (McKinney 1984).

[146] *Id.* §14.55.1.

[147] *Id.* §14.57.4.

[148] 164 F.2d at 525.

are given in the opinion to make a precise determination,[149] but one could distinguish between a drawing appearing as part of an advertisement and a drawing appearing outside of that context as an insertion in that magazine. The former would provide a better argument for "advertising or trade use," although in the latter case it could also be argued that the drawings were "advertising or trade use" because they were included to make the magazine more attractive to buyers. Assuming the drawings were not "advertising or trade use," the question becomes whether the New York statute allows waiver.[150] If the right of attribution is not waivable, Vargas would prevail.

In the second representative case, *Crimi*, the Rutgers Presbyterian Church contracted with the artist Alfred D. Crimi for the painting of a fresco on the rear chancel wall of the church. The Supreme Court of New York found that, under the contract, the fresco "would become a part of the church building," and that the copyright would be assigned to the church.[151] Upon completion, Crimi signed the mural. Eight years later, however, the church painted over the fresco mural, partly because some parishioners objected that "a portrayal of Christ with so much of His chest bare placed more emphasis on His physical attributes than on His spiritual qualities."[152] The court held that because all rights in the work passed to the church (pursuant to the contract), the artist had no legal basis for his claim of restoration or damages.[153]

Although the New York statute does not mention frescoes and murals specifically, presumably they fall within the definition of "painting."[154] The New York statute would not alter the result of the *Crimi* case, however, because after completely effacing the mural, the church was not guilty of publicly displaying an artwork in an "altered, defaced, mutilated or modified form."[155] *Crimi* underscores the inadequacy of the New York statute insofar as it fails to protect against complete destruction.

The third representative case, *Buffet v. Fersing*, was a French case decided after the enactment of the 1957 Law. Bernard Buffet painted six panels of a refrigerator, signed the work, and entitled the ensemble. The refrigerator was purchased at auction, and some months later only the top part was offered for sale. The artist sued to have the panels put back on the refrigerator. The trial court allowed the owner to keep the panels

---

[149] See *id.* at 523-25.

[150] See *supra* notes 84-85 and accompanying text.

[151] 194 Misc. 570, 571, 89 N.Y.S.2d 813, 814 (Sup. Ct. 1949).

[152] *Id.* at 571, 89 N.Y.S.2d at 815.

[153] *Id.* at 576-77, 89 N.Y.S.2d at 819.

[154] See N.Y. Arts & Cultural Affairs Law §14.51.5 (McKinney 1984).

[155] See *id.* §14.53; see also *supra* notes 61-62 and accompanying text.

in a dismantled state and permitted private disposition, but forbade any public exhibition or sale.[156] The appellate court was more severe. It forbade private disposition as well, but allowed the owner to keep the panels in a dismantled state in the privacy of his own home.[157] The highest French court, the Court of Cassation, upheld the decision of the court of appeals.[158]

If *Buffet* had arisen in New York, the artist would have had legal recourse. The refrigerator would fall in the "painting" category of the statute,[159] and the refrigerator as a whole, rather than each panel individually, would be the artwork since that was the artist's intention in signing it once and giving it one name. As such, a public display of one detached panel would be the public display of a work of fine art in an "altered, mutilated or modified form." [160] The artist, of course, still would have to prove that such display damaged his reputation.[161] Curiously, the question of public or private disposition would probably also arise in New York. The statute forbids "display in a place accessible to the public" or publishing of a work of fine art in an altered state.[162] A private sale arguably would not violate this provision since the owner could invite interested individuals into his own home and effect a sale in that manner. Therefore, the owner would be prohibited from public sale only, unless a private sale would constitute "publication," a highly ambiguous term as pre-1976 copyright litigation testifies.[163]

CONCLUSION

That the New York statute seeks to protect the artist's reputation while the California statute aims at preservation and personality protection indicates the ambivalence of American attitudes toward the purpose of protecting authors' rights. The acknowledged purpose of the French concept of droit moral, at least in the eyes of French legal scholars, is the protection of the *author's* personality rather than any public interest in preserving artwork.[164] Although the protection of the author's personality includes the element of reputation, personality is not limited to repu-

---

[156] Judgment of June 7, 1960, Trib. gr. inst., Paris, *aff'd* Judgment of July 6, 1965, Cass. civ. 1re, Fr., No. 644 (available on LEXIS, Prive library, Cass file).

[157] Judgment of May 30, 1962, Cour d'appel, Paris, 1962 D. Jur. 570.

[158] Judgment of July 6, 1965, Cass. civ. 1re, Fr., No. 644 (available on LEXIS, Prive library, Cass file).

[159] See N.Y. Arts & Cultural Affairs Law §14.51.5 (McKinney 1984).

[160] See *id.* §14.53.

[161] See *id.*

[162] *Id.*

[163] N. Boorstyn, *supra* note 8, §1:6, at 7-10.

[164] See *supra* note 68 and accompanying text.

tation.[165] Insofar as the New York statute was inspired by the droit moral, it is but a very pale reflection. The California statute, on the other hand, goes beyond the theoretical justification for droit moral to preserve art-work with the conscious object of furthering the public interest.[166]

The distinctions in the three legal theories animating these statutory schemes provide the key to understanding the differences among the three statutes. These differences are most clearly perceived in five areas: the work covered, whether destruction is covered, whether waiver is allowed, how stringent the duty of care is, and what the duration of protection is. The personal rights theory provides the best justification for extending the definition of protected works to the broadest practicable class. By contrast, the art preservation theory limits statutory coverage by determining which artworks ought to be preserved in the public interest, and the reputation protection theory limits protection to situations in which it is possible for reputation damage to occur — hence the public display requirement. Again, the personal rights and the art preservation theories distinguish themselves from the reputation protection theory with regard to destruction. The former must necessarily encompass it, while the latter prohibits destruction only by a problematic extension of reasoning. The art preservation theory and the personal rights theory also treat waiver differently. Although it would be impossible to enforce a contractual provision whereby the artist *bound* himself to allow alter-ation or destruction, under the personal rights theory, the artist can consent to such acts, or agree to perform them himself. Such is not the case with the art preservation theory, since the public interest would override even the author's wishes. In the case of the reputation protec-tion theory, the recognition of reputation protection waivers in the com-mon law generally may influence this yet unsettled issue. The duty of care — the duty to maintain the artwork in its original state — may be derived most easily from the art preservation theory, although there is no theoretical inconsistency in deriving it from the personal rights theory as well.[167] Neither is there a theoretical problem in inferring a duty of care from the reputation protection theory, although the public display re-quirement considerably lessens the possibility of liability.[168] Finally, the art preservation theory provides the best rationale for extending protec-

---

[165] See Pound, Interests of Personality, 28 Harv. L. Rev. 343, 349 (1915).

[166] Cal. Civ. Code §987(a) (West Supp. 1984).

[167] One can distinguish the duty of care to be exercised in maintaining a work from the duty of care to be exercised in restoring a work to its original state. See *supra* notes 88-103 and accompanying text.

[168] See *supra* notes 100-01 and accompanying text.

tion over artwork in perpetuity. Such protection under the personal rights and reputation protection theories is less certain, given the still controversial issue of post mortem personality protection.[169]

In sum, the personal rights and art preservation theories differ significantly in two particulars — the class of works protected and the freedom of the artist to consent to alteration or destruction. The two are not necessarily incompatible, however, since the personal rights theory indirectly serves the goal of art preservation if, as one assumes, the vast majority of artists would be loathe to alter or destroy their work or authorize such acts. Thus, no great violence would be done to the concept of the personal rights of authors by carving out a subset from the class of works protected and according them protection even against their creator if they are of substantial interest to the public.

Yet while the personal rights theory enshrined in French law provides an argument for expanding protection in each of the five areas noted, the reputation theory provides arguments for limiting protection — to public display, against destruction coverage, for waivability, against a duty of care for undisplayed works, and for limitation to the life of the artist. The New York statute, in comparison to the French, is not only flawed by ambiguities and seeming inconsistencies, but is also sterile in that its theoretical basis precludes development into more comprehensive protection. In contrast to the New York statute, the California statute, despite shortcomings of its own, does contain a theoretical basis from which broader protection may evolve. Thus, while the enactment of the New York Artists' Authorship Rights Act creates protection for artists, where once there was none, the inherent limits of reputation protection mean that the best hope for comprehensive protection of artists and artwork lies in supplanting rather than supplementing the New York statute.[170]

---

[169] See N.Y. Arts & Cultural Affairs Law §§14.57, 14.57.5 (McKinney 1984).

[170] The Berne Convention, for example, limits its protection of personal rights to the life of the author plus 50 years. Berne Convention, *supra* note 8, art. 7(1). In contrast, American courts are less likely to recognize the post mortem transferability of nonproperty rights. Cf. Ginsburg, Transfer of the Right of Publicity: Dracula's Progeny and Privacy's Stepchild, 25 Copyright L. Symp. (ASCAP) 1, 2-3 (1980) (Of four categories of invasion of privacy—intrusion of solitude, public disclosure of private facts, false light, and misappropriation of name or likeness — only the last survives death because, unlike the others, it implicates a pecuniary interest and not just a matter of "feeling."); Prosser & Keeton, *supra* note 103, at 778-79 ("[N]o civil action will lie for the defamation of one who is dead.") (footnote omitted). The 1957 Law, however, deems the droit moral to be perpetual.

§5.4.4. *Newmann v. Delmar Realty Co.:* First Test of the New York Statute

The New York moral right statute became effective on January 1, 1984. It made its first court appearance a few months later in *Newmann v. Delmar Realty Co., Inc.,* a case in which its relevance was — to say the least — somewhat oblique. The work of art that the artist sought to protect was not being displayed in an "altered, defaced, mutilated or modified form," the event that should trigger the statute; it was simply unfinished. Can the New York statute really be stretched that far? If a painter, for example, became incapacitated when partly through a mural project, could he obtain an injunction against his incomplete work being left on view? (Compare the claim of Dubuffet against the Renault Company, discussed in §5.2.3 *supra.*) In *Newmann,* however, the court did not have to go that distance. It was able to find a contract-based right that gave the artist the access necessary to finish his work (notwithstanding that the work might be obliterated promptly upon its completion). The Artists' Authorship Rights Act had only tangential application. It served to indicate a legislatively approved policy of protecting the "personal" interest of the artist rather than to provide any immediate remedy for the injury of which he was complaining.

Subsequent to the *Newmann* decision, which follows, the artist brought the defendant back to court, seeking civil and criminal contempt for willful violation of the preliminary injunction the court had entered. Newmann complained that

[t]o my utter amazement, I saw that two large holes had been broken through the south wall of the theatre and that I-beams were being passed through one of them by workers. Upon closer examination, I saw substantial construction activity taking place in the interior of the building. . . . One of the holes is approximately 3½ feet square, and is located in the exact place where my work is incomplete. Another hole is about one foot square, and is just adjacent to my work.[2]

Plaintiff thus claimed that the two holes constituted an alteration of the "negative space" surrounding his work — and, in effect, a modification of the work itself. Also submitted in support of Newmann's request was an affidavit of Thomas Hoving, editor-in-chief of Connoisseur Magazine and former director of the Metropolitan Museum of Art in New York, in support of the "negative space" argument. Mr. Hoving averred the following:

---

[2] Newmann v. Delmar Realty Co., No. 2955/84 (N.Y. Sup. Ct., Aug. 2, 1984) (affidavit of Newmann at 2).

A work of art only exists within a context, and what creates any work of art is the tension between the positive space — i.e., the objects, or the figure, and the negative space — i.e., the space surrounding the objects, or the ground. The concept is the same whether the work is on a canvas or on the side of a building.

This concept of positive and negative space is a central one in the history of art. For example, the use in ancient Chinese scroll paintings of blank areas of canvas or paper to create an effect of clouds or mists predates Western art by thousands of years. Since the development of abstract art, the relationship between positive and negative space has become more complex and equivocal, but is no less central to the idea of artistic creation.

It is clear that the rear wall represents the total space of Mr. Newmann's art work, and that he has created a deliberate tension between the image and the edges of the building.

Mr. Newmann's work is valuable, in my opinion, because it represents an unusual concept of mural art. It is not political, nor a trompe l'oeil, as are most wall murals visible around New York. Mr. Newmann's work is much more spiritual than exhortational, and I believe that it is much more valuable for the area because of its spirituality.

I am of the opinion that the damage done to Mr. Newmann's work by the two holes in the wall is irreparable, and has substantionally [sic] reduced its value. The fact that the holes are outside of the present image area is irrelevant. To rupture any part of the environment of a work of art, even if hardly noticeable, does damage to the artist's conception, and any damage drastically reduces the value of the work. Even if the removed bricks are replaced, the differences in tone will be obvious.

I fully support the policy behind the Artists' Authorship Rights Act. I believe that Mr. Newmann's rights have been violated, and I respectfully urge the Court to read the Act broadly, in accordance with its remedial purposes. The law must protect the *total* work of art, both the positive and negative spaces, if it is to have any meaning. Otherwise, the result could be disruptive to the artist's entire conception of future works of art. Moreover, Mr. Newmann's work is particularly in need of protection because of its public nature. Since the work does, in effect, belong to the public, the public will benefit as much as the artist by the protection of the law.[3]

Unfortunately for Newmann, the court disagreed, finding that the defendants' actions "do not rise to the level of contempt."[4]

The New York statute simply does not go this far. Such a claim, i.e., that the force of moral right extends beyond the limits of the artwork proper, is reminiscent of some of the arguments advanced in the matter of Richard Serra's *Tilted Arc* (discussed in §4.2.3 *supra*).

---

[3] Newmann v. Delmar Realty Co., No. 2955/84 (N.Y. Sup. Ct., Sept. 6, 1984) (affidavit of Hoving at 2-3).

[4] Newmann v. Delmar Realty Co., No. 2955/84 (N.Y. Sup. Ct., Aug. 8, 1984) (order denying motion for contempt, available at Spec. I Liber N67).

NEWMANN v. DELMAR REALTY CO.
No. 2955/84 (N.Y. Sup. Ct., March 2, 1984)

WILK, J.: Plaintiff, an established fine artist, moves to preliminarily enjoin defendants from interfering with the completion and integrity of an art work in progress, a mural on the south wall of the Palladium Theatre building at 126-128 East 14th Street in New York County.[1] Plaintiff received a grant from the National Endowment for the Arts (NEA) to create the work.

On February 9, 1982, plaintiff entered into a written agreement with defendant Delmar Realty Co., Inc. (Delmar) the owner of the building, and with the Public Art Fund, Inc. (PAF), a not-for-profit corporation. The unrecorded agreement recites that the parties "wish to provide for the continuing display of the Art Work for the benefit and enjoyment of owners of properties adjoining the Building, and the general public."

In the agreement, Delmar granted permission to plaintiff to create and display the work of art on the south wall of the building. The mural was to be completed by May 3, 1983 and to be displayed until March 3, 1988.

Paragraph 6 of the agreement provides that if Delmar leases or sells the building it will both notify plaintiff and use its best efforts to obtain the consent of the new lessee or owner to assume Delmar's obligations under the agreement.

On March 14, 1983, Delmar entered into a fifteen-year net lease, commencing June 1, 1983, with defendant Muidallap Corporation (Muidallap). A memorandum of the lease was recorded. Plaintiff alleges that he was not notified of the existence of the lease until after it had been executed. He additionally asserts that Delmar failed to use its best efforts to have Muidallap assume Delmar's obligations under its agreement with him.

The lease provides that the premises will be used for entertainment.[2] In paragraph 28 of the "Rider to Lease," Muidallap agrees to expend no less than $500,000 to improve the premises by June 1, 1984. An "illus-

---

[1] There are two identical motions before me, apparently because plaintiff was initially unable to effect service. It is unclear why the first motion was added to the calendar; it is deemed withdrawn.

[2] Paragraph 2 provides that

[t]enant shall use and occupy demised premises for a theatre and/or as a club presenting live contemporary rock music and/or any other type of music shows; and/or dance; and/or closed circuit telecasts; and/or opera; and/or motion picture; and/or stage shows; and/or right to operate concession stands including one or more bars serving liquor in connection therewith; and/or discotheque; and/or cabaret and night club; and/or restaurant; and/or teaching institution in connection with theatre and/or dance and/or music and/or recorded music; and/or recording and/or sound and/or T.V., and/or similar type of studio.

trative" list of items of improvement contained in the lease includes "alterations and repairs to the outside facade of the building."

Muidallap contends that because (1) plaintiff's contract with Delmar was not recorded and gave plaintiff only a revocable license and (2) its lease with Delmar made no reference to plaintiff's agreement, it is bound only by the terms of the lease. It contradicts Delmar's allegation that Delmar attempted to obtain Muidallap's consent to the display of the mural.

One who seeks a preliminary injunction has the burden of proving that (1) he is likely to succeed on the merits of his claim; (2) he will suffer irreparable injury if the injunction is denied and (3) the equities are balanced in his favor. (*Paine & Chriscott v. Blair House Associates*, 70 A.D.2d 571, 572.)

Muidallap intends to alter the facade of the building and alleges that such action is mandated by its lease with Delmar. It has expressed an intention to paint over the mural. In view of Muidallap's plan to obliterate this almost completed work of art, it is clear that the harm to plaintiff will be irreparable if injunctive relief is not granted.

While Muidallap claims the balance of the equities, the facts suggest otherwise. Plaintiff submitted a photograph of the south wall which verifies his claim that the mural, which has been created by sandblasting the exterior wall, is almost complete. It is equally apparent that in reliance upon his agreement with Delmar, plaintiff has already expended considerable time and effort in the production of the mural.

The only item listed in paragraph 28 that arguably is effected by granting plaintiff injunctive relief is "alterations and repairs to the outside facade of the building." This language is insufficiently specific to compel an interpretation of the contract as requiring any alteration to the south wall of the building. Moreover, a construction of this paragraph as mandating alterations to the south wall is wholly inconsistent with Delmar's contractual obligation to plaintiff to use its best efforts to insure the preservation of the mural. Thus, an injunction will not serve as an impediment to Muidallap's adhering to its contractual obligations to Delmar.

The remaining issue is whether it is likely that plaintiff will prevail on the merits of his suit. . . .

It is obvious that plaintiff's motive is not pecuniary gain, but the integrity of his work in progress and the protection of his reputation as an artist. Some wrongs cannot be redressed by money alone. Only equitable relief can prevent the harm plaintiff seeks to avoid.

Muidallap further maintains that plaintiff's failure to record his contract with Delmar is fatal to his position. The purpose of recording acts is to give notice, actual or constructive, to prospective recipients of an interest in real property that title to the property has been affected in some manner. (*Reid v. Town of Long Lake*, 44 Misc. 370; N.Y. Jur. Records and Recording Acts. Sec. 54 at p.280.) Actual notice obviates the need to rely upon a recording, (*Reed v. Barkley*, 123 Misc. 635).

Thus, one who rents premises with actual or constructive knowledge of a prior restrictive covenant agreed to by his or her lessor in favor of another is bound by the restriction. (*Weiss v. Mayflower Doughnut Corp.*, 1 N.Y.2d 310; *Reltron Corp. v. Voxakis Enterprises*, 57 A.D.2d 134.)

The facts strongly suggest that Muidallap had actual or constructive knowledge of plaintiff's interest in the property. Although there is no evidence that Delmar used its best efforts to persuade Muidallap to adopt the contract, Delmar alleges that it informed Muidallap of the existence of its contract with plaintiff.

Even if Delmar did not inform Muidallap of the contract, it appears that Muidallap had knowledge of plaintiff's interest in the property. It is unlikely that sophisticated business people negotiating so substantial a transaction would have failed to notice and inquire about the construction of a prominent mural on the south wall of the building.

A subsequent purchaser of land, or in this case a net lessee, cannot resist the assertion of claims on the property if the conditions giving rise to those claims are physically defined and apparent at the time of purchase. (See, *XAR Corp. v. DiDonato, supra; Hey v. Collman*, 78 A.D. 584 *aff'd*, 180 N.Y. 560.) Knowledge and notice of any condition on the property should at least lead the prudent person to inquire. (See, *487 Elmwood Inc. v. Hassett*, 83 A.D.2d 409; *Covey v. Niagra, Lockport & Ontario Power Co.*, 286 A.D. 341.) It would appear that Delmar and Muidallap contrived to ignore Delmar's contractual responsibility to plaintiff to use its best efforts to insure the completion and continued display of the mural.

Defendant also alleges that plaintiff failed to complete the work by May 3, 1983, as a consequence of which the agreement, by its terms, was terminable at the option of Delmar. Delmar fails to reveal if or how it notified plaintiff that the agreement was terminated.

Plaintiff states that his inability to complete the work on schedule was caused by defendants' obstructionism. He alleges that he was prepared to complete the work in early April, that he needed only one or two days' access to the wall, and that he telephoned Mr. Roth at Delmar to arrange an access date. Mr. Roth said that he had to check with Mr. Greenberg of Muidallap, the new lessee.

By late April, Roth had been unable to contact Greenberg and agreed to extend the date by which plaintiff could complete the mural. Plaintiff himself finally reached Greenberg on July 16. Plaintiff states that in August, Delmar and Muidallap agreed to extend his time to complete the work. Before the letter of extension could be executed, Greenberg changed his mind.

Under these circumstances, in which the conduct of Delmar, or Muidallap, or both, prohibited plaintiff from completing the work in a timely fashion, it is unlikely that defendants can prevail upon their assertion that Delmar's contract with plaintiff was terminated for reasons of untimely performance on plaintiff's part.

In view of the viability of plaintiff's action and its likelihood of success, the motion for a preliminary injunction is granted.

Plaintiff also maintains that he is protected by the recently enacted Article 228 of the General Business Law (Artists' Authorship Rights Act).[4]

The Artists' Authorship Rights Act has its antecedent in the concept of "droit moral," or "moral right" developed in Continental Europe. The recognition that artists have personal as well as economic rights in the works that they create gave rise to an attempt to protect them from having their works displayed in an altered or modified form.

Defendants' continued denial to plaintiff of access to the south wall results in a public display of his work in an unfinished and modified form to the probable detriment of plaintiff's reputation as an artist, and in a violation of the spirit and letter of the Artists' Authorship Rights Act. Accordingly, pending the resolution of plaintiff's claims, Delmar and Muidallap are enjoined from denying to plaintiff reasonable access to the south wall to complete his work. Whether plaintiff will choose to complete the work at the risk of its subsequent obliteration is for him to decide. He should not be compelled, however, to suffer the display of the mural in its current unfinished state.

As a condition of the preliminary injunction, plaintiff shall be required to post a bond in the amount of $1,000.

Settle order.

§5.4.5. Massachusetts Moral Right Statute: Based on the California Model

Massachusetts' moral right statute, which follows, was signed into law in January, 1985, and took immediate effect. While generally

---

[4] Section 228-n provides that:

no person other than the artist or a person acting with the artist's consent shall knowingly display in a place accessible to the public . . . a work of fine art of that artist . . . in an altered, defaced, mutilated or modified form if the work is displayed . . . as being the work of the artist, or under circumstances under which it would reasonably be regarded as being the work of the artist, and damage to the artist's reputation is reasonably likely to result therefrom.

based on the California statute (see §5.4.1. *supra*), it differs radically in the scope of its coverage.

MASSACHUSETTS MORAL RIGHT STATUTE
Mass. Gen. Laws Ann. ch. 231, §85S (West 1985)*

Section 85S. (a) The general court hereby finds and declares that the physical alteration or destruction of fine art, which is an expression of the artist's personality, is detrimental to the artist's reputation, and artists therefore have an interest in protecting their works of fine art against such alteration or destruction; and that there is also a public interest in preserving the integrity of cultural and artistic creations.

(b) As used in this section, the following words shall, unless the context clearly requires otherwise, have the following meanings: "Artist," the natural person who actually creates a work of fine art but not to include such art as is created by an employee within the scope of his employment. In case of a joint creation of a work of art, each joint creator shall have the rights of an artist with respect to the work of fine art as a whole.

"Fine art," any original work of visual or graphic art of any media which shall include, but not limited to, any painting, print, drawing, sculpture, craft object, photograph, audio or video tape, film, hologram, or any combination thereof, of recognized quality.

"Gross negligence," the exercise of so slight a degree of care as to justify the belief that there was an indifference to the particular work of fine art.

"Public view," means on the exterior of a public owned building, or in an interior area of a public building.

(c) No person, except an artist who owns or possesses a work of fine art which the artist has created, shall intentionally commit, or authorize the intentional commission of any physical defacement, mutilation, alteration, or destruction of a work of fine art. As used in this section, intentional physical defacement, mutilation, alteration, or destruction includes any such action taken deliberately or through gross negligence.

(d) The artist shall retain the right to claim and receive under his own

---

* See also, Mass. Gen. Laws Ann. ch. 260, §2C (West 1985), which governs the statute of limitations under the Massachusetts moral right statute and reads as follows:

Section 2C. Actions commenced under the provisions of section eighty-five S of chapter two hundred and thirty-one shall be commenced only within two years next after the cause of action accrues, or within one year next after the discovery of the act, whichever is later.

name or under a reasonable pseudonym or, for just and valid reason, to disclaim authorship of his work of fine art. Credit shall be determined in accord with the medium of expression and the nature and extent of the artist's contribution to the work of fine art.

(e) The artist or any bonafide union or other artists' organization authorized in writing by the artist for such purpose may commence an action in the superior court department of the trial court of the commonwealth without having as prerequisites to a suit any need for: (1) damages, already incurred, (2) a showing of special damages, if any, or (3) general damages in any monetary amount to recover or obtain any of the following (i) injunctive relief or declaratory relief, (ii) actual damages, (iii) reasonable attorneys' and expert witness fees and all other costs of the action, or (iv) any other relief which the court deems proper.

(f) In determining whether a work of fine art is of recognized quality, the court shall rely on the opinions of artist, art dealers, collectors of fine art, curators of art museums, restorers and conservators of fine art and other persons involved with the creation or marketing of fine art.

(g) The provisions of this section shall, with respect to the artist, or if any artist is deceased, his heir, legatee, or personal representative, continue until the fiftieth anniversary of the death of such artist, continue in addition to any other rights and duties which may now or in the future be applicable, and except as provided in paragraph (1) of subdivision (h) may not be waived except by an instrument in writing expressly so providing which is signed by the artist and refers to specific works with identification and such waiver shall only apply to work so identified.

The attorney general may, if the artist is deceased, assert the rights of the artist on the artist's behalf and commence an action for injunctive relief with respect to any work of art which is in public view.

(h) (1) If a work of fine art cannot be removed from a building without substantial physical defacement, mutilation, alteration, or destruction of such work, the rights and duties created under this section, unless expressly reserved by an instrument in writing signed by the owner of such building and properly recorded, prior to the installation of such art shall be deemed waived. Such instrument, if recorded, shall be binding on subsequent owners of such building.

(2) If the owner of a building wishes to remove a work of fine art which is a part of such building but which can be removed from the building without substantial harm to such fine art, the rights and duties created under this section shall apply unless the owner has diligently attempted without success to notify the artist, or, if the artist is deceased, his heir, legatee, or personal representative, in writing of his intended action affecting the work of fine art, or unless he did provide notice and that person failed within ninety days either to remove the work or to pay for its removal. If such work is removed at the expense of the artist, his heir,

legatee, or personal representative, title to such fine art shall be deemed to be in such person.

§5.4.6. The Expanding Definition of Fine Art: The Potential for Confusion

Whereas the moral right in its European origin is not limited to visual artist—it is enjoyed as well by musicians, poets, and playwrights—its development in the United States has thus far been wholly with respect to the fine arts. Curiously, however,—if not inexplicably—the scope of what the term fine art embraces has widened steadily since California enacted the first American moral right statute in 1979.

As initially adopted, the California statute applied only to original paintings, sculptures, and drawings (with the added requirements that these be of "recognized quality" and not prepared under contract for "commercial use"). By 1982, interested creative individuals then working in other media had succeeded in securing the adoption and then the amendment of §997 of the California Civil Code. This brought "porcelain painting" and "stained glass artistry" within the definition of "fine art" (the alternative, presumably, to classifying them as "crafts") for the purpose of *all* of California's art legislation, including, presumably, its moral right statute. (Given that it costs the legislature nothing to expand such a definition and given also the general lack of organized opposition, the only wonder is that the League of San Fernando Valley Senior Soap Carvers has not yet succeeded in further amending §997 to include "ornamental carvings in soap and other saponified fats." [5])

In New York, meanwhile, it was not so much the craftsmen who were pressing for recognition as it was the printmakers and photographers. They were successful. When the legislature adopted the New York State Artists' Authorship Rights Act in 1983, the media that the statute covered were broadened considerably. A "work of fine art" was defined to mean:

> any original work of visual or graphic art of any medium which includes, but is not limited to, the following: painting; drawing; print; photographic print or sculpture of a limited edition of no more than three hundred copies; provided however, that work of fine art shall not include sequential imagery such as that in motion pictures. [6]

---

[5] In at least one instance, however, an effort to expand coverage made directly through the courts was less successful. See Robert H. Jacobs, Inc. v. Westoaks Realtors, Inc., 159 Cal. App. 3d 637, 205 Cal. Rptr. 620 (1984), where an architect claimed that the California Resale Royalties Act covered architectural plans. The court disagreed, holding that the plans did not qualify as "fine art".

[6] See §5.4.2 *supra*.

When New York's Arts and Cultural Affairs Law was recodified in 1984 (see §3.2.2 *supra*) this provision was preserved in substance, although formulated differently.

Works of art prepared for use in advertising or trade were generally excluded by another section of the Act rather than by definition. The specific exclusion of motion pictures was no doubt added in response to the film industry's apprehension that the moral right might be judicially extended to cinematographers and set designers, if not directors and performers. Earlier, in California, the powers of Hollywood had made certain that the "fine art" definition adopted there was wholly restricted to tangible objects.

Despite such care, Massachusetts may nevertheless have now blown the whole field wide open. Under the moral right statute it adopted in 1985 — a statute that more or less follows the California model in interdicting such things as the mutilation or alteration of a work of art, rather than prohibiting its display in mutilated or altered form — "fine art" is defined to include "any original work of visual or graphic art of any media which shall include, but not [*sic*] limited to, any painting, print, drawing, sculpture, craft object, photograph, audio or video tape, film, hologram, or any combination thereof, of recognized quality."[7]

Such language offers considerable potential for litigation. In a world where one man's art may be another man's commerce, it will be left wholly to judges and juries to sort out the distinctions between, for example, video and films that are "fine art" and video and films that are merely commercial products. Worse still, it will also be up to the courts to adjudicate the competing artistic claims of joint creators, a problem compounded by the statute's provision that "[i]n case of a joint creation of a work of art, each joint creator shall have the rights of an artist with respect to the work of fine art as a whole."[8]

What then of the aggrieved painter who contributes the costume or set designs to a 33-minute "fine art" video tape that is subsequently cut (with the permission of its other joint creators) to fit a 29-minute time slot on a public television station? Whom can he sue, and for what? Moreover, if a film can be a work of "fine art" while a theatrical performance cannot, could the filming of such a performance bring it within the statute and turn the playwright into an artist? And would that diminish the rights of the painter who designed the sets from those of a sole creator to those of a joint creator? Such questions abound.

Another potential source of difficulty will be the exclusion of works of

---

[7] See §5.4.5 *supra*.
[8] *Ibid.*

art "created . . . within the scope of . . . employment" from the statute's coverage. Does "employment" here refer simply to the traditional master/servant relationship, or may it have the broader meaning that has been given to similar words in applying the "work made for hire" rule of the Copyright Revision Act of 1976? (Concerning the latter, see *Aldon Accessories, Ltd. v. Spiegel*, and *Peregrine v. Lauren Corporation* in Chapter 2.) Under the Copyright Act, the fact that something was created within the scope of employment may simply operate to shift the ownership of the copyright from the artist to the employer. Here, however, it appears to destroy the moral right altogether. Thus, a film made by a director, crew, and performers, all of whom were employed by a film company, would not be protected. Conversely, if the same film were made by a partnership consisting of the director, crew, and performers, each member thereof might assert a moral right to maintain the film's integrity. By the same token, a mural might or might not be protected, depending on the relationship between the muralist and the patron who commissioned the work.

While both California and New York seek to restrict the protection of their moral right statutes to works of art created for other than commercial purposes, they do so by addressing the intended *use* of the work rather than by making the distinction turn wholly on the basis of whether the work was prepared in the course of employment.

§5.4.7. Maine Moral Right Resolution: An Interim Contractual Solution

Unable thus far to enact moral right legislation in Maine, its proponents have meanwhile settled for the following resolution adopted in 1983. It contemplates an interim contractual solution under which form contracts embodying a moral right clause would be made available by the Maine State Commission on the Arts and the Humanities upon request to any "interested Maine artist, governmental entity or other interested persons."

MAINE MORAL RIGHT RESOLUTION
1983 Me. Acts 40

RESOLVE, Authorizing and Directing the
Maine State Commission on the Arts and the
Humanities to Prepare and Make Available
to Artists a Form Contract for the
Protection of Works of Art

Maine State Commission on the Arts and the Humanities is authorized and directed to prepare and make available certain form contracts. Resolved: That the Maine State Commission on the Arts and the Humanities is authorized and directed to:

1. Prepare a form contract that an artist and heirs of the artist may use and have executed by the owners of works of art by the artist. The contract shall provide for agreement by the owner not to physically deface, mutilate or destroy the work of art without permission of the artist or the heir of the artist;

2. Make the form contract available upon request to any interested Maine artist, governmental entity or other interested persons; and

3. Distribute the form contract to any artist or the heir of any artist and the contracting agency participating in the acquisition of works of art under the Percent for Art Act, Revised Statutes, Title 27, chapter 16.

§5.5. FINAL OBSERVATIONS ON THE CALIFORNIA AND NEW YORK MORAL RIGHT STATUTES

An advantage of drafting a statute is that by writing a set of rules against a historical background one can readily draw on the experiences of the past. An area where a series of general problems have arisen can be analyzed in terms of a theoretical number of issues and potential solutions; cases that were unpersuasively decided can be rectified.

With respect to the California and New York statutes, there has been a paradoxical result. When California enacted its moral right statute it could have drawn on the substantial European experience. Yet it can be readily seen that lawmakers selected only a small amount of that precedent. The statute's focus is on the "alteration" or "destruction" of a work of "fine art." Application of the law, however, is limited to works of "recognized quality," a concept that did not exist in the traditional view of the moral right of an artist. While the underlying rationale for this limitation was the fear that the statute might become a vehicle through which little-known artists could publicize their work, it nonetheless does not quite fit with the claimed justification for a moral right. New York, despite the recent enactment of the California statute, has moved in a different fashion. By contrast, the key assumption of the New York statute is that the work shall have been "publicly displayed or published." It is not relevant under the New York statute whether the work is deemed by persons other than the artist to be of "recognized quality."

If the underlying basis of the right is "moral," what significance attaches to the fact that the work may be of recognized quality? Similarly, what moral basis is there for saying that for a work to be protected it must be publicly displayed or published? Do not both the California and New York statutes, albeit in different ways, potentially protect economic rights rather than rights that would generally be deemed personal to the creator? Has not the California statute, by limiting the persons with standing to sue to those who have created works of "recognized quality," permitted the courtroom to be a forum where quality and one's view of artistic merit becomes the dominant issue? Would paintings once exhibited in the Salon des Refusés or Dada or graffiti art be subject to protection? The very term "recognized quality" speaks to a certain acceptance that transcends any personal injury or harm to the creator. Works of "recognized quality" may be very different from works that have substantial market value, either on initial sale or in the secondary market.

At another level, some statutes provide their own impediment. It may very well be that an artist who is considering instituting a suit in California would be well advised to avoid confronting the issue of whether his art is of recognized quality. Even if he proves all elements of his cause of action — other than recognized quality — will he not walk out of the courtroom with second thoughts about having instituted the litigation? While monetary damages may or may not be won in the California courts, personal affront is likely for an artist-plaintiff facing an inhospitable "trier of fact."

To some degree a similar situation prevails in New York, where actions or potential damage to the artist's reputation is necessary to state a cause of action. In such an action, the defense might well be that the artist-plaintiff has little or no reputation to damage. The New York statute functions as an extension of the law of defamation, and actions under it are subject to the same pitfalls as actions for libel or slander: The cure may be more painful than the disease.

CHAPTER SIX

Resale Rights

•

§6.1. Overview

§6.2. The European Perspective

§6.3. The Contractual Approach: A Valiant Effort

§6.4. The Legislative Approach

§6.5. The Practical Effects of Resale Royalty Statutes

§6.1. OVERVIEW

§6.1.1. Introduction

One of the most memorable art world incidents of the past two decades was the confrontation between the artist Robert Rauschenberg and the collector Robert Scull at a 1973 Sotheby Parke-Bernet Galleries auction. At the auction, the painting *Thaw* that Scull originally bought from Rauschenberg in 1958 for less than $1000 was sold by the collector for $85,000. Entitled to no share of Scull's profit, Rauschenberg was apparently angered at what he regarded as an unjust enrichment for Scull. Should artists share in such increases in value? If so, how? This is the topic examined in this chapter.

In March, 1978, Congressman Henry A. Waxman of California introduced into the U.S. House of Representatives H.R. 11403, the Visual Artists' Residual Rights Act of 1978. It was the high-water mark of a campaign that had been waged over a dozen or more years to create some mechanism through which American visual artists might derive an ongoing economic benefit from their work following its original sale.

Generally termed a "resale royalty," the right envisaged was similar to the *droit de suite*—literally the "follow-up right"—first established in France in 1920 and subsequently adopted (with substantial variations and varying rationales) by, among other countries, Belgium (1921), Czechoslovakia (1926), Poland (1935), Uruguay (1937), Italy (1941), Yugoslavia (1957), West Germany (1965), Morocco (1970), and Luxembourg (1972). The extent to which these predominately European statutes have or have not been successful is discussed in the article *Right of Artists: The Case of the Droit de Suite* in this chapter.

§6.1.2. Contractual Alternatives

In their attempts to establish an American resale royalty, its proponents have alternately urged that this be done by contract or through legislation. Interest in the contract alternative, an example of which appears in §6.3.1. *infra*, peaked in the early 1970s when several efforts were made to draft a model sales agreement that would provide to artists — along with several elements of the moral right (see Chapter 5) — the equivalent of a *droit de suite*. These drafts were put forward in the hope that they would either win a wide popular acceptance through moral suasion or, failing that, that artists would band together (in essence, unionize) to enforce their use by boycotting any other terms of sale.

The most widely circulated of these draft agreements was one prepared by Robert Projansky, a New York City lawyer. First published in 1971, it included an explanatory preface by Seth Siegelaub[1] — an art dealer and consultant who had involved himself as an advocate of the artists — which suggested why (in those anarchic days of Kent State and the Vietnam war protests) some of its sponsors considered the contractual approach more desirable than legislation. This route, wrote Mr. Siegelaub, involved "no organization, no dues, no government agency, no meetings, no public registration, no nothing — just your [i.e., the artist's] will to use it."[2]

Projansky's draft, sonorously titled *The Artist's Reserved Rights Transfer and Sale Agreement,* found only sporadic use. Its principal flaw was a condition to which virtually no purchaser — not even one otherwise prepared to pay the artist a "royalty" of 15 percent of the gross profit on the first resale of the work — would agree: that the only way a subject work of art could be resold (or otherwise transferred) was on condition that the original purchaser not only pay such a "royalty" but also guarantee that any subsequent purchasers (or other transferees) would enter into the same agreement. Any other form of transfer (including, specifically, by death!) would leave the original purchaser (or his estate) liable to a claim for damages. What the *Reserved Rights Transfer and Sale Agreement* contemplated was a chain of privity that would connect the artist to every subsequent owner and that would run not only for the artist's life but also for the lifetime of any surviving spouse and then for still another 21 years. This last link in the chain, Siegelaub explained, was to take care of any last-minute minor children.

In 1974, Projansky released a second draft of this agreement. Although simpler and briefer — the length was cut by half — this new edition nonetheless perpetuated what had been the chief difficulty of the earlier version: the burden placed on each purchaser to bind every subsequent purchaser to the "royalty" terms of the original agreement.[3] Recognizing this as the major stumbling block to any widespread adoption of Projansky's approach, Charles Jurrist — also a New York City lawyer — had meanwhile begun work on a different form of agreement that would, as he described it, "secure a somewhat more modest package

---

§6.1. [1] The 1971 Projansky Agreement with explanatory preface by Seth Siegelaub may be found in F. Feldman & S. Weil, Art Works: Law, Policy, Practice 81-94 (1974).

[2] *Id.* at 89.

[3] The 1974 draft may be found in L. D. Duboff, The Deskbook of Art Law, Appendix at 1138 (1977).

of rights for the artist." The Jurrist agreement, with explanation, is reproduced in §6.3.1 *infra*. While it continued Projansky's imposition of a
15 percent "royalty" on any gross resale profit — regardless of whether
or not any *net* profit was derived from the transaction — this payment
applied only to the first resale. Importantly, there was no provision
requiring the original purchaser to guarantee that a subsequent owner
bind himself to the same agreement.

§6.1.3. Legislative Alternatives

Whatever its merits, however, the Jurrist agreement was almost
wholly forgotten when the alternative, which generally had been considered remote, suddenly became a dazzling reality: that every artist, immediately, could be assured a "resale royalty" by legislative fiat instead of
one at a time through voluntary contract. In 1976, the state of California
unexpectedly enacted a resale royalties act, the first such law in the
United States. The California Act, a challenge to it on constitutional
grounds, and commentary on federal *droit de suite* legislation, is the topic
of §6.4 *infra*.

Although there had been several efforts to encourage such legislation
in the late 1950s, the first real impetus came from Diana B. Schulder's
1966 article *Art Proceeds Act: A Study of the "Droit de Suite" and a Proposed
Enactment for the United States.*[4]

The rationale for such legislation was that visual artists did not benefit
as did other types of creators, such as authors or composers, who derived
royalties from either the reproduction or performances of their work.
Closely examined, however, this implied parallel between visual artists
and other creators turns out not to be a parallel at all. While each additional copy of an author's book (or every performance of a composer's
composition) can be said to enlarge his total "output" — and thereby
serve as justification for additional compensation — the same cannot be
said of the successive resales of a work of art. What began as one painting
remains one painting. Whether still in the hands of its original purchaser
or sold and resold a dozen times, its theoretical fair market value at any
point will be the same. Given this, there seems no logic in the argument
that an artist should receive over time a greater economic benefit from a
painting that is periodically sold and resold than he should from one that
remains in the hands of its original purchaser. Such an analysis notwithstanding, this argument won a wide and sympathetic audience among

---

[4] 61 Nw. U.L. Rev. 19 (1966).

artists' rights advocates. It was one such advocate, State Senator Alan Sieroty, who introduced and engineered the quick passage of the California royalty law in 1976.

In structure, the California law steers an odd course among its various European prototypes. In common with the French and German laws, its 5 percent impost applies to the gross amount of a covered sale. In this, it stands in sharp contrast to other laws (those of Italy, Czechoslovakia, and Poland, for example) where the charge on any sale is levied (much like a capital gains tax) only against the increase in value since the previous sale. On the other hand, *unlike* the French and German laws, the California statute applies only to sales when the gross sales price is not less than the seller's previous purchase price. As with the Projansky and Jurrist agreements, this applies regardless of whether there is any *net* profit. The overall result is a series of anomalies. A painting originally purchased for $1,000 and resold for $10,000 would provide the artist with a royalty of $500; a painting originally purchased for $100,000 and resold for exactly the same amount would provide the artist with a royalty of $5,000; a painting originally purchased for the same $100,000 but resold for $99,000 would give the artist nothing.

Disturbed by what they felt was the precipitous and poorly considered passage of this royalty rights legislation, a group of California collectors and dealers undertook a lawsuit to test its validity. In *Morseburg v. Balyon* they claimed that the California statute violated both the contract and due process clauses of the U.S. Constitution. They also argued that it dealt with a matter that had been preempted by the federal 1909 Copyright Act. The court opinion, in which the Act was upheld, is reproduced in this chapter. On a final appeal in 1980 to the U.S. Supreme Court, certiorari was denied.

The protest against the California statute did, however, have several practical results. As originally drafted, it applied to sales by a dealer who had purchased a work directly from the artist. This has now been changed, as has the provision requiring payment to artists not living in the United States.

Emboldened by their success in California, the proponents of resale royalties moved quickly— even as the *Morseburg* case was working its way through the courts — to secure comparable legislation elsewhere. Bills to establish resale royalties were actually introduced into the legislatures of New York, Pennsylvania, and Ohio. In other states, notably Florida and Texas, the lobbying machinery was prepared for similar efforts. All these initiatives paled, however, against the awesome possibility that they might be able to secure federal legislation to create a national resale royalty.

In 1977, Congressman Waxman — whose home district overlapped that of State Senator Sieroty, the progenitor of the California act — agreed to sponsor such federal legislation. Assured at the beginning that there would be general art-world consensus favoring its passage, Congressman Waxman's staff was astonished by the vigorous opposition that almost immediately surfaced. California collectors and dealers — citing the haste and virtual secrecy in which they felt their own royalty act had been adopted — were particularly vocal. By 1978, when the legislation was finally introduced in the House — Congressmen Frederick Richmond of New York and Robert Drinan of Massachusetts served as its co-sponsors — Congressman Waxman had backed away from it by a considerable distance. In his introductory remarks, he suggested to his colleagues that they should proceed deliberately. A suitable preliminary step, he said, might perhaps be a study of the art market to understand what effect such legislation would actually have. He cautioned, however, that nothing should be rushed. Congressman Waxman's remarks appear in this chapter. The bill went to committee, where it died, and Congressman Waxman has since made no effort to revive it. Also dead — or at least, long quiet — are the various initiatives that were launched at the state level.[5]

Currently, the California resale royalty legislation still stands, but it stands alone. And so it may remain, as the practical implications of a *droit de suite* or similar right become better understood by the American art community.

The practical economic effect of a resale rights statute is the topic of §6.5 *infra*. A resale royalty does not bring any new money into the system. At best, it only redistributes the money already there. While it could undoubtedly provide some additional income for a small number of better-known artists, most commentators agree that it is probably from the lesser-known artists rather than from collectors or dealers that this additional income would be drawn.[6] As Monroe Price and Aimée Brown

---

[5] Resale rights legislation was recently reintroduced in New York; the future of the bill appears uncertain, given that as of this writing it had been languishing in committee since February 1985. See also §6.4.4 n.1 *infra*.

[6] See, for example, M. Asimow, Economic Aspects of the Droit de Suite, originally published in Legal Rights of the Artist (M. Nimmer ed. 1971), and reprinted in J. H. Merryman & A. E. Elsen 4-124 (1979); Bolch, Damon & Hinshaw, An Economic Analysis of the California Art Royalty Statute, 10 Conn. L.R. 689 (Spring 1978), reproduced at §6.5.1 *infra*; and Glucksman, Art Resale Royalties: Symbolic or Economic Relief for the Fine Artist, 1 Cardozo Arts & Entertain. L.J. 115 (Spring 1982).

Price concluded in the article reproduced in the next section, after examining the French *droit de suite* in operation, "to those who have shall more be given."

§6.2. The European Perspective

§6.2.1. The French Experience and Early American Doubts

Following Diana B. Schulder's 1966 proposal of an American *droit de suite*, the following article was prepared by the lawyer/art historian team of Monroe E. Price and Aimée Brown Price as an examination of how this concept worked in Europe and whether it might be applicable in the United States.

PRICE & PRICE, RIGHT OF ARTISTS: THE CASE OF THE *DROIT DE SUITE*
31 Art J. 144 (Winter 1971-72)

In that law of art, as in art itself, we innocents often look abroad for instruction. That process has been taking place with respect to the *droit de suite*, an addition to the copyright laws of France, Italy, and Germany, among other nations. Usually translated as an "art proceeds right," the *droit de suite* is a technique designed to furnish artists with a portion of the increase in the value of their works when they are resold. Sometimes, as in France, a flat fee is payable to the artist or his heirs on the public resale of all paintings, and the fee must be paid whether the painting rises in price or not. In Italy, on the other hand, the artist is entitled to a *droit de suite* only on the increase in value of the work of art. The techniques used differ with respect to the resale covered (auctions, dealer, or private), the percentage of the resale price the artist obtains (three per cent in France, one per cent in Germany), the minimum price the object must bring before the mechanism is brought into play at all, and the length of time during which the mechanism operates (sometimes the life of the artist plus 50 years).

The *droit de suite* springs from certain assumptions about the relationship between society and its artists, particularly painters and sculptors, and from a belief that the artist does not receive a fair price for his work. The current demand in the United States for an art proceeds right is buttressed by allegations that copyright schemes, including currently proposed revisions, do not provide just compensation for most painters and sculptors as compared, for example, with authors. It is also based on changes in the way artists look at their continuing property interests in their own work. This essay examines the assumptions underlying the *droit de suite*, tests their validity in the American context, and explores alternatives to an art proceeds right to determine if they better comport with the American temperament, the American art market, and the needs of American artists.

THE THEOLOGY OF THE *DROIT DE SUITE*

The *droit de suite* evolved, in large part, from a not wholly accurate but widely-held conception of art, the artist, and the way art is sold. At its core is a vision of the starving artist, with his genius unappreciated, using his last pennies to purchase canvas and pigments which he turns into a misunderstood masterpiece. The painting is sold for a pittance, probably to buy medicine for a tubercular wife. The purchaser is a canny investor who travels about artists' hovels trying to pick up bargains which he will later turn into large amounts of cash. Thirty years later the artist is still without funds and his children are in rags; meanwhile his paintings, now the subject of a Museum of Modern Art retrospective and a Harry Abrams parlor-table book, fetch small fortunes at Parke-Bernet and Christie's. The rhetoric of the *droit de suite* is built on this peculiar understanding of the artist and the art market. It is the product of a lovely wistfulness for the nineteenth century with the pure artist starving in his garret, unappreciated by a philistine audience and doomed to poverty because of the stupidity of the world at large. The *droit de suite* is *La Bohême* and *Lust for Life* reduced to statutory form. It is an expression of the belief that

(1) the sale of the artist's work at anything like its "true" value only comes late in his life or after his death;
(2) the postponement in value is attributable to the lag in popular understanding and appreciation;
(3) therefore the artist is subsidizing the public's education with his poverty;
(4) this is an unfair state of affairs;
(5) the artist should profit when he is finally discovered by the newly sophisticated market.

Despite the rewards our society provides those who rebel and innovate, the romantic image of the poor artist continues to dominate public thought. One reason for this fixation is suggested by Geraldine Pelles:

[T]he artist's intense commitment to a precarious occupation seems a counterbalance to the leveling of aspiration in the society of the Organization Man; he is regarded as one of the few who uphold values that others profess but negate in their work. Despite economic embarrassment, the artist seems to wield unpurchasable power as he manipulates an environment in the world of his painting.

Moreover, the romantic idea has been as important to artists as it has been to the audience for art. Poverty or its semblance, is a uniform which distinguishes the artist from his bourgeois audience. Lack of money is a celebration of sorts. Part of the burden of being a prophet in a philistine society is the burden of being misunderstood and neglected.

Society, it is thought, must pay for its thickheadedness; the artist should not support the entire maturing process. The *droit de suite* is exactly this kind of penance. It is a tax on the second generation for the lack of perception of its fathers. Or, more charitably, the *droit de suite* assumes that the current generation is as blind to the virtues of contemporary artists as the preceding generation was to its avant-garde. If each group post-pays, then some justice will ensue. Painters still may not get rich while they are painting — that is consonant with the romantic view of creation — but their retirement years will be more secure and their wives and children will have some profit. The special virtue of the *droit de suite* is that with one thrust it preserves the struggling artist, starving in his garret, while it salves society's conscience by paying a token to him or his estate when it finally recognizes the quality of his work. A weakness of the *droit de suite* is the narrow time span over which it operates as compared with the time it takes artistic taste to mature. If it is penance society is doing, and it is paying the penance within fifty years of the artist's death, then fashion must mature or begin to mature within that time. But it has not always been the case, even in this accelerated century, that the inflation in art values attaches to work painted in the twilight years of an artist's life or within fifty years after his death. If Impressionism or Post-Impressionism is the rage in the 1920's and after, then the model works, if creakingly. But when the fashion in 1970 becomes Rippl-Ronai, or the Ashcan school, or Vorticism, the *droit de suite* has little of the desired effect. In other words, if living artists are recognized during their productive period, the *droit de suite* is unnecessary; if they become fashionable more than fifty afters after their death, it is irrelevant. Thus the *droit de suite* model is confined to a special type of art market.

Legislation is also deemed necessary by advocates of the *droit de suite* because artists are seen at an inherent disadvantage in bargaining. There is the same motive for the *droit de suite* as for consumer protection laws or support of the trust responsibility exercised by the federal government over American Indians. Artists are children of trust.

The *droit de suite* is also an emblem of a society which has changed its view of the artist's role in the creation and destiny of his work. Around 1500 Isabella d'Este instructed Perugino to the minute detail in the program for a mural, including the size of the figures. The artist-executor was "free to make fewer (figures), but not to add anything else." Such arrangements were frequent when artists were viewed as skilled craftsmen. But times changed. Whistler wrote in 1900 of the ". . . ABSO-

LUTE RIGHT [his capitals] of the Artist to control the destiny of his handiwork—and, at all times, and in all circumstances, to refuse its delivery into unseemly and ridiculous keeping." The relationship between the artist and his work is largely a product of the cultural ambience; and whether a work of art is at all valued is a matter, of course, that varies from place to place.

Our own times are closer to Whistler's than to Perugino's. The artist's product ought not to be treated by the legal rules governing the transfer of mundane chattels — a chair, a lump of clay. The interest and concern of the artist in his work often should not end with the sale of the physical object; the law can recognize this fact. What happens to the work in terms of its resale, in terms of its treatment, in terms of its availability for exhibition is of profound and rightful concern to the artist. The notion of a *droit de suite* is compatible with our sense of the relationship between the artist and the collector.

THE *DROIT DE SUITE* IN CONTEXT

Proposals for an art proceeds right have a ring of neutrality. But it is impossible for the government to be wholly uninfluential in its effect on the artist's product, depending on the way the statute is constructed. Seemingly the market decides where the rewards will be. The state is a mere policeman. This neutral pose betrays a false modesty. To the extent that the *droit de suite* is effective, it is an incentive to produce work that can and will be resold. Besides, the extent to which an artist (and, when generalized, a whole school or generation of artists) will benefit from the *droit de suite* depends largely on the kind of work he creates: whether it is monumental sculpture or easel painting, auto-da-fé or laminated for preservation, whether, in fact, it is salable at all, too fragile to endure, or so massive that resales are unlikely.

The coverage of the *droit de suite* is usually limited to unique works of art like painting and sculpture. It is possible, however, that the concept of an "original" work itself is misleading and that artists are currently moving away from such concrete and unique embodiments of their creative conception. If fewer and fewer artists rely on something that resembles a masterpiece in oil for their livelihood, then the *droit de suite* loses significance as a tool for economic reward. Of course, the fact that an increasing number of artists may be producing multiple reproductions does not mean that the painter of an original oil should be stripped of art proceeds protection because his work is not produced in numerous copies like a book. But in assessing the even-handedness of the *droit de suite*, one must also take into account the increasing acceptance of the separation of invention from execution (or, indeed, of ending the process with invention). The artist formulates a project which others execute. The "original" may be a blueprint, a set of sketches and instructions to the craftsmen or even the promise of accepting bids for the yet undisclosed idea for a project. The tendency of artists to produce works of monumental scale also diminishes the force of the art proceeds right; such artists often wilfully reject a potential market by producing work that is so large or so expensive as to defy the likelihood of sale or resale.

The distribution system for works of art is as important in determining the relevance of the *droit de suite* model to the American art market as are issues of style. However the *droit de suite* is applied and enforced, there must be transactions which are more or less public. In France, the *droit de suite* is only applicable to resale at auction.* Such a rule in America would make an art proceeds benefit virtually useless since in this country auctions are a comparatively unimportant locus of sale and resale. Because of sale of works is more decentralized here than elsewhere, the art proceeds rights would be harder to enforce.

The workability of the *droit de suite* would also be affected by what appears to be the declining role of galleries, at least in the traditional sense, in the representation of artists and the sale of works of art. Works of art are now apparently held by single owners for longer spans of time. And the increase in the number of museum and corporate purchasers, and in purchases by the government, mean that a larger number of paintings will be held indefinitely by single purchasers making a *droit de suite* inapplicable.

As a tool for increasing the economic security of artists, the *droit de suite* suffers from a fatal dependence on the resale of works of art. Works have to change hands during the artist's lifetime for the copyright period to benefit him or his family. The likelihood that a painting or sculpture will change hands within the copyright period is small — though not meaningless — particularly if gifts and non-profit transactions are not included. Using *Art Prices Annual* reports for three years, some notion of the sales at auction of work subject to the *droit de suite* can be obtained.

	1963-1964	1964-1965	1965-1966
Total number of artists whose work was sold	1144	1261	1431
Number of artists living at the time of sale (percentage of all artists whose work was sold that year)	145 (13)	179 (14)	164 (12)
Artists dead less than 50 years before sale (percentage of all artists whose work was sold that year)	229 (20)	264 (21)	315 (22)

* [The *droit de suite* in France has been extended to cover sales by dealers, as well as auction sales. — Eds.]

What do these sales mean in terms of benefits to the artists? A few are rewarded handsomely; the proceeds for the rest are minimal. A 1964 report on the administration of the French *droit de suite* summarized the distribution for three years: one-fourth of the funds to living artists (about 15,000 francs) went to 10 artists; the rest went to 306. Among artists who were dead at the time of sale, the beneficiaries of 40 received 135,000 francs; beneficiaries of the remaining 174 received about the same amount. As is true in other contexts, to those who have shall more be given.

For all the hope and interest, there is good reason to believe that the assumptions underlying the *droit de suite,* based as they are on romantic nineteenth-century notions about the artist in society, are not valid in the United States. As a consequence, the charitable motive for an art proceeds right loses something of its emotional strength. This is not to say that young artists are prosperous, or that excellence is immediately appreciated, but that several factors have changed the relationship between the artist and society in a way which makes an art proceeds right less fitting than other means of protecting the artists and less necessary than it might have been at an earlier time. The "discovery" of the Impressionists and Post-Impressionists in the early twentieth century has altered patterns of acquisition by individuals and museums. Partly as a result of the surge in values in late nineteenth century non-academic work, collectors, galleries, and museums have hedged against the future by buying works of artists when they are less well-known and less expensive. This hedging operation has created a greater market for the lesser-known avant-garde artist thus leveling out the prices for his work over his lifetime. Finally, the value of a *droit de suite,* particularly as a way of contributing to the economic security of artists, can only be measured in relation to other techniques designed to accomplish the same objectives.

CONTRACTUAL ARRANGEMENTS

Convention and custom are often great barriers to change and we often look to legislation as a way of sweeping them away. But increased sophistication in contractual arrangements is a route to change which avoids some of the pitfalls and rigidities of legislation. There are few contracts now between artist and collector, or between institutions and artists. The Los Angeles County Museum's recent "Art and Technology" show is indicative. At great effort and expense, industries were cajoled into investing large amounts of money in the creation of interesting new works. The artists made sizeable commitments of time. The project was intricate in conception and execution. Yet, in the end, the rights to the work and control over their disposition remain unclear in several instances.

The range of issues which are or could be subjects for negotiation is quite large. The most obvious is reproduction rights. To the degree that the receipt of royalties makes a painter more like an author, such rights are a supplement to the *droit de suite*. Under American law, except in New York, the sale of the object carries with it the sale of the common law copyright unless the copyright is expressly retained.[†] That simple action, retaining the copyright, is taken by some artists and dealers, but extremely few. In some cases the dealer retains the copyright allowing him to make reproductions in the future without compensating the artist. There is some indication that museums would resist purchasing objects without purchasing copyrights, but such resistance would probably crumble in the face of demands by artists for their copyright rights. Indeed, museums have been known to embrace special conditions of a far more exotic nature when they are imposed by contributors.

As long as the artist retains ownership and possession of the work itself, he necessarily maintains control over its exhibition. Thus he can loan his work to others for exhibition to the public, and can, in certain cases, obtain compensation. Without bargaining, the right to obtain works for exhibit will almost certainly be lost. It is true that collectors are usually anxious to have their work exhibited; but contracts are drafted to take account of the unlikely and eccentric as well as the predictable.

A similar potential right of the artist relates to subsequent use of the work. Because the work of art is considered unique and because the painter or sculptor must rely on the continued existence and integrity of the work to exploit his other rights, there may be an implicit right in the artist to enjoin the distortion or ruin of his painting or sculpture. Although such a right is recognized in France (*droit moral*), there is again little case law to suggest whether it is also recognized in the United States.[*]

Other subjects for bargaining include *dealer practices*. The way in which the dealer deploys his budget has serious consequences for the artist. Changes in the advertising budget, the decision to keep a gallery open, the guarantee of exhibition, the turnover in shows — freedom in all these respects is permitted the dealer because he maintains his stock without strings. Few other dealers who have exclusive arrangements with suppliers can act with such immunity from supplier sanctions.

---

† [Section 202 of the Copyright Revision Act of 1976, enacted after the writing of this article, reverses this presumption and makes the transfer of ownership of the material object distinct from the conveyance of the copyright in the object. — Eds.]

* [Since the writing of this article, California, New York, and Massachusetts have adopted moral rights legislation; Maine has adopted a moral rights resolution. For a full discussion of *droit moral* in the United States, see Chapter 5. — Eds.]

When an artist agrees to be represented exclusively by a gallery he makes certain assumptions which might be articulated and made explicit in a contract for representation: for example, that there will be a maintenance of the existing advertising budget or that it will increase at a certain percentage each year. Also there could be a guarantee to certain artists who are represented that there will be one-man shows each 12 months and gallery group shows once a year. Two frequent complaints are that artists lose track of their work or fear that the gallery will be slow to pay them. Certain contractual techniques might alleviate these complaints. Artists could require that the gallery maintain, in an accessible place and at the gallery's expense, a registry of all work on hand by artists. This central file would be open to the artist for his inspection at set times. Artists could also require that a penalty clause be inserted which would add five per cent to the monies due for each three month delay in submitting payment.*

The art proceeds right concentrates on the immediate financial interest an artist has in the fate of his work. But various non-financial controls may be more important to the artist's welfare. For example, an artist has a great stake in the manner his work is displayed by the dealer. At present, the dealer has complete discretion over the placement of paintings within the gallery. If the gallery does not have shows, or reserves a section of the gallery for selections from artists represented, some assurance can be built into the contract that there be regular display of each artist's work of art. Furthermore, the artist may require the dealer to impose certain exhibition obligations on the purchaser, such as making the works available for display in museum shows. The artist might demand the right to limit the number of times a painting could be loaned and the duration of each loan. The artist might wish to exercise some censorship over the occasions on which his work is exhibited; there are related rights similar to the "moral rights" which exist in France and many other countries. The artist may wish to exercise contractual control over modifications of the work of art, such as changing its colors so that it will be a better match for the owner's furniture and wallpaper. The artist may seek contractual assurance that the purchaser will not mutilate or destroy the painting or that the purchaser will adequately protect the work, periodically relining it, for example, or the artist may even demand that the work be destroyed in a certain number of years.

Clearly, one of the harshest blows for artists occurs when a gallery decides to close. The artist may wish to protect himself by obtaining some

_____

* [For a discussion of artist-art dealer consignment statutes, governing to some extent the relationship between artist and dealer (and, for the most part, enacted after the writing of this article), see §3.2 *supra*. — Eds.]

assurance in his contract with the dealer that the gallery will continue to operate. For the artist, the choice of dealer is extremely important; his tie to one agent may foreclose other arrangements. He becomes closely identified with a certain market and certain purchasers. For him, the dealer's decision to close can be quite cruel. It may mean he has to find another dealer, which may be difficult, or fend for himself, which may be impossible. What protection is there? First, there ought to be a notice requirement. A contract could provide that a dealer must give at least three months notice before he closes up shop. This would give the artists involved some opportunity to persuade the dealer to change his mind, to encourage some quick additional financing, or to make other arrangements. Second, the artists may have some interest in the liquidation of the gallery's assets. In a sense, the artists have become quasi-partners; their continuous subsidy and investments in frames, materials, etc., have been a substantial factor in the gallery's financing. The artists may have considerable interest in the mailing list of the gallery and other records that may permit them to continue the business. They certainly have an interest in their paintings and in the gallery's accounts receivable, at least to the extent that their commissions depend on the monthly installment payments by the purchasers of their paintings. In sum, the contract with the gallery can provide for rights on liquidation. Because of custom, lack of experience, and a feeling of powerlessness, private contractual techniques for future participation in the increase in value in a work of art have not yet been adequately tested.

POWERLESSNESS AND CHANGE

Because of the strong influence of custom in the contractual practices of the parties, very few artists have given consideration to fashioning different arrangements with their dealers or ultimate customers. There are various explanations for the pervasive impact of existing practices. First, although it is a popular pastime for artists to complain about their dealers, they do not normally conceive of the need for intermediaries between them and the dealers. An analogy from the motion picture industry is apt: a show business personality does not depend on his producer or exhibitor to look out for his or her best interests; he hires an agent who negotiates the contract for exhibition. The agent tests the market for flexibility in various aspects of the producer-personality arrangement, bargains for better billing, for a different form of compensation and for artistic control over the end product. He is able to force the producer to differentiate among the various performers he employs. For better or for worse, the art dealer performs the role of exhibitor and agent. He may have short or long range interests that are different from and even conflict with those of the artist; he may be less concerned than the artist would be with increasing the artist's control over the use and disposition of a work of art that has left dealer through a sales transaction. For the dealer, enforcing the art proceeds right and coping with the sales resistance it creates only causes headaches. Similarly, any conditions imposed on the sale which lead to limitations on usage or requirements of display restrict the market.

A second theology relates to the "power" of artists. Many of the participants in the process think that artists and sculptors could not get changes in their arrangements even if they so desired. As a consequence, they give little thought to the form change might take. The prophecy of powerlessness is self-fulfilling. The various movements, dating from WPA and still lingering in the shape of artists' cooperative associations, have exceedingly little force in the marketplace. Indeed, the feeling of powerlessness extends to the point that even powerful individual artists do not exercise their strength, although it appears that they could exact such benefits as an art proceeds right, reproduction rights, exhibition rights and others. There seems to be no recorded instance of collective action which has changed the policies of a dealer, gallery, or local market. The attempts to exercise power have either been on an individual basis, or on a mass basis, like the Artists Equity movement. Part of the reason is that a large number of artists, including artists that have a certain reputation and power in the market, have only a fragmented idea of the sorts of matters they could negotiate about with their dealers. And even if the art proceeds right became a matter of negotiation, it would almost certainly be in the context of other sorts of contractual provisions which would furnish a spectrum of techniques of enhancing the economic security of the artist and the dealer.

Much is made of the inconvenience that attends retained reproduction rights. One way out is the method employed by the American Society of Composers, Authors and Publishers (ASCAP) — policing public performances of music; however, this is extremely expensive and would be suitable for artists only when reproductions become widespread and policing worth the cost. Other methods are less burdensome. For example, it is contended that retention of reproduction rights would create too much bother and confusion for people who wanted to reproduce the painting. But even now the reproducer must check with someone, normally the owner of the painting or the museum before he copies the work. Museums normally require that the reproducer establish a credit line as do collectors, although museums often waive any charge. An artist could require that the museum collect a certain fee for reproduction, perhaps geared to the size of the publication. At first, until it is clear how such a system would work, the artist could relieve the private collector or the museum from liability for non-collection of the royalty, leaving the arrangement up to the bona fides of the owner of the painting.

CONCLUSION

What do these changes in style and the marketing of art imply for government policy? First and most important, there is a need for vast improvement in the operation of the marketplace. The artist, ignorant of his rights, saddled with the concept of powerlessness, has by no means explored the limits of his contractual arrangements with dealer and purchaser. The government can play a crucial role in eliminating this informational gap. Just as the Department of Agriculture and the Small Business Administration do in their areas, some governmental agency, perhaps the National Endowment on the Arts, should provide technical assistance to artists and sculptors. Such technical assistance would include information about the income tax — in particular allowable deductions — information about new materials and new processes, information about the great variety of bargaining relationships among artists and dealers, information about firms that would reproduce their art, and information about new markets for works of art. At present, most artists, whether they are trained at universities, colleges or art schools, emerge with only the barest idea of any of these matters. They are saved from poverty by the general, though declining, level of prosperity in the nation. An educational role may seem trivial to a government that is better organized to pass a statute than to implement a policy, but it could be extremely worthwhile. Second, the government should expand the market for works of art, particularly contemporary American paintings and sculpture. The government can do this by increasing its own purchases of art or increasing, by regulation, the investment in works of art by others. The program of purchasing American art for embassies abroad might be extended to federal offices in this country. The policy of requiring a small percentage of public construction funds to be spent on murals, paintings, and sculpture should be more rigorously fostered and administered. Greater federal encouragement, particularly through the State Commissions on the Arts, should yield increased buying of contemporary works by state and municipal governments. The National Endowment for the Arts can encourage more elaborate aesthetic zoning, more parks and public places with room for sculpture gardens, better tax breaks for office buildings which are exemplars of good, rather than horrid, taste. The Endowment should explore in great depth the way in which the private art market presently functions and how current trends may modify the income patterns of various schools of American artists. More information is necessary about who the new purchasers are; whether individual collectors, corporate collectors or museums predominate; what is the extent of the market for paintings at various price levels; and what is the capability of the dealers to ferret out new markets for the artists they represent. Fourth, the government should explore and develop new avenues of participation for artists in architecture and city planning so that novel forms of creative expression have compensating outlets. In part this may involve subsidizing production facilities which require extraordinary capital outlays.

The *droit de suite* cannot function as the cornerstone of federal planning. The fashioning of government policy in the area of the arts is difficult enough without the additional paralysis of reliance on outmoded ideas of the production and distribution of art. The rude intrusion of technology into the craft of the parlor and the rampant extension of the artistic imagination is rendering obsolete such notions as "paintings," "originals," "authentic." The shape of the demand profile is also changing. The practices of periodic resales and passing works of art from generation to generation are growing less significant as institutional, government, and corporate buying begin to become a greater proportion of the market. The pervasive idea of distinguishing between books and paintings must fade somewhat as the market for reproductions doubles and redoubles. What is most clear is that the government cannot define its policy on the basis of a nineteenth century view — or any fixed view — of the art market at a time when standards, and styles, and methods of sale are so quickly changing. That is the plague of the *droit de suite*. True, it offers a small solution to the problems of some painters. Yet the administrative problems it produces would probably outweigh its benefits and the government could better direct its energy in channels calculated to improve the economic security of the artist. In terms of its articulated goals, the *droit de suite* rewards the wrong painters with probably inconsequential amounts of money at the wrong times in their lives.

§6.3. THE CONTRACTUAL APPROACH: A VALIANT EFFORT

The agreement (with its accompanying explanation) that follows was prepared by the New York City lawyer Charles Jurrist in the mid-1970s as a sort of last-gasp effort to salvage a contractual *droit de suite*. It was never widely employed, presumably because its terms were unpalatable to collectors. For a review of its history, see §6.1 *supra*.

C. JURRIST, FORM OF AGREEMENT BETWEEN ARTIST AND COLLECTOR

The following contract is loosely based on an earlier, and by now well-known contract which was prepared by Robert Projansky, Esq. Many of Mr. Projansky's ideas and some of his actual provisions are included. However, the present contract seeks to respond to an apparent need for a simpler and more practicable contract which achieves many of the results toward which the Projansky contract addressed itself. To the best of our ability, we have attempted to use clear and forthright language, and to avoid, to the greatest extent possible, internal cross-references.

Practical experience has shown that the vast majority of collectors are extremely reluctant to submit to any continuing contractual obligations to the artists from whom they purchase works of art; almost none, to our knowledge, have been willing to execute the Projansky contract as written. This contract would, we believe, achieve wider acceptance because it both seeks to secure a somewhat more modest package of rights for the artist, and it provides certain safeguards for the collector which direct experience has shown make the contract more palatable to collectors. The most important difference between this contract and the Projansky version is that this contract seeks to secure a royalty for the artist only on the first resale of the work. This eliminates the immensely complicated system of ongoing contracts envisioned by Projansky and it makes the contract substantially more acceptable to the collector in that it does not restrict the salability of the work. Under the Projansky system, the collector was entitled to sell only to a purchaser who would himself enter into a new contract with the artist.

Even in this reduced form, we do not expect that any substantial number of collectors will be willing to enter into such a contract. We do believe, however, that this contract represents a realistic starting point from which the artist may negotiate a package of contractual rights with the collector; he may have to agree to alter some of the provisions or even to omit some entirely. Nonetheless, any ongoing contractual obligation by the collector to the artist represents an advance over the state of affairs that has prevailed in the art world. For example, collectors have shown a willingness to contract to give artists the borrowing, restoration and reproduction rights which are set forth in this document.

Charles Jurrist

AGREEMENT, made this ____ day of _____ 19___, between _____ (hereinafter referred to as the "Artist"), residing at _____, and _____ (hereinafter referred to as the "Collector"), residing at _____ _____.

WITNESSETH:

WHEREAS the Artist has created a certain work of art (hereinafter referred to as the "Work"), which is fully described in Paragraph 1 below; and

WHEREAS the Collector desires to purchase the Work from the Artist and the Artist is willing to sell the Work to the Collector upon the terms set forth in this Agreement and not otherwise,

NOW, THEREFORE, in consideration of the mutual promises set forth in this Agreement, as well as other good and valuable consideration, the receipt of which is hereby mutually acknowledged, the parties do hereby covenant and agree as follows:

1. *The Transaction.* The Artist hereby sells to the Collector, and the Collector hereby purchases from the Artist, for a total price of $_____, the Work, which is described and identified as follows:

Medium: _____

Dimensions: _____

Title: _____

Date (or approximate period of creation): _____

Size of edition: _____

2. *Edition and Provenance.* (a) Unless otherwise indicated in the space "Size of edition" in Paragraph 1 of this Agreement, the Work is unique. If the Work is unique, the Artist hereby covenants that he shall not produce any exact duplicate of the Work; if the Work is one of an edition, the Artist hereby covenants that the size of the edition shall not be increased after the date of execution of this Agreement.

(b) Upon receipt of a written request from the Collector, the Artist shall provide the Collector with a written statement attesting to the authenticity of the Work and setting forth the size of the edition, if any, of which the Work is a part.

3. *Care of Work.* (a) So long as the Work remains in the Collector's possession, the Collector covenants to exercise reasonable care in maintaining the Work and further covenants not intentionally to alter or destroy the Work.

(b) If the Work is damaged in any manner, the Collector shall notify the Artist of the occurrence and the nature of the damage and shall afford the Artist a reasonable opportunity to conduct, or to supervise, the restoration of the Work.

(c) If the Artist does not take steps to commence the restoration of the Work within thirty (30) days after receipt of notice of damage from the Collector, the Collector shall be free to make whatever arrangements he deems appropriate for the restoration of the Work.

(d) Nothing contained in this Paragraph 3 shall be construed to require that the Collector cause or permit the Work to be moved from the place where it is usually kept in order to allow the Artist to conduct, or to supervise, its restoration.

4. *Artist's Right to Borrow.* (a) The Artist reserves the right, upon giving

the Collector reasonable notice of his intention to do so, to borrow the Work from the Collector in order to include it in a public exhibition of the Artist's works. The Collector shall have the right, before permitting the Artist to borrow the Work, to demand the submission, by the Artist or by the exhibiting institution, of documents evidencing adequate insurance coverage on the Work and prepayment of shipping charges to and from the exhibiting institution.

(b) The Artist shall not be entitled to borrow the Work more than once in any twelve-month period or for any single period longer than six (6) weeks.

(c) If the Artist borrows the Work for inclusion in a public exhibition, it shall be the Artist's responsibility to ensure that the exhibiting institution identifies the Work as belonging to the Collector.

5. *Notices to Be Supplied by Collector.* (a) If the Collector moves from the address set forth at the opening of this Agreement, he shall promptly notify the Artist of his new address. The Collector shall also promptly notify the Artist of any subsequent changes of address.

(b) If the Collector lends the Work to any museum, gallery, or other institution for purposes of exhibition or otherwise, the Collector shall promptly notify the Artist that the Work has been so lent. If the Work is to be publicly exhibited, such notice shall include the name of the exhibiting institution, the title of the exhibition, the dates of the exhibition, and the name of the curator or other person, if any, in charge of the exhibition.

6. *Reproduction.* (a) The Collector shall be entitled to permit the reproduction of the Work in books, art magazines, and exhibition catalogues, as he shall see fit.

(b) Except as provided in subparagraph (a), the Artist hereby reserves all rights whatsoever to copy or reproduce the Work and the Collector agrees not to permit such reproduction without first securing the written consent of the Artist.

(c) Nothing contained in this Paragraph 6 shall be construed as requiring that the Collector afford access to the Work for purposes of its being photographed, copied, or reproduced.

(d) (There may be inserted here a subparagraph governing the division between Artist and Collector of any fees received for a reproduction of the Work which the Artist authorizes pursuant to 6(b).)

7. *Transfer of Work.* (a) If the Collector, at any time after the execution of this Agreement, sells the Work, he shall pay to the Artist a sum equal to fifteen per cent (15%) of the excess of the gross amount realized from the sale of the Work over the price set forth in Paragraph 1 of this Agreement.

(b) If the Collector, at any time after the execution of this Agreement, exchanges, barters, or trades the Work for another work of art, he shall pay to the Artist a sum equal to fifteen per cent (15%) of the excess of the fair market value of the work of art which he receives over the price set forth in Paragraph 1 of this Agreement.

(c) The Collector may, at any time, donate the Work to a museum and, in the event of such donation, no payment shall be required to be made to the Artist. If, however, at any time after the execution of this Agreement, the Collector donates the Work to any institution other than a museum and takes a tax deduction in respect of such donation, he shall pay to the Artist a sum equal to fifteen per cent (15%) of the excess of the tax deduction so taken over the price set forth in Paragraph 1 of this Agreement.

(d) If the Collector, at any time after the execution of this Agreement, gives or transfers the Work to any person in any manner other than those enumerated in subparagraphs (a) through (c) of this Paragraph 7, he shall pay to the Artist a sum equal to fifteen per cent (15%) of the excess of the fair market value of the Work at the time of such transfer over the price set forth in Paragraph 1 of this Agreement.

8. *Duration and Effect.* This Agreement shall remain in full force and effect until five (5) years after the death of the Artist and shall operate to bind the parties as well as their heirs, legatees, executors, and administrators. However, the obligations imposed upon the Collector by Paragraphs 3(b) and 4 of this Agreement shall terminate immediately upon the death of the Artist.

9. *Construction.* This Agreement shall be construed in accordance with the laws of the State of _____.

10. *Headings.* Paragraph headings have been included in this Agreement solely for purposes of convenience and such headings shall not have legal effect or in any way affect the extent or interpretation of any of the terms of this Agreement

IN WITNESS WHEREOF the parties have signed this Agreement as of the date first above written.

_____
Artist
_____
Collector

§6.4. THE LEGISLATIVE APPROACH

§6.4.1. California Resale Royalties Act: A Lone Statute?

Hurriedly passed in 1976, California's statutory *droit de suite*, which follows, continues to be an American anomaly. Intended to cover both all sales within the state as well as any sales outside the state by California residents, its extraterritorial enforcement appears to be nil.

There are even questions about how widely it is actually observed within California, the difficulty being that artists are often reluctant to sue the collectors on whom they may rely for their livelihoods.

The statute was amended in 1982 to eliminate some of its more extravagant features, such as the conferral of richer benefits on such heavily valued foreign painters and sculptors as Marc Chagall and Henry Moore; California's own artists' works were selling at less lofty prices. The 1982 amendment also permitted artists to appoint agents to collect royalties on their behalf and extended the *droit de suite* for 20 years following the artist's death. This was applicable, however, only to artists who died after January 1, 1983.

CALIFORNIA RESALE ROYALTIES ACT
Cal. Civ. Code §986 (West Supp. 1985)

986. (a) Whenever a work of fine art is sold and the seller resides in California or the sale takes place in California, the seller or the seller's agent shall pay to the artist of such work of fine art or to such artist's agent 5 percent of the amount of such sale. The right of the artist to receive an amount equal to 5 percent of the amount of such sale may be waived only by a contract in writing providing for an amount in excess of 5 percent of the amount of such sale. An artist may assign the right to collect the royalty payment provided by this section to another individual or entity. However, the assignment shall not have the effect of creating a waiver prohibited by this subdivision.

  (1) When a work of fine art is sold at an auction or by a gallery, dealer, broker, museum, or other person acting as the agent for the seller the agent shall withhold 5 percent of the amount of the sale, locate the artist and pay the artist.

  (2) If the seller or agent is unable to locate and pay the artist within 90 days, an amount equal to 5 percent of the amount of the sale shall be transferred to the Arts Council.

  (3) If a seller or the seller's agent fails to pay an artist the amount equal to 5 percent of the sale of a work of fine art by the artist or fails to transfer such amount to the Arts Council, the artist may bring an action for damages within three years after the date of sale or one year after the discovery of the sale, whichever is longer. The prevailing party in any action brought under this paragraph shall be entitled to reasonable attorney fees, in an amount as determined by the court.

  (4) Moneys received by the council pursuant to this section shall be deposited in an account in the Special Deposit Fund in the State Treasury.

(5) The Arts Council shall attempt to locate any artist for whom money is received pursuant to this section. If the council is unable to locate the artist and the artist does not file a written claim for the money received by the council within seven years of the date of sale of the work of fine art, the right of the artist terminates and such money shall be transferred to the council for use in acquiring fine art pursuant to the Art in Public Buildings program set forth in Chapter 2.1 (commencing with Section 15813) of Part 10b of Division 3 of Title 2, of the Government Code.

(6) Any amounts of money held by any seller or agent for the payment of artists pursuant to this section shall be exempt from enforcement of a money judgment by the creditors of the seller or agent.

(7) Upon the death of an artist, the rights and duties created under this section shall inure to his or her heirs, legatees, or personal representative, until the 20th anniversary of the death of the artist. The provisions of this paragraph shall be applicable only with respect to an artist who dies after January 1, 1983.

(b) Subdivision (a) shall not apply to any of the following:

(1) To the initial sale of a work of fine art where legal title to such work at the time of such initial sale is vested in the artist thereof.

(2) To the resale of a work of fine art for a gross sales price of less than one thousand dollars ($1,000).

(3) Except as provided in paragraph (7) of subdivision (a), to a resale after the death of such artist.

(4) To the resale of the work of fine art for a gross sales price less than the purchase price paid by the seller.

(5) To a transfer of a work of fine art which is exchanged for one or more works of fine art or for a combination of cash, other property, and one or more works of fine art where the fair market value of the property exchanged is less than one thousand dollars ($1,000).

(6) To the resale of a work of fine art by an art dealer to a purchaser within 10 years of the initial sale of the work of fine art by the artist to an art dealer, provided all intervening resales are between art dealers.

(7) To a sale of a work of stained glass artistry where the work has been permanently attached to real property and is sold as part of the sale of the real property to which it is attached.

(c) For purposes of this section, the following terms have the following meanings.

(1) "Artist" means the person who creates a work of fine art and who, at the time of resale, is a citizen of the United States, or a resident of the state who has resided in the state for a minimum of two years.

(2) "Fine art" means an original painting, sculpture, or drawing, or an original work of art in glass.

(3) "Art dealer" means a person who is actively and principally engaged in or conducting the business of selling works of fine art for which business such person validly holds a sales tax permit.

(d) This section shall become operative on January 1, 1977, and shall apply to works of fine art created before and after its operative date.

(e) If any provision of this section or the application thereof to any person or circumstance is held invalid for any reason, such invalidity shall not affect any other provisions or applications of this section which can be effected, without the invalid provision or application, and to this end the provisions of this section are severable.

(f) The amendments to this section enacted during the 1981 – 82 Regular Session of the Legislature shall apply to transfers of works of fine art, when created before or after January 1, 1983, that occur on or after that date.

§6.4.2. *Morseburg v. Balyon:* A Constitutional and Copyright Challenge to the California Act

Morseburg, which follows, was a case brought to test the validity of California's *droit de suite*. Litigation costs for the plaintiff (who happened to be president of the Art Dealers Association of Southern California) were underwritten by a group of California dealers and collectors. In 1980, the Court of Appeals for the Ninth Circuit affirmed the lower court's rejection of plaintiff's challenges to the Act on constitutional and copyright grounds. Later that year, the U.S. Supreme Court denied certiorari. With respect to the copyright preemption challenge by *Morseburg*, even though the Court of Appeals found, inter alia, that the 1909 Copyright Act did not preempt the California law, some commentators have questioned whether a different result might result under the Copyright Revision Act of 1976, which was not applicable to the *Morseburg* action.[1]

---

§6.4. [1] One point that was not raised in the *Morseburg* litigation, and does not appear to have been discussed in the *droit de suite* dialogues (or treated in the form agreements that grew out of them), is a related principle applicable to the transfer of real property. More than one hundred years ago the New York Court of Appeals held in the leading case of DePeyster v. Michael, 6 N.Y. 467 (1852), that in a lease of land *in fee*, a condition that the grantee shall not transfer or sell the property without paying a sum of money to the grantor was an unlawful restraint on alienation, and therefore void. Said the court,

It was also said on the argument, that the quarter sale money, being reserved in the lease, was not the money of the lessee, but the money of the purchaser who buys from the lessee. If there be any force of this objection, it must rest on the ground that the

MORSEBURG v. BALYON

621 F.2d 972 (9th Cir. 1980), *cert. denied*, 449 U.S. 983 (1980)

Appeal from the United States District Court for the Central District of California.

Before SNEED, SCHROEDER and ALARCON, Circuit Judges.

SNEED, C.J.: Appellant is an art dealer. On March 24, 1977, he sold two paintings under such circumstances as to require him to pay royalties under the California Resale Royalties Act (California Act), which is set forth in full in the margin.[1] He thereupon brought suit challenging the Act's constitutionality, claiming that it is preempted by the 1909 Copyright Act[2] and that it violates due process and Contracts Clause of the Constitution. The lower court rejected these contentions. We affirm.

I. PREEMPTION UNDER THE 1909 COPYRIGHT ACT

Appellant's preemption argument has compelled us to review in some detail the preemption doctrine as applied by the Supreme Court and developments in copyright law during much of this century and, to some extent, even those of an earlier time. We shall not extend this opinion describing in detail our research but shall limit it to stating our reasoning in a direct and straightforward manner. Before commencing this statement we emphasize that this case concerns the preemptive effect of the 1909 Act only. We do not consider the extent to which the 1976 Act, particularly section 301(a) and (b), 17 U.S.C. §301(a) and (b), may have preempted the California Act. It is unavoidable that certain of our reasons will be weighed and measured to determine their applicability to the 1976 Act. Nonetheless, our holding, as well as our reasons, to repeat, are addressed to the 1909 Act only.

Appellant utilizes as the foundation to his argument portions of sec-

---

reservation takes nothing from the pocket of the tenant, and is, therefore, no injury to him. But this is clearly a mistake. We have already seen that the grant in fee carries with it the *inseparable* right of alienation, and the reservation is an attempt to separate from the thing granted an incident or quality which cannot be detached from it.

Id. at 507.

Is there any distinction to be drawn when tangible personal property, such as artwork, is sold? The teaching of the *DePeyster* court has extended to personalty; for example, it has been the general custom in the area of corporate law to draft agreements, principally shareholders' stock restriction agreements, in ways that do *not* indefinitely restrain alienation of shares of stock that may be involved. See in this connection §202 of the Delaware Corporation Law, which permits only certain specified restrictions on the sale of securities.

[1] [Footnote omitted.]

[2] [Footnote omitted.]

tions 1 and 27 of the 1909 Act. The selected portion of section 1 reads: "Any person entitled thereto, upon complying with the provisions of this title, shall have the exclusive right: (1) To print, reprint, publish, copy, *and vend* the copyrighted work." (Italics supplied.) The section 27 portion, after providing that the copyright was distinct from the object and that the latter's transfer did not of itself transfer the copyright, reads: "but nothing in this title shall be deemed to forbid, prevent, or *restrict the transfer* of any copy of a copyrighted work the possession of which has been lawfully obtained." (Italics supplied.)

On this foundation appellant asserts that the California Act impairs the artist's ability *to vend* his "work of fine art" when it is a "copyrighted work" within the meaning of section 1 of the 1909 Act. He also asserts that the California Act "restricts the transfer" of a copyrighted "work of fine art" when in the hands of one who lawfully obtained it, such as a purchaser from the artist. It follows, appellant contends, that the California Act conflicts with the 1909 Act. Under these circumstances, appellant concludes, the California Act is preempted by the 1909 Copyright Act.

To evaluate appellant's position we shall describe briefly certain aspects of the "works of fine art" market place as well as our perception of the current attitude of the Supreme Court with respect to preemption generally.

A. Aspects of the Market Place for "Works of Fine Art"

Turning to the market place for "works of fine art," it is frequently the case that such works are not copyrighted and that the sales proceeds realized by the artist upon its first sale are significantly less than the prices at which it subsequently changes hands. See Sheehan, *Why Don't Fine Artists Use Statutory Copyright? An Empirical and Legal Survey*, 22 Bull. Copyright Soc'y 242 (1975); Price and Price, *Right of Artists: The Case of the Droit de Suite*, Art Works: Law, Policy, Practice, 67 (Practising Law Inst. 1974). There are several explanations for both circumstances. The failure to utilize copyright protection has its source in, among other things, ignorance, a distaste for legal details, weak bargaining power, and the desire to avoid defacing the work with a copyright symbol. See Note, *Courting The Artist With Copyright: The 1976 Copyrights Act*, 24 Wayne L. Rev.1685-86 (1978). An increase in the price of an artist's works after they have left his hands may be the result of greater recognition of the artist, an increase in the overall demand for art works, inflation, unpredictable shifts in fashion and taste, or some combination of the above.

The California Act functions under these conditions. It is an American version of what the French call the *droit de suite*, an art proceeds right. See

Emley, *The Resale Royalties Act: Paintings, Preemption and Profit*, 8
Golden Gate Univ. L. Rev. 239, 240, n.9 (1978). It provides by force of
state law a conditional economic interest of a limited duration in the
proceeds of sales other than the initial one. Similar rights perhaps could
be obtained by contract. See Projansky and Siegelaub, *The Artist's Reserved Rights Transfer and Sale Agreement, Art Works: Law, Policy, Practice, supra* at 81. Opinions differ as to whether the existence of such an
interest, without regard to its source, will increase the incentives to produce available to the young and not well known artist. See Katz, *Copyright Preemption Under the Copyright Act of 1976: The Case of Droit de Suite*,
47 Geo. Wash. L. Rev. 200, 220-21 (1978). Some argue that only a few
artists will benefit, as appears to have been the French experience, while
others believe such an interest prevents exploitation of the artist's creativity. See Hauser, *The French Droit de Suite: The Problem of Protection for
the Underprivileged Artist Under the Copyright Law*, 6 Bull. Copyright
Soc'y 94 (1959). See Merryman & Elsen, Law, Ethics and the Visual Arts,
ch. IV *passim* (1979). Resolution of that dispute is not necessary for the
purposes of this opinion.

B. Preemption and the Supreme Court

With respect to preemption the Supreme Court's emphasis
varies from time to time. At times the preemption doctrine has been
applied with nationalistic fervor while during other periods with generous tolerance of state involvement in areas already to some extent the
subject of national concern. See Note, *The Preemption Doctrine: Shifting
Perspectives on Federalism and The Burger Court*, 75 Colum. L. Rev. 623
passim (1975). Without regard to the emphasis of the period certain basic
doctrinal notions repeatedly are used in applying preemption. Thus, the
extent to which the federal law has "occupied the field" and the presence
of "conflict" between the federal and state law have always been focuses
of analytic attention. The nature of the Court's emphasis at a particular
time is revealed by whether "occupation of the field," and "conflict" are
easily found to exist or not. "Occupation" can require no more than the
existence of a federal law generally applicable to a significant portion of
the area in question to no less than an express statement demonstrating
an intention to occupy the area duly enacted by Congress. "Conflict,"
likewise, can require no more than a mechanical demonstration of potential conflict between federal and state law to no less than a showing of
substantial frustration of an important purpose of the federal law by the
challenged state law. When the emphasis is to protect and strengthen
national power "occupation" and "conflict" are easily found while not so
easily found when the emphasis is to promote federalism.

Although there is a discernable cyclical character in the Supreme
Court's choice of emphasis, it is also true that, without regard to the
particular point in the cycle at which a preemption issue arises, the choice

of emphasis is heavily influenced by the area of the law in which the issue arises. Thus, when the area concerns foreign affairs, as in *Hines v. Davidowitz*, 312 U.S. 52, 61 S. Ct. 399, 85 L. Ed. 581 (1941), or labor relations, as in *San Diego Building Trades Council v. Garmon*, 359 U.S. 236, 79 S. Ct. 773, 3 L. Ed. 2d 775 (1959), the emphasis, not surprisingly, is on the national interest, while when the area is protection of consumers of commodities, as in *Florida Lime & Avocado Growers, Inc. v. Paul*, 373 U.S. 132, 83 S. Ct. 1210, 10 L. Ed. 2d 248 (1963), the emphasis understandably is upon the state's interest particularly and the imperatives of federalism generally. See Note, *The Preemption Doctrine: Shifting Perspectives on Federalism and The Burger Court, supra* at 638-39.

Fortunately, the Supreme Court provided clear guidance with respect to the emphasis proper for this case. This was done in *Goldstein v. California* 412 U.S. 546, 93 S. Ct. 2303, 37 L. Ed. 2d 163 (1973), in which the court held valid a California statute making it a criminal offense to "pirate" recordings produced by others, an activity against which the copyright holder at that time had no protection. The interests of California in particular and of federalism in general were given emphasis. The Court refused to read the Copyright Clause of the Constitution to foreclose the existence of all state power "to grant to authors the exclusive Right to their respective Writings." *Id.* at 560, 93 S. Ct. at 2311. Also it held that the 1909 Copyright Act did not preempt the California statute. In support of this conclusion the Court observed that Congress had not exercised its full power under the Copyright Clause and that it was not required to do so. In addition, Congress had evidenced no intent, either expressly or impliedly, to bar the states from exercising their power. As a consequence, the area was not fully occupied by the federal government. This was supported additionally by the Court's explicit conclusion that no conflict between the national and state law existed because state law regulated a matter not covered by the federal Copyright Act of 1909 in a manner that did not disturb a careful balance struck by Congress between those matters deserving of protection and those things that should remain free. *Id.* at 567-70, 93 S. Ct. at 2315-2316. Both *Sears, Roebuck & Co. v. Stiffel Co.*, 376 U.S. 225, 84 S. Ct. 784, 11 L. Ed. 2d 661 (1964), and *Compco Corp. v. Day-Brite Lighting, Inc.*, 376 U.S. 234, 84 S. Ct. 779, 11 L. Ed. 2d 669 (1964), cases in which state unfair competition laws were held to be preempted by the federal patent law, were distinguished on the ground that in each case the state law upset the federally struck balance between protection and freedom. Finally, the Court in *Goldstein* held that California's statute did not restrain the use or expression of knowledge, truths ascertained, conceptions, or ideas.

We hold the *Goldstein* governs this case. The Copyright Clause does not prevent the enactment by California of Resale Royalties Act. Nor has the Copyright Act of 1909 explicitly forbade the enactment of such an act by a state. A bar by implication cannot be found in the word "vend" in section 1 of the 1909 Act. Doubt concerning the correctness of this conclusion disappears when the rights of the artist who creates a work of fine art are analyzed. Prior to the initial sale he holds title to the work and, assuming proper steps have been taken, all rights given to him by reason of his copyright. None of these provide the right afforded to him by the California Resale Royalties Act. This is an additional right similar to the additional protection afforded by California's anti-pirating statute upheld in *Goldstein*. It is true that under the California Act the right it bestows cannot be waived or transferred. This limits the right created by state law but not any right created by the copyright law.

It would be proper to brand this conclusion as sophistry were it true that the right "to vend" provided by section 1 of the 1909 Act meant a right to transfer the works at all times and at all places free and clear of all claims of others. It is manifest that such is not its meaning. It merely means that the artist has "the exclusive right to transfer the title for a consideration to others." See *Bauer v. O'Donnell*, 229 U.S. 1, 11, 33 S. Ct. 616, 617, 57 L. Ed. 1041 (1912). The California Act does not impair this right; it merely creates a right *in personam* against a seller of a "work of fine art."

Nor can we conclude that section 27 of the 1909 Act by implication precludes the enactment of resale royalty acts by the states. Technically speaking such acts in no way restrict the transfer of art works. No lien to secure the royalty is attached to the work itself, nor is the buyer made secondarily liable for the royalty. The work can be transferred without restriction. The fact that a resale may create a liability to the creator artist or a state instrumentality and, at the same time, constitute an exercise of a right guaranteed by the Copyright Act does not make the former a legal restraint on the latter. It is true, of course, that the imposition of the royalty may well influence the duration of a purchaser's holding period of a work of fine art. To cover the royalty the holder may defer selling until the work's value has appreciated to a greater extent than otherwise might have been the case. The aggregate volume of business done by the relevant art markets may be diminished somewhat. Moreover, the possibility of the imposition by the state of very high royalty rates and more than one state "taxing" a single sale[3] suggests that resale royalty acts

---

[3] The California Act imposes its obligation when "a work of fine art is sold and the seller resides in California or the sale takes place in California." Cal. Civil Code §986(a). A similar statute enacted by another state could lead to a particular sale being construed as having been made in each state. Similar multiple application could occur if the statute of a state other than California imposed its obligation to protect resident artists whose works were sold within that state. A seller, who was a resident of California and who sold the work within the second state, would be confronted with the application of statutes of two states. Even if the second state adopted a statute identical to that of California, a sale by a California resident in the second state would result in multiple application.

under certain circumstances could make transfer of the work of fine art a practical impossibility. Without regard to how the preemption argument should fare under those circumstances, we are not confronted with them here. We explicitly restrict our holding to the facts before us.

These observations permit us to conclude that the 1909 Copyright Act has not occupied the area with which we are concerned and that the California Act is not in conflict with it. A resale royalty is not provided by the 1909 Act; no hostility toward such a royalty is expressed by the Act; and, on the facts before us, the obligation to pay a resale royalty does not impermissibly restrict resales by the owners of works of fine art. The teaching of *Goldstein* is not limited to situations in which the matter regulated by state law is not covered by the 1909 Act. *Kewanee Oil Co. v. Bicron Corp.*, 416 U.S. 470, 94 S. Ct. 1879, 40 L. Ed. 2d 315 (1974), makes this clear. The crucial inquiry is not whether state law reaches matters also subject to federal regulation, but whether the two laws function harmoniously rather than discordantly. We find no discord in this instance. For these reasons we distinguish *Sears* and *Compco* in the same manner as was done in *Goldstein*.

II. THE CONTRACTS CLAUSE AND DUE PROCESS ISSUE

Appellant also contends that even if the Resale Royalties Act is not preempted by federal copyright law, it violates either the Contracts Clause or the due process provisions of the Constitution. We hold otherwise.

A. The Contracts Clause Issue

The California Act with respect to initial sales by the artist subsequent to its enactment impairs only the power of the artist and his purchaser to contract. The exercise of the police power of states frequently has this effect and raises no Contracts Clause issue. See *Manigault v. Springs*, 199 U.S. 473, 480, 26 S. Ct. 127, 130, 50 L. Ed. 274 (1905). With respect to initial sales prior to enactment of the California Act a Contracts Clause issue lurks sufficiently close by to require discussion.

The economic interest bestowed on an artist, who previous to the Act's enactment has parted with his work, can be viewed as a benefit conferred upon him by the state because of its desire to promote artistic endeavor generally. So viewed no Contract Clause issue emerges. Appellant, however, contends that the California Act rewrites his contract with the person from whom he acquired the work to require payment to the creator of the work or the California Arts Council. This is not a compelling characterization of the operation of the Act. However, without regard to whether the California Act can be said to rewrite all pre-California Act sales contracts, the inescapable effect of the Act is to burden such a buyer of a work of fine art with an unbargained-for obligation to pay a royalty to the creator of that work or the Arts Council upon resale. The buyer's obligation is increased, and such an alteration no doubt requires that the Act be scrutinized under the Contracts Clause. See, e.g., *Allied Structural Steel Co. v. Spannaus*, 438 U.S. 234, 244-45, n.16, 98 S. Ct. 2716, 2723, 57 L. Ed. 2d 727.

This scrutiny reveals no unconstitutional impairment. The Contracts Clause is not absolute. "One whose rights, such as they are, are subject to state restriction, cannot remove them from the power of the State by making a contract about them." *Hudson County Water Co. v. McCarter*, 209 U.S. 349, 357, 28 S. Ct. 529, 531, 52 L. Ed. 828 (1908). Nor are all impairments of contracts improper. "The States must possess broad power to adopt general regulatory measures without being concerned that private contracts will be impaired, or even destroyed, as a result." *United States Trust Co. v. New Jersey*, 431 U.S. 1, 22, 977 S. Ct. 1505, 1517, 52 L. Ed. 2d 92 (1977). The degree to which a state may impair the obligations of contract varies with the public need for that impairment. *Allied Structural Steel v. Spannaus, supra*, 438 U.S. at 241-42, 98 S. Ct. at 2721. An insignificant impairment does not need the extensive justification that otherwise might be necessary. *Id.* at 245, 98 S. Ct. at 2723. Moreover, we should defer to the state legislature's determination of the public need whenever possible. *United States Trust Co. v. New Jersey, supra*, 431 U.S. at 22-23, 97 S. Ct. at 1517-1518, However, an impairment that is severe, permanent, irrevocable and retroactive and which serves no broad generalized economic or social purpose violates the Contracts Clause. See *Allied Structural Steel Co. v. Spannaus*, 438 U.S. 234, 250, 98 S. Ct. 2716, 2725, 57 L. Ed. 2d 727 (1978).

If impairment there be, which we are not prepared to concede, it is not of that magnitude. The obligation of the appellant created by the California Act serves a public purpose and is not severe. Under these circumstances the California Act survives a Contracts Clause challenge.

B. The Due Process Issue

Appellant's due process arguments fare no better. He asserts that he has lost a fundamental property right; that the Resale Royalties Act affects the very heart of the relationship between buyers and sellers of art; and that there is no public interest whatsoever to support such meddling. We reject these contentions.

We view the California Act, whatever its merits as a legislative matter, as economic regulation to promote artistic endeavors generally.

It is by now well established that legislative Acts adjusting the burdens and benefits of economic life come to the Court with a presumption of constitutionality, and that the burden is on one complaining of a due process violation to establish that the legislature has acted in an arbitrary and irrational way.

Usery v. Turner Elkhorn Mining Co., 428 U.S. 1, 15, 96 S. Ct. 2882, 2892,

49 L. Ed. 2d 752 (1976). The courts are not to act as "superlegislature[s] to judge the wisdom or desirability of legislative policy determinations made in areas that neither affect fundamental rights nor proceed along suspect lines. . . ." *City of New Orleans v. Dukes*, 427 U.S. 297, 303, 96 S. Ct. 2513, 2517, 49 L. Ed. 2d 511 (1976).

We would ignore a national characteristic were we to say that an act modeled upon a French law lacked a rational basis. Nor need we do so. The required rational basis exists. Moreover, the California Act is neither arbitrary nor capricious. In its present form it does not affect fundamental rights.

Appellant emphasizes that the California Act is retroactive, removing it from the sphere of the usual economic regulation. This is arguable because it is only applicable to sales made subsequent to the passage of the California Act. In any event, "legislation readjusting rights and burdens is not unlawful solely because it upsets otherwise settled expectations." *Usery v. Turner Elkhorn Mining Co.*, 428 U.S. 1, 16, 96 S. Ct. 2882, 2893, 49 L. Ed. 2d 752 (1976). Many laws upset some expectations regarding the legal consequences of prior conduct. Much legal business consists of assisting clients to adjust their affairs to the new laws. It has been said that "Only when such retroactive effects are so wholly unexpected and disruptive that harsh and oppressive consequences follow is the constitutional limitation exceeded." *Hazelwood Chronic & Convalescent Hospital, Inc. v. Weinberger*, 543 F.2d 703, 708 (9th Cir. 1976), accord, *Matter of U.S. Financial, Inc.*, 594 F.2d 1275 (9th Cir. 1979). The consequences of the California Act in its present form are not of that magnitude.

Affirmed.

§6.4.3. A Commentary

Until his death in 1985, the New York lawyer Ralph F. Colin served as an eloquent spokesman for this country's art dealers. He was instrumental in founding the Art Dealers Association of America in 1962 and served for many years as its administrative vice president. In 1977, he submitted the following statement at an informal meeting convened by Congressman Henry A. Waxman of California to discuss the possibility of creating a federal *droit de suite*. Colin found neither logic nor equity to an artist's sharing in the collector's profits from the resale of the artist's work. Pointing out, for example, that a surgeon did not forever share in the earnings of a football star whose knee he might have repaired, Colin asked why artist should be treated differently. He also challenged the logic of a proposal under which artists would share in gains, but have nothing to do with losses.

COLIN, STATEMENT ON BEHALF OF THE ART DEALERS
ASSOCIATION OF AMERICA ON THE SUBJECT OF
ARTISTS SHARING IN PROFITS OF RESALE
Submitted at a Meeting Called by Cong. Henry A. Waxman (July 21, 1977)

Ever since a much publicized confrontation between the artist
Robert Rauschenberg and the collector Robert Scull after a sale of paintings from the Scull Collection at the Sotheby Parke-Bernet Galleries on
October 18, 1973, there has been increased discussion of an alleged
equitable right of the artist to share in the resale profits of his works. The
confrontation involved a criticism by Rauschenberg of the fact that his
painting, purchased by Scull in 1958 for $900, had been resold by Scull
at the auction in 1973 for $85,000.

A typical discussion of the problem appeared in an article by Roy
Bongartz in the Arts and Leisure Section of the New York Times on
Sunday, February 2, 1975 under the inaccurate and misleading title
"Writers, Composers and Actors Collect Royalties — Why Not Artists."
That Times article contained false assumptions and false charges and,
therefore, false conclusions.

The article's headline and the carryover on a later page: "Should
Artists Collect Royalties?," did not accurately describe the contents of the
article. The main thrust of the article had nothing at all to do with
"royalties." It, and other discussions on the same subject, considered the
desirability and propriety of artists sharing in resale profits. In attempting
to justify such sharing by analogies to royalties, the author was comparing cherries and potatoes.

The definition of "royalty" in the *Random House Dictionary of the
English Language* is "an *agreed* portion of the *income* from the work paid to
its authors, composers, etc., usually a percentage *of the retail price* of *each
copy* sold." ([Emphasis] added) The definition of royalty in the *Oxford
Dictionary* is "a payment made to an author, editor or composer *for each
copy* of a book, piece of music, etc. *sold by the publisher* or *for the presentation* of a play." ([Emphasis] added)

In other words, a royalty is an *agreed* payment *for a future use,* on a *per
piece basis* and has nothing whatsoever to do with profit sharing. It is
payable to the creative artists for the authorized use of their products
whether or not the book publisher, music publisher or play producer
makes a profit or suffers a loss.

Visual artists already *have* that same right under the Copyright Law if
they would copyright their works as other creative artists do. But visual
artists, for reasons unknown, have, with few and minor exceptions,
failed to take the simple steps necessary to provide themselves with
copyright protection. The simplest way to accomplish this would be to
add the usual small c in a circle beside their signatures and the dates

where those appear on the work of art. Such additions would no more mar the work than do the signatures and dates under the current practice.

There is patently a distinction not only in size but also in kind between the sale of an object, such as a book or piece of sheet music, created from the start with the idea of its distribution in multiple copies, and the creation and sale of a unique object — a painting or sculpture. Books and sheet music are not originals; they are multiple reproductions. The true analogy to the book or piece of sheet music would be the sale of reproductions of the work of art for which, as has already been said, royalties could be collected. Artists need only copyright their work as do authors and composers. The true analogy, on the other hand, to the sale of an artist's painting or sculpture is the sale by an author or composer of his *original* manuscript. There has never been any suggestion or claim that a person who acquires the original manuscript of a book or score should share with the author or composer any profit realized from its resale.

There is, furthermore, a *practical* reason for the distinction in addition to that *logical* distinction. When an author or composer creates a work to be distributed in multiple at a unit cost to the buyer of anywhere from a dollar for a piece of sheet music to $7.95 or $10.00 for a book, his projected and expected income comes fom his per piece *royalty* on *each* sale. When painters or sculptors create and sell a unique work for anywhere from $1,500 to $25,000, as do successful artists today, they are looking for their profit to that single sale of that single work, and not to "royalties" on repeated sales of innumerable units thereafter. There is an essential difference in the nature of the creative product and the manner in which profits from it are to be realized.

Visual artists are not alone in failing to share in profits from future resale of works created by them. An architect, for instance, creates a set of plans for and supervises the construction of a building to cost, let us say, $100,000, for which he gets a fee of say 10 percent or $10,000. If the building is thereafter sold for $200,000, he does not share in the profit. If a surgeon repairs the knee of a professional athlete earning $50,000 a year, with the result that the athlete is able to negotiate a contract for $100,000 a year, the surgeon receives his single fee for the operation and no participation in the profit which results from his labors. The nature of the sale of a work of art, the preparation of architect's plans and the operation on a knee are simply different in kind from the service of the creator of a work designed to yield its profits in the form of royalties from the sale of multiple copies or from multiple theatrical or musical performances.

It is necessary to emphasize that his problem affects a mere handful of the tens, or possibly hundreds, of thousands of professional artists. For most artists are *not* in the "upper brackets" and their works do *not* create large resale profits: Their works probably have little or no resale market whatsoever. The requirement that buyers be obligated to share resale profits with the artists and that successive buyers thereafter be similarly obligated would be additional hurdles in the already difficult path of lesser known artists' efforts to sell their work. Such hurdles would be illogical in nature and impractical to enforce.

The fact is that even in the case of an artist, like Rauschenberg in the Scull case, who later becomes successful and "rich" and whose works sell for prices astronomically higher than those for which they were originally sold, the collector who bought early at what later proves to be a bargain price contributes to the economic welfare of the artist more than he would by sharing a profit after the artist is already successful. That spade money indicating confidence in a lesser known artist's work, and subsequent purchases by subsequent collectors at always increased prices, is what causes and supports the artist's ultimate success. On purely economic grounds, collectors who took chances in the beginning are entitled to the profit if their judgment proves sound. Just think of all of the collectors who purchase all of the works which never increase in value and which finally have no resale value whatsoever. They represent the typical buyer: Robert Scull and Robert Rauschenberg are as atypical as one in a hundred thousand.

Artists may want to share in economic success. Are they prepared to share in the buyers' economic failure? What if the buyers' resales result in losses? Are artists prepared to return a portion of the sales prices? Admittedly this [is] an academic question because regardless of any legal commitment, artists whose works are resold at a loss or cannot be resold at all would be in no position to carry out their legal commitments to refund a share of the buyers' purchase price.

The fact is, therefore, that there is neither logic nor equity to an artist's sharing in the collector's profits from the resale of the artist's work. Powerful practical reasons exist for not creating such a requirement which would cause an additional burden on most artists' efforts to sell their work.

§6.4.4. A Federal Response

As of 1985, Congressman Waxman's submission of the Visual Artists' Residual Rights Act of 1978 had been the only effort to create a *droit de suite* through federal legislation.[2] Submitted in March 1978, some

---

[2] In March 1986, however, the *droit de suite* again became a federal issue when a bill proposing its establishment, H.R. 4366, was introduced in the House by Cong. Thomas Downey. We understand that a resale royalty provision was also to be included in an omnibus visual artists' rights amendment to the Copyright law that Sen. Edward Kennedy was preparing to introduce in the Senate later that year.

eight months after the meeting in July 1977 at which Ralph F. Colin introduced the statement of the Art Dealers Association of America against such legislation, the Act was accompanied by the lengthy remarks of Waxman that follow. Waxman acknowledges that the art community is sharply divided over the issue and that "strenuous opposition . . . has been forcefully expressed by dealers, collectors, museum executives, and some artists as well." In introducing his bill, he said, he hoped to have the proposal "serve as a catalyst" for discussions that might lead to a "firm and broad consensus among all affected."

CONG. WAXMAN OF CALIFORNIA, REMARKS CONCERNING THE VISUAL ARTISTS' RESIDUAL RIGHTS ACT OF 1978
124 Cong. Rec. 32 (daily ed. March 8, 1978)

Mr. WAXMAN. Mr. Speaker, in 1976, the State of California enacted legislation which recognized for the first time the right of visual artists to a continuing economic interest and financial return on their work by providing for the payment of royalties on profitable resales of art. This right is known as *droit de suite*, or arts proceeds right, and has been incorporated for years into the laws of several Western European countries. Passage of this bill in California, which was sponsored by Senator Alan Sieroty, has prompted a vigorous and important national debate on the merits of this concept and its application.

I believe there is substantial justification for extending the concept of royalties to visual artists, and that this proposal deserves careful consideration by the Congress. However, at issue is not only the question of the fairness or justness of this principle, but the effect the payment of royalties will have on the art market. The benefits to be gained by visual artists by congressional recognition and enactment of royalties for them may be outweighed by the harm done the art market by virtue of their implementation.

In order to focus this debate more clearly, to provide a forum for its resolution on the national level, to enlist the guidance and resources of the National Endowment of the Arts, the U.S. Office of Copyrights, and all interested Government agencies, and to further discussion among affected constituencies on these questions, I am today introducing legislation that would provide for the payment of royalties to visual artists. Under this bill, visual artists would receive 5 percent of the price of a registered work which was profitably resold at over $1,000.

Although this proposal has been welcomed by many artists and legal scholars, there are difficulties which must be confronted before this legislation can be enacted. The bill's enjoyment of support of those directly affected by it — dealers, collectors, and other who would be paying royalties on visual art, no less than artists themselves — must be viewed as a precondition to approval by the Congress. I am committed toward working in good faith to develop such support. Similarly, this legislation must attract the endorsement of those who have traditionally extended their leadership, support, and encouragement to the arts — the patrons, both private and public, without whom art in America would languish. I urge them to give this proposal their fullest consideration.

This legislation represents a significant departure from measures which have previously received congressional approval. Rather than simply enhancing opportunities for support of the arts, or providing additional grants, or altering the incentives for the purchase or sale of art — rather than simply giving more to the arts, this bill would redistribute, from one party to another, financial proceeds from the sale of art.

The heightened political controversy over this legislation flows from this distinctive characteristic. It may well be that given the unique quality of this bill, with its potential for divisiveness among those concerned with the arts, that consideration should be deferred in favor of other, less controversial initiatives designed to aid visual artists, or provide incentives for the purchase of their work, in more traditional ways. On the other hand, its enactment would affirm a right many believe has been long due — and unjustly denied — visual artists.

There is strong justification for resale royalties. After the initial sale by an artist of a painting or sculpture, the artist does not participate in or enjoy any profits derived from the subsequent resale of the work. This places visual artists at a distinct disadvantage with respect to other artists — authors, composers, playwrights, film makers, and others — who are able to receive copyright royalties for the commercial use of their work. These creators' works almost always appear in multiple, with financial returns attached to each copy which is commercially used. Although the visual artist may, of course, copyright any work — and thereby control publication and any unauthorized use of that work as any other artist — the singular quality of painting and sculpture inherently precludes the generation of royalties as a function of multiple reproduction.

Thus it may be said that the copyright laws, whose justness and utility were recognized by the framers of the Constitution, and whose purpose is to provide a reward for past endeavors and an incentive to future creativity, have afforded inadequate protection to the visual artist.

The basic rationale for providing royalties to visual artists, therefore, lies in the desire to secure for them a continuing financial interest in their work in a manner commensurate with that conferred on other artists by our copyright laws. It reflects the belief that it is only just that visual artists share the benefits of profitable resales, which would otherwise remain solely in the possession of sellers in the market.

Although artists can seek to secure these rights through contracts with purchasers of their work , in reality this can be resorted to only by the most successful artists; others can hardly hope to attach such conditions to the sale of their creations. Indeed, the point of droit de suite is that it is not a contractual matter but an inherent right outside the bounds of any other financial arrangement agreed to between artist and purchaser and secondary buyer.

The classic transaction justifying resale royalties was captured in a film which records the sale of Robert Rauschenberg's "Thaw." Originally purchased by collector Robert Scull in the 1950's for $800, it was auctioned 20 years later for $85,000. Rauschenberg, who was present, could only exclaim to Scull, "I've been working . . . for you to make that profit?"

Strenuous opposition to resale royalties — both on the principle and the effects its implementation will have — has been forcefully expressed by dealers, collectors, museum executives, and some artists as well. Many argue not only that the payment of royalties will not benefit visual artists, but will prove harmful to their livelihood. First, it is contended that art is property and, as in all property transfers, all rights are and should be relinquished to each purchaser with each sale. It is argued, moreover, that artists do already benefit from profitable resales as their unsold works automatically appreciate as the artist's popularity increases — to the artist's benefit. Third, it has been contended that artists are more than justly compensated for their work, and that the most successful are paid much more for their paintings than authors or poets are paid for their manuscripts. Fourth, many analysts of the art market believe that dealers and collectors are not unjustly enriched by their purchases and resales — that in fact the proportion of art which increases significantly in real value, discounting inflation, insurance, and other costs of ownership, is marginal.

The most serious reservation to resale royalties, however, even among those who otherwise acknowledge its fairness, is that the royalty will act as a tax, and that as with any tax, its imposition will depress the art market, which is by nature fragile and volatile. Not only will the royalty increase prices and decrease sales, it is argued, but it will also decrease dealers' profits, which are used to subsidize the exhibition of promising but unknown artists. Therefore, opponents of this legislation conclude that initial sales will surely be hurt and that opportunities for aspiring artists may also be compromised.

In these circumstances, it is clear that neither the need for legal recognition of the right of visual artists to resale royalties nor the economic

arguments arrayed against it can be dismissed out of hand. Consideration of this concept is hampered by the lack of any authoritative data on
critical aspects of the art market — such as even a rough estimate of gross
primary sales and resales — by which to test these claims. Thoughtful
evaluation of the merits must be accompanied by the development of
relatively accurate economic information, which I very much hope will
be generated in the coming months.

My purpose in introducing the Visual Artists' Residual Rights Act of
1978, therefore, is to have this proposal serve as a catalyst for this debate,
which has already spread to several States throughout the Nation.

This draft bill is patterned after the law enacted in California in 1976.
My legislation provides for the creation of a National Commission on the
Visual Arts, which would administer the resale royalty program. Artists
would register the works they wish to qualify for royalties with the
Commission. Visual art is defined to include paintings, sculpture, photographs, prints, and other original works. Each seller of a work of visual
art sold for $1,000 or more would transmit a copy of the bill of sale to the
Commission along with a payment equal to 5 percent of the gross sales
price provided the work was resold for more than it was originally purchased. The bill enumerates certain exemptions from these payments.
The Commission is responsible for distributing payments to artists, and
has enforcement powers in this regard. If after 7 years the Commission
cannot locate the artist for payment of the royalty, it is kept by the
Commission. The bill authorizes Federal appropriations by the Commission. The bill authorizes Federal appropriations to cover the Commission's operating expenses.

The $1,000 trigger for payment of royalties is motivated by two con-
siderations. The paperwork involved in keeping track of all sales would
be enormous and unduly burdensome. Moreover, a 5 percent royalty on
anything less than $1,000 would approach the insignificant. To those
who would argue that such a formula will benefit only well-established
artists, it may be responded that today's most famed artists were yester-
day's unknowns. The opportunity for all to receive a royalty is protected
in this bill.

This legislation has removed the two most objectionable features of
the California law. First, it is not retroactive, and does not apply to any
works sold before the date of enactment. The constitutionality of the
retroactive nature of the California law is currently being reviewed by the
courts. My legislation has no such provision, and therefore avoids this
area of contention entirely. Second, enforcement of royalty payments
resides with the Commission and not, as under the California law, with
the artists themselves. In California, this has proved a severe impediment
to effective compliance with the law. Artists rarely have the resources to

pay for a legal challenge to secure payments due them. They should not, in my judgment, be handicapped in this manner.

Further, the California law applies only to residents of the State and to sales within it. It cannot pretend to be national in scope, although its enactment has prompted other States, including New York, Florida, and Texas, to consider similar legislation. However, the law may have had the effect of driving some portion of California's art market out of the State, to its competitive disadvantage. Clearly this is an issue, because of the effect on interstate commerce, which deserves resolution at the national level.

Finally, I wish to state that I consider all provisions in the bill open for modification. It may be desirable for this legislation to be administered not by a new, independent organization, but perhaps by the National Endowment for the Arts or the U.S. Office of Copyrights. Visual artists might also form an ASC[A]P-like organization, which serves other artists under copyright, for the collection and payment of royalties. Such an organization, known as SPADEM, exists in France. The bill was drafted solely so that the implementation of resale royalties might be presented in its purest form.

Additionally, alternative formulas for the calculation of royalties due have been suggested. Many argue that payment of 15 percent of the profit of a resale, rather than 5 percent of the gross sales price, would be more equitable by allowing the seller to more fully take into account the cost of commissions payments to agents and other costs before extracting the royalty. This is an approach which deserves further consideration.

It is not my intention to seek enactment without the development of a firm and broad consensus among all affected by this bill. I look forward to this process and welcome the involvement of my colleagues. . . .

§6.5. THE PRACTICAL EFFECTS OF RESALE ROYALTY STATUTES

§6.5.1. Do Artists Gain?

What are the practical effects of a resale royalty statute? Will it increase the monies that go to artists who have increased in stature? Will it have a chilling effect or, alternatively, an artificial inflationary effect on prices? What of the museum — could the not-for-profit collector compete for acquisitions under such a scheme? The following article examines some of the economic realities inherent in such a statute.

BOLCH, DAMON & HINSHAW, AN ECONOMIC ANALYSIS OF THE CALIFORNIA ART ROYALTY STATUTE
10 Conn. L. Rev. 689 (Spring 1978)*

I. INTRODUCTION

In 1976, California enacted a version of the *droit de suite*[1] designed to yield to artists a portion of the resale value of their works.[2] The statute provides that, for the life of the artist, whenever a work of "fine art"[3] is resold and the seller resides in California or the sale takes place in California, the seller or his agent must pay the artist or the artist's agent five percent of the amount of such sale.[4] While the artist may execute a written contract for a resale royalty in excess of five percent, the artist

---

*[Bolch, Ben W., & Damon, William W., & Hinshaw, C. Elton, An Economic Analysis of the California Art Royalty Statute, 10 Conn. L. Rev. 689 (Spring 1978). Mr. Bolch is president of The Bolch Group, Inc., a financial investment firm in Atlanta, Georgia; he is a former professor of Economics at Vanderbilt University. Mr. Damon is a professor of Economics at Vanderbilt University. Mr. Hinshaw is an associate professor of Economics at Vanderbilt University and the secretary of the American Economics Association. Reprinted with permission. — Eds.]

[1] Usually translated as the "right to art proceeds," the *droit de suite*, an addition to the copyright laws of certain European nations, is designed to furnish artists with a portion of the increase in value of their works when they are resold. By 1966, Belgium, Czechoslovakia, France, Germany, Italy, Poland, Sweden, Tunisia, and Uruguay had enacted *droit de suite* legislation, and Austria, Great Britain, Holland, Norway, Portugal, Spain, and Switzerland were considering doing so. Schulder, Art Proceeds Act: A Study of the Droit De Suite and a Proposed Enactment for the United States, 61 Nw. U.L. Rev. 19, 22 n.13 (1966).

In France, for example, a flat fee is payable to the artist or his heirs on the public resale of all paintings, and the fee must be paid whether the painting rises in price or not. In Italy, on the other hand, the artist is entitled to a *droit de suite* only on the increase in value of the work of art. The techniques used differ with respect to the methods of resale covered (auctions, dealer, or private), the percentage of the resale price the artist obtains, the minimum price the object must bring before the mechanism is brought into play at all, and the length of time during which the mechanism operates. See Price, Government Policy and Economic Security for Artists: The Case of the Droit de Suite, 77 Yale L.J. 1333, 1333-34 (1968).

[2] [See §6.4.1 *supra* for the text of the current California statute, Cal. Civ. Code §986 (West Supp. 1985). — Eds.]

[3] [See §6.4.1 *supra* for the statutory definition of "fine art," which has been amended since the writing of this article. — Eds.]

[4] *Id.* §986(a)(1). The statute exempts any transaction in which the gross sales price is less than $1,000 or where the resale price of the work of art is less than the seller's purchase price. *Id.* §986(b)(2), (4).

cannot accept less.[5] This article examines the probable economic impact of this legislation on the art market, museums, and the artist.[6]

The basic premise of the *droit de suite* is that an artist does not receive the true value of a work of art at its original sale. Proponents of the principle argue that true value is generally determined many years after the original sale and that the artist is exploited because any appreciation in value does not inure to the artist's benefit. The concept of the *droit de suite* is actually a variation on the more general doctrine of "just price," which posits that things have an objective, intrinsic value in and of themselves.[7] It is our belief that the notion of just price clouds the legal and economic analysis of the artist's right to a resale royalty.

II. AN ECONOMIC MODEL

One may identify two general motivations for the purchase of art. The connoisseur may purchase art with the intention of treating the art as a pure consumption good. No resale is foreseen at the time of purchase, and the buyer intends merely to enjoy a flow of nonmonetary utility which accrues from ownership. In contrast, an individual or institution may purchase art at least in part for investment reasons.[8] The California statute is directed primarily at the latter type of purchaser and our analysis, therefore, will be restricted to the investment aspect of art purchasing.

It may be useful, before looking at the art market, to review some elementary notions concerning decision rules for the purchase of any asset for investment purposes. Suppose that an instrument, such as a United States Treasury bill, is to be redeemed at a known price one time period from today. In the case of a Treasury bill, the instrument carries a

---

[5] *Id.* §986(a).

[6] The problems of enforcing the statute and determining its constitutionality are not treated in this article. For a consideration of these problems see Merryman, The California Royalty Bill: Milestone or Mistake? Am. Artist, Feb. 1977, at 60.

[7] The doctrine of just price posited that "there was such a thing as an objective value, something inherent in the commodity rather than in the minds of buyer and seller. We now have had enough experience and have made enough examination of the problem, of course, to know that no such objective value ever existed." Gras, Economic Rationalism in the Late Middle Ages, 8 Speculum 304, 305 (1933). Another writer has argued that Gras' characterization of just price is a vulgarization of that doctrine. See Dempsey, Just Price in a Functional Economy, 25 Am. Econ. Rev. 471, 472-73 (1935). Nevertheless, many proponents of the royalty statute appear to rely on the doctrine as it was defined by Gras.

[8] However, in recent years, investment in paintings has been shown to yield only "ordinary" returns when adjusted for risk. See Stein, The Monetary Appreciation of Paintings, 85 J. Pol. Econ. 1021 (1977).

face redemption value, or price, P_1. P_1 is the true value of the bill one period in the future.

The question that the investor wishes to answer concerns the price to pay today, P_0, for the right to receive P_1 one time period in the future. Suppose that a given investor is willing to pay $9433.96 for the right to receive $10,000 at the end of one time period. In this case, the investor has revealed that he requires a rate of return of six percent on the investment: $P_1/P_0 = \$10,000/\$9433.96 = 1.06$. In general, we call the required rate of return for investor i his internal discount rate, r_i. The bid price, P_0, the redemption price, P_1, and the discount rate, r_i, will be related as follows for the investor:

$$P_0 = P_1/(1 + r_i)$$

Table 1 shows the bid prices of five investors for a $10,000 redemption price after one time period. Notice that as discount rates increase, bid prices fall.

With this background in mind we are ready to turn to an analysis of sales of works of art. We begin by considering a single artist who wishes to sell an original and unique work of art for the first time. Since the given work cannot be expanded by further production,[9] the work will sell only if a buyer offers a price at least as high as the minimum price which is acceptable to the artist. In the language of economics, the selling price will be determined completely by prospective buyers, provided that some offer price is at least as high as the artist's reservation price. If the offer prices are all lower than the artist's reservation price, no sale will take place.[10]

Table 1. Bid Price in Terms of a Redemption Price of $10,000 at Selected Discount Rates

Investor i	Discount Rate r_i	Bid Price $P_0 = \$10,000/(1 + r_i)$
1	0.01	$9900.99
2	0.06	9433.96
3	0.10	9090.91
4	0.20	8333.33
5	0.50	6666.67

[9] In contrast, records, sheet music, books, and other reproducible forms of art may be expanded by additional production. It is precisely this distinction that makes unpersuasive an appeal to the argument that since reproducible art carries a royalty, so should nonreproducible art.

[10] A particular work of art might be offered for sale in a sealed bid auction, in a

Now let us assume that the artist is faced with a decision as to whether he should sell his art today or hold his art as an investment for one time period. Let us also assume that the artist and the bidders are in agreement as to the future price of the art one time period from today, P_1.[11] In this situation, both the artist and the prospective buyers have discount rates which will value consumption one period from today in terms of consumption today. If there are many prospective purchasers with different discount rates as in Table 1, then the purchaser with the lowest discount rate, which we shall call r_*, will offer the highest bid to the artist and, since we ignore risk, the bid will be $P_1/(1 + r_*)$. The artist, on the other hand, has the option of refusing to sell the work of art, and may prefer to invest in his own art and to receive its future price, P_1, after one time period. In this case, the artist will value the work of art at $P_1/(1 + r_A)$, where r_A is the artist's discount rate. The sale will take place whenever

$$P_1/(1 + r_*) > P_1/(1 + r_A) \qquad \text{Equation (1)}$$

which reduces to

$$r_A > r_* \qquad \text{Equation (2)}$$

Thus, a sale will take place if the artist has a greater present need for consumption than the buyer with the least present need for consumption among all prospective buyers.

To the extent that a "starving" artist is facing a "wealthy" buyer, the situation represented by equation (2) is likely to obtain. However, there is no exploitation of the artist in this situation. Although both the artist and the buyer agree on the future price of the work, they differ in their preferences for present consumption relative to future consumption. In a noncoerced exchange, both parties benefit. However, at some later time, because of increased wealth or for other reasons, the artist may have a lesser need for present consumption and may in retrospect view the sale

---

competitive bid auction, on display at a given price (which we would denote as the artist's reservation price) either subject to bargaining or not, or through any of several other institutional arrangements. Although the specific institutional arrangement may affect the ultimate transaction price, it will not affect the conceptual analysis of the economic impact of the statutory imposition of a royalty. Our assumption of a sealed bid market structure is motivated by clarity of exposition, rather than a belief that it is the most prevalent structure. All of our major conclusions hold under the more realistic, but more difficult to present, assumption that the artist sets the price of the work at his reservation price and buyers either take or refuse to take the work at that price; the only difference is that the artist will never be offered a price higher than his reservation price.

[11] The effect of this assumption of homogeneous expectations of the market participants is discussed at a later point in this article. See text following note 17 *infra*.

with regret, feeling that a just price was not obtained at the time of original sale.

III. THE CALIFORNIA STATUTE

The California statute levies a royalty of five percent upon the resale price of a work of art at the end of the buyer's holding period. Thus, the best offer that will be made for the art today is

$$(1 - t)P_1/(1 + r_*) \qquad\qquad \text{Equation (3)}$$

where $t = 0.05$, or 5%. Compared to equation (1), the offer has been reduced by the factor $(1 - t)$, or to 95% of the offer made without the royalty. This reduction is reasonable, since the buyer is clearly aware that upon resale he will realize only 95% of P_1, the other 5% being returned to the artist as a royalty. Under the statute, the artist will not only receive today the amount given by equation (3), but he will also earn tP_1 (5% of the resale price) at the end of the buyer's holding period. Given the discount rate of the artist, r_A, the future payment tP_1 will be worth $tP_1/(1 + r_A)$ to the artist today. The artist will compare the sum of the present and discounted future payment with the discounted amount that he may expect to receive by holding the art as an investment. A sale will take place whenever

$$\frac{(1 - t)P_1}{(1 + r_*)} + \frac{tP_1}{(1 + r_A)} > \frac{P_1}{(1 + r_A)} \qquad\qquad \text{Equation (4)}$$

As before, equation (4) implies a sale whenever $r_A > r_*$.

Let us now explore the meaning of equation (4). If there is no royalty, $t = 0$ and equation (4) reduces to equation (1), as it should. Furthermore, if there is a 100% royalty, $t = 1$, the entire resale price is returned to the artist, and the term $(1 - t)P_1/(1 + r_*)$ becomes zero. In this case the artist will never be able to sell his art to a rational investor. Therefore, as the royalty increases toward 100%, the bid price decreases. However, the situation in which the artist will prefer to sell the work rather than to hold it as an investment does not change as a result of the resale royalty. That is, the artist will prefer to sell his work as long as $r_A > r_*$, with or without the royalty. This fact is demonstrated by Table 2.

The price of the art at the end of the holding period, P_1, is assumed to be $10,000, and the discount rate of the highest bidder, r_*, is assumed to be six percent. Column (1) shows the present value of the future compensation that an artist may expect from holding his art at various discount rates, r_A, that is, the artist's reservation price.

Column (2) depicts the present compensation to the artist from a sale of the art in the absence of any resale royalty. We see that if $r_A = 0.01$, the artist will prefer to hold rather than sell his art; his reservation price in column (1) of $9900.99 exceeds the highest bid in column (2) of

Table 2. Alternative Compensation to the Artist From Holding or Selling Art, With and Without a 5% Royalty*

Hold Art		Sell Art			
		No Royalty	5% Royalty	5% Royalty	5% Royalty
	(1)	(2)	(3)	(4)	(5)
Artist's Discount Rate, r_A	Present Value of Future Compensation (Reservation Price)^a	Present Compensation (Highest Bid)^b	Present Compensation (Highest Bid)^c	Present Value of Future Resale Royalty^d	Total Present Value^e
0.01	$9900.99	$9433.96	$8962.26	$495.05	$9457.31
0.06	9433.96	9433.96	8962.26	471.70	9433.96
0.10	9090.91	9433.96	8962.26	454.55	9416.81
0.20	8333.33	9433.96	8962.26	416.67	9378.93
0.50	6666.67	9433.96	8962.26	333.33	9295.59

* $P_1 = \$10,000$, $r_* = 0.06$
^{a}) $\$10,000/(1 + r_A)$
^{b}) $\$10,000/(1.06)$
^{c}) $(.95)(\$10,000)/(1.06)$
^{d}) $(.05)(\$10,000)/(1 + r_A)$
^{e}) Col. (3) + Col. (4)

$9433.96. If $r_A = 0.06$ the artist is indifferent to the sale of his work, and if $r_A > 0.06$, selling is preferable to holding. Our previous hypothesis that selling is preferable to holding if $r_A > r_*$ is verified.

Columns (3) through (5) show the present and discounted compensation under the five percent California royalty statute. Again, if $r_A = 0.06$, the artist is indifferent to selling or holding. But, as column (5) shows, if $r_A > 0.06$, the artist always receives less total discounted compensation with the five percent royalty than he would without a royalty.

The following results are evident from Table 2:

1. If an artist sells his work, his discount rate is always equal to or larger than that of the buyer.
2. An artist who sells his work will always have a smaller discounted compensation under a scheme where there is a positive resale royalty than under a scheme where there is no resale royalty.

The obvious question is: Who does benefit from the statute? One answer is that any artist who sells his work before the market reflects the new price structure caused by the royalty statute and who lives to see his art sold at least once again stands to benefit. Such an artist will have received compensation at the initial sale that was not adjusted for the royalty and, in addition, will receive the undiscounted value of any royalties incident to any future resale(s). Therefore, under this model, a third result is apparent:

3. The California statute tends to benefit older established artists, not younger, less established artists.[12]

One probable impact of the statute will be to reduce the original bid prices for art works once buyers adjust to the existence of the resale royalty. Thus, as a result of the legislation, artists may be forced to invest in their own work, contrary to what they might consider to be in their own self interest. Because the artist cannot waive the "right" to receive at least five percent of the resale price of his art,[13] the statute, rather than extending the rights of the artist, may actually constrict those rights.

Result 2 implies that at the time of original sale, the California statute requires the artist who sells his work to accept a lower price now for the prospect of future compensation (i.e., a percentage of the later resale price). Thus, the statute implicitly forces the artist to invest in his own work. The artist must forego in current compensation the difference between the price in the absence of the statute and the lower bid price which will result from the statute. In return, he is promised some future compensation which results from the resale of the work. If the return to the artist on this implicit investment is equal to or greater than his discount rate, r_A, the artist is not adversely affected. In fact, the rate of return will be $r_* = (P_1 - P_0)/P_0$, and the implicit investment that the statute imposes is advantageous to the artist only if $r_* > r_A$. However, as we previously demonstrated, the artist will sell his work only if $r_A > r_*$. Thus, the two conditions necessary for the statute to benefit the artist at the time of the original sale are mutually exclusive.

Result 3 demonstrates that only established artists are likely to benefit from the statute and then only if their works were originally sold in the absence of the royalty provision when potential buyers did not adjust their bid prices downward to account for the royalty. According to the Art Dealers Association, only about fifty living artists have a resale market for their works, and ninety-nine percent of all art depreciates in value.[14]

---

[12] Results 2 and 3 verify criticism of the legislation to the effect that the artist who benefits is the one who has an established reputation and a secondary market for his work. See Hochfield, Legislating royalties for artists, Art News, Dec., 1976, at 52; Hochfield, Artists rights: Pros and cons, Art News, May, 1975, at 22.

[13] Cal. Civ. Code §986(a) (West Supp. [1985]). The statute clearly violates the maxim: *Quilibet potest renunciare juri pro se introducto* (Anyone may waive a right asserted in his behalf). See Burgettstown Nat'l Bank v. Nill, 213 Pa. 456, 460, 63 A. 186, 187 (1906).

[14] See Hochfield, Legislating royalties for artists, Art News, Dec., 1976, at 52.

Thus, if the statute benefits anyone, it benefits the select few who need protection the least.[15]

Our analysis of the impact of the California statute may appear to be excessively abstract. First, it treats art as though it were merely another form of investment, and even economists realize that an original Rauschenberg is different from a United States Treasury bill. However, the statute is intended to capture a portion of the returns accruing to the art investor and to transfer them to the artist. To the extent that art is bought for investment purposes its purchase can be analyzed using investment decision rules.

Second, the analysis assumes that art is sold on a sealed bid auction basis. However, our basic findings do not depend on the nature of the institutions in the marketplace. Rather they are based on assumptions about the behavior of buyers and sellers when an implicit tax is levied upon a future sale.[16]

Third, the analysis is based on a model that differs in three important respects from the actual market for art. It was implicitly assumed that the art work would be resold only once during the life of the artist, that all parties in the market held homogeneous expectations of the future selling price of a specific art work, and that all parties acted as though they were certain that this price would be realized one time period in the future.

To the extent that it is reasonable to assume that an art work will have multiple changes of ownership during the life of the artist, the preceding analysis is an understatement of the statute's full effect upon bid prices. An analysis of the case of multiple sales shows that: (a) The statute will lead to a more significant reduction in the current bid price of an art work than was demonstrated above; (b) that the burdens and benefits, though magnified, will be allocated as described above; and (c) that the conditions necessary for an exchange to take place between the artist and a buyer are the same as those described above.[17]

---

[15] An analysis of a capital gains royalty, whereby a percentage royalty would be imposed only on the increase in value at resale, reveals a similar impact upon the artist. The same three results can be shown to hold. The reduction in the original bid price, P_0, would be less substantial in the case of a capital gains royalty than would be the reduction with the resale royalty, if the percentage royalties were of equal size. Thus, a royalty on the increase in value would be less deleterious than the resale royalty. However, neither royalty proposal is to the advantage of the artist at the time of the original sale of his work. For an application of the capital gains royalty see Projansky & Siegelaub, The Artist's Reserved Rights Transfer and Sale Agreement, in Art Works: Law, Policy, Practice 81-94 (F. Feldman & S. Weil eds. 1974).

[16] See note 10 *supra* and accompanying text.

[17] The mathematical analysis necessary to verify these conclusions is simply an extension of the equations outlined above. The complete analysis is on file in the office of the Connecticut Law Review.

We are currently studying the implications of the more realistic assumption that the artist and buyers may hold different and uncertain beliefs about the future market price of a particular work. We do not anticipate that heterogeneous expectations and differing attitudes toward risk-bearing on the part of market participants will change the incidence of the burdens and benefits of the statute.

Finally, our formal model leads to conclusions which have been widely noted by those knowledgeable in the art market.[18] We view the consistency of these conclusions as a confirmation that it is not necessary to consider the specific institutional arrangements of the art market in order to predict the impact of the statute.

IV. THE STATUTE'S EFFECT ON MUSEUMS

One of the effects of the statute is to provide a windfall gain to artists whose works were sold at full market value before the market anticipated the resale royalty. Of course, the loss will be borne by the present owners of such art at resale. Since museums are active as both buyers and sellers of art, museums located in California will suffer some loss upon the resale of the works of any living artist.

In order to measure the full impact of the statute on a California museum, the differential effects upon categories of works must be identified. Since losses would only be incurred for works of living artists, the effect of the statute depends upon the proportion of the museum's collection devoted to living artists. Within this classification further differentiation is required since the extent of the decrease in market value will depend upon the number of times a work is expected to be sold within the lifetime of the artist.[19] Thus, the decline in market value of works by older artists would be smaller, proportionately, than the decline in market value for works of younger artists, since the expected number of transfers of ownership of the senior artist's works in his remaining lifetime would be smaller. Thus, the overall decline in market value of a museum's portfolio depends upon its relative investment in the works of living artists and the age distribution of artists represented in the collection. A collection devoted to young artists would be the most severely devalued.

Perhaps in anticipation of its effect upon large collections, the statute ameliorates the impact by providing that the royalty shall not apply:

To a transfer of a work of fine art which is exchanged for one or more works of fine art or for a combination of cash, other property, and one or more works of

---

[18] See, e.g., Elsen, The art bills: Pluses and minuses, Art News, Oct. 1977, at 52-54.

[19] For a discussion of this phenomenon see note 17 *supra* and accompanying text.

fine art where the fair market value of the property exchanged is less than one thousand dollars ($1,000).[20]

To the extent that California museums can finance their acquisitions of young artists' works with works currently in their collection by young artists, the reduced market values of the works to be traded would tend to offset one another. Such an exchange of works of comparable market value would not be subject to the royalty.

V. CONCLUSION

The California statute is a misguided attempt at paternalism which may afford windfall gains to a few living artists whose work was sold prior to market knowledge of the five percent resale royalty. For other artists, economic theory and common sense indicate that the market will on the average simply reduce the original selling price of the art to compensate for expected future royalties.

Because the legislation will result in lower bid prices at the time of a work's first sale, the artist will be forced to accept a lower current price in exchange for a promise of a portion of the future resale price. Since very little art has a secondary market, the net result will be to penalize the unknown, struggling artist. Only art sold before the enactment of the legislation will yield a net benefit, upon resale, to the artist. Once the market adjusts its expectations to include the royalty, artists will not benefit.

The positive net effect on an established artist may be small. Established artists benefit from any increase in the prices of their existing works because of the positive impact that such increases have on the value of their unsold and future works. Thus, while the California statute may afford windfall gains on previously marketed art, it should also reduce the market price of art sold in the future.

The windfall gains that accrue to living established artists are at the expense of losses to dealers, museums, and the major owners of art. Museums specializing in the work of contemporary artists will suffer the greatest damage. Currently, many museums buy portfolios of contemporary artists' works and hold them, in part, for investment reasons.* To the extent that the resale royalty discourages such behavior, the market for new art is damaged.

Profitable resale of art work is rare. Few artists have a secondary market and few works of art appreciate significantly in value. The resale royalty law will result in only a small economic gain to a few and an economic loss to many. It should be repealed for the sake of the artists affected.

---

[20] Cal. Civ. Code §986(b)(5) (West Supp. [1985]).

* [We respectfully disagree with Messrs. Bolch, Damon & Hinshaw that this practice is as widespread as they suggest. —Eds.]

CHAPTER SEVEN
Other Legislation
Protective of Artists

•

§7.1. Artists' Studios: Where May an Artist Both Live and Work?

§7.1.1. Live-Work Statutes

§7.1.2. New York Multiple Dwelling Law, Art. 7-B: Joint Living-Work Quarters for Artists

§7.1.3. *Matter of Marhoffer:* Who Is a Person "Regularly Engaged in the Fine Arts"?

§7.2. Artists' Materials: The Right to Be Warned

§7.2.1. Introduction

§7.2.2. California Legislation: Mandatory Labeling and Restricted Purchase of Toxic Art Supplies

§7.1. ARTISTS' STUDIOS: WHERE MAY AN ARTIST BOTH LIVE AND WORK?

§7.1.1. Live-Work Statutes

Among the urgent needs of most artists are inexpensive, large studio space as well as affordable housing. Often these needs are met by artists living and working in suitable commercial or manufacturing buildings. (This is particularly true in urban areas, where artists tend to cluster.) Unfortunately, however, the areas in which these buildings are located are often zoned against residential or mixed use.

Recognition both of these needs and the reality that artists were renovating — and drastically improving — these spaces and their environs prompted the passage in New York State of a "live-work" statute, sanctioning a renaissance that had already taken hold in New York City neighborhoods like Soho and Tribeca. Similar legislation was also adopted in California.[1] Several cities — Boston, Minneapolis, and Seattle — have also given recognition to this need of artists with a variety of programs. Such enactments empower local governments to establish areas in which artists can both live and work. The New York legislation, representative of the laws in the other states, is reproduced in this section.

One of the problematic issues under such statutes is who may legally occupy these artists' districts, requiring a determination of who is or is not a professional artist within the statutory definition. In January of 1985, New York faced this question in *Matter of Marhoffer*, reproduced in this section following the New York statute. In *Marhoffer*, the petitioner-artist sought to overturn the denial by the New York City Department of Cultural Affairs of his application for "professional artist" certification. Marhoffer, a photographer, needed the certification to live and work in the New York City artists' district. At issue was not only whether Marhoffer was an artist, but also whether he was a commercial artist, which would make him ineligible for certification under New York law. The basis for the department's denial was Marhoffer's application and the lack of recognition by others in the field. The department focused on the lack of evidence indicating Marhoffer's professional involvement in photography as a "fine art."

Marhoffer's request for a rehearing on the denial of his application was granted, and the New York court found that the Department of Cultural Affairs had failed to promulgate sufficiently clear guidelines by which certification as an artist was to be determined. Query as to whether that determination can ever be satisfactorily made.

§7.1.2. New York Multiple Dwelling Law, Art. 7-B: Joint Living-Work Quarters for Artists

New York has been a model for legislation by which local municipalities may designate certain districts as suitable for live-work spaces by professional artists. The New York legislation, with legislative findings (of particular interest for their review of the needs — both the artists' and the communities' — addressed by the statute), follows.

---

§7.1. [1] See Cal. Health & Safety Code §17958.11 (West 1984); see also Live/Work — The San Francisco Experience. Prepared by Barbara Kibbe for the San Francisco Arts Commission (April 1985).

JOINT LIVING-WORK QUARTERS FOR ARTISTS, OR GENERAL RESIDENTIAL OCCUPANCY OF LOFT, COMMERCIAL, OR MANUFACTURING BUILDINGS

N.Y. Mult. Dwell. Law, Art. 7-B, §§275 to 278 (McKinney Supp. 1986)*

§275. LEGISLATIVE FINDINGS

It is hereby declared and found that in cities with a population in excess of one million, large numbers of loft, manufacturing, commercial, institutional, public and community facility buildings have lost, and continue to lose, their tenants to more modern premises; and that the untenanted portions of such buildings constitute a potential housing stock within such cities which is capable, when appropriately altered, of accommodating general residential use, thereby contributing to an alleviation of the housing shortage most severely affecting moderate and middle income families, and of accommodating joint living-work quarters for artists by making readily available space which is physically and economically suitable for use by persons regularly engaged in the arts.

There is a public purpose to be served by making accommodations readily available for joint living-work quarters for artists for the following reasons: persons regularly engaged in the arts require larger amounts of space for the pursuit of their artistic endeavors and for the storage of the materials therefor and of the products thereof than are regularly to be found in dwellings subject to this article; that the financial remunerations to be obtained from pursuit of a career in the arts are generally small; that as a result of such limited financial remuneration persons regularly engaged in the arts generally find it financially impossible to maintain quarters for the pursuit of their artistic endeavors separate and apart from their places of residence; that the cultural life of cities of more than one million persons within this state and of the state as a whole is enhanced by the residence in such cities of large numbers of persons regularly engaged in the arts; that the high cost of land within such cities makes it particularly difficult for persons regularly engaged in the arts to obtain the use of the amounts of space required for their work as aforesaid; and that the residential use of the space is secondary or accessory to the primary use as a place of work.

It is further declared that the legislation governing the alteration of such buildings to accommodate general residential use must of necessity be more restrictive than statutes heretofore in effect, which affected only joint living-work quarters for artists.

It is the intention of this legislation to promulgate statewide minimum standards for all alterations of non-residential buildings to residential

---

* Formerly N.Y. Arts and Cultural Affairs Law §§27.01 to 27.07 (McKinney 1983).

use, but the legislature is cognizant that the use of such buildings for residential purposes must be consistent with local zoning ordinances. The legislature further recognizes that it is the role of localities to adopt regulations which will define in further detail the manner in which alterations should be carried out where building types and conditions are peculiar to their local environment.

§276. DEFINITION OF AN ARTIST

As used in this article, the word "artist" means a person who is regularly engaged in the fine arts, such as painting and sculpture or in the performing or creative arts, including choreography and filmmaking, or in the composition of music on a professional basis, and is so certified by the city department of cultural affairs and/or state council on the arts.

§277. OCCUPANCY PERMITTED

Any building in any city of more than one million persons which at any time prior to January first, nineteen hundred seventy-seven was occupied for loft, commercial, institutional, public, community facility or manufacturing purposes, may, notwithstanding any other article of this chapter, or any provision of law covering the same subject matter (except as otherwise required by the local zoning law or resolution), be occupied in whole or in part for joint living-work quarters for artists or general residential purposes if such occupancy is in compliance with this article. Such occupancy shall be permitted only if the following conditions are met and complied with:

1. (a) The exterior walls of the building shall be non-combustible and have a fire-resistive rating of at least three hours unless the exterior wall or walls, measured on a horizontal plane perpendicular to said exterior wall or walls, is a minimum of thirty feet distant in a direct unobstructed line from another structure, except that a wet pipe sprinkler system, with maximum sprinkler spacing of four feet, must be provided along such wall or walls to protect exposed, unrated columns or beams at the interior of the wall in non-fireproof buildings.

(b) Window openings in exterior walls shall conform wth the limitations of table 3-4 chapter twenty-six of the administrative code of the city of New York, unless such windows are fire protected and provided with either a minimum of one sprinkler head per window or window automatic closing devices, acceptable to the department of buildings.

2. The building is (a) of fireproof construction, as provided in section one hundred one of this chapter, or is of class two construction, as provided by the requirements of the building code and regulations of the city of New York in effect prior to December sixth, nineteen hundred sixty-eight; or

(b) if non-fireproof, does not exceed a height of six stories, and eighty-five feet measured to the ceiling of the highest floor in a depth of one hundred feet; or does not exceed a height of seven stories, and eighty-five feet and a depth of one hundred feet and is wet sprinklered throughout; and has a maximum floor area between the two hour rated partitions constructed in accordance with section C26-504. 2 of the administrative code of the city of New York of:

(i) three thousand square feet; or

(ii) five thousand square feet if the building is six stories or less in height and is fully wet sprinklered; or

(iii) five thousand square feet if the building is seven stories in height and is fully wet sprinklered and has a stand pipe system; or

(iv) ten thousand square feet if the building is fully wet sprinklered and has one hour rated ceilings.

(c) complies with the requirements of table 3-4 chapter twenty-six of the administrative code of the city of New York for J-2 occupancy.

3. Any part of the building may be occupied for manufacturing and commercial purposes (as permitted by local zoning law or resolution), provided, however, that only the second story and below may be occupied for uses listed as medium fire hazard in rules of the board of standards and appeals implementing the labor law unless the entire building is wet sprinklered; in addition, high fire hazard occupancies shall not be permitted in any portion of the building.

4. All areas occupied for manufacturing or commercial purposes shall be protected by an approved wet-pipe automatic sprinkler system. Such wet-pipe automatic sprinkler system shall extend to and include public hallways and stairways coincidentally serving residential occupancies.

5. All occupancies or tenancies shall be separated by a vertical fire separation, extending to the underside of the floor above and having a minimum fire-resistance rating of at least one hour and conform in all respects with applicable zoning regulations. No separation shall be required between the working and living portions of a joint living-work quarters for artists.

6. The building (a) complies with all requirements imposed on old-law tenements by sections two hundred twelve and two hundred sixteen of this chapter and on converted dwellings by sections one hundred eighty-five, one hundred eighty-six, one hundred eighty-eight, one hundred eighty-nine, one hundred ninety, one hundred ninety-one and one hundred ninety-four of this chapter, in addition to those provided in section two hundred seventy-eight of this article and (b) complies with the standards of lighting, ventilation, size of rooms, alcoves and balconies contained in section C26-1205.0 through and including sections C26-1205.5 and C26-1205.7 of the administrative code of the city of New York, except as otherwise provided in paragraph (d) of subdivision seven of this section.

7. Minimum light and air standards for joint living-work quarters for artists or general residential portions of lofts or manufacturing and commercial buildings altered to residential use shall comply with the following:

(a) Portions of such buildings which are occupied exclusively as joint living-work quarters for artists as permitted by local law shall comply with the following:

(i) The minimum size of a joint living-work quarters for artists shall be twelve hundred square feet of interior space, except as otherwise authorized by the zoning resolution of the city of New York, for units occupied for residential purposes on or before January first, nineteen hundred eighty-five.

(ii) Joint living-work quarters for artists shall conform to the standards for light and ventilation of sections C26-1205.0 through and including C26-1205.7 of the administrative code of the city of New York.

(b) Portions of such buildings which are occupied exclusively as residential units as permitted by local law shall comply with the following:

(i) Every dwelling unit shall have one or more windows:

A. which open onto a street, a court with a dimension of fifteen feet perpendicular to the windows and one hundred square feet minimum area above a setback or a thirty foot rear yard; or

B. for corner lots or lots within one hundred feet of a corner, where the minimum horizontal distance between such windows opening onto a rear yard and the rear lot line is at least twenty feet; or

C. for interior lots, where the minimum horizontal distance between such windows opening onto a rear yard and any wall opposite such windows on the same or another zoning lot is at least twenty feet and not less than a distance equal to one-third of the total height of such wall above the sill height of such windows; but need not exceed forty feet; or

D. for interior lots, where the minimum horizontal distance between such windows opening onto a rear yard and any wall opposite such windows on the same or another zoning lot is at least fifteen feet and the minimum size of such dwelling unit is twelve hundred square feet; or

E. in no event shall the distance between such windows and the rear lot line be less than five feet; and

F. yards and courts may be existing or may be new in buildings seven stories or less in height.

(ii) The minimum required ratio of window area opening onto a street, rear yard, or court to the floor area of every living room shall:

A. be ten percent where the floor area of such living room is less than five hundred square feet; or

    B. decrease, by one percent for every one hundred square feet greater than five hundred square feet of floor area of such living room, to a minimum of five percent; and

    C. in no event shall the distance between such window area and the rear lot line be less than five feet; and

    D. at least fifty percent of the required window area shall be openable.

(c) Ventilation of spaces other than living rooms, including enclosed work spaces for joint living-work quarters for artists shall be either in accordance with this section or in accordance with the administrative code of the city of New York.

(d) No building converted pursuant to this article shall be enlarged, except where the underlying zoning district permits residential use. Such an enlargement shall be in conformance with the bulk regulations for conforming residential use for new construction and shall be in conformance with the provisions of section twenty-six of this chapter. No interior floor area enlargement shall be permitted except that a mezzanine with a minimum headroom of seven feet shall be allowed within individual dwelling units, provided that the gross floor area of such mezzanine does not exceed one-third of the floor area contained within such dwelling unit. No mezzanine shall be included as floor area for the purpose of calculating the minimum required size of a living room or a dwelling unit or for calculating floor area devoted to dwellings. For the purpose of this article a mezzanine may be constructed above the level of the roof of a building as long as the aggregate area of roof structures does not exceed one-third of the total roof area and the roof structures conform with applicable building code requirements.

(e) The kitchen located within dwelling units and having a floor area of fifty-nine square feet or more shall have natural ventilation as prescribed in sub-article 1205.0 of chapter twenty-six of the administrative code of the city of New York. Open kitchens shall be considered as part of the adjacent space where forty percent of the area of the separation between the spaces is open and without doors. If the floor area of the combined space exceeds seven hundred fifty square feet, a separate bedroom shall not be required. When the floor area is less than fifty-nine square feet the kitchenette shall be ventilated by either of the following:

    (i) Natural means complying with sub-article 1205.0 of chapter twenty-six of the administrative code of the city of New York and further that the windows shall have a minimum width of twelve inches, a minimum area of three square feet, or ten percent of the floor area of the space, whichever is greater and be so constructed that at least one-half of their required area may be opened. When the space is located at the top story, the window or windows may be replaced with a skylight whose minimum width shall be twelve inches, whose minimum area shall be four square feet or one-eighth of the floor area of the space, whichever is greater and which shall have ventilation openings of at least one-half of the required area of the skylight.

(ii) Mechanical means exhausting at least two cubic feet per minute of air per square foot of floor area. Where doors are to be used to separate the space, the lower portion of each door shall have a metal grill containing at least forty-eight square inches of clean openings or in lieu of such grill, two clear opening spaces may be provided, each of at least twenty-four square inches, one between the bottom of each door and the floor and the other between the top of each door and the head jamb.

(f) When bathrooms and toilet rooms are ventilated by natural means, the natural ventilation sources shall comply with sub-article 1205.0 of chapter twenty-six of the administrative code of the city of New York and shall have an unobstructed free area of at least five percent of the floor area. In no case shall the net free area of the ventilation sources be less than one and one-half square feet. When bathrooms and toilet rooms are vented by mechanical means, individual vent shafts or ducts constructed of non-combustible materials with a minimum cross section area of one square foot shall be utilized, the exhaust system shall be capable of exhausting at least fifty cubic feet per minute of air. Means shall be provided for egress of air by louvers in doors, by undercutting the door, or by transfer ducts, grills or other openings. Toilet exhaust systems shall be arranged to expel air directly to the outdoors.

(g) A single station smoke detector shall be installed immediately outside each sleeping or bedroom area of each dwelling unit. Such device shall be designed and installed so as to detect smoke and activate an alarm, be reasonably free from false alarms and provide visible indication that the alarm is energized. Such device shall be directly connected to the lighting circuit of the dwelling or rooming unit with no intervening wall switch and shall provide a warning signal clearly audible in all sleeping quarters with intervening doors closed. Cord connected installations or smoke detectors which rely exclusively on batteries are not permissible. Such devices shall either be approved or listed by an acceptable testing service or laboratory.

8. All openings from apartments leading into a public hall or corridor shall be provided with fireproof doors and assemblies with the doors self-closing. Partitions between apartments on each floor shall be one hour fire rated partitions. All windows opening on fire escapes shall be provided with wire glass, unless such windows are protected by a wet pipe sprinkler head with a minimum of one head per window.

9. Such buildings, in regard to egress, shall comply with the following:

(a) In a non-fireproof building there shall be:

(i) one independently enclosed stairway and a fire escape from each dwelling unit; or

(ii) where the building is fully wet sprinklered and not in excess of seventy-five feet in height and not exceeding five thousand square feet in building area one independently enclosed stairway from each dwelling, and an independently enclosed hallway, of one hour fire rating where there are two or more tenants on a floor; or

(iii) a sprinklered enclosed hallway with access to two independently enclosed stairs.

(b) In a fireproof building, there shall be:

(i) an enclosed hallway and two independently enclosed stairs; or

(ii) an enclosed hallway and one independently enclosed stair and a screened exterior stair in conformance with section two hundred sixty-eight of the labor law with all glazed openings thereon equipped with wire glass; or

(iii) for buildings not exceeding seven stories or seventy-five feet in height, egress conforming with the provisions of paragraph (a) of this subdivision; or

(iv) egress conforming with the provisions of section one hundred two of this chapter.

(c) No more than two dwelling units shall open directly to a stair without an intervening enclosed hallway.

(d) Enclosed stairways shall have a one hour fire rating.

(e) Enclosed stairways shall be:

(i) one hour fire rated in non-fireproof buildings four stories or less in height; or

(ii) one hour fire rated and sprinklered in non-fireproof buildings six stories or less in height; or

(iii) one hour fire rated in non-fireproof, fully sprinklered buildings seven stories in height; or

(iv) two hour fire rated in all other cases.

(f) The travel distance to the means of egress shall comply with the administrative code of the city of New York.

(g) Wooden stairs permitted by section one hundred eighty-nine of this chapter may be retained only if, in addition to meeting all of the requirements set forth therein, they are within a fully wet-sprinklered enclosure, and the stair and landing soffit are fire retarded, notwithstanding any other provisions.

(h) Every required stair shall extend through the roof by a bulkhead, except that a scuttle may be used if the dwelling does not exceed four stories and except that no bulkhead or scuttle is required where the roof is a peak roof with a pitch of more than fifteen degrees.

(i) Mezzanines shall be provided with a stair at least two feet six inches wide terminating not more than twenty feet from an exit door or fire escape, and all portions of such mezzanines shall be not more than fifty feet from such exit door or fire escape.

10. In buildings in excess of two stories in height, stairways shall be

provided with skylights at least twenty square feet in area, glazed with plain glass with a wire screen over and under and provided with fixed or movable ventilators having a minimum open area of one hundred forty-four square inches. In lieu of the skylight and ventilators, a window of equal area may be provided with fixed louvers having a minimum open area of one hundred forty-four square inches installed in or immediately adjacent to the window.

11. Except as otherwise provided in this article, all shafts shall be enclosed with incombustible material of two hour fire rating and comply with the administrative code of the city of New York, provided, however, existing shaft enclosures constructed in part of combustible material may be retained if upgraded to obtain a two hour fire rating.

12. Every kitchen or kitchenette or cooking space in such building shall comply with the requirements imposed on multiple dwellings erected after April eighteenth, nineteen hundred twenty-nine by section thirty-three of this chapter.

13. Such building shall comply with all requirements imposed on multiple dwellings erected after April eighteenth, nineteen hundred twenty-nine by title three of article three of this chapter.

14. All interior iron columns in unsprinklered buildings shall be protected by materials or assemblies having a fire-resistive rating of at least three hours. Where sprinklers are provided for an exterior wall as provided in subdivision one of this section or in a fully wet sprinklered building such columns shall be protected by two sprinkler heads located eighteen inches or more away and each on opposite sides of such colmn but no further than four feet. Such sprinklers shall be provided at any interior column where fire protection is omitted in non-fireproof buildings.

15. The elevator shafts in such buildings shall be enclosed with incombustible material of two hour fire rating, except that existing elevator shaft enclosures constructed in part of combustible material may be retained if upgraded to obtain a two hour fire rating; and have fireproof doors and assemblies with (a) the doors self-closing; or (b) a vestibule the walls of which shall be of non-combustible material and have a minimum two hour fire resistive rating, with self-closing fireproof doors and be fire-stopped; or (c) where the elevator is manually operated in fully sprinklered buildings have fireproof doors, with approved interlock devices.

§278. APPLICATION OF OTHER PROVISIONS

1. The provisions of this article apply to buildings with residential, mixed or joint living-work quarters or artists' occupancy as herein provided and to such buildings only. In addition to the provisions of this article, the following enumerated articles and sections of this chapter shall, to the extent required therein, apply to such buildings:

Article   1. Introductory provisions: definitions
          2. Miscellaneous application provisions except subdivision two of section nine
          8. Requirements and remedies
          9. Registry of names and service of papers
          10. Prostitution
          11. Laws repealed; saving clause; effect
Section 28. Two or more buildings on same lot
          29. Painting of courts and shafts
          31. Size of rooms, subdivision six only
          37. Artificial hall lighting
          53. Fire-escapes
          55. Wainscoting, subdivision two only
          56. Frame buildings and extensions
          57. Bells; mail receptacles
          58. Incombustible materials
          59. Bakeries and fat boiling
          60. Motor vehicle storage
          61. Business uses (except paragraph c of subdivision one and subdivision three)
          62. Parapets, guard railings and wires

2. Failure to comply with any provision of this chapter other than this article and the above enumerated articles and sections shall not be grounds for refusal of a certificate of occupancy or compliance.

§7.1.3. *Matter of Marhoffer:* Who Is a Person "Regularly Engaged in the Fine Arts"?

Marhoffer, which follows, deals with the difficult if not impossible question of determining who is a person "regularly engaged in the fine arts . . . on a professional basis" for the purpose of securing certification to live in a live-work artists' district.[2]

---

[2] See also Pilgreen v. 91 Fifth Ave. Corp., 91 A.D.2d 565, 457 N.Y.S.2d 48 (1st Dept. 1982) (involving tenant photographers and a lack of certification as "artists" by the New York City Dept. of Cultural Affairs); and Lipkis v. Pikus, 96 Misc. 2d 581, 409 N.Y.S.2d 598, *aff'd,* 99 Misc. 2d 518, 416 N.Y.S.2d 694, *aff'd,* 72 A.D.2d 697, 421 N.Y.S.2d 825, *appeal dism'd,* 51 N.Y.2d 874, 433 N.Y.S.2d 1019, 414 N.E.2d 399 (1978) (involving artist-in-residence status and what constitutes a land board's consent to conversion). *Marhoffer, Pilgreen,* and *Lipkus* were decided under the Joint Living-Work Quarters statute, now appearing in N.Y. Mult. Dwell. Law, Art. 7-B, §§275 to 278 (McKinney Supp. 1986) and formerly appearing in N. Y. Arts and Cultural Affairs Law §§27.01 to 27.07 (McKinney 1983). The recodification of the law involved minor amendments.

MATTER OF MARHOFFER
N.Y.L.J., Jan. 14, 1985, at 13

SMITH, J. (City of New York) — This article 78 proceeding seeks, inter alia, an order reversing the decision of the respondent which denied petitioner artist certification pursuant to Multiple Dwelling Law §275 *et seq.*[1] and Zoning Resolution of the City of New York §§12-10 and 42-01.

The petitioner is a professional photographer and resident of a loft apartment located at 417 Lafayette Street, a building designated as an "interim multiple dwelling" pursuant to Multiple Dwelling Law §281. The loft is located in a district set aside for joint living-work quarters for artists pursuant to section 42-14D of the Zoning Resolution of the City of New York. Pursuant to sections 275 *et seq.* of the Multiple Dwelling Law and sections 42-01 and 42-14D of the Zoning Resolution of the City of New York, certification as an artist is necessary for an individual to qualify for joint living-work space in this district. In a letter dated May 18, 1982, respondent City of New York Department of Cultural Affairs denied petitioner's application. On Dec. 12, 1983 the Artists Certification Appeals Board upheld the initial decision.

The petitioner challenges the decision as (1) not being supported by substantial evidence; (2) contrary to the weight of the evidence; (3) in violation of lawful procedure; (4) arbitrary and capricious; (5) an unreasonable abuse of discretion and (6) conflicting with the Arts and Cultural Affairs Law and General Business Law. Respondent maintains that its decision was not arbitrary and capricious.

Both sections 275 and 276 of the Multiple Dwelling Law and section 42-01 of the Zoning Resolution of the City of New York provide that certification of artists for joint living-work space rests with the respondent New York City Department of Cultural Affairs. Multiple Dwelling Law §276 defines an artist as "a person who is regularly engaged in the fine arts, . . . on a professional basis, and is so certified by the city department of cultural affairs. . ." (McKinney's Supp. 1983-84). Respondent department allegedly utilizes the following guidelines in making its determination:

1. The individual is engaged in the fine arts, not the commercial arts,

---

[1] Effective Dec. 31, 1983 Multiple Dwelling Law §§275-278 were repealed. The provisions dealing with joint living-work quarters for artists now appear in the Arts and Cultural Affairs Law §27.01 *et seq.* Multiple Dwelling Law §§275 and 276 which will be referred to in this decision now appear in the Arts and Cultural Affairs Law §§27.01 and 27.03 respectively. [Effective Aug. 1, 1985, the Joint Living-Work Quarters statute was returned to the Multiple Dwelling Law where it now appears, with minor amendments, as Article 7-B, §§275 to 278 (McKinney Supp. 1986). — Eds.]

including but not necessarily limited to painting, sculpture, choreography, filmmaking and the composition of music, regularly and on a professional basis:

2. The individual demonstrates a serious, consistent commitment to his/her art form.
3. The individual is currently engaged in his/her art form.
4. The individual demonstrates a need for a large loft space in which to create his/her art. (See Respondent's Exhibit A)

In the petitioner's case, the respondent denied certification on the grounds that (1) his application failed to demonstrate a clear commitment to photography as a fine art and (2) the application failed to indicate a sufficient history of professional experience in fine art photography.

As part of the certification process, petitioner submitted an application with supporting documentation, including examples of his photographic work. Petitioner has annexed numerous photographs to his motion papers, including some which were published as book covers. (Petitioner's Exhibits G&H). Whether or not these are the samples which respondent considered is unclear. Also included as documentation is a resume in which petitioner claims to have held photographic exhibitions of his works (Petitioner's, Exhibit B). It appears to the Court that the petitioner is a professional photographer, a person at least within the art field. Whether he is in fact an artist within the statutory definition is a determination left to the respondent. In making that determination and denying certification the respondent appears to draw a subjective distinction not only between who is an "artist" and who is not, but also between who is an artist in the fine arts and who is an artist in the commercial arts. In a letter to plaintiff dated Jan. 27, 1984 respondent elaborates on its determination as follows:

> In the case of your application, although there is evidence of photography done on a commercial or work-for-hire basis, there is almost no indication of your professional involvement in photography as a fine art, nor recognition of this involvement by others in the field.

(Respondent's Exhibit M).

The problem here is that it is unclear what criteria the respondent city agency uses to determine whether certification as an artist should be granted. While the verified answer to the petition (paragraphs 19 and 20), as well as other papers submitted, speak in terms of specific criteria having been adopted, other documents of the agency make the fact of such adoption questionable. Thus the Department of Cultural Affairs of the City of New York has not promulgated any formal rules, regulations, or procedures to be followed in the determination of whether or not artist certification should be granted. In a January 27, 1984 response to a Freedom of Information Law Request by plaintiff, Howard Rubinstein,

Director of Management Services and Records Access Officer of Respondent Department of Cultural Affairs, wrote the following:

> In response to your request for rules and regulations governing the procedures followed by the Artist's Certification Committee, I should first note that the Department itself has no formal regulations regarding the artist's certification procedure. There do, however, exist informal regulations which were adopted by the Artist's Certification Committee ("ACC") to set guidelines for its own procedures. These regulations have never been the subject to promulgation by DCA; nor have they been formally approved by our Commissioner.

The same response went on to say that the agency had no documents which set forth criteria for "fine art photography" or which indicated what constitutes a "sufficient history of professional experience in fine art photography."

It is well settled that the construction given statutes and regulations by the agency responsible for their administration, if not irrational or unreasonable, should be upheld (*Matter of Howard v. Wyman*, 28 N.Y. 2d 434, 438 [1971]). The guidelines used by the respondent are not guidelines which have been adopted by the agency. Moreover they are too general, vague and prone to subjective analysis to be considered reasonable criteria in determining who is an artist for the purpose of determining eligibility for joint living-work quarters for artists. The need for more definite, objective guidelines is especially pronounced with reference to artist certification, as the consequence of denial will be the eventual eviction of the loft tenant.

For the foregoing reasons, petitioner's application is granted to the extent of remanding the matter for reconsideration under guidelines adopted by the agency. The petitioner's application is to be reconsidered under those new guidelines.

This decision constitutes the decision and order of the court.

§7.2. ARTISTS' MATERIALS: THE RIGHT TO BE WARNED

§7.2.1. Introduction

Industrial workers today are protected against exposure to toxic materials in the workplace by a whole maze of federal and local regulations. Until recently, artists — working alone in their studios, often using similarly toxic materials — have enjoyed no such protection. Under the prodding of such advocacy groups as the New York City Center for Occupational Hazards and the California Public Interest Research Group this situation has begun to change. Questions are being raised as to whether various fine-art materials are so potentially dangerous as to warrant state-mandated labeling laws and other warnings. Also being asked is whether the state should be obligated to go even further — i.e., become involved in the testing and/or banning of hazardous substances. As an alternative, might voluntary programs that are currently in effect suffice?

California was the first state to pass legislation on health hazards relating to fine-art supplies. Its law is reproduced in this section. Since then, Tennessee and Oregon have followed suit, enacting statutes based on California's.[1] Additionally, Illinois has passed a similar law, mandating the labeling of art materials used in schools.[2] (New York, Massachusetts, and New Jersey have introduced legislation that has yet to become law; Kentucky has also expressed an interest.)

Enacted in September of 1984, to be effective January 1, 1986, the California legislation involves two laws. The first is a labeling statute, the second a limitation on which school supplies may be purchased by the state. The labeling statute requires that art or craft materials containing certain toxic substances causing chronic illness (defined, in part, as substances that are even potentially carcinogenic to humans) be labeled according to specifications in the Act. Failure to label may result in seizure, and possible forfeiture, of misbranded or banned hazardous substances by the California State Department of Health Services; injunctive relief, to restrain violations of the Act, is also available to the state.

The consumer group the California legislature seeks to protect is broad-based: professional artists and craftspersons, art teachers, hobbyists, students (at all educational levels), and children. The group upon whom the duty to warn falls covers the entire span of the commercial chain: Those that manufacture, distribute, and sell art or craft materials must convey to the consumer information concerning the potential health hazards of their products.

More generally, manufacturers have attempted to enact a voluntary nationwide labeling program to avoid the potential complication of diverse state labeling laws, each requiring different information. Can this work or is federal legislation needed?

---

§7.2. [1] Tenn. Code Ann. §§49-50-1201 to 49-50-1204 (Supp. 1985); Or. Rev. Stat. §§453.205 to 453.275 (1985).

[2] The law, called the Toxic Art Supplies in Schools Act, will take effect June 1986. Ill. Ann. Stat., ch. 122, ¶1601, et seq. (Smith-Hurd Supp. 1986).

§7.2.2. California Legislation: Mandatory Labeling and Restricted Purchase of Toxic Art Supplies

By enacting the following law, California was the first state to recognize that artists working alone in studios did not have the benefit of an employment setting for receiving warnings about hazardous substances with which they might interact. The legislation was also in response to concern for school children who might also be exposed to these hazards in the classroom.

MANDATORY LABELING LAW
Cal. Health & Safety Code*

LEGISLATIVE COUNSEL'S DIGEST
AB 3438, Sher. Toxic substances: labeling of art or craft material.

(1) Existing law, in the California Hazardous Substances Act, requires that certain hazardous substances, as defined, or products which contain a hazardous substance, be labeled, as specified. That act permits the State Department of Health Services to seize misbranded or banned hazardous substances, and to bring forfeiture proceedings in the superior court. It also authorizes the department to bring an action for an injunction to restrain anyone from violating that act. A violation of any provision of the act is a misdemeanor.

This bill would impose a state-mandated local program by adding to the California Hazardous Substances Act provisions which would require that art or craft materials containing certain toxic substances causing chronic illness, as defined, be labeled, as specified. These provisions would become operative January 1, 1986.

(2) Article XIII B of the California Constitution and Sections 2231 and 2234 of the Revenue and Taxation Code require the state to reimburse local agencies and school districts for certain costs mandated by the state. Other provisions require the Department of Finance to review statutes disclaiming these costs and provide, in certain cases, for making claims to the State Board of Control for reimbursement.

---

* [The Mandatory Labeling Law was an act to amend §28758.5 of Chapter 13 of Division 22 of the Health and Safety Code; its purpose was also to add §§28741.5, 28744.5, and 28745.5 to the Code; further, it added Article 4 (commencing with §28794) to the Code. The restrictions on purchases of toxic art supplies was an act to add Article 5 (commencing with §49350) to Chapter 8 of Part 27 of the Education Code. — Eds.]

However, this bill would provide that no appropriation is made and no reimbursement is required by this act for a specified reason.

The people of the State of California do enact as follows:

SECTION 1. Section 28741.5 is added to the Health and Safety Code, to read:

28741.5 The term "art or craft material" means any raw or processed material or manufactured product marketed or being represented by the manufacturer, repackager or retailer as being suitable for use in any phase of the creation of any work of visual or graphic art of any medium. These mediums may include, but shall not be limited to, paintings, drawings, prints, sculpture, ceramics, enamels, jewelry, stained glass, plastic sculpture, photographs, and leather and textile goods. The term shall not include economic poisons subject to the Federal Insecticide, Fungicide, and Rodenticide Act (61 Stats. 163) or Chapter 2 (commencing with Section 12751) of Division 7 of the Food and Agricultural Code; or to drugs, devices, or cosmetics, which are subject to the Federal Food, Drug and Cosmetics Act (52 Stats. 1040) or Division 21 (commencing with Section 26000).

SEC. 2. Section 28744.5 is added to the Health and Safety Code, to read:

28744.5 The term "human carcinogen" means any substance listed as a human carcinogen by the International Agency for Research on Cancer.

The term "potential human carcinogen" means one of the following:

(1) Any substance which does not meet the definition of human carcinogen, but for which there exists sufficient evidence of carcinogenicity in animals, as determined by the International Agency fo Research on Cancer.

(2) Any chemical shown to be changed by the human body into a human carcinogen.

SEC. 3. Section 28745.5 is added to the Health and Safety Code, to read:

28745.5. The term "toxic substance causing chronic illness" means any of the following:

(1) Human carcinogens.

(2) Potential human carcinogens.

(3) Any substance included in the list of hazardous substances prepared by the Director of industrial Relations, pursuant to Section 6382 of the Labor Code, notwithstanding exemptions made for substances on the list which are used in particular forms, circumstances, or concentrations, if the health hazard presented by the substance is not the subject of label statements required by federal law.

SEC. 4. Section 28758.5 of the Health and Safety Code is amended to read:

28758.5. Notwithstanding any other provision of this chapter, no substance or article shall be deemed to violate any provision of this chapter except the provisions of Article 4 (commencing with Section 28794), if the substance or article complies with federal law.

SEC. 5. Article 4 (commencing with Section 28794) is added to Chapter 13 of Division 22 of the Health and Safety Code, to read:

Article 4. Art or Craft Materials

28794. For the purposes of this article, an art or craft material shall be presumed to contain an ingredient which is a toxic substance causing chronic illness if the ingredient, whether an intentional ingredient or an impurity, is 1 percent or more by weight of the mixture or product, or if the department determines that the toxic or carcinogenic properties of the art or craft material are such that labeling is necessary for the adequate protection of the public health and safety.

28795. The Legislature finds and declares that there exists a significant danger to the public health and safety from exposure to art or craft material which contains toxic chemicals. This health risk threatens not only professional artists and craftspersons, but art teachers, students at every educational level, hobbyists, and children. Toxic substances may be employed during the course and scope of creating art or craft objects of all varieties.

The Legislature additionally finds and declares that present labeling of ingredients and hazards of art or craft material is insufficient to adequately protect the consumers of this state from chronic adverse health effects. Because many persons do not know what toxic chemical substances they work with, proper precautionary actions cannot be taken. Disclosure of toxic ingredients, their possible adverse effects on health, and instructions for safe handling, will substantially minimize unnecessary exposure to excessive risk.

Additionally, the Legislature finds and declares that it is consistent to impose upon those who manufacture, repackage, distribute, and sell art or craft material a duty to convey to consumers information about the potential health hazards of the products they manufacture.

Therefore, the Legislature intends by this article to ensure that consumers be provided information concerning the nature of the toxic substances with which they are working and the known and suspected health hazards of these substances, and to ensure the uniformity of labeling standards, so that materials with similar hazards also have essentially similar labels.

28796. No person shall distribute, sell, offer for sale, or expose for sale any art or craft material containing toxic substances causing chronic illness on which the person:

(a) Has failed to affix a conspicuous label containing the signal word "WARNING," to alert users of potential adverse health effects.

(b) Has failed to affix a conspicuous label warning of the health-related dangers of the art or craft material.

(1) If the product contains a human carcinogen, the warning shall contain the statement: "CANCER HAZARD! Overexposure may create cancer risk."

(2) If the product contains a potential human carcinogen, and does not contain a human carcinogen, the warning shall contain the statement: "POSSIBLE CANCER HAZARD! Overexposure might create cancer risk."

(3) If the product contains a toxic substance causing chronic illness, the warning shall contain, but not be limited to, the following statement or statements where applicable:

(A) May cause sterility or damage to reproductive organs.

(B) May cause birth defects or harm to developing fetus.

(C) May be excreted in human milk causing harm to nursing infant.

(D) May cause central nervous system depression or injury.

(E) May cause numbness or weakness in the extemities.

(F) Overexposure may cause damage to (specify organ).

(G) Heating above (specify degrees) may cause hazardous decomposition products.

(4) If a product contains more than one chronically toxic substance, or if a single substance can cause more than one chronic health effect, the required statements may be combined into one warning statement.

(c) Has failed to affix on the label a list of ingredients which are toxic substances causing chronic illness.

(d) Has failed to affix on the label a statement or statements of safe use and storage instructions, conforming to the following list. The label shall contain, but not be limited to, as many of the following risk statements as are applicable:

(1) Keep out of reach of children.

(2) When using, do not eat, drink, or smoke.

(3) Wash hands after use and before eating, drinking, or smoking.

(4) Keep container tightly closed.

(5) Store in well ventilated area.

(6) Avoid contact with skin.

(7) Wear protective clothing (specify type).

(8) Wear NIOSH certified masks for dusts, mists, or fumes.

(9) Wear NIOSH certified respirator with appropriate cartridge for (specify type).

(10) Wear NIOSH certified supplied-air respirator.

(11) Use window exhaust fan to remove vapors and assure adequate ventilation (specify explosion proof if necessary).

(12) Use local exhaust hood (specify type).

(13) Do not heat above (specify degrees) without adequate ventilation.

(14) Do not use or mix with (specify material).

(e) Has failed to affix on the label a statement on where to obtain more information, such as "call your local poison control center for more health information."

(f) Has failed to affix on the label the name and address of the manufacturer.

(g) If all of the above information cannot fit on the package label, a package insert shall be required to convey all the necessary information to the consumer. In this event, the label shall contain a statement to refer to the package insert, such as "CAUTION: see package insert before use." For purposes of this section, "package insert" means a display of written, printed, or graphic matter upon a leaflet or suitable material accompanying the art supply. The language on this insert shall be non-technical and nonpromotional in tone and content.

Art or craft material offered for sale in containers which contain less than one fluid ounce (30 milliliters) or one ounce net (29 grams) shall be deemed to comply with this section if there is affixed on the container a precautionary label that includes the words "USE WITH CAUTION: Contains Hazardous Substances."

The requirements set forth in subdivisions (a) to (g), inclusive, shall not be considered to be complied with unless the required words, statements, or other information appear on the outside container or wrapper, or on a package insert which is easily legible through the outside container or wrapper and is painted in a color in contrast with the product or the package containing the product.

(h) Pursuant to Section 28778, the department may exempt a material from full compliance with this article. In considering this exemption, the department shall take into consideration the potential for reasonably forseeable misuse of a material by a child.

(i) If an art or craft material complies with labeling standards D-4236 of the American Society for Testing and Materials (ASTM), the material complies with the provisions of this article, unless the department determines that the label on an art or craft material does not satisfy the purposes of this article.

28797. (a) The manufacturer of any art or craft material sold, distributed, offered for sale, or exposed for sale in this state shall supply to a national poison control network approved by the director the formulation information required by that network for dissemination to poison control centers. Failure to file formulation information with an approved poison control network is a violation of this chapter.

(b) The requirements set forth in Section 28796 shall not be considered to be complied with unless all required words, statements, or other information accompany art or craft materials from manufacturer to consumer, not excluding any distributor, packager, repackager, or retailer.

SEC. 6. Sections 1 to 5, inclusive, of this act shall become operative January 1, 1986.

SEC. 7. No appropriation is made and no reimbursement is required by this act pursuant to Section 6 of Article XIII B of the California Constitution or Section 2231 or 2234 of the Revenue and Taxation Code because the only costs which may be incurred by a local agency or school district will be incurred because this act creates a new crime or infraction, changes the definition of a crime or infraction, changes the penalty for a crime or infraction, or eliminates a crime or infraction.

PURCHASE OF TOXIC ART SUPPLIES LAW
Cal. Educ. Code

LEGISLATIVE COUNSEL'S DIGEST
AB 3439, Sher. Schools: toxic art supplies.

(1) Existing law does not restrict the purchase of toxic art supplies in schools.

This bill would prohibit the purchase of specified toxic art supplies for use in kindergarten and grades 1 to 6, inclusive, and would impose a state-mandated local program by restricting the purchase of these materials for use in grades 7 to 12, inclusive, as specified.

(2) Article XIII B of the California Constitution and Sections 2231 and 2234 of the Revenue and Taxation Code require the state to reimburse local agencies and school districts for certain costs mandated by the state. Other provisions require the Department of Finance to review statutes disclaiming these costs and provide, in certain cases, for making claims to the State Board of Control for reimbursement.

This bill would provide that no appropriation is made by this act for the purpose of making reimbursement pursuant to the constitutional mandate or Section 2231 or 2234, but would recognize that local agencies and school districts may pursue their other available remedies to seek reimbursement for these costs.

(3) This bill would provide that, notwithstanding Section 2231.5 of the Revenue and Taxation Code, this act does not contain a repealer, as required by that section; therefore, the provisions of the act would remain in effect unless and until they are amended or repealed by a later enacted act.

(4) The bill would become operative June 1, 1986.

The people of the State of California do enact as follows:

SECTION 1. Article 5 (commencing with Section 49350) is added to Chapter 8 of Part 27 of the Education Code, to read:

Article 5. Toxic Art Supplies in Schools

49350. (a) The Legislature finds and declares that art supplies which contain toxic substances or which are potential human carcinogens pose a significant danger to the health and safety of school children. The Legislature also finds and declares that school children are not sufficiently protected by present health laws in so far as materials which may be seriously harmful are not so labeled and therefore children are not properly warned as to the dangers inherent in the use of those materials.

(b) The Legislature intends by this article to ensure that elementary school children are protected by prohibiting the sale of these toxic substances to schools and school districts for use in kindergarten and grades 1 to 6, inclusive, and that the toxic substances may be purchased by schools and school districts for students in grades 7 to 12, inclusive, only if the materials are properly labeled, as described in Section 49354.

49351. The term "art or craft material" means any raw or processed material or manufactured product marketed or being represented by the manufacturer or repackager as being suitable for use in the demonstration or the creation of any work of visual or graphic art of any medium. These media may include, but shall not be limited to, paintings, drawings, prints, sculpture, ceramics, enamels, jewelry, stained glass, plastic sculpture, photographs, and leather and textile goods.

49352. The term "human carcinogen" means any substance listed as a human carcinogen by the International Agency for Research on Cancer.

The term "potential human carcinogen" means one of the following:

(1) Any substance which does not meet the definition of human carcinogen, but for which there exists sufficient evidence of carcinogenicity in animals, as determined by the International Agency for Research on Cancer.

(2) Any chemical shown to be changed by the human body into a human carcinogen.

49353. The term "toxic substance causing chronic illness" means any of the following:

(1) Human carcinogens.

(2) Potential human carcinogens.

(3) Any substance included in the list of hazardous substances prepared by the Director of Industrial Relations, pursuant to Section 6382 of the Labor Code, notwithstanding exemptions made for substances on the list which are used in particular forms, circumstances, or concentrations, if the health hazard presented by the substance is not the subject of label statements required by federal law.

49354. (a) For the 1986-87 academic year and for each academic year thereafter, no art or craft material which is deemed by the State Department of Health Services to contain a toxic substance, as defined by the California Hazardous Substance Act, Chapter 13 (commencing with

Section 28740) of Division 22 of the Health and Safety Code, or a toxic substance causing chronic illness, as defined in this article, shall be ordered or purchased by any school or school district in California for use by students in kindergarten and grades 1 to 6, inclusive.

(b) Commencing June 1, 1986, any substance which is defined in subdivision (a) as a toxic substance causing chronic illness shall not be purchased or ordered by a school or school district for use by students in grades 7 to 12, inclusive, unless it meets the labeling standards specified in Section 49355.

(c) If the State Department of Health Services finds that, because the chronically toxic, carcinogenic, or radioactive substances contained in an art or craft product cannot be ingested, inhaled, or otherwise absorbed into the body during any reasonably foreseeable use of the product in a way that could pose a potential health risk, the department may exempt the product from these requirements to the extent it determines to be consistent with adequate protection of the public health and safety.

(d) For the purposes of this article, an art or craft material shall be presumed to contain an ingredient which is a toxic substance causing chronic illness if the ingredient, whether an intentional ingredient or an impurity, is 1 percent or more by weight of the mixture or product, or if the State Department of Health Services determines that the toxic or carcinogenic properties of the art or craft material are such that labeling is necessary for the adequate protection of the public health and safety.

49355. Warning labels for substances specified in Section 49354 shall meet all of the following standards:

(a) The warning label shall be affixed in a conspicuous place and shall contain the signal word "WARNING," to alert users of potential adverse health effects.

(b) The warning label shall contain information on the health-related dangers of the art or craft material.

(1) If the product contains a human carcinogen, the warning shall contain the statement: "CANCER HAZARD! Overexposure may create cancer risk."

(2) If the product contains a potential human carcinogen, and does not contain a human carcinogen, the warning shall contain the statement: "POSSIBLE CANCER HAZARD! Overexposure might create cancer risk."

(3) If the product contains a toxic substance causing chronic illness, the warning shall contain, but not be limited to, the following statement or statements where applicable:

(A) May cause sterility or damage to reproductive organs.

(B) May cause birth defects or harm to developing fetus.

(C) May be excreted in human milk causing harm to nursing infant.

(D) May cause central nervous system depression or injury.

(E) May cause numbness or weakness in the extremities.

(F) Overexposure may cause damage to (specify organ).

(G) Heating above (specify degrees) may cause hazardous decomposition products.

(4) If a product contains more than one chronically toxic substance, or if a single substance can cause more than one chronic health effect, the required statements may be combined into one warning statement.

(c) The warning label shall contain a list of ingredients which are toxic substances causing chronic illness.

(d) The warning label shall contain a statement or statements of safe use and storage instructions, conforming to the following list. The label shall contain, but not be limited to, as many of the following risk statements as are applicable:

(1) Keep out of reach of children.

(2) When using, do not eat, drink, or smoke.

(3) Wash hands after use and before eating, drinking, or smoking.

(4) Keep container tightly closed.

(5) Store in well-ventilated area.

(6) Avoid contact with skin.

(7) Wear protective clothing (specify type).

(8) Wear NIOSH certified masks for dust, mists, or fumes.

(9) Wear NIOSH certified respirator with appropriate cartridge for (specify type).

(10) Wear NIOSH certified supplied-air respirator.

(11) Use window exhaust fan to remove vapors and assure adequate ventilation (specify explosion-proof if necessary).

(12) Use local exhaust hood (specify type).

(13) Do not heat above (specify degrees) without adequate ventilation.

(14) Do not use/mix with (specify material).

(e) The warning label shall contain a statement on where to obtain more information, such as, "Call your local poison control center for more health information."

(f) The warning label, or any other label on the substance, shall contain the name and address of the manufacturer or repackager.

(g) If all of the above information cannot fit on the package label, a package insert shall be required to convey all the necessary information to the consumer. In this event, the label shall contain a statement to refer to the package insert, such as "CAUTION: See package insert before use." For purposes of this section, "package insert" means a display of written, printed, or graphic matter upon a leaflet or suitable material accompanying the art supply. The language on this insert shall be nontechnical and nonpromotional in tone and content.

(h) Art or craft material offered for sale in containers which contain less than 1 fluid ounce (30 milliliters) or 1 ounce net (29 grams) shall be deemed to comply with this section if there is affixed thereon a precautionary label that includes the signal works "USE WITH CAUTION: Contains Hazardous Substances," and a list of potentially harmful or sensitizing ingredients.

The requirements set forth in subdivisions (a) to (g), inclusive, shall not be considered to be complied with unless the required words, statements, or other information appear on the outside container or wrapper, or on a package insert which is easily legible through the outside container or wrapper and is painted in a color in contrast with the product or the package containing the product.

An art or craft material shall be considered to be in compliance with this section if Article 4 (commencing with Section 28794) of Chapter 13 of Division 22 of the Health and Safety Code requires labeling of the art or craft material, and if the material is in compliance with that article.

49356. The State Department of Health Services shall, by June 1, 1986, develop a list of those art or craft materials which cannot be purchased or ordered for use in kindergarten and in grades 1 to 6, inclusive, and a list of materials which, while not currently sold or manufactured, may be reasonably suspected to still exist at some schools. In developing the lists, the State Department of Health Services shall consult with manufacturers of art supplies, artists' groups, health organizations, and toxicologists as the State Department of Health Services deems appropriate.

The Superintendent of Public Instruction shall distribute the lists to all school districts in California, and shall make the lists available to preschools, childcare centers, and other businesses and organizations which involve children in the use of art or craft materials.

The superintendent shall inform school districts of the requirements of this article, and shall encourage school districts to dispose of art or craft material which may contain human carcinogens, potential human carcinogens, or chronically toxic substances, but which is not affected by this article.

SEC. 2. Notwithstanding Section 6 of Article XIII B of the California Constitution and Section 2231 or 2234 of the Revenue and Taxation Code, no appropriation is made by this act for the purpose of making reimbursement pursuant to these sections. It is recognized, however, that a local agency or school district may pursue any remedies to obtain reimbursement available to it under Chapter 3 (commencing with Section 2201) of Part 4 of Division 1 of that code.

SEC. 3. Notwithstanding Section 2231.5 of the Revenue and Taxation Code, this act does not contain a repealer, as required by that section; therefore, the provisions of this act shall remain in effect unless and until they are amended or repealed by a later enacted act.

SEC. 4. This act shall become operative June 1, 1986.

CHAPTER EIGHT

The Artist's Estate

•

§8.1. CONSEQUENCES OF THE ARTIST'S DEATH

§8.1.1. Introduction

The death of an artist has a number of important legal conse-quences. Among the parties who may be affected are those who had, or have, business relations with him, and his family or other heirs.

In terms of the subsequent market value of an artist's works, death makes a sharp distinction between the output of an artist who at the time he died was perceived as successful and the work of one who was not. For the latter, death may often mean the collapse of his primary market — and unrecognized artists rarely have a secondary one — a market fre-quently sustained through unceasing personal effort, a charismatic per-sonality, or the kindness of a loyal relative, personal friend, or corporate patron. With the artist no longer alive to "hustle" his work, its market value may very quickly evaporate.

For the artist considered successful, however, the impact of his death on sales may be exactly the opposite. By closing out his *oeuvre,* it forces the hands of those collectors who had continually postponed their purchases in order to see what he might do next. It also introduces a scarcity factor. Prices may be expected to rise, the primary market will dwindle as the last of a finite inventory is liquidated, and an active secondary market can be expected.

The two cases reproduced in the first part of this chapter involve works of art left by two American artists, the painter Franz Kline and the sculptor David Smith, recognized as leading members of the abstract expressionist generation at the time of their deaths. Kline's death in 1962 from a recurring heart ailment was to a degree expected; Smith died unexpectedly in 1965 from a violent accident. The market values for both of their works have escalated steadily ever since. Each of the deaths was followed by an important judicial decision addressing post-mortem controversies over the ownership or value of the artist's output, controversies that might have been anticipated for such "successful" artists. The courts' opinions are reproduced in this section together with our observations. A brief discussion follows concerning the special provisions that several states include in their estate tax statutes for visual artists.

Another of the changes brought about by an artist's death is a temporary substitution in the management of the sale and distribution of his work. Whether this substitution is brief or for a longer period will depend on what, if any, testamentary provisions the artist has made. During his lifetime the artist may be business-like or capricious, or both. Following his death, however, his personal representative — whether denominated as an administrator, executor, or trustee — must adhere to a fiduciary standard requiring both undivided loyalty and prudent care. Transactions with an artist's personal representative that involve the breach of either or both of these duties may have far-reaching legal consequences for everyone concerned. The role of the artist's fiduciary — particularly as exemplified in the cases of Kline and Smith's noted contemporary, the painter Mark Rothko, and the relatively unknown Arnold Friedman — is examined in the second part of this chapter.

§8.1.2. *Estate of Franz Kline:* The Role of the Dealer at the Artist's Death

Although Franz Kline's paintings had been seen earlier in several group exhibitions, it was not until 1950 that the dealer Charles Egan gave him his first one-man exhibition in New York. Kline showed again with Egan in 1951 and 1954. Notwithstanding that Kline later transferred to the more prestigious Sidney Janis Gallery, he remained grateful to Egan and provided in his will that the dealer might have two paintings of his own choosing. After Egan made his choice, Kline's executrix advised him that those particular paintings were not available, having been sold prior to the artist's death. Egan suspected this was not so and instituted a proceeding against the estate. The court's opinion follows.

ESTATE OF FRANZ KLINE

N.Y.L.J., Mar. 31, 1964, at 14, cols.6-7 (Surr. Ct. 1964)

Cox, Surr. The testator, who was a modern abstract artist of established reputation, bequeathed his "studio equipment, studio materials and two large paintings created by me to Charles Egan. . . ." This provision of the will also stated: "These paintings shall be selected by Mr. Egan prior to the disposition of my works by my executrix." When Mr. Egan selected two paintings known as "1960 New Year Wall Night" and "Shenandoah Wall 1961" he was advised by the executrix that these two works had been sold in the testator's lifetime and were not available to the legatee. Thereafter Mr. Egan instituted this proceeding to compel delivery to him of these paintings, his contention being that a sale of the paintings had not been accomplished prior to the testator's death. The answer of the executrix indicated that the facts relating to the disposition of the paintings were peculiarly within the knowledge of Sidney Janis who acted as the testator's sales representative and allegedly had negotiated the sale of one painting to the Art Institute of Chicago and himself had purchased the other painting. The motion of Mr. Janis to intervene in this proceeding was unopposed and was granted.

The essential facts, developed at the hearings, are not in dispute. In early March, 1962, Mr. Janis, acting as the agent of the testator shipped the painting known as *1960 New Year Wall Night* to the Art Institute of Chicago for its approval and offered to sell the painting at a net price of $18,000. A committee of the institute known as the Committee on Twentieth Century Painting and Sculpture met on May 9, 1962, and recommended the acquisition of the painting by the institute. The testimony of the representatives of the institute was that this committee's function was advisory and its authority was to recommend to the board of trustees appropriate purchases to be made by the institute. Concededly the board of trustees had the power to disapprove the recommendations of this committee and until action by the board of trustees, the advice of the committee was not a commitment of the institute under any provision of its bylaws. In actual practice the recommendations of the committee had not been regarded as conclusive. The function of this committee was defined not only in the testimony of the representatives of the institute but in correspondence with Mr. Janis in which Mr. Speyer, the curator of the institute, reported that the committee had "recommended to the trustees of the Art Institute of Chicago the purchase of your painting." While there was evidence that certain funds were particularly allocated for purchases within the field of art with which this committee was concerned, it does not appear that the committee had control of these funds and it is clear that the funds for the purchase of the testator's painting were made available through a donation of a member of the committee and the allocation of moneys from the Goodman Fund, which admittedly was not within the control of the committee.

Until such time as the board of trustees had accepted the recommendation of the committee and, by such act, had made funds available for the acquisition of the painting, the corporate action essential to a commitment of the institute had not been taken. The board of trustees did meet on May 14, 1962, and did approve the recommendation of the committee as to the purchase of the painting but the intervening fact was that on May 13, 1962, the testator had died. The testator's death was known to the institute at the time its board of trustees met and attempted to accomplish the purchase of the painting. The proof also was that, upon learning of the testator's death, Mr. Janis' son had made some attempt to withdraw the picture from sale.

A purported copy of an invoice from the Janis office, dated May 11, 1962, has not been substantiated and the court is satisfied that the only invoice in this transaction was a receipt invoice mailed to the institute to [by] Mr. Janis on May 17, 1962, a date subsequent to his actual receipt of the institute's check.

Upon these facts it is the position of the legatee that a sale was not consummated in the testator's lifetime and could not have been accomplished subsequent to his death because the authority of Mr. Janis to act as the testator's agent terminated on the latter's death. The position of the legatee is sound and it must be concluded that the authority of Mr. Janis terminated on May 13, 1962, when testator died.[1] On that date the necessary corporate action had not been taken to accomplish the purchase of the painting. The board of trustees could not effectively accept the Janis offer on May 14, 1962, a time when Mr. Janis did not have a principal for which to act. This conclusion rests upon the internal requirements of the corporation as to its functioning as distinguished from the view of a contracting party seeking to enforce a contract against the

---

[1] Vincent v. Rix, 248 N.Y. 76; Farmers' Loan & Trust Co. v. Winthrop, 238 N.Y. 477; Farmers' Loan & Trust Co. v. Wilson, 139 N.Y. 284; Matter of Tabbagh, 167 Misc. 156; Matter of Weber, 163 Misc. 81; Matter of Shuke, 165 Misc. 554; Matter of Zweig, 176 Misc. 770; Matter of Ihmsen, 253 App. Div. 472.

corporation. Although a contracting party may be in a position to enforce an unauthorized contract upon the basis of an estoppel or because of representations of a corporation employee or by reason of a holding out by the corporation, it does not follow that the corporation itself can take advantage of such acts to enforce an actually unauthorized contract.

It is held that this painting was available to the legatee under the terms of the will and the executrix will be required to deliver the painting to the legatee or to account to him for its value.

The respondent Janis contends that he purchased the painting *Shenandoah Wall 1961,* for himself and his wife on January 15, 1962, after an attempt[ed] sale to a customer had fallen through. All testimony by Mr. Janis with respect to his alleged purchase of the painting was barred by section 4519 of the Civil Practice Law and Rules. The evidence which may be considered in connection with this transaction is found in books and ledgers maintained in the regular course of business and established by an accountant and the testimony of a warehouseman. The testimony of the warehouseman gives no support to the claim of title made by Mr. Janis but establishes only that the painting was released to Mr. Janis pursuant to written instructions from the attorney for the executrix and upon presentation of an estate tax waiver. Prior to the testator's death Mr. Janis had [not] asserted ownership of the painting nor had he exercised any dominion or control over it.

There is some question as to the authenticity of book entries allegedly made in the regular course of business but, if these entries were accepted, they would not establish the alleged sale. There is no indication that the testator ever was apprised of the alleged purchase by Mr. Janis and this fact alone would vitiate any attempted sale. An agent employed to sell cannot, without disclosure to the principal, buy goods on his own account even though he pays a higher price than the principal could obtain otherwise (Restatement of Law: Agency 2d, sec. 389). The reason for the rule is evident and has been commented upon by our courts on numerous occasions. The duty of the agent is to act solely for the benefit of his principal and without any conflict of interest.[2]

The respondent Janis will be directed to return to the executrix the painting known as *Shenandoah Wall 1961,* and the executrix will be directed to turn over the painting to the petitioner.

Submit decree on notice.

The decision of the New York County Surrogate's Court in *Estate of Franz Kline* raises a number of danger signals concerning business prac-

---

[2] Matter of Clarke, 12 N.Y.2d 183; Matter of Hubbell, 302 N.Y. 246; Matter of People v. Bond & Mortgage Guar. Co., 303 N.Y. 423; Matter of Jones, 8 N.Y.2d 24; Meinhard v. Salmon, 249 N.Y. 458; Dutton v. Willner, 52 N.Y. 312.

tices that are sometimes considered "normal" in the art world. For those artists who prefer handshake agreements with their dealers (see, for example, the comments of Robert Rauschenberg and Robert Motherwell quoted at §3.1.1 *supra*), the case ought to be a particular caution as to what might happen when they die. An authorization to deal for an artist — unless embedded in some agreement binding on the artist's heirs or in some way coupled with a continuing interest on the dealer's part — is no different from any other agency that ends with the death of the principal.

Why should an artist care? Several reasons can be suggested. To begin with, the period immediately after his death might be an opportune moment for the sale of his work — not simply to gain posthumous glory, but to raise the funds that his family may need, for example, to substitute for a lost teaching salary, to pay the deceased's medical bills, or even to cover funeral costs and a possibly considerable estate tax. If there are delays in the appointment of a personal representative, a significant amount of time may pass before anyone can be empowered to deal with the artist's work. Thus, an important opportunity might be lost.

Consider the more extreme case of an artist without a written agreement with his dealer — or even the possibility of an artist who dies on the eve of an exhibition with a written agreement that does not contemplate substituting his estate as the dealer's principal. If the dealer must be newly appointed as agent for the estate — and that assumes that the artist has left a personal representative who is by then both empowered *and* willing to retain the dealer — would the dealer be bound to the same commission structure that the artist negotiated during his lifetime? Could he try to persuade the bereaved spouse that his percentage should be larger? (On the other hand, of course, the dealer might have already advanced funds to print catalogues, purchase advertisements, and ship a dozen two-ton sculptures from the other side of the globe. In such a case, a not-so-bereaved spouse might just as easily try to persuade the dealer that it is the estate's percentage which should be larger!) Given that death is inevitably a disruptive event, to the extent that an artist can temper this disruption through arrangements made in advance, the well-being of his heirs (and perhaps of his market, too) may be protected.

The *Kline* case also suggests the degree to which death may vitiate arrangements so casual — in this case the alleged sale of a painting to Sidney Janis and his wife — that they lack any documentary evidence. Under so-called deadman's statutes, testimony as to certain conversations with a person before his death (particularly conversations advantageous to the witness) may be inadmissible. In the *Kline* case, not even the best documentary evidence could have overcome the larger point: Without some evidence that the artist had known of and consented to the sale, it would not be recognized. While the agent's payment of the painting's full price (or even more) may not violate his fiduciary duty of prudent care, dealing on his own behalf *does* violate his duty of undivided loyalty. See in this connection the *Rothko* and *Friedman* cases in §8.2 *infra*. Again, if the parties had intended that the dealer be able to buy the artist's work, a written agreement could have made this possible. The right of an art dealer to purchase consigned paintings for his own account is too important a matter not to be settled at the formative stages of his relationship with the artist and memorialized in some admissible way. Equally, the manifest absence of a regular accounting procedure between the artist and the dealer here contributed, in the end, to the failure of the dealer's claim that he had purchased the painting himself. (As for the right of a dealer in New York to purchase a painting consigned to him by an artist, see Article 12 of the New York Arts and Cultural Affairs Law in §3.2.2 *supra*.)

Wholly aside from issues relative to the artist's death, the *Kline* case raises the question of where the authority lies within the organizational structure of a particular museum to conclude a purchase. This must generally be discovered by reference to the institution's by-laws. In some museums (as was the case here with the Art Institute of Chicago), only the Board of Trustees or other governing body can commit the institution to a purchase. In others, a Collections (or similar) Committee of the Board may have this authority. In still others, the director or even a curator may be empowered to buy. Further, even within a single museum, the determination of who is entitled to make a particular purchase may depend on the amount of the purchase price, the funds out of which the purchase price is to be paid, or still other factors. A prudent dealer or collector engaged in dealing with a museum — whether selling or buying from it — should always ascertain the precise authority of the representative with whom he is negotiating.

§8.1.3. *Estate of David Smith:* Fair Market Value at Death

The Tax Court's opinion in *Smith*, which follows, deals with two issues: the fair market value of the enormous body of sculpture that the artist left at his death in 1965, and whether (and, if so, to what extent) the selling commissions that his executors had paid to his gallery (now the Marlborough Gallery, but at that time named Marlborough-Gerson) in New York City were deductible as administration expenses in computing the federal estate tax due on his death. With respect to the latter issue, the court allowed the commissions to be deducted only with respect to those works of art that *had* to be sold in order to settle claims and to pay the decedent's debts, the expenses of administration, and taxes as finally adjudicated. This holding was subsequently affirmed by a divided court of appeals.[1] There is, however, authority that points in a different direction. In *Estate of Park v. Commissioner*[2] the Court of Appeals for the Sixth Circuit overruled the Tax Court and held that all selling expenses (in that case, real estate commissions) could be deducted as an administration expense and, accordingly, invalidated the Treasury regulations.[3] We have edited the *Smith* opinion to concentrate on the valuation question; on that point, it stands as a unique pronouncement.

ESTATE OF DAVID SMITH

57 T.C. 650 (1972),* *aff'd sub nom.* Lowe v. Commissioner, 510 F.2d 479 (2d Cir.), *cert. denied*, 423 U.S. 827 (1975)

TANNENWALD, J.: Respondent determined a deficiency of $2,444,629.17 in the Federal estate tax of the Estate of David Smith (hereinafter referred to as "Smith" or "decedent").

Several issues raised in the petition have been either resolved by agreement of the parties or abandoned by petitioner. The following issues remain for decision: (1) the fair market value of 425 sculptures created by Smith and in his possession at the time of his death; and (2) the deductibility of certain commissions incurred and paid by petitioner in the course of selling some of the aforementioned sculptures.

FINDINGS OF FACT

Some of the facts have been stipulated and, together with the exhibits attached thereto, are incorporated herein by this reference.

David Smith died from injuries sustained in an automobile accident on May 23, 1965. He was a citizen of the United States and a resident of Bolton Landing, New York, at the time of his death. Robert Motherwell, Clement Greenberg, and Ira M. Lowe qualified as co-executors of the decedent's estate. A Federal estate tax return was filed on August 24, 1966 with the district director of internal revenue in Albany, New York; the property included therein was valued as of the date of decedent's

---

§8.1.   [1] 510 F.2d 479 (2d Cir. 1975).

[2] 475 F.2d 673 (6th Cir. 1973), *rev'g* 57 T.C. 705 (1972).

[3] But cf. Marcus v. DeWitt, 704 F.2d 1227 (11th Cir. 1983); The Hibernian Bank v. United States, 581 F.2d 743 (9th Cir. 1978).

*[The Treasury acquiesced in the decision, 1974-2 C.B. 4.—Eds.]

death. A deficiency was agreed upon and paid on July 10, 1968. On August 7, 1969, respondent issued the notice of deficiency herein. At his death, Smith owned 425 pieces of sculpture created during various periods of his life. Of these sculptures, 291 were located at Bolton Landing, New York.

Smith began making metal sculptures in 1937. Most of his work is of the abstract, nonrepresentational variety and fashioned out of welded steel and other metals, a technique which Smith pioneered. The quality of Smith's sculptures varied according to the period in his life during which they were created. From 1940 to 1963, Smith was represented by two art galleries who endeavored to sell his works, albeit without much success. Between 1940 and 1956, Smith was represented by the Willard Gallery, during which time 53 of his works sold for $33,432.50 at prices ranging from $40 to $3,213. From 1957 until 1963, he was represented by the Otto Gerson Gallery, during which time 17 pieces were sold for $76,148.

On or about June 2, 1963, Smith and Marlborough-Gerson Galleries ("Marlborough") entered into an agreement which provided, in part, as follows:

The following shall constitute our agreement with respect to the sale by us of sculpture, drawings and graphics created by you (hereinafter referred to as "your work"):

1. During the period of 5 years commencing on the date hereof, we shall have the exclusive right, in any part of the world, to offer for sale and to authorize others to offer for sale all items of your work owned by you. You shall initially deliver each such item of your work to us at such location as we shall indicate.

2. During such period of 5 years, we shall also have the exclusive right to arrange and to authorize others to arrange the publication and/or sale, in any part of the world, of books and catalogues containing illustrated reproductions of your work.

3. During such period of 5 years, we shall arrange for exhibitions of your work in New York, London, Rome and such other places as you and we shall jointly determine. We shall be responsible for all of the expenses of such exhibitions (including advertising and catalogue costs) other than insurance and shall bear the entire cost of storing all items of your work delivered to us pursuant to this agreement.

4. You have furnished us with photographs of each item of your work owned by you on the date hereof. The price at which we shall offer each such item for sale shall not be less than the price set forth on the back of such photograph. We shall agree with you as to the minimum sale prices of those items of your work created in the future. Minimum prices may be changed from time to time in such manner as you and we shall jointly agree. . . .

6. Upon the sale by us of any item of your work, we shall reimburse ourselves from the actual net proceeds for any initial shipping costs and insurance cost advanced to you with respect to such item. In addition, as

compensation for our services, we shall retain ⅓ of the balance of such net proceeds. The remaining ⅔ of such balance, less any amounts due to us hereunder, shall be paid to you in United States dollars on a quarterly basis. . . .

8. This agreement shall be construed in accordance with the laws of the State of New York and shall be binding upon and inure to the benefit of your and our respective executors, administrators, successors and assigns.

This contract was renewed by Smith's estate on June 3, 1968.

Smith's sculptures were mostly sold at retail to museums and individual collectors during his lifetime.

Between June 2, 1963 and Smith's death on May 23, 1965, Marlborough's efforts (which included an exhibition of 29 selected works at Marlborough's Gallery in New York in October of 1964) resulted in the following sales:

Date	Pieces Sold	Total Sales Price	Commissions	Artist
November 20, 1963	1	$ 6,000	$ 2,000	$ 4,000
June 29, 1964	1	14,000	4,666	9,334
November 12, 1964	1	40,000	13,333	26,667
November 14, 1964	1	8,500	2,833	5,667
January 7, 1965	1	40,000	13,333	26,667

During the two years following Smith's death, Marlborough effected the following sales, presented below in summary fashion:

Period	No. of Works Sold	Total Sales Price	Commissions	Artist
5/23/65-5/23/66	16	$269,383.00	$ 89,795.00	$179,588.00
5/24/66-5/31/67	52	718,951.67	240,264.00	478,687.67

During his lifetime and at the time of his death, several factors militated against Smith's becoming a commercially successful artist. First, abstract sculptures attract far fewer buyers than do paintings, partly because the latter more easily fit into the decor of a buyer's household or of a museum. While Smith received mixed critical acclaim from his contemporaries and art critics, his work was not particularly appealing to the general public upon whom an artist must rely for the great bulk of his sales. Secondly, the size of his works (particularly those of the "Cubi" series, his most highly regarded series of sculptures), required a prospective buyer to have a great deal of space available for installation in order to properly exhibit them. Indeed, 185 of the 425 works in Smith's possession at his death were over 7 feet tall and comprised 80 percent of the total retail selling prices estimated by Smith's executors.

Finally, Smith's works were priced relatively high, and it was generally acknowledged in the art world that the lowering of an artist's prices signified a lack of confidence in the quality of the work.

Towards the end of Smith's life, Smith began to receive critical recognition of his work and honors commensurate with his status as one of the leading American abstract sculptors. He was appointed to the National Council of Art in 1964, the first such artist to receive this honor; he also participated in the 1962 Festival of Two Worlds in Spoleto, Italy, a guest of the Italian Government and American composer, Gian Carlo Menotti, as well as being awarded a major prize at the 1959 Sao Paulo Biennial of Modern Art. Upon his death, several national magazines which had hitherto ignored Smith noted his contribution to American art, catapulting him into national prominence.

Smith was a prolific sculptor and constantly created a larger number of sculptures than the market could readily absorb. He customarily produced series of between 10 and 30 sculptures which were similar in appearance, technique, and scale. The most prized of Smith's works were those of the "Cubi" series, which consisted of 28 or 29 works of welded, polished steel cubes ranging from 7 feet to 9 feet in height and being offered for sale for between $35,000 and $50,000. Smith's sculptures generally tended to be large and consequently expensive to transport and to warehouse.

At the time of Smith's death and for an undetermined period thereafter, the general public was not aware of how many of Smith's works were in his possession at the time of his death. Had the public been aware of this fact, and had all 425 pieces been made immediately available for sale, the estate and Marlborough could reasonably have expected to get substantially less money for them than if the works were slowly disseminated in the market over a period of years. It was also important to "hold back" certain works for sale at a future date (particularly the more desirable of Smith's works) in order to sustain interest in his works over the ten-year period of time envisioned by the estate as necessary to liquidate Smith's works.

In valuing the works of art included in the return, the executors first computed the price each piece would bring if sold individually at retail at the time of death, the total hypothetical price being $4,284,000. They then discounted this figure by 75 percent on the theory that these works could only be sold at the time of death to a bulk purchaser for resale, and then reduced this figure by one-third to cover Marlborough's commission. The resulting figure of $714,000 was reported as the date of death value of the sculptures. . . .

ULTIMATE FINDING OF FACT

The fair market value of the 425 sculptures at the time of Smith's death was $2,700,000.

OPINION

David Smith, a sculptor, died possessed of 425 pieces of non-representational metal sculptures created by his own efforts. The sculptures were valued at $714,000 in the estate tax return. Respondent, in his deficiency notice, determined that they should be valued at $5,256,918, but now concedes that they should be valued at not more than $4,284,000. It is this issue of valuation, together with a related question involving the deductibility of certain expenses, which the parties have placed before us for decision. We approach the task with considerable circumspection, recognizing that this case involves a highly unusual set of circumstances to which the usual, simplistic valuation approach may not be fully applicable and that, in the final analysis, our ultimate determination of value will necessarily constitute a "Solomon-like pronouncement." See *Morris M. Messing*, 48 T.C. 502, 512 (1967).

Initially, we are faced with certain broad assertions by petitioner, which attack this proceeding in its entirety. First, it argues that the number and nature of the sculptures, coupled with the limited scope and vagaries of the market in which they might be disposed of, make valuation as of the date of death impossible. Consequently, it argues that we should determine a zero value and that any other determination of value would be a violation of its constitutional rights.[1] We find this argument to be without merit. Valuation has been consistently recognized as an inherently imprecise process. See *Morris M. Messing, supra.* Difficulties encountered in determining value, e.g., the presence of a limited market or other restrictive elements, have never been considered a bar to accomplishment of that task, much less to have acquired a constitutional significance, although such elements are factors to be taken into account.[2] *Publicker v. Commissioner,* 206 F.2d 250 (C.A. 3, 1953); see also *George P. Fisher, Executor,* 3 B.T.A. 679 (1926). Moreover, the record herein shows clearly that the sculptures had value at the date of Smith's death, so petitioner's assertion that they had a zero value is factually baseless.

Petitioner next contends that the process by which respondent arrived at the valuation determined in his deficiency notice was "without foundation, unreasonable and arbitrary." This argument we also reject as without merit. Even if we were to decide that respondent's determination was erroneous, neither that consequence, nor the fact that respondent

---

[1] Petitioner claims the benefit of the "equal protection" doctrine, the freedom-of-expression principle embodied in the First Amendment, and the due-process clause of the Fifth Amendment.

[2] In an estate tax case, unlike an income tax case, there is an overriding necessity to determine a value. See Burnet v. Logan [2 USTC ¶736], 283 U.S. 404 (1931); Simpson, J., dissenting in Stephen H. Dorsey, 49 T.C. 606, 634-635 (1968).

has reduced his claimed valuation from that set forth in the deficiency notice, constitutes sufficient grounds for disregarding the deficiency notice of relieving petitioner of its burden of proof. *Jacob D. Farber,* 43 T.C. 407, 428-429 (1965). Nothing in this record permits the conclusion that respondent's action was so utterly unjustified as to fall within the ambit of *Helvering v. Taylor,* 293 U.S. 507 (1935). Moreover, it is well established that — at least where unconstitutional conduct is not involved — the courts will not inquire into the administrative policies and procedures employed by respondent prior to making his determination. *Arthur Figueiredo,* 54 T.C. 1508 (1970).

Finally, petitioner contends that payment of a prior proposed deficiency was tantamount to a closing agreement and should preclude respondent from asserting any further deficiency. This argument must also be rejected. There is no evidence that the requirements that a closing agreement be in writing and signed by the Secretary of the Treasury of his delegate have been met. Section 7121; section 301.7121-1, Proc. and Adm. Regs. Mere payment of an asserted deficiency does not satisfy those requirements. *Payson v. Commissioner,* 166 F.2d 1008 (C.A. 2, 1948); cf. *Helen Rich Findley,* 39 T.C. 580, 588-589 (1962), *affirmed in part and reversed in part on other issues,* 332 F.2d 620 (C.A. 2, 1964).

We now turn our attention to the critical issue in this case — the determination of the fair market value of the sculptures at the time of Smith's death. In the final analysis, this is essentially a question of fact. *Daniel S. McGuire,* 44 T.C. 801, 812 (1965). As we view the record herein, petitioner does not complain about the mathematical result of respondent's calculation of value, if it is determined that respondent accorded appropriate weight to the various elements involved. Indeed, the value attached by respondent to each piece of sculpture, if it had been sold separately, is identical with the value established by petitioner on the same basis. Where they part company is with respect to the weight to be accorded to the fact that each item would be sold on a market on which 424 other items would simultaneously be available. Respondent claims that such simultaneous availability would have no adverse impact and that the fair market value of each item should simply be determined by the price at which the item could be separately sold in the retail art market on a "one-at-a-time" basis in accordance with the provision of section 20.2031-1(b), Estate Tax Regs.[3] Petitioner asserts that this is totally unre-

---

[3] Sec. 20.2031-1 (b):

Valuation of property in general. The value of every item of property includible in a decedent's gross estate under sections 2031 through 2044 is its fair market value at the time of the decendent's death, except that if the executor elects the alternate valuation method under section 2032, it is the fair market value thereof at the date, and with the

alistic in this case; that the problem must be viewed in the context of what could be obtained if all 425 sculptures were offered for sale at the moment of death; that any purchaser under these circumstances could only be a person or syndicate acquiring the bulk of the sculptures for resale; that such person would be required to make a large cash investment which could be recouped with an acceptable profit only over a long period of time; and that such person would pay only 25 per cent of the separate "one-at-a-time" value which, after a further discounting by one-third to take into account the effect of the contract with Marlborough, results in a valuation of $714,000.

We find it unnecessary, in this unusual case, to make any hard and fast choice between the two approaches urged by the parties.[4] On the one hand, we think that the initial 75 percent discount, which petitioner has applied to the "one-at-a-time" value in order to determine the price which a purchaser would pay for all the sculptures, is too high. On the other hand, we think that respondent should have given considerable

---

adjustments, prescribed in that section. The fair market value is the price at which the property would change hands between a willing buyer and a willing seller, neither being under any compulsion to buy or to sell and both having reasonable knowledge of relevant facts. The fair market value of the particular item of property includible in the decedent's gross estate is not to be determined by a forced sale price. Nor is the fair market value of an item of property to be determined by the sale price of the item in a market other than that in which such item is most commonly sold to the public, taking into account the location of the item wherever appropriate. Thus, in the case of an item of property includible in the decendent's gross estate, which is generally obtained by the public in the retail market, the fair market value of such an item of property is the price at which the item or a comparable item would be sold at retail. . . . The value is generally to be determined by ascertaining as a basis the fair market value as of the applicable valuation date of each unit of property. For example, in the case of shares of stock or bonds, such unit of property is generally a share of stock or a bond. Livestock, farm machinery, harvested and growing crops must generally be itemized and the value of each item separately returned. Property shall not be returned at the value at which it is assessed for local tax purposes unless that value represents the fair market value as of the applicable valuation date. All relevant facts and elements of value as of the applicable valuation date shall be considered in every case. The value of items of property which were held by the decedent for sale in the course of a business generally should be reflected in the value of the business . . . (Emphasis added).

This regulation was amended to read as above on June 7, 1965, a date subsequent to Smith's death. See T.D. 6826, 1965-2 C.B. 367. Both parties have dealt with this case on the basis of the amended language nevertheless being applicable, and we have no reason to question this approach. See section 7805(b). Moreover, our ultimate decision as to the proper valuation would be the same, whichever regulation were applied.

[4] For a discussion of some of the difficulties involved in applying respondent's regulations on a broad-brush basis, see Federal Estate and Gift Taxation: Amended Regulations Change Valuation for Estate and Gift Taxes, 1966 Duke L.J. p.248 et seq.; Report of the Committee on Estate and Gift Taxes, Bulletin of the Section of Taxation of the American Bar Association, Vol. XIX, No. 4, p.71 (July 1966).

weight to the fact that each item of sculpture would not be offered in isolation. We think that, at the very least, each willing buyer in the retail art market would take into account, in determining the price he would be willing to pay for any given item, the fact that 424 other items were being offered for sale at the same time. The impact of such simultaneous availability of an extremely large number of items of the same general category is a significant circumstance which should be taken into account.[5] In this connection, the so-called "blockage" rule utilized in connection with the sale of a large number of securities furnishes a useful analogy. See *Maytag v. Commissioner*, 187 F.2d 962, 965 (C.A. 10, 1951), *affirming* a Memorandum Opinion of this Court; *Helvering v. Maytag*, 125 F.2d 55, 63 (C.A. 8, 1942), *affirming* a Memorandum Opinion of this Court *Helvering v. Safe Deposit & Trust Co. of Baltimore*, 95 F.2d 806, 811-812 (C.A. 4, 1938), *affirming* 35 B.T.A. 259 (1937); *Estate of Robert Hosken Damon*, 49 T.C. 108, 117 (1967). We think that a museum or individual collector of art objects would not completely ignore the resale value of a given item, although it obviously has far less significance than in the case of a dealer. Moreover, the "retail market" claimed by respondent may well encompass the use of an auction method of disposal (to be distinguished from the usual forced sale concept) for at least a part of the art objects;[6] in such a situation the presence of a large number of pieces on the market at one time would be a most material factor. Under the foregoing circumstances, we think that, in this case, the amount which an en bloc purchaser for resale would pay and the aggregate of the separate "one-at-a-time" values to be obtained by a variety of dispositions in the "retail market" would be the same.

We have taken into account certain other elements involved in the valuation process as they existed at the moment of death. These include[7] the fact that Smith's reputation as a sculptor had not fully blossomed; the relatively low level of acceptability of nonrepresentational sculpture in the market place; the distribution of the 425 items according to size, period in Smith's life during which they were created, and their expression, in relative terms, of the quality of Smith's work; Smith's tendency

---

[5] See section 20.2031-1(b), Estate Tax Regs., footnote 3, *supra:* "All relevant facts and elements of value as of the applicable valuation date shall be considered in every case." (Emphasis added.) Compare Bankers Trust Co. v. United States 284 F.2d 537 (C.A. 2, 1960); Old Kent Bank and Trust Company v. United States, 292 F. Supp. 48 (W.D. Mich. 1968).

[6] We note that art objects are frequently disposed of by way of auction (to be distinguished from a forced sale auction) and that estimates of prices to be obtained by a sale of such objects in this fashion are of some significance. See Eugene P. Mathias, 50 T.C. 994, 999 (1968).

[7] In listing such elements, we do not mean to imply that we have set forth every consideration which has influenced our decision herein.

to work in series and whether or not a given item was part of a complete series owned by Smith at his death, the number of sales by Smith (or his agents) in the 25 years before his death and the prices at which sales were made during the period immediately preceding and following death;[8] the fact that the bulk of the items was located at Bolton Landing, New York, which was relatively inaccessible, and that a large number of the items could not have been readily transported to a location more accessible to potential buyers.[9]

One element of value which petitioner urges be taken into account relates to its obligation to Marlborough by virtue of the exclusive agency contract which Smith made and which survived his death. Petitioner insists that any value based upon the gross sales price must be reduced by one-third to take into account the commissions to which Marlborough was entitled. We think any reduction in value with respect to this element is precluded by the decided cases. In *Publicker v. Commissioner, supra*, the court refused to permit the price which could be realized on the sale of a piece of jewelry to be reduced by the Federal excise tax which would have been payable. Cf. also *Estate of Frank Miller Gould*, 14 T.C. 414 (1950).[10] The measure of value laid down by these cases is what could be received on, not what is retained from, a hypothetical sale. Even if one may question the equating of "price" with the gross price including tax, in situations involving the excise tax, it cannot be gainsaid that the "price" herein is what a purchaser would pay for a piece of sculpture. Cases such as *Estate of Albert L. Salt*, 17 T.C. 92 (1951), relied upon by petitioner, are not in point. Concededly, they limit the value of property subject to a restrictive agreement, but they, too, look to what the estate of the decedent can obtain, not to the net it will retain when the property is sold. Nor does an examination of the contractual relationship between Smith and Marlborough reveal sufficient elements to construct a joint venture which might have given Marlborough an interest in the sculptures themselves with a consequent effect on the value at death (cf. RAUM, J., concurring, in *Harry C. Porter, Transferee*, 49 T.C. 207, 227 (1967) — an

---

[8] Provided they are not too far removed from the critical date, sales before and after such date may be used to corroborate the ultimate determination of value. In this case, we have given little weight to sales taking place more than two years after Smith's death. See Fitts' Estate v. Commissioner, 237 F.2d 729, 731 (C.A. 8, 1956), *affirming* a Memorandum Opinion of this Court. James Couzens, 11 B.T.A. 1040.1165 (1928); cf. sec. 20.2031-2(b), Estate Tax Regs.

[9] Compare section 20.2031-1(b), Estate Tax Regs., footnote 3, *supra*, which recognized the propriety of "taking into account the location of the item."

[10] While both Publicker and Gould are gift tax cases, the provisions relating to value in the gift and estate tax areas have been held to be in pari materia. Merrill v. Fahs, 324 U.S. 308, 311-313 (1945).

effect which we might add could have favorable as well as unfavorable aspects to a taxpayer in the valuation process.

Having carefully considered the entire record herein, we conclude that the fair market value of the 425 sculptures at the moment of Smith's death was $2,700,000. . . .

Reviewed by the Court.

Decision will be entered under Rule 50. . . .

TIETJENS, J., dissenting and concurring: This case was tried before Judge John W. Kern. Judge Kern died before he decided the case which then was assigned to me without objection.

I do not disagree on the valuation issue so far as the discussion of the legal principles to be applied is concerned. I would, however, give more weight to the actual sales prices of various pieces of statuary sold both before and after the sculptor's death as well as uncontested evidence of values placed on the separate pieces by both the respondent and petitioner if they had been sold separately. Accordingly I would find the fair market value of the 425 sculptures to be $4,284,000.

On the remaining issue I concur.

An artist's death is one of the few occasions on which it may be necessary to determine the fair market value of a large number of artworks that have all been created by a single hand. Inexact as the valuation of individual artworks may be, the valuation of bunches of hundreds is simply a form of speculation. Nevertheless, it must sometimes be done. The *Smith* case posed the question in its most blunt terms: If an artist is able to sell three works every year for $20,000 each, what would be the fair market value for federal estate tax purposes of 500 similar works remaining unsold at his death? That the answer is most decidedly *not* — as the IRS initially claimed on comparable facts in *Smith* — 500 times $20,000 (or $10 million) is one of the few small comforts that might be drawn from the case.

Aside from its recognition that "blockage" may be properly considered in valuing an artist's unsold production, the opinion in the *Smith* case is eminently unsatisfying. During two days of testimony before Judge Kern (who died before rendering a decision, the case subsequently being decided on the record by the Tax Court itself), the parties, through expert witnesses, advanced a number of hypotheses that if adopted might then and thereafter have served as guides to those who must plan for or deal with artists' estates. None of these found their way into the opinion that the court characterized as a "Solomon-like pronouncement." Rather, arriving at a valuation of $2,700,000 — approximately midway between (a) the average of the government's alternative figures of $5,250,418 and $4,284,000 and (b) the estate's figure of $714,000 — the court suggested a hypothesis of its own that bears little relation to the realities of the contemporary art market.

Lacking in the court's rationale is any recognition that, past a certain saturation point, there may be no significant market for an artist's work. In the 25 years before his death, David Smith had reportedly sold fewer than 100 pieces of sculpture. Of the 425 works remaining unsold at his death, 185 were welded steel constructions over seven feet in height. These, both parties agreed, constituted 80 percent in value of the artworks in the estate. While there is a primary market for such large scale works — museums and those few private collectors who maintain sculpture gardens — it is quickly exhausted and there is little beyond. That some number of such pieces can be sold at good prices after the artist's death does not necessarily prove that the remainder can be sold at all, or, more to the point, that the remainder had any substantial market value at the time of his death. The court's concentration on the psychology of each of 425 individual buyers assumes the very fact that it should theoretically have questioned — whether those buyers existed at all.

One hypothesis advanced by the government was that the estate might be liquidated in even dollar increments over a 10-year period and that a proper way to compute an estate tax value would be to discount the proceeds from such liquidation backwards to the date of death. The court rejected this. The subsequent facts did, however, support the government's instinct. A report, as of January 1, 1974 (approximately 8½ years after Smith's death), showed that the estate had realized approximately $4.5 million in sales, with half of the sculpture and all of the drawings still remaining unsold. Since that time, the demand for (and the prices of) Smith's work has continued to grow.

Although the court, in arriving at a date-of-death value, did admit evidence as to the prices at which post-death sales were made, it gave "little weight to sales taking place more than two years after Smith's death." Nevertheless, in considering these at all, the court missed the opportunity to decide what might have been the most interesting issue of all: whether, for estate tax purposes, the impact of an artist's death on the market value of his work can be taken into account in determining the fair market value *at* his death.

There is no question that Smith's death profoundly affected his market. He was an artist whose style was in constant evolution and whose prices were high. Buyers tended to hold back, waiting to see what he would do next. His death served to concentrate the critical acclaim that had been scattered while he was alive and, of course, to mark perma- nently his last works as his most "mature." Five pieces were sold in the two years before he died and sixty-eight in the first two years afterward. If the estate tax is levied on what a decedent owns at his death, then the instant before death would seem the appropriate time to make a valua- tion. Of course, in other contexts the moment after death is considered the critical date. Thus, in valuing the stock of a one-man corporation, the death of the "one man" is a significant factor in valuing the stock.

The impact of death has further relevance. Since the artist has died, should not the test of "value" be measured by what the heirs receive and not by what the decedent owned — i.e., should not the commissions payable to the dealer (in this instance, one-third of the selling price) be deducted from the theoretical gross proceeds? The court, relying on settled authority, answered the question in the negative: "The measure of value . . . is what could be received on, not what is retained from, a hypothetical sale." To reverse a customary aphorism, this is like eating half of a cake, and having only a quarter of it left.

Some partial information as to how the matter of blockage was han- dled in settling Alexander Calder's estate can be gleaned from the find- ings of fact in a 1985 gift tax case, *Calder v. Commissioner,*[4] which involved some transfers made by his widow subsequent to his death in 1976. Included in the artist's estate were 1,292 paintings in gouache. In their estate tax return, his executors contended that it would take the market approximately twenty-five years to absorb so great a number of paintings. Based on an average selling rate of roughly fifty-two sales annually, a formula was applied that produced a blockage discount suf- ficient to reduce the aggregate of the one-at-a-time values of these gouaches from $2,907,000 (based on an estimated selling price of $2,250 each) to $949,750 (an average of just over $735 each). Although the commissioner's own blockage formula produced a slightly higher value, the executor's figure was deemed within an reasonable range and ac- cepted.

The 1985 case involved, among other things, the blockage formula to be used in computing the value of a gift of some of these same gouaches by Louisa J. Calder to a series of trusts for the benefit of the artist's children and grandchildren. Given the benefit of hindsight, the court used a blockage formula based on the *actual* rate at which gouaches were sold by these trusts during the period 1977 to 1982. With an average of 60

---

[4] 85 T.C. No. 42 (1985).

sales annually, the total time estimated as necessary to liquidate them was found to be slightly shorter than in the estate tax calculation. Accordingly, for gift tax purposes the aggregate fair market value of the gouaches was found to be somewhat higher.

§8.1.4. Estate Tax Statutes: Paying with Art

Two states, Maine and New Mexico, permit death taxes on an artist's estate to be paid with works of art.[5] Under the Art Acceptance Act of New Mexico, an appraisal that is acceptable to the IRS must first be obtained; the work is then offered to the Museum of New Mexico for its collection.[6] The Board of Regents of the museum must then decide whether it would be "advantageous to the state" to accept the work; its decision is by law final and not appealable.[7] Among the criteria used are whether the work "encourages growth of the museum's collection,"[8] or whether it "furthers the preservation and understanding of the arts traditions which exist in New Mexico."[9]

Agreement on valuation between the decedent's estate representative and the New Mexico Taxation and Revenue Department must also be obtained.[10] Of particular interest is the limitation placed on the museum by the legislature: During any fiscal year the Board of Regents may not accept works having an aggregate value of more than $100,000 for the purposes of this section.[11] This would apparently apply to *all* works by *all* artists to be accepted during the year. If so, it would seem that the executor of an artist's estate should plan to offer payment early in the year (so that the $100,000 is not reached) or the board should wait until the end of the year to determine which works it will accept.

A related development has recently been reported in Spain.[12] In July 1985, it was announced that the widow of Spanish artist Joan Miró would be permitted to give Spain 24 of her husband's paintings in lieu of income taxes due from the late artist, who died in December 1983. According to

---

[5] Me. Rev. Stat. Ann. tit. 36, §3688 (1978 & West Supp. 1985); and N.M. Stat. Ann. §§7-7-15 to 7-7-20 (1983).

[6] *Id.* N.M. at §7-7-18.A.

[7] *Ibid.*

[8] *Id.* at §7-7-18.B.(1).

[9] *Id.* at §7-7-18.B.(2).

[10] *Id.* at §7-7-19.

[11] *Id.* at §7-7-20.B.

[12] Washington Post, July 17, 1985, at D9.

Spain's minister of culture, this is the first application of a recently enacted Spanish law that allows donations of art in place of money for income tax purposes. This parallels the arrangement made in France following Pablo Picasso's death in 1973 by which the Musée Picasso was established. Under a special law passed in France on December 31, 1968, the government was allowed to accept works of art in lieu of death duties.[13]

Michigan has a very liberal policy with respect to time of payment of estate taxes for professional artists. Upon the showing of reasonable cause, payment of the estate taxes (as well as interest on that tax) may be deferred for a period of 10 years without penalty or interest.[14] California has similar legislation; it provides, however, that the state controller may "for reasonable cause" extend the time payment of the tax, provided that he "finds that payment of the tax plus interest is adequately secured." [15] Compare the federal treatment, which in the very least requires that the artwork constitute at least a substantial percentage of the gross estate. (If it exceeds 35 percent of the adjusted gross estate, there is an election to pay in two or more — but not exceeding ten — equal installments. The first installment may be deferred for five years.)[16]

§8.2. THE ARTIST'S FIDUCIARIES

§8.2.1. The Role of Fiduciaries in Art Law

We have pointed out that problems following an artist's death often bring into focus the role of a person with whom the artist's estate has a fiduciary relationship. In the *David Smith* case, and even in the *Franz Kline* case, the executors, acting in their fiduciary capacity, were presumably trying to protect the estate; namely, to reduce estate taxes or to resist a beneficiary's claim. Often, however, the person who has that fiduciary status acts in conflict with the interests of the estate and the beneficiaries he is required to protect.

Notwithstanding the trauma that death brings, there is, in most jurisdictions, a very important and consoling feature: the courts that deal with

---

[13] Catalogue of the exhibition, "Picasso from the Musée Picasso, Paris" at the Walker Art Center, Minneapolis, at Foreward (1980).

[14] Mich. Comp. Laws Ann. §205.203(2) (West 1986).

[15] Cal. Rev. & Tax. Code §14180 (West Supp. 1986).

[16] I.R.C. §§6166 and 6601(j) (CCH 1984).

estates and conflicts arising after death. In New York, it is the Surrogate's Court. If there had not been a death, and the consequent overseeing activity of the court in New York, it is probable that the issues present in *In the Matter of Rothko* and *In the Matter of Wilhelmina Friedman*, both reproduced in this section, would not have found a forum in which they could be effectively raised and dealt with. Once death occurred, interests arose that demanded protection. It is very clear from these cases that the Surrogate's Court provided this protection very effectively.

The very special relationship of the art dealer to an artist is, of course, not confined to situations that involve a death. In Chapter 3, we detail various obligations imposed on the art dealer-artist relationship, principally by statute, but sometimes by contract.

§8.2.2. *In the Matter of Rothko:* The Obligations of the Executors

Rothko, which follows, is one of the major art law cases of recent times. In it we have a prime example of the conflict between the interests of the estate and those of the persons acting as fiduciaries. The case itself is so revealing about the obligations of persons appointed as executors of an artist's estate that little additional commentary is needed. One point worth mentioning, however, is that the hardship experienced by all of the parties involved could have been avoided. The executors could have petitioned the court for approval of their proposed transactions with the Marlborough Gallery; there is little doubt that if they had done so, much of their grief would have been eliminated and all of their commissions retained.

IN THE MATTER OF ROTHKO
43 N.Y.2d 305, 372 N.E.2d 291, 401 N.Y.S.2d 409 (1977)

COOKE, J. Mark Rothko, an abstract expressionist painter whose works through the years gained for him an international reputation of greatness, died testate on February 25, 1970. The principal asset of his estate consisted of 798 paintings of tremendous value, and the dispute underlying this appeal involves the conduct of his three executors in their disposition of these works of art. In sum, that conduct as portrayed in the record and sketched in the opinions was manifestly wrongful and indeed shocking.

Rothkos' will was admitted to probate on April 27, 1970 and letters testamentary were issued to Bernard J. Reis, Theodoros Stamos and Morton Levine. Hastily and within a period of only about three weeks and by virtue of two contracts each dated May 21, 1970, the executors dealt with all 798 paintings.

By a contract of sale, the estate executors agreed to sell to Marlborough AG., a Liechtenstein corporation (hereinafter MAG), 100 Rothko paintings as listed for $1,800,000, $200,000 to be paid on execution of the agreement and the balance of $1,600,000 in 12 equal interest-free installments over a 12-year period. Under the second agreement, the executors consigned to Marlborough Gallery, Inc., a domestic corporation (hereinafter MNY), "approximately 700 paintings listed on a Schedule to be prepared," the consignee to be responsible for costs covering items such as insurance, storage, restoration and promotion. By its provisos, MNY could sell up to 35 paintings a year from each of two groups, pre-1947 and post-1947, for 12 years at the best price obtainable but not less than the appraised estate value, and it would receive a 50% commission on each painting sold, except for a commission of 40% on those sold to or through other dealers.

Petitioner Kate Rothko, decedent's daughter and a person entitled to share in his estate by virtue of an election under EPTL 5-3.3, instituted this proceeding to remove the executors, to enjoin MNY and MAG from disposing of the paintings, to rescind the aforesaid agreements between the executors and said corporations, for a return of the paintings still in possession of those corporations, and for damages. She was joined by the guardian of her brother Christopher Rothko, likewise interested in the estate, who answered by adopting the allegations of his sister's petition and by demanding the same relief. The Attorney-General of the State, as the representative of the ultimate beneficiaries of the Mark Rothko Foundation, Inc., a charitable corporation and the residuary legatee under decedent's will, joined in requesting relief substantially similar to that prayed for by petitioner. On June 26, 1972 the Surrogate issued a temporary restraining order and on September 26, 1972 a preliminary injunction enjoining MAG, MNY, and the three executors from selling or otherwise disposing of the paintings referred to in the agreements dated May 21, 1970, except for sales or dispositions made with court permission. The Appellate Division modified the preliminary injunction order by increasing the amount of the bond and otherwise affirmed. By a 1974 petition, the Attorney-General, on behalf of the ultimate charitable beneficiaries of the Mark Rothko Foundation, sought the punishment of MNY, MAG, Lloyd and Reis for contempt and other relief.

Following a nonjury trial covering 89 days and in a thorough opinion, the Surrogate found: that Reis was a director, secretary and treasurer of MNY, the consignee art gallery, in addition to being a coexecutor of the estate; that the testator had a 1969 inter vivos contract with MNY to sell Rothko's work at a commission of only 10% and whether that agreement survived testator's death was a problem that a fiduciary in a dual position could not have impartially faced; that Reis was in a position of serious conflict of interest with respect to the contracts of May 21, 1970 and that his dual role and planned purpose benefited the Marlborough interests to the detriment of the estate; that it was to the advantage of coexecutor Stamos as a "not-too-successful artist, financially," to curry favor with Marlborough and that the contract made by him with MNY within months after signing the estate contracts placed him in a position where his personal interests conflicted with those of the estate, especially leading to lax contract enforcement efforts by Stamos; that Stamos acted negligently and improvidently in view of his own knowledge of the conflict of interest of Reis; that the third coexecutor, Levine, while not acting in self-interest or with bad faith, nonetheless failed to exercise ordinary prudence in the performance of his assumed fiduciary obligations since he was aware of Reis' divided loyalty, believed that Stamos was also seeking personal advantage, possessed personal opinions as to the value of the paintings and yet followed the leadership of his coexecutors without investigation of essential facts or consultation with competent and disinterested appraisers, and that the business transactions of the two Marlborough corporations were admittedly controlled and directed by Francis K. Lloyd. It was concluded that the acts and failures of the three executors were clearly improper to such a substantial extent as to mandate their removal under SCPA 711 as estate fiduciaries. The Surrogate also found that MNY, MAG and Lloyd were guilty of contempt in shipping, disposing of and selling 57 paintings in violation of the temporary restraining order dated June 26, 1972 and of the injunction dated September 26, 1972; that the contracts for sale and consigment of paintings between the executors and MNY and MAG provided inadequate value to the estate, amounting to a lack of mutuality and fairness resulting from conflicts on the part of Reis and Stamos and improvidence on the part of all executors; that said contracts were voidable and were set aside by reason of violation of the duty of loyalty and improvidence of the executors, knowingly participated in and induced by MNY and MAG; that the fact that these agreements were voidable did not revive the 1969 inter vivos agreements since the parties by their conduct evinced an intent to abandon and abrogate these compacts. The Surrogate held that the present value at the time of trial of the paintings sold is the proper measure of damages as to MNY, MAG, Lloyd, Reis and Stamos. He imposed a civil fine of $3,332,000 upon MNY, MAG and Lloyd, same being the appreciated value at the time of trial of the 57 paintings sold in violation of the temporary restraining order and injunction.[1] It was held that Levine was liable for $6,464,880 in damages, as he

---

[1] The decree of the Surrogate's Court, New York County, dated January 15, 1976, was amended in this respect pursuant to an order filed April 28, 1976 by substituting "63" for "57" as the number of paintings sold and disposed of and "$3,872,000" as the amount of the fine instead of "$3,332,000."

was not in a dual position acting for his own interest and was thus liable only for the actual value of paintings sold MNY and MAG as of the dates of sale, and that Reis, Stamos, MNY and MAG, apart from being jointly and severally liable for the same damages as Levine for negligence, were liable for the greater sum of $9,252,000 "as appreciation damages less amounts previously paid to the estate with regard to sales of paintings." The cross petition of the Attorney-General to reopen the record for submission of newly discovered documentary evidence was denied. The liabilities were held to be congruent so that payment of the highest sum would satisfy all lesser liabilities including the civil fines and the liabilities for damages were to be reduced by payment of the fine levied or by return of any of the 57 paintings disposed of, the new fiduciary to have the option in the first instance to specify which paintings the fiduciary would accept.

The Appellate Division, in an opinion by Justice Lane, modified to the extent of deleting the option given the new fiduciary to specify which paintings he would accept. Except for this modification, the majority affirmed on the opinion of Surrogate Midonick, with additional comments. Among others, it was stated that the entire court agreed that executors Reis and Stamos had a conflict of interest and divided loyalty in view of their nexus to MNY and that a majority were in agreement with the Surrogate's assessment of liability as to executor Levine and his findings of liability against MNY, MAG and Lloyd. The majority agreed with the Surrogate's analysis awarding "appreciation damages" and found further support for his rationale in *Menzel v List* (24 NY2d 91). Justice Kupferman, in an opinion styled "concurring in part and dissenting in part," stated that, although he had "expressed reservations with respect to various factors to be considered in the calculation of damages," he concurred "in the basic conclusion and, therefore, in order to resolve the matter for the purpose of appeal" voted to modify as per the Lane opinion (56 AD2d 499, 505-506). Justices Capozzoli and Nunez, in separate dissenting in part opinions, viewed *Menzel v List* as inapplicable and voted to modify and remit to determine the reasonable value of the paintings as of May, 1970, when estate contracts with MNY and MAG had their inception in writing.

Since the Surrogate's findings of fact as to the conduct of Reis, Stamos, Levine, MNY, MAG and Lloyd and the value of the paintings at different junctures were affirmed by the Appellate Division, if there was evidence to support these findings they are not subject to question in this court and the review here is confined to the legal issues raised (CPLR 5501, subd [b]; *Simon v Electrospace Corp.*, 28 NY2d 136, 139; *Matter of City of New York [Fifth Ave. Coach Lines]*, 22 NY2d 613, 620-621).

In seeking a reversal, it is urged that an improper legal standard was applied in voiding the estate contracts of May, 1970, that the "no further inquiry" rule applies only to self-dealing and that in case of a conflict of interest, absent self-dealing, a challenged transaction must be shown to be unfair. The subject of fairness of the contracts is intertwined with the issue of whether Reis and Stamos were guilty of conflicts of interest.[2] Scott is quoted to the effect that "[a] trustee does not necessarily incur liability merely because he has an individual interest in the transaction. . . . In *Bullivant v. First Nat. Bank* [246 Mass 324] it was held that . . . the fact that the bank was also a creditor of the corporation did not make its assent invalid, *if it acted in good faith and the plan was fair*" (2 Scott, *Trusts*, §170.24 p1384 [emphasis added]), and our attention has been called to the statement in *Phelan v Middle States Oil Corp.* (220 F2d 593, 603, *cert den sub nom. Cohen v Glass*, 349 US 929) that Judge Learned Hand found "no decisions that have applied [the no further inquiry rule] inflexibly to every occasion in which the fiduciary has been shown to have had a personal interest that might in fact have conflicted with his loyalty."

These contentions should be rejected. First, a review of the opinions of the Surrogate and the Appellate Division manifests that they did not rely solely on a "no further inquiry rule," and secondly, there is more than an adequate basis to conclude that the agreements between the Marlborough corporations and the estate were neither fair nor in the best interests of the estate. This is demonstrated, for example, by the comments of the Surrogate concerning the commissions on the consignment of the 698 paintings (see 84 Misc 2d 830, 852-853) and those of the Appellate Division concerning the sale of the 100 paintings (see 56 AD2d, at pp 501-502). The opinions under review demonstrate that neither the Surrogate nor the Appellate Division set aside the contracts by merely applying the no further inquiry rule without regard to fairness. Rather they determined, quite properly indeed, that these agreements were neither fair nor in the best interests of the estate.

To be sure, the assertions that there were no conflicts of interest on the part of Reis or Stamos indulge in sheer fantasy. Beside being a director and officer of MNY, for which there was financial remuneration, however slight, Reis, as noted by the Surrogate, had different inducements to favor the Marlborough interests, including his own aggrandizement of status and financial advantage through sales of almost one million dollars for items from his own and his family's extensive private art collec-

---

[2] In New York, an executor, as such, takes a qualified legal title to all personalty specifically bequeathed and an unqualified legal title to that not so bequeathed; he holds not in his own right but as a trustee for the benefit of creditors, those entitled to receive under the will and, if all is not bequeathed, those entitled to distribution under the EPTL, Blood v Kane, 130 NY 514, 517; see Bischoff v Yorkville Bank, 218 NY 106, 110-111; Bankers Sur. Co. v Meyer, 205 NY 219, 223-224; but see Restatement, Trusts 2d, §6; Bogert, Trusts [Hornbook Series — 5th ed], p31).

tion by the Marlborough interests (see 84 Misc 2d, at pp843-844). Similarly, Stamos benefited as an artist under contract with Marlborough and, interestingly, Marlborough purchased a Stamos painting from a third party for $4,000 during the week in May, 1970 when the estate contract negotiations were pending (see 84 Misc 2d, at p845). The conflicts are manifest. Further, as noted in Bogert, *Trusts and Trustees* (2d ed), "The duty of loyalty imposed on the fiduciary prevents him from accepting employment from a third party who is entering into a business transaction with the trust" (§543, subd [S], p573). "While he [a trustee] is administering the trust he must refrain from placing himself in a position where his personal interest or that of a third person does or may conflict with the interest of the beneficiaries" (Bogert, *Trusts* [Hornbook Series — 5th ed], p343. Here, Reis was employed and Stamos benefited in a manner contemplated by Bogert (see, also, *Meinhard v Salmon*, 249 NY 458, 464, 466-467; *Schmidt v Chambers*, 265 Md 9, 33-38). In short, one must strain the law rather than follow it to reach the result suggested on behalf of Reis and Stamos.

Levine contends that, having acted prudently and upon the advice of counsel, a complete defense was established. Suffice it to say, an executor who knows that his coexecutor is committing breaches of trust and not only fails to exert efforts directed towards prevention but accedes to them is legally accountable even though he was acting on the advice of counsel (*Matter of Westerfield*, 32 App Div 324, 344; 3 Scott, *Trusts* [3d ed], §201, p1657). When confronted with the question of whether to enter into the Marlborough contracts, Levine was acting in a business capacity, not a legal one, in which he was required as an executor primarily to employ such diligence and prudence to the care and management of the estate assets and affairs as would prudent persons of discretion and intelligence (*King v Talbot*, 40 NY 76, 85-86), accented by "[n]ot honesty alone, but the punctilio of an honor the most sensitive" (*Meinhard v Salmon*, 249 NY 458, 464, supra). Alleged good faith on the part of a fiduciary forgetful of his duty is not enough (*Wendt v Fischer*, 243 NY 439, 443). He could not close his eyes, remain passive or move with unconcern in the face of the obvious loss to be visited upon the estate by participation in those business arrangements and then shelter himself behind the claimed counsel of an attorney (see *Matter of Niles*, 113 NY 547, 558; *Matter of Huntley*, 13 Misc 375, 380; 3 Warren's Heaton, *Surrogates' Courts* [6th ed], §217, subd 3, par [b]).

Further, there is no merit to the argument that MNY and MAG lacked notice of the breach of trust. The record amply supports the determination that they are chargeable with notice of the executors' breach of duty.

The measure of damages was the issue that divided the Appellate Division (see 56 AD2d, at p500). The contention of Reis, Stamos, MNY and MAG, that the award of appreciation damages was legally erroneous and impermissible, is based on a principle that an executor authorized to sell is not liable for an increase in value if the breach consists only in selling for a figure less than that for which the executor should have sold. For example, Scott states:

"The beneficiaries are not entitled to the value of the property at the time of the decree if it was not the duty of the trustee to retain the property in the trust and the breach of trust consisted *merely* in selling the property for too low a price" (3 Scott, *Trusts* [3d ed], §208.3, p1687 [emphasis added]).

"If the trustee is guilty of a breach of trust in selling trust property for an inadequate price, he is liable for the difference between the amount he should have received and the amount which he did receive. He is not liable, however, for any subsequent rise in value of the property sold." (*Id.*, §208.6, pp1689-1690.)

A recitation of similar import appears in Comment *d* under Restatement, Trusts 2d (§205):

d. Sale for less than value. If the trustee is authorized to sell trust property, but in breach of trust he sells it for less than he should receive, he is liable for the value of the property at the time of the sale less the amount which he received. If the breach of trust consists *only* in selling it for too little, he is not chargeable with the amount of any subsequent increase in value of the property under the rule stated in Clause (c), as he would be if he were not authorized to sell the property. See §208.

(Emphasis added.) However, employment of "merely" and "only" as limiting words suggests that where the breach consists of some misfeasance, other than solely for selling "for too low a price" or "for too little," appreciation damages may be appropriate. Under Scott (§208.3, pp1686-1687) and the Restatement (§208), the trustee may be held liable for appreciation damages if it was his or her duty to retain the property, the theory being that the beneficiaries are entitled to be placed in the same position they would have been in had the breach not consisted of a sale of property that should have been retained. The same rule should apply where the breach of trust consists of a serious conflict of interest — which is more than merely selling for too little.

The reason for allowing appreciation damages, where there is a duty to retain, and only date of sale damages, where there is authorization to sell, is policy oriented. If a trustee authorized to sell were subjected to a greater measure of damages he might be reluctant to sell (in which event he might run a risk if depreciation ensued). On the other hand, if there is a duty to retain and the trustee sells there is no policy reason to protect the trustee; he has not simply acted imprudently, he has violated an integral condition of the trust.

If a trustee in breach of trust transfers trust property to a person who takes with notice of the breach of trust, and the transferee has disposed of the property . . . [i]t seems proper to charge him with the value at the time of the decree, since if it had not been for the breach of trust the property would still have been a part of the trust estate

(4 Scott, *Trusts* [3d ed], §291.2; see, also, *United States v Dunn*, 268 US 121, 132). This rule of law which applies to the transferees MNY and MAG also supports the imposition of appreciation damages against Reis and Stamos, since if the Marlborough corporations are liable for such damages either as purchaser or consignees with notice, from one in breach of trust, it is only logical to hold that said executors, as sellers and consignors are liable also pro tanto.

Contrary to assertions of appellants and the dissenters at the Appellate Division, *Menzel v List* (24 NY2d 91, *supra*) is authority for the allowance of appreciation damages. There, the damages involved a breach of warranty of title to a painting which at one time had been stolen from plaintiff and her husband and ultimately sold to defendant. Here, the executors, though authorized to sell, did not merely err in the amount they accepted but sold to one with whom Reis and Stamos had a self-interest. To make the injured party whole, in both instances the quantum of damages should be the same. In other words, since the paintings cannot be returned, the estate is therefore entitled to their value at the time of the decree, i.e., appreciation damages. These are not punitive damages in a true sense, rather they are damages intended to make the estate whole. Of course, as to Reis, Stamos, MNY and MAG, these damages might be considered by some to be exemplary in a sense, in that they serve as a warning to others (see *Reynolds v Pegler*, 123 F Supp 36, 38, *aff'd* 223 F2d 429, *cert den* 350 US 846), but their true character is ascertained when viewed in the light of overriding policy considerations and in the realization that the sale and consignment were not merely sales below value but inherently wrongful transfers which should allow the owner to be made whole (see *Menzel v List*, 24 NY2d 91, 97, *supra*; see, also, *Simon v Electrospace Corp.*, 28 NY2d 136, 144, *supra*).

The decree of the Surrogate imposed appreciation damages against Reis, Stamos, MNY and MAG in the amount of $7,339,464.72 — computed as $9,252,000 (86 works on canvas at $90,000 each and 54 works on paper at $28,000 each) less the aggregate amounts paid the estate under the two rescinded agreements and interest. Appellants chose not to offer evidence of "present value" and the only proof furnished on the subject was that of the expert Heller whose appraisal as of January, 1974 (the month previous to that when trial commenced) on a painting-by-painting basis totaled $15,100,000. There was also testimony as to bona fide sales of other Rothkos between 1971 and 1974. Under the circumstances, it was impossible to appraise the value of the unreturned works of art with an absolute certainty and, so long as the figure arrived at had a reasonable basis of computation and was not merely speculative, possible or imaginary, the Surrogate had the right to resort to reasonable conjectures and probable estimates and to make the best approximation possible through the exercise of good judgment and common sense in arriving at that amount (see *Story Parchment Co. v Paterson Co.*, 282 US 555, 562-563; *Eastman Co. v Southern Photo Co.*, 273 US 359, 379; *Wakeman v Wheeler & Wilson Mfg. Co.*, 101 NY 205, 209-210; *Alexander's Dept. Stores v Ohrbach's*, 269 App Div 321, 328-329; *Sutcliffe v Potts*, 88 NYS2d 55, 57, *aff'd* 277 App Div 751; cf. *Sheldon v Metro-Goldwyn Pictures Corp.*, 106 F2d 45, 51 [L. Hand, J.]). This is particularly so where the conduct of wrongdoers has rendered it difficult to ascertain the damages suffered with the precision otherwise possible (*Story Parchment Co. v Paterson Co.*, *supra*, at p563; *Eastman Co. v Southern Photo Co.*, *supra*, at p379). Significantly, the Surrogate's factual finding as to the present value of these unreturned paintings was affirmed by the Appellate Division and, since that finding had support in the record and was not legally erroneous, it should not now be subjected to our disturbance.

On February 21, 1969, decedent made a contract with MAG which provided that "Mark Rothko agrees not to sell any works of art for a period of eight years, except to Marlborough A.G. if a supplementary contract is made." A supplementary contract made that same day recited that "Mark Rothko has the option to sell to Marlborough A.G. an additional four paintings each year at prices not below Marlborough A.G.'s then current selling prices, the price to be paid being [90%] of the current selling prices." The Surrogate reasoned that the fact that the 1970 agreements for the sale and consignment of paintings were voidable because of self-dealing did not revive the 1969 inter vivos agreements and found that the parties by their conduct intended to abandon and abrogate these 1969 agreements. In turn and in effect, the Appellate Division agreed with this finding of abandonment (56 AD2d, at p501). "A voidable contract is one where one or more parties thereto have the power, by a manifestation of election to do so, to avoid the legal relations created by the contract; or by ratification of the contract to extinguish the power of avoidance" (Restatement, *Contracts*, §13). Where a contract is voidable on both sides, as where there has been a violation of the duty of loyalty and improvidence by executors knowingly participated in and induced by the other contracting parties (see 84 Misc 2d, at p858), the transaction is not wholly void, since in order to prevent the contract from having its normal operation the claim or defense must in some manner be asserted and also since the contract is capable of ratification, such a contract affects from the outset the legal relations of the parties (1 Williston, *Contracts* [3d ed], §15, pp28-29). The question of whether there has been an abandonment or abrogation of a contract is usually one of fact (see *Green v Doniger*, 300 NY 238, 245) and the circumstances disclosed by the record, including a showing of the new agreements in 1970, contained a sufficient basis for the finding of the abandonment or abrogation of those which came into being in 1969 (see *Schwartzreich v Bauman-Basch*, 231 NY 196, 203).

The Marlborough corporations and Lloyd contend that there was no violation of either the temporary restraining order or the preliminary injunction by the delivery of paintings sold prior to the court's restraints and that, therefore, the finding of contempt was erroneous. The Attorney-General in response contends that the "group" sales did not pass equitable ownership and that even if the invoices had been typed prior to said order and injunction no sale took place until after the injunction. In support of the latter position, the Uniform Commercial Code (§2-106, subd [1]; §§2-307, 2-401, subds [2], [3]) is cited for the proposition that as a matter of law the questioned sales took place on delivery to the purchasers which in all instances occurred after the injuction, the latter of the two court restraints. MNY, MAG and Lloyd counter with the argument that, under art market custom, invoices of paintings are sales and that the restraining order and preliminary injunction failed to clearly state what acts were prohibited. In any event, the plain and simple import of both the order and the injunction — not to sell or otherwise dispose of the paintings (cf. *Matter of Black*, 138 App Div 562, 565) - -was violated by dispositions of them. Consequently, it is immaterial how the applicable Uniform Commercial Code provisions might be interpreted. If MNY, MAG and Lloyd had invoiced paintings and were acting in good faith, they would have advised the court of their prior commitments.

We have considered the other alleged errors urged by the parties, and find those arguments to be without merit. In short, we find no basis for disturbing the result reached below.

Accordingly, the order of the Appellate Division should be affirmed, with costs to the prevailing parties against appellants, and the question certified answered in the affirmative.

Chief Judge BREITEL and Judges JASEN, GABRIELLI, JONES, WACHTLER and FUCHSBERG concur.

Order affirmed, etc.

§8.2.3. *Kate Rothko Prizel v. Karelsen*[1]: *Rothko's* Progeny

Following the decision in *In the Matter of Rothko*, Rothko's daughter and administratrix c.t.a. of his estate, Kate Rothko Prizel, filed

---

§8.2. [1] The full title of the action, filed in the U.S. District Court for the Southern District of New York (76 Civ. No. 2144), was Kate Rothko Prizel v. Karelsen, Karelsen, Lawrence & Nathan, Daniel Saidenberg and Saidenberg Gallery, Inc. See also 74 F.R.D. 134 (1977) for the court's decision on a hard-fought discovery issue.

suit in federal court in New York City against the attorneys for the estate and the gallery (along with its president) retained as appraiser for the estate. The suit alleged conspiracy to defraud the estate and breach of fiduciary duty by the executors removed by court decree several months prior. With respect to the Karelsen law firm, Prizel also alleged negligence and misconduct, inter alia, in seeking to conceal and cover up the fraud and breaches of fiduciary duty. Actions of misconduct alleged by the plaintiff included the preparation of an opinion letter by the Karelsen firm (a letter that was allegedly false), negotiations by the Karelsen firm with dealer Frank Lloyd for the sale of 100 paintings (negotiations that were allegedly neither bona fide nor at arm's length, purported to have been previously arranged by Bernard J. Reis, one of the original executors removed by court order), retention by the Karelsen firm of the Saidenberg Gallery for the appraisal (while allegedly knowing that the appraisal given would be false and fraudulent, the gallery supposedly having been preselected by Reis), and various other alleged acts relating to misconduct in relation to the preparation and suppression of documents. Plaintiff sought a multi-million dollar judgment. After discovery and motions addressed to discovery issues, the case was, according to the plaintiff's counsel, Edward J. Ross, "settled against all defendants with the parties agreeing that the amount of the settlement be kept confidential."[2]

§8.2.4. *In the Matter of Wilhelmina Friedman:* The Obligations of the Art Dealer

The *Friedman* case, which follows, is a variant of the fiduciary problem. There, the fiduciary, art dealer Charles Egan, was not the executor of the estate of artist Arnold Friedman, but a person who owed a significant obligation to the artist and his family. As in *Rothko*, overreaching and apparent greed combined to subordinate the interests that the fiduciary was required to protect to the economic interest of those in an adversarial relationship to the family of the artist. In both cases, it took a hard-fought court battle to sustain the interest of the beneficiaries of the artist's estate.

IN THE MATTER OF WILHELMINA FRIEDMAN
64 A.D.2d 70, 407 N.Y.S.2d 999 (1978)

MARGETT, J. Arnold Friedman was an important American artist who derived his style from Impressionism, but who expanded and tran-

---

[2] Interview with Edward J. Ross, Esq. (Summer 1985).

scended that idiom with his own unique personal style.[1] Friedman's biography reads like the classic (some might say stereotyped) tale of a struggling artist whose work was never appreciated in financial terms until well after his death. Born in 1874, Friedman grew up on the east side of Manhattan. His father—who had emigrated from Hungary with his wife — died in 1878, leaving his mother with three other small children to support. In his early teens Friedman became a wage earner, working at the Produce Exchange. At the age of 17 he was virtually the sole support of his family and began to work for the New York Post Office.

At age 32, while still employed by the Post Office, Friedman began to study art at the Art Students League in New York. In 1908, after three years of evenings at the League, he took a leave of absence from his job and traveled to Paris, where he lived for six months. While there he met his wife. Upon his return to New York, he continued to work six days a week, as many as 10 hours a day, at the New York Post Office. Two or three years after his marriage, with $25 coming in every week, he purchased a house in then rural Corona, Queens, complete with an attic studio. He worked there as time permitted. His daily routine of travel to and from the New York Post Office went on until his retirement on a meager pension in the 1930's.[2]

In terms of quantity, his production was limited by his job and by his responsibilities to his wife and four children. Friedman was 42 years old before he participated in his first group show and 52 before he had his first one-man show. Although a number of his paintings were sold to collectors and museums during his lifetime, his only assets when he died intestate in 1946 consisted of his work. Today, Friedman's legacy of over 300 works of art is worth approximately a half-million dollars.[3]

This appeal involves a dispute over the ownership of that legacy. The dispute is between Elizabeth Becque, Friedman's daughter and the administratrix of his widow's estate, and Charles Egan, an art dealer. The

---

[1] Impressionism was clearly the "dominant influence of his work," and Friedman himself wrote wryly on the back of one of his pictures: "Psst! Psst! Don't look now, mister, but your impressionism is showing. — Thanks" (Schack, The Ordeal of Arnold Friedman, Painter, Commentary, January, 1950. pp40-46). Friedman "create[d] an Impressionist vein of his own" (id. p42), and "attempt[ed] to carry Impressionism in the direction of abstraction while refusing, in the end, to go over into abstraction" (Kramer, New York Times, March 23, 1969). "[H]e carried his work to a plateau of feeling far removed from the orthodoxies of [Impressionism]" (id).

[2] The foregoing biographical material is drawn largely from an excellent article, The Ordeal of Arnold Friedman, Painter, By William Schack, in the January, 1950 issue of Commentary. An article by Thomas B. Hess in the February, 1950 issue of Art News (pp25-27, 59-60), Friedman's Tragedy and Triumph, also supplied a good deal of the material used.

[3] This value was conceded by appellant's counsel at the hearing before the Surrogate.

origin of this controversy is an agreement entered into in May, 1963 between the artist's widow, Renee (Wilhelmina) Friedman, and Charles Egan, "d/b/a EGAN GALLERY." The agreement recites that Renee's children have "duly assigned to . . . [her] all of their right, title and interest in and to the estate of their late father Arnold Friedman"; that Renee "is now the sole owner of the unsold works of the late Arnold Friedman"; that "Egan, who is conducting an art gallery at 313 E. 79th Street, New York, N.Y. was a friend and admirer of the late Arnold Friedman"; and that "Renee wishes to have her late husband's works properly distributed in the art world." It is then agreed that "Renee . . . sells, transferrs [sic] and assigns over to Charles Egan all of the works of the late Arnold Friedman now in her possession . . . absolutely and forever." The parties further agreed to make an inventory of the collection. The consideration for this "sale, transfer and assignment" is as follows:

> Egan agrees to accept the said works and properly prepare them for sale and exhibition, to put forth his best efforts to sell said works at prices which will be consonant with the merit of said works, and to pay to Renee, from time to time as said works are sold and payment therefor received, one half of the total received by him in the sale of any and all of the said works, it being understood that Renee's share of the proceeds of such sale is not to be diminished in any manner by expenses or charges of any kind.

However, the agreement further provided that Renee "shall have no voice in determining the manner of sale or exhibition . . . or the prices at which . . . [the paintings] will be sold." It is recited that "having parted with title to said works, Renee's interest is limited to the receipt of one half of the proceeds from the sale thereof." This "agreement" was prepared by Egan's lawyer.

Mrs. Friedman could not afford her own lawyer. She was about 75 years of age at the time. Although she had been employed since the 1950's doing light housework in exchange for room and board, she received no monetary compensation. Mrs. Friedman had been "completely devoted" during her entire life to giving her late "husband an opportunity to paint and she believed very much in the quality of his paintings." She wanted to see her husband's work exhibited and sold, but the bulk of the collection had been in the basement of a gallery which was closed or in the process of closing. In late 1961 or early 1962, Mrs. Friedman approached Egan, an experienced art dealer who had known her husband since 1939 or 1940. According to Egan, Mrs. Friedman wanted to "give . . . [him] the work with the idea that . . . [he] would take care of it." Egan did in fact take possession of the collection and he sold a small oil painting — a still-life — in 1962 for $300. He remitted $150 to Mrs. Friedman, since they "were on a fifty-fifty basis."

The following year, Mrs. Friedman and Egan went to the office of Egan's attorney, Samuel Duker, to see about having a written agreement drafted. At that meeting, it "came out" that Arnold Friedman had died intestate and Mr. Duker suggested to Mrs. Friedman that she have an attorney draw up assignments of her children's interests in the paintings. Duker testified that Mrs. Friedman told him she could not afford a lawyer and that he thereupon drafted such assignments for her. He gave these documents to Mrs. Friedman and told both her and Egan that they should notify him when the assignments were signed; he would then draft the "agreement" that they sought.[4]

Duker was subsequently notified by Egan that the assignments had been executed and he proceeded to draft the contract. When Mrs. Friedman and Egan arrived at his office for the execution of the contract, Duker "went over the agreement, word for word, and . . . [he] explained [it] to her and . . . [he] cleared up some misconceptions that she had about it." Duker testified that "at the end of the session . . . [he] said" to Mrs. Friedman: "Look, I'm Charlie's lawyer and, of course, he will pay me but I would like to have a picture and, in view of the fact that I drew this agreement — this assignment — and I had to go through this agreement and explain it to you word by word, would you mind if I picked out a small picture?" Mrs. Friedman gave Duker two paintings as a fee for his services.

For the next 14 years, Egan maintained exclusive custody of the Friedman collection.[5] During that period he held only one Arnold Friedman exhibition — in 1969. No sales resulted from that exhibition. According to petitioner, Elizabeth Becque, Egan failed to maintain any contact with Mrs. Friedman during the year immediately following the exhibition. Mrs. Becque testified that in 1970, in her mother's presence, she telephoned Mr. Egan to inquire as to his efforts to promote the paintings. Mrs. Becque stated that she mentioned her mother's need for money at the time. Mr. Egan allegedly told her that he was negotiating with a museum and that she should be patient. Mrs. Becque testified that Egan then said: "Look. You can have the paintings and see what you can do." Before she could respond, Egan added: "But, look, let's wait for the first of the year and we'll have an exhibition and see what happens then."

---

[4] Mr. Duker testified that he urged Mrs. Friedman to "get a lawyer because it makes it more difficult for one lawyer to handle a matter where there is only one lawyer in the picture and you have to be on guard to explain everything to the other side." However, "[s]he said she couldn't afford it."

[5] The decree appealed from, dated August 16, 1977, directs Egan to deliver the collection to the estate by September 15, 1977. Egan sought a stay of enforcement CPLR 5519, subd [a], par 4) pending the outcome of this appeal, but his motion was withdrawn after the parties stipulated that the collection should be held in joint custody at a room in the Morgan Manhattan warehouse until this court determines the appeal.

No exhibition was held in 1971, or thereafter. On the contrary, Egan closed his gallery in 1971 and began operating out of his apartment as a private dealer. Those Friedman works which were not in storage were hung on his apartment walls or stacked in a small room used as an office.

According to Elizabeth Becque, nothing was heard from Egan after her 1970 call, and she phoned him again in 1971 to ask about his promotional efforts. He allegedly repeated that he was still negotiating with museums and that if Mrs. Becque "thought . . . [she] could do better" she should "[t]ake the paintings and see what you can do."

In 1974 Mr. Egan did sell one painting to a noted collector for $1,000. Mrs. Friedman received a remittance of $500 on this sale. The sale price of $1,000 was considerably lower than the $3,000 to $15,000 range of prices at the 1969 exhibition. Mr. Egan explained at the trial that he wanted the collector "to buy a whole lot of . . . [Friedman's work] and wanted to make a very low price for him . . . but he . . . liked [only] one painting."

In 1974 or 1975 Mrs. Friedman entered a nursing home;[6] she died there on March 31, 1976. Shortly after her death, her estate demanded that Egan return the Arnold Friedman paintings (and memorabilia consisting of letters, etc.) in his possession. When Egan refused, the instant proceeding, pursuant to SCPA 2103, was commenced.

At the hearing before the Surrogate, three expert witnesses testified for petitioner as to the regular method of dealing ("usage of trade") between artists and art dealers. Virginia Zabriskie, an art dealer who has operated the Zabriskie Gallery in New York City for 22 years (and who also operates a gallery in Paris), testified that dealers generally take paintings on consignment or purchase them outright. In the former case, the consignment would normally be for two years because artists usually want to be shown at least every two years. Estates would consign paintings for a longer period of time and might be exhibited every three years. The longest consignment she had ever handled was five years, and she has never heard of a consignment lasting 14 years or more. When a dealer purchases paintings outright, the consideration is an "[a]bsolutely fixed sum" of money payable "[t]hen and there" or "over a period of time." The contract under consideration at bar is not customary in the art field because "[t]here is nothing in it for the artist" (Emphasis supplied). No objections were taken to any of this testimony.

Clement Greenberg, a gentleman who has been called by some the leading American art critic, testified that he has served as executor or trustee for the estates of two artists. Over objection he testified that the

---

[6] Irmgard Bartinieff, the lady with whom Mrs. Friedman had lived since the 1950's, testified that Mrs. Friedman left her home in about 1974. Petitioner states in her brief that her mother left Mrs. Bartinieff's household in early 1975.

agreements made by him in such fiduciary capacity were consignments, where the estate controlled the prices in consultation with the dealer. The estates would control or be consulted with respect to every decision the dealer made once a price had been fixed, aside from the "routine" ones involved in selling. On cross-examination, Mr. Greenberg elaborated. In terming the instant contract "a preposterous agreement," he observed:

> No provision is made for the valuation or appraising of the works of art. No provision is made to insure that a decent price be obtained in the sale of these pictures. It is left to the one to whom the title passes to sell a Thousand Dollar picture for Five Hundred should he be in need of money. . . . There is . . . no control over the person who received the title. . . . He is left all alone with his judgment and his own interests.

Gilbert Edelson, an attorney specializing in art law who has practiced for 22 years, testified over objection that the normal relationship between artist and dealer is that of principal and agent. The artist consigns art work to the dealer and, when the art work is sold, the dealer gets a commission. The dealer accounts periodically to the artist. The dealer not only exhibits the artist periodically — he promotes the artist's reputation as well. Promotion is accomplished by trying to interest museum curators in getting the works into museums, by trying to interest critics in writing articles and by trying to interest scholars in doing research. Some dealers have subsidized books on artists. In addition, catalogs are published in conjunction with, or even without, exhibitions. Many dealers will commission scholars, critics and art historians to write introductions to those catalogs. Exhibits are held every one to three years depending upon the quantity of work available.

On cross-examination, Mr. Edelson stated that the contract under consideration has elements of both a sale and a consignment. "This looks more to me at first glance like a consignment agreement because the works are going to be sold, the commission retained, and the proceeds paid which I think is the essence of the normal consignment agreement in the art world." However, he acknowledged that title never passes in a consignment.

Mr. Egan sought to introduce the testimony of Samuel Duker, the attorney who had prepared the contract. After brief testimony about Mr. Duker's background and about work he had done for Mr. Egan, counsel asked whether there came a time when Duker met Mrs. Friedman. An objection was taken to any testimony by Duker with respect to transactions concerning Mrs. Friedman. A voir dire followed, during which Duker testified generally with respect to his role in the execution of the subject contract. Following this voir dire the Surrogate granted a motion to exclude Duker's testimony with respect to the Egan-Friedman "agreement" on the ground that the attorney-client privilege had not been waived.

Following the luncheon recess, the Surrogate acknowledged that there was substantial authority for the lack of confidentiality where an attorney has been consulted by two or more persons in regard to a matter of common interest and where a controversy arises between such parties or their representatives. Nevertheless, the Surrogate adhered to his position on the ground of the inability of a party to a proceeding to prepare properly for cross-examination or to attempt to rebut the testimony of an attorney who represents both sides. In the words of the Surrogate, his ruling was "based on a strong feeling of equity and fairness to both sides," since "there is no way . . . [that] petitioner can attempt to meet the challenge of the testimony of a man who was in that room with Mr. Egan."

In an opinion dated August 1, 1977, Surrogate Laurino reasoned that although the "subject contract speaks in terms of an absolute conveyance of title, . . . [Egan's] duties thereunder were fiduciary in nature with complete accountability for proceeds of sale to the decedent." (*Matter of Friedman*, 91 Misc 2d 201, 204.) This "patent inconsistency" could only be resolved by resort to the acts of the parties and by the application of custom and usage. In reviewing the evidence adduced with respect to those standards, the Surrogate concluded (p205) that the contract was "a consignment arrangement."

The Surrogate noted that Egan has consistently acted, by his own testimony, as the "agent" for the decedent, collecting "sales commissions" on the two works of art that he did sell. Furthermore, the Surrogate credited petitioner's testimony that Egan had told her (p204), " 'Look. You can have the paintings back and see what you can do.' " The court concluded that these were not the words of a man who has full title and interest in the paintings.

On the issue of custom and usage, the Surrogate credited the expert testimony to the effect that "with the rare exception of an outright sale for a sum certain . . . the common practice in the trade is consignment of art works from artist to dealer for a specified period of time, normally 2 to 5 years." (91 Misc 2d 205.) The court also took note of subdivision 1 of section 219-a of the General Business Law (enacted as section 220 in 1966 [L 1966, ch 984]), which provides that

> whenever an artist delivers . . . a work of fine art of his own creation to an art dealer for the purpose of exhibition and/or sale on a commission, fee or other basis of compensation, the delivery to and acceptance thereof by the art dealer is deemed to be "on consignment," and (i) such art dealer shall thereafter . . . be deemed to be the agent of such artist.

While recognizing that the statute had been enacted subsequent to the date of the contract at issue, the court took note (p205) of authority for the proposition that the statute had been enacted " 'to clarify the inherently fiduciary character of the "consignment arrangement" in the artist-art dealer relationship' which had existed through custom and usage prior to the enactment of . . . [the] statute" (citing Memorandum of the State Department of Law, 2 McKinney's Session Laws of NY, 1969, pp2412-2413).[7]

Accordingly, the Surrogate held (p205) that the 1963 contract was "a consignment agreement which terminated on the date of death of decedent principal." He directed, inter alia, that "all the art works of the late Arnold Friedman presently in the possession of [Egan] . . . be turned over to petitioner." The resulting decree, dated August 16, 1977, is appealed by Egan. We affirm.

Appellant contends that the contract at issue is unambiguous and that it was error for the Surrogate to admit evidence of "custom and usage" or to credit testimony as to the conduct of the parties in his construction of the "agreement." Alternatively, it is argued that it was error for the court to exclude the testimony of Samuel Duker, the attorney who drafted the contract, with respect to the meeting at which the contract was executed.

"It is the rare writing that requires no interpretation" (*Bensons Plaza v Great Atlantic & Pacific Tea Co.*, 44 NY2d 791, 792-793). The contract before us is not that rare writing. Although the separate clauses of the "agreement" seem internally unambiguous, they diverge into inconsistency when the contract is read as a whole.

It is a fundamental canon of construction that a "contract must be read as a whole in order to determine its purpose and intent, and that single clauses cannot be construed by taking them out of their context and giving them an interpretation apart from the contract of which they are a part" (*Eighth Ave. Coach Corp. v City of New York*, 286 NY 84, 88). "The complete instrument with all its contextual meanings in 'the light of the obligation as a whole' is the main guide to construction" (*Nash v Gay Apparel Corp.*, 9 AD2d 345, 348), "Form should not prevail over substance and a sensible meaning of words should be sought" (*Atwater & Co. v Panama R.R. Co.*, 246 NY 519, 524; see, also, *City of New York v Pennsylvania R.R. Co.*, 37 NY2d 298, 300).

At bar, the Surrogate correctly concluded that there is a "patent inconsistency" between the language of absolute sale and the alleged purchaser's obligations thereunder, which are "fiduciary in nature with complete accountability for proceeds of sale to the decedent." We would agree with the opinion of one of petitioner's experts, that the contract has both the elements of a sale and the elements of a consignment. Accord-

---

[7] This memorandum, which was submitted in connection with further legislation in 1969 which strengthened the 1966 law, refers back to the "aim" of the original legislation. We note that the 1969 legislation (L 1969, ch 321), inter alia, brings a deceased artist's heirs or personal representatives under the protective umbrella of the section.

ingly, the Surrogate properly considered extrinsic evidence with respect to the intent of the parties and the purpose of the "agreement."

On the basis of the evidence received, the Surrogate's characterization of this contract as a consignment was the correct one. There was overwhelming evidence, uncontradicted by appellant, that consignments of art—not sales — are the prevalent business arrangement between artists, or their estates, and art dealers. This evidence is, of course, buttressed by the 1966 enactment of legislation which "deem[s]" an artist's delivery of fine art to a dealer "to be 'on consignment'" (General Business Law, §219-a). As noted by the Surrogate, that legislation was intended "to clarify the *inherently* fiduciary character of the 'consignment arrangement' in the artist-art dealer relationship" (see Memorandum of the State Department of Law, 2 McKinney's Session Laws of NY, 1969, p2413). The expert testimony at the hearing further established that when an outright sale from an artist to an art dealer occurs, the consideration paid is customarily an absolute sum of money. In addition, appellant's statements to petitioner, in 1970 and 1971, to the effect that she should take the paintings if she thought she could do a better job of selling them, are consistent with an understanding that he had the paintings on consignment. Those words would not be spoken by one who owned the paintings.

Well-established tenets of contract construction also support the Surrogate's conclusion. "[P]arties to an agreement are presumed to act sensibly . . . and an interpretation that produces an absurdly harsh result is to be avoided" (*River View Assoc. v Sheraton Corp. of Amer.*, 33 AD2d 187, 190). Since there exists, in every contract, an implied covenant of good faith and fair dealing, the courts may take into consideration the fact that one construction would make the contract unreasonable. Thus, courts "will endeavor to give the construction most equitable to both parties instead of one which will give one of the parties an unfair or unreasonable advantage over the other"(*Rush v Rush*, 19 AD2d 846). Furthermore, it is a "basic principle of contract law that a written document is to be construed against the party who prepared it where there are ambiguous or contradictory provisions" (*Gillette v Heinrich Motors*, 55 AD2d 841).

These standards uniformly point toward the interpretation of this "agreement" as a consignment. The harshness and inequity of this contract if viewed as a sale will be dealt with at length later in this opinion. Suffice it to say at this point that if this be viewed as a sale, the "consideration" given by appellant is rather indefinite. He must use his "best efforts" to sell the paintings and Mrs. Friedman is to receive 50% of the gross receipts. What if Egan had died prior to Mrs. Friedman? Would his estate be obliged to attempt to sell the paintings and to remit half the proceeds to Mrs. Friedman? If viewed as a sale under the circumstances at bar, must Egan continue to use his "best efforts" to sell and must he pay Mrs. Friedman's estate 50% of the total received by him? It would appear that the workable alternatives would be (a) to construe the "considera- tion" clause as providing consideration only until one of the parties died, or (b) to construe the "agreement" as a consignment, with the accompa- nying principal-agent relationship which would terminate upon the death of either. The former alternative could result in a situation where the "transferor" received nothing in the way of financial benefit even though such financial benefit was plainly contemplated. The latter alter- native would be more equitable to both parties and would substantially avoid the absurdly harsh result that one could "sell" more than 300 paintings with the possibility of getting nothing in return.[8]

Were it not for the exclusion of Samuel Duker's testimony, we would have no difficulty in affirming the decree upon the Surrogate's reason- ing. However, despite the fact that Duker's credibility might be subject to the greatest degree of suspicion,[9] his testimony was both competent and germane with respect to the intent of the parties. No attorney-client privilege could be invoked to exclude his testimony since "[i]f two or more persons consult an attorney in regard to a matter of common inter- est . . . nothing that is said by the parties or the attorney is deemed confidential, in an action arising subsequently thereto between the par- ties or their personal representatives" (Richardson, *Evidence* [10th ed], §413, and cases cited therein). Furthermore, in construing this ambigu-

---

[8] We reject a third possible alternative — that of deeming that the contract creates an agency coupled with an interest — as unworkable and well beyond the contemplation of the parties. Since neither the death of principal nor agent terminates an agency coupled with an interest (1 Mechem. Agency [2d ed], §§655, 672), the adoption of that alternative could lead to the potentially absurd result of one estate using its "best efforts" to promote the sale of these paintings for the other estate ad infinitum. Furthermore, the recitations in the contract (e.g., that "Egan, who is conducting an art gallery at 313 E. 79th Street, New York, N.Y., was a friend and admirer of the late Arnold Friedman") indicate that the parties contemplated that Egan would *personally* represent the Friedman collec- tion. In all probability, the parties contemplated that all the paintings would be sold within their lifetimes.

[9] It is a fair assumption that independent counsel retained by Mrs. Friedman would have strongly advised against her entering into the subject "agreement." In view of the fact that Mr. Duker testified that he explained the "agreement" to Mrs. Friedman "word for word," and that he "cleared up some misconceptions that she had about it," there would have been a definite motive for Mr. Duker to testify that Mrs. Friedman wanted Egan to own the paintings. Otherwise, be- cause of the language suggesting an absolute conveyance of title, Mr. Duker's claim of full disclosure would have been untrue. Conversely, Mr. Duker could not be expected to testify that a consignment was intended, since such a poorly drafted "consignment agreement" would border on malpractice. In short, Mr. Duker's testimony might well be influenced by his own role in this transaction.

ous contract, all evidence relevant to its execution should have been held admissible.

Having said that, we hold this error to be harmless. To the extent that the "agreement" purports to transfer ownership of the paintings to Egan, it is unconscionable on its face.

The doctrine of unconscionability has been discussed by the courts and the commentators at great length (see, e.g., *Industralease Automated & Scientific Equip. Corp. v R.M.E. Enterprises*, 58 AD2d 482; *Blake v Biscardi*, 62 AD2d 975; *Henningsen v Bloomfield Motors*, 32 NJ 358; *Williams v Walker-Thomas Furniture Co.*, 350 F2d 445; 14 Williston, *Contracts* [3d ed], §1632; Eddy, *On the "Essential" Purposes of Limited Remedies: The Metaphysics of UCC Section 2-719[2]*, 65 Cal L Rev 28) and we therefore limit our observations on the subject. The doctrine appears in section 2-302 of the Uniform Commercial Code (which became effective *after* the instant contract was executed [L 1962, ch 553, eff Sept. 27, 1964]), but the conclusion is inescapable that the Uniform Commercial Code simply codified the doctrine, which was used by the common-law courts to invalidate contracts under certain circumstances (*Industralease Automated & Scientific Equip. Corp. v R.M.E. Enterprises*, *supra*, p488; *Triple D & E v Van Buren*, 72 Misc 2d 569, 577, *aff'd sub nom. D & E Ind. Catering v Antinozzi*, 42 AD2d 840). The classic definition was a broad one. An unconscionable contract was one "such as no man in his senses and not under delusion would make on the one hand, and as no honest and fair man would accept on the other" (*Earl of Chesterfield v Janssen*, 2 Ves Sen 125, 155 [28 Eng Rep Reprint 82, 100]; cf. *Hume v United States*, 132 US 406, 411). A contractual clause would not be enforced where it was "so monstrous and extravagant that it would be a reproach to the administration of justice to countenance or uphold it" (*Greer v Tweed*, 13 Abb Prac [NS] 427,429).

The concept of unconscionability must necessarily be applied in a flexible manner depending upon all the facts and circumstances of a particular case. The courts have identified various elements of the unconscionable contract that may be characterized as substantive and procedural. Substantive elements of unconscionability appear in the content of the contract per se; procedural elements must be identified by resort to evidence of the contract formation process (*Industralease Automated & Scientific Equip. Corp. v R.M.E. Enterprises*, 58 AD2d 482, 489, n4, *supra*; see, also, *Nu Dimensions Figure Salons v Becerra*, 73 Misc 2d 140, 143). Inflated prices (i.e., grossly inadequate consideration given by the seller), unfair disclaimers of warranty and termination clauses have been deemed substantively unconscionable (*Industralease Automated & Scientific Equip. Corp. v R.M.E. Enterprises*, *supra*, p489, n4). High pressure sales tactics, misrepresentation and unequal bargaining position have been recognized as procedurally unconscionable (*Industralease Auto-*

mated & Scientific Equip. Corp. v R.M.E. Enterprises, supra, p489, n4). The foregoing examples of unconscionable elements are by no means exhaustive; nor would we attempt to define a hierarchy of importance for any particular element in all cases. The weight to be given to each factor is as variable as the facts of each individual case. Where the disparity in the consideration exchanged by the parties is overwhelming, that factor alone "may be sufficient to sustain [a finding that the contract is unconscionable]," since such disparity "itself leads inevitably to the felt conclusion that knowing advantage was taken of [one party]" (*Jones v Star Credit Corp.*, 59 Misc 2d 189, 192 [Wachtler, J.]).

At bar, the contract of the parties qua "sale" is grossly unconscionable in the substantive sense. In return for the stated conveyance of more than 300 works of art, Mrs. Friedman received neither the payment of a purchase price at the time of the "agreement" nor the right to receive a fixed price within a definite time in the future. Instead, she obtained only the uncertainty of payment to be made if and when sales were effected. Complete control over the timing of these "future sales" was placed in the hands of the dealer.

The "consideration" given by the dealer actually resulted in a situation where his interests were potentially adverse to the widow's. By holding out for a price far in excess of the fair market for the art works, the dealer could deny Mrs. Friedman any payment whatsoever. The dealer would, however, still retain title to the paintings. The incentive for the dealer to make any sales was therefore questionable. If he made no sales, he owned the collection outright. If he made sales, he would have to part with 50% of the purchase price.

This conflict of interest is reflected by the actual course of events over the last 15 years. From the date the contract was signed until Mrs. Friedman's death, Egan held only one exhibition of the Friedman paintings and made only one sale. Although the expert testimony established that dealers ordinarily seek to promote an artist's reputation through exhibits, catalogs and other efforts, Egan's own testimony was that he "protected," "watched" and "nursed" the paintings (at least during the period 1963-1969). It was certainly in his own self-interest to do that — and nothing more.

Viewed as a sale, the contract gave Egan similar latitude in the opposite direction. He could "dump" the paintings at a minimal price in order to raise immediate cash. While there is no indication that he did so, the opportunity for such abuse was present.[10]

---

[10] There are indications that the one painting which was sold in 1974 *was* sold at a low price. Egan testified that he wanted the collector "to buy a whole lot of . . . [Friedman's work] and wanted to make a very low price for him . . . but he . . . liked [only] one painting." Although the tactic of selling

In sum, the "consideration" given for this "sale" was so contingent and so dependent upon the discretion of one who had a "built-in" conflict of interest as to be grossly inadequate. This patent inadequacy so permeates the "agreement" as to render it unconscionable. As Virginia Zabriskie put it at the hearing, "[t]here is nothing in it for the artist."

Furthermore, although the substantive unconscionability here present predominates, there are elements of procedural unconscionability attendant upon the execution of this contract which negate the possibility of any salvation for this "agreement." At the time the "agreement" was entered into, Mrs. Friedman was about 75 years of age. Her only formal education had been at a convent in France. There was testimony at the hearing to the effect that she had no real business experience and that she displayed "an unworldly attitude" towards business matters. She did not have her own lawyer and professed that she could not afford one.

In contrast, when the agreement was executed, Charles Egan had been in business nearly 30 years and had spent 18 years as the owner of his own gallery. He was represented by his own attorney who had participated in previous transactions between Egan and other artists. His attorney drafted the agreement and "explained" it to the widow.

It strains credulity to believe that Mrs. Friedman was told the full ramifications of the document she was signing. Was she told, for instance, that the "consideration" given by Egan was subject to an inherent conflict of interest? True it is that there exists in every contract an implied covenant of good faith and that Egan promised to use his "best efforts" to promote the paintings. But the phrase "best efforts" is a slippery one in the absence of any checks on the promisor, and the potential for abuse here was so great, that it is difficult to conceive of any truly informed person entering into such an "agreement."

After 15 years of exile, Arnold Friedman's legacy should be returned to his family.

SHAPIRO, J.P., COHALAN and O'CONNOR, JJ., concur.

Decree of the Surrogate's Court, Queens County, dated August 16, 1977, affirmed insofar as appealed from, with costs to petitioner payable personally by appellant.

---

one painting "low" in order to arouse further interest in the artist's work is a valid business practice, it could verge on the unethical when one artist's work is sold "low" in order to promote the dealer's general inventory of works by other artists (at least where the "bait" is on consignment or the dealer is otherwise accountable to the artist for part of the sales price). There is no indication of any such impropriety in connection with the 1974 sale. However, once again, the potential for abuse was present if the "agreement" is considered a sale.

§8.2.5. Fiduciary Bond Statute: Ohio Provisions

The State of Ohio has a unique provision for fiduciaries and the bonds they must file on the estates they handle that involve artworks. Normally, a fiduciary in Ohio must file a bond no less than double the probable value of the estate in question prior to the issuance of his letters (unless, of course, the relevant instrument waives the requirement of bond).[3] An exception is made, however, for estates consisting in whole or in part of works of art suitable for exhibition in a museum or other similar institution.[4] Under this exception, the probate court may direct that the works be deposited with the institution (providing it has a net worth at least ten times the value of the works to be deposited) and may then reduce the amount of the bond due from the fiduciary so that the amount of the penalty is determined only on the balance of the estate.[5] Additionally, the fiduciary, if he has acted in good faith, is then relieved of any liability to the estate resulting from the deposit of the works.[6]

---

[3] Ohio Rev. Code Ann. §2109.04 (1978).
[4] *Id.* §2109.14.
[5] *Ibid.*
[6] *Ibid.*